Blackstone's Police Manual

General Police Duties

Blackstone's Police Manual

Volume 4

General Police Duties

2009

Glenn Hutton

BA, MPhil, FCIPD

and

Gavin McKinnon

LLB, LLM, MSc

Consultant Editors: Paul Connor and Fraser Sampson

OXFORD
UNIVERSITY PRESS

OXFORD
UNIVERSITY PRESS

Great Clarendon Street, Oxford OX2 6DP

Oxford University Press is a department of the University of Oxford.
It furthers the University's objective of excellence in research, scholarship,
and education by publishing worldwide in

Oxford New York

Auckland Cape Town Dar es Salaam Hong Kong Karachi
Kuala Lumpur Madrid Melbourne Mexico City Nairobi
New Delhi Shanghai Taipei Toronto

With offices in

Argentina Austria Brazil Chile Czech Republic France Greece
Guatemala Hungary Italy Japan Poland Portugal Singapore
South Korea Switzerland Thailand Turkey Ukraine Vietnam

Oxford ia a registered trade mark of Oxford University Press
in the UK and in certain other countries

Published in the United States
by Oxford University Press Inc., New York

First edition 1998
Eleventh edition 2008

British Library Cataloguing in Publication Data

Data available

Library of Congress Cataloging in Publication Data

Data available

Typeset by Laserwords Private Limited, Chennai, India
Printed in Italy
on acid-free paper by
Legoprint S.p.A

ISBN 978-0-19-954763-0

10 9 8 7 6 5 4 3 2 1

Foreword for 2009 Blackstone's Police Manuals

The role of a police officer has become more technical and more demanding over the last decades. To be properly qualified as a frontline officer, particularly a frontline supervisor and manager, there is a huge quantity of law, legal precedent and its interpretation that is required. Unlike a barrister, solicitor or judge, who has the books to hand or a website one click away with their mouse, a police officer frequently has to make crucial legal decisions with partial knowledge of all the facts, the pressure of time and events, and the presence of a none-too-cooperative citizen. It is a testimony to the training that officers receive that they get the decisions right most of the time.

However, the training is crucially dependent on the quality of the training materials. These manuals are the product of a partnership between the National Policing Improvement Agency (NPIA) and Blackstone's. The NPIA has a key role in promoting learning and the development of leadership in policing. It is building on more than two decades of national expertise in supporting learning for police officers, and now has responsibility for improving every aspect of learning in the policing profession from recruit training to the most senior ranks. Alongside Blackstone's we are committed to ensuring that the public is served by qualified, well trained and well led officers and police staff. These manuals are a key part of that mission.

Peter Neyroud QPM
Chief Constable and Chief Executive of the National Policing Improvement Agency

Preface

The *Blackstone's Police Manuals* are the only official study guides for the OSPRE® Part I Police Promotion Examinations: if the law is not in the Manuals, it will not be in the exams.

All the Manuals include explanatory keynotes and case law examples, providing clear and incisive analysis of important areas. As well as covering basic law and procedure they take full account of the PACE Codes of Practice and human rights implications. They can also be used as a training resource for police probationers, special constables and PCSOs, or as an invaluable reference tool for police staff of all ranks and positions.

By its very nature, policing covers a wide and widening range of activities. As society gets more complex and demanding, so too does the job of those who police it. Add to that the enormous political dimension, and it is no surprise that the legislative framework governing policing delivery has grown in depth and breadth. As a result, *General Police Duties* necessarily contains a wide range of powers, offences and considerations. Some parts of this Manual govern the practical application of the others in the series—an example is the Human Rights Act 1998 and the restrictions it places on the use of policing powers generally. Other areas involve the general powers of police constables and their CSO colleagues, the constitution of the police, the National Policing Plan, and the provisions governing misconduct and complaints. To that extent the areas of this Manual are absolutely fundamental to the effective delivery of policing across England and Wales.

The Manual also covers other areas of policing such as anti-social behaviour, harassment, public order and terrorism, firearms and gun crime, weapons, civil disputes, offences relating to land and premises, licensing, offences and powers relating to information, and diversity, discrimination and equality.

The 2009 edition has been extensively edited and updated to incorporate all recent legislative changes and the revised PACE Codes of Practice. The legislation containing significant changes to the contents of the Manual includes, the Violent Crime Reduction Act 2006, the Domestic Violence, Crime and Victims Act 2006, the Police and Justice Act 2006, the Equality Act 2006 and the Gambling Act 2005.

In addition to the very rapid and extensive changes in the law, these features mean that *General Police Duties* covers a lot of ground.

The aim of this Manual is to take this shifting and growing body of national and European law and analyse the essential elements in a practical and pragmatic context—without losing the specific meaning and applicability along the way. If we have achieved that, it is thanks to the contributions of the many police officers and staff, lawyers and practitioners who have helped in the development of this Manual, now in its eleventh edition; if we haven't, it is not for the want of trying.

Oxford University Press are always happy to receive any useful written feedback from any reader on the content and style of the Manual, especially from those involved in or with the criminal justice system. Please email this address with any comments or queries: police.uk@oup.com.

The law is stated as at 1 June 2008.

Acknowledgements

Blackstone's Police Manuals have become firmly established as a 'household name' in the context of police law for which they are the leading text in England and Wales. Their growth and refinement year on year is a result, not simply of Parliament and the legislators, but also of the many and varied contributions of the Manuals' wide readership.

Thanks are due to all (except perhaps the legislators) and there is never space to mention everyone individually.

In particular, thanks to the staff of the Legal Services Department of the National Policing Improvement Agency (NPIA) and Examinations and Assessment. The monthly Digest produced by Legal Services Department is an invaluable reference and the informative syllabus review conducted by Examinations and Assessment has helped to shape the content and style of the Manual.

Thanks to George Cooper (Northamptonshire Police), Stuart K. Fairclough (Metropolitan Police), Paul Murphy (Greater Manchester Police), and Kevin Whitehouse (West Midlands Police).

Our thanks, as always, to all the staff involved in the production of the Manual in the Academic and Professional Law Department at Oxford University Press, especially Peter Daniell, Lindsey Davis, Jodi Towler, Geraldine Mangley, Pam Birkby and Ashley Mackie. Special thanks also to Rosalie for her continued support and forbearance.

Glenn Hutton and Gavin McKinnon

Contents

Table of Cases

This table is a compilation of cases referred to in the *General Police Duties* volume of Blackstone's Police Manuals. Case law, containing the decisions of the courts, is one of the primary sources of law in England and Wales.

Cases are referred to by the names of parties. A full citation includes the abbreviation of the law report (of which there are many different series), the volume number and page numbers as follows:

Atkins *v* DPP [2000] 1 WLR 1427
[Names of parties, year case reported, volume no., publication name (Weekly Law Reports), page no.]

In criminal actions the single letter *R* (meaning Rex or Regina) comes first, indicating the state's role as prosecutor, followed by the name of the accused person (the defendant).

In some family cases the report may be headed '*In re Brown*' or, in more modern cases, *Re Brown*, meaning 'in the matter of'. *Ex parte Brown* may also be used, meaning 'Brown' is the name of the applicant for whom the case is heard. Where a single letter is used for one of the parties, e.g. T *v* DPP this means that one of the parties to the case cannot be named for legal reasons.

Cases in the table of cases below are listed alphabetically with references to the relevant paragraph number in this Manual.

Tables of Primary Legislation

These tables are a compilation of all references to Statutes (also known as Acts of Parliament) found in the *General Police Duties* volume of Blackstone's Police Manuals.

Statutes are usually referred to by their short title and date, e.g. Abortion Act 1967, and in many cases this Manual may refer to just one Part, section (s.) or Schedule (sch.) of an Act. This Manual states the current law as at 1 June 2008 (unless stated otherwise).

The Statutes below are listed alphabetically with references to the relevant paragraph number in this Manual.

UK Statutes

EC Legislation

Tables of Secondary Legislation

Secondary, subordinate or delegated legislation is legislation made by a body other than Parliament with powers conferred by Parliament through a specific Act. Secondary legislation is published in the Statutory Instruments (SI) series, and SIs are cited in the following way:

The Misuse of Drugs Regulations 2001 (SI 2001/2066)
[Title, year, number]

SIs deal with the detail of how legislation is to work in practice and they can be speedily amended or revoked as necessary. They may also be used to bring legislation into force. This Manual states the current law as at 1 June 2008 (unless stated otherwise).

The tables also contain Codes of Practice, which are not legislation but should be regarded as legally binding on the relevant parties unless exceptional circumstances prevail.

The legislation below is listed alphabetically with references to the relevant paragraph number in this Manual.

For further information on sources of law, please see chapter 2.1 Sources of Law in the *Evidence & Procedure* Manual 2009, pages 3–6.

UK Statutory Instruments, Rules and Regulations

Codes of Practice

Home Office Circulars

EC Secondary Legislation

How to use this Manual

Volume numbers for the Manuals

The 2009 Blackstone's Police Manuals each have a volume number as follows:

Volume 1: *Crime*
Volume 2: *Evidence & Procedure*
Volume 3: *Road Policing*
Volume 4: *General Police Duties*

The first digit of each paragraph number in the text of the Manuals denotes the Manual number. For example, paragraph 2.3 is chapter 3 of the *Evidence & Procedure* Manual and 4.3 is chapter 3 of the *General Police Duties* Manual.

All index entries and references in the Tables of Legislation and the Table of Cases, etc. refer to paragraph numbers instead of page numbers, making information easier to find.

Length of sentence for an offence

Where a length of sentence for an offence is stated in this Manual, please note that the number of months or years stated is the maximum number and will not be exceeded.

OSPRE® Rules & Syllabus Information

The rules and syllabus for the OSPRE® system are defined within the OSPRE® Rules & Syllabus document published by National Policing Improvement Agency (NPIA) Examinations and Assessment on behalf of the Police Promotions Examination Board (PPEB). The Rules & Syllabus document is published annually each September, and applies to all OSPRE® assessments scheduled for the calendar year following its publication. For example, the September 2008 Rules & Syllabus document would apply to all OSPRE® Part I and Part II assessments held during 2009.

The document provides details of the law and procedure to be tested within the OSPRE® Part I examinations, information on the Part II assessment centre, and also outlines the rules underpinning the OSPRE® system.

All candidates who are taking an OSPRE® Part I examination or Part II assessment centre are strongly encouraged to familiarise themselves with the Rules & Syllabus document during their preparation. The OSPRE® Part I rules also apply to candidates who take the Part I and then go on to apply for their force's work-based assessment promotion trials.

The document can be downloaded from the Recruitment, Assessment & Selection Section of the NPIA website, which can be found at www.npia.police.uk. Electronic versions are also supplied to all force OSPRE® contacts.

If you have any problems obtaining the Rules & Syllabus document from the above source, please email the OSPRE® Candidate Administration Team at:

exams.ospre@npia.pnn.police.uk

Usually, no further updates to the Rules & Syllabus document will be issued during its year-long lifespan. However, in exceptional circumstances, the NPIA (on behalf of the PPEB) reserves the right to issue an amended syllabus prior to the next scheduled annual publication date.

For example, a major change to a key area of legislation or procedure (e.g. the Codes of Practice) during the lifespan of the current Rules & Syllabus document would render a significant part of the current syllabus content obsolete. In such circumstances, it may be necessary for an update to the syllabus to be issued, which would provide guidance to candidates on any additional material which would be examinable within their Part I.

In such circumstances, an update to the Rules & Syllabus document would be made available through the NPIA website, and would be distributed to all force OSPRE® contacts. The NPIA will ensure that any syllabus update is distributed well in advance of the examination date, to ensure that candidates have sufficient time to familiarise themselves with any additional examinable material. Where possible, any additional study materials would be provided to candidates free of charge.

Please note that syllabus updates will only be made in *exceptional* circumstances, an update will not be made for every change to legislation included within the syllabus. For further guidance on this issue, candidates are advised to regularly check the NPIA website, or consult their force OSPRE® contact, during their preparation period.

PART ONE

Police

4.1 Police

4.1.1 Police Legislation

The two main pieces of legislation affecting the maintenance and operation of the police service in England and Wales are the Police Act 1996 and the Police Reform Act 2002.

The Police and Justice Act 2006 has brought about a number of changes to police legislation. It also creates a National Policing Improvement Agency to drive forward the police reform programme and develop the critical national policing infrastructure on behalf of the service.

The Police Act 1996 continues to set out key offences relating to police officers and is the source of the regulation of efficiency, conduct and complaints for officers of all ranks.

What this chapter sets out to do is to unravel some of the legislative provisions that lie beneath the whole complex business of policing in a broader sense, and that will drive policing policy and practice in the future.

4.1.2 Policing Services and Jurisdiction

There are many different policing bodies in England and Wales. The main forces can be divided into those coming under the provisions of the Police Act 1996 and the general jurisdiction of the Home Office, and other statutory forces (referred to as special police forces in the Serious Organised Crime and Police Act 2005). All of these main policing bodies are covered in more detail in this chapter.

4.1.2.1 Home Office Police Services

Police officers in Home Office services in England and Wales derive their jurisdiction from s. 30 of the Police Act 1996, which states:

> (1) A member of a police force shall have all the powers and privileges of a constable throughout England and Wales and the adjacent United Kingdom waters.

4.1.2.2 The Police Act 1997

The Police Act 1997 contains provisions in relation to:

- the Serious Organised Crime Agency;
- the National Policing Improvement Agency;
- the entry on and interference with property and wireless telegraphy in the prevention or detection of serious crime;
- the issue of certificates about criminal records; and
- the administrative provisions for the police.

4.1.2.3 Serious Organised Crime Agency

Chapter 1 of the Serious Organised Crime and Police Act 2005 created the Serious Organised Crime Agency (SOCA), which replaced the National Criminal Intelligence Service and the National Crime Squad.

Despite the references to 'serious organised crime' in its title, and elsewhere in the Act, SOCA may carry on activities in relation to other crime if they are carried on for the purposes of any of its functions (as to which see below). In particular SOCA may:

(i) institute criminal proceedings in England and Wales or Northern Ireland;
(ii) act in support of any activities of a police force (or 'special police force'—see below) or law enforcement agency, at the request of the chief officer or the agency;
(iii) enter into other arrangements for co-operating with bodies or people (in the United Kingdom or elsewhere) which it considers appropriate in connection with the exercise of its relevant functions.

SOCA may also give such assistance as it considers appropriate in response to requests made by any government or other body exercising functions of a public nature in any country or territory outside the United Kingdom, other than requests for help to obtain evidence under s. 13 of the Crime (International Co-operation) Act 2003 (s. 5(6)).

The Director-General of SOCA has general operational control of SOCA's activities and functions including which particular operations are to be mounted in the exercise of any of those functions and how such operations are to be conducted (s. 21). The Secretary of State may determine strategic priorities for SOCA (s. 9(1)) and issue codes of practice relating to the exercise by SOCA of any of its functions (s. 10(1)).

The functions of SOCA are:

(a) preventing and detecting serious organised crime, and
(b) contributing to the reduction of such crime in other ways and to the mitigation of its consequences.

However, given the nature of its work, SOCA will come into contact with other types of criminal activity in the course of its function at (a) above. Therefore the Act makes provision for such situations in relation to serious or complex fraud and the relationship with the Serious Fraud Office and HM Revenue and Customs (generally s. 2).

SOCA took on most of the work of the Assets Recovery Agency on 1 April 2008 with the exception of the ARA's training and accreditation functions, which transferred to the NPIA.

SOCA also has a key function in relation to the gathering, storing, analysing and disseminating of information relevant to:

(a) the prevention, detection, investigation or prosecution of offences, or
(b) the reduction of crime in other ways or the mitigation of its consequences.

In discharging this function, s. 3 provides that SOCA may disseminate such information to a wide range of people and organisations including:

- police forces in the United Kingdom, the States of Jersey, the Island of Guernsey and the Isle of Man Constabulary;
- 'special police forces', i.e. the Ministry of Defence Police, the British Transport Police, the Civil Nuclear Constabulary and the Scottish Drug Enforcement Agency;
- other law enforcement agencies (including any government department, the Scottish Administration, any other person who is charged with the duty of investigating offences or

charging offenders, or any other person who is engaged outside the United Kingdom in the carrying on of activities similar to any carried on by SOCA or a police force); and

- such others as it considers appropriate in connection with any of the matters at (a) or (b).

A key aspect of SOCA's operational functions is disseminating information and the Act makes a number of provisions for this. These cover what you can tell SOCA, what you *must* tell SOCA and what the consequences of disclosure will be.

Information obtained by SOCA in connection with the exercise of any of its functions may be disclosed by SOCA if the disclosure is for any permitted purposes. Permitted purposes are provided by s. 33(2) and include:

(a) the prevention, detection, investigation or prosecution of criminal offences;
(b) the prevention, detection or investigation of conduct for which non-criminal penalties are provided under the law of any country or territory inside or outside the United Kingdom;
(c) the exercise of any of SOCA's core functions;
(d) the exercise of any functions of any intelligence service within the meaning of the Regulation of Investigatory Powers Act 2000;
(e) the exercise of any functions under part 2 of the Football Spectators Act 1989;
(f) the exercise of any function designated by order of the Secretary of State.

Any disclosure under these provisions does not breach any obligation of confidence owed by the person making the disclosure, or any other restriction on the disclosure of information (however imposed) (s. 33(3)). However, nothing in the above provisions authorises disclosure, in contravention of any provisions of the Data Protection Act 1998 of personal data (**see para. 4.12.3**) which are not exempt from those provisions, a disclosure which is prohibited by part 1 of the Regulation of Investigatory Powers Act 2000 (**see para. 4.12.4**), or a disclosure in contravention of s. 35(2). Similarly, SOCA depends to a large extent on information it receives. Consequently, the Act provides that any person may disclose information to SOCA if the disclosure is made for the purposes of the exercise by SOCA of any of its functions (s. 34(1)).

The chief officer of a police force in Great Britain or special police force must keep SOCA informed of any information relating to crime in his/her police area that appears to him/her to be likely to be relevant to the exercise by SOCA of any of its functions (s. 36). In addition, every constable, officer of Her Majesty's Revenue and Customs and member of Her Majesty's armed forces or Her Majesty's coastguard has a statutory duty to assist SOCA in the exercise of its functions in relation to serious organised crime (s. 37).

It is anticipated that SOCA will work closely with police forces, and the Serious Organised Crime Act 2005 makes provision for some of the operational practicalities of such co-operative working. The Act allows for mutual assistance between SOCA and other law enforcement agencies—either for SOCA to provide assistance to a police force or law enforcement agency, or for SOCA to *receive* such assistance from those other bodies. The arrangements are generally divided into those that apply voluntarily and those arrangements that are directed (ss. 23 and 24).

Unlike its predecessors, SOCA will not appoint its own constables. Although its members can be endowed with the powers of a constable, an officer of Revenue and Customs or an immigration officer (see s. 43), SOCA is not a police force and its agents will not be police officers. Police officers can be seconded to SOCA, but where they do not resign from the police service they will be treated as having been suspended from that office until they return to the police service (s. 43(6)).

SOCA is liable in respect of unlawful conduct of any constable or other person who has been seconded to SOCA to serve as a member of its staff and any constable or other person who has been provided for the assistance of SOCA under the mutual assistance arrangements (see ss. 28 to 31).

4.1.2.4 Property Interference

A further measure introduced by the Police Act 1997 also makes provisions for the use of highly specialised and intrusive measures to combat crime. Part III provides for the appointment of a Chief Commissioner and other commissioners to oversee the operation of the powers under this part of the Act. It also identifies 'authorising officers' who may grant the relevant authority with the power to use intrusive surveillance techniques under the strict criteria set out in the Act. The whole area of surveillance and interference with property—particularly to the levels covered by part III—is acutely sensitive in the light of the Human Rights Act 1998. The law regulating the use of surveillance and interception of communications generally is addressed by the Regulation of Investigatory Powers Act 2000 (as to which **see para. 4.12.4**).

4.1.2.5 Criminal Records Certificates

Part V of the Police Act 1997 (as amended) provides for the creation of a Criminal Records Bureau which is able to access the data on the Police National Computer and which will issue different types of criminal conviction certificate in response to 'searches' on certain individuals. Requests for such certificates in respect of individuals who have criminal records are not restricted to police officers and are intended to help employers and others 'vet' applications for certain posts or positions. The 1997 Act provides for a code of practice (s. 122), and creates offences in relation to making a false certificate, altering or using it, with intent to deceive (s. 123), and disclosing information unless the disclosure is in the course of a person's duties (ss. 124 and 124A).

4.1.2.6 National Policing Improvement Agency

Section 1 of and sch. 1 to the Police and Justice Act 2006 established the National Policing Improvement Agency (NPIA) from 1 April 2007, and abolished Centrex and PITO from the same date. The NPIA takes on much of the work of the bodies it is replacing, as well as a number of policing policy functions from the Home Office and the Association of Chief Police Officers (ACPO). Schedule 1 to the Act sets out the agency's functions (described as 'objects'). These are:

- to identify, develop and promulgate good policy practice (this would be issued in the form of either non-statutory guidance by the Agency, or Codes of Practice made under s. 39 of the Police Act 1996, or as Regulations made under s. 53A of that Act);
- to provide expert operational advice and assistance to listed police forces (as defined by para. 3—essentially police forces in England and Wales and other law enforcement agencies operating throughout the United Kingdom);
- to identify and assess opportunities for and threats to police forces in England and Wales (this might include opportunities presented by new detection methods and threats posed by new crime patterns);
- to share policing issues with international partners; and

- to provide support to listed police forces in connection with the provision of IT, procurement and training services (such services might be provided directly by the Agency or by other providers under contract to the Agency).

Police officers seconded to the NPIA will initially come under the provisions of s. 97 of the Police Act 1996, but para. 19 of sch. 1 to the 2006 Act allows the Secretary of State to make Regulations for seconded constables and directly recruited constables. The Regulations will mirror those of a territorial police force. Direct recruitment of police officers was not available to any of the NPIA's precursor bodies.

4.1.2.7 Other Police Services

There are several other full-time police services in Great Britain with statutory policing functions. These include:

- British Transport Police (BTP)—see the Railways and Transport Safety Act 2003.
- Ministry of Defence Police (MDP)—see the Ministry of Defence Police Act 1987.
- Civil Nuclear Constabulary—see the Energy Act 2004.
- Ports Police—see, e.g., the Port of London Act 1968 and the Harbours, Docks and Piers Clauses Act 1847.

In relation to the arrangements for complaints and conduct matters, many of these forces have their own systems which are based largely upon the general provisions affecting the police (as to which **see para. 4.1.7**); provision is also made for the Independent Police Complaints Commission to have jurisdiction in relation to police officers, special constables and others under the direction and control of the relevant chief constables of some such forces (see the Independent Police Complaints Commission (Forces Maintained Otherwise than by Police Authorities) Order 2004 (SI 2004/672)).

The jurisdiction of the first two of these forces has been extended over recent years, e.g. by the Anti-terrorism, Crime and Security Act 2001. The Police Reform Act 2002 has made a number of further changes to the jurisdiction of both the BTP and the MDP. As well as opening up the opportunities for officers from these—and other—forces to join and be seconded to the Serious Organised Crime Agency, the Act makes many other changes, some of which are summarised below.

4.1.2.8 Ministry of Defence Police

Part 5 of the Police Reform Act 2002 is devoted to the MDP and introduces many changes affecting the force, including:

- a s. 2B in the Ministry of Defence Police Act 1987 extending the jurisdiction of MDP officers when serving under the direction and control of a Home Office force while on secondment to that force;
- changing the discipline framework to allow it to mirror, as far as possible, that applicable to Home Office forces;
- bringing the MDP within the inspection remit of Her Majesty's Inspector of Constabulary on a statutory basis;
- amending firearms legislation so as to enable MDP recruits/potential recruits to use firearms without the need for a certificate during training or assessment.

4.1.2.9 British Transport Police

Other sections of the Police Reform Act 2002 amend various legislative provisions affecting the BTP, including:

- bringing the chief constable into the definition of relevant authorities who can apply for Anti-social Behaviour Orders (ASBOs—**see chapter 4.5**) (s. 61);
- providing the Chief Constable with powers to accredit suitable people with limited policing powers under a Railway Safety Accreditation Scheme;
- extending the jurisdiction of officers of or above the rank of superintendent to exercise the powers under s.16 of the Crime and Disorder Act 1998 (removal of truants—**see Evidence & Procedure, chapter 2.6**);
- extending the relevant provisions of the Road Traffic Offenders Act 1988 relating to fixed penalty regime (as to which **see Road Policing, chapter 3.11**), allowing BTP officers to take part in the scheme within their own jurisdiction.

For details of the protocols between non-Home Office forces and other forces see Home Office Circulars 24/2002, 25/2002 and 26/2005.

4.1.2.10 Special Constables

The terms under which special constables may be appointed and deployed are set out in s. 30 of the Police Act 1996. However, the Police and Justice Act 2006 introduces significant amendments: para. 21 of sch. 2 to the Police and Justice Act 2006 allows special constables to use their constabulary powers in forces throughout England and Wales. These amendments bring special constables in line with regular officers, and allow greater flexibility in their deployment.

4.1.2.11 The Extended Police Family

The Police Reform Act 2002 brought with it the concept of the 'extended police family'. Some family members, such as the special constabulary (above), have been around for many decades, while other non-sworn members, such as street and neighbourhood wardens and police support volunteers, are a relatively new thing. However, as well as giving all these contributors to the wider policing service greater publicity, the Police Reform Act 2002 also gave some of them statutory powers—and created a few more family groups at the same time.

The status, powers and restrictions on the newer arrivals to the extended police family are discussed in the next chapter and also in other Manuals in this series. It suffices to say at this stage that the government's reforms in relation to policing are based partly on the premise that policing is far too complicated, important and widespread a business to be left entirely to the police. One of the key distinctions that help make sense of the many new policing roles put in place by the 2002 Act is whether the individual is a sworn constable or not. Full and part-time members of *any* police force who are sworn in as, and have the statutory powers of, a constable are generally unaffected by the fairly complex legislation extending the policing family.

4.1.3 The National Community Safety Plan and National Policing Plan

Following the passage of the Police Reform Act 2002, the first annual National Policing Plan (NPP) for England and Wales was introduced to Parliament in November 2002. Section 1 of the Act requires the Home Secretary to prepare an annual NPP and to publish it by 30

November each year. However, following the 2004 White Paper *Building Communities, Beating Crime: A Better Police Service for the 21st Century*, the government incorporated the NPP into the newly created National Community Safety Plan (NCSP).

4.1.3.1 National Community Safety Plan

The 2004 White Paper contained a commitment by the government to produce a community safety strategy in 2005. It was recognised that the police alone could not successfully deliver community safety and that broadly based partnerships were vital. To this end the government decided to move beyond an annual NPP to a NCSP.

The government has now set out its community safety priorities for 2008–2011 which outline a new approach to community safety and aim to manage a coherent community safety programme across government, providing people with a clear view of overall priorities. The priorities for community safety are built around five themes:

- Making communities stronger and more effective
- Further reducing crime and anti-social behaviour
- Creating safer environments
- Protecting the public and building confidence
- Improving people's lives, so they are less likely to commit offences or re-offend.

The NCSP is not limited to the work of the police, but defines the minimum expectations of each of the key partners involved in Crime and Disorder Reduction Partnerships (**see para. 4.1.4**).

4.1.3.2 National Policing Plan

Before the NPP there was no single document or central system co-ordinating and guiding all the various performance indicators, priorities and development plans of the many policing stakeholders. This situation, whereby the government, Police Authorities, chief officers and other key groups referred to different sources, focusing on different priorities and working to different timescales in setting out their various plans for the future, was seen as something of a weakness in the overall ability of the police service to plan strategically. The Plan's purpose, therefore, is to set out strategic national priorities for the police service as a whole, along with the indicators against which the service will be judged.

These Regulations supplement the provisions in s. 6ZB of the Police Act 1996 on policing plans by Police Authorities, and came into force in March 2008. They are also supplemented by Home Office Circular 4/2008.

The Regulations contain some transitional provisions which relate to the plan period beginning on 1 April 2008; these are that this policing plan:

- Shall be modified prior to publication, to include details of the performance of the police authority in the period 1 April 2005 to 31 March 2008 by reference to the statutory performance indicators for the police authority under s. 4 (performance indicators and standards) of the Local Government Act 1999.
- Shall be taken not to include any matters relating to the efficiency and effectiveness of the police force arising out of any inspection of the police force by Her Majesty's Inspectors of Constabulary, or raised with the police authority by the Secretary of State, and how the police authority intends to address such matters nor any local improvement target to which the police authority must have regard under s. 100 of the Local Government and Public Involvement in Health Act 2007.

The Regulations state that, before issuing a police plan, a police authority shall consider:

- Any performance targets established by the police authority, whether in compliance with a direction under s. 38 of the 1996 Act (performance targets) or otherwise, that relate to the plan period.
- Any matters relating to the efficiency and effectiveness of the police force arising out of any inspection of the police force by Her Majesty's Inspectors of Constabulary, or raised with the police authority by the Secretary of State.
- Any direction given to the police authority by the Secretary of State under s. 40(4)(d) of the 1996 Act (power to give directions in relation to police force) or any information given to the police authority of the grounds on which such a direction might be given.
- The strategies for the plan period formulated by the relevant responsible authorities under s. 6 (formulation and implementation of crime and disorder reduction strategies) of the Crime and Disorder Act 1998.
- Any local improvement target to which the police authority must have regard under s. 108 (duty to have regard to local improvement targets) of the 2007 Act.

The Regulations also state that in addition to the matters set out in s. 6ZB(1) (contents of policing plans) of the 1996 Act the policing plan of a police authority shall set out:

- Any strategic priorities determined by the Secretary of State under s. 37A (strategic priorities for police authorities) of the 1996 Act that relate to the plan period.
- Any performance targets established by the police authority, whether in compliance with a direction under s. 38 of the 1996 Act or otherwise, that relate to the plan period and how it is proposed to meet those targets.
- A statement of the financial resources the police authority expects to be available for the plan period and the proposed allocation of those resources.
- Any planned increases in efficiency and productivity of the police force during the plan period and how it is proposed such increases will be achieved.
- Any matters relating to the efficiency and effectiveness of the police force arising out of any inspection of the police force by Her Majesty's Inspectors of Constabulary, or raised with the police authority by the Secretary of State, and how the police authority intends to address such matters.
- Any direction given by the Secretary of State under s. 40 of the 1996 Act or any information given to the police authority of the grounds on which such a direction might be given and how the police authority intends to address such matters.
- The strategies formulated by the relevant responsible authorities under s. 6 of the 1998 Act for the plan period and how the police authority intends to implement those strategies.
- Any planned improvements in the ability of the police force to deliver protective services during the plan period and how it is proposed such improvements will be achieved.
- Details of the arrangements required to be made by the police authority in the exercise of functions conferred on it under s. 6ZA of the 1996 Act (power to confer particular functions on police authorities) for co-operation between the police force and other police forces.
- Details of any co-operation between the police force and other police forces that is taking place at the time the plan is issued, and is proposed for the plan period.
- Any local improvement target to which the police authority must have regard under s. 108 of the 2007 Act.

In respect of the publication of policing plans, the Regulations state that:

- A police authority shall arrange for every policing plan issued by it to be published in such manner as appears to it to be appropriate by 30 June of the financial year before the beginning of which it was issued, and shall send a copy of the plan to the Secretary of State.

4.1.3.3 Publication of Local Policing Summaries

Under s. 8A of the Police Act 1996, as soon as possible after the end of each financial year, every police authority shall issue a report for members of the public in the authority's area on matters relating to the policing of that area for the year.

This report (the 'local policing summary') must contain those matters specified by the Secretary of State and the police authority must arrange for every local policing summary issued by it to be published in such manner as appears to it to be appropriate, and for a copy of every such summary to be sent (by whatever means appear to the authority to be appropriate) to each household.

The Police Act 1996 (Local Policing Summaries) Order 2006 (SI 2006/122) specifies the matters which must be included in local policing summaries. These are:

- A statement of the police authority's priorities for the year.
- An assessment of the extent to which the police force met the priorities set for the previous year.
- An assessment of the extent to which the police force has met the strategic policing priorities (if any) set by the Secretary of State.

Police authorities must have regard to any guidance issued by the Secretary of State on the form and content of the local policing summary. Three documents have been produced by the Home Office containing such guidance.

4.1.3.4 Inter-Agency Operation

The National Policing Plan places strong emphasis on the establishment and maintenance of partnerships with local and national agencies and fits within a new framework being introduced by the government for the improved effectiveness and 'professionalisation' of the police.

4.1.3.5 Measuring Performance and Promoting Good Practice

Central to the latest changes in the way in which policing is managed are the features of performance measurement and the promotion of good practice across the service. These features are apparent in some earlier legislation, such as the Police (Efficiency) Regulations 1999 (SI 1999/732) (**see para. 4.1.10**) and the Best Value requirements under the Local Government Act 1999 (**see para. 4.1.5**). In furthering the broader ends of performance enhancement for policing generally, the Police Reform Act 2002 and the National Policing Plan build upon existing schemes.

4.1.3.6 Increased Accountability

In addition to the measures arising out of s. 1, the Police Reform Act 2002 also contains powers and procedures aimed at increasing the accountability, efficiency and effectiveness of the police service. But the aspects that gave rise to some of the lengthiest and fiercest exchanges were those that follow below as they were viewed by some as an erosion (if not wholesale abandonment) of the operational independence of chief officers. The legislation contains a number of procedural safeguards designed to preserve the tripartite structure of policing (chief officers, police authorities and the Home Office) that has been at the heart of policing in England and Wales for over 50 years.

4.1.3.7 HMIC Inspections

The Police Reform Act 2002 contains powers for the Secretary of State to order inspections of police forces (and *parts* of police forces), along with inspections of other policing organisations such as the Serious Organised Crime Agency. By amending the Police Act 1996, the 2002 Act empowers the Secretary of State to give directions to a police authority where an inspection report by Her Majesty's Inspector of Constabulary (HMIC) using the PPAF described above, is of the opinion that all or part of the force inspected is not efficient or effective, or will cease to be efficient or effective unless remedial measures are taken (see s. 40). In the event of any such report being received from the HMIC, the Secretary of State may direct the police authority to take 'remedial measures'. Any direction to this effect must be made by the Secretary of State in a report laid before Parliament and *only* after the police authority and the chief officer have been given sufficient information about the Secretary of State's grounds and an opportunity to make representations about them. In addition, the police authority must have been given the opportunity to make proposals for any remedial measures that would make any direction by the Secretary of State unnecessary. The Secretary of State must then consider all representations and proposals before he/she has the power to direct any remedial measure to be taken. If the Secretary of State considers that remedial measures are needed, he/she can direct the police authority to submit an action plan, drafted by the chief officer within a matter of weeks. The Secretary of State may make regulations setting out the specific procedure to be followed in these cases. These provisions are extended to include bodies such as the Serious Organised Crime Agency (see the Police Reform Act 2002, sch. 1).

In essence, the statutory procedure gives the chief officer and the relevant police authority notice of those areas highlighted for improvement and the opportunity to put things right before the Home Secretary can intervene.

Sections 28 to 32 of the Police and Justice Act 2006 now place a much greater emphasis on inspection across the criminal justice sector and require HMIC to co-operate with a list of bodies including the HM Inspectors of Prisons, the CPS, Probation, and Court Administration as well as Inspectorates focusing on health, children and education.

4.1.4 Crime and Disorder Strategies

Sections 5 and 6 of the Crime and Disorder Act 1998 placed a statutory responsibility on police services and local authorities to formulate and implement crime and disorder strategies for their respective areas. These sections sought to build upon the work that had already been done in the area of crime prevention before the 1998 Act was passed and follow some of the proposals put forward in the report commissioned by the Home Office Standing Conference on Crime Prevention, *Safer Communities: The Local Delivery of Crime Prevention through the Partnership Approach 1991* (the Morgan Report). Crime and Disorder Reduction Partnerships were set up under the Crime and Disorder Act 1998 and involved chief officers of police and local authorities formulating and implementing strategies to reduce crime and disorder in their areas. The statutory framework placed a duty on the police to co-operate with a number of other agencies such as the probation service.

A further duty to act in co-operation with other agencies was imposed by the Crime and Disorder Act 1998. Those bodies and agencies, which included:

- schools and educational institutions,
- the Crown Prosecution Service,
- youth services, and
- local stakeholder groups,

were similarly under an obligation to co-operate with the responsible authorities in exercising these functions. The list of those people and bodies who are either required to co-operate with, or who must be invited to participate with the responsible authorities as set out in s. 5(1) of the Act continues to grow, with recent additions to the former being NHS Trusts and parish councils and the latter including some non-Home Office police forces, Transport for London and other public transport operators.

Section 97 of the Police Reform Act 2002 extends these provisions in several ways. It includes police and fire authorities in the list of responsible authorities required to formulate and implement crime and disorder reduction strategies and adds the appropriate health organisations (Primary Care Trusts in England and the relevant health authority in Wales) to the list. The amended legislation also requires the formulation and implementation of strategies to combat substance misuse, placing the delivery of the National Drugs Strategy on a statutory footing and involving Drug Action Teams (DATs) in the case of England and Drug and Alcohol Action Teams (DAATs) in Wales.

As this legislation is concerned with matters affecting local government, various provisions are made to reflect the different constitutional positions and processes between England and Wales, with the Welsh Assembly being given relevant powers as appropriate.

Before formulating their strategies, the responsible authorities must have carried out a review of the levels and patterns of crime and disorder, taking into account the knowledge and experience of people in the area (s. 6(2)). They must then have published a report of that review and taken account of the views of any bodies and individuals prescribed by the Secretary of State on its contents.

Under s. 6(4) of the 1998 Act the strategy must contain at least:

- objectives to be pursued,
- long-term performance targets, and
- short-term performance targets.

The strategy must be published within the relevant area and must be kept under review with a view to monitoring its effectiveness, making any changes that appear necessary or expedient. The priorities for community safety, provided by the National Community Safety Plan (**see para. 4.1.3.1**) must also be considered by the Partnerships.

Section 19 of the Police and Justice Act 2006 extends the remit of local authorities to scrutinise the functioning of the local Crime and Disorder Reduction Partnership. It also introduces the 'community call for action' mechanism which allows members of the public who are dissatisfied with service provision to ask their local councillor to call for action from the local authority and its partners. Issues that cannot be resolved through normal mechanisms can be referred to Overview and Scrutiny Committees for consideration. At the moment, the community call for action proposals relate only to crime and disorder, but the powers are likely to become more wide reaching following the publication of the local government White Paper *Strong and Prosperous Communities*.

4.1.5 Best Value

Section 3 of the Local Government Act 1999 states:

> (1) A best value authority must make arrangements to secure continuous improvement in the way in which its functions are exercised, having regard to a combination of economy, efficiency and effectiveness.

Section 4 of the Police and Justice Act 2006 removes the requirement for police authorities as best value authorities to conduct best value reviews and removes the requirement for auditors to audit best value performance plans. Subsection (1)(d) provides that a police authority is not a best value authority for the purpose of certain provisions in part 1 of the 1999 Act. Those provisions are:

- section 5, under which a best value authority must conduct best value reviews of its functions;
- section 6, under which a best value authority must prepare a best value performance plan for each financial year;
- sections 7 to 9, which require best value performance plans to be audited and place a duty on the best value authority to publish the auditor's report; and
- sections 13(5) and 15(2)(a) and (b), which will no longer be relevant once a police authority does not have to prepare a best value performance plan.

Subsection (2) clarifies that references in other Acts to best value authorities will, if the context allows, continue to include police authorities.

The high-level duty set out in s. 3 of the Local Government Act 1999 will continue to apply to police authorities as best value authorities. Consequently, a police authority must continue to make arrangements to secure continuous improvement in the way in which its functions are exercised, having regard to a combination of economy, efficiency and effectiveness. Section 4 of the Local Government Act 1999 also continues to apply in respect of police authorities. Under that section the Secretary of State may, through an order, set out statutory performance indicators against which a best value authority's performance can be measured.

The Home Secretary will, by order, require police authorities to publish an abridged best value performance plan for the financial years ending 31 March 2008 and 31 March 2009. The abridged plan must set out:

- the performance indicators set in relation to the police authority's functions by the Home Secretary under s. 4(1)(a) of the Local Government Act 1999; and
- a summary of its assessment of its performance in the previous financial year against those indicators.

4.1.6 The Police Federation and Trade Union Membership

Part III of the Police Act 1996 makes provision for the establishment and maintenance of police representative institutions.

Section 59 provides for the continued existence of the Police Federation and specifies that it may represent a police officer in any proceedings brought under Regulations made under s. 50(3) (e.g. efficiency and conduct; see below) or an appeal from such proceedings.

The Secretary of State may make Regulations in relation to matters concerning the Federation (s. 60(1)), e.g. the Police Federation Regulations 1969 (SI 1969/1787), as amended.

Provision is made under s. 61 for a Police Negotiating Board to represent the interests of police authorities and members in relation to:

- hours of duty
- leave
- pay and allowances
- pensions
- clothing, equipment and accoutrements.

Section 64 of the Police Act 1996 states:

> (1) Subject to the following provisions of this section, a member of a police force shall not be a member of any trade union, or of any association having for its objects, or one of its objects, to control or influence the pay, pensions or conditions of service of any police force.

KEYNOTE

Where a person was a member of a trade union before becoming a member of a police service, he/she may, with the consent of the chief officer of police, continue to be a member of that union during the time of his/her service (s. 64(2)).

Section 64 also states:

> (5) Nothing in this section applies to membership of the Police Federations, or of any body recognised by the Secretary of State for the purposes of this section as representing members of police forces who are not members of those Federations.

4.1.7 Employment Status and Conditions of Police Officers

Police officers are not 'employees' for most purposes as they are not employed under contracts as such; they are public office holders (see *Fisher* v *Oldham Corporation* [1930] 2 KB 364; see also *Sheikh* v *Chief Constable of Greater Manchester Police* (1989) ICR 373). For this reason a significant number of the employment rights given to workers in other occupations do not apply to police officers. They cannot bring claims for wrongful dismissal because these are *contractual* claims. Similarly, they are prevented by statute from claiming unfair dismissal and some other protection that is given to ordinary employees by the Employment Rights Act 1996. However, for some purposes (e.g. sex and race discrimination) chief officers are treated *as if they are employers* of their officers. This has caused some technical difficulties in practice (**see chapter 4.13**). These categories have become blurred even further by recent events. So, for instance, some non-Home Office police officers *do have* a contract for service with their 'employer' (e.g. British Transport Police—see *Spence* v *British Railways Board* [2001] ICR 232). Similarly, the NPIA can have 'employed constable' by para. 17 of sch. 1 to the Police and Justice Act 2006. In addition, some of the Police Reform Act 2002 rules allow individuals who are employees in the strict sense to potentially be placed outside the full statutory protection for employees (by the Employment Rights Act 1996, s. 200) because they have the powers and privileges of constables. And for some purposes, statutes refer to the European concept of 'workers' which, being a wider concept than 'employees', often *does* apply to the police. An example of this expression can be found in the Working Time Regulations 1998 (SI 1998/1833). These Regulations are a good example of an important area in which police officers are treated as though they were employees working under a contract of employment. One effect of this is that (for highly technical reasons) officers can rely on the annual leave year that is agreed from time to time by the force—something which has a knock-on effect on issues such as pension entitlements (see *Hyman* v *Chief Constable of South Wales Police* (2003) 8 April, unreported).

'Workers'—which include a number of healthcare and emergency personnel—are generally protected under the Public Interest Disclosure Act 1998 and this is a further area of recent importance to police officers (see below).

The real practical importance of all this, however, lies in the fact that the police have had to be given their own statutory framework for dealing with complaints, conduct and efficiency—the subject of the next part of this chapter.

In April 1999 a number of very significant changes were made to the procedures governing the performance and conduct of, and complaints against, police officers. These changes have been further extended by amendments to the general employment laws (e.g. those relating to discrimination: **see chapter 4.13**) and changes to the police conduct and complaints framework.

The Police Regulations 2003 cover a number of areas that are central to the performance of police duties and good governance, as well as placing restrictions on the private lives of officers (**see para. 4.1.15.1**), including business interests (**see para. 4.1.15.2**).

4.1.7.1 Part-time Appointments

Regulation 5 of the Police Regulations 2003 allows a chief constable, after consultation with local representatives of the staff associations, to appoint an officer to perform part-time service in any rank. Part-time officers may give notice in writing of their intention to be re-appointed as a full-time member and will be appointed within one month of the date on which the notice is received by the police authority, where the authority has a suitable vacancy, or when three months have elapsed since the day the notice was received, or from an earlier date if reasonably practicable.

4.1.7.2 Personal Records

The Police Regulations 2003 place a requirement on the chief constable to keep a personal record of each member of their force. Regulation 15(2) specifies that the record must contain:

- a personal description of the member;
- particulars of the member's place and date of birth;
- particulars of their marriage or civil partnership (if any) and children (if any);
- if applicable a record of their service in any branch of the military or civil service;
- a record of service (if any) in any other police force and of transfers (if any) from one police force to another;
- a record of whether the officer passed or failed any qualifying examination at which they were a candidate;
- a record of their service in the police force and the date on which they ceased to be a member of the police force with the reason thereof.

The record must also include particulars of all promotions, postings, removals, injuries received, periods of illness, commendations, rewards, sanctions other than cautions imposed under reg. 31 of the Police (Conduct) Regulations 1999 or under reg.17 of the Police (Efficiency) Regulations 1999.

4.1.7.3 Periods of Duty and Travelling Time

Regulation 22 allows the Home Secretary to determine the normal periods of duty of a member of a police force. It also gives him/her the authority to specify the periods allowed for refreshment, the variable shift arrangements which may be brought into operation by a force, the manner and timing of the publication of duty rosters and the matters to be contained therein.

The circumstances in which 'travelling time' may be treated as duty can also be determined by the Home Secretary under reg. 22. In this context 'travelling time' means time spent by a member of a police force in travelling to and from their home where they are required to perform their normal daily period of duty in more than one tour of duty between two tours or where they are recalled to duty between two tours of duty, in consequence of their recall. The Home Secretary may confer on the chief officer discretion to fix a limit on the travelling time which is to be treated as duty and allow the police authority discretion to fix a limit on the amount of the expenses which may be reimbursed in respect of travelling time.

4.1.7.4 Overtime, Public Holidays and Rest Days

Regulation 25 permits the Home Secretary to determine the circumstances and manner in which a member of a police force shall be compensated in respect of overtime incurred when an officer begins work earlier than their rostered time without 'due notice' and has completed their normal daily period of duty, or remains on duty after their tour of duty ends, or is recalled between two tours of duty. For the purposes of this regulation, 'due notice' means notice given at least eight hours before the revised starting time of the rostered tour of duty in question. 'Recall' does not include a warning to be in readiness for duty if required.

The Home Secretary can confer on the chief officer discretion to fix the day on which a period commences for the purposes of the determination, to fix the period within which time off in compensation for overtime is to be granted, and the discretion to allow time in addition to that specified in the determination to be taken into account in computing any period of overtime.

Likewise, reg. 26 allows the Home Secretary to determine the circumstances and manner in which a member of a police force shall be granted leave or otherwise compensated in respect of time spent on duty on public holidays or rostered rest days.

4.1.8 The Public Interest Disclosure Act 1998 and 'Whistle Blowing'

The Public Interest Disclosure Act 1998 was introduced to help create an atmosphere where workers both feel and *are* able to report certain cases of wrongdoing at work, primarily to their employers, but to outside bodies or individuals if appropriate. Often described as 'whistle blowing', the reporting of criminal, unlawful, dangerous or damaging practices and situations has been protected by the 1998 Act for most workers for several years—provided the Act's conditions are complied with. The framework that the legislation creates distinguishes between internal disclosures to the relevant employer and disclosures made to external bodies or individuals including the police—with the emphasis firmly on *internal* disclosure. It would clearly not be appropriate for all occasions where an employee believes something is amiss at work for that to be reported to an outside body, for instance by selling the story to the press or passing the information straight to their MP. The Act therefore differentiates between different types of situation which may need to be reported. These distinctions are less important where the employer *is* the police but it is still necessary to consider the relevant statutory procedure. Many employers have published detailed reporting procedures for making disclosure. In some areas of employment, the Secretary of State has made regulations prescribing those people and bodies to whom some disclosures can be made where appropriate. Examples are the Independent Police Complaints Commission (IPCC) (**see para. 4.1.12.1**), the Inland Revenue, the Charity Commissioners and the Health and Safety Executive (see the Public Interest Disclosure (Prescribed Persons) Order 1999 (SI 1999/1549).

The Act works by inserting various provisions into the Employment Rights Act 1996 (ERA). This has resulted in a fairly complex piece of legislation and reference should be made to the full statutory text, along with any relevant regulations and guidance.

4.1.8.1 Protected Disclosures

The Act refers to 'protected disclosures'. These are generally disclosures made in accordance with the Act of information which, in the reasonable belief of the maker, tends to show *one or more* of the following:

- a criminal offence has been committed, is being committed or is likely to be committed;
- a person has failed, is failing or is likely to fail to comply with any legal obligation to which he is subject;
- a miscarriage of justice has occurred, is occurring or is likely to occur;
- the health or safety of any individual has been, is being or is likely to be endangered;
- the environment has been, is being or is likely to be damaged;
- information tending to show any matter falling within any one of the preceding paragraphs has been, is being or is likely to be deliberately concealed.

Clearly, although many of these things would be unusual in most employment contexts, the likelihood of some of the issues covered above arising is possibly greater in a policing or criminal justice environment than elsewhere.

It is immaterial that the relevant failure reported occurs or would occur outside the United Kingdom (ERA, s. 43B(2)). As discussed above, the disclosure should generally be made to the employer or other responsible or prescribed person. However, if:

- the employee reasonably believes that he/she will be subjected to a detriment by the employer if the disclosure is made, or
- there is no relevant or prescribed person and the employee reasonably believes that it is likely that evidence relating to the failure will be concealed or destroyed if a disclosure is made, or
- the employee has previously made a disclosure of substantially the same information to the employer or prescribed person

then he/she may make a protected disclosure to someone else. However, even if the above conditions are met, the employee must make any disclosure in good faith, must not be acting for personal gain and must reasonably believe that the information (and any allegation contained in it) is substantially true—and it must be reasonable in all the circumstances of the case for him/her to make the disclosure (see generally ERA, s. 43G). In determining whether it was reasonable to make the disclosure in all the circumstances here, regard will be had in particular to the identity of the person receiving it, the seriousness of the reported failure, any breach of confidentiality by the employee and the circumstances of any earlier disclosure.

If the relevant failure is of an exceptionally serious nature and the employee reasonably believes that the information (and any allegation contained in it) is substantially true, he/she may make a protected disclosure, in good faith and not for personal gain, to an external person provided it is reasonable in all the circumstances to do so (see ERA, s. 43H). Again, all the circumstances, and particularly the identity of the external party, will be relevant in determining whether it was reasonable to make the disclosure. It is important to note that, if the making of the disclosure would itself amount to an offence, the disclosure will not be protected. An example of where this might be the case is under the Regulation of Investigatory Powers Act 2000, s. 19—disclosing information as to the existence or non-existence of an interception warrant—**see para. 4.13.4**.

Initially the Public Interest Disclosure Act did not apply to the police but it is the government's clear intention to remove the statutory exception (see the Police Reform Act 2002, s. 37) and to bring the police into the 'whistle blowing' framework.

4.1.8.2 Practical Implications

As well as making the workplace safer and more open to scrutiny, the 1998 Act creates a number of key rights for individuals. For instance, it makes the dismissal of an employee automatically unfair if the reason (or principal reason if there is more than one) for the dismissal is that the employee made a protected disclosure (see ERA, s. 103A). While the Code of Conduct under the Police (Conduct) Regulations 2004 (as to which **see para. 4.1.11.4**) has always placed officers under a duty to report wrongdoing by fellow officers, there has not been any form of statutory protection for those who do so. In addition to being protected from dismissal, an employee also has the right under the Act not to be subjected to any other detriment by his/her employer (e.g. being disciplined, denied perks or promotion) on the grounds that he/she has made a protected disclosure (ERA, s. 47B). Employees can bring a complaint to the employment tribunal in respect of these matters and the usual statutory ceiling on the amount of the compensatory award that the tribunal can make is removed.

4.1.9 The Conduct, Complaints and Efficiency Framework

Under the Police Reform Act 2002, the Secretary of State may issue guidance to police authorities, chief officers and the members of their police services in respect of the discharge of their functions in matters of performance, conduct and complaints. The Home Office has issued police services with such guidance and its contents are admissible in any proceedings under the various Regulations. More importantly, the guidance specifies that its provisions must be followed unless there is good reasons for departing from them. However, the guidance does not form part of the Regulations and, if it is incompatible with the Regulations in any respect, the Regulations will prevail.

The sources of the changes are to be found mainly within the Police Act 1996 and the Police Reform Act 2002. What follows is an attempt to steer a path through many of those pieces of legislation. To this end, this part of the chapter is set out in four sections:

- unsatisfactory performance,
- complaints and conduct matters,
- the complaints framework, and
- appeals.

Note that there is a general duty for all police officers to obey lawful orders (see reg. 20 of the Police Regulations 2003 (SI 2003/527)).

4.1.10 Unsatisfactory Performance

The Regulations give police managers an objective structure by which to evaluate and address any suspected failures to meet the required standard of performance by their police staff.

4.1.10.1 Who?

These procedures are generally set out in the Police (Efficiency) Regulations 1999 (SI 1999/732), as amended. They do not apply to:

- officers above the rank of chief superintendent,
- probationers,
- cadets, and
- non-warranted (civilian) staff,

each of whom has their own specific procedures. For the provisions relating to probationary constables and their dismissal, see regs 12 and 13 of the Police Regulations 2003 (SI 2003/527). For special constables, see s. 27(2) of the Police Act 1996 and the Special Constables Regulations 1965 (SI 1965/536), as amended. Section 35 of the Police Reform Act 2002 allows the Secretary of State to make regulations in relation to the conduct and discipline of special constables (as to which **see para. 4.1.2**). For cadets, see s. 28(2) of the Police Act 1996 and the Police Cadets Regulations 1979 (SI 1979/1727), as amended.

Part 3 of the Police Reform Act 2002 has introduced measures for the removal, suspension, resignation and disciplining of chief officers. While legislation has for many years provided some extensive measures to deal with officers up to and including the rank of chief superintendent, the range of options open to police authorities and/or the Secretary of State has been very limited in relation to chief officers whose conduct or performance is in question. Former legislation meant that chief officers could be required to retire in the interests of effectiveness and efficiency, but there are two main reasons why this has not been entirely satisfactory. First is the fact that this is a very restricted option which will not always be appropriate under the circumstances (especially given the cost), and second is the fact that chief officers are being appointed at a younger age than in the past.

In essence, what the framework set up by the Police Reform Act 2002 does is to provide a system whereby officers of ACPO rank can be suspended or removed by their police authority, either of the authority's own volition or with the intervention of the Secretary of State. This highly controversial change to the constitutional position of chief officers is achieved by amending the Police Act 1996 and making specific regulations thereunder.

4.1.10.2 Why?

Although there are procedures for dealing with allegations of *misconduct* against police officers (**see para. 4.1.11**), there had previously been a lack of any formal structure by which police managers could address issues of perceived poor *performance*. The distinction here between conduct and performance is an important one. The complaints system is generally inadequate and often inappropriate in helping police managers tackle issues of performance, and it was clear for some time that another, separate mechanism, similar to those used by many other employers, was needed.

Even under the Code of Conduct (**see para. 4.1.11**) the focus is still on enforcement and punishment and the process follows more of a straight, linear path. In matters of perceived poor performance, however, the process is a cycle. The emphasis needs to be on the early identification of problems followed by discussion and agreement on action and an opportunity to improve. There should then be a monitoring period followed by a review of performance and further agreement and action as appropriate. This notion of providing the underperforming officer with opportunities to improve is a key feature of this process and can be found right up until after any formal inefficiency hearing has started. In other words, from the point of view of the officer, it is rarely 'too late' to show a sufficient improvement. Clearly there needs to be an end to the process somewhere and that final stage may well involve sanctions, but the general tenor of the process is ultimately developmental.

4.1.10.3 What?

Unlike several of the other Regulations covered in this chapter, the Police (Efficiency) Regulations 1999 have no equivalent predecessor. Made under s. 50 of the Police Act 1996, the Regulations establish procedures for the management—and ultimately the punishment—of officers whose performance is felt to be unsatisfactory. In the majority of cases, general managerial discretion and appropriate words of guidance will probably suffice. In other cases, however, there may be a need to invoke the formal procedures set out below.

4.1.10.4 The Police (Efficiency) Regulations 1999

Regulation 4 states:

(1) Where the reporting officer for a member of a police force is himself a member of that police force and is of the opinion that the performance or the attendance or both of that member is or are unsatisfactory, he may require the member concerned to attend an interview (in these Regulations referred to as a first interview) to discuss the performance or attendance (or both) of the member concerned.

(2) Where the reporting officer for a member of a police force is a person employed under section 15 of the 1996 Act and is of the opinion that the attendance of that member is unsatisfactory, he may require the member concerned to attend an interview (in these Regulations referred to as a first interview) to discuss the attendance of the member concerned.

(3) Where the reporting officer for a member of a police force is a person employed under section 15 of the 1996 Act, any other member of the force who has supervisory responsibility for that first member may, if he is of the opinion that the performance of that member is unsatisfactory, require him to attend an interview (in these Regulations referred to as a first interview) to discuss his performance, and in such a case references in these Regulations to a reporting officer shall be taken to include references to the member with that supervisory responsibility.

KEYNOTE

Throughout the Regulations, the officer whose performance is in question is referred to as the 'member concerned', i.e. the member of a police force in respect of whom proceedings are, or are proposed, to be, taken (reg. 3(1)). Although not defined in the Regulations or the parent Act, 'member of a police force' refers to a sworn police constable. Therefore, even though the reporting officer or countersigning officer (see below) may be a civilian member of staff, the regulations themselves only apply to the performance and attendance of a sworn police officer. This expression was formerly used in the conduct and complaints framework but has, in that context, been replaced (**see para. 4.1.11**). The efficiency framework applies to members of the Serious Organised Crime Agency.

The 'reporting officer' will be the person having immediate supervisory responsibility for the 'member concerned' (reg. 3(1)). In most instances involving constables, the 'reporting officer' will therefore be their sergeant. Where the officer's immediate supervisor is a civilian member of staff (appointed under s. 15 of the Police Act 1996), this person will be the reporting officer for these purposes. However, there is a distinction throughout the newly amended regulations as to when civilian reporting officers and countersigning officers (see below) may act. While reporting officers who are also sworn police officers (e.g. sergeants and inspectors) may implement all the various stages of the procedures in the regulations, *civilian* supervisors and managers may only do so where the relevant police officer's *attendance* (as opposed to performance) is at issue (see reg. 4(2) above).

The Regulations only require that the reporting officer be *of the opinion* that the performance of the member concerned is unsatisfactory. However, single instances of poor performance or attendance would not generally be enough to invoke these Regulations and, as discussed above, the instigation of formal proceedings would not normally happen before day-to-day supervisory discretion had been applied. Although the Regulations do not say so, it would seem fair that, in assessing the performance or attendance of the member concerned, nothing done before April 1999 is taken into account.

The source of the reporting officer's 'opinion' may be from internal observations and reports but it may also arise from members of the public. Although the procedures for performance and attendance improvement and the investigation of complaints (**see para. 4.1.12**) are quite separate, there may be cases where there is an overlap.

4.1.10.5 Arranging First Interview

Regulation 5 states:

(1) If the reporting officer decides to require a member of a police force to attend a first interview, he shall—
  (a) send a notice in writing to the member concerned—
    (i) requiring him to attend, at a specified time and place, an interview with the reporting officer or, if the member concerned so requests, the countersigning officer;
    (ii) stating the reasons why his performance or attendance is considered unsatisfactory;
    (iii) informing him that he may seek advice from a representative of his staff association and be accompanied at the interview by a member of a police force selected by him; and
  (b) send a copy of the notice to the countersigning officer,

(2) A member of a police force who receives a notice pursuant to paragraph (1) may, not later than 7 days (or such longer period as the reporting officer may permit when sending the notice under paragraph (1)(a)) after the date on which the notice was received by him, request by notice in writing that the interview be conducted by the countersigning officer; and if the member concerned so requests the interview shall be conducted by the countersigning officer.

KEYNOTE

The 'countersigning officer' will be the person having supervisory responsibility for the reporting officer (as to which, see reg. 4 above). Like the reporting officer, this can be a sworn police officer (in which case he/she must be senior in rank to the reporting officer) or a civilian member of staff. There is no requirement for the countersigning officer to have any direct responsibility for the member concerned.

It is important to note that any superintendent/chief superintendent or Assistant Chief Constable/ Commander who attends or *is otherwise involved in* the first interview is barred from appearing on the panel of any later inefficiency hearing involving the member concerned (see below).

The 'first interview' will be with the reporting officer unless the member concerned asks for it to be with the countersigning officer. There is, however, a general time limit on making that request (reg. 5(2)).

Unlike some of the other procedures in this chapter, there does not appear to be any restriction on the timing of the first interview.

The responsibility for sending out the notice containing the details set out at reg. 5(a)(i) to (iii) falls to the reporting officer. The notice, which must be copied to the countersigning officer, must advise the member concerned that he/she may seek advice from the relevant staff association representative *and* that he/she may select another officer, from any police service, to accompany him/her to the interview. This 'friend' is able to advise and assist the member concerned, to speak on the officer's behalf and to produce witnesses and exhibits where appropriate. The notice must also set out the *reasons* why the member's performance is considered to be unsatisfactory.

4.1.10.6 Procedure at First Interview

Regulation 6 states:

(1) The following provisions of this regulation apply to the procedure to be followed at the first interview.

(2) The interviewing officer shall—

(a) explain to the member concerned the reasons why the reporting officer is of the opinion that the performance or attendance of that member is unsatisfactory; and

(b) provide the member concerned, or the member of a police force who has accompanied him to the interview, or both of them, with an opportunity to make representations in response.

(3) If, after considering any representations made in accordance with paragraph (2) (b), the interviewing officer is satisfied that the performance or attendance of the member concerned has been unsatisfactory, he shall—

(a) inform the member concerned in what respect his performance or attendance is considered unsatisfactory;

(b) warn the member concerned of any specific action which he is required to take to achieve an improvement in his performance or attendance; and

(c) warn the member concerned that, if a sufficient improvement is not made within such reasonable period as the interviewing officer shall specify, he may be required to attend a second interview in accordance with regulation 9.

(4) The interviewing officer may, if he considers it appropriate, recommend that the member concerned seek assistance in relation to any matter affecting his health or welfare.

(5) The interviewing officer may adjourn the interview to a specified later time or date if it appears to him necessary or expedient to do so.

KEYNOTE

The 'interviewing officer' is the person conducting the first interview (reg. 3(1)) and could be either the reporting officer or the countersigning officer (see earlier Keynotes).

Having explained the reasons why the member's performance or attendance is unsatisfactory, the interviewing officer must provide the member, his/her 'friend' *or both*, with an opportunity to make representations in response. A reasonable amount of time must be allowed for the making of such representations.

Those representations must be 'considered' by the interviewing officer, not simply acknowledged or dismissed. The interviewing officer, having so considered the representations made, must carry out the actions set out in reg. 6(3)(a) to (c), provided he/she is 'satisfied' that the member's performance or attendance has been unsatisfactory.

The expression 'warn' at reg. 6(3)(b) seems odd in this context, particularly when the word 'inform' is used at the next stage (see below), but the 'warning' is referred to later in reg. 8. Whatever the terminology, the interviewing officer must tell the member concerned what he/she must do to achieve an improvement in his/her performance or attendance.

Under reg. 6(3)(c) the interviewing officer must specify a 'reasonable period' during which this improvement is to take place. This would appear to be normally no less than three, and probably no more than six months.

Regulation 6 says nothing about what must be done if the interviewing officer is *not* satisfied that the member's performance or attendance was unsatisfactory. Presumably the issue comes to a halt at this stage, although the reporting requirements under reg. 7 (see below) appear to apply irrespective of the outcome of the first interview.

4.1.10.7 After First Interview

Regulation 7 states:

(1) The interviewing officer shall, not later than 7 days after the date of the conclusion of the first interview—

(a) cause to be prepared a written record of the substance of the matters discussed at the interview; and

(b) send one copy or, where the member concerned was accompanied at the interview by a member of a police force selected by him, two copies of that record to the member concerned together with a notice in writing informing him that he may submit written comments, or indicate that he has no comment to make, not later than 7 days after the date on which the copy is received by him.

(1A) In a case where a member has been required to attend a first interview to discuss his attendance and he has failed to attend the interview, the interviewing officer shall, if he is satisfied that the attendance of the member has been unsatisfactory, not later than 7 days after the date on which the first interview was due to take place—

(a) cause to be prepared a written notice informing and warning the member of the matters mentioned in sub-paragraphs (a) to (c) of regulation 6(3);

(b) send one copy or, where a member of a police force selected by the member concerned attended the interview, two copies of that notice to the member concerned together with a notice in writing informing him that he may submit written comments, or indicate that he has no comments to make, not later than 7 days after the date on which the copy is received by him.

(2) Subject to paragraph (3), the member concerned shall be entitled to submit written comments in relation to the record of the interview to the interviewing officer not later than 7 days after the date on which the copy is received by him.

(3) The interviewing officer may, on the application of the member concerned, extend the period specified in paragraph (2) if he is satisfied that it is appropriate to do so.

KEYNOTE

The written record need not be a verbatim account of all that took place at the first interview but it must summarise the 'substance' of the matters discussed. If the member concerned does not agree with the record, he/she may raise this in the form of written comments submitted under reg. 7(2).

The requirement under reg. 7(1)(b), to *send* the member and his/her 'friend' a copy of the record, suggests that there is no need for personal service. The seven-day period for responding to the service of the documents begins when the copy of the record *is received by the officer*. This would mean that, if the officer were on annual leave or was otherwise unable to receive the posted documents at the place to which they were sent, he/she may not have 'received' them. If so, the time limit should not begin until he/she physically receives the documents. If the member concerned applies for the time period to be extended, the interviewing officer may do so if it seems appropriate. The interviewing officer cannot extend the time period of his/her own volition.

The interviewing officer *may* make a recommendation that the member concerned seeks help in relation to his/her health or welfare.

Where the first interview has been required in relation to the officer's *attendance*, and he/she fails to turn up, a further written notice must be issued in accordance with reg. 7(1A)(a) and (b) above if the interviewing officer is satisfied that the officer's attendance has been unsatisfactory. In effect, this is like having the first interview in the officer's absence.

Any written comments received by the interviewing officer must be retained with the record of interview (reg. 7(5)). Records of any stage of the unsatisfactory performance procedures will be expunged from an officer's personal record after two years have elapsed since the last action was taken (or the last review/appeal was heard (see below)).

Where a member has been required to attend a second interview this can only relate to the category or categories of behaviour that was or were the subject of the first interview (reg. 7(6)).

4.1.10.8 Other Copies

Regulation 7 goes on to state:

(4) The interviewing officer shall send a copy of the record of the interview, and of any written comments of the member concerned, to—
  (a) the senior manager;
  (b) the personnel officer; and
  (c) (i) if the interview was conducted by the reporting officer, the countersigning officer; or
    (ii) if the interview was conducted by the countersigning officer, the reporting officer.

KEYNOTE

'Senior manager' means the officer who is for the time being the supervisory officer of the countersigning officer (reg. 3(1)(a)). Although the Regulations do not specify that this person must be a police officer, this will generally be a chief inspector or superintendent. Where the member concerned is a superintendent, the 'senior manager' will be his/her supervising officer but again there is no stipulation that this must be a police officer (reg. 3(1)(b)).

'Personnel officer' means a person employed under s. 15 of the Police Act 1996 (a civilian) or a police officer who, in either case, has responsibility for personnel matters relating to members of the force to which the member concerned belongs (reg. 3(1)).

4.1.10.9 Second Interview

Regulation 8 states:

(1) Where the reporting officer is of the opinion that a member of a police force who was warned under regulation 6(3)(b) that he was required to improve his performance or attendance has, at the end of the period specified by the interviewing officer under regulation 6(3)(c), failed to

> make a sufficient improvement in his performance, or, as the case may be, in his attendance, he may refer the case to the countersigning officer.
>
> (2) Where a case is referred under paragraph (1) and the countersigning officer is a member of the police force concerned, he may, after consulting with the personnel officer, require the member concerned to attend a further interview (in these Regulations referred to as a second interview) to discuss the performance or the attendance (or both) of the member concerned.
>
> (3) Where a case is referred under paragraph (1) and the countersigning officer is a person employed under section 15 of the 1996 Act, he may, after consulting with the personnel officer, require the member concerned to attend a further interview (in these Regulations referred to as a second interview) to discuss the attendance of the member concerned.

KEYNOTE

It is not mandatory for the reporting officer to refer the case back to the countersigning officer if the member concerned has failed to make sufficient improvement. Regulation 8(1) says that he/she *may* do so.

All that is necessary in order to make such a referral is that the reporting officer *is of the opinion* that there has been insufficient improvement in the member's performance or attendance. This broadly drafted requirement gives the reporting officer a considerable degree of latitude but again the importance of general supervisory discretion should perhaps be reinforced here. Such a referral can only be made at the end of the specified period.

As with the procedure for first interviews (see earlier Keynote), the power for a civilian manager to require attendance at a second interview is limited to issues arising out of the officer's attendance.

Although the process is started by the reporting officer, the decision to hold a second interview will be made by the countersigning officer. Once again, there is no requirement to hold such an interview and the wording of reg. 8(2) is permissive rather than mandatory. What is mandatory, however, is that, in reaching his/her decision, the countersigning officer consult with the personnel officer (as defined above).

Note that where an officer has been required to attend a first interview in relation to his/her performance, attendance or both, any second interview can *only* relate to the same category (or categories) of behaviour that was the subject of the first interview (reg. 7(6)).

Regulation 9 states:

> If the countersigning officer decides to require a member of a police force to attend a second interview, he shall—
>
> (a) send a notice in writing to the member concerned—
>
> (i) requiring him to attend, at a specified time and place, an interview with the countersigning officer and the personnel officer;
>
> (ii) stating the reasons why his performance or attendance is considered unsatisfactory and that further action will be considered in the light of the interview; and
>
> (iii) informing him that he may seek advice from a representative of his staff association and be accompanied at the interview by a member of a police force selected by him; and
>
> (b) send a copy of the notice to the reporting officer, the senior manager and the personnel officer.

KEYNOTE

Once the decision is reached by the countersigning officer to hold a second interview, the responsibility to comply with the requirements of reg. 9 falls to him/her.

Again the notice must set out the reasons why the member's performance or attendance is considered unsatisfactory and must remind the member of his/her entitlement to consult the relevant staff association and to be accompanied by a 'friend' (police officer).

It is important to note that any superintendent or Assistant Chief Constable/Commander who attends *or is otherwise involved in* the second interview is barred from appearing on the panel of any later inefficiency hearing involving the member concerned (see below).

Regulation 10 states:

(1) The following provisions of this Regulation shall apply to the procedure to be followed at a second interview.
(2) The interview shall be conducted by the countersigning officer and the personnel officer.
(3) The countersigning officer shall—
   (a) explain to the member concerned the reasons why the reporting officer is of the opinion that the member concerned has failed to make a sufficient improvement in his performance or attendance; and
   (b) provide the member concerned, or the member of a police force who has accompanied him to the interview, or both of them, with an opportunity to make representations in response.

KEYNOTE

The personnel officer (as defined above) takes part in the second interview although it is clear from reg. 10(3) that the countersigning officer takes the lead in running the proceedings.

The countersigning officer must explain the grounds for the second interview and must provide the opportunity for the member, his/her 'friend' *or both* to make representations in response.

As with the first interview (see above) there will be an option of 'no further action', in which case any note of the procedure followed will be expunged from the member's personal record after two years have elapsed.

Regulation 10 goes on to state:

(4) If, after considering any representations made under paragraph (3), the countersigning officer is satisfied that the performance or attendance of the member concerned has been unsatisfactory during the period specified by the interviewing officer under regulation 6(3)(c), he shall—
   (a) inform the member concerned in what respect his performance or attendance is considered unsatisfactory;
   (b) warn the member concerned that he is required to improve his performance or attendance in any such respect;
   (c) inform the member concerned of any specific action which he is required to take to achieve such an improvement; and
   (d) warn the member concerned that, if a sufficient improvement is not made within such reasonable period as the countersigning officer shall specify, he may be required to attend an inefficiency hearing at which the officers conducting the hearing will have the power, if appropriate, to require the member concerned to resign from the force or to order reduction in rank.

KEYNOTE

Once again, the representations made under reg. 10(3)(b) must be considered by the countersigning officer (and presumably, though it does not say so, the personnel officer).

The member must be told of any specific action that he/she is required to take to achieve the necessary improvement in performance or attendance. He/she must also be warned at this stage that failure to achieve sufficient improvement by the set date *may* result in a further hearing and that such a hearing would have the power to require the member to resign or to reduce him/her in rank. The warning will also contain a timescale for improvement which, as with the first interview, will normally be not less than three and not more than six months from the time of the interview.

The countersigning officer may adjourn the second interview to a later time or a later date if it appears necessary or expedient to do so (reg. 10(5)).

4.1.10.10 After Second Interview

Regulation 11 states:

(1) The countersigning officer shall, not later than 7 days after the conclusion of the second interview—
   (a) in consultation with the personnel officer, prepare a written record of the substance of the matters discussed during the interview; and
   (b) send one copy or, where the member concerned was accompanied at the interview by a member of a police force selected by him, two copies of that record to the member concerned together with a notice in writing—
      (i) if a warning was given under regulation 10(4), confirming the terms of that warning; and
      (ii) informing him that he may submit written comments, or indicate that he has no such comments, not later than 7 days after the date on which the copy is received by him.

(1A) In a case where a member has been required to attend a second interview to discuss his attendance and he has failed to attend the interview, the countersigning officer shall, if he is satisfied that the attendance of the member has been unsatisfactory during the period specified by the interviewing officer under regulation 6(3)(c), not later than 7 days after the date on which the second interview was due to take place—
   (i) cause to be prepared a written notice informing and warning the member of the matters mentioned in sub-paragraphs (a) to (d) of regulation 10(4);
   (ii) send one copy or, where a member of a police force selected by the member concerned attended the interview, two copies of that notice to the member concerned together with a notice in writing informing him that he may submit written comments, or indicate that he has no comments to make, not later than 7 days after the date on which the copy is received by him.

(2) Subject to paragraph (3), the member concerned shall be entitled to submit written comments in relation to the record of the interview to the countersigning officer not later than 7 days after the date on which it was received by him.

(3) The countersigning officer may, on the application of the member concerned, extend the period specified in paragraph (2) if he is satisfied that it is appropriate to do so.

(4) If the countersigning officer receives any written comments under paragraph (2), he shall ensure that they are retained with the record of the interview.

(5) The countersigning officer shall send a copy of the record of the interview, and of any written comments by the member concerned, to the reporting officer, the personnel officer and the senior manager.

KEYNOTE

The written record must be prepared *in consultation with* the personnel officer. The written record of the interview again appears to be a summary of the substance rather than a verbatim account of what took place. The record must be accompanied by a written notice confirming the 'warning' if one was given under reg. 10(4). As the requirement refers to a singular warning (there are in fact *two* warnings under reg. 10(4)), that warning seems to be the one given in relation to the consequences of failing to improve (i.e. the warning at reg. 10(4)(d)). In practice, such a warning may only be given twice within a period of two years before resulting in a hearing. Once again, as with the first interview, there are requirements relating to the sending of copies to the relevant people concerned, together with the notice of opportunity to submit written comments within seven days. There are also similar requirements in relation to the retention of written responses and the countersigning officer may, on the application of the member concerned, extend the seven-day deadline.

Where the officer's *attendance* is in issue, the process above is, in effect, a repeat performance of the first interview provisions (see reg. 7 above) and the hearing can be determined in his/her absence.

As with the earlier provisions, where a member has been required to attend a second interview in relation to his/her performance, attendance or both, any inefficiency hearing can only relate to the category (or categories) of behaviour that formed the subject of the second interview (reg. 11(6)).

4.1.10.11 Assessment of Performance or Attendance

Regulation 12 states:

(1) Not later than 14 days after the date on which the period specified under regulation 10(4)(d) ends—
 (a) the countersigning officer shall, in consultation with the reporting officer, assess the performance or attendance of the member concerned during that period; and
 (b) the countersigning officer shall inform the member concerned in writing whether the reporting officer and the countersigning officer are of the opinion that there has been a sufficient improvement in performance or attendance during that period.

(2) If the countersigning officer is of the opinion that there has been an insufficient improvement, the member concerned shall also, within the period of 14 days mentioned in paragraph (1), be informed in writing that he may be required to attend, at a time (being not sooner than 21 days, but not later than 56 days, after the date on which the notification under this paragraph is received by him) to be notified separately, a hearing (in these Regulations referred to as an inefficiency hearing) to consider his performance.

(3) The countersigning officer shall refer any case in which the member concerned has been informed in accordance with paragraph (2) to the senior manager, who shall, if he thinks it appropriate to do so, direct that an inefficiency hearing be arranged under regulation 13.

KEYNOTE

The countersigning officer, *in consultation with* the reporting officer must assess the performance or attendance of the member concerned and this must be done no later than 14 days after the period set out in the warning under reg. 10(4)(d). The assessment must relate to the member's performance *during that period*. Following this assessment, the countersigning officer must inform the member in writing whether or not he/she considers that there has been a sufficient improvement in the member's performance or attendance. If there *has* been a sufficient improvement, however, there does not appear to be a specific requirement as to when the member must be so informed. Given the requirement at reg. 12(2)—to inform the member within the 14-day period that he/she may have to attend an inefficiency hearing—it would seem that, if the member has not heard anything from the countersigning officer within 14 days of the assessment period ending, he/she can assume that there must have been sufficient improvement in his/her performance or attendance.

If the countersigning officer feels that there has not been a sufficient improvement, he/she must refer the case to the 'senior manager' (as defined above) who then has the discretion to direct an inefficiency hearing to be held. As with the other stages of the process so far, this element is *discretionary* and there is no compulsion on the senior manager to direct that a hearing be held.

4.1.10.12 Inefficiency Hearing

Regulation 13 states:

(1) The personnel officer shall, not less than 21 days before the date fixed for the hearing, send a notice in writing to the member concerned—
   (a) requiring him to attend an inefficiency hearing at a specified time and place;
   (b) stating the reasons why his performance or attendance is considered unsatisfactory;
   (c) informing him that he may be represented at the hearing—
      (i) either by counsel or a solicitor; or
      (ii) by a member of a police force selected by him; and
   (d) warning him of the powers under regulation 17 which are available to the officers conducting the inefficiency hearing in the event that they find that the performance or attendance of the member concerned has been unsatisfactory.

(2) If the member concerned wishes to call any witnesses other than the person representing him at the inefficiency hearing, he shall, not later than seven days before the hearing, give notice in writing to the personnel officer of the names and addresses of those witnesses.

(3) In paragraph (2), the reference to the hearing includes a reference to any hearing under regulation 15; and in relation to such a hearing the period within which notice is to be given under that paragraph shall be such period as the chairman of the hearing may direct when he postpones or, as the case may be, adjourns the hearing.

KEYNOTE

The responsibility for sending out the relevant notice here falls to the personnel officer. Such a notice must be *sent*—though not necessarily received—not less than 21 days before the proposed date of the hearing.

The notice will advise the member that he/she may be represented at the hearing by a solicitor/counsel *or* a police officer. This right emanates from s. 84 of the Police Act 1996 which provides that an officer (of the rank of superintendent or below) may not be dismissed, required to resign or reduced in rank as a result of a hearing unless he/she has been given an opportunity to elect to be legally represented.

The requirement under reg. 13(2) is important as only those witnesses that are mentioned in the member's notification are *entitled* (under reg. 14(7)) to give evidence at the hearing (though the chair may admit them under his/her discretion even if they were not specified above). Notification of which witnesses the member wishes to call must be made to the *personnel officer.*

The inefficiency hearing must be conducted by three officers, one of whom will be:

- in the case of a provincial police force—an Assistant Chief Constable
- in the case of the Metropolitan Police—a Commander in that force
- in the case of the City of London Police—a Commander in that force (reg. 14).

This officer will chair the hearing (reg. 14(1)).

In practice the hearing will comprise any two superintendents/chief superintendents (subject to the rule under reg. 14(2) below) plus the chair.

Where the member concerned is a Metropolitan Police officer, the superintendents/ chief superintendents will be Metropolitan Police officers (reg. 14(3)(b)).

Where the member concerned is a superintendent/chief superintendent, the hearing will comprise two Assistant Chief Constables from outside the member's own force, together with an Assistant Chief Constable from the member's own force who will chair the hearing.

Where the member concerned is a Metropolitan Police superintendent/chief superintendent, the hearing will be chaired by a Commander from the member's own area with two Commanders from another area/other areas.

Where the member concerned is a City of London Police superintendent/chief superintendent, the hearing will be chaired by a City of London Police Commander or the Assistant Commissioner, with two Assistant Chief Constables or Metropolitan Police Commanders.

In any case, the chair and any of the officers assisting him/her must not have attended or otherwise been involved with the first or second interview held in relation to the member concerned (reg. 14(2)).

Regulation 14 goes on to state:

(4) As soon as the chief officer of police has appointed the chairman, the personnel officer shall arrange for a copy of any document—
  (a) which was available to the interviewing officer in relation to the first interview;
  (b) which was available to the countersigning officer in relation to the second interview; or
  (c) which was prepared or submitted under regulation 11, 12 or 13,

to be made available to the chairman; and a copy of any such document shall be sent to the member concerned.

KEYNOTE

The personnel officer must collate copies of any documents which were available to the interviewing officer and the countersigning officer at the first and second interview respectively and also copies of any document prepared or submitted under regs 11 to 13. The personnel officer must arrange to make these copies available to the chair of the hearing as soon as one has been appointed. These copies must also be sent to the member concerned, though there does not appear to be a specific time limit on this requirement.

Subject to the other provisions in reg. 14, the chair will determine the procedure to be followed at the inefficiency hearing (reg. 14(5)). As such, the chair might decide the 'batting order' for the respective parties and may call witnesses to the proceedings. This apparently wide discretion will, however, also be subject to the general principles of natural justice.

The inefficiency hearing will be held in private but may be in public *if both the chair and the member concerned agree* (reg. 14(6)).

The member concerned must be given the opportunity to make representations in relation to the matters referred to in the notice sent out by the personnel officer under reg. 13 (reg. 14(7)). A further effect of reg. 14(7) is that the member concerned is *entitled* to call any witnesses that he/she named in the notification to the personnel officer under reg. 13(2). There may be good reasons why the member failed to include details of potential witnesses in the reg. 13(2) notification and it would seem that the general discretion given to the chair under reg. 14(5) above would allow for other witnesses not previously named to be called.

Unlike the procedure to be followed at the first and second interview stages, a verbatim record must be made of the proceedings (reg. 14(8)).

4.1.10.13 Postponement and Adjournment

In addition to the general power to adjourn the proceedings under reg. 15(7), the chair may adjourn or postpone the hearing in a number of specified circumstances.

Additional period for assessment

The chair of the hearing may adjourn the proceedings if, having heard the representations from the member concerned, he/she considers it appropriate to allow a further period for assessment. Therefore, even after the hearing has begun, the member concerned may still be given the opportunity to address his/her shortcomings. Any further period under this regulation must not exceed three months. The time and date for the resumed hearing must be fixed by the chair and, within 14 days of the end of that period, the reporting officer and countersigning officer will prepare a report containing an assessment of the member's performance or attendance over that time (reg. 15(3)).

When the hearing resumes, the member concerned will be allowed to make representations on the matters referred to *in that latest report* and may call any of the original witnesses set out in the notification under reg. 13(2).

Regulation 15(6) makes provision for the situation where the chair of the inefficiency hearing is likely to be absent, incapacitated or suspended from duty when the hearing resumes.

Non-attendance

If the member concerned does not attend the inefficiency hearing and gives what the chair considers to be a 'good reason' for that non-attendance, the chair *must* postpone or adjourn the hearing (reg. 15(1)). This requirement does not apply where an attendance notice has been sent to the officer under the Regulations (see earlier). This seems to make sense, given that the whole issue of poor attendance is what will have caused the notices to be sent and the hearing convened in the first place. In such cases, however, the chair does not have to adjourn the hearing even where the officer *does have* good reason for not attending.

If the member concerned informs the chair that he/she will be unable to attend the hearing, it must also be postponed or adjourned. A strict reading of the wording of reg. 15(1) suggests that the requirement for a 'good reason' to be given is confined to cases of *non-attendance* rather than a prospective *inability* to attend. The result of such an interpretation, however, would allow for any number of stalling tactics to be used to avoid the hearing and may hold up what is supposed to be a quicker process for dealing with poor performance.

The hearing may proceed in the absence of the member concerned under reg. 14(9) but that option is 'subject to' the provisions of reg. 15(1) above.

Where any of the requirements under regs 14 or 15 cannot be complied with owing to the absence of the member concerned, the case may be proceeded with as if they had been complied with (reg. 14(10)). Again, this is intended to prevent the procedure from being obstructed or held back by the absence of the member concerned.

Ill health

An officer who is on sick leave may still appear at an inefficiency hearing (see the Police Regulations 2003, reg. 33). Nevertheless, if the state of the officer's health means that he/she is incapacitated to the extent that attendance at the hearing is not possible then, at least in cases where no attendance notice has been sent out, the hearing is likely to be postponed (under reg. 15(1) above).

4.1.10.14 The Finding

Regulation 16 states:

> (1) Subject to paragraph (2), at the conclusion of the inefficiency hearing, the officers conducting the hearing shall reach a decision whether the performance or attendance of the member concerned—
>
> (a) in the period referred to in regulation 10(4)(d); or
>
> (b) where the hearing was adjourned under regulation 15(2), over the whole of the period comprising the period referred to in regulation 10(4)(d) and the further period specified by the chairman under regulation 15(3)(a),
>
> has been satisfactory or not.
>
> (2) The chairman may, at the conclusion of the hearing, defer reaching a decision until a later time or date if it appears necessary or expedient to do so.

(3) The decision of the officers conducting the hearing shall state the finding and, where they have found that the performance or attendance of the member concerned has not been satisfactory, their reasons as well as any sanction which they impose under regulation 17.

(4) The chairman shall record the decision in writing, and shall, not later than three days after the finding is stated under paragraph (3), send a copy of it to—
   (a) the member concerned;
   (b) the senior manager; and
   (c) the personnel officer;

and the copy sent to the member concerned shall be accompanied by a notice in writing informing him of his right to request a review under regulation 19.

KEYNOTE

Unless the chair decides to defer the decision under reg. 16(2), the officers conducting the hearing must reach a conclusion as to whether the member's performance or attendance in the relevant period has been satisfactory or not. That decision—or a decision under reg. 17 below—need not be unanimous and may be based on a simple majority but this will not be indicated in the finding (reg. 16(5)). This appears to give the officers an equal say in the judgment with no special 'casting' vote being held by the chair.

Their decision must state their finding and, if the member's performance or attendance is found not to have been satisfactory, the decision must give reasons. The decision must also state the relevant sanction to be imposed. Although it is not explicit, there may of course be a finding that the member's performance or attendance has been satisfactory in which case there will be no further action and the relevant records will be removed from the member's personal file.

The record of the decision must be sent to the relevant parties no later than three days *after the finding is stated*. The copy sent to the member must also be accompanied by a notice in relation to the member's right to ask for a review under reg. 19.

4.1.10.15 Sanctions

Regulation 17 states:

(1) If the officers conducting the inefficiency hearing make a finding that the performance of the member concerned during the relevant period has been unsatisfactory, they may—
   (a) require the member concerned to resign from the force either one month after the date on which a copy of the decision sent under regulation 16(4) is received by him or on such later date as may be specified;
   (b) order reduction in his rank with immediate effect and issue a written warning to the member concerned that unless a sufficient improvement in his performance is made within such period as the chairman shall specify, he may, following consideration of his performance during that period in accordance with regulation 18, be required to attend a first interview in respect of that performance; or
   (c) issue such a written warning as is mentioned in sub-paragraph (b).

(2) Where the sanction under paragraph (1)(a) is imposed and where the member concerned has not resigned from the force in accordance with the requirement, then the effect of the decision shall be to dismiss the member concerned from the force as from the time referred to.

(3) If the officers conducting the inefficiency hearing make a finding that the attendance of the member concerned during the relevant period has been unsatisfactory, they may—
   (a) impose the sanction mentioned in paragraph (1)(a);
   (b) in a case where it is established that insufficient support has been given to the member concerned during the relevant period in order to assist him to return to work, specify such measures as must be taken in order to give him sufficient support in order to assist him to return to work;
   (c) issue a written warning to the member concerned that unless a sufficient improvement in his attendance is made within such period as is specified, he may, following consideration

of his attendance during that period in accordance with regulation 18A, be required to attend a second inefficiency hearing at which he may be required to resign from the force;
(d) in a case where it is established that the member's duties within the force contribute directly to his unsatisfactory attendance record, order the member to be redeployed to alternative duties (which may involve a reduction of rank) within the force with immediate effect.

(4) Where the steps under paragraph (3)(b) or (d) are taken, the member concerned shall be issued with a written warning that unless a sufficient improvement in his attendance is made within such period as is specified, he may, following consideration of his attendance during that period in accordance with regulation 18A, be required to attend a first interview, a second interview or an inefficiency hearing, as specified by the officers conducting the inefficiency hearing.

KEYNOTE

Any requirement for the member to resign cannot take effect before one month after the notice of the finding *was received* by the member. It may take effect at some later date. If the member has not resigned as required by the specified date, he/she will automatically be dismissed as of that date (reg. 17(2)).

Any reduction in rank must take effect 'immediately', an expression which presumably means immediately the finding is made as opposed to it being sent to, or received by, the member concerned. The instant effect of this finding will not be held up or deferred by any review or appeal process. In accordance with the developmental and ongoing nature of this process, a reduction in rank must be accompanied by a warning that a sufficient improvement is still required within a specified period. This indicates that the process is by no means over and that, under reg. 18 below, further reports as to the member's performance will be assessed.

A similar procedure involving a written warning followed by a further report is available as a third sanction without any reduction in rank.

Any sanction imposed under reg. 17 shall be expunged after two years if that period was free from any such sanction (reg. 15(4) of the Police Regulations 2003).

In cases arising out of poor *attendance*, the measures in reg. 17(3) may be invoked. These measures include issuing specific written warnings as to the effect of reg. 18A (below) after a further period of assessment. The measures also include a specific provision dealing with cases where the officer's duties have contributed to his/her poor attendance. In such cases, the officer may be redeployed and, if appropriate, reduced in rank in the process.

4.1.10.16 Further Period of Assessment

Regulation 18 states:

(1) This regulation applies where the member concerned has been given a written warning under paragraph (1)(b) or (c) of regulation 17.

(2) Not later than 14 days after the end of the period specified in the warning, the reporting officer shall—
(a) assess the performance of the member concerned during that period
(b) cause to be prepared a report on the performance; and
(c) send a copy of the report to the member concerned.

(3) Where the report prepared under paragraph (2)(b) concludes that the performance of the member concerned has been satisfactory during the period specified in the warning, no further action shall be taken in respect of that performance during that period.

(4) Where the report prepared under paragraph (2)(b) concludes that, in the opinion of the reporting officer, the performance of the member concerned has been unsatisfactory during that period, the reporting officer shall request the member concerned to attend a first interview in accordance with regulation 4; and these Regulations shall have effect for the purposes of the

performance of the member concerned during that period as if he had been invited to a first interview under regulation 4.

KEYNOTE

Regulation 18 applies where a written warning under reg. 17(1)(b) or (c) has been issued (performance). Unlike the other stages in the process, this stage makes specific provision for occasions where the member's performance is found to have been satisfactory. In such cases there is to be no further action in respect of *that* performance during *that* period. This does not necessarily mean that there can be no further action in relation to any performance during any other stage of the whole process.

If the 'reporting officer' is of the opinion that the member's performance during this most recent assessment period has been unsatisfactory, the reporting officer *must* request a 'first interview' and the whole cycle begins again. Unlike the original 'first interview' (see above), the wording of reg. 18 does not leave the request of the 'first interview' to the reporting officer's discretion.

Regulation 18A makes very similar provisions for assessing and reporting on the officer's progress in cases of poor attendance (under reg. 17(3)(c) or (4)). In cases of poor attendance, however, the final report is made by the countersigning officer (not the reporting officer) and if he/she concludes that the officer's attendance has been unsatisfactory or has made insufficient improvement, then:

- if the officer has been given a written warning under reg. 17(3)(c), he/she may be required to attend an inefficiency hearing, or
- if the officer has been given a written warning under reg. 17(4), he/she may be required to attend a first interview, second interview or an inefficiency hearing (see reg. 18A).

4.1.10.17 The Review

Regulation 19 states:

(1) Where the officers conducting the inefficiency hearing have imposed a sanction under regulation 17, the member concerned shall be entitled to request the chief officer of the police force concerned, or where the member concerned is a member of the Metropolitan Police force the Assistant Commissioner, ('the reviewing officer') to review the finding or the sanction imposed, or both the finding and the sanction.

(2) A request for a review must be made to the reviewing officer in writing within 14 days of the date on which a copy of the decision sent under regulation 16(4) is received by the member concerned unless this period is extended by the reviewing officer.

(3) The request for a review shall state the grounds on which the review is requested and whether a meeting is requested.

KEYNOTE

'Sanction' here would appear to mean any of the three options set out under reg. 17(1)(a) to (c). Therefore, the member concerned may request a review where the hearing only imposes a written warning without any further punishment.

The request will be made to the member's chief officer or, in the case of a Metropolitan Police officer, to the Assistant Commissioner.

Regulation 22 makes special provisions for situations where the chief officer or Assistant Commissioner is an 'interested party' or where there is an assistant chief officer deputising under s. 12A of the Police Act 1996.

For some reason the Regulations do not define 'interested party', but reg. 4 of the former Police (Conduct) Regulations 1999 (SI 1999/703) (**see para. 4.1.11**) since repealed, defines it as 'a witness or any person involved in the conduct which is the subject of the case or who otherwise has a direct interest in the case'. In cases falling under reg. 22, the review will be carried out by the Deputy Chief Constable. Where that Deputy Chief Constable is absent or is an interested party, the review will be carried out by the chief officer of another force.

Where the member concerned is a Metropolitan Police officer and the review officer is absent or an interested party, the review will be carried out by the designated Commander. If that Commander is absent or an interested party, the review may be carried out by another Assistant Commissioner (reg. 22(3)).

Where the member concerned is a City of London Police officer and the Commissioner is absent or an interested party, the review will be carried out by the chief officer of another force or an Assistant Commissioner in the Metropolitan Police (reg. 22(4)).

The request must be made to the reviewing officer in writing within 14 days of the date on which the member *receives* the notification sent out under reg. 16(4). The period may be extended by the reviewing officer without the need for the member to apply for such an extension.

The purpose of the review can be to consider the finding, the sanction or both. The reviewing officer may confirm the decision of the hearing or he/she may impose a different sanction. However, the reviewing officer may not impose a sanction greater than that imposed at the hearing (reg. 21(2)).

The request must state the grounds on which it is made and whether a meeting is requested. If a meeting is requested, the reviewing officer must hold one (reg. 20(1)). However, a review can be carried out without holding such a meeting. Where a meeting is held, the member may be accompanied by a 'friend' (police officer) and a solicitor/counsel (reg. 20(2)).

4.1.10.18 The Finding of the Review

The member concerned must be informed of the finding of the reviewing officer in writing and within three days of the completion of the review (reg. 21(1)).

The reviewing officer's decision is substituted for that of the hearing and takes effect from the same date (reg. 21(3)). If there is a finding that the performance of the member concerned had not been unsatisfactory the original sanction will be expunged forthwith (reg. 15(5)) of the Police Regulations 2003.

If the reviewing officer's decision results in the member concerned being required to resign or in his/her reduction in rank, the member must be notified of the right to appeal to a Police Appeals Tribunal (reg. 21(4)) (**see para. 4.1.13**).

4.1.11 Complaints and Conduct Matters

Part 2 of the Police Reform Act 2002 (along with schs 2 and 3) brings fundamental changes to the area of police complaints and misconduct.

4.1.11.1 Appropriate Authority

This expression is repeated throughout the text that follows and is of central importance to the complaints and discipline framework. Section 29 of the Act states that:

> 'the appropriate authority', in relation to a person serving with the police or in relation to any complaint, matter or investigation relating to the conduct of such a person, means—
> (a) if that person is a senior officer, the police authority for the area of the police force of which he is a member; and
> (b) if he is not a senior officer, the chief officer under whose direction and control he is.

In addition to performance and attendance management, it is also an important supervisory and managerial function to be alert to the way in which individuals conduct themselves. As with issues of performance and attendance (**see para. 4.1.10**), a great deal of supervisory and managerial discretion is called for in dealing with information concerning the conduct of individual officers. The exercise of supervisory and managerial discretion is generally a matter for local and organisational policy. Any such policy relating to the alleged misconduct of police officers is, however, subject to the legislative provisions discussed in this chapter.

It is, however, critical to note at the outset the observations of Lord Donaldson who said that an officer was not to be put in peril in respect of disciplinary proceedings unless there was *substantial compliance* with the regulations (see *Calveley* v *Chief Constable of Merseyside* [1989] 2 WLR 624 and *R* v *CC, ex parte Calveley* (1986) 2 WLR 144). This means that even relatively minor departures by investigators and managers from the framework which follows in the rest of this paragraph could result in any subsequent disciplinary proceedings being overturned by a court.

4.1.11.2 Who?

The legislative provisions relating to allegations of misconduct can be found in the Police (Conduct) Regulations 2004 (SI 2004/645). These Regulations apply to all police officers including senior (e.g. ACPO rank) officers and, for the first time, to special constables. As well as setting out the procedures to be followed in cases of alleged misconduct, the Regulations contain the Code of Conduct which replaced the former Discipline Code.

4.1.11.3 When?

The 2004 Regulations came into force on 1 April 2004 and specific provisions are made for cases which fall within the transitional period (see reg. 2).

4.1.11.4 The Code of Conduct

Schedule 1 to the 2004 Regulations states:

> 1. *Honesty and integrity*
> It is of paramount importance that the public has faith in the honesty and integrity of police officers. Officers should therefore be open and truthful in their dealings; avoid being improperly beholden to any person or institution; and discharge their duties with integrity.
>
> 2. *Fairness and impartiality*
> Police officers have a particular responsibility to act with fairness and impartiality in all their dealings with the public and their colleagues.
>
> 3. *Politeness and tolerance*
> Officers should treat members of the public and colleagues with courtesy and respect, avoiding abusive or deriding attitudes or behaviour. In particular, officers must avoid: favouritism of an individual or group; all forms of harassment, victimisation or unreasonable discrimination; and overbearing conduct to a colleague, particularly to one junior in rank or service.
>
> 4. *Use of force and abuse of authority*
> Officers must never knowingly use more force than is reasonable, nor should they abuse their authority.
>
> 5. *Performance of duties*
> Officers should be conscientious and diligent in the performance of their duties. Officers should attend work promptly when rostered for duty. If absent through sickness or injury, they should avoid activities likely to retard their return to duty.

6. *Lawful orders*
The police service is a disciplined body. Unless there is good and sufficient cause to do otherwise, officers must obey all lawful orders and abide by the provisions of Police Regulations. Officers should support their colleagues in the execution of their lawful duties, and oppose any improper behaviour, reporting it where appropriate.

7. *Confidentiality*
Information which comes into the possession of the police should be treated as confidential. It should not be used for personal benefit and nor should it be divulged to other parties except in the proper course of police duty. Similarly, officers should respect, as confidential, information about force policy and operations unless authorised to disclose it in the course of their duties.

8. *Criminal offences*
Officers must report any proceedings for a criminal offence taken against them. Conviction of a criminal offence or the administration of a caution may of itself result in further action being taken.

9. *Property*
Officers must exercise reasonable care to prevent loss or damage to property (excluding their own personal property but including police property).

10. *Sobriety*
Whilst on duty officers must be sober. Officers should not consume alcohol when on duty unless specifically authorised to do so or it becomes necessary for the proper discharge of police duty.

11. *Appearance*
Unless on duties which dictate otherwise, officers should always be well turned out, clean and tidy whilst on duty in uniform or in plain clothes.

12. *General conduct*
Whether on or off duty, police officers should not behave in a way which is likely to bring discredit upon the police service.

Notes

(a) The primary duties of those who hold the office of constable are the protection of life and property, the preservation of the Queen's peace, and the prevention and detection of criminal offences. To fulfil these duties they are granted extraordinary powers; the public and the police service therefore have the right to expect the highest standards of conduct from them.
(b) This Code sets out the principles which guide police officers' conduct. It does not seek to restrict officers' discretion: rather it aims to define the parameters of conduct within which that discretion should be exercised. However, it is important to note that any breach of the principles in this Code may result in action being taken by the organisation, which, in serious cases, could involve dismissal.
(c) Police behaviour, whether on or off duty, affects public confidence in the police service. Any conduct which brings or is likely to bring discredit to the police service may be the subject of sanction. Accordingly, any allegation of conduct which could, if proved, bring or be likely to bring discredit to the police service should be investigated in order to establish whether or not a breach of the Code has occurred and whether formal disciplinary action is appropriate. No investigation is required where the conduct, if proved, would not bring or would not be likely to bring, discredit to the police service.

KEYNOTE

In relation to para. 8 of the Code, this is an oddity in itself in that it requires the reporting of *proceedings* (or a caution), rather than a conviction for a criminal offence. It also requires an officer to report where they have received a fixed penalty notice for disorder. It therefore allows for further disciplinary action even where the officer has not been found guilty of a criminal matter; it also creates practical problems for chief officer reviews.

While the making of an Anti-social Behaviour Order (ASBO) is a civil matter that does not necessarily arise out of any criminal conduct (**see chapter 4.5**), it is questionable whether the passing of such an order in respect of a police officer means that he/she has necessarily fallen below the required standard—much would turn on the individual facts and circumstances of each case. It would plainly be wrong to treat every imposition of an ASBO on an officer as conclusive proof that his/her conduct had fallen below the required standard or that this amounted to proceedings for, or a conviction of, a criminal offence in accordance with para. 8 above.

In relation to 'sobriety' at para. 10 above, Home Office guidance suggests that superintendents/chief superintendents will be classed as being 'on duty' while they are formally 'on call'. They will not be 'on duty' by reason only of their general 24-hour responsibility for their own area of command or department. The guidance further provides that an officer who is *unexpectedly* called out for duty should be able, at no risk of discredit, to say that he/she has had too much to drink.

The Police (Amendment) Regulations 2005 (SI 2005/2834) have inserted a new reg. (19A) into the Police Regulations 2003. This provides that the chief officer of a police force (in accordance with procedures determined by the Secretary of State) may require any member of the force to give a sample of saliva or urine to be tested for evidence of controlled drugs, or a sample of breath to be tested for evidence of alcohol. This testing for drugs or alcohol can be carried out where there is reasonable suspicion of substance abuse, pre-employment screening, testing in the probationary period, and screening in specialist and safety critical areas, for example firearms officers. The Regulations also cover where a member gives the chief officer reasonable cause to suspect that he/she has used a controlled drug.

A proposed new Code of Professional Standards, to replace the current Code of Conduct, has been drawn up by a working party of the Police Advisory Board and was subject to a period of consultation. The new Code, which will apply to all police officers and special constables, sets out ten principles which reflect the expectations that the police service and the public have of how police officers should behave. It is intended that a similar Code for police staff will eventually be produced.

4.1.11.5 Suspension

The Police (Conduct) Regulations 2004

Regulation 4 states:

(1) Where it appears to the appropriate authority, on receiving a report, complaint or allegation which indicates that the conduct of a police officer does not meet the appropriate standard, that the officer concerned ought to be suspended from his office as constable and (in the case of a member of a force) from membership of the force, the appropriate authority may, subject to the following provisions of this regulation, so suspend him.

(2) The appropriate authority shall not so suspend a police officer unless it appears to it that either of the following conditions ('the suspension conditions') is satisfied—
- (a) that the effective investigation of the matter may be prejudiced unless the officer concerned is so suspended;
- (b) that the public interest, having regard to the nature of the report, complaint or allegation, and any other relevant considerations, requires that he should be so suspended.

KEYNOTE

The appropriate authority will generally be the officer's own chief officer (see reg. 3); for senior officers it is the police authority for the area. The chief officer may delegate the power to suspend to an officer of at least Assistant Chief Constable/Commander rank (reg. 4(8)).

The 'appropriate standard' means that set out in the Code of Conduct.

The power to suspend can only be used if one of the two suspension conditions at (a) or (b) is met.

The appropriate authority may generally exercise the power to suspend at any time from receipt of the report, complaint or allegation until:

- it is decided that the conduct of the officer concerned shall not be the subject of proceedings under reg. 11;
- the notification of a finding that the conduct of the officer concerned did not fail to meet the appropriate standard;
- a sanction has been imposed under reg. 35 and, in the case of an officer other than a senior officer, either the officer concerned has not requested a review within the period specified in reg. 40 or any such review has been completed (see reg. 4(5)).

There are further considerations where the officer to be suspended is a senior officer.

Where an officer is suspended, he/she will remain suspended until any of the events above or until the appropriate authority decides he/she shall cease to be suspended, whichever occurs first (reg. 4(6)). If the officer is required to resign, he/she will remain suspended until that requirement takes effect (reg. 4(7)).

There are separate provisions for the suspension of officers in urgent cases applying to senior officers under reg. 5.

The effect of suspension is that the officers no longer hold the office of 'constable' for the period of the suspension and, if they are regular police officers, their membership of their force is suspended. They will continue to be regarded as a 'member' of their force for the purposes of the Police Regulations 2003 (see reg. 3) but cease to enjoy the powers and privileges of the office of constable. A further effect is that the officer will not, under the Rules of the Police Promotion Examinations Board, be able to sit the qualifying examination(s) for promotion unless his/her chief officer expressly authorises it.

Generally, an officer who is suspended will continue to receive full pay (without any special allowances) unless their whereabouts are unknown or where they are in custody following conviction (see the Police Regulations 2003, sch. 2).

When deciding whether to use the power to suspend an officer or not, consideration must be given to the equality of the treatment being applied to all officers under investigation or subject to complaint. Failure to do so can lead to finding that such treatment was discriminatory (see *Virdi* v *Commissioner of Police for the Metropolis* (2000) LTL 5 February).

4.1.11.6 Outstanding Criminal Proceedings

Regulation 6 states:

> Where there are criminal proceedings outstanding against the officer concerned, proceedings under these Regulations, other than exercise of the power to suspend under regulations 4 and 5, shall not take place unless the chief officer concerned believes that in the exceptional circumstances of the case it would be appropriate for them to do so.

KEYNOTE

Although as a general rule disciplinary proceedings other than suspension will not be brought against an officer while there are any outstanding criminal proceedings against him/her, reg. 6 leaves it open to the chief officer to do so. That discretionary power to institute disciplinary proceedings is limited to 'exceptional circumstances' where the chief officer *believes* it to be appropriate.

4.1.11.7 Investigation Procedure

Supervising officer

Regulation 7 states:

(1) Subject to paragraph (2), where a report, complaint or allegation is received by the chief officer which indicates that the conduct of a police officer (other than a senior officer) did not meet the appropriate standard, the case may be referred by him to a police officer, who satisfies the conditions in paragraph (3), to supervise the investigation of the case.

(2) ...

(3) The supervising officer shall be—

(a) of at least the rank of chief inspector and at least one rank above that of the officer concerned;

(b) a member of, or a special constable appointed for the area of, the same force as the officer concerned; and

(c) not an interested party.

KEYNOTE

Regulation 7(1) does not apply where the case arises from a complaint the investigation of which is supervised, investigated or managed by the IPCC (**see para. 4.1.12.1**).

The supervising officer must meet all of the criteria set out at reg. 7(3)(a) to (c).

The 'supervising officer' is not the same as the 'investigating officer' (see below).

Investigating officer

Regulation 8 states:

(1) A supervising officer may appoint an investigating officer to investigate the case.

...

(7) In a case which concerns the conduct of an officer other than a senior officer, the investigating officer shall be—

(a) a member of the same police force as the officer concerned or, if the chief officer of some other force is requested and agrees to provide an investigating officer, a member of that other force;

(b) of at least the rank of sergeant;

KEYNOTE

The duty to appoint an investigating officer does not arise where the case arises from a complaint the investigation of which is supervised, investigated or managed by the IPCC (reg. 8(3)).

An investigating officer must be of at least the same rank as the officer concerned and must not be an interested party in the case (reg. 8(9)).

There are further considerations where the officer concerned is a senior officer. If the officer concerned is a superintendent or chief superintendent, the investigating officer must be at least an Assistant Chief Constable or Commander.

4.1.11.8 Notice of Investigation

Regulation 9 states:

The investigating officer shall as soon as is practicable (without prejudicing his own or any other investigation of the matter) cause the officer concerned to be given written notice—

(a) that there is to be an investigation in to the case;

(b) of the nature of the report, complaint or allegation;
(c) informing him that he is not obliged to say anything concerning the matter, but that it may harm his defence if he does not mention when questioned or when providing a written response something which he later relies on in any subsequent proceedings under these Regulations;
(d) informing him that he may, if he so desires, make a written or oral statement concerning the matter to the investigating officer or to the appropriate authority and that if he makes such a statement it may be used in any subsequent proceedings under these Regulations;
(e) informing him that he has the right to seek advice from his staff association or any other body; and
(f) informing him that he has the right to be accompanied by a police officer, who shall not be an interested party, to any meeting, interview or hearing.

KEYNOTE

It was a long time coming, but the law has now been changed to allow for adverse inferences to be drawn from an officer's failure to make a response when served with reg. 9 forms. The 'teeth' behind this provision above can be found in reg. 27 (see below) which allows any hearing to draw such inferences as appear proper from a relevant failure to give an explanation or make comment.

The written 'reg. 9' notice must be given 'as soon as is practicable'. Practicable has been accepted as meaning 'possible to be accomplished with known means or resources' (see *Adsett* v *K & L Steelfounders* [1953] 1 All ER 97). However, the giving of such a notice must not be to the prejudice of the investigation of the matter—whether by the investigating officer or someone else—therefore there may be some justifiable delay in the provision of a reg. 9 notice.

The wording 'cause to be given'—as opposed to 'sent'—suggests that personal service is required.

Although the above provision replaced the troublesome 'reg. 7' wording which caused a lot of legal argument over the years, the effect of failing to serve a correctly worded notice as soon as practicable should not be underestimated (see *R* v *Chief Constable of Merseyside, ex parte Merrill* [1989] 1 WLR 1077). The purpose of the notice under reg. 9 is to put the officer on '*very early notice*' that an allegation has been made (see *Calverley* v *Chief Constable of Merseyside* [1989] 2 WLR 624).The whole point of serving a reg. 9 notice is to allow the officer to put forward a denial or explanation and to enable him/her to collect and recollect evidence. Therefore both the issuing of the notice *and the wording contained within it* ought to reflect this (subject to the proviso of prejudicing any investigation). The responsibility for careful drafting and service of the form will become even more significant in light of the reduction in the officer's right to silence. The making of/declining to make a statement in response to the receipt of a reg. 9 notice is also of greater significance in this light, and very serious consideration ought to be given to exercising the right to consult with a staff association representative. For further discussion of the way in which inferences can be drawn in general criminal proceedings under s. 34 of the Criminal Justice and Public Order Act 1994 (and which, by extension, will be applied to conduct cases) **see Evidence & Procedure, chapter 2.7.**

4.1.11.9 Investigating Officer's Report

Regulation 10 states:

(1) At the end of his investigation the investigating officer shall as soon as practicable submit a written report on the case—
  (a) if the case concerns a senior officer, to the appropriate authority;
  (b) in any other case, to the supervising officer; and
  (c) if the Commission is managing or supervising the investigation, to the Commission.
(2) If at any time during his investigation it appears to the investigating officer that the case is one in respect of which the conditions specified in Part 1 of Schedule 2 are likely to be satisfied, he

shall, whether or not the investigation is at an end, submit to the appropriate authority (in the case of a senior officer) or supervising officer (in any other case)—

(a) a statement of his belief that the case may be one to which regulation 45 applies and the grounds for that belief; and

(b) a written report on the case so far as it has then been investigated.

KEYNOTE

If the investigation is being managed or supervised by the IPCC (**see para. 4.1.12.1**) the investigating officer must submit two reports: one to the supervising officer and one to the Commission.

If it appears to the investigating officer that the case is a 'special case' as provided for under reg. 45 (i.e. involving a serious allegation of an imprisonable offence; see below), the investigating officer must submit a report stating his/her belief and setting out the current position of the investigation. Given the seriousness of 'special cases', this report would probably need to be submitted immediately and reg. 10(2) makes it clear that the report does not need to be delayed until the end of the investigation.

Regulation 11 states:

(1) Subject to paragraphs (2) and (4) to (6), on receipt of the investigating officer's report the appropriate authority (in the case of a senior officer) or supervising officer (in any other case) may refer the case to a hearing.

(2) Where—

(a) the appropriate authority has a duty to take action, secure that disciplinary proceedings are proceeded with or to comply with a direction under paragraph 27 of Schedule 3 to the 2002 Act; or

(b) the officer concerned has received two written warnings about his conduct within the previous twelve months and has in a statement made under regulation 9 admitted that his conduct failed to meet the appropriate standard,

the appropriate authority (in the case of a senior officer) or supervising officer (in any other case) shall refer the case to a hearing.

KEYNOTE

Other than in those circumstances where there is a duty to bring disciplinary proceedings or a direction has been given by the IPCC (**see para. 4.1.12.1**), the appropriate authority has a discretion whether or not to refer the matter to a hearing. Where it decides not to do so, the officer concerned must be informed in writing as soon as possible (reg. 11(3)) and no reference to the case is to be made on the officer's personal record (reg. 11(7)).

If it is the supervising officer's opinion that the case satisfies the 'special case' conditions (see below), he/she must certify it as such and notify the officer concerned or, if appropriate, return the case to the investigating officer (see reg. 11(6)).

If the matter is to be referred to a hearing, the procedure under reg. 14 applies (see below) or, in the case of senior officers, reg. 13.

No sanction can be imposed without a hearing (reg. 15) except in the case of senior officers (see reg. 13—unlucky for some).

4.1.11.10 Withdrawal

Regulation 12 states:

(1) At any time before the beginning of the hearing the appropriate authority (in the case of a senior officer) or the supervising officer (in any other case) may direct that the case be

withdrawn, unless the appropriate authority has a duty to proceed under paragraph 27 of Schedule 3 to the 2002 Act.

(2) Where a direction is given under paragraph (1), the appropriate authority or supervising officer shall, as soon as possible, cause the officer concerned to be served with a written notice of the direction and the case shall be treated as if it had not been referred to a hearing.

KEYNOTE

For the cases where there is a 'duty to proceed' **see para. 4.1.12.8.**

Where a direction is made under reg. 12(1), the officer concerned must be notified in writing *as soon as possible.*

The effect of reg. 12(2) is that cases withdrawn before the beginning of a hearing will be treated as if they had never been referred in the first place and therefore no reference to them can be made on the officer's personal record (see reg. 11(7) above).

4.1.11.11 Referral of Cases to Hearing

Regulation 14 states:

(1) Where a case is to be referred to a hearing, as soon as practicable the officer concerned shall be given written notice of the decision to refer the case to a hearing, and at least 21 days before the date of the hearing he shall be supplied with copies of—
   (a) any statement he may have made to the investigating officer; and
   (b) any relevant statement, document or other material in each case obtained during the course of the investigation

(2) The notice given under paragraph (1) shall specify the conduct of the officer concerned which it is alleged failed to meet the appropriate standard and the paragraph of the Code of Conduct in respect of which the appropriate standard is alleged not to have been met.

KEYNOTE

The service of this notice is the next procedural step after the service of the reg. 9 notice discussed earlier. The notice under reg. 14 must be served on the officer as soon as practicable after the decision to refer the matter to a hearing. In addition, not less than 21 days before the date of the hearing, the officer concerned must be supplied with copies of the documents set out at reg. 14(1)(a) and (b), including a copy of any account or statement given verbally (reg. 14(3)).

In the case of senior officers there are specific provisions under regs 13 and 14 regarding notices of hearings.

4.1.11.12 Notice of Hearing

Regulation 16 states:

(1) The appropriate authority (in the case of a senior officer) or the supervising officer (in any other case) shall ensure that at least 21 days in advance the officer concerned is notified of the time, date and place of the hearing.

(2) In a case to which this paragraph applies the hearing may, if the appropriate authority or supervising officer considers it appropriate in the circumstances, take place before the expiry of the 21 days referred to in paragraph (1).

(3) Paragraph (2) applies where the officer concerned is given a written notice under regulation 14(1) of a decision to refer the case to a hearing and—

(a) at the time he receives such a notice he is detained in pursuance of the sentence of a court in a prison or other institution to which the Prison Act 1952 applies, or has received a suspended sentence of imprisonment; and

(b) having been supplied under regulation 14 with the documents therein mentioned he does not elect to be legally represented at the hearing.

KEYNOTE

Generally the officer concerned must be given at least 21 days' notice of the time, date and place of any proposed hearing. However, in the (very unusual) circumstances set out at reg. 16(3)(a) and (b), the appropriate authority or supervising officer may allow the hearing to take place earlier if they consider it appropriate in the circumstances.

If the supervising officer is of the opinion that the sanctions of:

- dismissal
- requirement to resign, or
- reduction in rank

should be available to the hearing, he/she *must* make sure that any officer concerned is given written notice at the same time as the notice of a hearing, that:

- they are entitled to elect legal representation at the hearing, and
- that the hearing cannot reduce the officer in rank, require them to resign or dismiss them unless they have been given the opportunity to elect such representation, and
- that unless they have so elected, they may only be represented at the hearing by a 'friend' (police officer) (reg. 17).

Similar provisions for the legal representation of special constables are set out in reg. 17(3)–(5).

Practically, this means that, if the opportunity to be legally represented is not given to the officer concerned, the only options open to the hearing are a fine, reprimand or caution under reg. 35.

The officer concerned will be 'invited' to state in writing:

- whether or not he/she accepts that his/her conduct did not meet the appropriate standard;
- whether he/she wishes to be legally represented (if reg. 17 applies);
- whether he/she proposes to call any witnesses (and if so, their names and addresses so that the supervising officer may secure their attendance) (reg. 18(1)).

Any such written response must be made within 14 days of the officer being 'notified' that the last of the documents under reg. 14(1) have been supplied (reg. 18(1)).

As with a statement made under reg. 9 (see above), any admission made under reg. 18 may have significant consequences for the officer concerned, particularly as an admission can, without more, amount to a finding against him/her (see below).

Any witnesses who are police officers will be ordered to attend the hearing (reg. 18(2)) and, if requested to do so, the supervising officer must cause any other witnesses to be notified that their attendance is required and to advise them of the time and place of the hearing (reg. 18(2)).

The officer concerned will also be ordered to attend the hearing (reg. 28(1)). If he/she fails to attend the hearing, it may proceed and be concluded in his/her absence (reg. 28(2)) and any requirement under these Regulations that cannot be complied with because the officer is absent will be dispensed with (reg. 28(4)). Similarly, a hearing can go ahead where any of the witnesses are unwilling or unable to attend (reg. 18(3)). In other words, the hearing does not *have* to be adjourned simply because the officer concerned or a witness is prevented from attending—either by ill health or any other cause—and may proceed to conclusion without him/her. If, however, the officer informs the officer presiding over the hearing in advance that he/she is unable to attend as a result of ill health, *or some other unavoidable reason*, the hearing *may* be adjourned (reg. 28(3)). In addition, the ordinary rules of natural justice may mean that the unavailability of a key witness on behalf of the officer would render any hearing unfair and the matter may have to be postponed.

If the hearing arises from a complaint or conduct matter falling under part 2 of the Police Reform Act 2002 (as to which **see para. 4.1.12**), the complainant or interested person will generally be entitled to attend the hearing up to the point where the decision on his or her conduct is made (reg. 29(2)). In addition the complainant or interested person may nominate up to three other people (or a higher number if the presiding officer allows it) to accompany them (reg. 29(3)). However, where the complainant or interested person is to be called as a witness they (and any person accompanying them) will not be allowed to attend before that person gives their evidence (reg. 29(4)).

4.1.11.13 The Hearing

For cases not involving senior (ACPO) officers, reg. 19 requires that the hearing be conducted by three officers who are not interested parties.

Subject to the regulation dealing with 'remission of cases' (see below), the 'presiding officer' at the hearing must be an Assistant Chief Constable or, in the case of a Metropolitan Police or City of London Police officer, a Commander (reg. 19(2)).

Generally, the other two assisting officers must be at least the rank of superintendent (reg. 19(3)). However, where the officer concerned is a superintendent/chief superintendent, the assisting officers must be Assistant Chief Constables (or Commanders in the case of Metropolitan and City of London officers) in different forces from that of the officer concerned (reg. 19(4)).

In a case where the hearing arises from a complaint or conduct matter which has been the subject of an investigation supervised, managed or investigated by the IPCC (as to which **see para. 4.1.12.1**), the presiding officer will be assisted by two people of whom one is a police officer of at least the rank of superintendent (or, if the officer concerned is a superintendent or chief superintendent, of at least the rank of an assisting officer under para. (4)) and the other is a person selected by the police authority for the force concerned from a list of candidates maintained by that authority (reg. 19(5)).

There are different provisions for hearings where the officer concerned is a senior officer (see reg. 20).

Where the officer concerned accepts, in accordance with reg. 18, that his/her conduct fell short of the 'appropriate standard' (i.e. the Code of Conduct), a summary of the facts of the case will be prepared and a copy supplied to the officer at least 14 days before the hearing (reg. 21(1)). If the officer does not agree with the summary, he/she may submit a response within seven days *of receiving it* (reg. 21(2)). If the officer has not accepted that his/her conduct fell short of the appropriate standard, no summary will be prepared (reg. 21(3)).

Where a summary of facts has been prepared, a copy of it will be supplied to the officers conducting the hearing in addition to a copy of the reg. 14 notice (reg. 22).

Unless the officer has given notice (under reg. 18) that he/she wishes to be legally represented, the *supervising officer* must appoint another police officer to present the case (reg. 23(1)). Where the officer concerned has elected to be legally represented, the case may be presented by a police officer or by a solicitor/counsel (reg. 23(2)).

The officer concerned may conduct his/her own case in person or by another police officer chosen by him/her. If the officer has given notice under reg. 18, he/she may then be represented by a solicitor/counsel (reg. 23(3)).

Under the provisions of sch. 3 to the Police Reform Act 2002 the IPCC can make a recommendation that disciplinary proceedings be brought in certain cases (**see para. 4.1.12.8**). Where it does so, the Commission may present the disciplinary case itself under reg. 25. In addition, if the officer concerned has elected to be legally represented or is a senior officer, the Commission may instruct a solicitor or counsel to present the case on its behalf (reg. 25(2)). Where this happens, the IPCC will notify all relevant parties except the officer concerned (who will be notified by the appropriate authority or supervising officer).

The officers conducting the hearing may adjourn from time to time if it appears to them to be necessary or expedient for the due hearing of the case (reg. 26(1)).

Where the case involves an officer other than a senior officer, any decision of the officers need only be based on a simple majority but must not indicate whether it was so decided or whether it was reached unanimously (reg. 26(2)). No provision is made for the presiding officer to have any form of 'casting vote' or for his/her view to carry any more weight than those of the assisting officers.

4.1.11.14 Procedure at Hearing

The officers conducting the hearing will, subject to the provisions of the Regulations, determine their own procedure (reg. 27(1)). Any question as to whether any evidence is admissible, or whether any question should be put to a witness will also be determined by the officers conducting the hearing (reg. 32(1)). These widely drafted discretionary powers will, however, be subject to general principles of law (e.g. natural justice). Additionally, the presiding officer may, *with the consent of the officer concerned*, allow any document to be adduced in evidence, even though no copy of it was supplied to the officer under reg. 14 (reg. 32(2)).

The officers conducting the hearing must not find that the officer's conduct failed to meet the appropriate standard unless the conduct is admitted by the officer or is proved by the person presenting the case *on the balance of probabilities* (reg. 27(3)). Thus, the standard of proof required in such hearings is that of an ordinary civil trial (and that required of a defendant where the burden of proof falls on him/her; **see Evidence & Procedure, chapter 2.7**). However, in assessing the balance, it is a general common law rule that the greater the consequences being faced by the defendant, the greater the degree of evidence that will be required to tip the balance of probabilities against him/her.

In arriving at this decision, reg. 27(4) and (5) are highly significant. Where evidence is given that the officer concerned, at any time after he/she was given a reg. 9 notice, on being questioned by an investigating officer failed to mention orally or in writing any fact relied on in his/her defence (being a fact which in the circumstances existing at the time the officer concerned could reasonably have been expected to mention when so questioned or when making a statement under reg. 9(d)), the officers conducting the hearing may draw such inferences from the failure as appear proper. This effectively dilutes the former 'right to silence' that officers still enjoyed even after the criminal law had been changed in this regard. This wording, while restricting the inferences drawn from failing to mention any fact relied upon in the officer's defence, gives the discipline panel considerable discretion (in much the same way as an employment tribunal) and makes the decision whether or not to make a verbal or written response in a discipline interview all the more important. Adverse inferences cannot be drawn in relation to a failure to mention a fact if the *failure to mention it* happened before 1 April 2004 (reg. 27(6)).

If they decide that the officer's conduct did not meet that standard, the officers must then decide whether it would be reasonable to impose a sanction under reg. 35 (reg. 27(7)).

They are not obliged to impose any sanction even after making a finding that the officer's conduct failed to meet the appropriate standard.

The hearing will generally be held in private (reg. 30(1)), although note the provisions in relation to the attendance of complainants and interested parties under reg. 9 discussed earlier. If it appears to the presiding officer that a witness may disclose in evidence information which, in the public interest, ought not to be disclosed to the public, he/she must require any member of the public (including complainants and their accompanying friends) to withdraw while the evidence is given (reg. 31).

In cases where there has been a complaint or a conduct matter under part 2 of the Police Reform Act 2002, or where it has supervised, managed or conducted the investigation, the IPCC is entitled to attend the hearing (reg. 30(2)). Where the case arises from a complaint or conduct matter which has been investigated by the IPCC and the Commission considers that because of its gravity or other exceptional circumstances it would be in the public interest to do so, it may (after consulting the appropriate authority, the officer concerned, the complainant and any witnesses), direct that the whole or part of the hearing will be held in public (reg. 30(5)). If such a direction is made, all the people consulted will be notified of the decision and the reasons for it within five days (reg. 30(6)).

The officer concerned may be accompanied at the hearing by another police officer and, at the discretion of the presiding officer as the case may be, by any other person. In a case where the complainant or an interested person is accompanied by a greater number of people (under reg. 29), the presiding officer may allow the officer to be accompanied by that number of people (reg. 30(3)). Additionally, the presiding officer may allow witnesses to be accompanied at the hearing by a relative or friend (reg. 30(4)).

The presiding officer may impose whatever conditions he/she sees fit in relation to witnesses and others attending the hearing (see reg. 30(8)). More specifically, where the officer concerned gives evidence, then, after the presenting officer has had an opportunity of cross-examining him/her, the presiding officer must put to him/her any questions which the complainant or interested person requests and which might have been properly put by the presenting officer or, at the presiding officer's discretion, may allow the complainant or interested person to put such questions to the officer concerned (reg. 29(5)).

No one must be allowed to intervene in or interrupt the hearing and, if anyone attending a hearing behaves in a disorderly or abusive manner, or otherwise misconducts him/herself, the presiding officer may exclude him/her from the hearing (reg. 30(7)).

A verbatim record of the proceedings must be taken and, if the officer concerned lodges notice of appeal (see below) and applies for a copy or transcript of the record within the time limit, it will be supplied to him or her (reg. 34).

4.1.11.15 Remission of Cases

Regulation 33 states:

> (1) The hearing of the case—
> (a) shall, in the circumstances mentioned in paragraph (2); or
> (b) may, in the circumstances mentioned in paragraph (5),
> be remitted by the presiding officer concerned to an officer of equivalent rank in the force concerned or to an officer of equivalent rank in another force who, at the presiding officer's request, has agreed to act as the presiding officer in the matter.
> (2) A case shall be so remitted if—
> (a) the presiding officer is an interested party otherwise than in his capacity as such; or
> (b) there would not, because the officer concerned was not given notice under regulation 17 of the opportunity to elect to be legally represented at the hearing, be available on a finding against him any of the sanctions referred to in that regulation, and it appears to the

presiding officer concerned that those sanctions ought to be so available and that accordingly it would be desirable for there to be another hearing at which the officer concerned could, if he so wished, be so represented.

KEYNOTE

Remission of a hearing really means passing it over to another officer of equivalent rank, either in the force concerned or of another force.

The hearing of a case *must* be remitted if:

- the presiding officer is an 'interested party'; or
- the officer was not given the opportunity to elect legal representation under reg. 17, thereby limiting the sanctions available to the hearing *and* the presiding officer feels that those sanctions ought to be available.

In addition, the hearing of a case *may* be remitted if, either before or during the hearing, the presiding officer considers it appropriate (reg. 33(5)).

If the case is remitted for the second reason bulleted above (failure to elect legal advice), the officer must be served in writing with a notice inviting him/her to elect *within 14 days of receipt*, to be legally represented. Further, in such cases, the officer remitting the case must not give any indication of his/her assessment of the case, nor of the sanction that might be imposed by the 'new' officer. Although this suggests that, in cases where the hearing is remitted under the other provisions, the presiding officer *may* indicate his/her assessment of the case so far, such action would be difficult to support and would be open to attack on grounds of fairness.

4.1.11.16 The Sanctions

Regulation 35 states:

(1) Subject to section 84(1) of the 1996 Act, the persons conducting the hearing in the case of an officer other than a senior officer may—
  (a) record a finding that the conduct of the officer concerned failed to meet the appropriate standard but take no further action; or
  (b) impose any of the sanctions in paragraph (2).

(2) Those sanctions are—
  (a) dismissal from the force;
  (b) requirement to resign from the force as an alternative to dismissal taking effect either forthwith or on such date as may be specified in the decision;
  (c) reduction in rank;
  (d) fine;
  (e) in the case of a special constable only, suspension from all or from operational duties only for a period of up to three months;
  (f) reprimand;
  (g) caution.

KEYNOTE

The reference to s. 84(1) of the Police Act 1996 is to the general prohibition on imposing a reduction in rank, requirement to resign or dismissal without having first given the officer an opportunity to elect legal representation.

Any of the sanctions under reg. 35(1) or (3), *except a requirement to resign*, will have immediate effect (reg. 35(5)). This immediate effect will not be delayed by any appeal procedure.

If a fine is imposed it is subject to a maximum limit (set out under reg. 35(6)). To work out the maximum amount of the fine you must first assume that it is to be recovered from the officer concerned by weekly deductions over the next 13 weeks. The overall sum—whether one fine or a number of fines—when spread across these 13 weeks must not exceed one-seventh of the officer's weekly pay.

In the case of senior officers the sanctions of reduction in rank and caution are not available.

In considering what sanction to impose, the officers conducting the hearing *must* have regard to the officer's service record (reg. 36(1)(a)). In doing so, they *may* receive evidence from witnesses if the officers are of the opinion that such evidence would help them.

The officer concerned must be given the opportunity to make oral or written representations in respect of any sanction (either in person or through his/her representative) (reg. 36(1)(b)).

At the end of the hearing the officer concerned must be informed *orally* of:

- the finding, and
- any sanction imposed.

He/she must also be provided with a *written notification* and a *summary of the reasons* within three days of the end of the hearing (reg. 37). The written notification must include (for regular police officers) notification of their right to appeal to the Police Appeals Tribunal and (other than for senior officers) the right to request a review (reg. 37(3)).

4.1.11.17 Review

As with the unsatisfactory performance process (**see para. 4.1.10**), the 2004 Regulations provide for a review of any sanction imposed under reg. 35 and for any sanction to be expunged if it is found that the officer concerned had not failed to meet the appropriate standard.

The appropriate regulations here are regs 40 to 43. Generally, the provisions relating to a review are the same as those for unsatisfactory performance.

In misconduct cases, the time by which the request for a review must be made to the reviewing officer is 14 days from receipt of the written summary of reasons under reg. 37 unless the period is extended by the reviewing officer. The officer concerned may be accompanied at any review meeting by a fellow officer but can only be additionally accompanied by a solicitor/counsel where reg. 17 (in relation to the availability of the sanctions of dismissal, requirement to resign or reduction in rank) applies (reg. 41(2)). In a case where the IPCC has made a direction to an Appropriate Authority (**see para. 4.1.12.8**), the reviewing officer must notify the Commission of the outcome of the review and provide it with a written record of the reasons for his/her decision (reg. 42(5)).

4.1.11.18 Special Cases

Regulation 45 makes provision for 'special cases' involving allegations of misconduct. There are three elements to qualify as a 'special case':

- the report, complaint or allegation must indicate that the conduct of the police officer concerned did not meet the appropriate standard;
- the appropriate officer (see above) has issued a certificate under reg. 11(6)(b)(i); and
- the conditions set out in part 1 of sch. 2 are satisfied (see below).

4.1.11.19 The Conditions

Part 1 of sch. 2 states:

> (1) The conditions referred to in regulation 45 are—
> (a) the report, complaint or allegation indicates that the conduct of the officer concerned is of a serious nature and that an imprisonable offence may have been committed by the officer concerned; and
> (b) the conduct is such that, were the case to be referred to a hearing under regulation 11 and the tribunal or officers conducting that hearing were to find that the conduct failed to meet the appropriate standard, they would in the opinion of the appropriate officer or appropriate authority be likely to impose the sanction specified in regulation 35(2)(a) or (4)(a) (dismissal from the force); and
> (c) the report, complaint or allegation is supported by written statements, documents or other material which is, in the opinion of the appropriate officer or appropriate authority, sufficient without further evidence to establish on the balance of probabilities that the conduct of the officer concerned did not meet the appropriate standard; and
> (d) the appropriate officer or appropriate authority is of the opinion that it is in the public interest for the officer concerned to cease to be a member of a police force, or to be a special constable, without delay.

KEYNOTE

All of the conditions set out under part I must be satisfied before a case can be designated a 'special case'.

The circumstances are such that any 'special case' will be very unusual and will be dealt with under legal advice at a very high organisational level. What constitutes conduct of a 'serious nature' is not clear but there must be an indication that the officer's alleged conduct involves an offence punishable with imprisonment (if committed by a person aged 21 years or over).

A further requirement for a case to be classified as 'special' is that, in the opinion of the appropriate officer, the officers conducting a hearing into the case would be likely to dismiss the officer from the force if the case were found proved. 'Special cases' must also be supported by evidence which, again in the appropriate officer's opinion, is enough by itself to establish that the officer's conduct did not meet the required standard (on the balance of probabilities).

The final requirement for a case to fall into this category is that, in the appropriate officer's opinion, it is in the public interest that the officer concerned ceases to be a police officer or special constable without delay.

The time when all these criteria are most likely to be met is when an officer has been caught 'red-handed' in the commission of a serious offence.

4.1.11.20 Modifications for Special Cases

The important difference between 'special cases' and other cases involving allegations of misconduct is that the former will be subject to a 'fast track' procedure, greatly reducing the overall time that it takes from first report to imposition of sanction. That procedure, which is set out at part 2 of sch. 2, changes a number of the key regulations above. Where a case does meet the special case criteria but is subsequently returned to the supervising officer, the unchanged regulations will then apply once more (reg. 45(3)). A special case may be so returned at any time before the beginning of the hearing.

Generally, the modifications shift many of the administrative responsibilities to the 'appropriate officer'. This means:

- where the officer concerned is a member of the Metropolitan Police or the City of London Police, or is a special constable appointed for the area of any one of those forces, a police officer of at least the rank of Commander *in that force*;
- in any other case, a police officer of at least the rank of Assistant Chief Constable (reg.3(1)).

4.1.12 The Complaints Framework

Part IV of the Police Act 1996 sets out the provisions for the recording and investigation of complaints against police officers. Every police authority and the HMIC is under a statutory duty to 'keep themselves informed' as to the workings of the relevant sections of the Act relating to the recording and investigation of complaints. Provisions are also made for the making of regulations in respect of non-Home Office police forces under the Police Reform Act 2002.

In the light of a number of perceived shortcomings in the police complaints system, part 2 of the Police Reform Act 2002 introduced some significant changes in this area, including a framework for the recording and investigation of police complaints.

In addition, the Serious Organised Crime and Police Act 2005 introduced further amendments to the 2002 Act: an accelerated procedure to bring disciplinary proceedings against a police officer where 'special' conditions are met; and a new category of 'death and serious injury matters (DSI)' under the jurisdiction of the IPCC.

4.1.12.1 The IPCC

Replacing the old Police Complaints Authority (PCA), the IPCC has far greater and more significant powers than its predecessor. The chair is appointed by the Queen, and the other Commissioners (of whom there must be at least ten) are appointed by the Secretary of State.

The whole purpose of having the IPCC is to increase public confidence in the *independence* of the investigative and complaints handling process. Therefore, certain people are automatically excluded from appointment to the IPCC Board—principally anyone who has held the office of constable in any part of the United Kingdom, anyone who has been a member of the Serious Organised Crime Agency (SOCA), or its previous equivalent, i.e. National Crime Intelligence Service or National Crime Squad (**see para. 4.1.2.3**). This also includes anyone who has held office with Her Majesty's Revenue and Customs (HMRC). The IPCC has very similar responsibilities towards HMRC as it has to the police and SOCA within the provisions of part 2 of the Police Reform Act 2002 (see the Revenue and Customs (Complaints and Misconduct) Regulations 2005 (SI 2005/3311)). The Police and Justice Act 2006, through the Independent Police Complaints Commission (Immigration and Asylum Enforcement Functions) Regulations 2008 (SI 2008/212) confers functions on the IPCC in relation to the exercise of specified enforcement functions by immigration officers and officials of the Secretary of State in relation to immigration or asylum.

Schedule 2 to the Police Reform Act 2002 makes further specific provisions in relation to the appointment, service and removal of IPCC members, including the appointment of its chief executive. Schedule 2 also provides for the appointment of staff by the IPCC and the secondment of officers from police forces. Matters of pay and conditions for its employees are left largely to the discretion of the IPCC; however, it will be liable for the wrongful conduct of any seconded officers in the course of the IPCC's functions in the same way as any other employer (para. 8).

In relation to complaints about its own staff see the Independent Police Complaints Commission (Staff Conduct) Regulations 2004 (SI 2004/660).

IPCC members are not servants or agents of the Crown and do not enjoy any such status, privileges or immunity; the IPCC's property is not Crown property.

The general functions of the IPCC are set out in the Police Reform Act 2002, s. 10. In summary these are:

(1) ...
- (a) to secure the maintenance by the Commission itself, and by police authorities and chief officers, of suitable arrangements with respect to the matters mentioned in subsection (2);
- (b) to keep under review all arrangements maintained with respect to those matters;
- (c) to secure that arrangements maintained with respect to those matters comply with the requirements of the following provisions of this Part, are efficient and effective and contain and manifest an appropriate degree of independence;
- (d) to secure that public confidence is established and maintained in the existence of suitable arrangements with respect to those matters and with the operation of the arrangements that are in fact maintained with respect to those matters;
- (e) to make such recommendations, and to give such advice, for the modification of the arrangements maintained with respect to those matters, and also of police practice in relation to other matters, as appear, from the carrying out by the Commission of its other functions, to be necessary or desirable;
- (f) to such extent as it may be required to do so by regulations made by the Secretary of State, to carry out functions in relation to bodies of constables maintained otherwise than by police authorities which broadly correspond to those conferred on the Commission in relation to police forces by the preceding paragraphs of this subsection;
- (g) to carry out functions in relation to the Serious Organised Crime Agency which correspond to those conferred on the Commission in relation to police forces by paragraph (e) of this subsection; and
- (h) to carry out functions in relation to the National Policing Improvement Agency which correspond to those conferred on the Commission in relation to police forces by paragraph (e) of this subsection.

(2) Those matters are—
- (a) the handling of complaints made about the conduct of persons serving with the police;
- (b) the recording of matters from which it appears that there may have been conduct by such persons which constitutes or involves the commission of a criminal offence or behaviour justifying disciplinary proceedings;
- (ba) the recording of matters from which it appears that a person has died or suffered serious injury during, or following contact with a person serving with the police;
- (c) the manner in which any such complaints or any such matters as are mentioned in paragraph (b) or (ba) are investigated or otherwise handled and dealt with.

KEYNOTE

The IPCC has a duty to exercise its powers and functions 'in the manner it considers best calculated for the purpose of securing the proper carrying out of its functions' above. In addition (subject to any other express provisions in part 2) the IPCC 'may do anything which appears to it to be calculated to facilitate, or is incidental or conducive to, the carrying out of its functions' (s. 10(6)). This clearly provides the investigative and overseeing body with very wide discretion in the conduct of its affairs. However, in addition to the general restrictions imposed on public authorities by the Human Rights Act 1998, the IPCC is also prevented from carrying out functions which relate to the direction or control of a police force or the Serious Organised Crime Agency (s. 10(8)). Additionally, the IPCC must enter into arrangements with Her Majesty's Chief

Inspector of Constabulary for securing co-operation with the Inspectorate and to provide HM Inspectors with such assistance and co-operation as may be required under those arrangements. The IPCC must submit an annual report to the Secretary of State and such other reports as the Secretary of State may require of it. The annual report will be sent to every relevant police authority and service authority. The IPCC can also, of its own volition, submit reports to the Secretary of State which it considers should be drawn to his or her attention—copies of any such report will also be sent to any police authority, service authority and chief officer that appears to be concerned. Further specific provisions relating to the role, powers and responsibilities of the IPCC are set out in statutory instrument (see in particular the Police (Complaints and Misconduct) Regulations 2004 (SI 2004/643), including the detailed requirements in relation to one of their key functions: ensuring that the relevant people are kept informed at various stages).

Statutory guidance under part 2 of the Police Reform Act 2002 has been produced by the IPCC under the banner 'Making the new police complaints system work better' and took effect from 1 December 2005. As a consequence of the IPCC issuing this guidance, a new Home Office Circular has been produced dealing with the handling of complaints following the introduction of the Police Reform Act (Home Office Circular 51/2005, *Guidance on Police Unsatisfactory Performance, Complaints and Misconduct Procedures*).

4.1.12.2 Complaints and Conduct Matters

When considering the complaints framework it is necessary to 'separate complaints' from other matters relating to police conduct. There are three specific classifications that need to be understood in this regard—this is because they each bring about practical considerations regarding the recording and handling of the matter being considered.

These three classifications are:

- complaints;
- conduct matters, or death and serious injury matters; and
- recordable conduct matters, or death and serious injury matters.

They are discussed in greater detail below.

4.1.12.3 Complaints

For the purposes of part 2 of the Police Reform Act 2002, references to 'complaints' mean:

- any complaint about the conduct of *a person serving with the police*. This means a sworn constable, an employee under the direction or control of a chief officer or a special constable (s. 12(7)).

That complaint will amount to a part 2 'complaint' where it is made—in writing or otherwise—by:

- a member of the public who claims to be the person in relation to whom the conduct took place; or
- a member of the public who claims to have been adversely affected by the conduct or to have witnessed the conduct; or
- any person acting on behalf of any of the above (s. 12(1)).

Not every report from a member of the public claiming to have been adversely affected by, or to have witnessed, alleged police conduct will qualify as a part 2 complaint. Generally, simply having seen or heard the conduct or effects of the conduct will not bring the person under these categories. The relevant member of the public has to have been physically present nearby when the conduct took place or when the effects took place and, as a result, was able to see or hear the conduct or the effects of it in order to make a part 2 complaint under this category. Therefore, simply seeing live TV coverage of police misconduct will not—thankfully—be enough to go and report a complaint against the people involved. Similarly, where potential complainants claim to have witnessed the alleged conduct, their complaint will only be a part 2 complaint if they acquired knowledge in a manner that would make them a competent witness capable of giving admissible evidence in criminal proceedings or they have in their possession or control anything that would amount to admissible evidence in such proceedings (e.g. video footage or an exhibit).

If a person is claiming to make a complaint on behalf of another, the person must be designated (under the relevant regulations) or have been given *and be able to produce* written consent from that other person (s. 12(6)).

Note that the wording of the relevant provisions here does not refer to alleged conduct as you might expect—that is because the definition of conduct includes alleged conduct (s. 29).

4.1.12.4 Conduct Matters and Death and Serious Injury Matters

The revised complaints regime introduced several concepts, one of which is that of a 'conduct matter'. A conduct matter is, generally speaking, any matter which is not and has not been the subject of a complaint but where there is *indication* that a person serving with the police may have committed a criminal offence or behaved in a manner which would justify the bringing of disciplinary proceedings (s. 12(2)).

A death and serious injury (DSI) matter is any circumstances in or in consequence of which a person has died or sustained serious injury and where the following requirements are satisfied:

- the dead or seriously injured person had been arrested by a person serving with the police and had not been released from that arrest, or was otherwise detained in the custody of a person serving with the police;
- at or before the time of the death or serious injury the person had contact (of whatever kind, and whether direct or indirect) with a person serving with the police who was acting in the execution of his/her duties; and there is an indication that the contact may have caused (whether directly or indirectly) or contributed to the death or serious injury. (s. 12(2A) to (2C)).

4.1.12.5 Recordable Conduct Matters

The framework includes a number of novel provisions. For instance, the Police (Complaints and Misconduct) Regulations 2004 (SI 2004/643) allow for the recording of complaints where the officer has ceased to serve with the police and also for the recording of complaints where the identity of the officer is unknown.

Section 29 states that a 'recordable conduct matter' means (subject to any regulations under s. 23(2)(d)):

(a) a conduct matter that is required to be recorded by the appropriate authority under paragraph 10 or 11 of Schedule 3 or has been so recorded; or
(b) except in sub-paragraph (4) of paragraph 2 of Schedule 3, any matter brought to the attention of the appropriate authority under that sub-paragraph.

4.1.12.6 Handling Complaints, Conduct Matters and DSI Matters

The definitions of complaints, conduct matters and DSI matters are set out above: the practical provisions for dealing with such issues are to be found in part 2 of the Act and also in sch. 3.

Schedule 3 to the Police Reform Act 2002 states:

1.—(1) Where a complaint is made about the conduct of a chief officer, it shall be the duty of the police authority maintaining his force to secure that all such steps as are appropriate for the purposes of Part 2 of this Act are taken, both initially and from time to time after that, for obtaining and preserving evidence relating to the conduct complained of.

(2) Where—

(a) a complaint is made to a chief officer about the conduct of a person under his direction and control, or

(b) a chief officer becomes aware that a complaint about the conduct of a person under his direction or control has been made to the Commission or to a police authority,

the chief officer shall take all such steps as appear to him to be appropriate for the purposes of Part 2 of this Act for obtaining and preserving evidence relating to the conduct complained of.

(3) The chief officer's duty under sub-paragraph (2) must be performed as soon as practicable after the complaint is made or, as the case may be, he becomes aware of it.

(4) After that, he shall be under a duty, until he is satisfied that it is no longer necessary to do so, to continue to take the steps from time to time appearing to him to be appropriate for the purposes of Part 2 of this Act for obtaining and preserving evidence relating to the conduct complained of.

(5) It shall be the duty of a police authority to comply with all such directions as may be given to it by the Commission in relation to the performance of its duty under sub-paragraph (1).

(6) It shall be the duty of a chief officer to take all such specific steps for obtaining or preserving evidence relating to any conduct that is the subject-matter of a complaint as he may be directed to take for the purposes of this paragraph by the police authority maintaining his force or by the Commission.

KEYNOTE

These provisions place an obligation on a police authority (in the case of a complaint about a chief officer) and on chief officers in other cases to obtain and preserve relevant evidence. This duty is not confined to evidence *against* the person complained about and will apply equally to evidence tending to support the person's innocence or defence. The duty is a continuing one.

The chief officer has an additional duty to takes steps in response to proper directions of his/her police authority.

The next duty to arise on receiving a complaint will depend on who the complaint was made to. Where a complaint is made to the IPCC, it must:

- ascertain whether the complainant is content for the police authority or appropriate chief officer to be notified and, if so,
- notify that police authority or chief officer.

If a complainant is not content for the police authority or chief officer to be notified of the complaint, the IPCC can bring the *subject matter* of the complaint to the Appropriate Authority if it considers it is in the public interest to do so. Thereafter the complaint will be dealt with as a recordable conduct matter or DSI matter.

Where a complaint is made to a police authority or chief officer, they must:

- determine whether they are the 'Appropriate Authority' and, if not,
- notify the person or body who is (Police Reform Act 2002, sch. 3, para. 2).

Where the IPCC, police authority or a chief officer makes a notification under the above provisions, they must also notify the complainant, saying what the notification contained or that the matter has been brought to the Appropriate Authority's attention to be dealt with otherwise than as a complaint.

Where the IPCC, police authority or a chief officer decides that they are the Appropriate Authority on receiving a complaint they must record it—unless they are satisfied that the matter has been or is being dealt with by means of criminal or disciplinary proceedings against the person whose conduct is involved or that the complaint has been withdrawn.

If a police authority or chief officer decides not to notify the Appropriate Authority as above or to record *the whole or part* of the complaint, they must inform the complainant stating what decision has been taken, the grounds for taking it and the fact that the complainant has a right of appeal.

4.1.12.7 Appeal

In such cases (where the police authority or chief officer receiving the complaint decides not to notify the Appropriate Authority or to record the *whole* complaint), the complainant has a right of appeal to the IPCC (para. 3(3)). On appeal, the IPCC must decide whether any relevant action relating to notification or recording of the complaint should have been taken. If it finds in the complainant's favour, the IPCC may give such directions as it considers appropriate to the police authority or chief officer. The police authority or chief officer then has an obligation to comply with those directions.

The Secretary of State may make regulations governing the practicalities of this appeals process (see the Police (Complaints and Misconduct) Regulations 2004 (SI 2004/643)).

4.1.12.8 Referral of Complaints

In some cases the Appropriate Authority *must* refer a complaint to the IPCC, whereas in others there is some discretion whether or not to do so. The rules for referral are summarised as follows:

- **Mandatory**—if:
  (a) the complaint is one alleging that the conduct complained of has resulted in death or serious injury;
  (b) the complaint is of a description specified for the purposes of this sub-paragraph in regulations made by the Secretary of State; or
  (c) the IPCC notifies the Appropriate Authority that it requires the complaint in question to be referred to it for its consideration.

  Those specified under (b) are set out in the Police (Complaints and Misconduct) Regulations 2004 (SI 2004/643) and include:
  (i) a serious assault, a serious sexual offence and serious corruption, in each case as defined in guidance issued by the Commission;
  (ii) a criminal offence or behaviour which is liable to lead to a disciplinary sanction and which in either case was aggravated by discriminatory behaviour on the grounds of a person's race, sex, religion, or other status identified in guidance by the Commission; and
  (iii) an offence for which the sentence is fixed by law, or an offence for which a person of 18 years or over (not previously convicted) could be sentenced to seven years' imprisonment or more (inserted by the Serious Organised Crime and Police Act 2005, (Powers of Arrest) (Consequential Amendments) Order 2005 (SI 2005/3389)).

- **Voluntary**—if the Appropriate Authority or police authority considers that it would be appropriate to do so by reason of:
  (a) the gravity of the subject-matter of the complaint; or
  (b) any exceptional circumstances.
- **'Called in'**—if the IPCC notifies the Appropriate Authority that it requires the complaint in question to be referred to it for its consideration.

(See generally sch. 3.)

Any reference must be made within the relevant time as set out in the regulations and the power to refer/call in is exercisable irrespective of whether the complaint is already being investigated or has already been considered by the IPCC.

Where a complaint is referred to it, the IPCC has a duty to decide whether or not it is necessary for the complaint to be investigated. Where the IPCC decides it is not necessary for a complaint to be investigated, it may refer the matter back to the Appropriate Authority to deal with it. In such cases the IPCC must notify the complainant and (unless it might prejudice the possible future investigation of *that complaint*), notify the person complained against.

The majority of complaints will not involve a referral to the IPCC under any of the above methods (mandatory, voluntary or 'calling in'). In most cases, or in cases where the IPCC has referred a complaint back to the Appropriate Authority, that Appropriate Authority will deal with the complaint itself; in doing so, it must comply with the requirements of sch. 3 and any relevant regulations.

The first thing that sch. 3 requires the Appropriate Authority to do in such cases is to decide whether the matter is suitable for 'local resolution'. If the complaint is suitable, appropriate arrangements must be made; if it is not, then it must be investigated.

4.1.12.9 Local Resolution

Replacing the old informal resolution, this method of dealing quickly with complaints that are at the lower end of the scale is already familiar to the police service.

In relation to whether a complaint is suitable for local resolution, sch 3, para. 6 states:

> (3) A determination that a complaint is suitable for being subjected to local resolution shall not be made unless either—
> (a) the appropriate authority is satisfied that the conduct complained of (even if it were proved) would not justify the bringing of any criminal or disciplinary proceedings; or
> (b) the IPCC, in a case falling within sub-para. (4), has approved the use of local resolution.
>
> (4) The IPCC may approve the use of local resolution in the case of any complaint if, on an application by the appropriate authority, the IPCC is satisfied—
> (a) that the following two conditions are fulfilled—
> (i) that the conduct complained of (even if it were proved) would not justify the bringing of any criminal proceedings; and
> (ii) that any disciplinary proceedings the bringing of which would be justified in respect of that conduct (even if it were proved) would be unlikely to result in a dismissal, a requirement to resign or retire, a reduction in rank or other demotion or the imposition of a fine;
>
> or
>
> (b) that it will not be practicable (even if the complaint is thoroughly investigated) for either of the following to be brought—
> (i) criminal proceedings in respect of the conduct to which it relates that would be likely to result in a conviction; or

(ii) disciplinary proceedings in respect of that conduct that would be likely to result in a dismissal, a requirement to resign or retire, a reduction in rank or other demotion or the imposition of a fine.

Note that no more than one application may be made to the IPCC for the purposes in respect of the same complaint.

Before a complainant can give consent for the purposes of this paragraph to the local resolution of their complaint they must have been informed of their rights of appeal. Once given, however, a consent for these purposes is not capable of being withdrawn at any time after the procedure for the local resolution of the complaint has begun (para. 6(7)).

The Appropriate Authority may appoint a person to secure the local resolution of a suitable complaint. This person must be a person 'serving with the police' (**see para. 4.1.12.3**) and under the direction and control of the relevant chief officer (para. 8).

The procedures set out in the regulations must be followed.

Any statement made for the purposes of a local resolution of a complaint is not admissible in any subsequent criminal, civil or disciplinary proceedings. This general safeguard is only relaxed where the statement concerned consists of an admission relating to a matter that has not been subjected to local resolution (see para. 8(3)).

If, after attempts have been made to resolve a complaint using local resolution, it appears to the Appropriate Authority:

- that the resolution of the complaint in that manner is impossible, or
- that the complaint is, for any other reason, not suitable for such resolution,

the Appropriate Authority must make arrangements for the complaint to be investigated by that authority on its own behalf (para. 8(4)).

The local resolution of any complaint must be discontinued if it is referred to the IPCC under any of the avenues for referral.

A person who has participated in any attempt to resolve a complaint using local resolution is disqualified for appointment under any provision of sch. 3 to investigate that complaint, or to assist with the carrying out of the investigation of that complaint (para. 8(6)).

4.1.12.10 Appeals against Local Resolutions

In some circumstances, complainants may appeal against the local resolution procedure. Provisions governing these appeals are set out in sch. 3 and the relevant regulations (see the Police (Complaints and Misconduct) Regulations 2004 (SI 2004/643), reg. 9).

The first thing to note with this process is that the appeal is only against the *conduct* of the local resolution. This means that the appeal is about the *process*, not the result of the resolution. As a consequence, the IPCC—to whom the right of appeal exists—will review the extent to which there have been any contraventions of the procedural requirements relating to the local resolution.

In hearing any appeal, the IPCC must give the person complained against and the Appropriate Authority the opportunity to make representations about the matters under appeal.

If the IPCC finds in favour of the complainant it must give such directions as it considers appropriate to the Appropriate Authority regarding the future handling of that complaint (including an investigation of it) and the Appropriate Authority must comply with those directions.

The IPCC will notify all parties of any relevant decision it makes in hearing an appeal.

4.1.12.11 Conduct Matters and DSI Matters

Where a conduct matter or DSI matter (as defined by s. 12(2)) and (2A) to (2D) comes to the attention of the Appropriate Authority and it appears to meet the criteria of a recordable conduct matter or DSI matter, the Appropriate Authority must record it as such—that much is pretty obvious. Having recorded the matter, the Appropriate Authority must then decide whether referral to the IPCC is required or appropriate. There is no need to record the matter again if it has already been or is being dealt with by means of criminal or disciplinary proceedings.

If the matter comes first to the attention of the IPCC rather than the Appropriate Authority, the IPCC will direct that the matter be recorded as such if that has not already been done.

As with 'complaints', there is a duty on the Appropriate Authority to take such steps as are appropriate to obtain and preserve evidence relating to the recordable conduct matter or DSI matter and this duty is a continuing one (sch. 3, paras 12 and 14B).

Similarly, recordable conduct matters may—and in some circumstances must—be referred to the IPCC. Schedule 3, para. 13(1)(a)–(c) provides that the Appropriate Authority is under a duty to refer a recordable conduct matter where:

- that matter relates to any incident or circumstances in or in consequence of which any person has died or suffered serious injury;
- that matter is of a description specified for the purposes of this sub-paragraph in regulations made by the Secretary of State (these are generally the same as those requiring mandatory referral of complaints as described above); or
- the IPCC notifies the appropriate authority that it requires that matter to be referred to the IPCC for its consideration;

and it may do so where it is considered appropriate to do so by reason of the gravity of the matter or any exceptional circumstances. Schedule 3, para. 14C(1) requires that all DSI matters be referred to the IPCC.

The IPCC may also 'call in' a recordable conduct matter or DSI matter under its general powers. Where a recordable conduct matter or DSI matter is referred to the IPCC, the person whose conduct is involved will be notified by the Appropriate Authority unless it considers that to do so might prejudice a possible future investigation *of that matter* (para. 13(6)).

Where a recordable conduct matter or DSI matter is referred, the IPCC must decide whether it is necessary for it to be investigated. If it decides that investigation is not necessary, the IPCC may refer the matter back to the Appropriate Authority to deal with it as that authority thinks fit.

4.1.12.12 Investigations

Part 3 of sch. 3 to the Police Reform Act 2002 sets out the relevant provisions covering the investigation of complaints or recordable conduct matters or DSI matters.

On the completion of an investigation, the Investigating Officer will submit a report to the Appropriate Authority and, if relevant, to the IPCC.

No criminal or disciplinary proceedings can be brought in relation to any matter which is the subject of an investigation under sch. 3 until a report has been submitted, either to the IPCC or to the Appropriate Authority (para. 20). Schedule 3 to the 2002 Act was amended by the Serious Organised Crime and Police Act 2005 and provides for an accelerated procedure in relation to 'special cases'. This is where a person appointed or designated to investigate a complaint or recordable conduct believes that 'special conditions' apply (para. 20A(1)). These special conditions are provided by para. 20A(7) which states:

(a) the person whose conduct is the subject matter of the investigation may have committed an imprisonable offence and that person's conduct is of a serious nature;
(b) there is sufficient evidence, in the form of written statements or other documents, to establish on the balance of probabilities that conduct justifying dismissal took place; and
(c) it is in the public interest for the person whose conduct is the subject matter of the investigation to cease to be a member of a police force, or to be a special constable, without delay.

KEYNOTE

'Imprisonable offence' means an offence punishable with imprisonment in the case of a person aged 21 or over, and 'conduct justifying dismissal' means conduct which is so serious that disciplinary proceedings brought in respect of it would be likely to result in a dismissal (para. 20A(8)(a) and (b)).

Where it is believed the special conditions apply, a report is submitted to the appropriate authority who, if they determine that the special conditions are satisfied, certify the case as a special case for the purposes of reg. 11 of the Police (Conduct) Regulations 2004, subject to the agreement of the DPP (para. 20B(3)). The DPP may request the appropriate authority not to bring disciplinary proceedings without his/her prior agreement, if the DPP considers that bringing such proceedings might prejudice any future criminal proceedings. The appropriate authority is required to notify the IPCC of a certification under sub-para. (3) (para. 20B(6)). Where the appropriate authority considers the special conditions are not satisfied or (as the case may be) that they are so satisfied, but the circumstances are such as to make it inappropriate at present to bring disciplinary proceedings, a memorandum setting out its reasons is submitted to the IPCC (para. 20B(7) and (8)). The IPCC may accept the recommendation or direct the appropriate authority to certify the case (para. 20H(7)).

The DPP may bring criminal proceedings in any case where it appears to him/her that there are exceptional circumstances that make a delay in bringing proceedings undesirable. In 'special cases' the DPP may request the appropriate authority not to bring disciplinary proceedings without his/her prior agreement (para. 20G(1)).

4.1.12.13 Investigations involving the IPCC

Where a case has been referred to the IPCC and it has decided that an investigation is necessary, the IPCC must decide the form that any investigation will take, having regard to the seriousness of the matter and the public interest.

The investigation may take one of four forms, with the IPCC's involvement being at an ascending level, namely:

- An investigation carried out by the Appropriate Authority itself on its own behalf (Level One).
- An investigation carried out by the Appropriate Authority but under the *supervision* of the IPCC (Level Two).
- An investigation carried out by the Appropriate Authority but under the *management* of the IPCC (Level Three).
- An investigation carried out by the IPCC itself (Level Four).

The IPCC may at any time change the level of the investigation. The features of each level are considered further below.

4.1.12.14 Level One

Investigations under Level One are carried out by the Appropriate Authority on its own behalf. These may come about as the result of an initial decision by the Appropriate Authority itself on recording the matter or on referral to it by the IPCC. As such these will be fairly conventional investigations occurring in the majority of investigated complaints or conduct matters.

4.1.12.15 Level Two—Supervised Investigations

These investigations will be familiar to those who worked under the former system where matters were brought under the supervision of the PCA.

The key differences in features from those of the straightforward Level One investigations generally relate to the Investigating Officer. These differences are:

- The IPCC may require that no Investigating Officer is appointed or allowed to continue without its approval.
- If the IPCC is not satisfied with the Investigating Officer, it can require the Appropriate Authority to appoint another one.
- The Investigating Officer must comply with all requirements in relation to the carrying out of the investigation as may be imposed by the IPCC in accordance with the relevant regulations.

At the conclusion of a Level Two investigation the Investigating Officer must submit a report to the IPCC and send a copy to the Appropriate Authority (para. 22).

4.1.12.16 Level Three—Managed Investigations

These investigations will still be carried out by the Appropriate Authority but will be actively managed by the IPCC. In addition to all the requirements and conditions that apply to Level Two investigations, in managed investigations the Investigating Officer is under the direction and control of the IPCC. So far as the involvement of an independent body is concerned, this is a stage further than anything formerly allowed under the old system. This represents a significant increase in the level of control exercisable in an investigation into police conduct.

At the conclusion of a Level Three investigation the Investigating Officer must submit a report to the IPCC and send a copy to the Appropriate Authority (para. 22).

4.1.12.17 Level Four—IPCC Investigations

The highest level of independent investigation available into reported police conduct is to be found in this category. These investigations are a wholly new concept for the police and have been introduced in response to growing pressure for a mechanism whereby some matters of reported police conduct can be investigated by a body completely independent of the police endowed with appropriate powers and resources. Under such investigations the IPCC will designate one of its members to be the Investigating Officer, along with such others as are needed to assist.

The Investigating Officer will have all the powers and privileges of a constable throughout England and Wales (para. 19(7)) and the Secretary of State may specify that certain provisions of the Police and Criminal Evidence Act 1984 will apply (with modifications) to the investigation of offences under this level. In addition, the Commission's officers and employees have been given significant powers under the Police Act 1997 and the Regulation of Investigatory Powers Act 2000 (**see para. 4.12.4**) to gather intelligence and evidence (see the Independent Police Complaints Commission (Investigatory Powers) Order 2004 (SI 2004/815)).

At the conclusion of a Level Four investigation the Investigating Officer must submit a report to the IPCC (para. 22).

4.1.12.18 Action on Receiving a Report

On receiving a report from the Investigating Officer, the IPCC and the Appropriate Authority have overlapping responsibilities. Generally they must decide whether that report indicates that a criminal offence may have been committed by the person whose conduct was the subject-matter of the investigation and, if so, must notify the DPP (sending a copy to him/her) and notifying the Appropriate Authority (para. 23).

If criminal proceedings are brought in respect of any matters dealt with in a report from it to the DPP, the IPCC must notify:

- in the case of a complaint, the complainant and every person entitled to be kept properly informed in relation to the complaint under s. 21; and
- in the case of a recordable conduct matter or DSI matter, every person entitled to be kept properly informed in relation to that matter under that section.

If the IPCC:

- decides that there is no indication of a criminal offence;
- is notified by the DPP that he/she proposes to take no action in respect of any matters dealt with in the report; or
- is satisfied that all likely criminal proceedings in respect of matters dealt with in the report have been brought to a conclusion,

it must notify the Appropriate Authority, requiring it to decide what action (if any) it will take.

The Appropriate Authority must then arrive at its own decision and send a memorandum to the IPCC setting out what it proposes to do and, if it proposes not to bring disciplinary proceedings against the person whose conduct was reported on, it must give the reasons.

The IPCC must then consider the memorandum, decide whether or not to make its own recommendations and, if so, make them—notifying the relevant parties of its decision, the findings of the report and any recommended action (para. 23).

If the DPP decides to bring criminal proceedings against *any person* in respect of any matters dealt with in a report sent to him/her, the Appropriate Authority must notify all relevant parties (see para. 24(5)).

As with the IPCC above, if the Appropriate Authority has decided that there is no indication that a criminal offence has been committed, is notified by the DPP that he/she proposes to take no action in respect of any matters dealt with in the report, or is satisfied that all likely criminal proceedings in respect of matters dealt with in the report have been brought to a conclusion, the Appropriate Authority must decide what action (if any) to take. On deciding, the Appropriate Authority must notify all relevant parties of the findings of the report, any action it has decided to take and also of the complainant's right of appeal (see paras 24 and 24A to 24C).

4.1.12.19 Appeals

In cases involving an investigation by the Appropriate Authority (Level One) or one that is supervised by the IPCC (Level 2), the complainant has a right of appeal under sch. 3, para. 25 of which states:

> (1) This paragraph applies where a complaint has been subjected to—
> (a) an investigation by the appropriate authority on its own behalf; or
> (b) an investigation under the supervision of the Commission
> (2) The complainant shall have the following rights of appeal to the Commission—
> (a) a right to appeal on the grounds that he has not been provided with adequate information—
> (i) about the findings of the investigation; or
> (ii) about any proposals of the appropriate authority to take, or not to take, action in consequence of the report;
> (b) a right to appeal against the findings of the investigation; and
> (c) a right of appeal against any proposal of the appropriate authority to take, or not to take, action in respect of any of the matters dealt with in the report of the investigation;
> and it shall be the duty of the Commission to notify the appropriate authority, every person entitled to be kept properly informed in relation to the complaint under section 21 and the person complained against of any appeal brought under this paragraph.

KEYNOTE

The IPCC may require the Appropriate Authority to submit a memorandum to the IPCC which:

- sets out whether the Appropriate Authority is proposing to take any action in respect of the matters dealt with in the report and, if so, what;
- if the Appropriate Authority has decided in relation to any person whose conduct is the subject-matter of the report that disciplinary proceedings should not be brought against that person, sets out its reasons for so deciding;

and it is the duty of the Appropriate Authority to comply with any relevant requirement under this paragraph.

If the IPCC requires it on the bringing of an appeal in the case of an investigation by the Appropriate Authority on its own behalf, that Appropriate Authority must provide the IPCC with a copy of the report of the investigation (para. 25(4)).

On an appeal under para. 25, the IPCC will decide:

- whether the complainant has been provided with adequate information;
- whether the findings of the investigation need to be reconsidered; and
- whether the Appropriate Authority is proposing to take the action that the IPCC considers appropriate in consequence of the report.

If, on an appeal, the IPCC decides that the complainant has not been provided with adequate information about any matter, it will give the Appropriate Authority all such directions as it considers appropriate for making sure that the complainant is properly informed (para. 25(6)).

If the IPCC decides that the findings of the investigation need to be reconsidered, it will either review those findings without an immediate further investigation or direct that the complaint be re-investigated (para. 25(8)).

If the IPCC decides that the Appropriate Authority is not proposing to take the action in consequence of the report that the IPCC considers appropriate, the IPCC will decide whether or not to make recommendations (under para. 27), making any such recommendations as it thinks fit.

The IPCC will give notification of any decisions and recommendation under this paragraph to the Appropriate Authority, the complainant, every person entitled to be kept properly informed in relation to the complaint under s. 21 and, *except in a case where the IPCC decides that to do so might prejudice any proposed review or re-investigation of the complaint*, to the person complained against (see para. 25(10) and (11)).

The Secretary of State may make regulations governing the appeal procedure (see the Police (Complaints and Misconduct) Regulations 2004 (SI 2004/643)).

Where the IPCC conducts a review on appeal, it may generally uphold the findings in whole or in part or it may give the Appropriate Authority such directions in relation to the giving of information or handling of the matter as it thinks fit.

If it directs a re-investigation, the IPCC may require any level of investigation (1 to 4) and the whole process as set out earlier in this chapter essentially starts again.

The IPCC will notify all relevant parties of its decision in an appeal process.

4.1.12.20 Dispensation

An Appropriate Authority may apply to the IPCC for permission to handle a complaint differently from the prescribed conditions set out in sch. 3.

Provided the Appropriate Authority considers that, for whatever reasons, it should handle a complaint otherwise than in accordance with sch. 3 *and* the complaint falls within the categories set out in the regulations, the Appropriate Authority can apply for permission to handle that complaint in any manner it thinks fit. The relevant provisions can be found in the Police (Complaints and Misconduct) Regulations 2004 (SI 2004/643), reg. 3. Broadly dispensation can be granted where the appropriate authority considers that:

- more than 12 months have elapsed between the incident, or the latest incident, giving rise to the complaint and the making of the complaint and either that no good reason for the delay has been shown or that injustice would be likely to be caused by the delay;
- the matter is already the subject of a complaint;
- the complaint discloses neither the name and address of the complainant nor that of any other interested person and it is not reasonably practicable to ascertain such a name or address;
- the complaint is vexatious, oppressive, repetitious (specific guidance is given in reg. 3 as to what will amount to 'repetitious') or otherwise an abuse of the procedures for dealing with complaints; or
- it is not reasonably practicable to complete the investigation of the complaint or any other procedures under sch. 3.

Any such application must follow the provisions of the regulations and the IPCC will notify the Appropriate Authority and the complainant of its decision. If permission is not granted, no further applications can be made in relation to that complaint and the Appropriate Authority must decide whether to investigate the complaint or deal with it by way of local resolution.

4.1.12.21 Civil Proceedings

Where a chief officer or police authority receives notification that any civil proceedings have been brought by a member of the public against them (or it appears that such proceedings are likely to be brought) and it appears at any time that the proceedings involve a conduct matter, the chief officer or police authority has further specific obligations—apart from anything else, because this is a 'recordable conduct matter' (**see para. 4.1.12.5**).

In such cases, sch. 3 and the relevant regulations require the chief officer or police authority first to establish who is the Appropriate Authority in relation to the conduct matter involved. That Appropriate Authority must then record the matter but, before doing so, the Appropriate Authority must decide whether referral to the IPCC is either required or appropriate. If referral to the IPCC is not required or felt not to be appropriate, the matter may be dealt with in any manner that the Appropriate Authority decides.

If the matter has been, or is being, dealt with by means of criminal or disciplinary proceedings against the relevant person, there is no need to record the matter again under these provisions.

The IPCC can order the discontinuance of an investigation if the complaint falls within one of the categories set out in the relevant regulations. If it does so, the IPCC must notify all relevant parties and may give the Appropriate Authority relevant directions as set out in the regulations.

4.1.12.22 IPCC Duties in Disciplinary Proceedings

Under sch. 3, the IPCC may, in some circumstances, recommend that disciplinary proceedings (either generally or specific charges) be brought against, or modified in relation to, a person serving with the police (see para. 27). Where the IPCC makes such a recommendation, the Appropriate Authority must notify the IPCC saying whether it accepts the recommendation or not. If the Appropriate Authority does not take steps to secure that *full effect* is given to the recommendations the IPCC may direct the Appropriate Authority to take steps for that purpose and it is the duty of the Appropriate Authority to comply with the direction (para. 27(4)). Where the IPCC gives the Appropriate Authority a direction under this provision, it will supply the Appropriate Authority with a statement of its reasons for doing so.

Where disciplinary proceedings have been brought in accordance with a recommendation or direction under this provision, the authority has a duty to ensure that they are proceeded with to a proper conclusion (para. 27(7)).

The Appropriate Authority has a duty to keep the IPCC informed of its actions and decisions in these cases. Similarly, the IPCC has a duty to notify the relevant parties and keep them properly informed at each stage of this process.

4.1.13 Appeals

Where an officer has been:

- dismissed
- required to resign, or
- reduced in rank

following a hearing/chief officer's review in relation to unsatisfactory performance or misconduct, that officer has a right of appeal.

4.1.13.1 Police Appeals Tribunal

The Police Appeals Tribunal is made up of a number of people drawn by the relevant police authority from a list maintained by the Home Office. The tribunal will comprise:

- a legally qualified chairperson;

- a member of the police authority (or, in cases involving Metropolitan Police officers, a member of the Metropolitan Police Committee);
- a serving or former chief officer (not from the appellant's force);
- a retired officer of appropriate rank (i.e. a superintendent/chief superintendent where the appellant was a superintendent, otherwise a chief inspector or below).

A tribunal does not need to have a hearing in all cases (Police Act 1996, sch. 6, para. 6). It may determine an appeal without the formality of a hearing, provided the appellant and respondent are given the opportunity to make representations as to the holding of a hearing and provided also that those representations have been considered.

4.1.13.2 The Rules

Section 85 of the Police Act 1996 empowers the Secretary of State to make regulations in respect of appeals from hearings. After consultation with the statutory body that oversees all tribunals, the Council on Tribunals, the Secretary of State made the Police Appeals Tribunals Rules 1999 (SI 1999/818), which came into force on 1 April 1999.

Other than in cases brought under the old Police Discipline Regulations, the 1999 Rules revoke the former Police (Appeals) Rules 1985.

Any expression used in the Rules which also appears in the Police (Conduct) or Police (Efficiency) Regulations 1999 generally has the same meaning as it does in those Regulations (r. 3(2)).

4.1.13.3 Notice of Appeal

Rule 5 of the 1999 Rules states:

> (1) Subject to rule 7 and paragraph (2), the time within which notice of an appeal under section 85 of the Act shall be given is 21 days from the date on which the decision appealed against was notified to the appellant in pursuance of regulations made in accordance with section 50(3) of the Act.
>
> (2) In a case to which regulation 39 of the Police (Conduct) Regulations 1999 or regulation 25 of the Police (Conduct) (Senior Officers) Regulations 1999 applies where the decision appealed against was given in pursuance of those Regulations as modified by Part II of Schedule 2 or, as the case may be, by Part II of the Schedule to those Regulations, the time within which notice of an appeal under section 85 of the Act shall be given is 28 days from—
>
> (a) the conclusion of any criminal proceedings in which the appellant is charged with an offence in respect of the conduct to which the decision appealed against related; or
>
> (b) a decision that no such criminal proceedings will be instituted or taken over by the Director of Public Prosecutions has been communicated to the appellant.

KEYNOTE

Notice of the appeal must be given within 21 days of the date *on which the decision appealed against was notified to the member concerned.* It would seem that this means the date on which the member concerned actually received the notification of the decision. This time limit may, however, be extended by the 'relevant police authority' under r. 7(1) (see below). The relevant police authority will be the police authority for the member's force. In the case of Metropolitan Police officers, the authority will be the designated Home Office official of the Metropolitan Police Committee.

In 'special cases' (**see para. 4.1.11.18**) under reg. 45 of the Police (Conduct) Regulations 2004—or its equivalent for senior officers—the time limit is 28 days from:

- the end of any related criminal proceedings against the appellant; or

- the date when a decision from the Director of Public Prosecutions not to institute any such proceedings has been communicated to the appellant.

The notice of appeal must be in writing and a copy must be sent to the 'respondent' (r. 5(3)).

The 'respondent' is simply the chief officer of the appellant's force (or, where the appellant is a senior officer, a person designated for that purpose by the relevant police authority) (r. 4).

4.1.13.4 Procedure

Rule 6 states:

> (1) As soon as practicable after receipt of a copy of the notice of appeal, the respondent shall provide to the relevant police authority—
> (a) a copy of the report of the person who made the decision appealed against;
> (b) the transcript of the proceedings at the original hearing; and
> (c) any documents which were made available to the person conducting the original hearing.

KEYNOTE

The 'original hearing' is the conduct or inefficiency hearing which concluded that the appellant failed to meet the appropriate standard or that his/her performance was unsatisfactory (r. 3(1)).

A copy of the transcript referred to at r. 6(1)(b) must, at the same time, be sent to the appellant (r. 6(2)). Receiving this transcript provides the trigger for the 28-day time limit for the appellant to submit the various statements and documents under r. 6 (see below).

These copies must be provided/sent 'as soon as practicable' after the notification of appeal has been received.

Rule 6 goes on to state:

> (3) Subject to rule 7, the appellant shall, within 28 days of the date on which he receives a copy of the transcript mentioned in paragraph (1)(b), submit to the relevant police authority—
> (a) a statement of the grounds of appeal;
> (b) any supporting documents; and
> (c) either—
> (i) any written representations which the appellant wishes to make under paragraph 6 of the Schedule 6 to the Act or, as the case may be, any request to make oral representations under that paragraph; or
> (ii) a statement that he does not wish to make any such representations as are mentioned in paragraph (i):
>
> Provided that, in a case where the appellant submits a statement under sub-paragraph (c)(ii), nothing in this paragraph shall prevent representations under paragraph 6 of the Schedule 6 to the Act being made by him to the chairman of the tribunal.

KEYNOTE

The appellant must, within the time limit, submit a statement setting out the grounds of his/her appeal and any supporting documentation to the relevant police authority. This time limit may also be extended by the 'relevant police authority' under r. 7(1) (see below).

He/she must also submit either:

- any written representations or a request to make oral representations (where there is to be no hearing); or

- a negative statement (i.e. that he/she does not wish to make any such representations).

Submission of a negative statement does not, however, prevent an appellant from making representations to the chair of the tribunal where it has been decided to proceed without a hearing (r. 6(3)).

The documents set out above must also be copied, as soon as practicable, to the members of the tribunal and to the 'respondent' (r. 6(4)).

Rule 6 goes on to state:

> (5) The respondent shall, not later than 21 days from the date on which he receives the copy documents sent to him under paragraph (4), submit to the relevant police authority—
> (a) a statement of his response to the appeal;
> (b) any supporting documents; and
> (c) either—
> (i) any written representations which the respondent wishes to make under paragraph 6 of Schedule 6 to the Act or, as the case may be, any request to make oral representations under that paragraph; or
> (ii) a statement that he does not wish to make any such representations as are mentioned in paragraph (i):
>
> Provided that, in a case where the respondent submits a statement under sub-paragraph (c)(ii), nothing in this paragraph shall prevent representations under paragraph 6 of Schedule 6 to the Act being made by him to the chairman of the tribunal.

KEYNOTE

The respondent must submit similar documents to those required of the appellant under r. 6(3) above and must do so no later than 21 days from the date on which he/she receives the copies of the appellant's documents.

The documents submitted by the respondent must also be copied to the members of the tribunal (r. 6(7)).

Only those documents set out in r. 6(5)(a) and (c) must be *copied* to the appellant but a list of any supporting documents must be sent to him/her (r. 6(6)).

Again, a negative statement in relation to the making of representations will not prevent the respondent from making representations to the chair of the tribunal where it has been decided to proceed without a hearing.

4.1.13.5 Extension of Time Limits

Rule 7 allows the police authority to extend the time limits under rr. 5 and 6(3) where:

- the appellant applies for an extension, and
- the authority is satisfied that it is just to grant such an extension
- the special circumstances of the case require it.

Where an appellant makes a request for an extension and that request is turned down, the authority must give him/her written notice setting out the reasons (r. 7(2)). That notice must also advise the appellant of the right of appeal against this decision. The appellant can then appeal, within 14 days of receiving this notice, to the chair of the tribunal against the decision not to grant an extension. The chair may then grant an extension under r. 7.

4.1.13.6 Procedure at Hearing

Rules 8 to 10 regulate the procedure to be followed at a hearing.

Under r. 8 the appellant must generally be given at least 28 days' notice of the date of a hearing. However, this may be reduced provided both parties agree (r. 8(1)).

The provisions of the Local Government Act 1972 (giving powers in relation to local inquiries) are applied where relevant to hearings under these Rules.

There is no need for the appellant or the respondent to be present at the hearing which may proceed without either of them if it appears just and proper to do so (r. 8(3)).

The hearing may also be adjourned 'from time to time' as may appear necessary for the due hearing of the case (r. 8(3)).

Subject to the Rules (and also the general principles of law), the procedure at the hearing will be determined by the tribunal (r. 8(4)).

The hearing will be in private, though the tribunal has discretion to allow people it considers 'desirable' to attend the whole or part of the hearing (r. 9(1)).

A complainant will be also allowed to attend the hearing where the appeal is not simply against the sanction imposed earlier. In cases where the complainant is allowed to be present, that entitlement extends only to occasions *while witnesses are being examined and cross-examined about the facts alleged* (r. 12). This would not appear to give a complainant any entitlement to be present during the giving of any antecedents, mitigation or extraneous background evidence relating to the appellant. The complainant may be allowed to be accompanied by a friend or relative *who is not going to be called as a witness*, where appropriate (r. 12(3)).

If the complainant is going to give evidence, he/she must not attend before giving that evidence and, if the tribunal feels that a witness is going to give information that ought not to be disclosed to the public, it must require the complainant (and anyone accompanying him/her) to withdraw (r. 12(3)).

Generally, the respondent will 'open the batting', but the tribunal can determine otherwise (r. 10(1)). All oral evidence will be given under oath and the tribunal will decide what evidence is admissible or what questions can be put to a witness.

A verbatim record must be made of all evidence given at the hearing and this record must be kept for at least seven years after the end of the hearing (unless the chair asks for a transcript to be made) (r. 10(5)).

The tribunal may allow evidence to be submitted in a written statement in lieu of admissible oral evidence (r. 11).

4.1.13.7 Findings

A Police Appeals Tribunal may make an order which:

- appears to it to be *less* severe than the decision appealed against; and
- which could have been imposed by the person making that decision (Police Act 1996, s.85(2)).

The chair of the tribunal must prepare a written statement of its findings, together with reasons (r. 13(1)). That statement must be submitted to the relevant police authority (and the Secretary of State where the appellant is a senior officer) 'within a reasonable period' after the determination of the appeal. So too must a record of any order the tribunal makes under its powers under s. 85(2).

The relevant authority must copy the statement and record to the appellant and respondent as soon as practicable (r. 13(3)).

Where the decision appealed against arose from a complaint, the relevant police authority must also notify the complainant of the outcome of the appeal (r. 13(4)).

Although the Regulations relating to efficiency and misconduct specify that any decision may be reached by a simple majority (see above), the Appeals Rules make no such provision.

4.1.14 Vicarious Liability of Chief Officers

Section 88 of the Police Act 1996 originally provided that a chief officer will be vicariously liable for the 'torts' (civil wrongs) of his/her officers committed in the performance (or purported performance) of their duties. This meant that the chief officer was responsible for the payment of any damages arising out of a civil claim in respect of such a tort (for the situation regarding discrimination and other employment matters generally, **see chapter 4.13**). The extent of this vicarious liability was wider than that imposed on employers generally (see comments of the Court of Appeal in *Weir* v *Chief Constable of Merseyside Police* [2003] ICR 708).

However, despite the fact that the vicarious liability of chief officers was broader than that of any ordinary employer, its limitation to strictly actionable civil wrongs was felt to have led to some inequities, denying remedies to individuals while failing to impose full accountability on the relevant chief officers. The Police Reform Act 2002 has clarified the position and amends s. 88 to provide that chief officers will be liable for the 'unlawful conduct' (as opposed to purely civil wrongs) of their officers and employees when acting as such (s. 102). Section 88 does not apply in the case of officers seconded to central services such as the Serious Organised Crime Agency or the Central Police Training and Development Authority. However, s. 102 makes parallel amendments to the liability of the relevant Directors-General and other individuals in such cases.

4.1.15 Other Regulations

In addition to the specific provisions for conduct, complaints and efficiency, there are several other sources of regulation that govern the employment and deployment of police officers.

4.1.15.1 Restrictions on Private Lives

The Police Regulations 2003 (SI 2003/527) impose restrictions on the private lives of officers. Regulation 6 provides that the restrictions contained in sch. 1 shall apply to all members of a police force. It also provides that no restrictions other than those designed to secure the proper exercise of the functions of a constable shall be imposed by the police authority or the chief officer of police on the private lives of members of a police force except such as may temporarily be necessary or such as may be approved by the Secretary of State after consultation with the Police Advisory Board for England and Wales.

Schedule 1

Schedule 1 provides that a member of a police force:

- Shall at all times abstain from any activity which is likely to interfere with the impartial discharge of his duties or which is likely to give rise to the impression among members of the public that it may so interfere.
- Shall in particular—
  (a) not take any active part in politics;
  (b) not belong to any organisation specified or described in a determination of the Secretary of State.

  For this purpose the Secretary of State has determined that no member of a police force may be a member of the British National Party (BNP), Combat 18 or the National Front.
- Shall not reside at premises which are not for the time being approved by the chief officer of police.
- Shall not, without the previous consent of the chief officer of police, receive a lodger in a house or quarters with which he/she is provided by the police authority, or sub-let any part of the house or quarters.
- Shall not, unless he/she has previously given written notice to the chief officer of police, receive a lodger in a house in which he/she resides and in respect of which he/she receives an allowance under sch. 3, or sub-let any part of such a house.
- Shall not wilfully refuse or neglect to discharge any lawful debt.

4.1.15.2 Business Interests

Some business interests preclude people from applying to be a police constable (reg. 9 of the Police Regulations 2003).

Regulation 7 provides that, if a member of a police force or a relative included in his/her family proposes to have, or has, a 'business interest', the member shall forthwith give written notice of that interest to the chief officer of police unless that business interest was disclosed at the time of the officer's appointment as a member of the force.

On receipt of such a notice, the chief officer shall determine whether or not the interest in question is compatible with the member concerned remaining a member of the force and shall notify the member in writing of his/her decision within 28 days.

Within 10 days of being notified of the chief officer's decision (or within such longer period as the police authority may in all the circumstances allow), the member concerned may appeal to the police authority against that decision by sending written notice to the police authority.

If a business interest is felt to be incompatible, the chief officer may dispense with the member's services after giving them an opportunity to make representations, and subject to any earlier appeal to the police authority.

Regulation 8 provides that a member of a police force or relative has a business interest if:

- the member holds any office or employment for hire or gain or carries on any business;
- a shop is kept or a like business carried on by the member's spouse (not being separated) at any premises in the area of the police force in question or by any relative living with him/her at the premises where he/she resides; or
- the member, his/her spouse (not being separated) or any relative living with them has a pecuniary interest in any licence or permit granted in relation to liquor licensing,

refreshment houses or betting and gaming or regulating places of entertainment in the area of the police force in question.

'Relative' includes a reference to a spouse, parent, son, daughter, brother or sister.

A police officer must notify his/her chief officer of any changes in a business interest. The above regulations also apply to chief officer ranks but the relevant authority in such cases is the police authority (reg. 8(4)).

4.1.16 Offences

The following criminal offences relate to the general abuse of public office and specific offences relating to police officers or impersonation of officers or officials.

4.1.16.1 Misconduct in a Public Office

OFFENCE: **Misconduct in a public office—*Common law***

- Triable on indictment • Imprisonment at large

It is a misdemeanour at common law for the holder of a public office to do anything that amounts to a malfeasance or a 'culpable' misfeasance (*R* v *Wyatt* (1705) 1 Salk 380).

KEYNOTE

This offence has also been described as 'A man accepting an office of trust concerning the public is answerable criminally to the King for misbehaviour in his office . . . by whomsoever and in whatever way the officer is appointed' (*R* v *Bembridge* (1738) 3 Dougl 327).

Such offences can only be tried on indictment and the court has a power of sentence 'at large', that is, there is no limit on the sentence that can be passed. This ancient common law oddity is both a civil wrong (tort) giving rise to an action for damages in the county and High Court, and a criminal offence which is triable on indictment and punishable by an unlimited term of imprisonment.

Given the very wide scope of the 'offence' element, misfeasance can cover a multitude of transgressions by police officers, from mistreating prisoners to the improper use of criminal intelligence. The conduct can be separated into occasions of *mal*feasance and *mis*feasance. The first requires some degree of wrongful motive or intention on the part of the officer while the second is more likely to apply where there has been some form of wilful neglect of duty: both are notoriously difficult to prove.

The essence of both is generally an abuse of public power in bad faith (*Thomas* v *Secretary of State for the Home Department* (2000) LTL 7 August). There must at least be some real connection between the alleged misconduct and the public office—for instance where a man employed by a local council as a maintenance manager dishonestly caused his employees to carry out works on his girlfriend's premises (*R* v *Bowden* [1996] 1 WLR 98). Therefore, simply behaving badly while off duty would not of itself make a public office holder (such as a police officer) guilty of this offence (see *Elliott* v *Chief Constable of Wiltshire* (1996) *The Times*, 5 December—disclosure of previous convictions from PNC to a newspaper capable of amounting to misfeasance). It may, however, make the relevant *chief officer* vicariously liable under other heads of law if the off-duty officer was purporting to rely on his/her status as a constable (for a good example see *Weir* v *Chief Constable of Merseyside* [2003] ICR 708). After some blurring of the precise ingredients and what they actually mean in the context of policing, the key elements of the offence so far as it applies to public office holders (such as police officers) were set out by the Court of Appeal in *Attorney-General's Reference (No. 3 of 2003)* [2004] EWCA Crim 868). That case arose out of a death in police custody and the officers were charged with manslaughter by gross negligence, along with the alternative offence of misconduct in a public office.

In that case it was argued that misconduct in a public office is a 'conduct' crime, i.e. one where the acts (or omissions) themselves were the real consideration and not the consequences which those acts/omissions brought about (**see Crime, chapter 1.2**). Although reluctant to try to give an exhaustive definition of the offence, the Court of Appeal identified the elements of conduct and state of mind that must be proved in order to convict an officer of misfeasance, holding the main ingredients to be:

- Conduct (or omission) which involved the public office holder *acting as such*. In other words, this would need to arise from the actions (or omissions) of a police officer while acting in his/her capacity as a constable. A purely personal matter arising while the officer was off duty would not normally meet this first criterion.
- Evidence of wilful neglect and/or wilful misconduct. Simple inadvertence or accidental action/omission without more will not be enough.
- The degree of wilful neglect/misconduct must be such as to amount to an abuse of the public's trust in the office holder.
- Proof that the officer acted/omitted to act without any reasonable excuse or justification.

In the civil setting, even though there might be circumstances where officers could be criticised for failures including incompetence, excess of zeal and even serious negligence, the absence of bad faith or deliberate misuse of power would generally mean that there is not enough to support an allegation of misfeasance (see *Ashley* v *Chief Constable of Sussex* [2005] EWHC 415).

The ingredients of the civil wrong are fully set out in *Three Rivers District Council* v *Governor and Company of the Bank of England (No. 3)* [2000] 2 WLR 1220. Their application, especially in the case of police officers, was discussed at length by the Court of Appeal in reviewing the relevant authorities in *Cornelius* v *London Borough of Hackney* (2002) *The Times*, 27 August. In *Three Rivers*, Lord Steyn confirmed that the civil and criminal wrongs bore some resemblance. Although many of the earlier cases involved an element of corruption, this is not a requirement for the offence (*R* v *Dytham* [1979] 2 QB 722). This offence might be committed where a police officer wilfully neglects to prevent a criminal assault (as in *Dytham*), or possibly where a supervisory officer fails to intervene in a situation where one of his/her officers is carrying out an unlawful act.

From the many authorities (especially the Court of Appeal in *Bowden*) it is arguable that this offence could be extended in appropriate circumstances to misconduct of non-sworn employees such as those designated (or perhaps even those accredited) under the Police Reform Act 2002 (as to which **see chapter 4.2**).

The Court of Appeal has held that, where the police wrote to the registered keepers of vehicles believed to have been stolen in another country, informing those keepers that they may not be the legal owners, the person who imported and sold the vehicles *might* be able to bring a claim for misfeasance—much would depend on the state of mind and intentions of the relevant individual in acting as they did—*R Cruikshank Ltd* v *Chief Constable of Kent* (2002) *The Times*, 27 December.

4.1.16.2 Offences Relating to Impersonation

OFFENCE: **Impersonating a police officer—*Police Act 1996, s. 90(1)***

• Triable summarily • Six months' imprisonment

(No specific power of arrest)

The Police Act 1996, s. 90 states:

> (1) Any person who with intent to deceive impersonates a member of a police force or special constable, or makes any statement or does any act calculated falsely to suggest that he is such a member or constable, shall be guilty of an offence and liable ...

KEYNOTE

This is a crime of 'specific intent' (**see Crime, chapter 1.1**). The intention to deceive must be proved.

OFFENCE: **Wearing or possessing uniform—*Police Act 1996, s. 90(2) and (3)***

- Triable summarily • Fine

(No specific power of arrest)

The Police Act 1996, s. 90 states:

(2) Any person who, not being a constable, wears any article of police uniform in circumstances where it gives him an appearance so nearly resembling that of a member of a police force as to be calculated to deceive shall be guilty of an offence ...

(3) Any person who, not being a member of a police force or special constable, has in his possession any article of police uniform shall, unless he proves that he obtained possession of that article lawfully and has possession of it for a lawful purpose, be guilty of an offence ...

KEYNOTE

'Article of police uniform' means:

- any article of uniform, or
- any distinctive badge or mark, or
- any document of identification

usually issued to members of police forces or special constables (s. 90(4)).

OFFENCE: **Impersonating designated or accredited person—*Police Reform Act 2002, s. 46(3)***

- Triable summarily • Six months' imprisonment and/or a fine

(No specific power of arrest)

The Police Reform Act 2002, s. 46 states:

(3) Any person who, with intent to deceive—
  (a) impersonates a designated person, an accredited person or an accredited inspector,
  (b) makes any statement or does any act calculated falsely to suggest that he is a designated person, that he is an accredited person or that he is an accredited inspector, or
  (c) makes any statement or does any act calculated falsely to suggest that he has powers as a designated or accredited person or as an accredited inspector that exceed the powers he actually has,

is guilty of an offence.

KEYNOTE

These offences are based on the corresponding offences for police officers. They are offences of specific intent (**see Crime, chapter 1.1**). If the impersonation, deception etc. is done with a view to committing a further offence (e.g. theft or burglary), the relevant offences of going equipped and criminal deception (**see Crime, chapter 1.11**) ought to be considered.

4.1.16.3 Causing Disaffection amongst the Police

OFFENCE: **Causing disaffection—*Police Act 1996, s. 91(1)***

• Triable either way • Two years' imprisonment on indictment • Six months' imprisonment and/or a fine summarily

(No specific power of arrest)

The Police Act 1996, s. 91 states:

> (1) Any person who causes, or attempts to cause, or does any act calculated to cause, disaffection amongst the members of any police force, or induces or attempts to induce, or does any act calculated to induce, any member of a police force to withhold his services, shall be guilty of an offence . . .

4.1.17 Health and Safety

Because police officers are not 'employees' in the conventional legal sense (they are holders of the office of constable), many of the statutory provisions regulating the workplace do not apply directly to them. The health and safety regime that was set up mainly by the Health and Safety at Work etc. Act 1974 applies principally to 'employees' and therefore did not cover police officers (though it clearly covers their non-sworn support colleagues who *are* employees). However, the Police (Health and Safety) Act 1997 made certain changes to the legislation by treating police officers for certain purposes relating to health and safety as if they were employees. Briefly, these areas include:

- the application of part 1 of the 1974 Act to the police;
- the right of police officers not to be subjected to a detriment in relation to health and safety issues (e.g. not to be punished for raising appropriate health and safety issues or undertaking duties as health and safety representatives—see s. 49A of the Employment Rights Act 1996);
- the right of police officers not to be unfairly dismissed in relation to health and safety issues—see s. 134A of the Employment Rights Act 1996.

Under the Health and Safety at Work etc. Act 1974, any prosecution of a chief officer of police for an offence under that Act will be brought against the office of chief constable rather than against the individual him/herself. This change to the law (brought in by the Serious Organised Crime and Police Act 2005) brings the position of a chief officer into line with that of police authorities and their liability for breaches of health and safety legislation in respect of police staff (who are their employees). However, a chief officer may also be prosecuted in a personal capacity if it can be shown that he/she personally consented to the commission of an offence or personally connived in its commission, or was personally negligent.

4.2 Extending the Policing Family

4.2.1 Introduction

A further feature of the Police Reform Act 2002 (**see chapter 4.1**) lies in what has been called the 'extended police family'. There has been a recognition within and outside the police service that police officers spend too much time tied up with administrative or non-core tasks. Civilian support staff employed to help with these and some front-line functions do not have the powers to carry out their roles effectively. Creating specific roles of detention and escort officers, and giving them relevant powers to let them carry out their jobs, has the potential to free up police officers to concentrate on the core policing tasks that require the full range of powers and training that they offer. Similarly, training people and giving them the relevant powers to deal with low-level disorder and anti-social behaviour (such as Trading Standards Officers under ss. 15 and 16 of and sch. 7 to the Police and Justice Act 2006), can spread the policing burden and increase policing capacity.

4.2.2 Extending Policing Powers

Part 4 of the Police Reform Act 2002 introduces some novel developments in the law regulating policing powers by potentially extending some of those powers to a whole range of non-police individuals. These individuals will be designated in a particular role(s) or title(s) specifically used in the legislation. They will be given a number of different titles, including the titles specifically used in the legislation (such as Investigating Officers and Detention Officers). Some forces refer to these individuals collectively as police auxiliaries. The particular title applied to each of these individuals is largely irrelevant—what matters is the extent of the designation or accreditation conferred on the person by the chief officer. The whole system works by allowing the relevant chief officer to confer certain powers on different groups of people by designating or accrediting them. The chief officer does not *have* to confer any powers on any such groups and he/she can decide to confer only a reduced number of powers or to place further limitations on those powers: the Act simply gives the chief officer the freedom and flexibility to do so.

4.2.2.1 Who Manages or Employs People with Police Powers?

When approaching these powers and their applicability to different individuals a good starting point is to consider who the relevant person's employer is. Some roles created under the Act (such as Police Community Support Officers and Investigating Officers) can only be carried out by police employees; if you do not work directly for the police, you cannot have these powers or perform these roles. In other roles (Detention Officers and Escort Officers), the person does not necessarily have to be employed by the police. If the person is not employed by the force, then their employer must have a contract with the relevant police authority. These people will have their powers contained in a 'designation' from the relevant chief officer. Another group of people who can have powers conferred on them by a chief officer are not employees of either the police or a police authority contractor. These people are 'accredited' with powers that can only come from their accreditation under a statutory Community Safety Accreditation Scheme. And in order to perform *any* of the roles and exercise *any* of the powers under part 4 of the Act, an individual must be employed by somebody because it is through the person's employer that the chief officer or the relevant police authority can exercise a degree of control over those auxiliary staff who are not directly employed by the police. Therefore, if you are unemployed or self-employed, the legislation will not allow you to have these powers or to carry out any of the relevant functions.

4.2.2.2 The 'Chain of Control'

Another feature to note at the outset is that there is a sort of 'chain of control' linking the auxiliary or individual to a chief officer or police authority. The further along the chain a person is, the less control a chief officer or police authority has over them—and therefore the fewer powers they can be given under the Act. In the case of staff directly employed by a particular police force, they will have a contract of employment with their own force as will any member of non-sworn civilian staff. Moving down the chain of control, you find individuals who are not police employees but are employed by an outside organisation which itself has a contract with a police authority. Examples would be security companies providing prisoner escort services. These employees can be given more limited powers and roles under the Act. Further still along the chain of control are people employed by entirely independent non-police organisations. These people could be working for any number of local businesses or organisations within a police area and the Act allows a chief officer to accredit their employees with limited policing powers.

4.2.3 Designated Police Employees

The first group of people who can be empowered under part 4 of the Police Reform Act 2002 are people employed by the police authority maintaining that force and under the direction and control of their chief officer. These police employees can be 'designated' under s. 38 by their chief officer as *one or more* of the following:

- Police Community Support Officers (PCSOs)
- Investigating Officers
- Detention Officers
- Escort Officers.

No one may be designated in these roles unless the chief officer (or Director-General) is satisfied that they are a suitable person to carry out the designated functions, are capable of carrying out those functions effectively and that they have received adequate training. Adequate training is not defined but it would have to cover the exercise and performance of the relevant powers and duties to be conferred on the person (see s. 38(4)). Considerable weight was given to these safeguards—and the restrictions on any use of force (see below)—during the passage of the Police Reform Bill through Parliament and the provision of effective training was seen as an essential measure to the proper functioning of this new framework.

Because these designated staff are employees of the relevant force, the chief officer is responsible for dealing with reports of misconduct and complaints against them in the normal way. However, the Independent Police Complaints Commission (IPCC) also has jurisdiction over any such allegations or complaints.

4.2.3.1 Powers Conferred on Designated Police Employees

The specific powers that can be conferred by the chief officer on these designated employees depend on which designated role(s) they are given. The powers, which were extended by the Serious Organised Crime and Police Act 2005 and the Police and Justice Act 2006, are set out in sch. 4 to the Act. Schedule 4 is itself divided into further parts, 1–4, with each part containing a number of statutory powers. Helpfully the parts of sch. 4 correspond to the four roles set out in the list above so that the respective powers under parts 1–4 and the relative designated employee roles look like this:

Person	Powers
PCSO	Part 1
Investigating Officer	Part 2
Detention Officer	Part 3
Escort Officer	Part 4

The powers set out in sch. 4 are many and various but they do follow a degree of common sense when you consider the practical requirements of the roles they cover. For example, it makes sense for an Investigating Officer to be given investigative powers such as powers of entry, search and seizure, along with powers to arrest suspects during an interview where further offences are revealed. Similarly, Detention Officers need powers to fingerprint and search prisoners. People already employed by the police in certain roles can be designated under this part of the Act (e.g. scenes of crime officers can be given powers of entry and search).

The Police and Justice Act 2006 at s. 7 allows for a standard set of Community Support Officer (CSO) powers and duties. The powers will be determined by an order from the Secretary of State. Section 8 inserts a new power on dealing with truants into the list set out in sch. 4 to the Police Reform Act 2002 of powers that may be conferred on persons designated as CSOs. If designated with the power set out at para. 4C, CSOs now have the power that constables already have under s. 16 of the Crime and Disorder Act 1998 to deal with truants. This power would allow CSOs to remove from specified areas young people of school age that they believe are absent from school without lawful authority and to take them either to their school or to a place which has been specified by the local authority.

Also, s. 9 of the Police and Justice Act 2006 introduces sch. 5 which makes various amendments to provisions in the Police Reform Act 2002. Paragraph 2(3) inserts a subsection (5B) into s. 38 of the 2002 Act so that when a chief constable first designates a person as a PCSO, he/she is required to ensure that the person has received adequate training in the exercise of the standard powers that are in force at that time. The effect of para. 3 of the schedule is to amend s. 42 of the 2002 Act so that CSOs, when exercising powers or duties, must produce on demand, evidence of their designation as a CSO and of any non-standard power which they exercise that has been conferred on them by their chief officer under s. 38.

Accordingly, CSOs will not have to carry with them details of all the standard powers which have been conferred upon them by an order under s. 38A. The requirement to produce evidence of a designation could be satisfied by production of the designation itself, but could also be satisfied by something less, such as some form of document or card.

The full list of powers is summarised at **appendix 4.4.**

4.2.4 Employees of Contracted-Out Businesses

Moving another link along the chain of control from a chief officer and the relevant employee you come across the next group of people who can be granted powers under sch. 4 to the Police Reform Act 2002. Although their employee status is the source of control over these employees' activities and performance, the first thing to note is that they are *not* employed by the police force. Where a police authority has entered into a contract for the provision of services relating to the detention or escorting of people in custody, s. 39 allows the chief officer to designate employees *of the contractor* as either Detention Officers or Escort Officers or both. As such these people may be given some or all of the powers of those roles set out in parts 3 and 4 of sch. 4 to the Act (**see appendix 4.4**). These contracted-out personnel cannot be given the powers of PCSOs and Investigating Officers as they are not police employees—they are employees of the contractor. This slightly unconventional arrangement raises some interesting questions as to whether or not they are performing a public role such that they would come within the parameters of the Human Rights Act 1998 (**see para. 4.3.3.3**).

Before designating anyone under this part of the Act, a chief officer must be satisfied that the person:

- is a suitable person to carry out the functions for which he/she is to be designated;
- is capable of effectively carrying out those functions; and
- has received adequate training in the carrying out of those functions and in the exercise of those powers and duties to be conferred on him/her (s. 39(4)).

As with the police employees given powers under parts 1–4 of sch. 4, a great deal of emphasis was placed on these safeguards in securing the passage of the Police Reform Bill through Parliament and, in particular, the provision of effective training was seen as an essential measure to the proper functioning of the new measures. Further weight was given to the reassurances provided by the restrictions on the use of force (see below).

If an employee stops being an employee of the contractor, or the contract between the employer and the police authority comes to an end, any designation ceases to have effect (s. 39(13)). Section 39 also allows for regulations to be made regarding the handling of complaints and misconduct issues arising out of the functions of designated employees.

4.2.4.1 Accredited Employees

Moving further still along the chain of control linking the force with the employee brings you to those people who are simply employed by local businesses and employers in the relevant police area. Those businesses do not have to have an existing contract with the police authority and their employees only gain their accreditation from powers conferred under a Community Safety Accreditation Scheme (CSAS).

A CSAS is a scheme set up and maintained by a chief officer for the purposes of:

- contributing to community safety and security;
- combating crime and disorder, public nuisance and other forms of anti-social behaviour.

4.2.4.2 Community Safety Accreditation Schemes

Before establishing a CSAS, a chief officer must consult with the police authority maintaining that force and every local authority any part of whose area lies within his/her force (s. 40(4)). In the case of the Metropolitan Police Force the commissioner must also consult with the Mayor of London. Any CSAS must also appear in the policing plan of any force (as to which **see chapter 4.1**). A CSAS must contain provisions for making arrangements with local employers carrying on business (including those carrying out statutory functions) for the supervision of any of their employees who become accredited under the scheme (s. 40(8)). In addition, it is the duty of the chief officer to ensure that the employers of the persons on whom powers are conferred have established and maintain satisfactory arrangements for handling complaints relating to the carrying out of functions under the scheme (s. 40(9)). This is all the more important as the accredited employees will have no formal individual link with the force, either directly (as in the case of designated police employees under parts 1 to 4 of sch. 4 above) or indirectly (as with employees of contracted-out businesses whose employees are designated under parts 3 and 4 of the schedule).

Under a CSAS, s. 41 of the Police Reform Act 2002 allows a chief officer to accredit people with certain policing powers. These powers are set out in sch. 5 to the Act and at **appendix 4.4**.

Photographing of persons given fixed penalty notices—paragraph 9ZA

Under this paragraph an Accredited Employee will, within the relevant police area, have the power of a constable under s. 64A(1A) of the Police and Criminal Evidence Act 1984 (as to which **see Evidence & Procedure, para. 2.10.12**) to take a photograph, elsewhere than at a police station, of a person to whom the accredited person has given a penalty notice (or as the case may be a fixed penalty notice) in exercise of any power mentioned in para. 1(2).

OFFENCE: **Failing to comply with requirements—*Police Reform Act 2002, sch. 5, para. 2(2)***

- Triable summarily • Fine

(No specific power of arrest)

The Police Reform Act 2002, sch. 5, para. 2 states:

> (2) A person who fails to comply with a requirement under sub-paragraph (1) is guilty of an offence.

KEYNOTE

The reference to 'a requirement' under sub-para. (1) above refers to the requirement for the person to give their name and address to the accredited employee (see earlier discussion of para. 2).

This offence is similar to those created by sch. 4 (**see para. 4.2.3**). In making the requirement it will be critical that the accredited person produces their authority and that, if relevant, they are in the correct uniform and wearing the proper badge etc.

The Police and Justice Act 2006 inserted s. 41A and sch. 5A into the 2002 Act, relating to the accreditation of weights and measures inspectors (Trading Standards Officers) and s. 41B allowing the Secretary of State to add other types of persons to whom accreditation could be granted.

4.2.4.3 General Considerations for Designated or Accredited Employees

A designated or accredited employee empowered under the Police Reform Act 2002 exercising any powers granted thereunder in relation to any person must produce their authority to that person if requested to do so (s. 42(1)). Their powers are only exercisable if the employee is wearing the relevant uniform as determined or approved by the chief officer and identified or described in the designation/accreditation (s. 42(2)). Any designation or accreditation will specify the extent, nature and duration of the powers conferred by it and also any uniform that the employee is required to wear. In the case of an accredited employee (i.e. acting under the authority of sch. 5 of the Act), he/she must also be wearing an appropriate badge as specified by the Secretary of State in the manner or place specified (s. 42(2)). Given the nature of some investigative functions carried out by investigating officers, a police officer of or above the rank of inspector may direct an investigating officer not to wear a uniform for the purposes of a particular operation (s. 42(2A). If such a direction is given, subs. (2) will not apply in relation to *that* investigating officer for the purposes of *that* operation. The officer giving this direction not to wear uniform must be from the same force as the chief officer who appointed the investigating officer under s. 38.

A chief officer of police may modify or withdraw an employee's designation or accreditation *at any time* simply by giving the employee notice (s. 42(3)). This power of revocation or amendment is absolute and there is no requirement for any misconduct or poor performance on the part of the employee. If a designation or accreditation is modified or withdrawn, the chief officer must send a copy of the notice to the relevant employer (see s. 42(5) and (6)). The Secretary of State can add to the relevant police powers that are extended to designated or accredited employees in a much simpler and quicker format in some circumstances and reference should be made to the most up-to-date version of the various schedules.

Any liability for civil wrongs (torts) arising out of conduct in the course of an employee's designation or accreditation will be apportioned jointly between the police authority, the employer and the individual (see s. 42). This should make life interesting, particularly in the areas of remedies and the application of the Human Rights Act 1998.

4.2.5 Use of Force

The use of force by police officers is a contentious area that has kept—and will no doubt continue to keep—the courts, litigants and their representatives busy for decades. The use of force by non-sworn personnel carrying out policing functions (the 'extended policing family' members) is likely to be at least as contentious, if not more so. There are two main sources of a designated employee's power to use reasonable force. The first source is the specific power granted under sch. 4 to the Police Reform Act 2002 as set out earlier. The second source is to be found in s. 38(8) of the Act. This provides that if a designated employee has a power which, if exercised by a constable, would have a further power to use reasonable force then the designated employee will also have the same entitlement to use reasonable force. For instance, where a constable is exercising powers under the Police and Criminal Evidence Act 1984 where the consent of another person other than a police officer is not needed (e.g. most powers of arrest, search and seizure), s. 117 gives the officer a power to use reasonable force if necessary (**see para. 4.4.6.3**). If an Investigating Officer designated under part 2 of sch. 4 to the Police Reform Act 2002 uses a power to enter premises following an arrest (per sch. 4, para. 18), he or she will be entitled to use reasonable force if necessary because a constable using the same power to enter and search would also have the power to use reasonable force. However, given the sensitivities around the use of force by the police and other agents of the State, there are further restrictions on the use of force by a designated employee. If, as in the above example, the designated employee uses force to enter premises, that power can *only* be used:

- in the company *and* under the supervision of a constable, or
- for the purpose of saving life or limb or preventing serious damage to property (s. 38(9)).

The accompanying constable in such circumstances can expect to be closely questioned over the extent and effectiveness of their 'supervision' in the event that the matter comes to trial or is investigated following a complaint, report or allegation of misconduct. It is unlikely that the requirements of s. 38(9) would be satisfied by a merely passive physical presence by a constable at a time when the power is exercised and the legislation envisages some form of active and effective supervision by the constable. Similarly, any designated employee using these powers will need to be able to show how the various criteria were met by the particular circumstances at the time.

The general rules and restrictions on the use of force will apply in these cases (**see para. 4.4.6.3**) and any use of force by a designated employee will come under close scrutiny—particularly where that person is a Detention Officer or Escort Officer employed by a contracted-out business under s. 39.

4.3 Human Rights

4.3.1 Introducing Human Rights

The European Convention on Human Rights and the Human Rights Act 1998 have been included in this chapter in some detail because of the effect they have on the use of policing powers. What follows is an introduction to some of the key features and principles.

Procedural and constitutional issues affecting the Convention and the Act within the administration of justice system are largely dealt with in **Evidence & Procedure**. Other matters affecting substantive law and the particular effects of the Human Rights Act 1998 on existing legislation have been included throughout the relevant chapters of each Manual in this series.

4.3.1.1 Human Rights Legislation—Why Have It?

Why do we need human rights legislation?

That is a good question—and not everyone in the administration of justice system agrees on the answer. One response is that the traditional freedom of individuals to do anything other than that which is expressly forbidden by law may have resulted in a permissive, democratic society. However, such a system gives no protection against the *misuse* of legal powers by the State. Neither does it provide protection for individuals from the acts or omissions of other public bodies that, although allowed by statute or common law, contravene basic human rights. Both of these shortcomings in our legal system were pointed out by the Lord Chancellor during the second reading of the Human Rights Bill in the House of Lords. Unlike many countries that have a written constitution or a Bill of Rights, our law has made no distinction between a breach of some contractual duty (such as a shopkeeper selling you a faulty TV) and the infringement of a basic human right (such as a breach of your right to meet with friends in public). Until now there has been no 'inalienable right' to meet with others freely any more than there is an inalienable right not to be sold dodgy electrical goods. In either case above, you would have to rely on the prevailing statutory and common law for redress. True, you could petition the European Court of Human Rights in certain circumstances where you felt that your fundamental rights had been interfered with, but the decisions of that Court cannot overrule our domestic laws or overturn national judgments. In addition, the Court is in Strasbourg and applications can take anything up to nine years before being heard!

Incidentally, one of the products of the Human Rights Act 1998 (see below) is that the government began to pass domestic legislation to bolster the rights of individuals generally. As a result, the Regulation of Investigatory Powers Act 2000 now provides a very clear legal framework within which to pursue claims against the police (**see para. 4.12.4**).

A final reason for introducing specific human rights legislation is to create a *positive* obligation on public authorities such as the police to protect the rights of others. Such others might be victims of stalking, domestic violence or anti-social behaviour generally. In the spirit of human rights legislation, it is no longer enough for public authorities to say 'we haven't breached anyone's rights ourselves'; police services and others have to consider whether they have taken reasonable and legitimate steps positively to protect the rights of individuals under appropriate circumstances.

4.3.1.2 The European Convention on Human Rights—What is It?

The European Convention for the Protection of Human Rights and Fundamental Freedoms is a Treaty between governments. It was signed in 1950 by the governments of those countries making up the Council of Europe and was intended to give full legal protection to the most fundamental rights and freedoms necessary in democratic societies. At the time the Convention was drawn up, many European countries were trying to come to terms with the total disregard for many of those rights and freedoms in the wake of the Second World War. It is important to bear this in mind when reading the Convention as it was written against the backdrop of a war-ravaged Europe and an emerging Soviet Union. This background explains some of the wording used within the Convention.

The Convention came into force in 1953, has been adopted by a majority of countries throughout Europe—including some former communist States—and has been used as a constitutional template by a great many others.

What *was* relatively new as a concept was the Human Rights Act 1998 itself (see below) which specifically enshrined most—though not all—of the Convention rights within our domestic legislation for the first time. Even though the Act is still fairly new, its preamble reiterates that it is intended to give *further effect* to the rights and freedoms already guaranteed by the Convention.

The Convention is part of *international* law, and consequently creates rights against the State (government) and not against other individuals (however, see below). Since 1966, people in the United Kindom have been able to go to Strasbourg and seek the help of the Court or (until November 1998) the European Commission of Human Rights where their civil liberties have been infringed by the State and where no domestic remedy has been available. The Court or the Commission could find that the government had violated the rights of the individual, but there were few practical remedies available even if the applicant was successful.

There have been a number of significant cases affecting the United Kingdom that have already appeared before the European Court of Human Rights using this avenue of individual petition. Actions brought via this—and other—domestic routes are important as they have influenced developments in our law within England and Wales. More importantly, they have created a body of case law that helps in gauging how our domestic courts may interpret the Convention in the future. Indeed, under s. 2 of the Human Rights Act 1998 our courts and tribunals have a duty to take such decisions into account. Less helpfully, those cases do not have to be followed in the same way as cases within the 'domestic' courts of England and Wales do and they may have a limited 'shelf life'. In other words, past results are no guarantee of future performance—as financial advisers might say.

4.3.2 Key Features of the Convention

The Convention sets out to protect most of what might be seen as the fundamental civil liberties within a democratic society. However, it is a very different concept from an Act of Parliament. There are several key features that need to be understood when considering the Convention and its effects. Those key features include:

- The balancing of competing rights and needs.
- Limitations and restrictions—the 'three tests'.
- The Convention as a 'living' instrument.
- The 'margin of appreciation'.
- Derogations and reservations.

Each of these features will now be considered.

4.3.2.1 Balancing Competing Rights and Needs

Some of the Convention's provisions are *absolute*, that is, they do not permit any infringement under any circumstances. An example would be the right to freedom from torture under Article 3 (**see para. 4.3.6**). Other rights are often limited or restricted in some way, such as the right to liberty under Article 5 (**see para. 4.3.8**). These rights have to be restricted if the 'democratic society' is going to work. If a person is lawfully arrested or detained, his/her right to liberty has been infringed, but the Convention takes account of such situations and imposes limitations on that right. Similarly, there will be times when the freedom of an individual conflicts with the general public interest—the right to freedom of assembly (protected under Article 11) and the need to maintain public order for instance. A perfect example of the balancing act required in a policing context can be seen in the powers to seize and retain a motor vehicle that is being used in an anti-social manner (**see paras 4.5.5.9 and 4.5.6.14**). Here, the owner's rights to enjoy his/her personal possessions have to be balanced with the rights of the general population to enjoy their private and family lives, and the Police Reform Act 2002 created policing powers to deal with the situation where the two sets of rights collide—the real trick is exercising those powers lawfully, proportionately and sensibly. These categories of rights are generally referred to as 'qualified' rights and the areas of potential conflict they raise are of particular significance to the police and other law enforcement agencies.

In some cases, the rights of individuals may directly compete with one another. An example would be one person's right to freedom of expression (Article 10) and another person's freedom to respect for their private life (Article 8). The potential for such rights to conflict, particularly in the areas of communications (**see chapter 4.5**) and civil disputes (**see chapter 4.9**) is painfully clear to most police officers.

What the Convention—and the European Court of Human Rights—sets out to do is to *balance* these rights against each other and against the needs of the democratic society within which they exist. For this reason many of the Convention's Articles include any relevant limitations or exceptions. Although each is different, a helpful practical approach when interpreting their extent is to apply the 'three tests'.

4.3.2.2 The Three Tests

Where the Convention gives individuals a particular right, any qualification or limitation on that right will be carefully defined and cautiously applied. Otherwise the effect of the Convention would be diluted by a series of 'get out' clauses or circumstances where the right could be easily overridden. This is particularly the case where the balancing of 'qualified' rights is concerned (see above).

Very generally, any limitations on a Convention right must be:

- prescribed by law
- intended to achieve a legitimate objective
- proportionate to the end that is to be achieved.

Each of these areas has a significant impact on the work of police officers and needs to be examined in turn.

Test one—prescribed by law

Any interference with a Convention right must first be traceable to a clear legal source (e.g. the Police and Criminal Evidence Act 1984). A person whose rights have allegedly been infringed is entitled to ask *'where did you get the power to act as you did?'* The public body concerned, whether it is a police service or a local authority or whatever, will have to point to a clear legal source and say *'that's where our authority to act in this way comes from'*. The source of this authority can be statutory or the common law; it can also be contractual (e.g. in matters relating to employment). This is one of the reasons why the need for police officers and anyone exercising policing powers to be able to identify the legal source of any power that they use has become even more important. If no such lawful authority can be identified, the consequent interference with a Convention right will be a violation of the Convention, *irrespective of any other justification*. Therefore if the relevant public authority (see below) cannot point to a legal regulation that allows it to interfere with a Convention right, it will be in breach of its obligations (see e.g. the case involving the tapping of a senior police officer's telephone at work—*Halford* v *United Kingdom* (1997) 24 EHRR 523). The circumstances surrounding this decision and the implications for intercepting communications generally prompted the Regulation of Investigatory Powers Act 2000 (as to which, **see para. 4.12.4**).

However, it is not enough that such a source of legal authority exists; it must also be readily accessible to the people of the relevant State (see *The Sunday Times* v *United Kingdom* (1979) 2 EHRR 245). This means that the law must be clearly and precisely defined and publicised so that people can make themselves aware of it and regulate their conduct accordingly. Acts of Parliament and statutory instruments would invariably meet this requirement. Our common law (**see Evidence & Procedure**) will probably meet this requirement in most cases (see the *Sunday Times* case above) although it is arguable that there is so much lack of clarity in some areas that all aspects of this requirement are not met by our common law system. A good historical example is in the area of 'lawful chastisement' in relation to punishment of children (as to which, **see Crime, chapter 1.7**). In a case involving an allegation of assault by a stepfather on his stepson, the European Court of Human Rights held that the United Kingdom was in breach of its obligation to protect individuals from inhuman or degrading punishment (under Article 3) because our law in the area of what was 'reasonable' chastisement was not clear enough (*A* v *United Kingdom* (1999) 27 EHRR 611).

Test two—legitimate objective

In addition to being authorised by a clear and accessible legal regulation, restrictions or limitations of qualified Convention rights must generally be directed at achieving a legitimate objective as set out under the Articles themselves. Such an objective might be the prevention of crime, the protection of the public and their property or the upholding of the rights of others. Given the broad nature of these objectives it should be relatively easy for a public authority, *when acting lawfully*, to meet this requirement.

Test three—proportionality and necessity

The test of proportionality asks *'were the measures you took necessary in a democratic society and in proportion to the ultimate objective?'* It is in this area that the 'balancing' of competing rights and needs takes place. It is also in this area that the use of police powers may be challenged most frequently. Any interference with a Convention right must be shown to have been relevant and proportional to the legitimate aim pursued (*Handyside* v *United Kingdom* (1976) 1 EHRR 737). A good example here would be police actions taken to prevent crime—forcibly entering and searching premises for instance. Clearly the prevention of crime would usually amount to a legitimate objective but *the means employed by the officers would have to be in proportion to the crime that was to be prevented.*

If the manner and extent of an operation were shown to have infringed someone's Convention rights in a way that was out of all proportion to the legitimate aim being pursued, there would almost certainly have been a violation of those rights. As the authors of *Blackstone's Guide to the Human Rights Act 1998* put it 'the State cannot use a sledgehammer to crack a nut'.

It can be seen then that this test has significant implications for those who supervise, manage and carry out law enforcement operations.

Although the decisions of public authorities, such as police services, have been open to the process of judicial review (**see Evidence & Procedure, para. 2.2.5.3**) for some considerable time, the 'proportionality' test adopted by the European Court of Human Rights represents a much tighter constraint on the activities of public authorities than anything that has gone before. Generally under the judicial review procedure, the courts will not interfere with a decision of a public authority unless it can be shown to meet one of two criteria: unlawful or irrational (in short 'wrong' or 'daft'). Under the *proportionality* test the Court in Strasbourg has taken a different approach and looks for a 'pressing social need' behind the actions complained of. If no such need can be found, the interference may be a violation of the Convention. It is for this reason that legislation in Northern Ireland outlawing consensual buggery between men was held to be an unnecessary interference by the State with an individual's right to privacy (*Dudgeon* v *United Kingdom* (1983) 5 EHRR 573); it is also the reason why a number of new legislative restrictions such as the Anti-social Behaviour Order (**see chapter 4.5**) and the Sexual Offences Prevention Order (**see Crime, chapter 1.9**) were challenged under the Human Rights Act 1998.

The overall practical result of the three tests means, in short, that the 'ways and means Act' has been repealed once and for all.

4.3.2.3 Discrimination

One final, generic test that will be applied to any limitation or restriction on Convention rights is whether the limitation or restriction is discriminatory, i.e. *'did the difference in treatment of the individuals affected have any objective and reasonable justification'* (*Belgian Linguistic Case (No. 1)* (1967) 1 EHRR 241).

Discrimination within the context of Convention rights is covered specifically by Article 14 (**see para. 4.3.17**). A good example of where UK legislation and practice have been held to contravene the principles in the three tests above and to be discriminatory is *A* v *Secretary of State for the Home Department* [2004] UKHL 56. That case involved the prolonged detention without charge of suspects under s. 23 of the Anti-terrorism, Crime and Security Act 2001. As the detention provisions were only used against *foreign nationals* suspected of being international terrorists, and not UK nationals similarly suspected, it was argued that the practice discriminated on grounds of nationality. The House of Lords accepted that there was discrimination on grounds of nationality and that this had not been the subject of the derogation (**see para. 4.3.2.6**) in force at the time. Slightly ironically, the reason why foreign nationals were detained in the first place was because they could not be deported to their country of origin as it was believed they would be tortured or killed and therefore deportation would have amounted to a breach of their Convention rights under Article 3 (**see para. 4.3.6**).

4.3.2.4 The Convention as a 'Living Instrument'

As discussed, the Convention is a creature of international law and is therefore different from the Acts of Parliament that appear elsewhere in this book. One difference is that the courts will interpret it in a 'purposive' way, i.e. in a way that gives effect to its central purposes, namely to protect the human rights of individuals and the ideals and values of a democratic society. Any such rights and ideals must not be theoretical, but practical and effective features of the lives of individuals within our democratic society. The Convention is also a 'living' instrument which must be interpreted in the light of present-day conditions (*Tyrer* v *United Kingdom* (1978) 2 EHRR 1). This means that its interpretation will develop alongside society without the need for older cases to be specifically overruled. If the acceptable standards within society become more tolerant (say, of consensual sexual activity or of behaviour in public), then the Convention should be interpreted and applied accordingly. Interestingly, this is the same test that has now been adopted in relation to assessing the appropriateness of a police officer's off-duty conduct under the discipline regulations (**see chapter 4.1**). Unlike our domestic common law where very old cases become well-established precedents, older case law relating to the Convention will not be followed slavishly by the courts and will therefore need to be considered carefully. This is not particularly helpful to practitioners; it is even less helpful to exam candidates. Nevertheless, it is a significant feature of the Convention.

4.3.2.5 What is the 'Margin of Appreciation'?

As social, economic, political and cultural conditions in the many countries that have signed up to the Convention vary, there must be some latitude in the interpretation of the Convention. As anyone travelling through mainland Europe discovers, behaviour that is socially acceptable in one country may not be so acceptable in another. One country may be more vulnerable to a particular type of threat, e.g. terrorism, and may therefore need to impose restrictions on some freedoms that in another country, where there is no such threat, might be unnecessary. Sensibly, the European Court of Human Rights has accepted that such local distinctions are best made by the relevant governments—albeit under its close supervision. For that reason, the Court will allow governments what is termed a 'margin of appreciation' when deciding to what extent the Convention has been violated by public policy.

An example of how this concept works can be seen in the litigation around transsexuals in the United Kingdom. The government has relied upon its 'margin of appreciation' to avoid changing the law in England and Wales to allow transsexuals to change their gender for certain legal and administrative purposes. The government originally declined to change domestic laws in order to recognise the particular status of transsexuals (e.g. in relation to birth record systems and the right to marry). In finally settling the matter, however, the European Court of Human Rights has said that the government could no longer claim that such matters fell within its margin of appreciation (see *Goodwin* v *United Kingdom* [2002] 35 EHRR 18). As a result, the various failures of the United Kingdom to provide recognition and protection for transsexuals' rights amounted to breaches of the relevant Convention articles (see below) and our domestic legislation has been altered.

As an international law concept, it has been held that the margin of appreciation has no application in domestic proceedings (see *R* v *DPP, ex parte Kebilene* [1999] 3 WLR 972).

4.3.2.6 What are Derogations and Reservations?

Article 15 allows governments to 'derogate' from their obligations under the Convention *in time of war or other public emergency threatening the life of the nation.*

This provision allows governments to restrict the freedoms of individuals under such circumstances but *only to the extent that it is strictly necessary to do so.* Any government availing itself of this provision must inform the Secretary-General of the Council of Europe of any measures it is taking in this regard and must make similar notification once those measures have ceased. Even so, some of the individual rights protected by the Convention cannot be derogated from at all—these are Article 2, Article 3, Article 4(1) and Article 7.

The original derogation that existed at the time when the Human Rights Act 1998 was passed related to the ongoing unrest in Northern Ireland. With the political developments in Northern Ireland, that derogation was removed but, since the events of 11 September 2001, the United Kingdom has passed a further derogation arising out of the Anti-Terrorism, Crime and Security Act 2001 and the powers thereunder. As those powers are, on the face of them, incompatible with some of the Convention rights of individuals, the government issued derogations in accordance with sch. 3 to the Human Rights Act 1998. While any derogations are controversial, the particular one that attracted a great deal of public interest was that allowing for the detention without charge of suspected international terrorists, inserted by the Anti-Terrorism, Crime and Security Act 2001. As a result of judicial and political pressure, on 16 March 2005, the UK government informed the Secretary-General of the Council of Europe under Article 15 that the derogation was being withdrawn (see the Human Rights Act 1998 (Amendment) Order 2005 (SI 2005/1071)). The relevant detention provisions were repealed by s. 16(2)(a) of the Prevention of Terrorism Act 2005. However, the area of terrorism and how best to deal with the threat posed by certain individuals while still observing the relevant Convention principles remains controversial. One specific example that is relevant to policing arises in the form of the control order (under the Prevention of Terrorism Act 2005).

The United Kingdom has attached a 'reservation' to its acceptance of one of the protocols to the Convention in relation to education (Protocol 1, Article 2). Article 2 says that no one shall be denied the right to education, and the reservation (which has also been registered by several other States) simply adds an amendment about compatibility with domestic provisions and unreasonable public expenditure.

4.3.2.7 Incorporation—International Law becomes our Law

While many of the signatories to the Convention chose to incorporate its provisions directly into their own domestic law, successive governments in the United Kingdom have felt that such incorporation was unnecessary. Many believed (and still do) that the 'permissive' system in England and Wales described above, already provides enough protection for the rights and freedoms of individuals. Although the avenue of individual petition resulted in several cases being brought against the UK government, the Convention itself was never incorporated into the domestic law of England and Wales. However, there were many politicians, lawyers and commentators who felt that there was a need for a specific Bill of Rights for the United Kingdom, going beyond even the direct incorporation of the Convention into our legal system and the issues were debated for years.

Eventually, in December 1996, the Labour Party published a paper entitled *Bringing Rights Home* setting out its own arguments in favour of incorporating the Convention into our domestic law—and including a pledge in its manifesto to do just that. Following victory in the general election of 1997, the Labour government published a White Paper, *Rights Brought Home* (Cm 3782), in which it explained the proposals contained within the Human Rights Bill and the Human Rights Act received Royal Assent in November 1998.

4.3.3 The Human Rights Act 1998

The Human Rights Act 1998 came into force in October 2000. Although there are many academic debates around the niceties of it all, to most intents and purposes the 1998 Act effectively incorporates what are often called an individual's 'Convention rights' into our domestic law. These Convention rights are set out in the various Articles and Protocols of the Convention which appear in sch. 1 to the Act.

4.3.3.1 How Important is the Human Rights Act?

The 1998 Act is a very significant piece of legislation—particularly for police officers and the wider 'policing family'. Not only does it give effect to the rights contained within the Convention, the Act also affects the way in which all other legislation will be interpreted and applied. Section 3 requires that, wherever possible, statutory provisions *and the common law* be read and given effect in a way that is compatible with Convention rights (**see Evidence & Procedure, chapter 2.1**). This requirement, which also applies to new legislation, will have an impact on all courts and tribunals in every jurisdiction, whether criminal or civil, where Convention rights are in issue.

A good example of this in action can be seen in a case involving the rights of a partner in a homosexual relationship to remain in their property when one partner died. Had the relationship been *heterosexual*, the survivor would have automatically become a statutory tenant entitled to remain in the home on the death of his partner. The House of Lords held that the relevant legislation should be read down and given effect in a way that was compatible with the Convention. The law as it stood discriminated against individuals on the basis of their sexuality (thereby breaching Article 14—**see para. 4.3.17**), within the context of their right to respect for their home as guaranteed by Article 8 (**see para. 4.3.11**). As a result, the statute in question (the Rent Act 1977) was read and applied in a way that allowed the surviving partner to receive an assured tenancy and to remain in the property—*Mendoza* v *Ghaidan* [2004] UKHL 30.

As discussed above, the Convention was aimed at securing rights against the State and public authorities—and the 1998 Act does the same. Although it creates avenues of redress against 'public authorities' (see below), the Act does not create any new rights in private matters between individuals. Just because someone next to you on the tube infringes your right to a private life by playing dance music on their stereo does not mean that you can now take them to court. Neither can disaffected workers complain that their private sector employers have stifled their freedom of speech by stopping them going to board meetings. However, the definition of 'public authorities' includes the courts (s. 6(3)) and therefore imposes an obligation for a court *in any matter*, criminal or civil, private or public, to give effect to the Act. This is why it is said that there will be occasions where the Act will be of 'indirect effect' as between individuals.

Although it makes changes to the procedures in getting redress locally for human rights infringements, the 1998 Act still allows for occasions where an individual will need to petition the European Court of Human Rights in Strasbourg (**see Evidence & Procedure, chapter 2.2**).

4.3.3.2 Article 13—Real and Effective Remedy

It should be noted that Article 13—which requires States to ensure that individuals have a 'real and effective remedy' if their Convention rights are violated—has *not* been incorporated into the Human Rights Act 1998. It was the government's view that the introduction of the Act itself is enough to meet these requirements. Nevertheless, because Article 13 is very important in the case decisions of the European Court of Human Rights and s. 2 of the Act requires courts in England and Wales to have regard to those decisions made in Strasbourg, Article 13 will still have some significance in practice.

4.3.3.3 Breach of the Act—What Can You Do About It?

The Human Rights Act 1998, s. 6 states:

> (1) It is unlawful for a public authority to act in a way that is incompatible with a Convention right.

KEYNOTE

As discussed above, the rights provided by the Convention are intended to be directly enforceable against 'public authorities'. Therefore, if it can be established that a person or organisation is a 'public authority' (as defined below), the Convention rights can be used directly against them in a number of ways. These ways include:

- Bringing proceedings against the public authority, e.g. for false imprisonment.
- Using the public authority's actions as a ground for judicial review (**see Evidence & Procedure, chapter 2.2**).
- Using the public authority's actions as a defence to any action brought by it, e.g. someone charged with an offence of obstructing a police officer (as to which, **see Crime, chapter 1.7**).

The first two ways of seeking a remedy are often referred to as using the Convention as a 'sword' while the last can be seen as making use of the Convention as a 'shield'. In using the Convention as a 'shield' in any legal proceedings, the person can do so *whenever the act complained of took place.* This will include citing acts by the public authority that have already taken place before the 1998 Act came into force. Where a person seeks to rely on their Convention rights as a 'sword', the restrictions and time limits under s. 7 will apply (**see para. 4.3.3.6**).

A good example of how the Convention can be used to launch a wide range of attacks on legislation and policing powers can be seen in *R (On the Application of Fuller and Secretary of State for the Home Department)* v *Chief Constable of Dorset Police* [2003] QB 480 (**see chapter 4.10**). There are many other examples throughout the text of the following chapters, particularly in the areas of public order, terrorism and anti-social behaviour.

In all cases where a person wishes to rely on the relevant Convention right in any proceedings (either as a sword or as a shield), they must meet the requirements of s. 7 (**see para. 4.3.3.6**).

If the person or organisation allegedly violating the individual's Convention rights cannot be shown to be a 'public authority', then there is no *direct* remedy against them (but, see below). An 'act' will include a failure to act under certain circumstances (see below).

4.3.3.4 Exceptions

Section 6 goes on to state:

(2) Subsection (1) does not apply to an act if—

(a) as the result of one or more provisions of primary legislation, the authority could not have acted differently; or

(b) in the case of one or more provisions of or made under, primary legislation which cannot be read or given effect in a way which is compatible with the Convention rights, the authority was acting so as to give effect to or enforce those provisions.

KEYNOTE

The 1998 Act is drafted in such a way as to preserve the concept of parliamentary sovereignty whereby Parliament's expressed intentions cannot be overruled. For this reason, s. 6(2) provides for circumstances where a public authority has acted in a way that is incompatible with a Convention right *but it only did so because it had no choice as a result of other legislation.* This means that if a public authority has a statutory duty to do something and, in so doing, cannot avoid acting in a way that is incompatible with a Convention right, it does not commit a breach of s. 6(1) above. An example might be where there is a statutory requirement to pass on information, as under the Vehicle Excise and Registration Act 1994 and that requirement is enforced by the police or the DVLA. If an individual successfully claimed that such a requirement unnecessarily infringed his/her Convention right to privacy (Article 8), the actions of the police and the DVLA (as 'public authorities') may well be protected by s. 6(2). The proper remedy in such a case would be to seek a declaration from a higher court that the legislation concerned was in fact incompatible with the Convention (**see Evidence & Procedure, chapter 2.1**). This represents a key difference between the Human Rights Act 1998 and the legislation of the European Union. If there is a conflict between the domestic law of a Member State and the law of the European Union, the latter is able to override the domestic legislation even if it appears in a lawfully enacted Act of Parliament (see s. 2 of the European Communities Act 1972). In such circumstances, the courts in England and Wales are also under an obligation to disapply the inconsistent local legislation and give effect to European Union law (see e.g. *R* v *Secretary of State for Employment, ex parte Equal Opportunities Commission* [1995] 1 AC 1).

The effect of s. 6(2) only extends to *legislation*; it does not therefore appear to exempt the acts of people who are obeying, say, a court order such as a warrant. Moreoever, the wording of s. 6(2)(a) suggests that it only applies where the legislation leaves the public authority no choice in the matter. Therefore this would not seem to apply to the exercise of *discretionary* powers such as powers of arrest, search and seizure. The bottom line is that an act or failure to act by a public authority will not be unlawful if:

- it is *not* incompatible with Convention rights;
- the authority could not have acted differently given the relevant primary legislation; or
- the authority acted so as to give effect to, or to enforce provisions made under, incompatible primary legislation.

4.3.3.5 Public Authorities

Section 6 goes on to state:

(3) In this section 'public authority' includes—

(a) a court or tribunal, and

(b) any person certain of whose functions are functions of a public nature, but does not include either House of Parliament or a person exercising functions in connection with proceedings in Parliament.

(4) In subsection (3) 'Parliament' does not include the House of Lords in its judicial capacity.

(5) In relation to a particular act, a person is not a public authority by virtue only of subsection (3)(b) if the nature of the act is private.

(6) 'An act' includes a failure to act but does not include a failure to—

(a) introduce in, or lay before Parliament a proposal for legislation; or

(b) make any primary legislation or remedial order.

KEYNOTE

It can be seen from the text above that there is no conclusive definition of what a public authority is; rather there is a description of the functions that will make a person/organisation a 'public authority'. It can also be seen that there will be two groups of 'public authorities'—those who are named or who are concerned solely with discharging functions of a public nature ('pure' public authorities) and those who have *some* public functions ('quasi-public' authorities).

In the first category (pure public authorities) would be:

- courts and tribunals (including the House of Lords when sitting as such)
- police, fire and ambulance services
- local authorities and the Independent Police Complaints Commission.

These organisations, and the people working for them, have a duty to conform to the Convention rights of individuals when exercising *any and all* of their functions. Therefore a police service must act in conformity with the Convention in relation to its operational functions (preservation of law and order) and also in relation to its other functions (e.g. as an employee or contractor).

From the definition above it can be seen that not only are police *organisations* public authorities, but so are individual police officers—whether they are regular officers or special constables—and others who are employed by the police to exercise policing powers. Whether the courts will extend the provisions to cover non-police employees who are designated or accredited with policing powers under the Police Reform Act 2002 (as to which **see para. 4.2.3**) remains to be seen but there is a strong argument for their inclusion in principle.

As courts and tribunals are specified within s. 6(3), judges, magistrates and people chairing tribunals will be under a duty to ensure conformity with the Convention in deciding *any legal issue*—even if the hearing is one of private law between two individuals (e.g. a landlord and tenant dispute or a purely contractual matter).

As the law has not yet been fully tested in the courts, it is difficult to identify accurately all the organisations that would fall into the second category. However, they might include a number of commercial or private organisations charged with some functions of a public nature, e.g.:

- Network Rail
- security companies running prisons/prisoner escort services
- government contractors
- other bodies such as the BBC.

The important thing to establish with such groups is whether they were, at the material time, acting within the scope of their public functions or whether their actions were carried out purely within the ambit of their private functions. It would seem from the wording of s. 6(5) that quasi-public authorities will be accountable for acting in a way that is incompatible with the Convention *only while they are carrying out their public functions.* An example of this distinction might be a surgeon who both works for the NHS and has a private practice. While working for the NHS—an organisation having functions of a public nature—the surgeon's acts would probably be caught by s. 6(1). While acting in an entirely private capacity in his/her practice, the surgeon's acts would probably be excluded from the provisions of s. 6(1) by the wording of s. 6(5). This second category of organisations will be important to police services as the growth in public and private partnerships continues. In such cases the police service may be liable for acts committed by private partners in certain circumstances. This distinction will be particularly important where employees of private companies who have no other 'public' functions have been accredited under the Police Reform Act 2002.

4.3.3.6 Who Can Bring Proceedings?

The Human Rights Act 1998, s. 7 states:

(1) A person who claims that a public authority has acted (or proposes to act) in a way which is made unlawful by section 6(1) may—
  (a) bring proceedings against the authority under this Act in the appropriate court or tribunal, or
  (b) rely on the Convention right or rights concerned in any legal proceedings, but only if he is (or would be) a victim of the unlawful act.

(2) ...

(3) If the proceedings are brought on an application for judicial review, the applicant is to be taken to have a sufficient interest in relation to the unlawful act only if he is, or would be, a victim of that act.

KEYNOTE

Although the application of the 1998 Act is not restricted to natural persons and could include organisations, s. 7 limits the occasions where such 'people' can rely on Convention rights. To so rely on a Convention right, the person must be a 'victim'. The test to see if a person is a 'victim' for these purposes is taken directly from Article 34 of the Convention (which is not included in the Act) (s. 7(7)).

In order to qualify as a 'victim', a person must satisfy the same requirements as they would have to in order to bring a case before the Court in Strasbourg. These requirements are found in the case law from the European Court of Human Rights and principally mean that the person must show that he/she is:

- directly affected or
- at risk of being directly affected

by the act/omission complained of.

There is no need for the person to have actually *been* affected by the act/omission, as long as the person can show a real risk of him/her being directly affected by it in the future. An example can be seen in *Dudgeon* v *United Kingdom* (1983) 5 EHRR 573, where the petitioner was able to challenge the law proscribing consensual homosexual activity even though he had not been prosecuted under that legislation himself.

This limitation on 'victims' means that public interest groups will be excluded from bringing human rights actions directly, as will government organisations and local authorities.

The expression 'victim' is of particular relevance to people who are challenging the lawfulness of their arrest or detention under Article 5 (see below).

There are significant restrictions on police officers relying on the Convention rights in the context of recruitment and disciplinary procedures. As the European Court of Justice regards police officers in Member States as being government servants, they cannot generally rely on their Convention rights against their employer (see *Pellegrin* v *France* (2001) 31 EHRR 26). Purely private matters such as police pensions disputes are, however, not precluded in this way and there are other examples of officers' Convention rights being taken into consideration by the courts (**see para. 4.3.5**).

The wording of s. 7(3) means that, if an application for judicial review is brought (**see Evidence & Procedure, para. 2.2.5.3**) on human rights grounds, the applicant will have to meet the requirements of a 'victim' under s. 7 or he/she will not be allowed to bring the case *even though he/she might have sufficient legal standing under the rules governing judicial review generally.*

Whether interest groups such as trade unions and the Police Federation will be held to qualify as 'victims' and therefore allowed to bring human rights actions remains to be seen.

Time limits

Section 7 goes on to state:

> (5) Proceedings under subsection (1)(a) must be brought before the end of—
> (a) the period of one year beginning with the date on which the act complained of took place; or
> (b) such longer period as the court or tribunal considers equitable having regard to all the circumstances,
>
> but that is subject to any rule imposing a stricter time limit in relation to the procedure in question.

KEYNOTE

Any proceedings brought against a public authority under s. 7(1)(a) must be brought within one year from the date on which the act complained of took place (subject to the discretion of the relevant court/tribunal).

As the time for judicial review is three months, this stricter time limit will still apply in cases involving allegations of Convention rights infringement.

This time limit does not prevent people from raising the issue of Convention rights as a 'shield' in any other proceedings, neither does it affect the courts' general duty (under s. 3) to give effect to the Convention when interpreting and applying the law.

4.3.4 What are the 'Convention Rights'?

Having considered some of the key concepts and features of the Convention and the provisions of the Human Rights Act 1998, we can now examine some of the specific rights protected by them. Those rights are also referred to throughout the relevant text of this Manual and the other Manuals in the series.

As Article 1 is simply a statement of the duty of governments signing up to the Convention to secure the relevant rights and freedoms to everyone within their jurisdiction, the starting point for the content of the Convention is Article 2.

4.3.5 Article 2—The Right to Life

Article 2 of the Convention states:

> 1. Everyone's right to life shall be protected by law. No one shall be deprived of his life intentionally save in the execution of a sentence of a court following his conviction of a crime for which this penalty is provided by law.
> 2. Deprivation of life shall not be regarded as inflicted in contravention of this Article when it results from the use of force which is no more than absolutely necessary:
>   (a) in defence of any person from unlawful violence;
>   (b) in order to effect a lawful arrest or to prevent the escape of a person lawfully detained;
>   (c) in action lawfully taken for the purpose of quelling a riot or insurrection.

KEYNOTE

Article 2 provides what must be one of the most important and fundamental rights of individuals, namely the right to life. There are two 'arms' to this Convention right, namely:

- a prohibition on the State from *taking* life, and
- a positive duty placed upon the State to *protect* life

(see *X* v *United Kingdom* (1978) 14 DR 31).

The European Court of Human Rights said of Article 2 that it 'ranks as one of the most fundamental provisions in the Convention—indeed one which in peacetime admits of no derogation under Art. 15. Together with Art. 3 . . . it also enshrines one of the basic values of the democratic societies making up the Council of Europe . . . as such its provisions must be strictly construed' (*McCann* v *United Kingdom* (1995) 21 EHRR 97 at 160).

In a case concerning withholding medical treatment, the High Court considered the positive and negative duties under Article 2. The court held that the negative obligation was to refrain from taking a life intentionally. It held that this obligation was not breached by a decision made in the patient's best interests to withdraw life support facilities. The intentional deprivation of life had to involve a deliberate act as opposed to an omission. In relation to the positive obligation, the court held that this required the relevant public authority to take adequate and appropriate steps to safeguard life. Again, the taking of a responsible clinical decision to withhold treatment that was not in the patient's best interests met the State's positive obligation under Article 2 (*NHS Trust A* v *M* [2001] 1 All ER 801). (In this judgment the court reaffirmed the pre-Convention decision (*Airedale NHS Trust* v *Bland* [1993] AC 789) to the same effect.)

Duties under Article 2 can arise in various practical policing situations such as deaths in police care and fatal shootings by officers. An example of where Article 2 was relied upon by police officers was *R (On the Application of A and B)* v *HM Coroner for Inner South District of Greater London* [2004] EWCA Civ 1439, where a coroner refused to allow officers involved in a fatal shooting of a suspect to give evidence anonymously at the inquest. The Divisional Court held that the risk of serious harm to the officers and their families was sufficient to engage Article 2 and the coroner ought to have protected the anonymity of the officers until the verdict or the occurrence of some other event requiring their identities to be disclosed in the interests of justice.

4.3.5.1 Taking Life

It can be seen from the wording of the first paragraph that Article 2 does not prohibit the taking of life by a lawful imposition of the death penalty.

It can be seen that the Article allows for a number of limited exceptions when the taking of life by the State may not be a violation of this Convention right. All of the situations covered by the exceptions are generally concerned with protecting life, preventing crime and preserving order. The exceptions include actions taken in defending another person (not property) from unlawful violence (**see Crime, chapter 1.4**) and effecting a lawful arrest (**see para. 4.4.6**). Therefore the Convention acknowledges that there will be occasions where the State is compelled to take the life of an individual, such as where a police officer has to use lethal force to protect the life of another.

However, while limited in themselves, these exceptions will also be subject to very restrictive interpretation by the courts. Given that Article 2 protects one of the most fundamental of all Convention rights, any claimed exceptions to the Article are likely to be very carefully examined by the courts.

When a life is taken under any of the three situations set out at para. 2(a)–(c) above, the force used must be shown to have been *no more than absolutely necessary*—a more stringent test than the general test imposed in our domestic criminal law by s. 3 of the Criminal Law Act 1967 (as to which, **see Crime, chapter 1.4**). This very strict test was examined by the European Commission on Human Rights in a case where a young boy was killed by a baton round fired by a soldier during an outbreak of serious disorder (*Stewart* v *United Kingdom* (1985) 7 EHRR CD 453). There the Commission held that force will be absolutely necessary only if it is strictly proportionate to the legitimate purpose being pursued. In order to meet those criteria, regard must be had to:

- the nature of the aim being pursued,
- the inherent dangers to life and limb from the situation, and
- the degree of risk to life presented by the amount of force employed.

This test applies, not only to cases where there has been an intentional taking of life, but also where there has been a permitted use of force that has led to the death of another. The test has been held to be a stricter one than even the general requirement of 'proportionality' that runs throughout the Convention (as to which, **see para. 4.3.2**) (*McCann* v *United Kingdom* (1995) 21 EHRR 97).

This area is of critical importance to police officers in general, but to police supervisors and managers in particular. This is because, not only are the courts concerned with any individual actions that directly lead to the death of another, but also because they will take into account 'other factors' surrounding and leading up to the incident that caused the loss of life.

Such other factors are likely to include:

- the planning and control of the operation,
- the training given to the officers concerned, and
- the briefing/instructions that they received.

Where the use of force by the police results in the deprivation of life, the training, briefing, deployment and overall competence of everyone involved in the relevant operation will potentially come under the scrutiny of the court. These considerations, which were made very clear by the European Court of Human Rights in the *McCann* case (a case involving the shooting of three terrorists by the SAS in Gibraltar in 1988), were applied by the Court to an incident when police officers shot and killed a gunman and his hostage (*Andronicou* v *Cyprus* (1997) 25 EHRR 491). In that case, the Court found that the police operation had been planned and managed in a way that was intended to minimise the risk to life, even though the officers ultimately made a mistake as to the extent of the gunman's weapons and ammunition when they took the decision to open fire. The Court found that the exceptional requirements of Article 2(2) had been made out and that there had been no violation of Article 2 by the Cyprus police.

4.3.5.2 Protecting Life

A further area of importance for the police in Article 2 lies in the second arm—that of protecting the lives of others. This area was considered in the case of *Osman* v *United Kingdom* (2000) 29 EHRR 245. In this case a man had been killed by a person who had become fixated with him. The dead man's relatives claimed that they had warned the police about the killer's fixation and tried to sue them for negligence in failing to protect Mr Osman. The High Court dismissed the relatives' action on grounds of public policy and the relative took their case to the European Court of Human Rights, claiming that the State had violated the second arm of Article 2 by failing to protect the life of Mr Osman. Although the Court held that there had been no such violation on the facts of the case, it went on to examine the positive obligation of the State under Article 2.

The positive obligation on the State to protect life is not an absolute one. In *Osman* the European Commission said that Article 2 must be interpreted as requiring preventive steps to be taken to protect life from *known and avoidable dangers* (emphasis added). The Commission went on to say that the extent of this obligation (which is clearly of the first importance to those tasked with investigating and preventing crime) will vary 'having regard to the source and degree of danger and the means available to combat it' (at 115). The European Court of Human Rights said in Osman (at 305) that it will be enough for an applicant to show that the authorities did not do all that could reasonably be expected of them to avoid a *real and immediate risk to life* (emphasis added) of which they have or ought to have knowledge. As such, whether a police officer or police force has failed in this positive obligation to protect life will only be answerable in the light of all the circumstances of a particular case. This requirement is therefore very similar to the test for negligence at civil law in England and Wales.

Under some circumstances, this requirement could make the police power to detain a person suffering from mental illness in a public place (**see para. 4.3.8**) a duty to do so.

4.3.6 Article 3—Torture

Article 3 of the Convention states:

> No one shall be subjected to torture or to inhuman or degrading treatment or punishment.

KEYNOTE

Torture was made a specific criminal offence under s. 134 of the Criminal Justice Act 1988 (**see Crime, chapter 1.8**) but, whereas that offence has a statutory defence of 'lawful authority, justification or excuse', the prohibition contained in Article 3 is absolute. Irrespective of the prevailing circumstances, there can be no derogation from an individual's absolute right to freedom from torture, inhuman or degrading treatment or punishment.

However, in a case where a French police officer kneed a prisoner, causing a ruptured testicle, the European Court of Human Rights accepted that general exceptions to criminal offences such as self-defence (**see Crime, chapter 1.4**) can apply (*RIVAS* v *France* (2004) Application No. 59584/00).

The European Court of Human Rights has described Article 3 as enshrining one of the basic values of our democratic society and that, as such, its provisions must be strictly construed (see *McCann* v *United Kingdom* (1995) 21 EHRR 97 and Article 2 above).

'Degrading treatment' has been held to mean, in the interrogation of suspects, 'ill treatment designed to arouse in victims feelings of fear, anguish and inferiority, capable of humiliating and debasing them (see *Ireland* v *United Kingdom* (1978) 2 EHRR 25).

The behaviour envisaged by Article 3 therefore goes far beyond the traditional image of 'torture' and its three features can be identified as having the following broad characteristics:

- Torture—deliberate treatment leading to serious or cruel suffering
- Inhuman treatment—treatment resulting in intense suffering, both physical and mental
- Degrading treatment—treatment giving rise to fear and anguish in the victim, causing feelings of inferiority and humiliation

(see generally *Ireland* v *United Kingdom* above).

It has been held by the European Commission of Human Rights that causing mental anguish without any physical assault could be a violation of Article 3 (see *Denmark* v *Greece* (1969) 12 YB Eur Conv HR special vol.). Given the advances made in our own common law relating to assault since that date (**see Crime, chapter 1.7**), it is likely that courts within the United Kingdom would accept that words alone might amount to inhuman or degrading treatment.

As with the preceding Article, Article 3 has two 'arms' to it, namely the duty of the State not to inflict torture etc. upon an individual and the correlative duty to prevent others from doing so.

It can be seen from the various categories of treatment above, Article 3 may be breached, not only by the deliberate application of pain and suffering to an individual, but also by a range of other behaviour. Oppressive interrogation techniques such as sleep deprivation, exposure to continuous loud noise and forcing suspects to adopt uncomfortable postures for prolonged lengths of time have been held to fall within the second and third categories of inhuman and degrading treatment (*Ireland* v *United Kingdom*). In each case, it must be shown that the prohibited behaviour went beyond the 'minimum level of severity. In determining whether the behaviour did go beyond that level, and under which particular category that behaviour falls, the courts will take into account factors such as the age, sex, state of health and general life experience of the victim.

Where an individual was alleged to have been punched and kicked by police officers and pulled along by his hair, the Court found that there had been a violation of Article 3 in the form of inhuman and degrading treatment (*Ribitsch* v *Austria* (1995) 21 EHRR 573). In future, courts may consider the denial of drugs or medical treatment to prisoners under certain circumstances a violation of Article 3, along with the deliberate misuse of CS spray, speed-cuffs or other police equipment.

The government's positive duty to prevent individuals from suffering torture or inhuman and degrading treatment has been raised against proceedings to extradite a murder suspect to the United States where it was argued that he would face a long period awaiting the death penalty (*Soering* v *United Kingdom* (1989) 11 EHRR 439). It has also been used to prevent the deportation of a political activist to India where it was argued that he would be subjected to inhuman treatment by the authorities (*Chahal* v *United Kingdom* (1996) 23 EHRR 413). In each of these cases, the reasonable likelihood of ill-treatment at the hands of the State was held to be capable of giving rise to the positive obligation of the United Kingdom to prevent the extradition/deportation.

In a case before the Special Immigration Appeals Commission it was held that if, on the balance of probabilities, it was concluded that any evidence had been obtained by torture, then it should not be admitted (*A* v *Secretary of State for the Home Department* [2005] 3 WLR 1249).

4.3.7 Article 4—Slavery and Forced Labour

The prohibition on slavery under Article 4 is another Convention right that cannot be derogated from. Slavery is not defined within the Convention and, at the time of writing, no authoritative reports have been published.

4.3.8 Article 5—The Right to Liberty and Security

Article 5 of the Convention states:

1. Everyone has the right to liberty and security of person. No one shall be deprived of his liberty save in the following cases and in accordance with a procedure prescribed by law:
   (a) the lawful detention of a person after conviction by a competent court;

(b) the lawful arrest or detention of a person for non-compliance with the lawful order of a court or in order to secure the fulfilment of any obligation prescribed by law;
(c) the lawful arrest or detention of a person effected for the purpose of bringing him before the competent legal authority on reasonable suspicion of having committed an offence or when it is reasonably considered necessary to prevent his committing an offence or fleeing after having done so;
(d) the detention of a minor by lawful order for the purpose of educational supervision or his lawful detention for the purpose of bringing him before the competent legal authority;
(e) the lawful detention of persons for the prevention of the spreading of infectious diseases, of persons of unsound mind, alcoholics or drug addicts or vagrants;
(f) the lawful arrest or detention of a person to prevent his effecting an unauthorised entry into the country or of a person against whom action is being taken with a view to deportation or extradition.

KEYNOTE

This Article is of paramount importance to police officers.

The starting point is the general right to liberty and security of person. Although another fundamental right within a democratic society, this right to liberty is qualified under Article 5 and can be derogated from under Article 15 at certain times (see below). However, a person can only be deprived of his/her general right to liberty under one of the conditions set out on the permitted grounds in Article 5(1)(a)–(f), and even then that deprivation must be carried out in accordance with *a procedure prescribed by law.* As noted at the beginning of this chapter, not only must the 'procedure' be set out in the domestic law of the country; it must also be recorded in such a way that people can appreciate the possible consequences of their actions and adapt their behaviour accordingly. If the legal authority used to deprive a person of his/her liberty is ambiguous or unclear, that may well provide grounds for challenge under Article 5.

Even if a lawful power is sufficiently clear and well established, the list of permitted grounds in Article 5(1)(a) to (f) will have to be construed narrowly by the courts (*Winterwerp* v *Netherlands* (1979) 2 EHRR 387).

That said, the House of Lords has ruled that, unlike part of Article 5(1)(c), 5(1)(f) does not require that detention has to be *necessary* in order to be justified. As a result, the temporary detention of asylum seekers pending their application to remain in the United Kingdom, is not of itself unlawful (*R (On the Application of Shayan Barom)* v *Secretary of State for the Home Department* (2002) LTL 31 October).

4.3.8.1 Permitted Grounds

Each of the situations envisaged in Article 5(1)(a) to (f) will now be examined. It should be noted at this point that Article 5 does not provide any *power* to arrest or detain; it simply sets out certain circumstances where the general right to liberty may be interfered with *by some existing lawful means.*

4.3.8.2 Lawful Detention after Conviction

This exception allows a person to be detained after their conviction by a 'competent court', i.e. a court having the jurisdiction to try that particular case. Article 6 provides a right to a fair trial (**see para. 4.3.9**). Those people who have been so convicted may be detained in accordance with the order of the court. Clearly if the court does not have the power to pass the relevant order, the exception at Article 5(1)(a) will not apply and any detention will potentially amount to a violation of Article 5.

4.3.8.3 Lawful Arrest or Detention for Non-Compliance

The exception under Article 5(1)(b) allows for the detention or arrest of a person who has failed to comply with the *lawful* order of a court. Failing to pay a fine or to observe the conditions of an injunction would be examples of such non-compliance. The exception also extends to the arrest or detention in order to secure the fulfilment of any obligation prescribed by law. Such an obligation might include an obligation to provide a roadside breath specimen or to surrender documents relating to a vehicle (as to which, **see Road Policing**) or an obligation to attend a police station in order to give samples or body impressions (**see Evidence & Procedure, chapter 2.11**). Once again the circumstances of any arrest or detention will be examined by the courts who will need to consider whether the person was given a reasonable opportunity to comply with the order/obligation. The court will also need to consider whether the arrest or detention was a reasonable way to make sure that the order/obligation was met.

4.3.8.4 Lawful Arrest/Detention in Relation to an Offence

There are several aspects to the permitted grounds under Article 5(1)(c). The arrest/detention must first be lawful in itself. Any arrest/detention that is later shown to have been *unlawful* cannot be saved under any of the other headings. The implications of Article 5 for custody officers are discussed in **Evidence & Procedure, chapter 2.10**. Even a lawful arrest/detention will only meet the requirements of Article 5(1)(c) if it can be shown to have been:

- effected for the purpose of bringing the person before the relevant 'competent legal authority' (i.e. a judge or magistrate) on reasonable suspicion that the person had committed an offence; or
- reasonably considered necessary to prevent the person committing an offence or from fleeing afterwards.

Where a person has been lawfully arrested for the purpose of bringing him/her before a competent legal authority, it is not necessary to show that he/she actually *was brought* before that authority (*Brogan* v *United Kingdom* (1988) 11 EHRR 117). It is the *purpose* of the arrest at the time that is relevant as opposed to its ultimate achievement. This interpretation appears to accord with the provisions of s. 30(7) of the Police and Criminal Evidence Act 1984 which require an arrested person to be released if the grounds for detaining him/her cease to exist (**see para. 4.4.10**). Given the statutory status of a custody officer (**see Evidence & Procedure, chapter 2.10**), he/she would probably not be a 'competent legal authority' for this purpose which seems to be judicial in nature and requiring a degree of independence from the arresting authorities. However, it is hard to see how the expression 'competent legal authority' can be limited to judges and magistrates because Article 5(3) goes on to use a more restrictive expression (*judge or other officer authorised by law to exercise judicial power*) to define just such people (see below). The lack of fit here between the wording and our own police and judicial roles is caused partly by the fact that those roles are different in nature from those in many other European Union countries.

'Reasonable suspicion' here will be assessed objectively and the court will look for 'the existence of facts or information which would satisfy an objective observer that the person may have committed the offence' (see *Fox* v *United Kingdom* (1990) 13 EHRR 157). Other tests applied to powers of arrest will need to be read in conjunction with this provision, as will powers to detain in connection with searches (as to which, **see para. 4.4.4**).

4.3.8.5 Lawful Detention of Minors

This ground refers solely to 'detention' rather than arrest, although Article 5 seems to use the two expressions interchangeably in places (e.g. Article 5(4) below) and there may be occasions where the two are difficult to distinguish anyway. As with Article 5(1)(c) above, the initial detention must be lawful. A minor for these purposes is a person who has not attained the age of 18.

4.3.8.6 Lawful Detention of Others

Article 5(1)(e) also refers to 'detention' of certain people, in this case those who have various physical or mental ailments. It also extends to 'vagrants'. The reasoning behind Article 5(1)(e) is that the people described may need to be detained in their own interests. The permitted grounds set out here appear to allow the detention of people under the Mental Health Act 1983 (as to which, **see Crime, chapter 1.9**). Although there is a power under s. 34 of the Criminal Justice Act 1972 for a person to be taken after arrest to an approved alcohol treatment centre (**see para. 4.11.8.9**), it is unlikely that Article 5(1)(e) would apply as there is no further power to *detain* such a person once he/she arrives at the centre. In such cases, the permitted grounds under Article 5(1)(c) above, would be more appropriate.

Whatever its extent, Article 5(1)(e) is likely to be very narrowly applied by the courts and the mere fact that an individual has, for example, an infectious disease, will not of itself justify his/her 'detention'.

4.3.8.7 Lawful Arrest/Detention for Deportation or Extradition

The House of Lords has ruled that, unlike part of Article 5(1)(c), 5(1)(f) does not require the detention to be *necessary* in order to be justified (*R (On the Application of Shayan Barom)* v *Secretary of State for the Home Department* (2002) LTL 31 October). In that case it was held that the temporary detention of asylum seekers pending their application to remain in the United Kingdom, was not unlawful simply by reason of it not being strictly necessary.

Article 5(1)(f) is concerned with the unauthorised entry into the country and also the deportation/extradition of a person from the country. Such cases will invariably be dealt with by the relevant immigration authorities and advice should be sought from the Home Office.

4.3.8.8 Procedure

Article 5 goes on to state:

2. Everyone who is arrested shall be informed promptly, in a language which he understands, of the reasons for his arrest and of any charge against him.
3. Everyone arrested or detained in accordance with the provisions of paragraph 1(c) of this Article shall be brought promptly before a judge or other officer authorised by law to exercise judicial power and shall be entitled to trial within a reasonable time or to release pending trial. Release may be conditioned by guarantees to appear for trial.
4. Everyone who is deprived of his liberty by arrest or detention shall be entitled to take proceedings by which the lawfulness of his detention shall be decided speedily by a court and his release ordered if the detention is not lawful.
5. Everyone who has been the victim of arrest or detention in contravention of the provisions of this Article shall have an enforceable right to compensation.

KEYNOTE

The right to be informed of the reason for arrest is already enshrined in our domestic law under s. 28 of the Police and Criminal Evidence Act 1984 (**see para. 4.4.6.1**). The wording of Article 5(2) strengthens that requirement by specifying that the information must be given in a language that the person understands. For the comparable right (under Article 6) to be given information on being charged with a criminal offence, **see para. 4.3.9**.

The reason for requiring this information to be given would appear to be to allow the arrested person to challenge the arrest and subsequent detention (*X* v *United Kingdom* (1981) 4 EHRR 188). The ability to challenge the lawfulness of that detention (and presumably, the arrest) is itself a Convention right under Article 5(4).

Article 5(3) clearly envisages the extension of bail where appropriate and for a discussion of this, together with the other implications of Article 5(3) and (4), **see Evidence & Procedure, chapters 2.4 and 2.10**.

Article 5(5) gives a person who is the 'victim' of an arrest or detention in contravention of the rest of the Article an enforceable right to compensation. This right applies not only to the people concerned in the arrest/detention itself, but is specifically extended to include the courts (see s. 9 of the Human Rights Act 1998). The expression 'victim' is defined at s. 7(7) of the Act itself (see above).

Where a person was being extradited to Spain, the hearing was entitled to conclude that a delay of over five years between an individual's arrest and their extradition did not render the extradition unjust or oppressive (*Owalabi* v *Court Number Four at the High Court of Justice in Spain* [2005] EWHC 2849 (Admin)).

4.3.9 Article 6—The Right to a Fair Trial

Article 6 of the Convention states:

1. In the determination of his civil rights and obligations or of any criminal charge against him, everyone is entitled to a fair and public hearing within a reasonable time by an independent and impartial tribunal established by law. Judgment shall be pronounced publicly but the press and public may be excluded from all or part of the trial in the interest of morals, public order or national security in a democratic society, where the interests of juveniles or the protection of the private life of the parties so require, or to the extent strictly necessary in the opinion of the court in special circumstances where publicity would prejudice the interests of justice.
2. Everyone charged with a criminal offence shall be presumed innocent until proved guilty according to law.

KEYNOTE

Article 6 addresses another fundamental right within a democratic society and can be expected to be given a wide interpretation by the courts. The provisions of Article 6 affect both civil and criminal proceedings, although the Article goes on to provide specific safeguards in relation to criminal matters. For the general effects of these safeguards within the administration of justice in England and Wales, **see Evidence & Procedure**.

The key features of Article 6 are:

- a fair and public hearing
- held within a reasonable time
- by an independent and impartial legal tribunal.

Even a perception that the relevant court or tribunal is partial or biased can result in a breach of Article 6(1), reviving Lord Hewart's famous dictum that it is not enough that justice be done; it must manifestly be *seen* to be done.

Article 6 is restricted, however, to *procedural* issues and not to matters of fairness of the substantive law (see e.g. *R* v *Gemmell and Richards* [2002] Crim LR 926).

It has been held that Article 6 applies to professional disciplinary proceedings (*Wickramsinghe* v *United Kingdom* [1998] EHRLR 338), and there is an argument for its provisions being applied to police disciplinary hearings (**see para. 4.1.11**). However, where an officer is to be interviewed for a *purely disciplinary* matter, he/she has no free-standing right to access to a lawyer, even if being interviewed under caution (*Lee* v *United Kingdom* (2000) LTL 22 September).

The Article allows for the right to a public hearing to be restricted under certain circumstances, but requires any judgment to be publicly pronounced.

Article 6 has been interpreted as creating a requirement for 'equality of arms' in any civil or criminal proceedings (*Neumeister* v *Austria* (1968) 1 EHRR 91). Equality of arms requires that both parties be afforded the same opportunities to present their case and to cross-examine the other side. Additionally, both parties should be given the opportunity to be legally represented.

An example of where Article 6 has been used (unsuccessfully) as a 'shield' can be seen in the Scottish case of *Jardine* v *Crowe* 1999 SLT 1023. There the defendant refused to give details of the driver of his vehicle after a relevant offence when required to do so by the police under s. 172 of the Road Traffic Act 1988 (as to which, **see Road Policing, para. 3.2.11**). He argued that the requirement infringed Article 6 on the grounds that it forced him to incriminate himself. This argument was disposed of in the English and Welsh courts in *DPP* v *Wilson* [2002] RTR 6.

4.3.10 Article 7—No Punishment without Crime

Article 7 of the Convention states:

1. No one shall be held guilty of any criminal offence on account of any act or omission which did not constitute a criminal offence under national or international law at the time when it was committed. Nor shall a heavier penalty be imposed than the one that was applicable at the time the criminal offence was committed.
2. This Article shall not prejudice the trial and punishment of any person for any act or omission which, at the time when it was committed, was criminal according to the general principles of law recognised by civilised nations.

KEYNOTE

The main purpose of Article 7 is to provide a safeguard against retrospective criminal legislation whereby a government passes laws that render previously lawful behaviour unlawful. It also prohibits the imposition of a heavier penalty for a crime than that which was available at the time the crime was committed. Both of these provisions are in accordance with the key principles underpinning the Convention, namely that people should be able to look at the law and to adapt their behaviour in the full knowledge of what may happen to them if they break it.

In one case which illustrates the point, a defendant claimed that the change in the common law relating to marital rape (as to which, **see Crime, para. 1.9.3**) violated Article 7 because he could not have foreseen that the law would be extended to protect wives. The European Court of Human Rights held that this did not amount to a violation of the Article (*SW* v *United Kingdom* (1995) 21 EHRR 363).

Claims that football banning orders (see para. 4.6.13.3) breached this Article have been unsuccessful (see *Gough* v *Chief Constable of Derbyshire Constabulary* [2002] 2 All ER 985).

Article 7(2) is aimed at maintaining the rule *of* law rather than the rule *by* law. It provides for the situation where a person carries out activities that would be classified as 'crimes' according to the general principles of law among civilised nations but which were not necessarily criminal offences under the domestic law of that country (e.g. acts persecuting minority groups carried out with the acquiescence of the government). This very limited exception prevents States from legitimising what would otherwise be criminal acts by passing or repealing criminal laws.

4.3.11 Article 8—Right to Private Life

Article 8 of the Convention states:

1. Everyone has the right to respect for his private and family life, his home and his correspondence.
2. There shall be no interference by a public authority with the exercise of this right except such as is in accordance with the law and is necessary in a democratic society in the interests of national security, public safety or the economic well being of the country, for the prevention of disorder or crime, for the protection of health or morals, or for the protection of the rights and freedoms of others.

KEYNOTE

The provisions of Article 8 extend a right to respect for a person's:

- private life,
- family life,
- home, and
- correspondence.

The main aim of the Article is to protect these features of a person's life from the arbitrary interference by 'public authorities' (as to which, see above) (*Kroon* v *Netherlands* (1994) 19 EHRR 263). This is a new concept as there is no statutory 'law of privacy' under the domestic law of England and Wales. However, the Convention does allow for individuals to raise issues of unjustified interference with their private lives and the courts have held that even celebrities have a basic right to privacy which will be protected by Article 8 (see *Campbell* v *Mirror Group Newspapers* [2004] UKHL 22); similar arguments (in a somewhat less genteel context) can be found in *Theakston* v *Mirror Group Newspapers* [2002] EMLR 22. The development of the law in this area has. been given far more impetus by changes in the laws on data protection (see chapter 4.12). A good practical example of how this Article can impact upon the actions of public authorities and decision-makers is *R (On the Application of Evans)* v *First Secretary of State* [2005] EWHC 149. In that case a planning inspector refused an application to develop a gypsy caravan site in what was a green belt area. The appellant claimed that, as a 'gypsy', his special status and associated rights under Article 8 should have been preferred over any other considerations by the planning inspector and the Secretary of State on his appeal. The Divisional Court disagreed and held that, while the appellant's rights under Article 8 should be considered as part of the balancing process, gypsy status alone could not in effect be used to trump any other considerations in this way.

Once again this Article is of considerable importance to police officers and managers for a number of reasons. First, the State is under a duty not to interfere with these features of a person's life except in accordance with Article 8(2). Many police activities such as entry onto premises, surveillance and the seizure of property, touch upon the features covered by Article 8. Once it can be shown that they have done so, the police must be able to point to:

- a legal authority allowing the interference,
- a legitimate objective behind their actions, and
- a 'pressing social need' for that interference (the 'three tests').

An individual's Article 8 rights are among the key reasons behind the introduction of the Regulation of Investigatory Powers Act 2000 (as to which, **see para. 4.12.4**).

Article 8 was also at the heart of the changes to the Sexual Offences Act 1956 as the European Court of Human Rights found that the law prohibiting consensual sexual acts between more than two men in private (s. 13) was an unjustifiable interference with Article 8 (see *ADT* v *United Kingdom* (2001) 31 EHRR 33). For the offences under the 1956 Act generally, **see Crime, chapter 1.9**.

The Consultancy Service Index maintained by the Secretary of State for the Department of Health providing access to employers' records on people considered to be unsuitable for work with children has been held not to infringe the human rights of those included on it (*R* v *Worcester County Council, ex parte W* [2000] 3 FCR 174). The maintenance of the list was held, by the Divisional Court, to be proportionate to the lawful objective sought (*R* v *Secretary of State for Health, ex parte L(M)* [2001] 1 FLR 406).

A second reason why this Article is of importance to police services is that the State also has a positive obligation to prevent others from interfering with an individual's right to private life (see *Stjerna* v *Finland* (1994) 24 EHRR 194). How far the police would have to go in order to discharge this obligation is unclear, but Article 8 will be relevant in areas such as those set out in Part 2 of this Manual (community safety), together with other areas such as civil disputes (as to which, **see chapter 4.9**).

It is here that the notion of balancing the rights and freedoms of individuals against each other and against those of the community at large can be seen most acutely. Article 8—and in particular the requirement for 'proportionality'—provides one of the main arguments that have been raised against the lawfulness of Anti-social Behaviour Orders (**see chapter 4.5**) and Sexual Offences Prevention Orders (**see Crime, chapter 1.9**).

A final reason that Article 8 is so important is that the Article appears to include the right to establish relationships with others, the right to privacy even within an office environment and the right to set up home, all of which have a significant impact on general supervisory and managerial functions. Failing to protect an individual from the unwanted advances of others, searching through an employee's office or directing an employee as to where he/she can and cannot live would all potentially fall within the remit of Article 8.

The European Court of Human Rights has held that there is no justification for barring transsexuals from enjoying rights conferred on others (such as the right to marry—see below) or to recognise their specific status and that to do so is a violation of Article 8 (*Goodwin* v *United Kingdom* [2002] 35 EHRR 18). This issue has been addressed in part by the Civil Partnerships Act 2004 (**see para. 4.13.10.1**) and the Gender Recognition Act 2004 (**see para. 4.13.9**).

Article 8 also has implications for the law in relation to data protection and computer misuse (**see chapter 4.12**), and the lack of legal regulation governing the use of CCTV cameras has been raised with the European Commission (*R* v *Brentwood Borough Council, ex parte Peck* [1998] EMLR 697 December 1997).

4.3.12 Article 9—Freedom of Thought

Article 9 of the Convention protects the right to freedom of thought, conscience and religion.

4.3.13 Article 10—Freedom of Expression

Article 10 of the Convention states:

1. Everyone has the right to freedom of expression. This right shall include freedom to hold opinions and to receive and impart information and ideas without interference by public authority and regardless of frontiers. This Article shall not prevent States from requiring the licensing of broadcasting, television or cinema enterprises.
2. The exercise of these freedoms, since it carries with it duties and responsibilities, may be subject to such formalities, conditions, restrictions or penalties as are prescribed by law and are necessary in a democratic society, in the interests of national security, territorial integrity or public safety, for the prevention of disorder or crime, for the protection of health or morals, for the protection of the reputation or rights of others, for preventing the disclosure of information received in confidence, or for maintaining the authority and impartiality of the judiciary.

KEYNOTE

Article 10 protects the freedom:

- of expression,
- to hold opinions, and
- to receive and impart information and ideas

in each case without interference by a public authority.

'Expression' here includes the creation of pictures and images (*Stevens* v *United Kingdom* (1986) 46 DR 245).

Although not providing a general 'right to freedom of information', Article 10 has been used in a number of different settings including the protection of artistic, political and economic expression. It has been used to protect journalists' sources (see *Goodwin* v *United Kingdom* (1996) 22 EHRR 123).

As the right to express freely has to be balanced against the rights of others and the needs of democratic society generally, this area of Convention rights has generated some considerable problems and is often intermingled with issues of freedom of thought, conscience and religion (under Article 9).

In a case where the defendant damaged the perimeter fence of a Trident defence base, the Divisional Court held that her acts could be characterised as an expression of her opinion under Article 10 but that the Convention required the expression of that opinion to be proportionate. There were other ways in which the defendant could have expressed her opinion without committing a crime and therefore her conviction for criminal damage **(see Crime, chapter 1.13)** was upheld (*Hutchinson* v *DPP* (2000) *The Independent*, 20 November).

Article 10(1) is drafted to allow for State licensing of broadcasts, television and cinema performances but, as you might expect, the courts will be unlikely to tolerate interference with the freedom of expression without compelling reasons. Once again, the courts will look for a 'pressing social need' and indeed one of the main cases setting out the requirement for proportionality (*Handyside* v *United Kingdom* (1976) 1 EHRR 737) involved an action under Article 10. A good example of how Article 10 can operate is the case in the Republic of Ireland where, although it was shown that injunctions used to prevent women from receiving information about abortion services were issued for a legitimate aim, the overall effect of such legal remedies was found to be disproportionate (*Open Door Counselling and Dublin Well Woman* v *Ireland* (1992) 15 EHRR 244).

Article 10(2) clearly allows for an individual's freedom of expression to be curtailed under a number of circumstances including the prevention of disorder or crime and the protection of morals. Balancing these competing needs is one area where the European Court of Human Rights has allowed a reasonable 'margin of appreciation' (see above). Nevertheless, any restrictions on an individual's freedom of expression will be narrowly construed and closely scrutinised. Demonstrators may be able to rely on Article 10 as a defence to a charge under the Public Order Act 1986 (**see chapter 4.6**) and hunt saboteurs bound over to keep the peace by magistrates have been able to show that their rights have thereby been unjustifiably restricted (see *Hashman* v *United Kingdom* (2000) 30 EHRR 241). It has also been held that the exercise of the right to free speech could fall within the concept of harassment for the purposes of the Protection from Harassment Act 1997 where the ingredients for the offence were present (*Howlett* v *Harding* [2006] EWHC 41).

The rights under this Article are subject to the restrictions allowed by Article 16 (political activities by aliens).

4.3.14 Article 11—Freedom of Assembly and Association

Article 11 of the Convention states:

1. Everyone has the right to freedom of peaceful assembly and to freedom of association with others, including the right to form and to join trade unions for the protection of his interests.
2. No restrictions shall be placed on the exercise of these rights other than such as are prescribed by law and are necessary in a democratic society in the interests of national security or public safety, for the prevention of disorder or crime, for the protection of health or morals or for the protection of the rights and freedoms of others. This Article shall not prevent the imposition of lawful restrictions on the exercise of these rights by members of the armed forces, of the police or of the administration of the State.

KEYNOTE

Article 11 is closely related to Article 10 and is often raised in conjunction with it, particularly in situations involving the arrest of demonstrators and protestors. In addition to refraining from interference with the individual's right to peaceful assembly, the State is also under a positive duty to prevent others from doing so. The assembly must, however, be *peaceful* and any intention to use violence or to cause disorder may take the individuals actions outside the protection of Article 11.

As with Article 10, there are allowances for reducing rights of assembly etc. under certain conditions including the prevention of disorder and crime and the interests of national security and public safety.

This Article may require changes to the current guidelines on picketing which restrict the number of pickets that may lawfully be allowed to gather at a workplace (**see para. 4.9.3.1**).

The right to freedom of association and to join trade unions means, among other things, that trade unions may be victims for the purposes of bringing an action under this Article. The State can impose 'lawful restrictions' on the exercise of these rights by 'members of the police'. It is not clear whether this refers only to attested constables (as under s. 64 of the Police Act 1996) or to all employees of a police service including unsworn civilian staff (**see chapter 4.1**). Neither is it clear what would amount to 'lawful restrictions' on officers forming collectives for the protection of their shared interests.

The rights under this Article are subject to the restrictions allowed by Article 16 (political activities by aliens).

4.3.15 Article 12—The Right to Marry

Article 12 of the Convention gives the right to marry and have a family.

4.3.16 Article 13—The Right to an Effective Remedy

Article 13 of the Convention states:

> Everyone whose rights and freedoms as set forth in this Convention are violated shall have an effective remedy before a national authority notwithstanding that the violation has been committed by persons acting in an official capacity.

KEYNOTE

Article 13 is *not* included within sch. 1 to the Human Rights Act 1998. However, it will be of relevance to our courts because it has been so prominent within the case law that has grown up through Convention jurisprudence and, under s. 2 of the 1998 Act, those courts are obliged to take that case law into account.

Article 13 is generally used in conjunction with another Convention right (i.e. the right for which there is allegedly no 'effective remedy'). What Article 13 means is that everyone must have an effective remedy in their national courts to protect their rights irrespective of any official capacity in which the person violating those rights was acting. In one case the Commission held that the police complaints procedure (as to which, **see chapter 4.1**) did not provide an 'effective remedy' for those whose Convention rights has been violated (*Govell* v *United Kingdom* (1997) 23 EHRR CD 101). It is not clear how far the current avenues of redress for police officers who are the victims of unfounded or malicious complaints and investigations (**see chapter 4.1**) would meet these requirements. It is interesting to note that the police complaints system generally has been held not to amount to an 'effective remedy' for complaints (*Govell* v *United Kingdom*).

4.3.17 Article 14—Prohibition of Discrimination in Convention Rights

Article 14 of the Convention states:

> The enjoyment of the rights and freedoms set forth in this Convention shall be secured without discrimination on any ground such as sex, race, colour, language, religion, political or other opinion, national or social origin, association with a national minority, property, birth or other status.

KEYNOTE

Article 14 simply provides a guarantee that access to the Convention's other provisions must be enjoyed equally by everyone under the jurisdiction of the particular State. The list set out in the Article is not exhaustive and other categories of people or grounds of discrimination may be added by the courts (and have been added by the European Court of Human Rights). A person claiming a breach of Article 14 must show that his/her own individual circumstances are similar to those of another person who has been treated differently in relation to the enjoyment of Convention rights.

Examples of Article 14 in practice can be found in a number of high profile cases. One such case was the challenge to the prolonged detention without charge of suspects under s. 23 of the Anti-terrorism, Crime and Security Act 2001 (now repealed). Because the detention was only used against *foreign nationals* suspected of being international terrorists and not UK nationals, the practice was held by the House of Lords to discriminate on grounds of nationality—*A* v *Secretary of State for the Home Department* [2004] UKHL 56.

The open-ended wording of Article 14 means that a wide range of categories of people who can be grouped by reference to their status may be protected. That protection certainly extends to a person's sexuality, an area that has generally not been protected in our domestic law (see *Mendoza* v *Ghaidan* [2004] UKHL 30).

However, it does not make express provision for *indirect* discrimination (as to which **see chapter 4.13**) and the Divisional Court has expressed considerable doubt as to whether Article 14 provides protection against indirect, as opposed to direct, discrimination (see *R (On the Application of Barber)* v *Secretary of State for Work and Pensions* [2002] 2 FLR 1181).

Some commentators take the view that the partial or uneven application of police powers such as stop and search may amount to a breach of Article 14 (**see para. 4.4.4**).

The rights under this Article are subject to the restrictions allowed by Article 16 (political activities by aliens).

4.3.18 Article 15—Derogation in Time of Emergency

Article 15 of the Convention states:

1. In time of war or other public emergency threatening the life of the nation any High Contracting Party may take measures derogating from its obligations under this Convention to the extent strictly required by the exigencies of the situation, provided that such measures are not inconsistent with its other obligations under international law.
2. No derogation from Article 2, except in respect of deaths resulting from lawful acts of war, or from Articles 3, 4 (paragraph 1) and 7 shall be made under this provision.
3. Any High Contracting Party availing itself of this right of derogation shall keep the Secretary General of the Council of Europe fully informed of the measures which it has taken and the reasons therefore. It shall also inform the Secretary General of the Council of Europe when such measures have ceased to operate and the provisions of the Convention are again being fully executed.

KEYNOTE

As discussed above, Article 15 allows a State to derogate from some of its obligations under the Convention during times of war or other public emergency threatening the life of the nation. This is a very narrow restriction and even under those extreme circumstances the derogation may only be made to the extent that is strictly required by the exigencies of the situation.

The strict application of this requirement can be seen in the case involving detention of suspected international terrorists who were non-UK nationals. In that case the House of Lords held that the derogation made under the Anti-terrorism, Crime and Security Act 2001 went further than was strictly required by the exigencies of the situation and that, if the threat presented to national security by UK residents suspected of being al-Qaeda terrorists could be addressed without infringing their Convention rights, then so could the threat posed by non-UK residents similarly suspected—*A* v *Secretary of State for the Home Department* [2004] UKHL 56.

As also discussed above (**see para. 4.3.2**) the original derogation lodged by the United Kingdom at the time when the Act was passed permitted longer detention of terrorist suspects before charge. That derogation related to the ongoing unrest in Northern Ireland. With political developments in Northern Ireland, that derogation was removed but, since 11 September 2001, the United Kingdom lodged a further derogation under the Anti-terrorism, Crime and Security Act 2001 and the powers thereunder. Because those powers are potentially incompatible with parts of the Convention, Parliament passed the Human Rights (Amendment No. 2) Order 2001 (SI 2001/4032), giving effect to the derogation set out in part I of sch. 3 to the Human Rights Act 1998.

4.3.19 Protocol 1, Article 1—Protection of Property

Protocol 1, Article 1 to the Convention states:

> Every natural or legal person is entitled to the peaceful enjoyment of his possessions.
> No one shall be deprived of his possessions except in the public interest and subject to the conditions provided for by law and by the general principles of international law.
> The preceding provisions shall not, however, in any way impair the right of a State to enforce such laws as it deems necessary to control the use of property in accordance with the general interest or to secure the payment of taxes or other contributions or penalties.

KEYNOTE

The Convention itself has been extended by the addition of a number of Protocols, not all of which have been incorporated by the Human Rights Act 1998. Article 1 of the First Protocol sets out the right to peaceful enjoyment of one's possessions. This leaves room for the State to deprive a person of his/her possessions 'in the public interest' (e.g. by nationalisation of an industry) and courts are likely to allow a wide margin of appreciation (see above) in such cases. Broadly, to prove a violation of this part of Protocol 1, it must be shown that the State has:

- interfered with the applicant's peaceful enjoyment of possessions, or
- deprived him/her of those possessions, or
- subjected those possessions to some form of control.

Clear examples of where such State activity can be found is in the seizure of property by HM Revenue and Customs and the police. The term 'possessions' is likely to be interpreted very widely and, under European case law, has extended to land, contractual rights and intellectual property. Restrictions on the use of firearms (**see chapter 4.7**), premises (**chapter 4.10**) and even animals may provide grounds for alleging a violation of this Convention right.

A different example of how this right might be used against a public authority can be seen in *AO* v *Italy* (2001) 29 EHRR CD 92. In that case the Italian police were held to have violated the applicant's right to peaceful enjoyment of his property when they continually failed to send any officers to his flat which he was trying to repossess from squatters. Although the action for repossession had been going on for over four years, this case illustrates one way in which private law matters can become issues of liability for public authorities such as police services.

4.4 Policing Powers

4.4.1 Introduction

Police officers are entrusted with many powers and privileges. The most important of these powers, both practically and constitutionally, are the powers of arrest, search, entry and seizure.

In addition to the far-reaching effects of the human rights provisions discussed above, using powers improperly can result in officers and their employers being liable, both at civil and criminal law; it can also lead to evidence being excluded and otherwise meritorious prosecutions being dropped. Even where police powers are exercised *lawfully*, the manner or frequency of their use might be perceived by the community as a source of oppression and discrimination, leading to a reduction in confidence in the police and the creation of an atmosphere of distrust. The risk of lawfully employed police powers being perceived in this way was highlighted very clearly in the Stephen Lawrence Inquiry (Cm 4262-I, see para. 46.31 and recommendation 61).

It is worth noting that where police officers act on the authority of a properly sworn warrant issued by a magistrate, they are protected against legal action by the Constables Protection Act 1750. This protection does not apply where the warrant has been issued by the High Court.

4.4.2 Acting Ranks

Many of the police powers considered in this—and subsequent—chapters are restricted to officers holding particular ranks. In particular, there are occasions where the Police and Criminal Evidence Act 1984 requires officers of certain ranks to perform roles. The 1984 Act recognises that there may be occasions where officers of the appropriate rank are not readily available and so in limited circumstances allows officers of a lower rank to perform their roles.

Section 107 of the Police and Criminal Evidence Act 1984 sets out occasions where an officer of a lower rank can perform the functions of that required by a higher rank.

Section 107 states:

(1) For the purpose of any provision of this Act or any other Act under which a power in respect of the investigation of offences or the treatment of persons in police custody is exercisable only by or with the authority of a police officer of at least the rank of superintendent, an officer of the rank of chief inspector shall be treated as holding the rank of superintendent if—
   (a) he has been authorised by an officer holding a rank above the rank of superintendent to exercise the power or, as the case may be, to give his authority for its exercise, or
   (b) he is acting during the absence of an officer holding the rank of superintendent who has authorised him, for the duration of that absence, to exercise the power or, as the case may be, to give his authority for its exercise.

(2) For the purpose of any provision of this Act or any other Act under which such a power is exercisable only by or with the authority of an officer of at least the rank of inspector, an officer of the rank of sergeant shall be treated as holding the rank of inspector if he has been authorised by an officer of at least the rank of superintendent to exercise the power or, as the case may be, to give his authority for its exercise.

KEYNOTE

Section 107 originally made reference to both superintendents and chief superintendents. This was amended by the Police and Magistrates' Courts Act 1994 to reflect the changes in rank structures within the police service. However, many police services have reintroduced the rank of chief superintendent in spite of the 1994 Act and the Criminal Justice and Police Act 2001 puts it back again. Although that part of the 2001 Act is now in force (see s. 125) and our deputies and chief superintendents have returned, it has not affected the above situation regarding acting ranks.

The only mention of officers performing the higher rank of sergeant in the Police and Criminal Evidence Act 1984 is to be found in s. 36. Section 36 states:

(3) No officer may be appointed a custody officer unless he is of at least the rank of sergeant.
(4) An officer of any rank may perform the functions of a custody officer at a designated police station if a custody officer is not readily available to perform them.

However, in *Vince* v *Chief Constable of Dorset Police* [1993] 1 WLR 415, Steyn LJ (as he was then) made it clear that s. 36(4) should only be an exception:

For my part I would start from the provisional premise that the legislature intended to introduce an effective system for the care and protection of detained suspects by custody officers. And on this basis section 36(4), which allows an independent officer of any rank to perform the function of a custody officer at a designated police station 'if a custody officer is not readily available to perform them', can be viewed as a concession to practicality in the light of the problems which will inevitably occur in a busy police station. In other words, there is much to be said for the view that it was not intended that chief constables would be entitled to arrange matters so that as a matter of routine officers below the rank of sergeant performed the functions of custody officers.

4.4.2.1 Temporary Promotion

Regulation 6 of the Police (Promotion) Regulations 1996 (SI 1996/1685) deals with temporary promotion. Regulation 6 states:

(1) A member of a police force who is required to perform the duties of a higher rank may, even if there is no vacancy for that rank, be promoted temporarily to it, but, in the case of promotion to the rank of sergeant or inspector only if he is qualified for the promotion under regulation 3.
(2) A member of a police force who is successful in the written paper under Part I of the qualifying assessment, and who has commenced the period of work-based assessment under Part IIB of the qualifying assessment, shall, at the commencement of the work-based assessment, be temporarily promoted to the rank of sergeant or inspector as the case may be.

4.4.3 Disorder Penalty Notices

Although the police have had the power to issue fixed penalty notices as an alternative to conventional prosecution in some road traffic offences for many years (**see Road Policing, chapter 3.11**), the Criminal Justice and Police Act 2001 introduced a whole new concept of police powers for fast-track resolution of some lower-level criminal offences. This system also relies on the issuing of penalty notices, though they are generally referred to as disorder penalty notices rather than fixed penalty notices. The powers in relation to some fixed penalty notices for low-level disorder are among those that can be given to Police Community Support Officers.

The offences which are subject to the fixed penalty scheme are set out in s. 1, along with the relevant penalties which are set out in the relevant statutory instrument issued under the 2001 Act. This has been amended several times since the initial Order was made in 2002 and the most up-to-date version should be consulted.

Part I Offences Attracting Penalty of £80 for People 16 and Over, or £40 for People under 16

Offence creating provision	*Description of offence*
Section 80 of the Explosives Act 1875	Throwing fireworks in a thoroughfare
Section 5(2) of the Criminal Law Act 1967	Wasting police time or giving false report
Section 91 of the Criminal Justice Act 1967	Disorderly behaviour while drunk in a public place
Section 1 of the Theft Act 1968	Theft
Section 1(1) of the Criminal Damage Act 1971	Destroying or damaging property
Section 5 of the Public Order Act 1986	Behaviour likely to cause harassment, alarm or distress
Section 141 of the Licensing Act 2003	Sale of alcohol to a person who is drunk
Section 146(1) and (3) of the Licensing Act 2003	Sale of alcohol to children
Section 149(3) and (4) of the Licensing Act 2003	Purchase of alcohol on behalf of children
Section 151 of the Licensing Act 2003	Delivery of alcohol to children or allowing such delivery
Section 127(2) of the Communications Act 2003	Using a public electronic communications network in order to cause annoyance, inconvenience or needless anxiety
Section 11 of the Fireworks Act 2003	Contravention of a prohibition or failure to comply with a requirement imposed by or under fireworks regulations or making false statements
Section 49 of the Fire and Rescue Services Act 2004	Knowingly giving a false alarm to a person acting on behalf of a fire and rescue authority

Part II Offences Attracting Penalty of £50 for People 16 and Over, or £30 for People under 16

Offence creating provision	*Description of offence*
Section 12 of the Licensing Act 1872	Being drunk in a highway, other public place or licensed premises
Section 55 of the British Transport Commission Act 1949	Trespassing on a railway
Section 56 of the British Transport Commission Act 1949	Throwing stones etc. at trains or other things on railways

Offence creating provision	*Description of offence*
Section 87 of the Environmental Protection Act 1990	Depositing and leaving litter
Section 12 of the Criminal Justice and Police Act 2001	Consumption of alcohol in designated public place
Section 149(1) of the Licensing Act 2003	Purchase of alcohol by children
Section 150 of the Licensing Act 2003	Consumption of alcohol by children or allowing such consumption

KEYNOTE

Section 3 sets out the form of the fixed penalty notice and the amounts permissible. The Secretary of State may add to this list by statutory instrument and may specify different amounts for people of different ages (s. 3(1A)).

There are restrictions on those occasions where theft and criminal damage can be dealt with by way of penalty notice (**see Crime, chapters 1.11 and 1.13** respectively).

Note the difference in the penalty payable by a person who was under the age of 16 at the time of the offence. For the additional provisions where offenders are under 16 **see para. 4.4.3.2**.

The heading to s. 1 in the statute refers to 'on the spot' penalties. This is inaccurate as no payment will be required before 21 days (under s. 5). While it might be in keeping with the media portrayal of offenders being frogmarched to a hole-in-the-wall cash dispenser by a police officer who would then accept payment in return for the offender's release, it is nevertheless misleading.

Just as misleading is the description of the offence under s. 12 of the 2001 Act (described as *'consumption of alcohol in a public place'*); this offence is wider than that (**see chapter 4.11**).

The other offences listed above are set out in the relevant parts of this and other Manuals and are indicated in the respective Keynotes.

4.4.3.1 Form of Penalty Notice

Section 3 of the 2001 Act requires any notice to:

- be in the prescribed form (see the Penalties for Disorderly Behaviour (Form of Penalty Notice) Regulations 2002 (SI 2002/1838) (as amended));
- state the alleged offence;
- specify the 'suspended enforcement period' (21 days beginning with the date when the notice was given);
- state the amount of the penalty (which may not be more than a quarter of the maximum fine available for that offence);
- state to whom and where the payment must be made; and
- inform the person of his/her right to be tried and explain how that right might be exercised.

All this information will be set out on any approved form.

4.4.3.2 Power to Issue Penalty Notices

The power to issue such notices in respect of the s. 1 offences is set out at s. 2. Basically, s. 2 allows a police officer in uniform (if away from a police station) or one that has been authorised by their chief officer (if at a police station) to give a person aged 10 or over a penalty notice if he/she has reason to believe that the person has committed a s. 1 offence. A person given a penalty notice will have the option of requesting to be tried in the normal way or of paying the penalty within the suspended enforcement period. The right to request trial is intended as a safeguard of the defendant's right to a fair trial under Article 6 of the European Convention (**see para. 4.3.9**). If the person fails to pay within that period, a sum of one and a half times the amount of the penalty may be enforced against them as a fine. After the suspended enforcement period ends, proceedings may be brought against the person in the normal way for the relevant offence(s). Where a penalty notice is given to a person under the age of 16, the relevant chief officer of police must notify such parent or guardian as he/she thinks fit (see the Penalties for Disorderly Behaviour (Amendment of Minimum Age) Order 2004 (SI 2004/3166)). Any such notification must be in writing and must include a copy of the penalty notice and may be served by giving it to the parent or guardian personally or sending it to the parent or guardian at their usual or last-known address by first-class post before the end of the period of 28 days beginning with the date on which the penalty notice was given (see article 3 of the 2004 Order).

If it transpires that a notification has been sent to a person who is not a parent or guardian of the person receiving the penalty notice (or that it would have been more appropriately sent to someone else), the chief officer can cancel the original notification and send out a fresh one (article 4).

Where a parent or guardian of a young penalty recipient is notified in this way, then (unless the notification is cancelled) they are liable to pay the penalty under the original notice (article 5). Full details surrounding the proposed operation of the whole scheme is available in the form of guidance from the Home Office under s. 6.

The power to issue penalty notices is among those that can be conferred on a designated person under sch. 4 to the Police Reform Act 2002 (**see para. 4.2.3**).

4.4.4 Stop and Search

There are many specific statutory authorities providing the police (and others) with powers to stop people and vehicles and search them (**see appendix 4.1**). There is also a general power for police officers to stop and search people and vehicles under the Police and Criminal Evidence Act 1984 (PACE). Both this general power to stop and search and those authorised by most other statutes must be carried out in accordance with Code A of the PACE Codes of Practice. (There are exceptions for certain powers under the Aviation Security Act 1982 and those exercised by statutory undertakers.) There has been a great deal of discussion and debate over the use of police stop and search powers, not least as a result of the government figures which have consistently shown a disproportionate number of black and ethnic minority people being stopped and searched when compared to white European groups.

While it has been acknowledged that some of this reported disproportionality arises from matters that are beyond the control of the police, the government set up a Stop and Search Action Team (SSAT) to consider the wider use of these powers and to identify and disseminate good practice. The SSAT has published a Stop and Search Manual containing guidance and research findings. In addition, following recommendation 61 of the Stephen Lawrence Inquiry and a number of regional trials, all 'stops' by the police are now being recorded in order to monitor their use and ensure that the policing powers are being used proportionately, reasonably and only to the extent necessary. To assist with the operational application of this policy, the SSAT has released a chart to assist in identifying the occasions where a record must be submitted (reproduced below); this is supplemented by a further flowchart issued by the Home Office to assist supervisors and managers in meeting the requirements for scrutinising and monitoring the recording of stops.

KEYNOTE

Her Majesty's Chief Inspector of Constabulary, Sir Ronnie Flanagan, was asked to conduct a fundamental review of policing by the Home Secretary. He published his final report on 7 February 2008, which focused on the need to manage the risks better in order to reduce the threat to the public and reduce the harm caused by crime. This is approached by:

- freeing up space by improving and strengthening the structures and systems that support policing
- improving performance and developing the workforce through better management of resources
- freeing up space by reducing unnecessary bureaucracy
- delivering in partnership through neighbourhood policing and involving local people.

A recommendation has been made that the Stop and Account form should be abolished, and the Stop and Search form streamlined. However, at the time of writing it is not clear if the tripartite partners that govern policing will accept these recommendations.

No.	Circumstances	Classification	Statutory Requirement to Record, Monitor and Report?
1.	An officer has reasonable grounds so stops, detains and physically searches a person.	STOP & SEARCH	Yes
2.	An officer has reasonable grounds so stops, detains but does not search because during questioning the need to search is negated.	A 'STOP'	Yes
3.	An officer 'encounters' a person and asks them to account for their actions, behaviour, presence in an area or possession of something.	A 'STOP'	Yes
4.	An officer engages with a group of witnesses to establish the background to an incident.	NOT A 'STOP'	No
5.	An officer carries out a search under s. 60 of the Criminal Justice and Public Order Act 1994.	STOP & SEARCH	Yes
6.	An officer stops a vehicle (using powers under the RTA 1988) and asks the driver/passengers to account for their actions, behaviour, presence in an area or possession of something.	A 'STOP'	Yes
7.	An officer stops a vehicle (using powers under the RTA 1988) as it has committed a moving traffic offence or the officer requires the production of driving documents and a HORT/1, VDRS or EFPN **is not** issued.	NOT A 'STOP'	No
8.	An officer stops a vehicle (using powers under the RTA 1988) as it has committed a moving traffic offence or the officer requires the production of driving documents and a HORT/1, Vehicle Defect Rectification Scheme Notice (VDRS) or Endorsable Fixed Penalty Notice (EFPN) is issued, or an officer requires a specimen of breath under s. 6.	NOT A 'STOP'	No

Before considering the specific statutory powers under the Police and Criminal Evidence Act 1984—and then the other main stop and search legislation—it is necessary to consider some general points arising from Code A. It is also worth noting that, as well as applying to these powers of search, Code A applies to some powers that allow the searching of people in the exercise of a power to search *premises*. For instance, the power to enter school premises and conduct searches of people for bladed articles and weapons under s. 139B of the Criminal Justice Act 1988 (as to which **see chapter 4.8**) will be governed by Code A (see para. 2.27). So, too, will the power to search people for controlled drugs under a warrant issued by virtue of s. 23 of the Misuse of Drugs Act 1971 (as to which **see Crime**).

4.4.4.1 Use of Stop and Search Powers

The power to stop and search members of the community is one of the most controversial of all the powers available to the police. Therefore it must be used fairly and responsibly, with respect for the individual and without unlawful discrimination (**see chapter 4.13**). Paragraph 1 of Code A points out the benefits of properly conducted stop and search practices as an effective policing tool, but emphasises the need for officers to be able to justify using their powers. The primary purpose of stop and search powers is, as Code A reinforces, to enable police officers to allay or confirm suspicions about individuals without exercising their powers of arrest. Code A goes on to point out the potential harm to public confidence in the police that can be brought about by the improper or insensitive use of stop and search powers, as well as setting out a timely reminder that misuse can result in disciplinary action. As discussed in earlier parts of this chapter, the fact that a power is lawfully available does not necessarily mean that its use is appropriate or justified in every case. Parliament has given these discretionary powers to constables (and, on limited occasions, some others who are assisting them) and it is the responsibility of each individual officer to determine not only whether a power *exists* in the particular circumstances, but also whether its use best serves the overall objectives of his/her police service. Conversely, Code A now specifically provides that, if there is no power to search a person, then an officer must not do so *even where the person being searched consents* (para. 1.5).

A key part of retaining public confidence and ensuring the proper functioning of the stop and search provisions lies in their monitoring and management. Code A imposes clear responsibilities on supervising officers to monitor the use of stop and search powers and, in particular, the possibility that they are being exercised on the basis of stereotyped images or other inappropriate generalisations (para. 5). Code A requires supervising officers to monitor the use of stop and search powers, to examine search records for any trends or patterns giving cause for concern and to take the appropriate action as necessary. This supervision and monitoring must be supported by the compilation of comprehensive statistical records of stops and searches at force, area and local level (para. 5.3). Any apparently disproportionate use of powers by particular officers or groups of officers, or their use in relation to specific sections of the community should be identified and investigated.

In addition to supervisors, Code A places a requirement on senior officers with area or force-wide responsibilities to monitor the 'broader use' of stop and search powers and, where necessary, to take action at the relevant level (para. 5.2). Code A also requires arrangements to be made for stop and search records to be scrutinised by representatives of the community (subject to confidentiality issues—Note 19) and for the use of these powers to be explained to the community at local level (para. 5.4).

4.4.4.2 General Stop and Search Powers

The law regulating the general police powers of stop and search is set out under part I of the Police and Criminal Evidence Act 1984 as discussed below. The Act imposes a number of detailed requirements and limits on the availability and use of these powers, while Code

A adds further practical detail that officers, their supervisors and managers will need to take into account.

Section 1 of the Police and Criminal Evidence Act 1984 states:

(1) A constable may exercise any power conferred by this section—
 (a) in any place to which at the time when he proposes to exercise the power the public or any section of the public has access, on payment or otherwise, as of right or by virtue of express or implied permission; or
 (b) in any other place to which people have ready access at the time when he proposes to exercise the power but which is not a dwelling.

(2) Subject to subsection (3) to (5) below, a constable—
 (a) may search—
  (i) any person or vehicle;
  (ii) anything which is in or on a vehicle,
  for stolen or prohibited articles or any article to which subsection (8A) below applies or any firework to which subsection (8B) below applies; and
 (b) may detain a person or vehicle for the purpose of such a search.

KEYNOTE

The above power applies where the officer has 'reasonable grounds for suspecting' that he/she will find stolen or prohibited articles or articles falling under s. 139 of the Criminal Justice Act 1988 (bladed or sharply pointed articles; **see chapter 4.8**) or any firework to which subsection (8B) applies (s. 1(3) of the 1984 Act). For a discussion of reasonable grounds, see below.

The power under s. 1 does not authorise the officer to stop a vehicle (s. 2(9)(b)). For the general power of police officers in uniform to stop vehicles, **see Road Policing**. Compare this aspect of the stop and search power with that provided by s. 60 of the Criminal Justice and Public Order Act 1994 below.

The power is restricted to those places set out in s. 1(1)(a) or (b). This does not mean that the search itself must be carried out there; in fact Code A, paras 3.5 and 3.6 require certain searches to be carried out away from public view.

Code A no longer allows the routine searching of people with their consent and only permits very limited use of the power as a condition of entry (e.g. to a sports ground) (para. 1.5). This means that the practice of conducting 'voluntary' searches in the street or other public places has gone.

4.4.4.3 Reasonable Grounds

The issue of when an officer has reasonable grounds for suspicion has been developed by the courts for many years. This common law development is now supported by the inclusion of specific guidance on search powers that require reasonable grounds for suspicion (see Code A, paras 2.2 to 2.4).

Generally, the courts have held that 'suspicion' requires a lower degree of certainty than 'belief'. The distinction between the two expressions has been held to be a significant one, intended by Parliament (see *Baker* v *Oxford* [1980] RTR 315). In that particular case—involving road traffic offences—the court held that the statutory requirement for a reasonable *belief* imposed a greater degree of certainty on the officers concerned. Accordingly, police officers using powers that impose such an extra requirement must be prepared to justify their belief. Suspicion, on the other hand, has been described by Lord Devlin as '. . . a state of conjecture or surmise when proof is lacking' (*Shaabin Bin Hussein* v *Chong Fook Kam* [1970] AC 492). That suspicion can be based on any evidence, even if the evidence itself would be inadmissible at trial (e.g. because it is hearsay) (**see Evidence & Procedure, chapter 2.7**). In fact Code A provides for occasions where a police officer has reasonable grounds to suspect that a person is in innocent possession of stolen or prohibited articles or other items which give rise to a power to search the person even though there would be no power of arrest, or no offence committed by that person.

The Court of Appeal has reiterated the principle in *Hussein* (above) in the context of an arrest of a person mistakenly thought to have been involved in an offence. The Court went on to say that a state of mind of 'being suspicious but uncertain' would provide reasonable grounds to support an arrest where reasonable suspicion was required (*Parker (Graham Charles)* v *Chief Constable of Hampshire Constabulary* (1999) *The Times*, 25 June, defendant seen in a car used in an earlier shooting incident in another part of the country). Confirmation that the source of reasonable grounds for suspicion can arise from intelligence or other information is supported by the entry in Code A, paras 2.2 and 2.4.

The courts have accepted that reasonable grounds for suspicion can arise from information given to the officer by a colleague, an informant or even anonymously (see *O'Hara* v *Chief Constable of the Royal Ulster Constabulary* [1997] 1 All ER 129).

Whether, in the case of the above powers, there were reasonable grounds for suspecting that the relevant articles would be found during the search is a question of fact that will have to be decided in the light of all the circumstances (see Code A, para. 2.2). The courts have held that it must be shown that any such grounds on which an officer acted would have been enough to give rise to that suspicion in a 'reasonable person' (*Nakkuda Ali* v *Jayaratne* [1951] AC 66).

However, the mere existence of such circumstances or evidence is not enough. The officer must actually *have* a 'reasonable suspicion' that the relevant articles will be found. If, in fact, the officer knows that there is little or no likelihood of finding the articles, the power could not be used (*R* v *Harrison* [1938] 3 All ER 134).

Reasonable suspicion can never be founded on the basis of purely personal factors such as a person's colour, age or appearance (Code A, para. 2.2) and grounds for suspicion cannot be provided retrospectively by questioning a person who the officer had no reason to stop.

However, Code A, para. 2.6 makes provision for the searching of members of gangs or groups who habitually carry:

- knives unlawfully or
- weapons or
- controlled drugs

and wear a distinctive item of clothing or other means of identifying themselves with such a gang or group, but only where there is reliable information or intelligence that members of a group or gang do so.

While there is no power to stop or detain a person in order to *find* grounds for a search (Code A, para. 2.11), in the case of searches under ss. 43 and 44 of the Terrorism Act 2000 (**see chapter 4.6**) this general restriction is modified to reflect the whole purpose of such searches. Similarly, Code A recognises that there are many reasons why police officers may be speaking to members of the public and, if during the course of any such non-stop-and-search encounter reasonable grounds for suspicion arise, the officer may then use his/her powers to search—even though no grounds existed at the beginning of the encounter. In order to make the position absolutely clear, Code A states that if an officer *is* detaining someone for the purpose of a search, he/she should tell the person *as soon as detention begins*.

The whole issue is best summed up at para. 2.5 of Code A which notes that searches are more likely to be more effective, legitimate and secure public confidence when reasonable suspicion is based on a range of factors and that the overall use of such powers is more likely to be effective when up-to-date, accurate intelligence and information are used.

If, in the course of a s. 1 search, the officer does find a stolen, prohibited or 'section 139' article, he/she may seize it (s. 1(6)).

If there are any grounds to suspect that the person has committed any offence, he/she must be cautioned before any questions are put to him/her about his/her involvement in the offence(s) if any answers, *or his/her silence,* are to be used in evidence (Code C). For a full discussion of these provisions, **see Evidence & Procedure, chapter 2.7.**

For the requirements and restrictions on conducting these searches **see para. 4.4.4.6.**

4.4.4.4 Prohibited Articles

Section 1 of the 1984 Act also states:

> (7) An article is prohibited for the purposes of this Part of this Act if it is—
> (a) an offensive weapon; or
> (b) an article—
> (i) made or adapted for use in the course of or in connection with an offence to which this sub-paragraph applies; or
> (ii) intended by the person having it with him for such use by him or by some other person.
>
> (8) The offences to which subsection (7)(b)(1) above applies are—
> (a) burglary;
> (b) theft;
> (c) offences under section 12 of the Theft Act 1968 (taking motor vehicle or other conveyance without authority); and
> (d) fraud (contrary to section 1 of the Fraud Act 2006).
> (e) offences under section 1 of the Criminal Damage Act 1971 (destroying or damaging property).
>
> (8A) This subsection applies to any article in relation to which a person has committed, or is committing or is going to commit an offence under section 139 of the Criminal Justice Act 1988.
>
> (8B) This subsection applies to any firework which a person possesses in contravention of a prohibition imposed by fireworks regulations.
>
> (8C) In this section—
> (a) 'firework' shall be construed in accordance with the definition of 'fireworks' in section 1(1) of the Fireworks Act 2003; and
> (b) 'fireworks regulations' has the same meaning as in that Act.
>
> (9) In this Part of this Act 'offensive weapon' means any article-
> (a) made or adapted for use for causing injury to persons; or
> (b) intended by the person having it with him for such use by him or by some other person.

KEYNOTE

For a full discussion on the law relating to offensive weapons and bladed/sharply pointed articles, **see chapter 4.8**, and for the relevant definitions and offences involving fireworks **see para. 4.5.6.**

For the offences listed at s. 1(8), **see Crime.** Note the addition of articles for causing criminal damage.

4.4.4.5 Search in Garden, Yard or Land Connected to Dwelling

Section 1 of the 1984 Act also states:

> (4) If a person is in a garden or yard occupied with and used for the purposes of a dwelling or on other land so occupied and used, a constable may not search him in the exercise of the power conferred by this section unless the constable has reasonable grounds for believing—
> (a) that he does not reside in the dwelling; and
> (b) that he is not in the place in question with the express or implied permission of a person who resides in the dwelling.

(5) If a vehicle is in a garden or yard occupied with and used for the purposes of a dwelling or on other land so occupied and used, a constable may not search the vehicle or anything in or on it in the exercise of the power conferred by this section unless he has reasonable grounds for believing—
   (a) that the person in charge of the vehicle does not reside in the dwelling; and
   (b) that the vehicle is not in the place in question with the express or implied permission of a person who resides in the dwelling.

KEYNOTE

If the person to be searched is in a garden, yard or other land occupied with and used as part of a dwelling, the power to search will not apply unless the officer has 'reasonable grounds for believing' that the person does not live there *and* that he/she is not there with the permission (express or implied) of any person who does live there.

If the garden or yard is attached to a house that is not so 'occupied', the restriction at s. 1(4) would not appear to apply.

Similar restrictions are placed on the searching of vehicles found in such places by s. 1(5). For the meaning of 'in charge' of a vehicle, **see Road Policing, chapter 3.1**. For these purposes 'vehicle' includes vessels, aircraft and hovercraft (s. 2(10) of the 1984 Act).

4.4.4.6 Conducting the Search

In keeping with the rest of Code A, the provisions regulating the conduct of searches apply not just to searches under s. 1 of the Police and Criminal Evidence Act 1984, but are of general application. Some of the main provisions of Code A are summarised below but the full text (**see appendix 4.1**) should always be consulted.

A good starting point is para. 3.1 which states that all stops and searches must be carried out with courtesy, consideration and respect for the person concerned and that every reasonable effort must be made to minimise the embarrassment that the person being searched may experience. In addition, the co-operation of the person being searched must be sought (this is not the same as requiring their *consent*—**see para. 4.4.4.1**) and forcible searches may be made only if it has been established that the person is unwilling to co-operate or they resist (para. 3.2).

It is important to note the requirements with regard to the information that must be brought to the attention of the person to be searched *before any search is commenced* (**see para. 4.4.4.7**).

The length of time that a person (or vehicle) is detained should be reasonable and kept to a minimum and the extent and thoroughness of the search must be related to the object of it and the relevant suspicion (para. 3.3). This means that, if you have reasonable suspicion only that the person has something concealed in a particular pocket, the search must be confined to that pocket.

Any search must be carried out *at or near* the place where the person or vehicle was first detained (para. 3.4). The predecessor of this provision in the first Code of Practice caused some confusion and now Note 6 sets the position out more clearly. While the search can take place at a nearby police station or elsewhere, the relevant place should be located within a reasonable travelling distance by car or on foot as appropriate. This applies to *all* such searches, not simply those involving the removal of clothing or which need to be conducted out of public view. If the search amounts to a 'strip search', Code C, Annex A will apply (**see Evidence & Procedure**).

Generally there is no power to require a person to remove any clothing in public other than an outer coat, jacket or gloves (except under s. 45(3) of the Terrorism Act 2000 which also allows for the removal of headgear and footwear. For further discussion of these powers **see chapter 4.6**; and under s. 60AA of the Criminal Justice and Public Order Act 1994 which allows for the removal of items used to conceal identity—as to which **see para. 4.4.4.14**). Code A imposes further restrictions on searches in public (para. 3.6 and Notes 4,7 and 8). Searches involving the removal of more than outer coats, jackets, gloves, footwear or headwear must not be carried out by, or in the presence of, someone of the opposite sex to the person being searched (para. 3.6). Searches under s. 43(1) of the Terrorism Act 2000 must be carried out by a person of the same sex as the person being searched. Searches involving the exposure of intimate parts must not be routinely carried out simply because nothing was found on the original search and they must not be carried out in public view or in a police vehicle (para. 3.7).

4.4.4.7 Information to be Provided by Officer

Before carrying out a search, the officer must take reasonable steps to give the person the following information:

- that they are being detained for that purpose;
- the officer's name (except terrorism cases or other cases where the officer reasonably believes that this might put him/her in danger—a warrant or identification number must be given in these cases) and police station. If the officer is not in uniform, he/she must show their warrant cards;
- the legal power that is being used;
- a clear explanation of the purpose, any relevant reasonable suspicion that is needed or the relevant authorisation (see generally Code A, para. 3.8).

Before conducting the search the officer must tell the person (or owner/person in charge of the vehicle) of their entitlement to a copy of the search record (**see para. 4.4.4.8**). If the person does not appear to understand what is being said, or there is any doubt about their ability to understand English, the officer must take reasonable steps to bring all the relevant information to the person's attention (see para. 3.11).

Having summarised the general rules regarding the conduct of searches, the specific requirements of s. 2 of the Police and Criminal Evidence Act 1984 can now be considered.

Section 2 of the Police and Criminal Evidence Act 1984 states:

(1) A constable who detains a person or vehicle in the exercise—
  (a) of the power conferred by section 1 above; or
  (b) of any other power—
    (i) to search a person without first arresting him; or
    (ii) to search a vehicle without making an arrest,
  need not conduct a search if it appears to him subsequently—
    (i) that no search is required; or
    (ii) that a search is impracticable.

(2) If a constable contemplates a search, other than a search of an unattended vehicle, in the exercise—
  (a) of the power conferred by section 1 above; or
  (b) of any other power, except the power conferred by section 6 below and the power conferred by section 27(2) of the Aviation Security Act 1982—
    (i) to search a person without first arresting him; or
    (ii) to search a vehicle without making an arrest,
  it shall be his duty, subject to subsection (4) below, to take reasonable steps before he commences the search to bring to the attention of the appropriate person—

(i) if the constable is not in uniform, documentary evidence that he is a constable; and
(ii) whether he is in uniform or not, the matters specified in subsection (3) below;

and the constable shall not commence the search until he has performed that duty.

(3) The matters referred to in subsection (2)(ii) above are—
(a) the constable's name and the name of the police station to which he is attached;
(b) the object of the proposed search;
(c) the constable's grounds for proposing to make it; and
(d) the effect of section 3(7) or (8) below, as may be appropriate.

KEYNOTE

As set out above, a person or vehicle may only be detained for such time as is reasonably necessary to permit a search to be carried out either at the place where the person or vehicle was first detained or nearby (s. 2(8)).

Having stopped a person for the purposes of searching them, there is no requirement for the officer to conduct the search if it appears that to do so is not necessary or that it is impracticable.

The officer carrying out the search must *take reasonable steps* to bring the matters at s. 2(3)(a) to (d) to the person's attention *before starting the search*. This information must be given whether it is requested or not. Whether reasonable steps have been taken to communicate information will ultimately be a question of fact for the court to decide and what is 'reasonable' will vary with the particular circumstances of each search (e.g. what is reasonable outside a busy city centre nightclub may well be different from that which is required on a rural public footpath). The courts have taken a very firm position in interpreting and applying these requirements. For example, the requirements for officers to provide details of their names and police stations still apply even though that information is discernible from the officers' uniform; failure to provide the information in such circumstances will make any subsequent search unlawful and will mean that the person being searched may use reasonable force to resist it (*Osman* v *DPP* (1999) *The Times*, 28 September). In a further case, the Divisional Court held that the officers conducting the stop and search had not informed the suspect of their intention to search him at an early enough stage before laying their hands on him. The suspect—who was standing with his hands in his pockets and who was suspected of drugs offences—had struggled with the officers when they took hold of him and had been arrested. The magistrates' court held that, where it was obvious that the people apprehending a suspect were police officers and where an officer was genuinely concerned for the safety of a fellow officer, it was not essential to comply with all the requirements of s. 2(3). However, the Divisional Court *disagreed*, quashing the conviction and holding that, where police officers contemplated a statutory search, they were required (by s. 2(2) above) to comply with s. 2(3) *before* commencing the search—*Bonner* v *DPP* [2004] EWHC 2415 Admin. The principle was restated in *R* v *Bristol* [2007] EWCA Civ Crim 3214.

In enquiries related to the investigation of terrorism, or where the officer reasonably believes that giving his/her name might put him/her in danger, the requirement for an officer to give his/her name is removed (see Code A, para. 3.8).

The 'effect of section 3(7) or (8)' referred to in s. 2(3)(d) means the person's entitlement to a copy of any search record made.

The 'appropriate person' is the person to be searched or the person in charge of the vehicle to be searched (s. 2(5)).

4.4.4.8 Action after Search

Section 3 of the Police and Criminal Evidence Act 1984 and Code A, para. 4 make certain requirements following any search of a person or vehicle (other than one not covered by s. 1 (**see para. 4.4.4.6**)). The first requirement is that the officer makes a written record of the search. While s. 3(1) makes an exception where it is not practicable to fill out such a record, Code A narrows the exception down to occasions where there are exceptional circumstances making it *wholly impracticable*. This very narrow exception will only be met if there was virtually no chance of the officer being in a position to make the record (e.g. by being called to an emergency immediately after the search). If the exception does apply, the officer must make the record as soon as practicable after the search has been completed (s. 3(2) and Code A, para. 4.1).

Section 3 of the Police and Criminal Evidence Act 1984 states:

(6) The record of a search of a person or a vehicle—
   (a) shall state—
      (i) the object of the search;
      (ii) the grounds for making it;
      (iii) the date and time when it was made;
      (iv) the place where it was made;
      (v) whether anything, and if so what, was found;
      (vi) whether any, and if so what, injury to a person or damage to property appears to the constable to have resulted from the search; and
   (b) shall identify the constable making it.

KEYNOTE

Where a search record has been made, the person searched, the owner or the person who was in charge of any vehicle that was searched, will be entitled to a copy of the record if he/she requests one within 12 months (s. 3(7), (8) and (9)). Code A requires that a copy of any record made *at the time* must be given immediately to the person who has been searched and the officer must ask for the name, address and date of birth of the person but there is no obligation to provide this information and no power to detain the person if they do not (para. 4.2).

Under the provisions of s. 2(3) (**see para. 4.4.4.7**), a person must be advised of his/her entitlement to a copy of the relevant search record unless it appears to the officer searching that it will not be practicable to make the record (s. 2(4)).

The requirements of s. 3 will apply to the searches of vehicles, vessels, aircraft and hovercraft (s. 3(10)).

The search record should contain the person's name but, if the officer does not know the name of the person, he/she cannot detain that person simply to find it out (s. 3(3)) and a description should be recorded instead (s. 3(4)). The record must also contain the information set out at Code A, para. 4.3 which includes a note of the person's self-defined ethnic background (see Note 18), the time when the person or vehicle was first detained, the outcome of the search, and the details of any other officer involved in the search (see Note 15). A record of a vehicle search must include a description of the vehicle (s. 3(5)) and the registration number (see Code A, para. 4.3 and Note 16).

A record is required for each person and each vehicle searched. However, if a person is in a vehicle and both are searched *and the object and grounds of the search are the same*, only one search record need be completed (Code A, para. 4.5). If more than one person in a vehicle is searched, separate records for each person must be made. Where a person is detained with a view to a search being carried out but no search is carried out as a result of the grounds being eliminated by questioning, a record must still be completed (para. 4.7).

It has been held that a failure to make a record of a search does not thereby render the search unlawful (*Basher* v *DPP* [1993] COD 372). However, it is not only the lawfulness of a search that is of concern to police officers and the general principles set out in Code A should be borne in mind at all times (**see para. 4.4.4.1**).

4.4.4.9 Action after Searching Unattended Vehicles

In the case of unattended vehicles, s. 2 of the Police and Criminal Evidence Act 1984 states:

> (6) On completing a search of an unattended vehicle or anything in or on such a vehicle in the exercise of any such power as is mentioned in subsection (2) above a constable shall leave a notice—
> (a) stating that he has searched it;
> (b) giving the name of the police station to which he is attached;
> (c) stating that an application for compensation for any damage caused by the search may be made to that police station; and
> (d) stating the effect of section 3(8) below.
>
> (7) The constable shall leave the notice inside the vehicle unless it is not reasonably practicable to do so without damaging the vehicle.

KEYNOTE

The requirements in relation to notice on unattended vehicles that are searched are also set out in Code A, para. 4. The requirements apply to the search of anything *on* an unattended vehicle as well as the vehicle itself. The notice must also state the police station where a copy of the search record can be obtained (para. 4.9) and, if practicable, the vehicle must be left secure (para. 4.10).

4.4.4.10 Road Checks

The power to stop vehicles generally is provided under s. 163 of the Road Traffic Act 1988 (officers exercising the power must be in uniform). Having caused a vehicle to stop, there are then certain other powers which may be employed by a police officer (or other authorised people).

Among those powers are the powers set out in the Police and Criminal Evidence Act 1984, s. 4 in relation to 'road checks'.

A road check is where the power under s. 163 of the Road Traffic Act 1988 is used in any locality in such a way as to stop all vehicles or vehicles selected by any criterion (s. 4(2) of the 1984 Act). That general power for uniformed officers to stop vehicles might be used in a particular geographical area to stop all vehicles on the road or all vehicles of a certain make, model or colour, or only those vehicles containing a certain number of adult occupants. In all these cases, there would be a 'road check' for the purposes of s. 4.

The power to carry out road checks following the appropriate authorisation under s. 4 of the Police and Criminal Evidence Act 1984 below is among those that can be conferred on a Police Community Support Officer designated under sch. 4 to the Police Reform Act 2002 (**see chapter 4.2**). In exercising this power, any such officer may also be given the power of a uniformed constable to stop vehicles (under s. 163 of the Road Traffic Act 1988).

Section 4 of the Police and Criminal Evidence Act 1984 states:

> (1) This section shall have effect in relation to the conduct of road checks by police officers for the purpose of ascertaining whether a vehicle is carrying—
> (a) a person who has committed an offence other than a road traffic offence or a vehicle excise offence;
> (b) a person who is a witness to such an offence;
> (c) a person intending to commit such an offence; or
> (d) a person who is unlawfully at large.
>
> (2) . . .
>
> (3) Subject to subsection (5) below, there may only be such a road check if a police officer of the rank of superintendent or above authorises it in writing.

(4) An officer may only authorise a road check under subsection (3) above—
   (a) for the purpose specified in subsection (1)(a) above, if he has reasonable grounds—
      (i) for believing that the offence is an indictable offence; and
      (ii) for suspecting that the person is, or is about to be, in the locality in which vehicles would be stopped if the road check were authorised;
   (b) for the purpose specified in subsection (1)(b) above, if he has reasonable grounds for believing that the offence is an indictable offence;
   (c) for the purpose specified in subsection (1)(c) above, if he has reasonable grounds—
      (i) for believing that the offence would be an indictable offence; and
      (ii) for suspecting that the person is, or is about to be, in the locality in which vehicles would be stopped if the road check were authorised;
   (d) for the purpose specified in subsection (1)(d) above, if he has reasonable grounds for suspecting that the person is, or is about to be, in that locality.

KEYNOTE

Road checks may only be authorised for the purposes set out at s. 4(4) and for the duration set out at s. 4(11) (see below). They must, subject to s. 4(5) (see below), be authorised in writing by an officer of superintendent rank or above (s. 4(3)).

For 'indictable offence' see Evidence & Procedure, para. 2.2.2.2.

The locality in which vehicles are to be stopped must also be specified (s. 4(10)).

If it appears to an officer below the rank of superintendent that a road check is required as a matter of urgency for one of the purposes in s. 4(1), he/she may authorise such a road check (s. 4(5)). What amounts to 'urgency' is not defined, but it would appear to be a somewhat subjective requirement based on the apprehension of the officer concerned. Where such an urgent road check is authorised, the authorising officer must, *as soon as is practicable to do so*, make a written record of the time at which the authorisation is given and must cause an officer of superintendent rank or above to be informed of the authorisation (s. 4(6) and (7)). Where this occurs, the superintendent (or more senior officer) may authorise, *in writing*, that the road check continue (s. 4(8)). If the officer considers that the road check should not continue, he/she must make a written record that it took place as well as the purpose for which it took place (including the relevant 'indictable offence' (s. 4(9) and (14)).

Under s. 4(13), every written authorisation for a road check must include:

- the name of the authorising officer
- the purpose of the road check—including any relevant 'indictable offence'
- the locality in which vehicles are to be stopped.

4.4.4.11 Duration of Road Check

Section 4 of the 1984 Act goes on to state:

(11) An officer giving an authorisation under this section, other than an authorisation under subsection (5) above—
   (a) shall specify a period, not exceeding seven days, during which the road check may continue; and
   (b) may direct that the road check—
      (i) shall be continuous; or
      (ii) shall be conducted at specified times,
   during that period.

(12) If it appears to an officer of the rank of superintendent or above that a road cheek ought to continue beyond the period for which it has been authorised he may, from time to time, in writing specify a further period, not exceeding seven days, during which it may continue.

KEYNOTE

In recording the purpose for the road check under s. 4(13), the officer must specify a period not exceeding seven days during which the road check is to run.

The road check may run continuously through that specified period or it may be carried out at specific times.

The road check may be extended—in writing—a number of times for further periods up to a total of seven days by a superintendent if it appears to him/her that it 'ought' to continue. There is no restriction of 'reasonableness' or requirement for the existence of particular grounds here and it seems that the judgement may be an entirely subjective one by the superintendent.

Where a vehicle is stopped during a road check, the person in charge of it is entitled to a written statement of the purpose of that road check if he/she applies for one no later than the end of the 12-month period from the day on which the vehicle was stopped (s. 4(15)).

4.4.4.12 Stop and Search under the Criminal Justice and Public Order Act 1994

In addition to the powers above, police officers may stop and search pedestrians or vehicles under the Criminal Justice and Public Order Act 1994.

Section 60 of the 1994 Act states:

(1) If a police officer of or above the rank of inspector reasonably believes—
- (a) that incidents involving serious violence may take place in any locality in his area, and that it is expedient to give an authorisation under this section to prevent their occurrence, or
- (b) that persons are carrying dangerous instruments or offensive weapons in any locality in his police area without good reason,

he may give an authorisation that the powers conferred by this section shall be exercisable at any place within that locality for a specified period not exceeding 24 hours.

(2) (repealed)

(3) ...

(3A) ...

(4) This section confers on any constable in uniform power—
- (a) to stop any pedestrian and search him or anything carried by him for offensive weapons or dangerous instruments;
- (b) to stop any vehicle and search the vehicle, its driver and any passenger for offensive weapons or dangerous instruments.

KEYNOTE

The practical operational aspects of these powers are regulated by the Police and Criminal Evidence Act 1984 Code of Practice (**see appendix 4.1 and para. 4.4.4**). In particular, paras 2.12–2.14 of Code A and Notes 10–13 apply.

Note 10 makes it very clear that the above powers are separate from, and additional to the general stop and search powers discussed earlier in this chapter. The overall purpose of the above powers is to prevent serious violence and the widespread carrying of weapons that might otherwise lead to serious injury, by empowering the police to disarm potential offenders *in circumstances where other powers would not be sufficient.* Therefore these powers should not be used to replace or get round the normal powers for dealing with routine crime problems (Note 10). There will be occasions where s. 60 is used in conjunction with other preventive policing powers (e.g. ss. 12 and 14 of the Public Order Act 1986—**see para. 4.6.11**—and/or the common law powers to prevent an imminent breach of the peace—**see para. 4.6.2.2**).

Section 60(1)(a) has a generally preventive function in relation to the apprehension of incidents that will involve serious violence. Section 60(1)(b), however, is a much broader provision triggered by the officer's 'reasonable belief' that people are carrying dangerous instruments or offensive weapons. Serious violence is not defined in the 1994 Act but, although violence could relate to property, the whole tenor of the section suggests that it is aimed at tackling violence against people.

'Dangerous instruments' are bladed or sharply pointed instruments, while offensive weapons have the same meaning as that under s. 1(9) of the Police and Criminal Evidence Act 1984 (**see para. 4.4.4.4**). For a full discussion of the law relating to weapons generally, **see chapter 4.8**.

Confusingly, for the purposes of s. 60, 'carrying' will mean 'having in your possession' (s. 60(11A)), a much wider meaning than carrying usually conveys (**see chapter 4.8 and also Crime, chapter 1.11**). Why the legislators did not simply use the term 'possession' is not clear.

The person authorising the exercise of the powers under s. 60(1)(a) must reasonably *believe* that it is expedient to do so in order to prevent the occurrence of the incidents involving serious violence. This is a more onerous requirement than reasonable grounds to 'suspect' (**see para. 4.4.4.3**). The reasonable belief must have an objective basis such as intelligence or a history of antagonism between particular groups or previous incidents of violence connected with certain locations or event (see Note 11). Code A also cites a significant increase in knife-point robberies within an area as being another example of an objective basis for such belief.

The initial period during which the authorisation can last must be no longer than appears to be reasonably necessary to prevent incidents of serious violence or to deal with the problem of carrying dangerous instruments/weapons *and in any event* must not exceed 24 hours (Code A, para. 2.13). Any such authorisation must be in writing and must set out the grounds, locality and period of operation of the authorisation. If an inspector gives an authorisation, he/she must, as soon as practicable, inform an officer of or above the rank of superintendent.

If it appears to an officer of or above the rank of superintendent that:

- having regard to offences that have been, or are reasonably suspected to have been, committed
- in connection with any activity falling within the authorisation and
- it is expedient to do so

he/she may authorise the continuation of the authority to exercise the powers under s. 60(1) for a further period of 24 hours (s. 60(3) and Code A, para. 2.14).

This authorisation must be in writing, signed by the officer giving it, and must specify:

- the grounds on which it is given
- the locality in which it is to operate, and
- the period during which the powers are exercisable

and any direction for the authorisation to continue must also be given in writing at the time or reduced into writing as soon as it is practicable to do so (s. 60(9)). Such a direction for the authorisation to continue may only be given once; thereafter a new authorisation must be sought (Code A, Note 12).

It is for the authorising officer to determine the period of time over which the authorisation will take effect. Not only should the officer set the *minimum* time considered necessary, but he/she should also set the geographical parameters no wider than necessary and it is important that officers taking part in the stop and search exercise are properly briefed as to these limits (see generally Code A, Notes 12 and 13).

If the power is to be used in response to a threat or incident that straddles police force areas, the relevant authority will have to be given by an officer from each of the forces concerned (Code A, Note 13).

A significant difference between this power and the general powers of stop and search (which are not affected by the granting of this power (s. 60(12))), is that it does not require any grounds at all for the officer to suspect that the person/vehicle is carrying offensive weapons or dangerous instruments (s. 60(5)).

A further difference is that the power under s. 60 authorises officers in uniform to stop vehicles in order to search them and their occupants (but not in relation to the removal and seizure of face coverings; see below).

The power allows the stopping and searching of pedestrians, vehicles (including caravans, aircraft, vessels and hovercraft) and passengers. If a dangerous instrument or anything reasonably suspected to be an 'offensive weapon' (**see chapter 4.8**) is found during the search, the officer may seize it (s. 60(6)). There is also provision for the removal and seizure of face coverings (see below). For the disposal of items seized under s. 60 see Police (Retention and Disposal of Items Seized) Regulations 2002 (SI 2002/1372).

Note the general requirements governing searches imposed by Code A (**see para. 4.4.4.6**).

Failing to stop (or to stop a vehicle) when required to do so under this power is a summary offence punishable with one month's imprisonment and/or a fine (s. 60(8)(a)). A power of arrest may be available under the legislation dealing with obstruction of a police officer (Police Act 1996, s. 89; **see Crime, chapter 1.7**).

Where a vehicle is stopped under s. 60, the *driver* (as opposed to the person 'in charge'; **see paras 4.4.4.8 and 4.4.4.10**) is entitled to a written statement *that the vehicle was so stopped* (as opposed to the 'purpose' for which it was stopped; **see para. 4.4.4.10**). That statement must be provided if the driver applies for one no later than the end of the 12-month period from the day on which he/she was stopped (s. 60(10)). A person who is searched under this section is also entitled to a statement stating that he/she was so searched if he/she applies for one no later than the end of the 12-month period from the day on which he/she was stopped (s. 60(10A)). However, note the more stringent recording requirements imposed by Code A, para. 4.

For the police powers to disperse groups under the Anti-social Behaviour Act 2003 **see chapter 4.6**.

4.4.4.13 Stop and Search Powers under the Aviation Security Act 1982

Section 12 of the Police and Justice Act 2006 inserts a new s. 24B in part 3 of the Aviation Security Act 1982 (policing of aerodromes). This enables a police constable to stop and search, without warrant, any person, vehicle or aircraft in any area of an aerodrome (excluding a dwelling house), whether designated or non-designated, for stolen or prohibited articles, where he has reasonable grounds to suspect that he/she will find such articles. Designation takes place under part 3 of the Aviation Security Act 1982. If applied to an aerodrome, it allows police constables additional powers that are not available at non-designated aerodromes. The term 'aerodrome', as defined by s. 38(1) of the 1982 Act, is used rather than 'airport', as it has wider meaning and covers major airports as well as airfields used only by private flying clubs.

The new s. 24B(4) enables a constable to seize items discovered during a search which he/she reasonably suspects to be stolen or prohibited articles. Section 24B(5) defines a prohibited article as something made or adapted for use in the course of or in connection with criminal conduct, or an article intended for such use by the person having it with him/her or by some other person. 'Criminal conduct' under the 1982 Act is defined as conduct which constitutes an offence in the part of the United Kingdom in which the aerodrome is situated or conduct which would constitute an offence in that part of the United Kingdom if it occurred there.

4.4.4.14 Powers to Require Removal of Disguises

In a provision that is modelled on the powers in the previous paragraph, the Anti-terrorism, Crime and Security Act 2001 added a further section to the Criminal Justice and Public

Order Act 1994. This section replaced the former s. 60(4A). Section 60AA of the Criminal Justice and Public Order Act 1994 states:

(1) Where—
  (a) an authorisation under section 60 is for the time being in force in relation to any locality for any period, or
  (b) an authorisation under subsection (3) that the powers conferred by subsection (2) shall be exercisable at any place in a locality is in force for any period,

  those powers shall be exercisable at any place in that locality at any time in that period.

(2) This subsection confers power on any constable in uniform—
  (a) to require any person to remove any item which the constable reasonably believes that person is wearing wholly or mainly for the purpose of concealing his identity;
  (b) to seize any item which the constable reasonably believes any person intends to wear wholly or mainly for that purpose.

(3) If a police officer of or above the rank of inspector reasonably believes—
  (a) that activities may take place in any locality in his police area that are likely (if they take place) to involve the commission of offences, and
  (b) that it is expedient, in order to prevent or control the activities, to give an authorisation under this subsection,

  he may give an authorisation that the powers conferred by this section shall be exercisable at any place within that locality for a specified period not exceeding twenty-four hours.

KEYNOTE

These provisions are wider than those under s. 60 in that they are not restricted to anticipated outbreaks of serious violence. The above is not simply a preventative power and can be used where the 'activities' are already under way.

The above powers are governed by Code A of the PACE Codes of Practice (**see appendix 4.1**) and therefore the general requirements imposed by Code A must be borne in mind (**see paras 4.4.4–4.4.4.8**). More specifically, paras 2.15–2.18 of Code A impose additional requirements on the authorisation and use of these powers. The intention of these powers is to prevent those involved in intimidatory or violent protests using face coverings to conceal identity (Code A, Note 10). Any officer exercising the above powers must reasonably *believe* (not merely 'suspect'—**see para. 4.4.4.3**) that the person wearing the item is doing so *wholly or mainly for the purpose of concealing his or her identity* (Code A, para. 2.15). Therefore if the person is a cyclist wearing a face mask to prevent the inhalation of traffic fumes, or a motorcyclist wearing a crash helmet, the fact that its *effect* is to conceal their identity will not be enough—concealing their identity has to be the purpose/main purpose of the wearer.

Unlike s. 60, there is no specific power under this section to stop vehicles but, given that this is a power for police officers in uniform, the general power under s. 163 of the Road Traffic Act 1988 could be used.

The requirements in relation to the further authority of a superintendent (or above) and the manner and form in which any authority is to be given are broadly similar to those set out in s. 60 (see previous Keynote). The limitations and requirements as to the time and geographical extent of any authorisation are the same (see previous Keynote).

There is no power to *search* for face coverings etc. under this power. The Divisional Court has held that the predecessor to this power (the old s. 60(4A)) neither involved nor required a 'search' and that therefore the provisions of s. 2 of the Police and Criminal Evidence Act 1984 did not apply (*DPP* v *Avery* [2002] 1 Cr App R 31). The Court went on to hold that, although the power amounted to a significant interference with a person's liberty, it was justified by the type of situation envisaged by the legislators whereby the police may need to call upon the law.

Clearly if an item is found during a lawful search for other articles (say under s. 60(4)) which does not require any 'reasonable belief' by the officer, face coverings and masks could then be seized under subsection (b).

The very stringent requirements of Code A in relation to the conduct and recording of searches must be borne in mind (**see paras 4.4.4–4.4.4.8**). Further, the specific guidance as to the religious sensitivities that may arise when asking someone (for instance Sikh, Hindu and Muslim men and women) to remove head or face coverings must be considered where appropriate (Code A, Note 4).

The expression 'item' is very wide and would clearly include balaclavas, scarves and crash helmets. It is not specifically restricted to face coverings and would appear to extend to anything that could be worn wholly or mainly for the purpose of concealing identity (e.g. where offenders swap clothing after an offence). Although the purpose of the legislation is primarily to ensure that people are not allowed to commit offences anonymously in situations of public disorder, it is unclear whether other methods that hinder identification—such as face paint—would be caught by this power as it may be difficult to show that such materials amounted to 'an item' which is capable of being seized.

4.4.4.15 Failing to Comply with Requirement to Remove Items

OFFENCE: **Failing to comply with requirement to remove items—*Criminal Justice and Public Order Act 1994, s. 60AA(7)***

- Triable summarily • One month's imprisonment and/or a fine

Section 60AA of the Criminal Justice and Public Order Act 1994 states:

(7) A person who fails to remove an item worn by him when required to do so by a constable in the exercise of his power under this section shall be liable . . .

KEYNOTE

The wording of this offence is absolute. There is no requirement that the person failed *without reasonable excuse* or *without good reason* etc.; simply that he/she failed to remove an item worn by him/her. However, it must be shown that:

- the requirement was made (and presumably understood)
- it was made by a police officer in uniform
- in the exercise of powers authorised under s. 60

in the reasonable belief that the person was wearing the item wholly or mainly for the purpose of concealing his/her identity.

4.4.4.16 Retention and Disposal of Seized Items

The procedure to be followed in relation to the retention and disposal of items seized under s. 60 is set out in the Police (Retention and Disposal of Items Seized) Regulations 2002 (SI 2002/1372).

4.4.5 Stop and Search Powers to Combat Terrorism

In addition to the other general statutory powers discussed above, there are further specific powers given to the police to enable them to stop, search and control the movement of people and vehicles in connection with terrorist investigations. These provisions are now contained in the Terrorism Act 2000 and the Terrorism Act 2006 (as to which, **see chapter 4.6**).

4.4.5.1 Cordons

Section 33 of the Terrorism Act 2000 empowers the police to set up cordons if it is considered expedient to do so for the purposes of a terrorist investigation. Under s. 32, 'terrorist investigation' means generally an investigation of:

- the commission, preparation or instigation of acts of terrorism;
- an act which appears to have been done for the purposes of terrorism;
- the resources of a proscribed organisation (**see chapter 4.6**);
- the commission, preparation or instigation of an offence under the 2000 Act or under part 1 of the Terrorism Act 2006 other than an offence under s. 1 or 2 of that Act.

Section 34 of the Terrorism Act 2000 states:

> (1) Subject to subsections (1A), (1B) and (2), a designation under section 33 may only be made—
> (a) where the area is outside Northern Ireland and is wholly or partly within a police area, by an officer for the police area who is of at least the rank of superintendent, and
> (b) ...
> (1A) A designation under section 33 may be made in relation to an area (outside Northern Ireland) which is in a place specified in section 31(a) to (f) of the Railways and Transport Safety Act, by a member of the British Transport Police Force who is of at least the rank of superintendent.
> (1B) A designation under section 33 may be made by a member of the Ministry of Defence Police who is of at least the rank of superintendent in relation to an area outside or in Northern Ireland—
> (a) if it is a place to which subsection (2) of section 2 of the Ministry of Defence Police Act 1987 (c. 4) applies,
> (b) if a request has been made under paragraph (a), (b) or (d) of subsection (3A) of that section in relation to a terrorist investigation and it is a place where he has the powers and privileges of a constable by virtue of that subsection as a result of the request, or
> (c) if a request has been made under paragraph (c) of that subsection in relation to a terrorist investigation and it is a place described in subsection 1A of this section.
> (1C) But a designation under section 33 may not be made by—
> (a) a member of the British Transport Police Force, or
> (b) a member of the Ministry of Defence Police,
> in any other case.
> (2) A constable who is not of the rank required by subsection (1) may make a designation if he considers it necessary by reason of urgency.

KEYNOTE

This power is designated to be *investigative* in its nature; contrast the *preventive* powers provided under s. 44 (see below). *The powers to designate under this section were extended to the non-Home Office police forces shown by the Anti-terrorism, Crime and Security Act 2001.*

If the superintendent (or higher-ranking officer) makes the designation orally, he/she must confirm it in writing as soon as reasonably practicable. If the designation is made by another officer under the urgency provisions of s. 34(2) and (3), that officer must, as soon as is reasonably practicable:

- make a written record of the time at which the designation was made, and
- ensure that a police officer of at least the rank of superintendent is informed (s. 34(3)).

On being so informed, the superintendent must confirm or cancel the designation. If he/she cancels the designation, he/she must make a written record of the cancellation and the reason for it (s. 34(4)).

However, if the designation is made, the person making it must arrange for the demarcation of the cordoned area, so far as is reasonably practicable by means of tape marked with the word 'police', or in such other manner as any police officer considers appropriate (s. 33(4)).

The period of designation begins at the time the order is made (i.e. it cannot be made to begin at some time in the future) and ends on the date specified in the order.

The initial designation cannot extend beyond 14 days from the time the order is made (s. 35(2)). However, the period during which a designation has effect may be extended in writing from time to time by the person who made it, or an officer of at least superintendent rank (s. 35(3)). Any extension must specify the additional period during which the designation is to have effect. Section 35(5) places a limit of 28 days on extended designations; this appears to mean an *overall limit of 28 days* beginning with the day on which the order is made (as opposed to an initial maximum period of 14 days plus a further extension period of 28 days).

4.4.5.2 Police Powers

Specific police powers in relation to terrorist investigations are addressed in sch. 5 to the 2000 Act. Other, more general, police powers appear in the main body of the Act. One such power is under s. 36, which states:

(1) A constable in uniform may—
- (a) order a person in a cordoned area to leave it immediately,
- (b) order a person immediately to leave premises which are wholly or partly in or adjacent to a cordoned area,
- (c) order the driver or person in charge of a vehicle in a cordoned area to move it from the area immediately,
- (d) arrange for the removal of a vehicle from a cordoned area,
- (e) arrange for the movement of a vehicle within a cordoned area,
- (f) prohibit or restrict access to a cordoned area by pedestrians or vehicles.

KEYNOTE

The officer giving the order or making the arrangements and prohibitions set out here must be in uniform. Therefore detectives or other plain clothes officers involved in the terrorist investigation will not have these powers available to them.

The powers under s. 36 are among those that can be conferred on a Police Community Support Officer designated under sch. 4 to the Police Reform Act 2002 (see para. 4.2.3).

Failing to comply with an order, prohibition or restriction under this section is a summary offence punishable by three months' imprisonment and/or a fine (s. 36(2) and (4)).

This wording will presumably cover refusal. There is a defence if the person can show that he/she had a reasonable excuse for the failure.

The Police and Justice Bill contains provisions which will allow a superintendent or above to request passenger, crew or service information from the owner or agent of an aircraft or ship travelling within the United Kingdom. This extends provisions contained within the Immigration, Asylum and Nationality Act 2006 which, when in force, will enable the request for information on ships or aircraft travelling to or from outside the United Kingdom.

4.4.5.3 Stop and Search Authorisations

The Terrorism Act 2000 also gives the police specific powers to authorise stop and search operations under certain conditions.

The exercise of these powers is governed by Code A of the Police and Criminal Evidence Act 1984 Codes of Practice (as to which **see paras 4.4.4–4.4.4.8**). Code A (**see appendix 4.1**) contains specific provisions that relate to the use of these powers, as well as the general guidance that applies to all stops and searches.

Where it appears to any officer of or above the rank of Assistant Chief Constable/ Commander (in relation to provincial forces and the Metropolitan/City of London Police respectively) that it is expedient to do so, in order to prevent acts of terrorism, he/she may authorise the use of stop and search powers in a locality for a period not exceeding 28 days (ss. 44 and 46). The area or place mentioned in the authorisation may include the internal waters adjacent to that area or place or such area of those internal waters specified in the authorisation (s. 44(ZA)). An authorisation under s. 44 may be extended by an officer of the specified rank(s). These powers—which replaced those under the former s. 13 of the Prevention of Terrorism (Temporary Provisions) Act 1989—are subject to PACE Code A. Where an officer gives such an authorisation, he/she must take immediate steps to send a copy of the authorisation to the National Joint Unit, Metropolitan Police Special Branch who in turn will forward it to the Secretary of State. If the Secretary of State does not confirm the authorisation within 48 hours of its being given, the authorisation 'runs out' after the 48 hours are up. The unit will inform the force within 48 hours whether the Secretary of State has confirmed, cancelled or reduced the period of the authorisation (Code A, para. 2.23 and Note 14). The authorisation may be given orally but, if so, it must be confirmed in writing as soon as reasonably practicable (s. 44(5)). Similar powers are given to officers of the specified ranks to impose prohibitions or restrictions on parking in a specified area (s. 48). If the driver or person in charge of a vehicle:

- permits it to remain at rest in contravention of any such prohibition or restriction, or
- fails to move the vehicle when ordered to do so by a constable *in uniform*

he/she commits a summary offence (s. 51).

It should be noted that these provisions are *preventive* whereas those relating to the setting up of cordons (see above) are *investigative*. An authorisation under these provisions empowers police officers *in uniform* to stop vehicles and search them and any occupants (s. 44(1)); it also allows such officers to stop and search pedestrians and anything carried by them (s. 44(2)). The authorities under each of these subsections can be combined (Code A, para. 2.19). These searches must be for the purpose of searching for articles of a kind which could be used in connection with terrorism only. The 2000 Act specifically provides that police officers may use reasonable force when exercising these powers (s. 114); however, the general limitations on the use of police powers under the Human Rights Act 1998 must also be borne in mind. The Divisional Court has confirmed that this legislation confers a broad discretion on the senior officer involved and envisages that an authority given under this section could cover a whole police area under certain circumstances (e.g. the threat posed by terrorist activity to London). However, great care must be taken to ensure that the authority is not used arbitrarily or against a particular group in the community (*R (On the Application of Gillan)* v *Commissioner of Police for the Metropolis* (2003) *The Times*, 5 November).

The same applies to the provisions of Code A. If the authorisation is given orally in the first instance, it must be confirmed in writing by the officer who gave it as soon as reasonably practicable (Code A, para. 2.20). When giving any authorisation under these powers, the officer must specify the geographical limits of the authority as well as the time and date when it will expire (Code A, para. 2.21). It is also important to note that a constable may only exercise the powers under s. 44 for the purpose of searching for articles of a kind that could be used in connection with terrorism but can do so whether or not there are any grounds for suspecting the presence of such articles (Code A, para. 2.24; see also s. 45(1)(b)). This is very different from the general requirements for reasonable suspicion that apply to most other aspects of Code A (**see para. 4.4.4.3**). Furthermore, although Code A states that officers must take particular care not to discriminate against members of minority ethnic groups, it acknowledges that there may be circumstances where it is appropriate for officers to take account of a person's ethnic origin in selecting people to be stopped *in response to a specific terrorist threat* (Code A, para. 2.25). The powers must only be used in a way that reflects an objective assessment of a threat posed by various terrorist groups in Great Britain. The requirements for officers to reveal their identities in search records is relaxed slightly when s. 44 powers are used (see Code A, para. 4.4) and there is no provision to extend an authorisation after the original one has expired (Note 12).

In hearing an appeal in the *Gillan* case, the Court of Appeal has held that the 2000 Act and its stop and search powers were entirely compatible with the Human Rights Act 1998 but, while the courts would respect the view of the relevant authorities (such as the police) on matters of security, they did retain a role in relation to *proportionality* and ultimately this was a question for them. Although there was clearly a disadvantage to individuals affected by an authorisation given by a senior officer under s. 44, that was outweighed by the possibility of a terrorist attack being avoided or deterred by the use of the power. The Court of Appeal went on to stress the importance of the police being able to demonstrate that any such powers were being used carefully and in a considered way (*R (On the Application of Gillan)* v *Commissioner of Police for the Metropolis* [2005] 1 All ER 970).

The powers of a constable in uniform under s. 44 in relation to the stopping and searching of vehicles, passengers and pedestrians, along with the powers of seizure, are among those that can be conferred on a Police Community Support Officer (PCSO) designated under sch. 4 to the Police Reform Act 2002 (**see para. 4.2.3**). However, a PCSO cannot exercise any power of stop, search or seizure under this provision unless he/she is in the company *and* under the supervision of a constable (Police Reform Act 2002, sch. 4, para. 15(2)).

People and vehicles may be detained for the purpose of carrying out the search (s. 45(4)). The extent of the search and the entitlement of people to be given a statement to the effect that they were so searched are subject to similar conditions to those under the Criminal Justice and Public Order Act 1994 (**see para. 4.4.4.12**). Failing to stop when required or wilfully obstructing an officer in the exercise of these powers is a summary offence punishable with six months' imprisonment and/or a fine (s. 47).

For the additional powers to 'seize and sift' under s. 51 of the Criminal Justice and Police Act 2001 **see para. 4.4.17**.

4.4.6 Powers of Arrest

An arrest involves depriving a person of his/her liberty to go where he/she pleases (*Lewis* v *Chief Constable of South Wales Constabulary* [1991] 1 All ER 206). In a criminal context an arrest will usually be to answer an alleged charge, but occasionally an arrest may be preventive (such as where a person is arrested in connection with a breach of the peace), it may be to take samples or fingerprints, or it may be to return someone to prison or bring them before a court.

The Football (Disorder) Act 2000 introduced a further concept in police powers; that of a statutory power to detain a person in order to issue a s. 21B notice requiring him/her to attend a magistrates' court for the purpose of ascertaining whether he/she should become subject to a football banning order.

While the courts may issue warrants ordering the arrest of certain individuals on occasions, police officers are not under any general duty to arrest without warrant and should always consider the use of alternative methods of dealing with the incident or matter.

The source of a power of arrest may come from:

- the conditions at the time (allowing an arrest under the Police and Criminal Evidence Act 1984, s. 24; **see para. 4.4.7.1**);
- the provisions of the particular Act (e.g. Bail Act 1976, s. 7, absconding from bail; **see Evidence & Procedure, para. 2.4.11.2**);
- the provisions of an order (e.g. a court order or warrant; **see Evidence & Procedure, para. 2.3.7**);
- common law (e.g. breach of the peace; **see para. 4.6.2**).

An arrest begins at the time when the arresting officer informs the person of it or when his/her words or actions suggest that the person is under arrest (*Murray* v *Ministry of Defence* [1988] 1 WLR 692).

It was held in *R* v *Fiak* [2005] EWCA Crim 2381 that an arrest had not been rendered unlawful by the police officer's failure to use the word 'arrest' until after a brief investigation into the defendant's story was completed.

Every arrest must be lawful, that is, the person carrying it out must be able to point to some legal authority which allows it; otherwise an arrest will be unlawful and actionable as an assault or a civil wrong (see *Spicer* v *Holt* [1977] AC 987). This position has been significantly reinforced by the Human Rights Act 1998 and the ability to challenge the lawfulness of detention and arrest is itself a Convention right under Article 5(4), while Article 5(5) gives a person who is the 'victim' of an arrest or detention in contravention of the rest of the Article an enforceable right to compensation (**see para. 4.3.8**).

Any unlawful arrest will also carry implications for the officer if he/she is assaulted during the course of making it, for their organisation, and for public confidence. Therefore an understanding of the legal powers and concepts underpinning arrests are critical to professional policing.

Where a power of arrest exists, any lawful arrest must be made for a proper purpose. In the past the courts have allowed the police a wide latitude in what amounts to a proper purpose, including bringing the person to a police station (*Holgate-Mohammed* v *Duke* [1984] AC 437), to obtain a confession even after a complainant has withdrawn his/her initial complaint (*Plange* v *Chief Constable of Humberside* (1992) *The Times*, 23 March) and arresting someone on a 'holding' offence (*R* v *Chalkley* [1998] QB 848). The courts have even accepted an arrest based on force policy (*Mohammed Al Fayed* v *Commissioner of Police of the Metropolis* [2004] EWCA Civ 1579). However, all of these decisions will need to be reviewed in light of the changes to police powers of arrest under s. 24 of the Police and Criminal Evidence Act 1984 (**see para. 4.4.7.1**).

The practice of arresting someone on a 'holding' offence was accepted by the Court of Appeal in *R* v *Chalkley* [1998] 3 WLR 146, *provided the arresting officers had reasonable grounds for suspecting that the person had actually committed that offence*. If that suspicion is present then the fact that the officers making the arrest are doing so with the intention of investigating another, more serious offence does not render the arrest unlawful. If, however, there are no such grounds to suspect that the person had in fact committed the offence, or the officers know at the time of the arrest that there is no possibility of the person actually being charged with it, the arrest will be unlawful.

Section 30(7) of the Police and Criminal Evidence Act 1984 (in keeping with common law) requires that, if the grounds for detaining a person cease to exist before reaching a police station, the person must be released (see below).

4.4.6.1 Information to be Given and Recorded on Arrest

Whether an arrest is made under the Police and Criminal Evidence Act 1984 or not, s. 28 makes clear provision for the information that *must* be given to a person on arrest. Section 28 states:

(1) Subject to subsection (5) below, where a person is arrested, otherwise than by being informed that he is under arrest, the arrest is not lawful unless the person arrested is informed that he is under arrest as soon as is practicable after his arrest.
(2) Where a person is arrested by a constable, subsection (1) above applies regardless of whether the fact of the arrest is obvious.
(3) Subject to subsection (5) below, no arrest is lawful unless the person arrested is informed of the ground for the arrest at the time of, or as soon as is practicable after, the arrest.
(4) Where a person is arrested by a constable, subsection (3) above applies regardless of whether the ground for the arrest is obvious.
(5) Nothing in this section is to be taken to require a person to be informed—
  (a) that he is under arrest; or
  (b) of the ground for the arrest,
  if it was not reasonably practicable for him to be so informed by reason of his having escaped from arrest before the information could be given.

KEYNOTE

The right to be informed of the reason for arrest is enshrined in our domestic law under s. 28 of the Police and Criminal Evidence Act 1984. The wording of Article 5(2) of the European Convention on Human Rights strengthens that requirement by specifying that the information must be given in a language that the person understands (see para. 4.3.8.8).

The formula used by courts in determining whether this has been properly carried out is taken from *Fox, Campbell and Hartley* v *United Kingdom* (1991) 13 EHRR 157, which stated:

> Any person arrested must be told in simple, non-technical language, that he/she can understand, the essential legal and factual grounds for their arrest so as to be able, if they see fit, to apply to a Court to challenge its lawfulness.

Therefore the key reason for requiring this information to be given is to allow the arrested person to challenge the arrest and subsequent detention (see also *X* v *United Kingdom* (1982) 4 EHRR 188).

Code C of the Police and Criminal Evidence Act 1984 also imposes requirements in this area.

The practical reality is that for certain types of offence (particularly those involving violence or disorder), it will be impractical to give each person arrested detailed particulars of the case against them. Whether or not the information actually given to a person on arrest was adequate for the purposes of the above legislation will have to be assessed objectively, *having regard to the information that was reasonably available to the arresting officer* (see *Taylor* v *Chief Constable of Thames Valley* [2004] EWCA Civ 858). It might suffice in some cases—such as the violent disorder in *Taylor*—for the police officer to tell the person they were being arrested on suspicion of taking part in violent disorder at a certain time and place.

Section 28 clearly makes provision for situations when the person cannot be told or would not be capable of understanding the information. However, as the failure to comply with s. 28 makes any arrest unlawful (see e.g. *Dawes* v *DPP* [1994] Crim LR 604), it is perhaps better to 'err on the side of caution'.

In relation to the requirement at s. 28(2) and (3), particular care should be taken when giving a suspect details of exactly why he/she is being arrested. The Court of Appeal has held that it had been unfair—and unlawful—for an arresting officer to withhold facts which had led him to arrest the suspect on suspicion of having committed an offence (*Wilson* v *Chief Constable of Lancashire Constabulary* (2000) 1 POLR 367). In that case the Court held that an arresting officer's minimum obligation was to give a suspect 'sufficient information as to the nature of an arrest to allow the suspect sufficient opportunity to respond'.

The reasons given for the arrest must be the *real* reasons in the officer's mind at the time (see *Christie* v *Leachinsky* [1947] AC 573) and he/she must clearly indicate to the person the fact that he/she is being arrested. This requirement might be met by using a colloquialism, provided that the person is familiar with it and understands its meaning (e.g. 'you're locked up' or 'you're nicked'; see *Christie* v *Leachinsky* above). It does not matter that the words describe more than one offence (e.g. 'burglary' or 'deception'), provided that they adequately describe the offence for which the person has been arrested (*Abbassy* v *Metropolitan Police Commissioner* [1990] 1 WLR 385).

As for the records of arrest, Code G provides that:

4.1 The arresting officer is required to record in his/her pocket book or by other methods used for recording information:

- the nature and circumstances of the offence leading to the arrest
- the reason or reasons why the arrest was necessary
- the giving of the caution
- anything said by the person at the time of the arrest

...

4.4 The custody record will serve as a record of the arrest.

4.4.6.2 Caution

The Police and Criminal Evidence Act 1984 Code of Practice, Code C, para. 10.4 (**see Evidence & Procedure**) requires that a person must be cautioned on arrest or further arrest. There is no longer a requirement that the arrest be for an 'offence'. As with the requirements under s. 28 of the 1984 Act, there are exceptions to the requirement to administer the caution and these are:

- where it is impracticable to do so by reason of the person's condition or behaviour at the time; or
- where he/she has already been cautioned immediately before the arrest in accordance with Code C, para. 10.1 (requirement to caution where there are grounds to suspect commission of an offence).

The wording of the general caution is set out at Code C, para. 10.5. Note, however, that there is a different form of words relating to some interviews (Code C, Annex C) and that the giving of the appropriate caution will determine whether or not adverse inferences can be drawn by a court under the Criminal Justice and Public Order Act 1994. Paragraph 10.7 of Code C provides that minor deviations from the words of *any* caution will not amount to a breach of the Code provided that the sense of the relevant caution is preserved. It goes on to provide that if a person does not appear to understand the caution, the officer who has given it should go on to explain it in his/her own words (Note 10D). There will be occasions where someone involved with the custody and care of prisoners will overhear remarks by a defendant or will have comments made to them, which may be of relevance to the case in which the defendant is prosecuted. While such people may not be under a strict duty to administer the caution in the same way as police officers, the admissibility of the evidence will be tested against the general requirements of fairness and it might be appropriate to give a caution and/or to make a record of such comments as soon as possible (see *R* v *Ristic* [2004] EWCA Crim 2107—prison officer giving evidence of incriminating remarks overheard by a defendant). For further details of cautioning generally, **see Evidence & Procedure**.

Where police officers are themselves being interviewed or investigated, it used to be that a separate caution was needed prior to any discipline matters being put to the officer. As the police conduct framework (**see para. 4.1.12**) has diluted an officer's right to silence, the caution used in such cases will follow the general criminal one from Code C, with the inclusion of an element relating to a failure to make a written statement.

4.4.6.3 Force

Section 117 of the Police and Criminal Evidence Act 1984 allows the use of reasonable force when making an arrest. Section 3 of the Criminal Law Act 1967 also allows the use of such force as is reasonably necessary in the arrest of people and the prevention of crime.

Whether any force used is 'reasonable' will be determined by the court in the light of all the circumstances, including the circumstances as the arresting officer believed them to be at the time. Such force may even be lethal to the defendant. Where serious harm is caused by an arrest, the courts will consider the time that was available to the officer to reflect on his/her actions and whether or not he/she believed that the danger presented to others by failing to arrest the person outweighed the harm caused to the person by the arrest (see *Attorney-General for Northern Ireland's Reference (No. 1 of 1975)* [1977] AC 105). This situation has been reinforced by the European Convention on Human Rights (see above) and the test for justifying the use of force has become more stringent (**see Crime, chapter 1.7**).

For the general power of search on arrest, **see para. 4.4.13**.

Use of excessive force, while amounting to possible misconduct (**see chapter 4.1**) and assault (**see Crime, chapter 1.7**), does not render an otherwise lawful arrest unlawful (*Simpson* v *Chief Constable of South Yorkshire* (1991) *The Times*, 7 March).

4.4.7 Arrest without Warrant

For almost 40 years, the main powers of arrest without warrant used by police officers in everyday policing were linked to the concept of 'arrestable offences'. Confusingly these were not offences for which there was a power of arrest, but rather offences that either carried a substantial term of imprisonment or were designated as being 'arrestable' by various statutes. The Police and Criminal Evidence Act 1984 extended these provisions and also introduced the concept of 'general arrest conditions'. These were conditions that would allow an officer to arrest the suspect or offender, irrespective of the offence committed or suspected.

The Serious Organised Crime and Police Act 2005, s. 110, changed this situation by replacing s. 24 (arrest without warrant for 'arrestable offences') and s. 25 (general arrest conditions) of the Police and Criminal Evidence Act 1984 with new ss. 24 and 24A. Section 24 deals with a constable's power of arrest, and s. 24A deals with the power of arrest by others.

The intended purpose of s. 110 was to standardise a constable's power of arrest, in effect giving them a power of arrest for both summary and indictable offences subject to a 'necessity test'.

In addition to the revised PACE Codes of Practice, the Home Office Police Leadership and Powers Unit has published a guidance document on the implementation of the new powers. This document accepts each individual officer's right to decide as to when to arrest but does stress that: 'When considering whether arrest is necessary the officer ... must identify the need for his actions and be able to justify why the arrest is necessary rather than deal with the case by way of a summons or fixed penalty notice ... should also consider ... street bail ...'. The document goes on to identify the key 'arrest drivers' as being the needs of the victim and achieving a successful outcome.

The power of summary arrest can now only be exercised if a constable has reasonable grounds for believing it is necessary for any of the reasons set out in the new s. 24(5) of the Police and Criminal Evidence Act 1984.

Further guidance is given in the new Code of Practice, Code G (**see appendix 4.3**).

4.4.7.1 Constable's Power of Arrest

The primary power of arrest available to police officers is set out in s. 24 of the Police and Criminal Evidence Act 1984.

The first part of the power deals with the factors involving the *person* to be arrested and is in subss. (1) to (3).

Section 24 of the Police and Criminal Evidence Act 1984 states:

(1) A constable may arrest without a warrant—
   (a) anyone who is about to commit an offence;
   (b) anyone who is in the act of committing an offence;
   (c) anyone whom he has reasonable grounds for suspecting to be about to commit an offence;
   (d) anyone whom he has reasonable grounds for suspecting to be committing an offence.

(2) If a constable has reasonable grounds for suspecting that an offence has been committed, he may arrest without a warrant anyone whom he has reasonable grounds to suspect of being guilty of it.

(3) If an offence has been committed, a constable may arrest without a warrant—
   (a) anyone who is guilty of the offence;
   (b) anyone whom he has reasonable grounds for suspecting to be guilty of it.

KEYNOTE

In keeping with the earlier legislation, the above power applies in three circumstances.

The first set of circumstances is where, as a matter of fact, the person:

- is about to commit
- is in the act of committing or
- is guilty of

any offence.

Given that there is often some defence, denial or mitigating factor and the question of *guilt* is not determined until the matter has been before a court, this set of circumstances is not likely to occur very often. In day-to-day policing the other two sets of circumstances are therefore more likely to be relevant.

The second set of circumstances is where the officer has *reasonable grounds for suspecting* the person:

- is about to commit
- is committing or
- to be guilty of

any offence.

Finally there is the situation where it is not certain whether or not an offence has been committed but the officer has *reasonable grounds for suspecting* that an offence has been committed. In such cases he/she may arrest without a warrant anyone whom he/she has *reasonable grounds to suspect* is guilty of it.

4.4.7.2 Reasonable Grounds to Suspect

Central to the criteria set out in s. 24 is the concept of 'reasonable grounds for suspecting'. This expression has been developed by the courts over many years and, while the revised wording of s. 24 has yet to be developed by the courts, the interpretation of and approach to the pre-existing legislation are helpful in understanding the concepts involved.

Tests of 'reasonableness' impose an element of objectivity and the courts will consider whether, in the circumstances, a reasonable and sober person might have formed a similar view to that of the officer. Failing to follow up an obvious line of enquiry (e.g. as to the ownership of property found in the possession of the defendant) may well provide grounds for challenging the exercise of a power of arrest (see e.g. *Castorina* v *Chief Constable of Surrey* below).

The *Castorina* test

The key test for establishing the lawfulness of an arrest without warrant is set out by the Court of Appeal in *Castorina* v *Chief Constable of Surrey* (1996) 160 LG Rev 241.

The *Castorina* test effectively has three stages:

(1) Did the arresting officer suspect that the person who was arrested was guilty of the offence (or about to commit etc.)?
(2) If so, was there reasonable cause (i.e. reasonable grounds) for the arresting officer's suspicion?
(3) Was the arresting officer's exercise of his/her discretion reasonable in all the circumstances?

The first stage in the *Castorina* test above is a subjective one in that it depends entirely on what was in the officer's mind at the time.

The test of 'reasonable suspicion' is lower than that of requiring an officer to provide *prima facie* evidence of guilt. It is (per Lord Devlin in *Hussein* v *Chong Fook Kam* [1970] AC 942): 'A state of conjecture or surmise where proof is lacking. It is for the Police to show on a balance of probabilities in relation to each arrested person that the arresting officer had reasonable grounds to suspect the commission of the offence(s) in question'.

Another way of putting it is that a suspicion can be reasonable even if it is uncertain; this can provide reasonable grounds for a lawful arrest (see the Court of Appeal's decision in *Parker* v *Chief Constable of Hampshire* (1999) *The Times*, 25 June.

Note that suspicion can take into account matters that could not be put in front of a court as 'evidence' at all (e.g. intelligence from the National Intelligence Model—see *Mohammed Al Fayed* v *Commissioner of Police for the Metropolis* [2004] EWCA Civ 1579).

The second stage of the *Castorina* test is a purely objective one to be determined by the judge on facts found by the jury/court. This element means that it is not enough for the officer to claim reasonable suspicion in his/her own mind—a court will go on to look at whether there were reasonable grounds to suspect that an offence had been committed and that the person had committed it.

There is no need, however, for the officer to discount every possible defence or to seek complete proof of the relevant facts or circumstances before effecting an arrest (*Ward* v *Chief Constable of Avon and Somerset Constabulary* (1986) *The Times*, 26 June). However, the test that the courts will apply in assessing the lawfulness of an arrest where an offence is suspected is partly subjective. The arresting officer must have formed a genuine suspicion that the person being arrested was guilty of an offence, as well as having reasonable grounds for forming such a suspicion (*Jarrett* v *Chief Constable of the West Midlands Police* (2003) *The Times*, 28 February).

It is not uncommon for police officers to be called to a situation where, while there might be only one or two people responsible for an offence, it is unclear which of a group of people is the culprit. The Court of Appeal has confirmed that where an offence has been committed and one of only a small number of people could have committed it, there is no reason why each or all of the group cannot be arrested (*Cumming* v *Chief Constable of Northumbria Police* [2004] ACD 42). In the absence of any information that could or should enable the police to reduce the number further, the fact that a person is in a small group, one of whom must have committed the offence, can amount to reasonable grounds for suspecting him/her.

What about the opposite case where only one person had the opportunity to commit the offence? Is 'opportunity' alone enough to justify reasonable grounds for suspicion? The view of Auld J in the *Al Fayed* case was that 'there is nothing in principle which prevents opportunity from amounting to reasonable grounds for suspicion. Indeed in some circumstances opportunity may be sufficient to found a conviction'.

However, merely being told to arrest someone by a more senior officer is not a reasonable ground for doing so (see *O'Hara* v *Chief Constable of the Royal Ulster Constabulary* [1997] AC 286).

4.4.7.3 Necessity Criteria

Even where the above criteria are met, the power of arrest is not available to a police officer unless further conditions apply. This is where the legislation differs from previous powers of arrest.

Section 24 of the Police and Criminal Evidence Act 1984 goes on to state that:

> (4) But the power of summary arrest conferred by subsection (1), (2) or (3) is exercisable only if the constable has reasonable grounds for believing that for any of the reasons mentioned in subsection (5) it is necessary to arrest the person in question.

KEYNOTE

The need to show *reasonable grounds for believing* that the arrest was *necessary* is a significant development in the law governing police powers.

While necessity has been a feature of a number of powers since the Human Rights Act 1998, it has only been a partial requirement for the exercise of a power of arrest (under the former 'general arrest conditions'). Now the need to show 'necessity' will apply to all arrests made under the power granted by s. 24.

There is no specific and absolute requirement under the Human Rights Act 1998 for all arrests to be 'necessary', though reference is made to necessity in Article 5 (The Right to Liberty and Security) (**see para. 4.3.8**). Strangely, there are clearly some other statutory powers of arrest where there is no requirement for necessity and which might be used as alternatives to the general power for this reason. However, as they involve the use of a discretionary power by a public authority on behalf of the state, all arrests should be justified and proportionate.

Necessary means 'required to be done, achieved or present' (*Oxford English Dictionary*). That suggests that there is a need to consider all viable alternatives before resorting to the power of arrest under s. 24.

Therefore the arresting officer needs to be able to show why he/she believed that arrest (rather than some other form of disposal) was necessary and to point to the grounds on which that belief was reasonably based.

Code G gives further guidance in relation to the necessity criteria.

The officer must have reasonable grounds for *believing*—a higher test than mere suspicion—that the arrest is necessary for one of the statutory reasons. This is more stringent than the former legislation that required simply that the officer showed that it appeared to him/her that proceeding by way of summons was impracticable or inappropriate.

4.4.7.4 Reasons Making Arrest Necessary

Section 24 of the Police and Criminal Evidence Act 1984 sets out the possible reasons that may make an arrest necessary.

(5) The reasons are—
- (a) to enable the name of the person in question to be ascertained (in the case where the constable does not know, and cannot readily ascertain, the person's name, or has reasonable grounds for doubting whether a name given by the person as his name is his real name);
- (b) correspondingly as regards the person's address;
- (c) to prevent the person in question—
  - (i) causing physical injury to himself or any other person;
  - (ii) suffering physical injury;
  - (iii) causing loss of or damage to property;
  - (iv) committing an offence against public decency (subject to subsection (6)); or
  - (v) causing an unlawful obstruction of the highway;
- (d) to protect a child or other vulnerable person from the person in question;
- (e) to allow the prompt and effective investigation of the offence or of the conduct of the person in question;
- (f) to prevent any prosecution for the offence from being hindered by the disappearance of the person in question.

(6) Subsection (5)(c)(iv) applies only where members of the public going about their normal business cannot reasonably be expected to avoid the person in question.

KEYNOTE

Refusing or failing to give an accurate or true name and address is not necessarily an offence here.

The wording of subs. 5(a) and (b) means that the person can be arrested if this is *necessary* to enable his/her name or address to be ascertained (where the officer does not know, and cannot readily ascertain it), or where the officer has reasonable grounds for doubting whether a name or address given by the person is his/her real one.

The advances in identification technology (such as portable fingerprinting equipment) and the extension of powers to take photographs away from a police station may reduce the number of occasions where these criteria make an arrest necessary.

For the powers to take fingerprints in order to ascertain an arrested person's details **see Evidence & Procedure, para. 2.11.3.1.**

An address will be sufficient if the person will be at it for a sufficiently long period for it to be possible to serve him/her with a summons; or, if some other person at that address specified by the person will accept service of the summons on their behalf (Code G, para. 2.9(b)). This is in keeping with the decision in *DPP* v *McCarthy* [1999] RTR 323 where the address of a person's solicitor was held to be sufficient for complying with obligations in relation to reportable road traffic accidents.

The remainder of the list of reasons (c) to (d) (mirroring the former s. 25) are relatively self-evident.

The wording of (e) is very wide and allows for the investigation, not only of the suspected offence, but also of the conduct of the person arrested. These are not the same thing, with the latter being very broad and potentially covering conduct before and after any offence (e.g. to show motive, guilty knowledge etc.).

Code G, para. 2.9 states:

This may include cases such as:

(i) Where there are reasonable grounds to believe that the person:
- has made false statements;
- has made statements which cannot be readily verified;
- has presented false evidence;
- may steal or destroy evidence;
- may make contact with co-suspects or conspirators;

- may intimidate or threaten or make contact with witnesses;
- where it is necessary to obtain evidence by questioning; or

(ii) when considering arrest in connection with an indictable offence, there is a need to:
- enter and search any premises occupied or controlled by a person
- search the person
- prevent contact with others
- take fingerprints, footwear impressions, samples or photographs of the suspect

(iii) ensuring compliance with statutory drug testing requirements.

The reason at (f) is very specific and must relate to the prosecution of the offence involved being hindered by the person's likely *disappearance*.

Taken together, these two subsections provide investigators with significant powers to bring a person to a police station, particularly in light of s. 110(4) of the Serious Organised Crime and Police Act 2005 which states that the above powers are to have effect in relation to 'any offence whenever committed'. After arrest, however, the grounds on which their detention can be authorised are set out elsewhere in the Act (see Evidence & Procedure, para. 2.10.6).

In summary, the power to arrest is given to each police officer individually and the decision to exercise that power must be made and explained by the officer. As Code G reminds us:

2.4 It remains an operational decision at the discretion of the arresting officer as to:
- what action he or she may take at the point of contact with the individual;
- the necessity criterion or criteria (if any) which applies to the individual; and
- whether to arrest, report for summons, grant street bail, issue a fixed penalty notice or take any other action that is open to the officer.

2.8 In considering the individual circumstances, the constable must take into account the situation of the victim, the nature of the offence, the circumstances of the suspect and the needs of the investigative process.

4.4.7.5 Arrest by Others

The Police and Criminal Evidence Act 1984 also makes provision for the so-called citizen's arrest powers. Far narrower than the police powers, these powers of arrest are set out in s. 24A.

Section 24A of the Police and Criminal Evidence Act 1984 states:

(1) A person other than a constable may arrest without a warrant—
   (a) anyone who is in the act of committing an indictable offence;
   (b) anyone whom he has reasonable grounds for suspecting to be committing an indictable offence.

(2) Where an indictable offence has been committed, a person other than a constable may arrest without a warrant—
   (a) anyone who is guilty of the offence;
   (b) anyone whom he has reasonable grounds for suspecting to be guilty of it.

KEYNOTE

Unlike the powers of arrest available to police officers (which apply to any and every offence), the citizen's power of arrest only applies where the relevant offence is *indictable*. This power is available to police staff and others in the wider policing family such as Police Community Support Officers (see para. 4.2.3).

Under s. 24A(3), an indictable offence must have been committed; it is not enough to suspect or even believe that such an offence has been committed, even if there are very good grounds for that suspicion or belief. This can cause difficulties for the person carrying out the arrest if the 'offender' is subsequently acquitted at court (see *R* v *Self* [1992] 3 All ER 476).

In addition to the criteria regarding the person's guilt/suspected guilt of an indictable offence (or their being about to commit one), there are two further elements to this power (see s. 24A(3)). These are:

(a) the person making the arrest must have *reasonable grounds for believing* that, for any of the reasons mentioned in subs. (4), it is necessary to arrest the person in question (for the meaning of these expressions **see paras 4.4.7.2 and 4.4.7.3**), and
(b) it appears to the person making the arrest that it is not reasonably practicable for a constable to make the arrest instead.

The specified reasons are to prevent the person in question:

(a) causing physical injury to him/herself or any other person;
(b) suffering physical injury;
(c) causing loss of or damage to property; or
(d) making off before a constable can assume responsibility for him/her (s.24A(4)).

Racial and religious hatred offences provided by the Racial and Religious Hatred Act 2006 do not apply to this section (s. 24A(5)).

4.4.7.6 Preserved Powers of Arrest

Section 26 of the Police and Criminal Evidence Act 1984 repealed all other powers of arrest without warrant which existed before the 1984 Act except those listed in sch. 2. This list has been further reduced by the provisions of the Serious Organised Crime and Police Act 2005.

The common law power of arrest for breach of the peace has been preserved by s. 26 of the 1984 Act (*DPP* v *Orum* [1989] 1 WLR 88).

4.4.7.7 Absentees and Deserters

Section 186 of the Army Act 1955 and the Air Force Act 1955 provide a power of arrest without warrant where a constable has reasonable cause to suspect a person has deserted or is absent without leave. The Acts also make provision for the issuing of arrest warrants in respect of absentees/deserters, and give a power of arrest to forces personnel in respect of absentees/deserters where no constable is available.

Similar provisions for arresting Royal Navy personnel exist under s. 105 of the Naval Discipline Act 1957.

Where suspected absentees or deserters have been arrested, they must be taken directly to a magistrates' court and the appropriate service authority should be informed. Magistrates' courts may remand absentees or deserters until they can be collected by a service escort. If the escort is likely to be provided soon after the person's appearance at court, the magistrates may remand that person to a police station and must issue a certificate which must be given to the service escort. Most police services have local arrangements in respect of military personnel who surrender themselves to police stations as being absent without leave.

4.4.7.8 Fingerprinting

For the power of arrest under s. 27 of the Police and Criminal Evidence Act 1984 to take a person's fingerprints, **see Evidence & Procedure, chapter 2.11**.

4.4.7.9 Failure to Answer Police Bail

Section 46A of the Police and Criminal Evidence Act 1984 states:

(1) A constable may arrest without a warrant any person who, having been released on bail under this Part of this Act subject to a duty to attend at a police station, fails to attend at that police station at the time appointed for him to do so.

(1A) A person who has been released on bail under section 37, 37C(2)(b) or 37CA(2)(b) above may be arrested without warrant by a constable if the constable has reasonable grounds for suspecting that the person has broken any of the conditions of bail.

(2) A person who is arrested under this section shall be taken to the police station appointed as the place at which he is to surrender to custody as soon as practicable after the arrest.

(3) For the purposes of—
(a) section 30 above (subject to the obligation in subsection (2) above), and
(b) section 31 above,
an arrest under this section shall be treated as an arrest for an offence.

KEYNOTE

The offence will be treated as if the person had been arrested for the original offence for which bail was granted. For a detailed discussion on bail, **see Evidence & Procedure, chapter 2.4.**

4.4.7.10 Arrest to Take Samples

Section 63A of the Police and Criminal Evidence Act 1984 provides a power of arrest without warrant in respect of people:

- who have been charged with/reported for a recordable offence and who have not had a sample taken or the sample was unsuitable/insufficient for analysis;
- who have been convicted of a recordable offence and have not had a sample taken since conviction;
- who have been so convicted and have had a sample taken before or since conviction but the sample was unsuitable/insufficient for analysis.

This is simply a summary of s. 63A and reference should be made to the 1984 Act for the exact wording. For further detail, **see Evidence & Procedure, chapter 2.11.**

4.4.7.11 Cross-Border Arrest without Warrant

The Criminal Justice and Public Order Act 1994 (ss. 136 to 140) makes provision for officers from one part of the United Kingdom to go into another part of the United Kingdom to arrest someone there in connection with an offence committed within their jurisdiction and gives them powers to search on arrest.

Under the 1994 Act an officer from a police service in England and Wales may arrest a person in Scotland where it appears to the officer that it would have been lawful for him/her to have exercised their powers had the suspected person been in England and Wales or where it would be impracticable to serve a summons for the same reasons which would justify an arrest in England and Wales.

A Scottish officer may arrest someone suspected of committing an offence in Scotland who is found in England, Wales or Northern Ireland if it would have been lawful to arrest that person had he/she been found in Scotland. In such a case the officer must take the person to a designated police station in Scotland or to the nearest designated police station in England or Wales (see s. 137(7)).

The 1994 Act sets out where a person arrested outside the relevant country should be taken on arrest (see s. 137(7)). The Act also provides wide powers of search in connection with arrests (see s. 139).

4.4.7.12 Mentally Disordered People

There is a power to remove a person who is apparently suffering from a mental disorder from a public place to a place of safety (**see Crime, para. 1.9.6.7**). This power is aimed at protecting the person's best interests rather than bringing him/her before a court to answer a charge.

4.4.8 Arrest under Warrant

Arrest warrants may be issued by magistrates (generally under s. 1 of the Magistrates' Courts Act 1980 as amended) and the Crown Court (under the Supreme Court Act 1981, s. 80(2)) where the statute in question, together with the powers of the court allow. Warrants of arrest may also be issued to secure the attendance of witnesses (see s. 97 of the Magistrates' Courts Act 1980 and s. 4 of the Criminal Procedure (Attendance of Witnesses) Act 1965).

The police owe defendants a duty of care when drawing up and enforcing the contents of warrants. Therefore, where officers put the wrong date on an arrest warrant issued by a magistrates' court and, as a result, the defendant was not released by the Prison Service when he should have been, the police were liable in damages for the defendant's unlawful imprisonment (*Clarke* v *Chief Constable of Northamptonshire Police* (1999) *The Times*, 14 June). The creation of civilian enforcement officers (CEOs) and approved enforcement agencies (AEAs) has meant that there are a significant number of people who, though not employed by the police, are nevertheless empowered to execute arrest warrants in certain circumstances. Generally CEOs and AEAs will be able to execute warrants in connection with court matters such as failure to appear, breaching some bail conditions, or securing the attendance of the defendant at trial. CEOs and AEAs are also given further powers—including some powers to enter and search premises for the purposes of executing warrants—under the Domestic Violence, Crime and Victims Act 2004. The details of these specific provisions are beyond the scope of this Manual.

Warrants issued in relation to an offence may be backed for bail in which case the person is then granted bail in accordance with the conditions on the warrant. If not backed for bail, the warrant will specify where the person is to be brought (i.e. before the next sitting of the court).

For bail generally, **see Evidence & Procedure, chapter 2.4**.

Warrants issued in England, Wales, Scotland or Northern Ireland may be executed by officers from the country where they are issued or in the country where the person is arrested (see s. 136 of the Criminal Justice and Public Order Act 1994).

Warrants from the Republic of Ireland (provided they are not issued for political offences) may be executed in England and Wales if so endorsed (s. 125 of the Magistrates' Courts Act 1980), as indeed may warrants issued in the Isle of Man or the Channel Islands if so endorsed (s. 13 of the Indictable Offences Act 1848).

Warrants issued in connection with 'an offence' do not need to be in the possession of the officer executing them at the time. The majority of warrants issued for the arrest of a person in England and Wales arise from matters such as failure to appear at court, breaching bail conditions' or failing to pay fines. All of these were once a significant source of policing activity, but they are now enforceable by civilian enforcement officers and approved enforcement agencies.

The requirement under s. 28 of the Police and Criminal Evidence Act 1984 to tell a person why they are being arrested applies to arrests under warrant.

For the law relating to warrants generally, **see Evidence & Procedure, chapter 2.3.**

The long-awaited arrival of a European Arrest Warrant is covered by Council Framework Decision 2002/584. The detail of this new procedure is outside the scope of this Manual.

4.4.9 Voluntary Attendance at a Police Station

There are occasions where a person attends at a police station in a voluntary capacity. This could arise where the person is a suspect, by pre-arrangement with the officers in the case or where the person learns that the police want to speak to him/her; alternatively it can arise where the person attends the police station in a different capacity—e.g. as a witness—and they become suspected of involvement in an offence. There will be those occasions where a person has elected to accompany a Police Community Support Officer to a police station rather than awaiting the arrival of a constable (**see para. 4.2.3**).

So far as the common law principles regarding arrest set out earlier are concerned (**see para. 4.4.6**), there is no distinction between a person being arrested at a police station after attending voluntarily, and a person arrested elsewhere, provided the arresting officers acted appropriately and reasonably (see *Al Fayed* v *Metropolitan Police Commissioner* [2004] EWCA Civ 1579).

However, there are certain statutory provisions with regard to the entitlements and treatment of people who are 'voluntary attenders' and these are set out below.

Section 29 of the Police and Criminal Evidence Act 1984 states:

> Where for the purpose of assisting with an investigation a person attends voluntarily at a police station or at any other place where a constable is present or accompanies a constable to a police station or any such other place without having been arrested—
> (a) he shall be entitled to leave at will unless he is placed under arrest;
> (b) he shall be informed at once that he is under arrest if a decision is taken by a constable to prevent him from leaving at will.

KEYNOTE

The person's attendance at a police station or other place must be for the purpose of 'assisting with an investigation', which would, on a strict interpretation, encompass witnesses and victims. The main principle behind s. 29 (and see also Code C, para. 3.2.1) is to avoid the situation where people find themselves at a police station (or any other place where there is a police officer present) and feel compelled to remain there but without the attendant procedural protection that follows a formal arrest. Section 29(b) is unusual in that it (along with s. 31 below) imposes an obligation on a police officer to make an arrest, an activity that is usually entirely within his/her discretion. The time when the need to arrest the person arises is when the officer takes the decision to prevent the person from leaving (e.g. the time when the officer decides him/herself)—it is not the time when the person is actually prevented from leaving or even when they are told of the decision.

If such a person is cautioned (under PACE Code C, para. 10), they must also be told that they are free to leave the police station. Although not in police detention (see s. 118), voluntary attenders should be given the opportunity to seek legal advice if they wish and should be given the appropriate notice (see Code C).

Section 31 of the 1984 Act goes on to state:

> Where—
> (a) a person—
> (i) has been arrested for an offence; and
> (ii) is at a police station in consequence of that arrest; and
> (b) it appears to a constable that, if he were released from that arrest, he would be liable to arrest for some other offence,
>
> he shall be arrested for that other offence.

KEYNOTE

Like s. 29 above, this section also imposes an obligation to make an arrest under certain circumstances. In *R* v *Samuel* (1988) 87 Cr App R 232, the Court of Appeal said that the purpose of the s. 31 requirement was to prevent the release and immediate re-arrest of an offender—therefore, the Court noted, s. 31 did not prevent any further arrest from being delayed until the release of the prisoner for the initial arrest was imminent. This decision would now have to be considered in the light of the Human Rights Act 1998. However, the Divisional Court has held that, where officers who had arrested a man for a breach of the peace failed to arrest him formally for the further offence of assault on the police, their omission did not impact on the magistrates' decision that there was a case to answer in respect of the assault charge—*Blench* v *DPP* [2004] EWHC 2717.

The power (though not, on the strict wording, the *obligation*) to arrest a person at a police station for a further offence under s. 31 is among those that can be conferred on an Investigating Officer designated under sch. 4 to the Police Reform Act 2002 (**see para. 4.2.3**). Where this power is exercised by a designated Investigating Officer, the provisions of s. 36 of the Criminal Justice and Public Order Act 1994 (failing to account for objects etc.—**see Evidence & Procedure**) will apply.

Where a person is re-arrested under this provision, the power of search under s. 18 of the Police and Criminal Evidence Act 1984 apply (**see para. 4.4.13**).

4.4.10 After Arrest

Section 30 of the Police and Criminal Evidence Act 1984 provides for the procedure to be adopted after a person has been arrested. Section 30 states:

> (1) Subsection (1A) applies where a person is, at any place other than a police station—
> (a) arrested by a constable for an offence, or
> (b) taken into custody by a constable after being arrested for an offence by a person other than a constable.
> (1A) The person must be taken by a constable to a police station as soon as practicable after the arrest.
> (1B) Subsection (1A) has effect subject to section 30A (release on bail) and subsection (7) (release without bail).
> (2) Subject to subsections (3) and (5) below, the police station to which an arrested person is taken under subsection (1A) above shall be a designated police station.
> (3) A constable to whom this subsection applies may take an arrested person to any police station unless it appears to the constable that it may be necessary to keep the arrested person in police detention for more than six hours.
> (4) Subsection (3) above applies—
> (a) to a constable who is working in a locality covered by a police station which is not a designated police station; and

(b) to a constable belonging to a body of constables maintained by an authority other than a police authority.

(5) Any constable may take an arrested person to any police station if—

(a) either of the following conditions is satisfied—

(i) the constable has arrested him without the assistance of any other constable and no other constable is available to assist him;

(ii) the constable has taken him into custody from a person other than a constable without the assistance of any other constable and no other constable is available to assist him; and

(b) it appears to the constable that he will be unable to take the arrested person to a designated police station without the arrested person injuring himself, the constable or some other person.

(6) If the first police station to which an arrested person is taken after his arrest is not a designated police station, he shall be taken to a designated police station not more than six hours after his arrival at the first police station unless he is released previously.

(7) A person arrested by a constable at any place other than a police station must be released without bail if the condition in subsection (7A) is satisfied.

(7A) The condition is that, at any time before the person arrested reaches a police station, a constable is satisfied that there are no grounds for keeping him under arrest or releasing him on bail under section 30A.

KEYNOTE

When arrested at a place other than a police station, the person must be taken to a designated police station unless the conditions under s. 30(5) and (6) apply.

As discussed above (**see para. 4.4.6**), under s. 30(7) and (7A), the officer *must* de-arrest a person if he/she is satisfied, before reaching the police station, that there are no grounds for detaining that person. This may happen where the person has been arrested under one of the general arrest conditions and the particular condition has ceased to apply (e.g. the person gives a suitable name and address having originally failed to do so). An officer who releases a prisoner under s. 30(7) and (7A) must record the fact that he/she has done so and must make that record as soon as practicable after the release (s. 30(8) and (9)).

Section 30(10) allows the officer to delay taking the arrested person to a police station where his/her presence elsewhere is *necessary in order to carry out such investigations as it is reasonable to carry out immediately*. Where there is such a delay, the reasons for it must be recorded when the person first arrives at the police station (s. 30(11)).

Escort Officers designated under sch. 4 to the Police Reform Act 2002 may be authorised to take people who have been arrested by a constable in the relevant police area to a police station under the provisions of s. 30(1) above. The provisions for taking a prisoner to a non-designated police station (see s. 30(3) and 4(a)), and also the provisions allowing a delay in taking the prisoner to a police station (s. 30(10)) will also apply to any exercise of the powers by a designated Escort Officer (see the Police Reform Act 2002, sch. 4, part 4). Escort Officers are subject to a number of further provisions in relation to the transfer and detention of people in police detention (**see Evidence & Procedure, chapter 2.10**).

Other exceptions in the application of subsection 1 to terrorism and immigration are made by s. 30(12).

The delay permitted under s. 30(10) and (11) will only apply if the matter requires *immediate* investigation; if it can wait, the exception will not apply and the person must be taken straight to a police station (*R* v *Kerawalla* [1991] Crim LR 451).

Taking an arrested person to check out an alibi before going to a police station may be justified in some circumstances (see *Dallison* v *Caffery* [1965] 1 QB 348).

4.4.11 Entry, Search and Seizure

Police powers to enter premises, search them and seize evidence and property are governed mainly by the Police and Criminal Evidence Act 1984 and Code B (**see appendix 4.2**). The 1984 Act covers entry, search and seizure both with and without a warrant.

4.4.11.1 Officer in Charge

Whenever premises are to be searched under the provisions of Code B, one officer must be appointed to act as the officer in charge of the search (para. 2.10). The duties of this officer (who will normally, but not always, be the most senior officer present—see Note 2F) are set out throughout the Code. Searches carried out by employees designated under the Police Reform Act 2002 (**see chapter 4.2**) are also subject to the provision of Code B (para. 2.11).

4.4.11.2 Persons Searched during Search of Premises

Where a *person* is searched during a search of premises without being arrested, that search should take place in accordance with Code A (**see para. 4.4.4**).

4.4.11.3 Application to Claim Property

Any person claiming property seized by the police generally may make an application to the magistrates' court under the Police Property Act 1897 and should be advised of this procedure (Code B, Note 7A). There are special provisions where the property has been seized under the extended powers of the Criminal Justice and Police Act 2001 (**see para. 4.4.17**).

4.4.12 Powers of Search and Seizure under Warrant

There are many statutes which make provision for a court to issue a search warrant to police officers and other investigators, many of which are covered within this Manual under the relevant headings. Some non-police investigators enjoy specific powers based upon amended versions of the following provisions (see e.g. the Police and Criminal Evidence Act 1984 (Department of Trade and Industry Investigators) Order 2002 (SI 2002/2326)).

The application for and execution of warrants is governed by the 1984 Act, which was amended by the Serious Organised Crime and Police Act 2005, and the Codes of Practice. The amendments made by the 2005 Act related to the issue of warrants to search premises and seize evidence. It also introduced an extension to the specific premises warrant to cover more than one set of premises and provided new safeguards for applications for search warrants. The Codes of Practice do not affect any directions in a search warrant or order requiring seized items to be handed over to the police or other authority (Code B, para. 2.6).

4.4.12.1 Application for Warrant

Section 15 of the Police and Criminal Evidence Act 1984 states:

(1) This section and section 16 below have effect in relation to the issue to constables under any enactment, including an enactment contained in an Act passed after this Act, of warrants to enter and search premises; and an entry on or search of premises under a warrant is unlawful unless it complies with this section and section 16 below.

(2) Where a constable applies for any such warrant, it shall be his duty—

(a) to state—
(i) the ground on which he makes the application;
(ii) the enactment under which the warrant would be issued; and
(iii) if the application is for a warrant authorising entry and search on more than one occasion, the ground on which he applies for such a warrant, and whether he seeks a warrant authorising an unlimited number of entries, or (if not) the maximum number of entries desired;
(b) to specify the matters set out in subsection (2A) below; and
(c) to identify, so far as is practicable, the articles or persons to be sought.

(2A) The matters which must be specified pursuant to subsection (2)(b) above are—
(a) if the application relates to one or more sets of premises specified in the application each set of premises which it is desired to enter and search; and
(b) if the application relates to any premises occupied or controlled by a person specified in the application —
(i) as many sets of premises which it is desired to enter and search as it is reasonably practicable to specify;
(ii) the person who is in occupation or control of those premises and any others which it is desired to enter and search;
(iii) why it is necessary to search more premises than those specified under sub-paragraph (i); and
(iv) why it is not reasonably practicable to specify all the premises which it is desired to enter and search.

(3) An application for such a warrant shall be made ex parte and supported by an information in writing.

(4) The constable shall answer on oath any question that the justice of the peace or judge hearing the application asks him.

(5) A warrant shall authorise an entry on one occasion only unless it specifies that it authorises multiple entries.

(5A) If it specifies that it authorises multiple entries, it must also specify whether the number of entries authorised is unlimited, or limited to a specified maximum.

(6) A warrant—
(a) shall specify—
(i) the name of the person who applies for it;
(ii) the date on which it is issued;
(iii) the enactment under which it is issued;
(iv) each set of premises to be searched, or (in the case of an all premises warrant) the person who is in occupation or control of premises to be searched, together with any premises under his occupation or control which can be specified and which are to be searched; and
(b) shall identify, so far as is practicable, the articles or persons to be sought.

(7) Two copies shall be made of a warrant (see section 8(1A)(a) above) which specifies only one set of premises and does not authorise multiple entries; and as many copies as are reasonably required may be made of any other kind of warrant.

(8) The copies shall be clearly certified as copies.

KEYNOTE

Sections 15 and 16 (see below) apply to *all* warrants to enter and search premises, including those issued to and executed by an Investigating Officer designated under sch. 4 to the Police Reform Act 2002 (as to which **see para. 4.2.3**). 'Premises' include any place, and in particular, (a) any vehicle, vessel, aircraft or hovercraft; (b) any offshore installation; (c) any renewable energy installation; (d) any tent or moveable structure (s. 23).

Section 15 has been amended as a result of changes introduced by the Serious Organised Crime and Police Act 2005, and sets out the new safeguards for applications for search warrants. This new s. 15 sets out what must be included in an application for a 'specific premises warrant' or an 'all premises warrant'. In particular, the applicant must set out the grounds on which a multiple entry warrant has been sought.

If the provisions of these sections are not complied with, any entry and search made under a warrant will be unlawful. Although the officers executing the warrant may have some protection from personal liability where there has been a defect in the *procedure* by which the warrant was issued, failure to follow the requirements of ss. 15 and 16 may result in the exclusion of any evidence obtained under the warrant (**see Evidence & Procedure, chapter 2.8**). The details of the extent of the proposed search should be made clear in the application and the officer swearing the warrant out must be prepared to answer *any* questions put to him/her on oath under s. 15(4). Many courts will go into background detail about the particular premises, or part of the premises, and who is likely to be present on the premises at the time the warrant is executed (e.g. children). The action to be taken in relation to the swearing out of a warrant is set out in PACE Code B, para. 3.

Applications for all search warrants must be made with the written authority of an officer of at least the rank of inspector (Code B, para. 3.4). However, in cases of urgency where no such officer is 'readily available', the senior officer on duty may authorise the application.

If an application for a warrant is refused, no further application can be made unless it is supported by additional grounds.

Details of the information needed in applying for a warrant are set out at Code B, para. 3.6. This paragraph makes provision for the warrant to authorise other people to be present during the search (para. 3.6 (f)) but such a person has no authority to force entry, to search for or seize property (Note 3C).

4.4.12.2 Execution of Warrant

Section 16 of the Police and Criminal Evidence Act 1984 states:

(1) A warrant to enter and search premises may be executed by any constable.

(2) Such a warrant may authorise persons to accompany any constable who is executing it.

(2A) A person so authorised has the same powers as the constable whom he accompanies in respect of—
- (a) the execution of the warrant, and
- (b) the seizure of anything to which the warrant relates.

(2B) But he may exercise those powers only in the company, and under the supervision, of a constable.

(3) Entry and search under a warrant must be within three months from the date of its issue.

(3A) If the warrant is an all premises warrant, no premises which are not specified in it may be entered or searched unless a police officer of at least the rank of inspector has in writing authorised them to be entered.

(3B) No premises may be entered or searched for the second or any subsequent time under a warrant which authorises multiple entries unless a police officer of at least the rank of inspector has in writing authorised that entry to those premises.

(4) Entry and search under a warrant must be at a reasonable hour unless it appears to the constable executing it that the purpose of a search may be frustrated on an entry at a reasonable hour.

(5) Where the occupier of premises which are to be entered and searched is present at the time when a constable seeks to execute a warrant to enter and search them, the constable—
- (a) shall identify himself to the occupier and, if not in uniform, shall produce to him documentary evidence that he is a constable;
- (b) shall produce the warrant to him; and
- (c) shall supply him with a copy of it.

(6) Where
- (a) the occupier of such premises is not present at the time when a constable seeks to execute such a warrant; but

(b) some other person who appears to the constable to be in charge of the premises is present, subsection (5) above shall have effect as if any reference to the occupier were a reference to that other person.

(7) If there is no person present who appears to the constable to be in charge of the premises, he shall leave a copy of the warrant in a prominent place on the premises.

(8) A search under a warrant may only be a search to the extent required for the purpose for which the warrant was issued.

(9) A constable executing the warrant shall make an endorsement on it stating—

(a) whether the articles or persons sought were found; and

(b) whether any articles were seized, other than articles which were sought; and

unless the warrant is a warrant specifying one set of premises only, he shall do so separately in respect of each set of premises entered and searched, which he shall in each case state in the endorsement.

(10) A warrant shall be returned to the appropriate person mentioned in subsection (10A) below—

(a) when it has been executed; or

(b) in the case of a specific premises warrant which has not been executed, or an all premises warrant, or any warrant authorising multiple entries, upon the expiry of the period of three months referred to in subsection (3) above or sooner.

(10A) The appropriate person is—

(a) if the warrant was issued by a justice of the peace, the designated officer for the local justice area in which the justice was acting when he issued the warrant;

(b) if it was issued by a judge, the appropriate officer of the court from which he issued it.

KEYNOTE

Although s. 16 allows for other people to be included in the warrant, authorising them to accompany the officer, some warrants *require* the presence of other people when a warrant is executed (e.g. under s. 135 of the Mental Health Act 1983; see Crime, chapter 1.9).

Section 16 was amended as a result of the changes made by the Serious Organised Crime and Police Act 2005. Note that under s. 16(3B), where a warrant authorises multiple entries, any subsequent entries must be authorised in writing by an officer of the rank of inspector or above.

Failure to comply with the requirements under s. 16 will make the entry and subsequent seizure of property unlawful. Therefore, where officers failed to provide the occupier of the searched premises with a copy of the warrant (under s. 16(5)(c)), they were obliged to return the property seized during the search (*R* v *Chief Constable of Lancashire, ex parte Parker* [1993] Crim LR 204).

Very minor departures from the letter of the warrant, however, will not render any search unlawful (see *Attorney-General of Jamaica* v *Williams* [1998] AC 351).

If the execution of the warrant is likely to have an adverse effect on community relations, the community liaison officer must be informed unless the case is urgent, in which case that officer must be advised as soon as practicable after the search—see Code B, paras 3–5.

Code B goes on to make further provisions for the execution of the warrant.

If a warrant itself is invalid for some reason, any entry and subsequent seizure made under it are unlawful (*R* v *Central Criminal Court and British Railways Board, ex parte AJD Holdings Ltd* [1992] Crim LR 669). After a warrant has been executed, or if it has not been used within three months (or sooner) from its date of issue, it must be returned to the designated officer for the local justice area in which the justice of the peace issued the warrant, or where it was issued by a judge to the appropriate officer of the court from it was issued (subss. (10) and (10A)).

4.4.12.3 Search Warrants for Indictable Offences

Section 8 of the Police and Criminal Evidence Act 1984 states:

(1) If on an application made by a constable a justice of the peace is satisfied that there are reasonable grounds for believing—
  (a) that an indictable offence has been committed; and
  (b) that there is material on premises mentioned in subsection (1A) below which is likely to be of substantial value (whether by itself or together with other material) to the investigation of the offence; and
  (c) that the material is likely to be relevant evidence; and
  (d) that it does not consist of or include items subject to legal privilege, excluded material or special procedure material; and
  (e) that any of the conditions specified in subsection (3) below applies in relation to each set of premises specified in the application.

he may issue a warrant authorising a constable to enter and search the premises.

(1A) The premises referred to in subsection (1)(b) above are—
  (a) one or more sets of premises specified in the application (in which case the application is for a "specific premises warrant"); or
  (b) any premises occupied or controlled by a person specified in the application, including such sets of premises as are so specified (in which case the application is for an 'all premises warrant').

(1B) If the application is for an all premises warrant, the justice of the peace must also be satisfied—
  (a) that because of the particulars of the offence referred to in paragraph (a) of subsection (1) above, there are reasonable grounds for believing that it is necessary to search premises occupied or controlled by the person in question which are not specified in the application in order to find the material referred to in paragraph (b) of that subsection; and
  (b) that it is not reasonably practicable to specify in the application all the premises which he occupies or controls and which might need to be searched.

(1C) The warrant may authorise entry to and search of premises on more than one occasion if, on the application, the justice of the peace is satisfied that it is necessary to authorise multiple entries in order to achieve the purpose for which he issues the warrant.

(1D) If it authorises multiple entries, the number of entries authorised may be unlimited, or limited to a maximum.

(2) A constable may seize and retain anything for which a search has been authorised under subsection (1) above.

(3) The conditions mentioned in subsection (1)(e) above are—
  (a) that it is not practicable to communicate with any person entitled to grant entry to the premises;
  (b) that it is practicable to communicate with a person entitled to grant entry to the premises but it is not practicable to communicate with any person entitled to grant access to the evidence;
  (c) that entry to the premises will not be granted unless a warrant is produced;
  (d) that the purpose of a search may be frustrated or seriously prejudiced unless a constable arriving at the premises can secure immediate entry to them.

(4) In this Act 'relevant evidence', in relation to an offence, means anything that would be admissible in evidence at a trial for the offence.

(5) The power to issue a warrant conferred by this section is in addition to any such power otherwise conferred.

KEYNOTE

Section 8 has also been amended by the Serious Organised Crime and Police Act 2005. This section now provides that a constable can apply for two different types of search warrant: a 'specific premises warrant' for the search of one set of premises; and an 'all premises warrant' when it is necessary to search all premises occupied or controlled by an individual, but where it is not reasonably practicable to specify all such premises at the time of applying for the warrant. The warrant allows access to all premises occupied or controlled by that person, both those which are specified on the application, and those which are not. Note that new subss. (1C) and (1D) provide that a warrant (either an 'all premises warrant' or a 'specific premises warrant') may authorise access on more than one occasion, and if multiple entries are authorised these may be unlimited or limited to a maximum.

The officer applying for a warrant under s. 8 must have reasonable grounds for believing that material which is *likely to be of substantial value to the investigation of the offence* is on the premises specified. Therefore, when executing such a warrant, the officer must be able to show that any material seized thereunder fell within that description (*R* v *Chief Constable of the Warwickshire Constabulary, ex parte Fitzpatrick* [1998] 1 All ER 65). Possession of a warrant under s. 8 does not authorise police officers to seize all material found on the relevant premises to be taken away and 'sifted' somewhere else (*R* v *Chesterfield Justices, ex parte Bramley* [2000] 2 WLR 409) (this matter is now addressed by s. 50 of the Criminal Justice and Police Act 2001, **see para. 4.4.17**). This means that material which is solely of value for *intelligence* purposes may not be seized under a s. 8 warrant. The limits imposed by this decision on the extent of authority granted by a s. 8 warrant is the reason behind the extended powers of sift and seizure introduced by the Criminal Justice and Police Act 2001 (**see para. 4.4.17**).

The power to apply for and execute a warrant under s. 8 and to carry out the actions under s. 8(2) are among those powers that can be conferred on a person designated as an Investigating Officer under sch. 4 to the Police Reform Act 2002 (**see para. 4.2.3**).

The conditions set out under s. 8(1)(e) are part of the *application* process, not part of the general execution process (which is set out at s. 16 above). Therefore the officer swearing out a s. 8 warrant will have to satisfy the court that any of those conditions apply.

Where the search includes information contained in a computer, the provisions of s. 20 apply (**see para. 4.4.15.2**).

4.4.13 Entry, Search and Seizure Powers without Warrant

Apart from a general power of entry to prevent a breach of the peace (**see chapter 4.6**), all common law police powers of entry were abolished by the Police and Criminal Evidence Act 1984. The Act introduced wide powers of entry, search and seizure particularly when made in connection with an arrest. Note the importance of the general principles and specific content of Code B in relation to these searches (**see appendix 4.2**).

4.4.13.1 Power to Search after Arrest for Indictable Offence

Section 18 of the Police and Criminal Evidence Act 1984 states:

(1) Subject to the following provisions of this section, a constable may enter and search any premises occupied or controlled by a person who is under arrest for an indictable offence, if he has reasonable grounds for suspecting that there is on the premises evidence, other than items subject to legal privilege, that relates—
 (a) to that offence; or
 (b) to some other indictable offence which is connected with or similar to that offence.

(2) A constable may seize and retain anything for which he may search under subsection (1) above.

(3) The power to search conferred by subsection (1) above is only a power to search to the extent that is reasonably required for the purpose of discovering such evidence.

(4) Subject to subsection (5) below, the powers conferred by this section may not be exercised unless an officer of the rank of inspector or above has authorised them in writing.

(5) A constable may conduct a search under subsection (1)—
(a) before the person is taken to a police station or released on bail under section 30A; and
(b) without obtaining an authorisation under subsection (4),
if the condition in subsection (5A) is satisfied.

(5A) The condition is that the presence of the person at a place (other than a police station) is necessary for the effective investigation of the offence.

(6) If a constable conducts a search by virtue of subsection (5) above, he shall inform an officer of the rank of inspector or above that he has made the search as soon as practicable after he has made it.

(7) An officer who—
(a) authorises a search; or
(b) is informed of a search under subsection (6) above, shall make a record in writing—
(i) of the grounds for the search; and
(ii) of the nature of the evidence that was sought.

(8) If the person who was in occupation or control of the premises at the time of the search is in police detention at the time the record is to be made, the officer shall make the record as part of his custody record.

KEYNOTE

This power has been amended to apply where the evidence relates to an indictable offence for which the person was arrested or some other indictable offence, as opposed to an 'arrestable' offence, a term repealed by the Serious Organised Crime and Police Act 2005.

For items that relate to legal privilege, see para. 4.4.16.

The premises must be occupied or controlled by the arrested person. This expression is not defined but it is a *factual* requirement, i.e. it is not enough that the officer suspects or believes that the premises are occupied or controlled by that person.

The search is limited to evidence relating to the indictable offence for which the person has been arrested or another indictable offence which is similar or connected; it does not authorise a general search for anything that might be of use for other purposes (e.g. for intelligence reports). The extent of the search is limited by s. 18(3). If you are looking for a stolen fridge-freezer, you would not be empowered to search through drawers or small cupboards. You would be able to, however, if you were looking for packaging, receipts or other documents relating to the fridge-freezer.

The search authority must be given in writing and only by an officer of or above the rank of inspector (Code B, para. 4.3). The authorising officer must be satisfied that the necessary grounds exist. If possible he/she should record the authority on the Notice of Powers and Rights given to the occupier, while a record of the grounds for the search and the nature of evidence sought should be made in the custody record (if there is one); otherwise in the officer's pocket book or the search record. That authority is for a search which is lawful *in all other respects*, that is, the other conditions imposed by s. 18 must be met. An inspector cannot make an otherwise unlawful entry and search lawful simply by authorising it (*Krohn* v *DPP* [1997] COD 345).

In addition to the general conditions of Code B above, where officers carry out a search under s. 18 they must, so far as is possible under the circumstances, explain to the occupier(s) the reason for it. If officers attempt to carry out an authorised search under s. 18 without attempting to explain to an occupier the reason, it may mean that the officers are not acting in the execution of their duty and their entry may be lawfully resisted (*Lineham* v *DPP* (1999) *The Independent*, 22 November).

The provision under s. 18(5) relates to cases where the presence of the person *is in fact necessary* for the effective investigation of the offence. This is a more stringent requirement than merely reasonable suspicion or grounds to believe on the part of the officer concerned. If such a search is made, the searching officer must inform an inspector (or above) as soon as practicable after the search.

If the person is in police detention after the arrest, the facts concerning the search must be recorded in the custody record. Where a person is re-arrested under s. 31 **(see para. 4.4.9)** for an indictable offence, the powers to search under s. 18 begin again, that is, a new power to search is created in respect of each indictable offence. Where the search includes information contained in a computer, the provisions of s. 20 apply **(see para. 4.4.15.2)**.

4.4.13.2 Powers to Search after Arrest for Other Offences

Where a person is arrested for any other offence, s. 32 of the Police and Criminal Evidence Act 1984 provides a number of general powers of entry, search and seizure.

Section 32 states:

(1) A constable may search an arrested person, in any case where the person to be searched has been arrested at a place other than a police station, if the constable has reasonable grounds for believing that the arrested person may present a danger to himself or others.

(2) Subject to subsections (3) to (5) below, a constable shall also have power in any such case-
- (a) to search the arrested person for anything—
  - (i) which he might use to assist him to escape from lawful custody; or
  - (ii) which might be evidence relating to an offence; and
- (b) ...

(3) The power to search conferred by subsection (2) above is only a power to search to the extent that is reasonably required for the purpose of discovering any such thing or any such evidence.

(4) The powers conferred by this section to search a person are not to be construed as authorising a constable to require a person to remove any of his clothing in public other than an outer coat, jacket or gloves but they do authorise a search of a person's mouth.

(5) A constable may not search a person in the exercise of the power conferred by subsection (2)(a) above unless he has reasonable grounds for believing that the person to be searched may have concealed on him anything for which a search is permitted under that paragraph.

KEYNOTE

The power to search the arrested person under s. 32(1) is a general one relating to safety. For the power to search at a police station, **see Evidence & Procedure, chapter 2.10.**

Section 32(2)(a) then goes on to provide a power to search the person in relation to anything that the arrested person might use to escape from lawful custody and anything that 'might be' evidence relating to *an offence*. There are restrictions placed on the extent and circumstances of the search (s. 32(3) and (4)) and the officer must have reasonable grounds to *believe* (as opposed to mere suspicion) that the person may have such things concealed on him/her (s. 32(5)). Nevertheless, this is still a very wide power. Some years ago the House of Lords confirmed that the police have a common law power to search for and seize property after a lawful arrest (*R* v *Governor of Pentonville Prison, ex parte Osman* [1990] 1 WLR 277). This decision was confirmed recently by the House of Lords in *R (On the Application of Rottman)* v *Commissioner of Police of the Metropolis* [2002] 2 AC 692. In *Rottman* their Lordships held that it was a well-established principle of the common law that an arresting officer had the power to search a room in which a person had been arrested (*per Ghani* v *Jones* [1970] 1 QB 693). This extended power is not limited to purely 'domestic' offences, but also applies to cases involving extradition offences.

Section 32 goes on to state:

(9) A constable searching a person in the exercise of the power conferred by subsection (2)(a) above may seize and retain anything he finds, other than an item subject to legal privilege, if he has reasonable grounds for believing—
- (a) that he might use it to assist him to escape from lawful custody; or

(b) that it is evidence of an offence or has been obtained in consequence of the commission of an offence.

4.4.13.3 Search of Premises after Arrest

Section 32 also provides that a constable shall have the power in such a case to enter and search any premises in which the person was when arrested or immediately before being arrested for an indictable offence (s. 32(2)(b)). The search may be conducted for the purpose of finding evidence relating to the offence for which the person was arrested.

Section 32 also states:

(6) A constable may not search premises in the exercise of the power conferred by subsection (2)(b) above unless he has reasonable grounds for believing that there is evidence for which a search is permitted under that paragraph on the premises.

(7) In so far as the power of search conferred by subsection (2)(b) above relates to premises consisting of two or more separate dwellings, it is limited to a power to search—

(a) any dwelling in which the arrest took place or in which the person arrested was immediately before his arrest; and

(b) any parts of the premises which the occupier of any such dwelling uses in common with the occupiers of any other dwellings comprised in the premises.

(8) A constable searching a person in the exercise of the power conferred by subsection (1) above may seize and retain anything he finds, if he has reasonable grounds for believing that the person searched might use it to cause physical injury to himself or to any other person.

...

(10) Nothing in this section shall be taken to affect the power conferred by section 43 of the Terrorism Act 2000.

KEYNOTE

Both 'reasonable grounds' and 'immediately' are questions of fact for a court to determine. It has been held that the power under s. 32(2)(b) is one for use at the time of arrest and should not be used to return to the relevant premises some time after the arrest in the way that s. 18 (see above) may be used (*R* v *Badham* [1987] Crim LR 202).

Officers exercising their power to enter and search under s. 32 must have a genuine belief (i.e. more than mere suspicion) that there is evidence on the premises; it is not a licence for a general fishing expedition (*R* v *Beckford* [1991] Crim LR 918).

The Divisional Court has refused to allow s. 32 to be used in a situation where the arrested person had not been in the relevant premises (where he did not live) for a period of over two hours preceding his arrest and where there were no reasonable grounds for believing that he presented a danger to himself or others (*Hewitson* v *Chief Constable of Dorset Police* [2003] EWHC 3296).

Code B sets out the procedure to be followed after searches have been carried out (paras 8 and 9).

4.4.13.4 Other Powers of Entry without Warrant

Just as there are many statutes which provide the police (and others) with powers to apply for warrants, there are as many statutes which provide a power of entry without warrant (an example would be s. 6 of the Scrap Metal Dealers Act 1964 which allows a constable entry at all reasonable times, onto a scrap metal dealer's premises to inspect the register and any scrap metal). Other examples are the power to enter:

- any land other than a dwelling house in order to search for crossbows (under s. 4 of the Crossbows Act 1987) **(see chapter 4.8)**;

- *any place* for the purpose of carrying out a search under s. 47 of the Firearms Act 1968 (**see chapter 4.7**);
- school premises in connection with weapons under s. 139B of the Criminal Justice Act 1988 (**see chapter 4.8**); and
- relevant premises in connection with a direction to leave and remove vehicles etc. under s. 62 of the Criminal Justice and Public Order Act 1994 (**see chapter 4.10**).

The Police and Justice Act 2006 amended the Aviation Security Act 1982 and this will give a constable the power to stop and search any person, vehicle or aircraft in any area of an aerodrome for stolen or prohibited articles.

The only common law power of entry without warrant is for dealing with a breach of the peace (**see chapter 4.6**). This power is preserved by s. 17(6) and only applies where officers have a genuine and reasonable belief that a breach of the peace is happening or is about to happen in the immediate future (*McLeod* v *Commissioner of Police for the Metropolis* [1994] 4 All ER 553).

Where police officers enter premises *lawfully* (including where they are there by invitation), they are on the premises for *all lawful purposes* (see *Foster* v *Attard* [1986] Crim LR 627). This means that they can carry out any lawful functions while on the premises, even if that was not the original purpose for entry. For instance, if officers entered under a lawful power provided by the Misuse of Drugs Act 1971 (**see Crime, chapter 1.6**), they may carry out other lawful functions such as enforcing the provisions of the Gaming Act 1968.

If officers are invited onto premises by someone entitled to do so, they are lawfully there unless and until that invitation is withdrawn. Once the invitation is withdrawn, the officers will become trespassers unless they have a power to be there, and the person may remove them by force (*Robson* v *Hallett* [1967] 2 QB 939). If that invitation is terminated, the person needs to communicate that clearly to the officer; it has been held that merely telling officers to 'fuck off' is not necessarily sufficient (*Snook* v *Mannion* [1982] RTR 321 (**see Road Policing, chapter 3.5**).

Once officers are lawfully on premises they may exercise the powers of seizure under s. 19 of the Police and Criminal Evidence Act 1984 (**see para. 4.4.15.1**).

4.4.13.5 Power of Entry: Police and Criminal Evidence Act 1984

Section 17 of the Police and Criminal Evidence Act 1984 states:

(1) Subject to the following provisions of this section, and without prejudice to any other enactment, a constable may enter and search any premises for the purpose—
 (a) of executing—
  (i) a warrant of arrest issued in connection with or arising out of criminal proceedings; or
  (ii) a warrant of commitment issued under section 76 of the Magistrates' Courts Act 1980;
 (b) of arresting a person for an indictable offence;
 (c) of arresting a person for an offence under—
  (i) section 1 (prohibition of uniforms in connection with political objectives) of the Public Order Act 1936;
  (ii) any enactment contained in sections 6 to 8 or 10 of the Criminal Law Act 1977 (offences relating to entering and remaining on property);
  (iii) section 4 of the Public Order Act 1986 (fear or provocation of violence);
  (iiia) section 4 (driving etc when under influence of drink or drugs) or 163 (failure to stop when required to do so by constable in uniform) of the Road Traffic Act 1988;
  (iiib) section 27 of the Transport and Works Act 1992 (which relates to offences involving drink or drugs);
  (iv) section 76 of the Criminal Justice and Public Order Act 1994 (failure to comply with interim possession order);

(v) any of sections 4, 5, 6(1) and (2), 7 and 8(1) and (2) of the Animal Welfare Act 2006 (offences relating to the prevention of harm to animals);

(ca) of arresting, in pursuance of section 32(1A) of the Children and Young Persons Act 1969, any child or young person who has been remanded or committed to local authority accommodation under section 23(1) of that Act;

(caa) Of arresting a person for an offence to which section 61 of the Animal Health Act 1981 applies;

(cb) of recapturing any person who is, or is deemed for any purpose to be, unlawfully at large while liable to be detained

(i) in a prison, remand centre, young offender institution or secure training centre, or

(ii) in pursuance of section 92 of the Powers of Criminal Courts (Sentencing) Act 2000 (dealing with children and young persons guilty of grave crimes), in any other place;

(d) of recapturing any person whatever who is unlawfully at large and whom he is pursuing; or

(e) of saving life or limb or preventing serious damage to property.

(2) Except for the purpose specified in paragraph (e) of subsection (1) above, the powers of entry and search conferred by this section—

(a) are only exercisable if the constable has reasonable grounds for believing that the person whom he is seeking is on the premises; and

(b) are limited, in relation to premises consisting of two or more separate dwellings, to powers to enter and search—

(i) any parts of the premises which the occupiers of any dwelling comprised in the premises use in common with the occupiers of any other such dwelling; and

(ii) any such dwelling in which the constable has reasonable grounds for believing that the person whom he is seeking may be.

(3) The powers of entry and search conferred by this section are only exercisable for the purposes specified in subsection (1)(c)(ii) or (iv) above by a constable in uniform.

(4) The power of search conferred by this section is only a power to search to the extent that is reasonably required for the purpose for which the power of entry is exercised.

(5) Subject to subsection (6) below, all the rules of common law under which a constable has power to enter premises without a warrant are hereby abolished.

(6) Nothing in subsection (5) above affects any power of entry to deal with or prevent a breach of the peace.

KEYNOTE

This section has been amended to apply where the proposed arrest relates to an indictable offence as opposed to an 'arrestable' offence, a term repealed by the Serious Organised Crime and Police Act 2005. The powers have also been extended to include: driving under the influence of drink or drugs (s. 17(1)(c)(iiia)), workers on transport systems being over the prescribed limit (s. 17(1)(c)(iiib)), and provisions relating to the control of rabies (s. 17(1)(caa)).

For the offences listed under s. 17, the references to the specific areas of the Manuals dealing with the legislation are:

- s. 17(1)(c)(i)—see para. 4.6.10
- s. 17(1)(c)(ii)—see para. 4.10.9.3 (s. 6), see para. 4.8.5 (s. 8)
- s. 17(1)(c)(iii)—see para. 4.6.7
- s. 17(1)(c)(iiia)—see Road Policing, chapter 3.5 (s. 4)
- s. 17(1)(c)(iiib)
- s. 17(1)(c)(iv)—see para. 4.10.8.3
- s. 17(1)(ca)
- s. 17(1)(caa)
- s. 17(1)(cb)

Section 10 of the Criminal Law Act 1977 contained in s. 17(1)(c)(ii) is not within the scope of the Manuals and relates to the obstruction of court officers executing any process issued by the High Court or county court.

In a case where police had been called to an address by an abandoned 999 call, the officers had to move a man away from the front door in order to gain entry under s. 17. The Queen's Bench Divisional Court held that the officers had the power to use reasonable force in order to do so (*Smith (Peter John)* v *DPP* (2001) 165 JP 432). The source of the power to use force here is s. 117 of the Police and Criminal Evidence Act 1984 (as to which, **see para. 4.4.6.3**).

'Unlawfully at large' does not have a particular statutory meaning; it can apply to someone who is subject to an order under the Mental Health Act 1983, or someone who has escaped from custody. The pursuit of the person must be 'fresh', that is, the power will only be available while the officer is actually 'pursuing' the person concerned (*D'Souza* v *DPP* (1993) 96 Cr App 278).

Force may be used in exercising the power of entry where it is necessary to do so. Generally, the officer should first attempt to communicate with the occupier of the premises, explaining by what authority and for what purpose entry is to be made, before making a forcible entry. Clearly though, there will be occasions where such communication is impossible, impracticable or even unnecessary; in those cases there is no need for the officer to enter into such an explanation (*O'Loughlin* v *Chief Constable of Essex* [1998] 1 WLR 374).

The officer must have reasonable grounds to *believe* that the person is on the premises in all cases except saving life and limb at s. 17(1)(e). This expression is narrower than 'reasonable cause to suspect' and you must be able to justify that belief before using this power (although see *Kynaston* v *DPP* (1987) *The Times*, 4 November, where the court accepted reasonable cause to *suspect*).

Note the requirement for an officer to be in uniform for the purposes of s. 17(1)(c)(ii) and (iv), and the restrictions on the power of *search* under s. 17(4) (i.e. that any such search is limited to the extent that is reasonably required *for the purpose for which you entered the premises in the first place*).

Code B regulates the way in which these powers of entry will be executed.

Again this section contains restrictions on the extent of any searches made (**see para. 4.4.4**).

The power to enter and search any premises in the relevant police area for the purpose of saving life or limb or preventing serious damage to property above is among those that can be conferred on a designated person under sch. 4 to the Police Reform Act 2002 (**see para. 4.2.3**).

4.4.14 Fire

The principal piece of legislation governing the powers and offences arising out of fires is the Fire and Rescue Services Act 2004. The Act provides employees of a fire and rescue authority who are authorised in writing by their authority, with some wide emergency powers. One such power is the power to do *anything they reasonably believe to be necessary* if they reasonably believe a fire to have broken out (or to be about to break out) for the purpose of extinguishing or preventing the fire or protecting life or property (s. 44).

4.4.15 Powers of Seizure under the Police and Criminal Evidence Act 1984

The Police and Criminal Evidence Act 1984 provides many powers for the seizure of property.

4.4.15.1 General Powers of Seizure under the Police and Criminal Evidence Act 1984

Section 19 of the Police and Criminal Evidence Act 1984 states:

(1) The powers conferred by subsections (2), (3) and (4) below are exercisable by a constable who is lawfully on any premises.
(2) The constable may seize anything which is on the premises if he has reasonable grounds for believing—
  (a) that it has been obtained in consequence of the commission of an offence; and
  (b) that it is necessary to seize it in order to prevent it being concealed, lost, damaged, altered or destroyed.
(3) The constable may seize anything which is on the premises if he has reasonable grounds for believing—
  (a) that it is evidence in relation to an offence which he is investigating or any other offence; and
  (b) that it is necessary to seize it in order to prevent the evidence being concealed, lost, altered or destroyed.
(4) The constable may require any information which is stored in any electronic form and is accessible from the premises to be produced in a form in which it can be taken away and in which it is visible and legible or from which it can readily be produced in a visible and legible form if he has reasonable grounds for believing—
  (a) that—
    (i) it is evidence in relation to an offence which he is investigating or any other offence; or
    (ii) it has been obtained in consequence of the commission of an offence; and
  (b) that it is necessary to do so in order to prevent it being concealed, lost, or destroyed.
(5) The powers conferred by this section are in addition to any power otherwise conferred.
(6) No power of seizure conferred on a constable under any enactment (including an enactment contained in an Act passed after this Act) is to be taken to authorise the seizure of an item which the constable exercising the power has reasonable grounds for believing to be subject to legal privilege.

KEYNOTE

For this very wide power to apply, the officer concerned must be on the premises lawfully (**see para. 4.4.13** and also PACE Code B). If the officers are on the premises only with the consent of the occupier, they become trespassers once that consent has been withdrawn (**see para. 4.4.13.4**). Once the officers are told to leave, they are no longer 'lawfully' on the premises—even though they must be given a reasonable opportunity to leave—and cannot then seize any property that they may find. For this reason, it is far safer to exercise a power where one exists, albeit that the *co-operation* of the relevant person should be sought.

The power of seizure only applies where the officer has 'reasonable grounds for believing' that:

- the property has been obtained in consequence of the commission of an offence, or
- the property is *evidence* in relation to an offence, *and*

in each case, that its seizure is *necessary* to prevent the property being concealed, lost or destroyed.

Where the 'premises' searched is a vehicle (see s. 23), the vehicle can itself be seized (*Cowan* v *Commissioner of Police for the Metropolis* [2000] 1 WLR 254). In *Cowan* it was argued that the powers given by ss. 18 (as to which, **see para. 4.4.13**) and 19 authorise the seizure of anything in or on the premises but not the *premises* themselves. The Court of Appeal disagreed, holding that the power to seize 'premises', where it was appropriate and practical to do so, was embodied in both ss. 18 and 19 and also at common law and the defendant's claim for damages following the seizure of his vehicle after his arrest for serious sexual offences was dismissed. This decision is now acknowledged in Code B, Note 7B.

Unless the elements above are satisfied, the power under s. 19 will not apply. Therefore, the power does not authorise the seizure of property purely for intelligence purposes (**see also para. 4.4.12**).

Section 19(5) expressly preserves any common law power of search and seizure; however, in *R (on the application of Rottman)* v *Commissioner of Police for the Metropolis* [2002] 2 All ER 865, the House of Lords held that s. 19 was confined to 'domestic' offences (e.g. and did not extend to extradition offences). The same applies to powers under s. 18 of the Police and Criminal Evidence Act 1984 (**see para. 4.4.13**).

If the warrant under which entry or seizure was made is invalid, the officers will not be on the premises lawfully (**see para. 4.4.12**).

The power of seizure under s. 19(1), along with the power to require information stored in any electronic form to be made accessible under s. 19(4), are among those that can be conferred on an Investigating Officer designated under sch. 4 to the Police Reform Act 2002 (**see chapter 4.2**). The safeguards provided by s. 19(6) in relation to privileged material also apply to the exercise of these powers by designated Investigating Officers.

4.4.15.2 Powers of Seizure and Information in Electronic Form

Section 20 states:

(1) Every power of seizure which is conferred by an enactment to which this section applies on a constable who has entered premises in the exercise of a power conferred by an enactment shall be construed as including a power to require any information stored in any electronic form and accessible from the premises to be produced in a form in which it can be taken away and in which it is visible and legible or from which it can readily be produced in a visible and legible form.

(2) This section applies—
   (a) to any enactment contained in an Act passed before this Act;
   (b) to sections 8 and 18 above;
   (c) to paragraph 13 of Schedule 1 to this Act; and
   (d) to any enactment contained in an Act passed after this Act.

KEYNOTE

This provision applies to:

- powers conferred under pre-PACE statutes;
- powers exercised under a s. 8 warrant (for 'indictable offences');
- powers exercised under s. 18 (following arrest for an indictable offence);
- powers under sch. 1 ('excluded' or 'special procedure material');
- powers exercised under s. 19 (officers lawfully on premises);
- powers of seizure exercised by Investigating Officers designated under sch. 4 to the Police Reform Act 2002 (as to which **see para. 4.2.3**).

See also PACE Code B, para. 7.6 which reinforces the power to require electronically stored information to be produced in a visible and legible form that can be taken away or reproduced (**appendix 4.2**).

The increased use of electronic media to facilitate criminal activity has meant that more conventional police powers of search and seizure have not been adequate for the needs of the police and other investigatory agencies. This is particularly true where data or information that may be of evidential value in a criminal enquiry has been 'encrypted'—that is, where some form of code or password has been used to prevent access to it. Part III of the Regulation of Investigatory Powers Act 2000 addresses these problems by providing a power to serve written notices requiring the holders of 'protected information' to disclose either the information in an intelligible format or, if relevant, the 'key' to it. Protected information in this context is generally electronic data that cannot be accessed readily or put into an intelligible form without a key (s. 56). The power to serve a notice (given by s. 49) generally applies to protected information that has been obtained or seized by some lawful means, for example where a computer has been taken under the authority of a warrant or voluntarily handed in to the police or the Serious Organised Crime Agency. At the time of writing, this part of the Act had not been brought into force.

Which person will have appropriate permission under the 2000 Act to issue the relevant s. 49 notice will depend largely on how the protected information was come by. Broadly, sch. 2 to the Act lists the people who may issue such notices and, just as importantly, appropriate circumstances under which they may do so. A circuit judge in England and Wales will have appropriate permission to grant police applications in all cases. Others included in the schedule are the Secretary of State and chief officers of police (under the appropriate circumstances). As with other areas of the 2000 Act (**see chapter 4.12**), the power to issue s. 49 notices will be restricted to occasions where its use is both necessary and proportionate to the interests of national security, the prevention or detection of crime and the economic well-being of the United Kingdom. In addition, a s. 49 notice cannot be issued unless it is not reasonably practicable for the person with appropriate permission to obtain the protected information in an intelligible form in any other way. Part III of the Act imposes certain requirements for reporting the use of the s. 49 powers to the Chief Surveillance Commissioner and creates safeguards for the storage and use of any keys and data obtained thereby. Knowingly failing to comply with a s. 49 notice will be, under appropriate circumstances, an offence triable either way and attracting an unlimited fine in the Crown Court (s. 53). There is also to be a more serious offence of 'tipping off' another person where a s. 49 notice has been authorised and that notice contains an express requirement for secrecy (s. 54).

This discussion is merely a summary of the key aspects of this power. To find the full extent of the powers and duties under this Part of the 2000 Act, the statutory text should be used along with the relevant code of practice in force at the time.

For other powers and offences involving data and information, **see chapter 4.12**.

4.4.15.3 Supply of Copies of Seized Material

Section 21 of the 1984 Act makes provision for the supplying of copies of records of seizure to certain people after property has been seized. If requested by the person who had custody or control of the seized property immediately before it was seized, the officer in charge of the investigation must allow that person access to it under police supervision. The officer must also make provisions to allow for the property be to photographed or copied by that person or to supply the person with photographs/copies of it within a reasonable time. Such a request need not be complied with if there are reasonable grounds to believe that to do so would prejudice any related investigation or criminal proceedings (s. 21(8)).

4.4.15.4 Retention of Seized Material

The provisions for accessing and copying of seized material as set out in ss. 21 and 22 of the Police and Criminal Evidence Act 1984 also apply to powers of seizure exercised by Investigating Officers designated under sch. 4 to the Police Reform Act 2002 (as to which **see para. 4.2.3**).

Section 22 of the 1984 Act makes provision for the retention of seized property. Section 22(1) provides that anything seized may be retained for as long as necessary in all the circumstances. However, s. 22(2) allows for property to be retained for use as evidence in a trial, forensic examination or further investigation *unless a photograph or copy would suffice*. This is reinforced generally by PACE Code B, para. 7.5. Seized property may be retained in order to establish its lawful owner (s. 22(2)(b)). Once this power to retain property is exhausted, a person claiming it can rely on his/her right to possession at the time the property was seized as giving sufficient title to recover the property from the police. This situation was confirmed by the Court of Appeal in a case where the purchaser of a stolen car was allowed to rely upon his possession of the car at the time it was seized. As it could not be established that anyone else was entitled to the vehicle, the Court allowed the claimant's action for return of the car to him (*Costello* v *Chief Constable of Derbyshire Constabulary* [2001] 1 WLR 1437). Clearly any claim based on previous possession where it would be unlawful for the police to return the property (e.g. a controlled drug) could not be enforced. Provisions amending this area of legislation are now contained in the Criminal Justice and Police Act 2001. There is no specific provision under s. 22 for the retention of property for purely intelligence purposes.

The importance of police officers being able to point clearly to the need for retaining property either in order to establish its owner or as a necessary part of the investigative or law enforcement process when relying on the above powers, was highlighted by the Court of Appeal in *Gough* v *Chief Constable of the West Midlands Police* (2004) *The Times*, 4 March. In that case it was clear that neither of these purposes was being served and therefore the officers could not rely on the statutory power for retaining the property.

Property seized simply to prevent an arrested person from using it to escape or to cause injury, damage etc. cannot be retained for those purposes once the person has been released (s. 22(3)). This includes car keys belonging to someone who is released from police detention having been detained under the relevant drink driving legislation (**see Road Policing, chapter 3.5**).

4.4.15.5 Prohibitions on Reuse of Information Seized

Information gained as a result of a lawful search may be passed on to other individuals and organisations for purposes of investigation and prosecution. It must not be used for private purposes (*Marcel* v *Commissioner of Police for the Metropolis* [1992] Ch 225; also **see chapter 4.1** for the requirements as to confidentiality in the Code of Conduct for police officers).

4.4.15.6 Disposal of Property in Police Possession

For the provisions regarding the disposal of property in police possession, see the Police (Property) Act 1897.

4.4.16 Protected Material

Some material cannot be seized, either under the Police and Criminal Evidence Act 1984 or any other enactment; certain other material can only be seized under special circumstances set out in the Act (and the extended 'seize and sift' powers under the Criminal Justice and Police Act 2001—**see para. 4.4.17**).

4.4.16.1 Legally Privileged Material

Material which falls within the definition in s. 10 of the 1984 Act is subject to legal privilege which means that it cannot be searched for or seized.

Section 10 states:

(1) Subject to subsection (2) below, in this Act 'items subject to legal privilege' means—
  (a) communications between a professional legal adviser and his client or any person representing his client made in connection with the giving of legal advice to the client;

(b) communications between a professional legal adviser and his client or any person representing his client or between such an adviser or his client or any such representative and any other person made in connection with or in contemplation of legal proceedings and for the purposes of such proceedings; and

(c) items enclosed with or referred to in such communications and made—
  (i) in connection with the giving of legal advice; or
  (ii) in connection with or in contemplation of legal proceedings and for the purposes of such proceedings,

when they are in the possession of a person who is entitled to possession of them.

KEYNOTE

Items held with the intention of furthering a criminal purpose are no longer subject to this privilege (s. 10(2)). However, when making an application for a warrant to search for and seize such material the procedure under sch. 1 should be used. Occasions where this will happen are very rare and would include instances where a solicitor's firm is the subject of a criminal investigation (see *R* v *Leeds Crown Court, ex parte Switalski* [1991] Crim LR 559). However, it may be possible during a search to ascertain which material is subject to legal privilege and which might be lawfully seized under the warrant being executed. Therefore, although a warrant cannot authorise a search for legally privileged material, the fact that such material is inadvertently seized in the course of a search authorised by a proper warrant does not render the search unlawful (*HM Customs & Excise, ex parte Popely* [2000] Crim LR 388).

4.4.16.2 Excluded Material

Access to 'excluded material' can generally only be gained by applying to a judge for a production order under the procedure set out in s. 9 of, and sch. 1 to the 1984 Act and PACE Code B. That strict statutory procedure also applies to the application for and execution of warrants by Investigating Officers designated under sch. 4 to the Police Reform Act 2002 (as to which **see para. 4.2.3**).

Section 11 of the 1984 Act states:

(1) Subject to the following provisions of this section, in this Act 'excluded material' means—
  (a) personal records which a person has acquired or created in the course of any trade, business, profession or other occupation or for the purposes of any paid or unpaid office and which he holds in confidence;
  (b) human tissue or tissue fluid which has been taken for the purposes of diagnosis or medical treatment and which a person holds in confidence;
  (c) journalistic material which a person holds in confidence and which consists—
    (i) of documents; or
    (ii) of records other than documents.

(2) A person holds material other than journalistic material in confidence for the purposes of this section if he holds it subject—
  (a) to an express or implied undertaking to hold it in confidence; or
  (b) to a restriction on disclosure or an obligation of secrecy contained in any enactment, including an enactment contained in an Act passed after this Act.

(3) A person holds journalistic material in confidence for the purposes of this section if—
  (a) he holds it subject to such an undertaking, restriction or obligation; and
  (b) it has been continuously held (by one or more persons) subject to such an undertaking, restriction or obligation since it was first acquired or created for the purposes of journalism.

> **KEYNOTE**
>
> Medical records and dental records would fall into this category, as might records made by priests or religious advisers.
>
> 'Personal records' are defined under s. 12 of the 1984 Act and include records relating to the physical or mental health, counselling or assistance given to an individual who can be identified by those records.
>
> 'Journalistic material' is defined under s. 13 as material acquired or created for the purposes of journalism.

4.4.16.3 Special Procedure Material

Special procedure material can be gained by applying for a search warrant or a production order under sch. 1 to the 1984 Act.

Section 14 of the 1984 Act states:

> (1) In this Act 'special procedure material' means—
> (a) material to which subsection (2) below applies; and
> (b) journalistic material, other than excluded material.
>
> (2) Subject to the following provisions of this section, this subsection applies to material, other than items subject to legal privilege and excluded material, in the possession of a person who—
> (a) acquired or created it in the course of any trade, business, profession or other occupation or for the purpose of any paid or unpaid office; and
> (b) holds it subject—
> (i) to an express or implied undertaking to hold it in confidence; or
> (ii) to a restriction or obligation such as is mentioned in section 11(2)(b) above.

> **KEYNOTE**
>
> For items subject to 'legal privilege' and 'excluded material', see the Keynotes above.
>
> The person believed to be in possession of the material must have come by it under the circumstances set out at s. 14(2)(a) *and* must hold it under the undertakings or obligations set out at s. 14(2)(b).

4.4.17 Seize and Sift Powers

One of the practical problems faced by operational officers when seizing certain types of material is that of sorting the 'wheat from the chaff'—sifting out those documents or computer-stored data that are pertinent to the case from the general mass of material within which they are found. Part 2 of the Criminal Justice and Police Act 2001 now provides the police with specific powers to 'seize and sift' under strict conditions and subject to a number of rigid procedural safeguards. One such safeguard is the specific application of Code B of the Police and Criminal Evidence Act 1984 Codes of Practice (**see appendix 4.2**).

4.4.17.1 Extended Powers

The first point to note about these seize and sift powers is that they will be rarely used and, even then, those using them will have to be able to show that it was *essential* (rather than simply convenient or preferable) to do so (Code B, para. 7.7). The second thing to note about these powers is that they only extend the scope of *some other existing power*.

In other words, they do not provide free-standing powers to seize property—rather they supplement other powers of search and seizure where the relevant conditions and circumstances apply. The full list of these powers is set out in sch. 1 to the Act and includes all the relevant powers under the Police and Criminal Evidence Act 1984, along with those under other key statutes such as the Firearms Act 1968 and the Misuse of Drugs Act 1971. If there is no existing power of seizure other than the Criminal Justice and Police Act 2001, then there is no power.

The Criminal Justice and Police Act 2001 powers allow officers to remove materials from the premises being searched where there are real practical difficulties in not doing so—e.g. because there will be insufficient time to examine all the material properly, where special equipment is needed to examine it or where the material is stored on a computer.

In summary, s. 50 of the Act provides the extended powers to seize material where it is not reasonably practicable to sort through it at the scene of the search. The factors that can be taken into account in considering whether or not it is reasonably practicable for something to be determined, or for relevant material to be separated from other materials, are set out in s. 50(3); these include the length of time and number of people that would be required to carry out the determination or separation on those premises within a reasonable period, whether that would involve damage to property, any apparatus or equipment that would be needed and (in the case of separation of materials) whether the separation would be likely to prejudice the use of some or all of the separated seizable property. Section 50 also allows for the seizure of material that is reasonably believed to be legally privileged (**see para. 4.4.16**) where it is not reasonably practicable to separate it. In some cases, the power to 'seize' will be read as a power to take copies (see s. 63).

Section 51 provides for extended seizure of materials in the same vein as above but where the material is found on people who are being lawfully searched.

One of the main purposes behind this legislative framework is to balance the competing needs of the criminal justice system with the individual rights of the person owning the property (see Code B, paras 7.7 and 7.8). Seizing large volumes of material and removing them from the owner's premises can have considerable consequences, particularly where they are taken from business premises. Therefore there are many strict requirements imposed on the police, not only in seizing the property in the first place, but also after the property has been lawfully seized by virtue of the powers. The first of these is the duty to carry out an initial examination.

4.4.17.2 Initial Examination

Where any property has been seized under ss. 50 or 51, the officer in possession of it is under a duty to make sure that a number of things are done (s. 53). These include ensuring that an initial examination of the property is carried out *as soon as reasonably practicable* after the seizure. In determining the earliest practicable time to carry out an initial examination of the seized property, due regard must be had to the desirability of allowing the person from whom it was seized (or a person with an interest in it) an opportunity of being present, or of being represented, at the examination (s. 53(4)).

The officer must also ensure that any such examination is confined to whatever is *necessary* for determining how much of the property:

- is property for which the person seizing it had power to search when making the seizure but is not property that has to be returned (by s. 54—see below);
- is property authorised to be retained (by s. 56—see below); or

- is something which, in all the circumstances, it will not be reasonably practicable, following the examination, to separate from the property above (see generally s. 53(3)).

The officer must ensure that anything found not to fall within the categories above is separated from the rest of the seized property and *is returned as soon as reasonably practicable* after the examination of all the seized property. That officer is also under a duty to ensure that, until the initial examination of all the seized property has been completed and anything which does not fall within the categories above has been returned, the seized property is kept separate from anything seized under any other power. There are special provisions where the property is inextricably linked to relevant material (e.g. where the 'innocent' material is completely mixed up with or inseparable from the material that is properly the subject of the investigation). However, those provisions place very strict limits on what use can be made of this inextricably linked material (see s. 62).

While there are great sensitivities over the use of widespread powers of seizure such as these in any event, those sensitivities are increased even further where legally privileged or special procedure material is involved (as to which **see para. 4.4.16**). Accordingly the Act imposes specific duties on the police in relation to these materials.

4.4.17.3 Protected Material

If, at any time, after a seizure of anything has been made in exercise of *any statutory power of seizure*, it appears that the property is subject to legal privilege (or it has such an item comprised in it), s. 54 imposes a general duty on the officer in possession of the property to ensure that the item is returned as soon as reasonably practicable after the seizure. This general duty is subject to some exceptions (e.g. where in all the circumstances it is not reasonably practicable for that item to be separated from the rest of that property without prejudicing the use of the rest of that property—see s. 54(2)) but is otherwise very wide-ranging and absolutely clear. A similar duty is generally imposed in relation to property that appears to be excluded material or special procedure material (as to which **see para. 4.4.16**)—s. 55.

4.4.17.4 Retention of Property

The Act authorises the retention of certain seized property by the police. In order to be retained, the property must have been seized on any premises by a constable who was lawfully on the premises, by a person authorised under a relevant statute (see s. 56(5)) who was on the premises accompanied by a constable, or by a constable carrying out a lawful search of any person (s. 56). Generally property so seized will fall within these categories if there are reasonable grounds for believing:

- that it is property obtained in consequence of the commission of an offence; or
- that it is evidence in relation to any offence; *and* (in either case)
- that it is necessary for it to be retained in order to prevent its being concealed, lost, altered or destroyed

(for full details see s. 56(2) and (3)). Note, so far as s. 56(2) is concerned, property may be retained if it is necessary to prevent its being 'damaged', in addition to the other factors listed.

These are fairly wide provisions and, if the property fits the above description, it may be retained even if it was not being searched for. Section 57 goes on to make certain provisions for the retention of property under other statutes including s. 22 of the Theft Act 1968 (**see Crime**) and s. 5(4) of the Knives Act 1997 (**see para. 4.8.7**). Further guidance on retention of property is set out in Code B, paras. 7.14–7.15.

4.4.17.5 Notice

Where a person exercises a power of seizure conferred by ss. 50 or 51, that person will be under a duty, on doing so, to give the occupier or person from whom property is seized a written notice (s. 52). That notice will specify:

- what has been seized and the grounds on which the powers have been exercised;
- the effect of the safeguards and rights to apply to a judicial authority for the return of the property (see below);
- the name and address of the person to whom notice of an application to a judge and an application to be allowed to attend the initial examination should be sent.

Where it appears to the officer exercising a power of seizure under s. 50 that the occupier of the premises is not present at the time of the exercise of the power, but there is some other person present who is in charge of the premises, the officer may give the notice to that other person (s. 52(2)). Where it appears that there is no one present on the premises to whom a notice can be given, the officer must, before leaving the premises, attach a notice in a prominent place to the premises (s. 53(3)).

4.4.17.6 Return of Property Seized

There are specific obligations on the police to return property seized under these powers—particularly where the property includes legally privileged, excluded or special procedure material. The general rule is that any extraneous property initially seized under these provisions must be returned—usually—to the person from whom it was seized unless the investigating officer considers that someone else has a better claim to it (see ss. 53–58).

Any person with a relevant interest in the seized property may apply to the appropriate judicial authority, on one or more of the grounds in s. 59(3) for the return of the whole or a part of the seized property. Generally those grounds are that there was no power to make the seizure or that the seized property did not fall into one of the permitted categories (see s. 59). Where a person makes such an application, the police must secure the property in accordance with s. 61 (e.g. in a way that prevents investigators from looking at or copying it until the matter has been considered by a judge). There are other occasions where protected material is involved that will give rise to the duty to secure the property under s. 61 too. What will amount to 'securing' will vary depending on the type of property and the circumstances and may involve 'bagging up' property and controlling access to it in many cases (see Code B, Note 7F). The 'judicial authority' (at least a Crown Court judge) will be able to make a number of wide-ranging orders in relation to the treatment of the seized property, including its return or examination by a third party. Failure to comply with any such order will amount to a contempt of court (s. 59(9)).

For further details on the extent and use of these powers, see Home Office Circular 19/2003.

PART TWO

Community Safety

4.5 Harassment, Hostility and Anti-Social Behaviour

4.5.1 Introduction

There is a growing list of measures available to police staff and the wider police family to help them preserve safety and quality of life within the community.

This chapter, and the rest of Part 2, aims to set out the key areas of legislation and common law that are available to address public and individual anxiety, threats to personal safety and anti-social behaviour.

4.5.2 Racially and Religiously Aggravated Offences

Sections 28 to 32 of the Crime and Disorder Act 1998 did not so much create *new* offences, but rather took *existing* offences and set out circumstances under which those offences will be deemed to be 'aggravated'. Those offences are:

- wounding or grievous bodily harm—Offences Against the Person Act 1861, s. 20
- causing actual bodily harm—Offences Against the Person Act 1861, s. 47
- common assault—Criminal Justice Act 1988, s. 39

(**see Crime, chapter 1.7**)

- 'simple' criminal damage—Criminal Damage Act 1971, s. 1(1)

(**see Crime, chapter 1.13**)

- causing fear or provocation of violence—Public Order Act 1986, s. 4
- intentional harassment, alarm or distress—Public Order Act 1986, s. 4A
- causing harassment, alarm or distress—Public Order Act 1986, s. 5

(**see chapter 4.6**)

- harassment—Protection from Harassment Act 1997, s. 2
- putting people in fear of violence—Protection from Harassment Act 1997, s. 4

(**see para. 4.5.4**).

This area of the law was changed once again after the terrorist attacks of 11 September 2001 by the Anti-terrorism, Crime and Security Act 2001. Part 5 of that Act amended the Crime and Disorder Act 1998, extending the provisions of what were 'racially aggravated' offences to include 'racially *or religiously* aggravated' offences (as to which, see below).

In order to prove these offences there must be proof of the relevant, substantive offence (e.g. common assault) together with further proof of the aggravating circumstances. Once both conditions have been made out, the offences attract greater maximum penalties and powers. For that reason the specific effects of this legislation are dealt with under the relevant chapters in this Manual.

4.5.2.1 'Racially or Religiously Aggravated'

The test for racial or religious aggravation is set out at s. 28 of the Crime and Disorder Act 1998:

(1) An offence is racially or religiously aggravated for the purposes of sections 29 to 32 ... if—
   (a) at the time of committing the offence, or immediately before or after doing so, the offender demonstrates towards the victim of the offence hostility based on the victim's membership (or presumed membership) of a racial or religious group; or
   (b) the offence is motivated (wholly or partly) by hostility towards members of a racial or religious group based on their membership of that group.

(2) In subsection (1)(a) above—
   'membership', in relation to a racial or religious group, includes association with members of that group; 'presumed' means presumed by the offender.

(3) It is immaterial for the purposes of paragraph (a) or (b) of subsection (1) above whether or not the offender's hostility is also based, to any extent, on any other factor not mentioned in that paragraph.

(4) In this section 'racial group' means a group of persons defined by reference to race, colour, nationality (including citizenship) or ethnic or national origins.

(5) In this section 'religious group' means a group of persons defined by reference to religious belief or lack of religious belief.

KEYNOTE

The aggravating factors for the purposes of s. 28 can be divided into:

- *demonstration* of hostility by the defendant
- *motivation* by hostility of the defendant.

The second type of situation, where the defendant is *motivated* by racial or religious hostility, is the type at which the government's policies to tackle racism are aimed; it is also by far the harder of the two to prove, even though the relevant offence need only be *partly* motivated by racial or religious hostility.

The revised wording of s. 28 (amended after the events of 11 September 2001) now includes 'religious groups'. These will include groups of people defined, not only by their religious belief, but also their *lack* of any such belief. An example of where this element has been proved is a case where a juvenile used the words 'bloody foreigners' immediately before smashing the window of a kebab shop. The Divisional Court held that this was capable of amounting to an expression of hostility based on a person's membership or presumed membership of a racial group for the purposes of the Crime and Disorder Act 1998, s. 28(1)(a)—*DPP* v *M* [2004] 1 WLR 2758.

In a case involving the abuse and assault of a doorman, the Administrative Court held that a racial insult uttered a few moments before an assault was enough to make the offence racially aggravated for the purposes of s. 29 of the Crime and Disorder Act 1998. The Court also held that the victim's own perception of the words used was irrelevant, as was the fact that he was not personally upset by the situation. Similarly, the fact that the defendant might have been motivated to utter the words merely by frustration rather than racism was also irrelevant (*DPP* v *Woods* [2002] EWHC Admin 85).

4.5.2.2 Hostility

Common to both factors under s. 28(1)(a) and (b) is the notion of hostility.

Hostility is not defined. However, in comparison to the problematic expression of 'racial hatred' used in the Public Order Act 1986 (**see para. 4.5.3**), hostility may well be much easier to identify and prove. The *Oxford English Dictionary* defines 'hostile' as 'of the nature or disposition of an enemy; unfriendly, antagonistic'. It would seem relatively straightforward to show that someone's behaviour in committing the relevant offences was 'unfriendly or antagonistic'. The difficult bit will come when trying to show that the hostility was *based on* the relevant person's membership of a racial or religious group.

A further difficulty for the courts will be making sure they do not confuse the two tests (see *DPP* v *M* [2004] 1 WLR 2758 where the youth court inadvertently mixed the two tests of hostility and motivation (under s. 28(1)(b)) as a result of which M's appeal against conviction was allowed).

4.5.2.3 Racial Groups

In each case the hostility must be based on the relevant person's membership of a racial group, i.e. membership of a group of people defined by reference to:

- race
- colour
- nationality (including citizenship)
- ethnic origins
- national origins (s. 28(4)).

This definition is the same as that used in the Public Order Act 1986 (see below). It is also very similar to that used in the Race Relations Act 1976. In determining whether or not a group is defined by *ethnic origins*, the courts will have regard to the judgment in the House of Lords in *Mandla* v *Dowell Lee* [1983] 2 AC 548. In that case their Lordships decided that Sikhs were such a group (for the purposes of the Race Relations Act 1976) after considering whether they as a group had:

- a long shared *history*;
- a *cultural tradition* of their own, including family and social customs and manners, often, but not necessarily, associated with religious observance;
- either a *common geographical origin* or descent from a small number of *common ancestors*;
- a *common language*, not necessarily peculiar to that group;
- a *common literature* peculiar to that group;
- a *common religion* different from that of neighbouring groups or the general community surrounding the group; and
- the characteristic of being a *minority* or an *oppressed* or a *dominant* group within a larger community.

Lord Fraser's dictum suggests that the first two characteristics above are essential in defining an 'ethnic group', while the others are at least relevant. His Lordship also approved a decision from New Zealand to the effect that Jews are a group with common ethnic origins (*Kings-Ansell* v *Police* [1979] 2 NZLR 531).

KEYNOTE

When considering whether an offence was racially motivated under s. 28, hostility demonstrated to people who were foreign nationals simply because they were 'foreign' could be just as objectionable as hostility based on some more limited racial characteristic. This was clarified by the Court of Appeal in *R* v *Rogers* [2006] 1 Cr App R 14 where the defendant had called three Spanish women 'bloody foreigners' and told them to 'go back to your own country'. The prosecution case was that the defendant had demonstrated hostility based on the women's membership of a racial group. The court held that, for an offence to be aggravated under s. 28 the defendant had first to form a view that the victim was a member of a racial group (within the definition in s. 28(4) and then had to say or do something that demonstrated hostility towards the victim based on membership of that group.

4.5.2.4 Religion

Lord Fraser's sixth point above refers to religion as a possible defining characteristic of an ethnic group. Although this was a notable omission from the ambit of *racial groups* as defined under the original s. 28(4) of the Crime and Disorder Act 1998, religious groups have now been included as a result of the Anti-terrorism, Crime and Security Act 2001. In addition, there are now specific regulations dealing with the area of less favourable treatment by employers on grounds of religious belief (**see chapter 4.13**). This means that the former case law (mostly arising in an employment context) over whether religious groups could also be regarded as racial groups is largely irrelevant. The change means that a purely religious group such as Rastafarians (who have been held not to be members of an ethnic group *per se* (*Dawkins* v *Crown Suppliers (Property Services Agency)* (1993) *The Times*, 4 February; [1993] ICR 517) are now covered by the aggravated forms of offences. In reality, a number of racial groups will overlap with religious groups in any event—Rastafarians would be a good example. An attack on a Rastafarian might be a racially aggravated offence under s. 28 because it was based on the defendant's hostility towards a *racial group* (e.g. African-Caribbeans) into which many Rastafarians fall. Alternatively, an attack might be made on a white Rastafarian based on the victim's religious beliefs (or lack of religious beliefs), i.e. his 'membership of a religious group'. Muslims have also been held not to be a racial group (*J.H. Walker* v *Hussain* [1996] ICR 291) but Muslims are clearly members of a religious group and, as such, are now covered by the Act.

Note that there is some disparity here between the recognition of religion for these specific purposes and those that appear under Article 9 of the European Convention on Human Rights.

4.5.2.5 Other Racial Groups

Traditional 'gypsies' (as opposed to travellers) are capable of being a racial group on the basis of ethnic origin (*Commission for Racial Equality* v *Dutton* [1989] QB 783). English and Scottish people have been held to constitute groups defined by reference to national origins and thus as members of 'racial groups' in the broad sense as defined and protected from discrimination under the Race Relations Act 1976 (*Northern Joint Police Board* v *Power* [1997] IRLR 610). This decision ought logically to extend to Irish and Welsh people. In *Attorney-General's Reference (No. 4 of 2004), sub nom Attorney-General* v *D* [2005] 1 WLR 2810 the use of the word 'immigrant', in its simple implication that a person was 'non-British', was specific enough to denote membership of a 'racial group' within its meaning in the Crime and Disorder Act 1998, s. 28(4).

4.5.2.6 Membership

An important extension of 'racial or religious groups' lies in the inclusion of people who associate with members of that group. 'Membership' *for the purposes of s. 28(1)(a)* will include *association* with members of that group (a slightly circular definition) (s. 28(2)). This means that a white man who has a black female partner would potentially fall within the category of a 'member' of her racial group—and vice versa. Moreover, people who work within certain racial or religious groups within the community could also be regarded as members of those groups for these purposes.

For the purposes of s. 28(1)(a), 'membership' will also include anyone *presumed by the defendant* to be a member of a racial or religious group. Therefore, if a defendant wrongly presumed that a person was a member of a racial or religious group, say a Pakistani Muslim, and assaulted them as a result, the defendant's *presumption* would be enough to make his/her behaviour 'racially or religiously aggravated', even though the victim was in fact an Indian Hindu.

Such a presumption would not extend to the aggravating factors under s. 28(1)(b). The only apparent reason for this would seem to be that the s. 28(1)(a) offence requires hostility to be demonstrated towards a particular person ('the victim') while the offence under s. 28(1)(b) envisages hostility towards members of a racial or religious group generally and does not require a specific victim.

Section 28(3) goes on to provide that it is immaterial whether the defendant's hostility (in either case under s. 28(1)) is also based to any extent on *any other factor*.

This concession in s. 28(3) only prevents the defendant pointing to another *factor* in order to explain his/her behaviour in committing the relevant offence (assault, criminal damage, etc.). Although it removes the opportunity for a defendant to argue that his/her behaviour was as a result of other factors (e.g. arising out of a domestic dispute), the subsection does not remove the burden on the prosecution to show that the defendant either demonstrated racial or religious hostility or was motivated by it.

4.5.2.7 Demonstration of Hostility

Under s. 28(1)(a) it must be shown that the defendant *demonstrated* the required hostility:

- at the time of the offence
- immediately before, or
- immediately after committing the offence.

No guidance is given as to how 'immediately' will be interpreted. It is submitted that whether a defendant's demonstration of hostility came immediately before or after the relevant offence will be a question of fact to be decided in light of all the circumstances.

In deciding the issue of immediacy the courts will have to consider the degree of proximity between the defendant's demonstration of racial or religious hostility and the relevant offence itself. It is submitted that the degree of proximity will have to be very high before the defendant's hostility could be shown to have been *immediately* before or after the *actus reus* of the offence. This might cause problems with offences that are said to be 'continuing' or 'ongoing'.

The courts have shown that they are prepared to adopt a wide approach when interpreting this important legislation. In the context of criminal damage (as to which **see Crime, chapter 1.13**), the Divisional Court has confirmed that the relevant hostility can be demonstrated even if the victim is no longer present—*DPP* v *Parry* [2004] EWHC 3112. However, the need for any such hostility to be demonstrated *immediately* means that it must be shown to have taken place in the immediate context of the offence.

In the context of the offence under s. 4 of the Public Order Act 1986 (**see para. 4.6.8**) the Divisional Court held that, where a court finds that the defendant has committed an offence under s. 4 and used racist, threatening and abusive words, it is immaterial for the purposes of s. 28(1)(a) of the 1998 Act that the defendant might have had additional reasons for using that language (*DPP* v *McFarlane* [2002] EWHC 485).

It is also necessary, for the purposes of s. 28(1)(a), to show that the defendant demonstrated his/her hostility *towards the victim of the offence*. Again this may be problematic in relation to certain offences, e.g. criminal damage (**see Crime, chapter 1.13**).

Racially or religiously aggravated offences can be committed where the aggravating behaviour is directed at or towards a police officer and police officers are entitled to the protection offered by this offence in the same way as any other person (see *R* v *Jacobs* (2000) *The Times*, 28 December).

4.5.3 Other Offences involving Racial and Religious Hatred

The Racial and Religious Hatred Act 2006 inserts part 3A into the Public Order Act 1986 which provides new offences of stirring up hatred against persons on religious grounds. This section provides a summary of the offences introduced by the 1986 Act aimed at addressing incidents specifically motivated by racial hatred, and the new offences, created by the Racial and Religious Hatred Act 2006, motivated by religious hatred.

For the purposes of the offences contrary to ss. 18 to 23 of the 1986 Act, 'racial hatred' means hatred against a group of persons defined by reference to colour, race, nationality (including citizenship) or ethnic or national origins (s. 17).

For the purposes of the new offences contrary to ss. 29B to 29G of the 2006 Act, 'religious hatred' means hatred against a group of persons defined by reference to religious belief or lack of religious belief (s. 29A).

4.5.3.1 Use of Words, Behaviour or Display of Written Material

OFFENCE: **Use of words or behaviour or display of written material—*Public Order Act 1986, s. 18***

- Triable either way • Seven years' imprisonment and/or a fine on indictment
- Six months' imprisonment and/or a fine summarily

The Public Order Act 1986, s. 18 states:

> (1) A person who uses threatening, abusive or insulting words or behaviour, or displays any written material which is threatening, abusive or insulting, is guilty of an offence if—
> (a) he intends thereby to stir up racial hatred, or
> (b) having regard to all the circumstances racial hatred is likely to be stirred up thereby.
>
> (2) An offence under this section may be committed in a public or a private place, except that no offence is committed where the words or behaviour are used, or the written material is displayed, by a person inside a dwelling and are not heard or seen except by other persons in that or another dwelling.

KEYNOTE

This, and the other offences under this part of the Act, may not be prosecuted without the consent of the Attorney-General (or Solicitor-General).

Generally, in order to prove these offences, you must show that a defendant:

- *intended* to stir up racial hatred; or
- that he/she *intended* the relevant words, behaviour or material to be threatening, abusive or insulting; or

- that he/she *was aware* that the relevant words/behaviour/material might be threatening, abusive or insulting.

This offence does not apply to broadcasts in a programme (but see below) and there are exemptions in the case of fair and accurate reports of parliamentary or court proceedings.

4.5.3.2 Defence

The Public Order Act 1986, s. 18 states:

> (4) In proceedings for an offence under this section it is a defence for the accused to prove that he was inside a dwelling and had no reason to believe that the words or behaviour used, or the written material displayed, would be heard or seen by a person outside that or any other dwelling.

4.5.3.3 Publishing or Distributing Written Material

OFFENCE: **Publishing or distributing written material—*Public Order Act 1986, s. 19***

- Triable either way • Seven years' imprisonment and/or a fine on indictment
- Six months' imprisonment and/or a fine summarily

The Public Order Act 1986, s. 19 states:

> (1) A person who publishes or distributes written material which is threatening, abusive or insulting is guilty of an offence if—
> (a) he intends thereby to stir up racial hatred, or
> (b) having regard to all the circumstances racial hatred is likely to be stirred up thereby.
> (2) ...
> (3) References in this Part to the publication or distribution of written material are to its publication or distribution to the public or a section of the public.

KEYNOTE

The Anti-terrorism, Crime and Security Act 2001 increased the penalty for this offence due to the prominence it was attracting. Prosecution of this offence needs the consent of the Attorney-General (or Solicitor-General).

4.5.3.4 Defence

The Public Order Act 1986, s. 19 states:

> (2) In proceedings for an offence under this section it is a defence for an accused who is not shown to have intended to stir up racial hatred to prove that he was not aware of the content of the material and did not suspect, and had no reason to suspect, that it was threatening, abusive or insulting.

4.5.3.5 Use of Words, Behaviour or Display of Written Material

OFFENCE: **Use of words or behaviour or display of written material—*Public Order Act 1986, s. 29B***

- Triable either way • Not exceeding seven years' imprisonment and/or a fine on indictment • Not exceeding six months' imprisonment and/or a fine summarily

The Public Order Act 1986, s. 29B states:

(1) A person who uses threatening words or behaviour, or displays any written material which is threatening, is guilty of an offence if he intends thereby to stir up religious hatred.
(2) An offence under this section is committed in a public or private place, except that no offence is committed where the words or behaviour are used, or the written material is displayed, by a person inside a dwelling and are not heard or seen except by other persons in that or another dwelling.

KEYNOTE

This differs from the other sections under the 1986 Act which have no specific power of arrest since the provisions of the Serious Organised Crime and Police Act 2005 were introduced.

All of the new offences are similar to that under s. 18 in that they require the consent of the Attorney-General before proceedings can be taken (s. 29L), and the same defences apply to this particular section—no reason to believe the words or behaviour, etc., would be heard or seen outside the dwelling (s. 29B(4)), or where used solely for the purpose of being included in a programming service (s. 29B(5)).

Section 29J of the Act provides that the offences of stirring up religious hatred are not intended to limit or restrict discussion, criticism or expressions of antipathy, dislike, ridicule or insult or abuse of particular religions or belief systems or lack of religion or of the beliefs and practices of those who hold such beliefs or to apply to persons newly converted to a religious faith, evangelism or the seeking to convert people to a particular belief or to cease holding a belief.

4.5.3.6 Publishing or Distributing Material

OFFENCE: **Publishing or distributing written material—*Public Order Act 1986, s. 29C***

• Triable either way • Not exceeding seven years' imprisonment and/or a fine on indictment • Not exceeding six months' imprisonment and/or a fine summarily

The Public Order Act 1986, s. 29C states:

(1) A person who publishes or distributes written material which is threatening is guilty of an offence if he intends thereby to stir up religious hatred.
(2) References in this Part to the publication or distribution of written material are to its publication or distribution to the public or a section of the public.

4.5.4 Protection from Harassment

The Protection from Harassment Act 1997 was introduced after a number of highly publicised cases of stalking. Although intended for such situations, the Act's extensive provisions have been applied—and interpreted—widely. In passing the legislation set out below, the government anticipated the number of prosecutions under the 1997 Act to be only several hundred; in fact, many thousands of prosecutions have been brought and the following legislation can be a useful and potent tool for the police.

4.5.4.1 The Offences

OFFENCE: **Harassment—*Protection from Harassment Act 1997, ss. 1 and 2***

• Triable summarily • Six months' imprisonment and/or a fine

OFFENCE: **Racially or religiously aggravated harassment—*Crime and Disorder Act 1998, s. 32(1)(a)***

- Triable either way • Two years' imprisonment and/or a fine on indictment
- Six months' imprisonment and/or a fine summarily

The Protection from Harassment Act 1997, ss. 1 and 2 state:

1.—(1) A person must not pursue a course of conduct—
(a) which amounts to harassment of another, and
(b) which he knows or ought to know amounts to harassment of the other.
(1A) A person must not pursue a course of conduct—
(a) which involves harassment of two or more persons, and
(b) which he knows or ought to know involves harassment of those persons, and
(c) by which he intends to persuade any person (whether or not one of those mentioned above)—
(i) not to do something that he is entitled or required to do, or
(ii) to do something that he is not under any obligation to do.

2.—(1) A person who pursues a course of conduct in breach of section 1(1) or (1A) is guilty of an offence.

KEYNOTE

Unlike some of the other racially or religiously aggravated offences (see below and **Crime, chapters 1.7 and 1.13**), provisions are specifically made for alternative verdicts in relation to harassment (see s. 32(5)). A full explanation of the meaning of 'racially or religiously aggravated' can be found in **para. 4.5.2**.

'Person' here does not include companies or corporate bodies and therefore they cannot apply for injunctions under this part of the legislation. However, their employees can do so if appropriate (*Daiichi UK Ltd* v *(1) Stop Huntingdon Cruelty, and (2) Animal Liberation Front* [2004] 1 WLR 1503). For injunctions relating to companies **see para. 4.5.4.9**.

'Harassment' includes alarming the person or causing them distress (s. 7(2) of the 1997 Act). The inclusion of harm and distress is significant as it has been held that a person, in this case a police officer, can be alarmed for the safety of another (*Lodge* v *DPP* [1989] COD 179).

The subs. (1A) offence was introduced by the Serious Organised Crime and Police Act 2005 specifically to protect employees working for certain companies from harassment by animal rights protestors. Because of the courts' strict interpretation of the elements of the s. 1 offence (as discussed above) it was unclear how far such employees could be protected by this provision when they had not previously been harassed *individually* even where fellow employees had been. Subsection (1A) makes it an offence for a person to pursue a course of conduct involving the harassment of two or more people on separate occasions which the defendant knows or ought to know involves harassment. The purpose of such harassment is to persuade *any person* (not necessarily one of the people being harassed) not to do something he/she is entitled to do—such as going to work—or to do something he/she is not under any obligation to do—such as releasing animals or passing on confidential information.

The sort of behaviour envisaged by the offence would be the making of threats and intimidation which forces an individual or individuals to stop doing lawful business with another company or with another person. The subsection is not intended to outlaw peaceful protesting or lobbying. For instance, a person simply distributing leaflets outside a shop would not commit this offence unless they threatened or intimidated the people to whom they were handing their leaflets and that person felt harassed, alarmed or distressed. There would also need to be at least two separate incidents amounting to 'a course of conduct'.

The meaning of 'course of conduct' provided in s. 7 of the Act was amended by the Serious Organised Crime and Police Act 2005 and states:

> (3) A 'course of conduct' must involve—
> (a) in the case of conduct in relation to a single person (see s. 1(1)), conduct on at least two occasions in relation to that person, or
> (b) in the case of conduct in relation to two or more people (see s. 1(1A)), conduct on at least one occasion in relation to each of those people.
>
> (3A) A person's conduct on any occasion shall be taken, if aided, abetted, counselled or procured by another—
> (a) to be conduct on that occasion of the other (as well as conduct of the person whose conduct it is); and
> (b) to be conduct in relation to which the other's knowledge and purpose, and what he ought to have known, are the same as they were in relation to what was contemplated or reasonably foreseeable at the time of the aiding, abetting, counseling or procuring.
>
> (4) 'Conduct' includes speech.
>
> (5) References to a person, in the context of the harassment of a person, are references to a person who is an individual.

KEYNOTE

As with the similarly worded offence under the Public Order Act 1986 (**see para. 4.6.7**), it appears that doing something remotely which has the desired effect on the victim—such as deliberately making a dog bark at someone—could form part of a 'course of conduct' for the purposes of an offence under the 1997 Act (see *Tafurelli* v *DPP* (2004) unreported). However, simply *failing* to stop a dog barking is a different matter and one that the Divisional Court in *Tafurelli* did not resolve.

Home Office Circular 34/2005 provides guidance on the introduction of the changes to this section and s. 1(1A). Examples of 'course of conduct' provided in the Circular include:

> Where an animal rights extremist sends a threatening letter on one occasion to an individual who works for a company and the same extremist sends a threatening email on another occasion to another individual who works for the same company, and his intention is to persuade the individuals that they should not work for that company because of the work that company does, or the contract that it has with other companies, he would commit an offence.
>
> Where an animal rights extremist send a threatening letter on one occasion to an individual who works for company A and the same extremist send a threatening email on another occasion to another individual who works for company B, and his intention is to persuade the individuals that they should not work for these companies because both companies supply company C, or he intends by his actions to persuade companies A and B not to supply company C, he would commit an offence.

In both these examples, if the letters or emails were sent by separate extremists, yet it could be proved that they were acting together, they both would be guilty of an offence. Additionally, under the new s. 3A both an individual employee or a company can apply for an injunction (**see para. 4.5.4.9**).

Not all courses of conduct will satisfy the offence of harassment. *Lau* v *DPP* [2000] Crim LR 580 involved a battery (slapping across the face) against the complainant on one occasion, followed sometime later by a threat being made to the complainant's boyfriend in her presence. The court held that the evidence of a 'course of conduct' by the defendant was insufficient to convict. It stated that regard should be had to the number of incidents and the relative times when they took place—the fewer the incidents and the further apart in time that they took place, the less likely it was that a court would find that harassment had taken place.

There are some incidents that do not amount to harassment. Where a defendant approached the victim to strike up conversations and had sent her a gift, this was insufficient to constitute harassment. However, such incidents could provide a background to later behaviour that included covertly filming the victim and rummaging through her rubbish (*King* v *DPP* [2001] ACD 7).

On occasions the courts have accepted that two instances of behaviour by the defendant several months apart will suffice. Where a defendant wrote two threatening letters to a member of the Benefits Agency staff, he was convicted of harassment even though there had been four and a half months' interval between the two letters (*Baron* v *CPS* (2000) 13 June, unreported). The opposite course of conduct was found to amount to harassment where a defendant made several calls to the victim's mobile phone in the space of five minutes. In this case the several abusive and threatening messages were left on the victim's voicemail facility and later replayed one after the other (*Kelly* v *DPP* (2002) 166 JP 621). The court held that it was enough that the victim was alarmed or distressed by the course of conduct as a whole rather than by each act making up the course of conduct. This is a different requirement from the more serious offence under s. 4 (**see para. 4.5.4.7**) where the victim must be caused to fear violence on at least two occasions. In relation to that more serious offence, a magistrates' court has been allowed to regard a defendant's conduct on the second occasion as almost retrospectively affecting previous conduct on the first occasion (**see para. 4.5.4.7**).

There is no specific requirement that the activity making up the course of conduct be of the same nature. Therefore two distinctly different types of behaviour by the defendant (e.g. making a telephone call on one occasion and damaging the victim's property on another) may suffice. In a case involving the racially or religiously aggravated offence, the aggravating element will need to be proved in relation to both instances of the defendant's conduct.

Some behaviour will be sufficiently disturbing or alarming for two instances alone to suffice' (e.g. the making of overt threats). If sufficiently alarming or distressing, the behaviour may also amount to an offence in itself under some other legislation (**see Crime, chapter 1.7**). Other behaviour, however, may not be sufficient to establish 'harassment' after only two occasions (e.g. the sending of flowers and gifts) and may require more than the bare statutory minimum of two occasions.

Although it may be helpful in terms of proving the occurrence of two or more acts amounting to 'a course of conduct', the practice in some police areas of issuing warnings and maintaining a register of the same (particularly in relation to their own officers) is not a specific requirement of the Act and may raise some issues of procedural fairness.

A limited company cannot be the 'victim' of harassment, although an individual employee or a clearly defined group of individuals could be—*DPP* v *Dziurzynski* (2002) 166 JP 545. However, in *Majrowski* v *Guy's and St Thomas's NHS Trust* [2005] QB 848, the Appeal Court held that a company could be a 'person' capable of harassing 'another' within the meaning of the Act. This ruling could therefore have implications in relation to the self-employed, customers and suppliers of businesses and members of the public in general. Where it can be shown that the conduct was carried out in the course of employment the employer could be held to be vicariously liable for that conduct.

The definition of harassment in s. 7 of the Protection from Harassment Act 1997 is an inclusive but not exhaustive list. Although the words used in s. 7 are 'alarm *and* distress', the Divisional Court has held that they should be taken disjunctively and not conjunctively, that is, the court need only be satisfied that the behaviour involved one or the other; alarm *or* distress (*DPP* v *Ramsdale* (2001) *The Independent*, 19 March).

All in all this has turned out to be a very prosecution-friendly piece of legislation extending to behaviour far beyond that which was probably envisaged by its authors.

The repeated commission of other offences (say, public order offences or offences against property) involving the same victim may also amount to harassment. In such cases the advice of the CPS should be sought as to which *charge(s) to prefer.*

In short, in order to prove the s. 1 offence you must show that:

- the defendant pursued a 'course of conduct',
- the course of conduct amounted to harassment as defined in s. 7(1), and
- the defendant knew, or ought to have known, that his/her conduct amounted to harassment.

To avoid the practical difficulties of proving the subjective *intention* of the defendant, the offence focuses on an objective test.

4.5.4.2 What a Reasonable Person Would Think Amounts to Harassment

In addition, s. 1 states:

(2) For the purposes of this section, the person whose course of conduct is in question ought to know that it amounts to or involves harassment of another if a reasonable person in possession of the same information would think the course of conduct amounted to or involved harassment of the other.

KEYNOTE

Section 1(2) requires the jury/court to consider whether the defendant ought to have known that his/her conduct amounted to or involved harassment by the objective test of what a 'reasonable person' would think. Section 1(3)(c) also imposes an objective test as to whether that conduct was reasonable in the judgment of the jury/court. As a result, the Court of Appeal has held that no characteristics of the defendant can be attached to the word 'reasonable' (*R* v *Colohan* [2001] Crim LR 845).

Although the defendant's mental illness may be relevant to sentence, the protective and preventative nature of the Act together with the objective nature of the tests above means that such illness does not provide a defence. (Contrast the relevance of a defendant's personal characteristics in the defences of duress and provocation—**see Crime, chapter 1.4**.)

4.5.4.3 Aiding and Abetting

As a result of incidents against the directors and staff of life science research companies, the Protection from Harassment Act 1997 was amended (see the Criminal Justice and Police Act 2001, s. 44). Those changes mean that if someone aids, abets, counsels or procures another to commit an offence under the 1997 Act, the conduct of the 'primary' defendant will be taken to be the conduct of the aider, abettor, counsellor or procurer of the offence. This does not prevent the primary defendant's conduct from being relevant; what it does is to make the aider, abettor, etc. of the offence liable for the conduct which he/she has facilitated. The 2001 Act also makes provision for determining the knowledge and intention of aiders, abettors, etc. Although the Act refers to this area as 'collective harassment', it overlaps with the whole concept of incomplete offences (**see Crime, chapter 1.3**) and the advice of the CPS should be sought in formulating appropriate charges.

4.5.4.4 Defences

If the person concerned in the course of conduct can show that he/she did so:

- for the purpose of preventing or detecting crime, or

- under any enactment or rule of law to comply with a particular condition or requirement, or
- in circumstances whereby the course of conduct was reasonable

the offence under s. 1(1) and (1A) will not apply (s. 1(3)).

The burden of proving any of these features or circumstances lies with the defendant (on the balance of probabilities, **see Evidence & Procedure, chapter 2.7**).

Examples might be police or DSS surveillance teams, or court officers serving summonses. (See also the defence under s. 12 below.)

Whether a course of conduct is 'reasonable' will be a question of fact for a court to decide in the light of all the circumstances. The wording of s. 1(2) suggests that such a test might be an *objective* one (i.e. as a reasonable bystander) and not one based upon the particular belief or perception of the defendant otherwise the main effect of the 1997 Act would be considerably diluted.

KEYNOTE

In *KD* v *Chief Constable of Hampshire* [2005] EWHC 2550 (QB) a police officer obtained from a female interviewee, over the course of several visits to her home, detailed explicit information about her sexual conduct. The interviewee was the mother of a complainant who had been allegedly raped and assaulted. The court held that the information obtained was not for the purpose of preventing or detecting crime under s. 1(3)(a) but to satisfy the officer's prurient interest.

4.5.4.5 Restraining Order and Injunctions

The courts have two significant sources of power available to them to deal with harassment under the 1997 Act. These are injunctions and restraining orders. Injunctions are issued in the ordinary way of any civil injunction and are governed by s. 3 (**see para. 4.5.4.9**), whereas restraining orders follow a *conviction* for an offence under ss. 2 or 4 of the Act and are governed by s. 5 (**see para. 4.5.4.11**).

4.5.4.6 Civil Claims for Harassment

Under s. 3(1) conduct or apprehended conduct falling within s. 1(1) and (1A) may be the subject of a civil claim by the victim/intended victim. This creates a 'statutory tort' of harassment in addition to the criminal offence.

4.5.4.7 Putting People in Fear of Violence

OFFENCE: **Putting people in fear of violence—*Protection from Harassment Act 1997, s. 4***

- Triable either way • Five years' imprisonment and/or a fine on indictment
- Six months' imprisonment and/or a fine summarily

OFFENCE: **Racially or religiously aggravated—*Crime and Disorder Act 1998, s. 32(1)(b)***

- Triable either way • Seven years' imprisonment and/or a fine on indictment
- Six months' imprisonment and/or a fine summarily

The Protection from Harassment Act 1997, s. 4 states:

(1) A person whose course of conduct causes another to fear, on at least two occasions, that violence will be used against him is guilty of an offence if he knows or ought to know that his course of conduct will cause the other so to fear on each of those occasions.

KEYNOTE

'Course of conduct' is discussed above.

The defendant's course of conduct must cause the victim to fear that violence *will* (rather than might) be used against him or her. This is quite a strict requirement and showing that the conduct caused the victim to be seriously frightened of what might happen in the future is not enough (*R* v *Henley* [2000] Crim LR 582).

You must show that the defendant knew, or ought to have known that their conduct would cause the other person to fear violence. This may be shown by any previous conversations or communications between the defendant and the victim, together with the victim's response to the defendant's earlier behaviour (e.g. running away, calling the police, etc.).

The fear of violence being used against the victim must be present on both occasions. If it is present on one occasion but not the other, the offence under s. 2 above may be appropriate. As with other parts of this legislation, this is not necessarily as straightforward as it may seem. What if the defendant's conduct on the first occasion (e.g. a threat to burn the victim's house down) did not cause the victim undue concern, but a second threat some time later to do the same thing *did* put the victim in fear of violence, partly because this was the second time the threat had been made? These were the circumstances in *R (On the Application of A)* v *DPP* [2004] EWHC 2454, where the defendant argued that the victim had only been put in fear of violence by his threats to burn her house down on the second occasion and that therefore the offence had not been made out. The Divisional Court disagreed and held that the magistrates were entitled to find as a matter of fact that the two incidents had put the victim in fear of violence, notwithstanding her admission that, on the first occasion, she had not been too concerned.

The course of conduct for the purpose of s. 4 has to cause a person to fear, on at least two occasions, that violence would be used against *him/her* rather than against a member of their family (*Mohammed Ali Caurti* v *DPP* [2002] Crim LR 131).

For a full explanation of the meaning of 'racially or religiously aggravated', **see para. 4.5.2.**

Unlike some of the other racially or religiously aggravated offences (**see Crime, chapters 1.7 and 1.13**), provisions are specifically made for alternative verdicts in relation to harassment (see s. 32(6)). Where the racially or religiously aggravated form of the offence is charged, the aggravating element of the defendant's conduct must be shown in relation to both instances.

As with the s. 2 offence, a single instance of behaviour may be enough to support a charge for another offence (e.g. assault, **see Crime, chapter 1.7**, or threats to kill, see below).

Again, this offence is not one of *intent* but one which is subject to a test of reasonableness against the standard of an ordinary person in possession of the same information as the defendant.

For the powers of a court to issue a restraining order or injunction in relation to this offence, see below.

For the police power to give directions in relation to the behaviour of people in the vicinity of dwellings, **see chapter 4.6.**

Section 4 goes on to state:

(2) For the purposes of this section, the person whose course of conduct is in question ought to know that it will cause another to fear that violence will be used against him on any occasion if a reasonable person in possession of the same information would think the course of conduct would cause the other so to fear on that occasion.

4.5.4.8 Defence

Section 4 states:

> (3) It is a defence for a person charged with an offence under this section to show that—
> (a) his course of conduct was pursued for the purpose of preventing or detecting crime,
> (b) his course of conduct was pursued under any enactment or rule of law or to comply with any condition or requirement imposed by any person under any enactment, or
> (c) the pursuit of his course of conduct was reasonable for the protection of himself or another or for the protection of his or another's property.

KEYNOTE

There is a slight difference in the wording of the defence when compared with that under s. 1(3) above. There, the defendant may show that his/her conduct was reasonable in the particular circumstances. In relation to the more serious offence under s. 4, the defendant must show that his/her conduct was reasonable *for the protection of themselves, another person or their own/another's property.* These are the only grounds on which the defendant may argue reasonableness in answer to a charge under s. 4. He/she could not therefore argue, say, that the pursuit of the course of conduct was 'reasonable' in order to enforce a debt or to communicate with the victim.

In addition, s. 12 allows for the Secretary of State to certify that the conduct was carried out by a 'specified person' on a 'specified occasion' related to:

- national security,
- the economic well-being of the United Kingdom, or
- the prevention or detection of serious crime

on behalf of the Crown. If such a certification is made, the conduct of the specified person will not be an offence under the 1997 Act.

4.5.4.9 Injunctions

Under ss. 3 and 3A of the Protection from Harassment Act 1997, the High Court or a county court may issue an injunction in respect of civil proceedings brought in respect of an actual or apprehended breach of s. 1(1) and (1A). The effect of this is that a defendant may be made the subject of an injunction even though his/her behaviour has not amounted to an offence under the 1997 Act.

Section 3 also states:

> (3) Where—
> (a) in such proceedings the High Court or a county court grants an injunction for the purpose of restraining the defendant from pursuing any conduct which amounts to harassment, and
> (b) the plaintiff considers that the defendant has done anything which he is prohibited from doing by the injunction,
> the plaintiff may apply for the issue of a warrant for the arrest of the defendant.

The Serious Organised Crime and Police Act 2001 introduced a new s. 3A to the 1997 Act in relation to injunctions to protect persons from harassment within s. 1(1A) (**see para. 4.5.4.1**). The person who is the victim of the course of conduct, or any person at whom the persuasion is aimed, may apply for an injunction. Therefore, where people who work for a life science or fur company are being harassed in order to persuade them not to work for that company, or in order to persuade the company not to supply another company, either the employees themselves or the company in question could apply for an injunction.

Section 3A states:

(1) This section applies where there is an actual or apprehended breach of section 1(1A) by any person ('the relevant person').

(2) In such a case—

(a) any person who is or may be a victim of the course of conduct in question, or

(b) any person who is or may be a person falling within section 1(1A)(c),

may apply to the High Court or the county court for an injunction restraining the relevant person from pursuing any conduct which amounts to harassment in relation to any person or persons mentioned or described in the injunction.

(3) Sections 3(3) to (9) apply in relation to an injunction granted under subsection (2) above as they apply in relation to an injunction granted as mentioned in section 3(3)(a).

KEYNOTE

Anyone arrested under a warrant issued under s. 3(3)(b) may be dealt with by the court at the time of his/her appearance. Alternatively, the court may adjourn the proceedings and release the defendant, dealing with him/her within 14 days of his/her arrest provided the defendant is given not less than two days' notice of the adjourned hearing (see the Rules of the Supreme Court (Amendment) 1998 (SI 1998/1898) and the County Court (Amendment) Rules 1998 (SI 1998/1899)).

This is in contrast to some other injunctions (e.g. under the Family Law Act 1996 (**see chapter 4.9**) and the Housing Act 1996 (**see chapter 4.10**)). In a case involving an injunction restraining the actions of an anti-vivisection group, the Divisional Court held that the 1997 Act was not a means of preventing individuals from exercising their right to protest over issues of public interest. Eady J said that such an extension of the law had clearly not been Parliament's intention and that the courts would resist any attempts to interpret the Act widely (*Huntingdon Life Sciences Ltd* v *Curtin* (1997) *The Times*, 11 December).

The application for an injunction is essentially a private matter being pursued by an individual (rather than a public authority as is the case with Anti-social Behaviour Orders—**see para. 4.5.5**). The point at which the matter becomes of concern to policing is where the injunction is breached without reasonable excuse (**see para. 4.5.4.10**). The civil standard of proof (balance of probabilities—**see Evidence & Procedure, chapter 2.7**) will apply to injunction applications—*Hipgrave* v *Jones* [2004] EWHC 2901.

In harassment cases the High Court can grant an interlocutory injunction under s. 37(1) of the Supreme Court Act 1981. This injunction can restrain conduct which is not in itself tortious or unlawful but is reasonably necessary to protect the legitimate interests of others. This includes the power to impose an exclusion zone when granting a non-molestation injunction (*Burris* v *Azadani* [1995] 1 WLR 1372). However in *Hall* v *Save Newchurch Guinea Pigs (Campaign)* (2005) *The Times*, 7 April, the court held that a 200 km^2 exclusion zone was not reasonably necessary for the protection of the protected person's rights.

4.5.4.10 Breach of Injuctions

Of far greater significance is the offence created by s. 3(6) of the Protection from Harassment Act 1997.

OFFENCE: **Breach of injunction—*Protection from Harassment Act 1997, s. 3(6)***

- Triable either way • Five years' imprisonment and/or a fine on indictment
- Six months' imprisonment and/or a fine summarily

The Protection from Harassment Act 1997, s. 3 goes on to state:

(6) Where—

(a) the High Court or a county court grants an injunction for the purpose mentioned in subsection (3)(a), and

(b) without reasonable excuse the defendant does anything which he is prohibited from doing by the injunction, he is guilty of an offence.

KEYNOTE

Civil injunctions generally will only involve the police where a power of an arrest has been attached (e.g. under s. 3(3) above). In these cases the role of the police will be to bring the defendant before the court in order that he/she can explain his/her behaviour. There is therefore no investigative or prosecuting function on the part of the officers. Section 3(6), however, creates a specific offence of breaching the terms of an injunction. Like the Anti-social Behaviour Order (ASBO) (see below) and Sexual Offences Prevention Order (SOPO) (**see Crime, chapter 1.9**) this marked a new concept in the criminal law.

If a defendant breaches an injunction and commits the offence under s. 3(6) above, he/she will be dealt with in the way of any other prisoner brought into police detention and will face a prison sentence of five years.

It is important to distinguish the offence under s. 3(6), breaching an injunction, from the provisions of s. 5 which deal with restraining orders.

4.5.4.11 Restraining Orders

Section 5 states:

(2) The order may, for the purpose of protecting the victim or victims of the offence, or any other person mentioned in the order, from conduct which—
(a) amounts to harassment, or
(b) will cause a fear of violence,
prohibit the defendant from doing anything described in the order.

KEYNOTE

The power to make a restraining order is, at the time of writing, restricted to a defendant who had been convicted of an offence under s. 2 or 4 of the Act; this restriction will be removed when the relevant parts of the Domestic Violence, Crime and Victims Act 2004 come into effect. In addition, a court before which a person is *acquitted* of an offence will, if it considers it necessary to do so to protect a person from harassment by the defendant, be able to make an order prohibiting the defendant from doing anything described in the order under s. 5A when in force. This will clearly amount to a considerable broadening of the scope of restraining orders.

Unlike the injunction under s. 3(3), restraining orders can be made in a criminal court.

The order may be made for the protection of the victim or anyone else mentioned and it may run for a specified period or until a further order. Any order must identify by name the parties it is intended to protect (*R* v *Mann* (2000) 97(14) LSG 41).

In a case arising out of protests against fur retailers, the Divisional Court held that restraining orders under the 1997 Act did not generally breach the right to freedom of speech and association as protected by Articles 10 and 11 of the European Convention (as to which, **see chapter 4.3**) (*Silverton* v *Gravett* (2001) LTL 31 October).

The prosecutor, the defendant or anyone else mentioned in the order may apply to the court that made it to have the order varied or discharged (s. 5(4)). The courts have the power to vary an order made for a specified period of time so as to extend the expiry date of the order (*DPP* v *Hall* (2006) 170 JP 11). In *R* v *Debnath* [2005] EWCA Crim 3472 an order prohibiting an offender from publishing information indefinitely was held to be lawful and not in breach of Article 10 (Freedom of Expression) of the European Convention on Human Rights.

Breach of a restraining order without reasonable excuse will amount to a significant criminal offence (**see para. 4.5.4.12**). A practical example of how restraining orders can operate can be seen in *R* v *Evans (Dorothy)* (2005) 169 JP 129. In that case the appellant had been convicted of harassing her neighbours and a restraining order under (s. 5(5)) had been made by the court. Among other things, the order prohibited the appellant from 'using abusive words or actions' towards her neighbours. Some time into the life of the order, the neighbour called a plumber out to their house and he parked his van in the street. It was alleged that the appellant then moved her own car—which was also parked in the street—into such a position that it effectively blocked the plumber's van. The appellant was convicted of the offence of breaching the order (see below) and appealed, partly on the basis that her conduct could not properly be said to have amounted to 'abusive action'. The Court of Appeal held that such matters should be approached in the same way as specific legislation which outlaws abusive conduct (e.g. the Public Order Act 1986—**see para. 4.6.4**) and that a jury was entitled to conclude that, as she had been motivated by spite, the appellant's actions could be 'abusive' for this purpose.

4.5.4.12 Breach of Restraining Order

OFFENCE: **Breach of restraining order—*Protection from Harassment Act 1997, s. 5(5)***

- Triable either way • Five years' imprisonment and/or a fine on indictment
- Six months' imprisonment and/or a fine summarily

The Protection from Harassment Act 1997, s. 5 states:

(5) If without reasonable excuse the defendant does anything which he is prohibited from doing by an order under this section, he is guilty of an offence.

KEYNOTE

The above offence is one of strict liability (**see Crime, chapter 1.1**) and therefore whether the defendant believed that the order was no longer in force is only relevant to the extent that he/she may have a reasonable excuse—*Barber* v *CPS* (2004) EWHC 2605 Admin. The prosecution needs simply to prove the existence and terms of the order (which it can do by an admission from the defendant in interview) and the doing of anything prohibited by it. Once that is done the offence is complete.

For an example of the practical operation and interpretation of this offence **see para. 4.5.4.11**. In the case of *R* v *Evans (Dorothy)* (2005) 169 JP 129, the Court of Appeal held that harassment takes many forms and therefore the courts need to be able to prohibit conduct in fairly wide terms (e.g. in the wording of the order). It is, however, unclear just how far the defendant's subjective understanding of the terms of the order will be relevant. If a defendant honestly believed that his/her conduct did not breach the terms of the order, this would certainly be relevant when considering whether or not he/she had a 'reasonable excuse'.

The fact that restraining orders can only be made after a conviction for one of the offences under s. 2 or 4 may affect decisions when selecting appropriate charges arising out of an incident. Substituting or failing to include a charge under s. 2 or 4, removes the court's powers to make a restraining order which may be the main remedy sought by a victim. In any cases of doubt the guidance of the CPS should be sought.

4.5.5 Anti-Social Behaviour

In aiming to create communities which are safer and which feel safer, the government introduced a form of restraint that can be imposed on the behaviour of some members of those communities—the Anti-social Behaviour Order (ASBO). (See also the remedies under the Protection from Harassment Act 1997, **para. 4.5.4**.)

A significant feature of ASBOs lies in the fact that they are civil orders, made under the procedure set out in the Magistrates' Courts Act 1980. This point was confirmed by the Court of Appeal in a case where it was held that the purpose behind ASBOs was the protection of an identified section of the community, not 'crime and punishment' and that this purpose had to be borne in mind when determining the compatibility of ASBO proceedings with the Human Rights Act 1998 (*R (On the Application of M (a child))* v *Manchester Crown Court* [2001] 1 WLR 1084). In a case involving a sex offenders order (under earlier legislation) the Divisional Court reiterated that these proceedings are *civil* in nature for the purposes of Article 6 of the European Convention (**see chapter 4.3**) (see *B* v *Chief Constable of Avon & Somerset Constabulary* [2001] 1 WLR 340. Although applications for ASBOs are civil (not criminal) in nature, the House of Lords has held that although the standard of proof in civil proceedings (the balance of probabilities) should apply to applications for ASBOs, the criminal standard of proof (beyond reasonable doubt) should apply where allegations are made which, if proved, would have serious consequences for the defendant (*R (On the Application of McCann)* v *Manchester Crown Court* [2003] 1 AC 787). For the standard of proof in civil and criminal proceedings **see Evidence & Procedure, para. 2.7.4**. It also means that the procedural requirements of Article 6(2) and (3) of the European Convention do not apply. While any proceedings have to be 'fair' in accordance with Article 6(1) and any restriction on the defendant's liberty in an order is an 'interference' with their private life (under Article 8), the whole point of such proceedings is to try and predict how far past behaviour gives reasonable cause to believe that an order is necessary under the circumstances to curb future misconduct (*Jones (Peter)* v *Greater Manchester Police Authority* [2002] ACD 4).

In *S* v *Poole Borough Council* [2002] EWHC 244, a juvenile, who was the subject of an ASBO application, had already been convicted of several offences under the Education Act 1996. He objected to the same material being used from his criminal trial to support the application for an ASBO, arguing that the use of the ASBO had been intended as an alternative to criminal prosecution. Hearing the appeal by way of case stated, the Divisional Court held that it was 'perfectly proper' to use the same material in this way and that the ASBO is akin to an injunction.

One of the benefits of an ASBO lies in its potential effect as a deterrent to others. This benefit will only be realised if there is sufficient publicity given to the issuing of the order and the circumstances of it. The extent to which the police (and local authorities) can use such publicity and include a photograph of the person made the subject of an ASBO, was clarified by the Divisional Court in *R (On the Application of Stanley)* v *Metropolitan Police Commissioner, Brent London Borough and the Secretary of State for the Home Department* [2005] EMLR 3. In that case ASBOs had been made against a number of youths, all of whom had previous convictions. The local authority posted details of the proceedings on its website, there was extensive press coverage of the case, and the police approved publication of leaflets bearing photographs of the youths which were distributed in the area specified in the ASBOs. The youths challenged the decisions to publish their ASBOs in this way. The Divisional Court held that ASBOs required publicity in order to be effective as a civil remedy. If publicity intended to reassure members of the community, to inform, to assist in reinforcement and to deter others, was to be effective, it needed photographs, names and at least parts of addresses. The court found that people living in the community had been subjected to significant criminal behaviour for several years and, as the ASBOs had been obtained to bring that behaviour to an end, the material publicising it could say so. Although the court accepted that it was always necessary to consider the Human Rights Act issues in the area of post-ASBO publicity, it held that there was a need here for readers to know the identities of the people against whom the orders had been made—if only to avoid misidentification—and even the 'colourful language' used in the publicity material might be necessary in order to attract the attention of readers. This decision does *not* mean that so-called 'name and shame' campaigns will be lawful—rather it means that those behind the publicising of the ASBO (or part of it) must be able to show a link between the publicity and the practical effectiveness of the ASBO.

4.5.5.1 The Anti-social Behaviour Order (ASBO)

The Anti-social Behaviour Order (ASBO) is a central feature of the government's community safety strategy. Some 50 areas across England and Wales have been designated 'TOGETHER Action Areas' which, among other things, will receive extra help in tackling wider anti-social behaviour.

The Crime and Disorder Act 1998, s. 1 states:

(1) An application for an order under this section may be made by a relevant authority if it appears to the authority that the following conditions are fulfilled with respect to any person aged 10 or over, namely—
- (a) that the person has acted, since the commencement date, in an anti-social manner, that is to say, in a manner that caused or was likely to cause harassment, alarm or distress to one or more persons not of the same household as himself; and
- (b) that such an order is necessary to protect relevant persons from further anti-social acts by him.

...

(1A) In this section and sections 1B, 1CA, 1E and 1F 'relevant authority' means—
- (a) the council for a local government area;
- (aa) in relation to England, a county council;
- (b) the chief officer of police of any police force maintained for a police area;
- (c) the chief constable of the British Transport Police Force;
- (d) any person registered under section 1 of the Housing Act 1996 (c 52) as a social landlord who provides or manages any houses or hostel in a local government area; or
- (e) a housing action trust established by order in pursuance of section 62 of the Housing Act 1988.

(1B) In this section 'relevant persons' means—
- (a) in relation to a relevant authority falling within paragraph (a) of subsection (1A), persons within the local government area of that council;
- (aa) in relation to a relevant authority falling within paragraph (aa) of subsection (1A) persons within the county of the county council;
- (b) in relation to a relevant authority falling within paragraph (b) of that subsection, persons within the police area;
- (c) in relation to a relevant authority falling within paragraph (c) of that subsection—
  - (i) persons who are within or likely to be within a place specified in section 31(1)(a) to (f) of the Railways and Transport Safety Act 2003 in a local government area; or
  - (ii) persons who are within or likely to be within such a place;
- (d) in relation to a relevant authority falling within paragraph (d) or (e) of that subsection—
  - (i) persons who are residing in or who are otherwise on or likely to be on premises provided or managed by that authority; or
  - (ii) persons who are in the vicinity of or likely to be in the vicinity of such premises

(2) ...

(3) Such an application shall be made by complaint to a magistrates' court.

(4) If, on such an application, it is proved that the conditions mentioned in subsection (1) above are fulfilled, the magistrates' court may make an order under this section (an 'anti-social behaviour order') which prohibits the defendant from doing anything described in the order.

The Crime and Disorder Act 1998, s. 1A states:

(2) The Secretary of State may by order—
  (a) provide that a person or body of any other description specified in the order is, in such cases and circumstances as may be prescribed by the order, to be a relevant authority for the purposes of such of sections 1 above and 1B, 1CA, 1E and 1F below as are specified in the order; and
  (b) prescribe the description of persons who are to be 'relevant persons' in relation to that person or body.

KEYNOTE

Although ASBOs are prohibitory in their nature (in that they order people *not* to do certain things rather than to do certain things), the purpose of the prohibition is not to punish but to prevent anti-social behaviour and to protect members of the public from further instances of it. Therefore, there is nothing legally wrong with including a curfew provision in an ASBO if it is necessary for such protection (*Lonergan* v *Lewes Crown Court* [2005] EWHC 457).

In order to apply for an ASBO it must appear to the relevant authority that:

- a relevant person acted in a manner that caused, or was likely to cause harassment, alarm or distress to one or more people who are not of the same household as the relevant person, and
- that such an order is necessary to protect people from further anti-social acts by that person. The 'relevant authority' for the purposes of an ASBO is the local authority or the chief officer of police, any part of whose police area lies within the area of that local authority. However, the chief constable of the British Transport Police may also apply for an ASBO to protect people from anti-social behaviour within the force's jurisdiction and 'registered social landlords' (under the Housing Act 1996, s. 1) may apply for orders in relation to such behaviour on or in the vicinity of premises owned by them. The Secretary of State may also add to this list of relevant authorities (see s. 1A).

However, the person against whom an application for an order is being considered has no legal right to be consulted (*Wareham* v *Purbeck District Council* (2005) *The Times*, 28 March).

A general requirement for local authorities and chief officers to consult before applying for an ASBO is imposed by s. 1E, meaning that, in practice, both of these sources of authority will have to work together in bringing any application for an ASBO. Applications by other relevant authorities must be made in consultation with the local chief officer and the local council in the area in which the person lives or appears to live. This imposition of multiple responsibility, which effectively enforces a collaborative approach between the police and local authorities, is another key feature of the 1998 Act (see also ss. 5 and 6, chapter 4.1).

It would seem that chief constables can delegate or devolve the functions set out in s. 1(1) and (2) of the Act to any officer(s) judged suitable by them—*R (On the Application of Chief Constable of West Midlands Police)* v *Birmingham Magistrates' Court* [2003] Crim LR 37. Under s. 1F, inserted by the Serious Organised Crime and Police Act 2005, local authorities can make arrangements for the contracting out of their ASBO functions subject to the relevant order made by the Secretary of State.

The Drugs Act 2005 inserted ss. 1G and 1H into the 1998 Act and these relate to intervention orders. This type of order can be made alongside an ASBO when drug misuse has been a cause of the behaviour that led to the ASBO being made. An intervention order sets out the specified activities and attendance requirements of a defendant, and the duration of the order cannot exceed six months (s. 1G). The breach of an order is a summary offence (s. 1H).

For these purposes, the relevant local government areas are:

- in relation to England, a district or London borough, the City of London, the Isle of Wight and the Isles of Scilly;
- in relation to Wales, a county or county borough (s. 1(12)).

In these circumstances it is the relevant authority who makes the application for an ASBO, thereby removing from the 'victim' of the conduct the burden of seeking a remedy themselves (contrast this with the remedy using an injunction in cases of harassment; **see para. 4.5.4.9**).

The proviso at s. 1(1)(a)—which excludes people from the same household—shows that the ASBO is not intended as a remedy for domestic disputes (as to which, **see chapter 4.9**).

Chief constables can delegate or devolve the functions set out in s. 1(1) and (2) of the Act to any officer(s) judged suitable by them—*R (On the Application of Chief Constable of West Midlands Police)* v *Birmingham Magistrates' Court* [2003] Crim LR 37.

An application may be made in respect of the behaviour of any person aged 10 or over. This is another significant departure from the earlier law and, together with the abolition of the presumption of *doli incapax* (**see Crime, chapter 1.4**), is consistent with the government's expressed intention to impose criminal responsibility on older children.

Local councils and chief officers may now make applications to protect people in their respective areas whether or not the original anti-social behaviour occurred in that area or elsewhere.

Criminal courts can also make an ASBO in respect of a defendant where he or she has been convicted of an offence (s. 1C). The court can make such an order of its own volition, irrespective of whether any specific application has been made but it can only be made *in addition* to any sentence or conditional discharge (s. 1C(4)). This illustrates that the order is, as under the other methods of application, a preventive measure rather than a punishment. If the defendant is detained in legal custody (e.g. given a custodial sentence or remanded into police custody), the order may be suspended until he/she is released (see s. 1C(5)).

Criminal courts can also make an ASBO in respect of a defendant where he or she has been convicted of an offence (s. 1C). However, in *R (On the Application of Mills)* v *Birmingham Magistrates' Court* [2005] EWHC 2732 it was held that cases of theft, including shoplifting, would not automatically fall within the criteria of s. 1. However, there may be circumstances where some thefts or acts of shoplifting could cause harassment, alarm or distress and so fall within this section.

The court may adjourn any proceedings in relation to an order under this section even after sentencing the offender (s. 1C(4A)). If the offender does not appear for any adjourned proceedings, the court may further adjourn the proceedings, or it may issue a warrant for his/her arrest but not unless it is satisfied that he/she has had adequate notice of the time and place of the adjourned proceedings (s. 1C(4B) and (4C)).

Under s. 1CA a relevant authority or the CPS can apply to vary or discharge an Anti-Social Behaviour Order made on conviction. No s. 1C order will be discharged before two years have passed since the date of the order without the consent of the defendant and the DPP (s. 1CA(7)).

4.5.5.2 ASBOs and Exclusion Orders in Court Proceedings

Section 1B of the Crime and Disorder Act 1998 allows relevant authorities to apply to a county court where they are, or have become, a party to the proceedings and similar conditions apply to such orders as those made by magistrates' courts.

In relation to criminal courts, s. 40A of the Powers of Criminal Courts (Sentencing) Act 2000 allows a court, on convicting a person, to make an exclusion order which can prevent the person from entering a specified area for a period of not more than three months. Such orders, which can be for a total period of time or for certain days (e.g. weekends) are quite flexible and, although not ASBOs, can be used for preventing anti-social behaviour.

Section 40A states:

> Where a person [aged under 16] is convicted of an offence, the court by or before which he is convicted may (subject to [sections 148, 150 and 156 of the Criminal Justice Act 2003]) make an order prohibiting him from entering a place specified in the order for a period so specified of not more than three months.

4.5.5.3 Interim Orders

Either the magistrates' or the county court may make an interim ASBO under the provisions of s. 1D if it considers that it is just to do so. Courts have the power to grant an interim order in relation to an application for an order under s. 1 or 1B (**see para. 4.5.5.2**) or a request under s. 1C (**see para. 4.5.5.1**) pending a full hearing. Interim orders can be made in this way pending the determination of the main application and any such order must be for a fixed period; it can be varied, renewed or discharged and ceases to have effect once the main application has been determined (e.g. once a full ASBO has been made or the application refused (s. 1D(4)).

Section 1(5) states:

> For the purpose of determining whether the condition mentioned in subsection (1)(a) above is fulfilled, the court shall disregard any act of the defendant which he shows was reasonable in the circumstances.

Section 1(6) states:

> The prohibitions that may be imposed by an anti-social behaviour order are those necessary for the purpose of protecting persons (whether relevant persons or persons elsewhere in England and Wales) from further anti-social acts by the defendant.

KEYNOTE

This requirement clearly places the burden of showing the reasonableness of his/her behaviour on the defendant.

4.5.5.4 Power to Direct a Person to Leave a Place

The Serious Organised Crime and Police Act 2005, s. 112 states:

> (1) A constable may direct a person to leave a place if he believes, on reasonable grounds, that the person is in the place at a time when he would be prohibited from entering it by virtue of—
> (a) an order to which subsection (2) applies, or
> (b) a condition to which subsection (3) applies.
> (2) This subsection applies to an order which—
> (a) was made, by virtue of any enactment, following the person's conviction of an offence, and
> (b) prohibits the person from entering the place or from doing so during a period specified in the order.
> (3) This subsection applies to a condition which—
> (a) was imposed, by virtue of any enactment, as a condition of the person's release from a prison in which he was serving a sentence of imprisonment following his conviction for an offence, and
> (b) prohibits the person from entering the place or from doing so during a period specified in the condition.
> (4) A direction under this section may be given orally.

KEYNOTE

Prior to the introduction of this section the police could only ask an offender in breach of an exclusion order to leave the area and had no power of arrest if he/she refused. However, s. 112 provides the police with a new power to direct a person to leave an exclusion area if they reasonably believe that the person is prohibited from entering the area. In knowingly failing to obey that direction the person commits a new offence of contravening a direction to leave a place (**see para. 4.5.5.5**).

The power only applies to a breach of those exclusion orders imposed as part of an:

- Exclusion order (s. 112(1)).
- Community sentence.
- Suspended sentence.
- Licence condition on release from custody (s. 112(3)).

Exclusion imposed as part of a civil order, such as an Anti-social Behaviour Order or a restraining order, are not included.

Notification of a breach of an exclusion requirement may be made by a person who is aware the offender is in breach of his or her exclusion requirements or by electronic monitoring. Pilot schemes testing the use of satellite tracking technology are currently being conducted by three forces in England.

Home Office Circular 29/2005 explains the new power under this section.

4.5.5.5 Contravening a Direction to Leave a Place

OFFENCE: **Contravening a direction to leave a place—*Serious Organised Crime and Police Act 2005, s. 112(5)***

- Triable summarily • 51 weeks' imprisonment or a fine

The Serious Organised Crime and Police Act 2005, s. 112 states:

(5) Any person who knowingly contravenes a direction given to him under this section is guilty of an offence.

4.5.5.6 Duration of Anti-social Behaviour Order

An ASBO has a minimum period of two years' duration (s. 1(7)). Although an ASBO has to run for a minimum of two years, it does not follow that every prohibition within the order must endure for the life of the order. In many cases it is possible that a period of curfew could properly be set at less than the full life of the order or, in light of behavioural progress, an application to vary the curfew could be made under s. 1(8) of the 1998 Act (*Lonergan* v *Lewes Crown Court* [2005] EWHC 457).

For the duration of interim orders **see para. 4.5.5.3.**

Under s. 1(8) of the 1998 Act, either the applicant or the defendant may apply to have the order varied or discharged but, under s. 1(9), no ASBO shall be discharged before the end of two years except with the consent of both parties.

4.5.5.7 Breach of an Anti-social Behaviour Order

OFFENCE: **Breaching an Anti-social Behaviour Order—*Crime and Disorder Act 1998, s. 1(10)***

- Triable either way • Five years' imprisonment and/or a fine on indictment
- Six months' imprisonment and/or a fine summarily

The Crime and Disorder Act 1998, s. 1 states:

(10) If without reasonable excuse a person does anything which he is prohibited from doing by an anti-social behaviour order, he is guilty of an offence and liable—
  (a) on summary conviction, to imprisonment for a term not exceeding six months or to a fine not exceeding the statutory maximum, or to both; or
  (b) on conviction on indictment, to imprisonment for a term not exceeding five years or to a fine, or to both.

KEYNOTE

The above offence applies to all ASBOs including interim orders and those made by the county court.

In proceedings for an offence under subs. (10), a copy of the original ASBO, certified as such by the proper officer of the court which made it, is admissible as evidence of its having been made and of its contents to the same extent that oral evidence of those things is admissible in those proceedings (s. 1(10C)).

As the punishment provided by a conditional discharge (under the Powers of Criminal Courts (Sentencing) Act 2000) has the same general effect as an ASBO, a court cannot impose a conditional discharge on a defendant found guilty of committing an offence under s. 1(10) above (s. 1(11)).

Given the breadth of an ASBO, which may restrain a defendant from communicating with a particular person or from creating noise or nuisance, the behaviour required to commit this offence could be relatively minor. The advice of the CPS may need to be sought in cases involving what appear to be innocuous but technical breaches of such an order.

It appears from the wording of the 1998 Act that a person might have an ASBO made against him/her in his/her absence. Although a magistrates' court has the power to issue a summons and then a warrant (under the Magistrates' Courts Act 1980) in order to compel the person to come to court when an application for an ASBO is being heard, it does seem that the court can go on to make an ASBO *ex parte* (in the absence of the other party). Again, if this is the case, there are serious human rights implications which may allow the procedure to be challenged.

Councils that are relevant authorities, along with councils for the local government area in which a person in respect of whom an ASBO has been made resides, can also bring proceedings for an offence under the above section (s. 1(10A)).

The Serious Organised Crime and Police Act 2005 amended the 1998 Act in relation to reporting restrictions for a child or young person convicted of breaching an ASBO. This amendment disapplied reporting restrictions under s. 49 of the Children and Young Persons Act 1933 and s. 45 of the Youth Justice and Criminal Evidence Act 1999. However, courts still retain the discretion to apply reporting restrictions (see s. 1(10D) and (10E)).

4.5.5.8 Appeal

The Crime and Disorder Act 1998, s. 4 states:

(1) An appeal shall lie to the Crown Court against the making by a magistrates' court of an anti-social behaviour order, an individual support order, an order under section 1D above,...
(2) On such an appeal the Crown Court—
  (a) may make such orders as may be necessary to give effect to its determination of the appeal; and
  (b) may also make such incidental or consequential orders as appear to it to be just.

KEYNOTE

The right of appeal process above applies to both full ASBOs and interim orders made by a magistrates' court; it does not apply to ASBOs made by the county court in civil proceedings under s. 1B.

There is no right of appeal open to the local authority or chief officer against a decision of a court not to make an order. That would not preclude the applicant from requiring the court to 'state a case' for consideration by the Divisional Court in appropriate circumstances.

4.5.5.9 People Acting in an Anti-social Manner

In addition to the ASBO system above, the police have other specific powers to deal with anti-social behaviour. If a constable in uniform has reason to believe that a person has been, or is, acting in an anti-social manner (within the meaning of s. 1 of the Crime and Disorder Act 1998—**see para. 4.5.5.1**), the constable may require the person to give their name and address (Police Reform Act 2002, s. 50). This power is among those that can be conferred on a Community Support Officer designated under sch. 4 to the Police Reform Act 2002 and a person accredited under sch. 5 to that Act (**see chapter 4.2**).

Where motor vehicles are involved, there are further specific powers to stop the vehicle and to seize it (**see Road Policing**).

Note that s. 91 of the Anti-social Behaviour Act 2003 allows a local authority to request a power of arrest to be attached to any provision of an injunction obtained under s. 222 of the Local Government Act 1972 where the injunction is to prohibit anti-social behaviour. The Police and Justice Act repealed s. 91 but the replacement provision still includes the power to attach a power of arrest. However, changes will be made as to the procedure following such an arrest.

OFFENCE: **Failing to comply with requirement to give name and address—*Police Reform Act 2002, s. 50(2)***

- Triable summarily • Fine

The Police Reform Act 2002, s. 50 states:

(2) Any person who—
 (a) fails to give his name and address when required to do so under subsection (1), or
 (b) gives a false or inaccurate name or address in response to a requirement under that subsection, is guilty of an offence ...

KEYNOTE

This provision creates a specific offence of failing to give a name and address under the circumstances outlined. There is no specific statutory power of arrest accompanying this offence but the arrest provisions contained in s. 24 of the Police and Criminal Evidence Act 1984 may always be considered.

The wording of the offence suggests that it will be complete if either the name *or* address given is false or inaccurate, not both. As with all such powers, you will need to show that the person both heard and understood the requirement—and that you both heard and noted the response. Just how 'inaccurate' the details given would need to be before the offence is committed remains to be seen.

4.5.6 Nuisance and the Environment

There are many forms of behaviour which, although not falling within some of the more 'serious' offences discussed elsewhere in this Manual, are nevertheless a source of annoyance or disquiet to the community. Some of these activities are usefully classified as 'nuisances', while others come under 'environmental' legislation. What follows is a brief summary of some of the main areas covered by both types of legislation.

4.5.6.1 Public Nuisance

Although many of the activities dealt with in this chapter are described as 'nuisances', there is a specific offence of creating or being responsible for a public nuisance, an offence that overlaps with some other aspects of criminal behaviour.

The common law concept of nuisance is separated into public and private nuisance. Private nuisance is dealt with under civil law as a *tort* ('wrong'). Public nuisance, however, can also be dealt with under criminal law.

A public nuisance is an unlawful act or an omission to discharge a duty which, in either case, obstructs or causes inconvenience or damage to the public in the exercise of their common rights (see *Attorney-General* v *PYA Quarries Ltd (No. 1)* [1957] 2 QB 169).

Although there is no 'magic number' of people who must suffer from the annoyance or obstruction in order for it to amount to a *public nuisance*, you must show that the act or omission affected the public in general as opposed to a small group of people (such as the employees of a firm). Therefore, in *R* v *Madden* [1975] 1 WLR 1379, where a person made a hoax bomb call to an organisation (**see paras 4.5.7.1 to 4.5.7.2**), it was held that such behaviour could in theory amount to a public nuisance, although in *Madden* it did not as the annoyance/obstruction was limited in its effect.

People who entered school premises for the purpose of glue sniffing were held to have committed a public nuisance by unduly interfering with the comfortable and convenient enjoyment of the land, even though the school was empty (*Sykes* v *Holmes* [1985] Crim LR 791). (For offences and powers in relation to educational premises specifically, **see chapter 4.10.**)

Given that the courts have unlimited sentencing power in relation to this offence, there may well be advantages in considering its application to cases where the only other offences disclosed would be summary offences. An example is the case of *R* v *Johnson* [1997] 1 WLR 367 where the defendant made several hundred obscene telephone calls to women across a county over a period of five years.

4.5.6.2 Offence of Public Nuisance

OFFENCE: **Public nuisance—*Common Law***

• Triable either way • Unlimited powers of sentence on indictment • Statutory maxima apply summarily

It is an offence at common law for a person to cause a public nuisance.

KEYNOTE

As this offence is a common law 'misdemeanour', a court may pass sentence at its discretion on indictment, that is, its sentencing powers are unlimited.

Although the typical and obvious causes of public nuisance are now the subject of express statutory prohibition, the common law offence still exists and is not in breach of Article 7 (No Punishment without Crime) of the European Convention on Human Rights (*R* v *Rimmington; R* v *Goldstein* [2005] 3 WLR 982).

The behaviour of the defendant must interfere with the material rights enjoyed by a class of Her Majesty's subjects (*R* v *Johnson* [1997] 1 WLR 367).

It is not necessary to prove that every member within a class of people in the community has been affected by the defendant's behaviour; simply that a representative cross-section has been so affected (*Attorney-General* v *PYA Quarries Ltd (No. 2)* [1961] 2 QB 169). Such a cross-section might include members of a housing estate or users of a public transport facility such as a main-line railway station.

In Lord Denning's view (also in the *PYA* case), a nuisance would need to be 'so widespread in its range or so indiscriminate in its effect' that it would not be reasonable to expect one person to bring proceedings on his/her own to put a stop to it.

There is no need to show that the defendant intended his/her actions or omission to cause a public nuisance and, as with the offence of harassment (**see para. 4.5.4**) it will be enough that he/she knew or ought to have known that the conduct would bring about a public nuisance (*R* v *Shorrock* [1994] QB 279).

A good practical example of how the law of public nuisance can be used in a policing context can be seen in *R* v *Harvey* [2003] EWCA Crim 112. In that case the defendant was convicted of causing a public nuisance after following different groups of children in his car, sounding the horn and smiling at them. Evidence was adduced to show that he presented a real threat to children with the possibility of his luring them into his car for unlawful purposes. Although the defendant was originally sentenced to life imprisonment, that was later reduced in the absence of features of sex or violence, to three years.

Other examples of criminal public nuisances have included:

- Allowing a rave to take place in a field (*R* v *Shorrock* [1994] QB 279).
- Making hundreds of nuisance telephone calls to at least 13 women (*R* v *Johnson* [1997] 1 WLR 367).
- Contaminating 30 houses with dust and noise from a quarry (*Attorney-General* v *PYA Quarries Ltd (No. 2)* [1961] 2 QB 169).
- Selling meat which was unfit for consumption (*R* v *Stephens* (1866) LR 1 QB 702).

In addition, the Environmental Protection Act 1990, s. 79 sets out a list of 'statutory nuisances', any of which would potentially be capable of amounting to a criminal offence if it met the relevant conditions.

4.5.6.3 Defence

Statutory authorisation for a person's conduct (e.g. building a road or a railway), will be a defence provided the behaviour is specifically permitted by that statute (*Hammersmith and City Railway Co.* v *Brand and Louisa* (1868) 4 QB 171, 34 JP 36).

4.5.6.4 Enforcement

In addition to providing powers of arrest and sentencing for tackling public nuisance through the criminal process, there is always the preventive measure of a court injunction available. Historically, the Attorney-General has sought injunctions on behalf of the public at large. However, local authorities have the power to apply for a public nuisance injunction under the Local Government Act 1972 (see *Stoke-on-Trent City Council* v *B & Q (Retail) Ltd* [1984] AC 754) and there appears to be no reason why chief officers should not do the same.

4.5.6.5 Fireworks

The former legislation regulating fireworks has been updated, mainly for practical reasons. The powers of the Secretary of State to make regulations under previous legislation (namely the Consumer Protection Act 1987) were limited to the supply of fireworks rather than the *use* to which they were put. At the same time, some of the other available legislation dealt with gunpowder and explosives and dated back to the nineteenth century.

The Fireworks Act 2003 regulates the sale and use of fireworks under certain circumstances and makes provision for further regulations by the Secretary of State. The principal regulations in this regard are the Fireworks Regulations 2004 (SI 2004/1836). The relevant aspects of this legislation affecting practical policing are summarised below.

4.5.6.6 Controls on Supplying Fireworks

Sections 2 and 3 of the Fireworks Act 2003 allow for regulations to ensure that there is no risk that the use of fireworks will lead to death, injury, or distress to people and animals or the destruction of, or damage to, property.

Generally 'fireworks' mean fireworks for the purposes of the British Standard Specification published on 30 November 1988 (BS 7114) or any British Standard Specification replacing it. The regulations go on to categorise specific types of firework according to the danger they present. These range from caps and party poppers to the elaborate pyrotechnic devices as used in public displays.

4.5.6.7 Possession of Fireworks

OFFENCE: **Possession of fireworks—*Fireworks Regulations 2004, regs 4 and 5***
- Triable Summarily • Six months' imprisonment and/or a fine

Regulations 4 and 5 state:

> **4.**—(1) Subject to regulation 6 below, no person under the age of eighteen years shall possess an adult firework in a public place.
>
> ...
>
> **5.** Subject to regulation 6 below, no person shall possess a category 4 firework.

KEYNOTE

The first offence prevents people under 18 from possessing an adult firework in a public place, while the second prohibits the possession of any category 4 firework generally. 'Public place' has the usual meaning of any place to which at the material time the public have or are permitted access, whether on payment or otherwise (reg. 3(2)). An 'adult firework' is broadly any firework which does not comply with the relevant requirements of Part 2 of BS 7114 (except for a cap, cracker snap, novelty match, party popper, serpent, sparkler or throwdown). A category 4 firework is one specified as such in BS 7114.

The exemptions in reg. 6 generally cover people who have such fireworks in the course of their work or business or who are properly authorised to conduct displays.

Note the specific offence of possessing fireworks during the period of designated sporting events (see para. 4.6.13.11).

Fireworks, as defined in s. 1(1) of the Fireworks Act 2003 and in the Regulations, are 'prohibited articles' for the purposes of s. 1 of the Police and Criminal Evidence Act 1984 (general stop and search powers, see para. 4.4.4.4).

When enacted, the Fireworks (Amendment) Bill will extend the types of fireworks that are prohibited under the Regulations. The Bill concentrates on category 3 fireworks which are specified as those that are excessively loud. The relevant prohibitions imposed by regs 5, 7 and 8 will be either modified or extended to include category 3 fireworks.

4.5.6.8 Prohibition of Use of Certain Fireworks at Night

Regulation 7 states:

(1) Subject to paragraph (2) below, no person shall use an adult firework during night hours.

KEYNOTE

For the general definition of an 'adult firework' **see para. 4.5.6.7.**

'Night hours' are the period beginning at 11 pm and ending at 7 am the following day (reg. 7(3)).

The exception referred to in reg. 7(2) deals with three main types of firework display, namely a 'permitted fireworks night', a firework display by a local authority, and a national public celebration or a national commemorative event.

Taking the first exception, the above restriction on using adult fireworks will not apply to use during permitted fireworks nights—an exception that has been built into the legislation to take account of the various festivals and celebrations that traditionally involve fireworks. The expression 'permitted fireworks night' means a period:

- beginning at 11 pm on the first day of the Chinese New Year and ending at 1 am the following day;
- beginning at 11 pm and ending at midnight on 5 November;
- beginning at 11 pm on the day of Diwali and ending at 1 am the following day; or
- beginning at 11 pm on 31 December and ending at 1 am the following day (see reg. 7(3)).

The other two exceptions—a firework display by a local authority or a national public celebration/commemorative event—*only* apply to a person who is employed by a local authority.

As with the regulations governing possession (**see para. 4.5.6.7**), breach of this regulation will be an offence under s. 11 of the 2003 Act (**see para. 4.5.6.10**).

4.5.6.9 Other Fireworks Regulations

Sections 4 and 5 of the Act allow for regulations to prohibit the supply of fireworks in certain circumstances or the supply of certain types of firework (such as excessively loud fireworks which are defined and regulated by reg. 8 of the 2004 Regulations). In addition, reg. 9 imposes a general requirement for anyone supplying adult fireworks (or exposing them for supply) to be licensed. However, this requirement does *not* apply:

- on the first day of the Chinese New Year or on the day of Diwali and the three days immediately preceding it;
- during the period beginning on 15 October and ending on 10 November; or
- during the period beginning on 26 December and ending on 31 December.

These exemptions are designed to work in conjunction with 'permitted fireworks nights' (**see para. 4.5.6.8**).

'Supplying' includes selling, exchanging and giving fireworks (even as prizes) but does not include supplying otherwise than in the course of business (see s. 1(3)). People licensed by the local authority to supply adult fireworks have to comply with certain conditions.

Where the supply or exposure for supply takes place on premises, the person must display in a prominent position a notice of the prescribed size stating that it is illegal to sell adult fireworks to anyone under the age of 18 and that it is illegal for anyone under the age of 18 to possess adult fireworks in a public place (reg. 10). There are also further requirements under reg. 10 for suppliers to provide full details as to their own suppliers and customers in cases of larger transactions of *any* fireworks (not just adult fireworks) and an absolute restriction on importing *any* fireworks unless certain information has been given to the Commissioners of Customs and Excise (see reg. 11).

The Act goes on to make provision for the regulation of public fireworks displays, the requirement of suppliers to attend training courses, the licensing of suppliers and the provision of information about fireworks generally.

4.5.6.10 Breach of Fireworks Regulations

OFFENCE: **Breach of regulations—*Fireworks Act 2003, s. 11***

- Triable summarily • Six months' imprisonment and/or a fine

The Fireworks Act 2003, s. 11 states:

(1) Any person who contravenes a prohibition imposed by fireworks regulations is guilty of an offence.
(2) Any person who fails to comply with a requirement imposed by or under fireworks regulations to give or not to give information is guilty of an offence.
(3) Where a requirement to give information is imposed by or under fireworks regulations, a person is guilty of an offence if, in giving the information, he—
(a) makes a statement which he knows is false in a material particular; or
(b) recklessly makes a statement which is false in a material particular.

KEYNOTE

There is some overlap between regulations made under the Consumer Protection Act 1987 and this offence and both pieces of legislation should be checked.

In particular, the general defence of due diligence (under s. 39 of that Act) will apply to offences at (1) and (2) above.

The regulations are amended regularly and reference should be made to the latest version when considering the enforcement of their provisions. Many of the regulations are concerned with the way in which fireworks are advertised, displayed and sold.

In relation to the supply of, offer or agreement to supply fireworks to a child or young person, s. 11(8) creates a defence for the defendant to show that he/she had no reason to suspect that the person was under the relevant age.

The sections of the Consumer Protection Act 1987 allowing for enforcement measures such as test purchases and powers of search, generally apply to the above offences.

The power to stop and search for prohibited fireworks is included in s. 1 of the Police and Criminal Evidence Act 1984 (see para. 4.4.4.4).

OFFENCE: **Throwing fireworks into highway or street—*Explosives Act 1875, s. 80***

- Triable summarily • Fine

The Explosives Act 1875, s. 80 states:

If any person throw, cast, or fire any fireworks in or into any highway, street, thoroughfare, or public place, he [shall be guilty of an offence and liable...

> **KEYNOTE**
>
> This offence is a 'penalty offence' for the purposes of s. 1 of the Criminal Justice and Police Act 2001 (see para. 4.4.3).
>
> For other offences involving explosives, see para. 4.6.14.8.

4.5.6.11 Noise

The creation of noise is another environmental issue that can severely affect quality of life in the community. As a result, there are several statutory provisions allowing the relevant agencies to address problems associated with noise and its sources.

Under the Anti-social Behaviour Act 2003 the chief executive of a relevant local authority can apply to a court for an order to close licensed premises in certain circumstances involving noise (**see chapter 4.10**).

In addition to the above legislation, the Noise Act 1996 provides powers to allow local authorities to tackle the problems of noise within their community. For instance, ss. 2 and 3 of the 1996 Act allow for the serving of warning notices in relation to 'excessive noise' emanating from one house which can be heard in another at night. Night is defined as being between 11 pm and 7 am (s. 2(6)). The Clean Neighbourhoods and Environment Act 2005 has extended s. 2 to include noise emitted from any premises in respect of which a premises licence (Licensing Act 2003—**see para. 4.11.4.1**), or a temporary event notice (Licensing Act 2003—**see para. 4.11.6.1**) has been issued, that can be heard in a dwelling (s. 2(2)(b) of the 1996 Act). The noise level must be measured using an 'approved device' (s. 6). Any warning must be served on the person who appears to be responsible for the noise or by leaving the warning notice at the 'offending premises' (s. 3(3)). (Note that, under the Environmental Protection Act 1990 there is no requirement for evidence of acoustic measurements and a court may convict on other evidence (e.g. evidence from an environmental enforcement officer of excessively loud music being played—*Lewisham Borough Council* v *Hall* [2003] Env LR 4).)

OFFENCE: **Where noise from a dwelling exceeds permitted level after service of notices—*Noise Act 1996, s. 4(1)***

- Triable summarily • Fine

The Noise Act 1996, s. 4 states:

> (1) If a warning notice has been served in respect of noise emitted from a dwelling, any person who is responsible for noise which—
> (a) is emitted from the dwelling in the period specified in the notice, and
> (b) exceeds the permitted level, as measured from within the complainant's dwelling,
> is guilty of an offence.
>
> (2) It is a defence for a person charged with an offence under this section to show that there was a reasonable excuse for the act, default or sufferance in question.

OFFENCE: **Where noise from other premises exceeds permitted level after service of notice—*Noise Act 1996, s. 4A(1)***

- Triable summarily • Fine

The Noise Act 1996, s. 4A states:

> (1) If—
> (a) a warning notice has been served under section 3 in respect of noise emitted from premises,
> (b) noise is emitted from the premises in the period specified in the notice, and

(c) the noise exceeds the permitted level, as measured from within the complainant's dwelling, the person responsible in relation to the offending premises at the time at which the noise referred to in paragraph (c) is emitted is guilty of an offence.

KEYNOTE

The 'permitted level' may be set or varied under regulations made by the Secretary of State (s. 5).

Sections 8 and 9 provide for the local authority to implement a 'fixed penalty procedure' whereby liability to prosecution under s. 4 above can be avoided by paying the fee (currently £100) within the prescribed period. Under s. 4A the current fee is £500.

Section 10 provides powers of entry to local authority officers where a warning notice has been served in respect of the offending premises and excessive noise is still measured as having come therefrom. There is also a power to seize any sound equipment involved, together with a power to apply for a warrant for local authority officers to enter premises.

Obstruction of anyone exercising these powers is a summary offence (s. 10(8)) and the provisions for the seizure and disposal of any equipment are set out in the schedule to the 1996 Act.

4.5.6.12 Litter

The law regulating the roles of local authorities in controlling litter can be found in the Litter Act 1983. The 1983 Act makes allowances for actions by 'litter authorities' (i.e. local councils, see s. 10) to discourage the dropping of litter and for the provision of litter bins.

Removing or interfering with local authority litter bins or litter notices is a summary offence under s. 5(9).

The remainder of the provisions regulating the dropping of litter are in the Environmental Protection Act 1990.

The law in this area has been extended recently by the Anti-social Behaviour Act 2003 and the Clean Neighbourhoods and Environment Act 2005. The Clean Neighbourhoods and Environment Act 2005 makes further provisions with regard to litter in public places and the use of fixed penalty notices to deal with litter offences. This has increased the powers of litter authorities and extended the powers of local authorities for dealing with unlawfully deposited waste.

OFFENCE: **Leaving litter—*Environmental Protection Act 1990, s. 87(1)***

- Triable summarily • Fine

The Environmental Protection Act 1990, s. 87 states:

(1) A person is guilty of an offence if he throws down, drops or otherwise deposits any litter in any place to which this section applies and leaves it.

KEYNOTE

This section applies to *any place* in the area of a principal litter authority which is open to the air (i.e. a local council etc.), other than a place to which the public does not have access (with or without payment) (see s. 87(3)).

This offence applies equally to the depositing of litter on land or in water (s. 87(4)).

No offence is committed under subs. (1) above where the depositing of the litter is authorised by law or done by or with the consent of the owner, occupier or other person having control of the place where it is deposited (s. 87(4A)).

A telephone kiosk enclosed on all sides with a six inch gap around the bottom was held not to be a 'public open place' in *Felix* v *DPP* [1998] Crim LR 657.

'Litter' can include animal droppings for this purpose (Litter (Animal Droppings) Order 1991 (SI 1991/961)). The Clean Neighbourhoods and Environment Act 2005 provides that local authorities and parish councils may make an order providing for an offence or offences relating to the control of dogs in respect of any land in its area (s. 55(1)). Such an order is known as a 'dog control order' (s. 55(2)). An offence relates to the control of dogs if it involves one of the following matters: fouling of land by dogs and the removal of dog faeces; keeping dogs on leads; excluding dogs from land; restricting the number of dogs a person can take on to any land (s. 55(3)). The procedure to be followed is contained in the Dog Control Orders (Procedures) Regulations 2006 (SI 2006/798).

Section 59 of the 2005 Act allows authorised officers to issue a fixed penalty notice in respect of any offence under s. 55.

Similarly, s. 88 of the Environmental Protection Act 1990 makes provision for the issuing of fixed penalty notices in respect of the general litter offence above. Section 88 provides that, where a notice setting out the prescribed details is given to an offender, by an authorised officer of a litter authority, no proceedings can be instituted against that person for 14 days. Payment of the fixed penalty will prevent the person's prosecution for that offence. Where the offender pays by posting the required amount properly to the relevant address, payment will be regarded as having been made at the time of the expected *delivery* (not the time the letter is posted) in the normal course of post (s. 88(4)).

The power to issue fixed penalty notices in relation to the Clean Neighourhoods and Environment Act and the Environmental Protection Act are among those that can be conferred on a Community Support Officer designated under sch. 4 to the Police Reform Act 2002 and a person accredited under sch. 5 to that Act, along with the relevant power to require the person to give their name and address (for a full discussion of these and related powers **see chapter 4.2**).

The Clean Neighbourhoods and Environment Act 2005, clarifies that 'litter', for the purposes of part 4 of the Environmental Protection Act 1990, specifically includes cigarettes, cigars and like products and discarded chewing gum (including bubble gum).

Under s. 91 of the 1990 Act, a magistrates' court may act on a complaint of anyone who is aggrieved by the defacement by litter or refuse of any relevant road, highway or land occupied by relevant statutory undertakers or educational institutions. Before doing so, the court must notify the occupier of the complaint. The court may then issue a litter abatement order requiring the relevant person to remedy the situation and failure to comply with such an order is a summary offence under s. 91(9).

Section 99 and sch. 4 to the 1990 Act give local authorities powers to deal with problems involving the abandonment of shopping trolleys and luggage trolleys. Schedule 4 allows local authorities (after abiding by the procedure in s. 99) to seize, retain and ultimately dispose of such trolleys. The Clean Neighbourhoods and Environment Act 2005 has extended the powers of local authorities and they can now charge the person believed to be the owner of an abandoned shopping or luggage trolley for its removal, storage and disposal.

Section 87 (4A) also states:

(4A) No offence is committed under subsection (1) above where the depositing of the litter is—
- (a) authorised by law; or
- (b) done by or with the consent of the owner, occupier or other person having control of the place where it is deposited.

4.5.6.13 Begging

The Vagrancy Act 1824, s. 3 creates the ancient offence of begging or gathering alms in streets and public places. This summary offence is still relevant and the activities of so-called beggars have attracted increased interest over recent years. It has been held that the mischief to which the 1824 Act was directed was conduct that forces passers-by to deal with the defendant's activities (*Mathers* v *Penfold* [1915] 1 KB 514) and there is authority to suggest that a single act of approaching one person and asking for money is not, without more, enough to raise a *prima facie* case of begging (*R* v *Dalton* [1982] Crim LR 375). Where the person seeking money is doing something in exchange, such as singing as a busker, it has been held that this conduct does not amount to begging (see *Gray* v *Chief Constable of Greater Manchester Police* [1983] Crim LR 45).

There is a further summary offence of 'persistent' begging, and both offences (s. 3 and s. 4) are 'trigger offences' for the purposes of the Criminal Justice and Court Service Act 2000. This has a number of consequences for those charged with such an offence. The principal consequence is that he/she will come within the provisions of s. 63B of the Police and Criminal Evidence Act 1984. This effectively allows (in certain circumstances) for a sample of urine or a non-intimate sample to be taken for the purpose of ascertaining the presence of any specified Class A drug in his/her body (**see Evidence & Procedure, chapter 2.10**).

4.5.6.14 Vehicles Used for Causing Harassment etc.

Section 59 of the Police Reform Act 2002 gives a constable in uniform powers in relation to motor vehicles that he/she has reasonable grounds for believing are being, or have been, used in a manner which:

- contravenes s. 3 or 34 of the Road Traffic Act 1988 (careless and inconsiderate driving and prohibition of off-road driving), *and*
- is causing, or is likely to cause, alarm, distress or annoyance to members of the public.

Those powers include the power to order the person driving it to stop the vehicle, to seize and remove the motor vehicle and to enter any premises on which he/she has reasonable grounds for believing the motor vehicle to be. However, the powers are subject to a system of warnings and limitations. For a full discussion of these provisions **see Road Policing, chapter 3.2**.

4.5.7 Offences involving Communications

As with many areas of criminal law and policing, the terrorist attacks on and after 11 September 2001 dramatically increased the relevance of the offence below. The making of direct threats to people's lives or their property is covered by a number of statutes. There are, however, specific offences which deal with the making of general threats and other communications which are intended to cause alarm or anxiety among people receiving them.

4.5.7.1 Placing or Sending Material

OFFENCE: **Placing or sending substances—*Anti-terrorism, Crime and Security Act 2001, s. 114***

• Triable either way • Seven years' imprisonment on indictment • Six months' imprisonment and/or a fine summarily

The Anti-terrorism, Crime and Security Act 2001, s. 114 states:

(1) A person is guilty of an offence if he—
(a) places any substance or other thing in any place; or
(b) sends any substance or other thing from one place to another (by post, rail or any other means whatever);
with the intention of inducing in a person anywhere in the world a belief that it is likely to be (or contain) a noxious substance or other noxious thing and thereby endanger human life or create a serious risk to human health.

OFFENCE: **Placing or sending articles—*Criminal Law Act 1977, s. 51(1)***

• Triable either way • Seven years' imprisonment on indictment • Six months' imprisonment and/or a fine summarily

The Criminal Law Act 1977, s. 51 states:

(1) A person who—
(a) places any article in any place whatever; or
(b) dispatches any article by post, rail or any other means whatever of sending things from one place to another,
with the intention (in either case) of inducing in some other person a belief that it is likely to explode or ignite and thereby cause personal injury or damage to property is guilty of an offence.

In this subsection 'article' includes substance.

KEYNOTE

The definitions above are very wide. The Criminal Law Act 1977 offence relates specifically to bomb threats while the 2001 offence (which is modelled on the earlier offence) is far broader and applies to creating a belief in someone anywhere in the world. For the purposes of the Anti-terrorism, Crime and Security Act 2001, 'substance' here includes any biological agent and any other natural or artificial substance (whatever its form, origin or method of production (s. 115(1)). The 'article' concerned in s. 51(1) can also be anything at all.

It is the inducing of a relevant belief in someone else that is the key element to the first offence not any actual endangering of life or risk to human health. You do not have to show that the defendant had any particular person in mind in whom he/she intended to induce the belief in question (see the Anti-terrorism, Crime and Security Act 2001, s. 115(2) and the Criminal Law Act 1977, s. 51(3)).

Both offences are offences of 'specific intent', **see Crime, chapter 1.1**.

For the summary offences of making nuisance communications via public communications networks **see para. 4.5.7.8**.

The Home Office guidance to the Anti-terrorism, Crime and Security Act 2001 offence gives examples of acts which, though at one time would not have been seen as threatening, would now amount to an offence under this section—examples such as scattering white powder in a public place or spraying water droplets around in an underground train, in each case with the requisite intent.

4.5.7.2 Threats or False Information on Dangerous Items

OFFENCE: **Threats involving noxious substances or things—*Anti-terrorism, Crime and Security Act 2001, s. 114***

• Triable either way • Seven years' imprisonment on indictment • Six months' imprisonment and/or a fine summarily

The Anti-terrorism, Crime and Security Act 2001, s. 114 states:

(2) A person is guilty of an offence if he communicates any information which he knows or believes to be false with the intention of inducing in a person anywhere in the world a belief that a noxious substance or other noxious thing is likely to be present (whether at the time the information is communicated or later) in any place and thereby endanger human life or create a serious risk to human health.

OFFENCE: **Communicating false information—*Criminal Law Act 1977, s. 51(2)***

• Triable either way • Seven years' imprisonment on indictment • Six months' imprisonment and/or a fine summarily

The Criminal Law Act 1977, s. 51 states:

(2) A person who communicates any information which he knows or believes to be false to another person with the intention of inducing in him or any other person a false belief that a bomb or other thing liable to explode or ignite is present in any place or location whatever is guilty of an offence.

KEYNOTE

The essence of these offences is the communication of information which the defendant knows or believes to be false. Again, the 1977 Act offence relates specifically to bomb hoaxes while the 2001 Act offence is far wider and applies to creating a belief in someone anywhere in the world. The meaning of 'substance' for the 2001 Act offence is the same as in the Keynote above and, in neither case is there a need to show that the defendant had any particular person in mind. Under the Criminal Law Act 1977 it has been held that while the information communicated need not be specific, a message saying that there is a bomb somewhere has been held to be enough, even though no location was given (*R* v *Webb* (1995) 92(27) LSG 31).

The wording of the 1977 Act offence is in the *present* tense which suggests that a message threatening to place a bomb etc. sometime in the *future* would not suffice, while the 2001 Act specifically allows for such a situation.

The use of some form of code word is not a prerequisite of the offence but it does go towards proving the defendant's intention that the threat etc. be taken seriously; it may also be taken into account when passing sentence.

The 'communication' can be in any form (including, it would seem, on the internet) and can be direct (e.g. to a railway station or department store where the bomb or device is alleged to be) or indirect (to a radio station switchboard).

There is no need for the person making the communication to have any particular person in mind at the time (s. 51(3)).

4.5.7.3 Misuse and Obstruction of Postal Services

OFFENCE: **Interfering with mail—*Postal Services Act 2000, s. 84***

• Triable summarily • Six months' imprisonment and/or a fine

The Postal Services Act 2000, s. 84 states:

(1) A person commits an offence if, without reasonable excuse, he—
 (a) intentionally delays or opens a postal packet in the course of its transmission by post, or
 (b) intentionally opens a mail-bag

(2) ...

(3) A person commits an offence if, intending to act to a person's detriment and without reasonable excuse, he opens a postal packet which he knows or reasonably suspects has been incorrectly delivered to him.

KEYNOTE

The Postal Services Act 2000 was introduced to make the extensive changes in the law that were required by the 'privatisation' of the Post Office and its functions.

The Act creates two offences in relation to interfering with the mail, along with a further offence of opening someone else's mail that has been incorrectly delivered.

The first general offence, under s. 84(1) above, applies to anyone. There is a second offence (under s. 83) which specifically applies to postal workers and which is triable either way, carrying a maximum of two years' imprisonment. Under the second, more specific, offence, you have to prove the same elements as the above offence but also need to show that the person was engaged in the business of a postal operator and that he/she was acting contrary to his/her duty.

To prove the above offence you must show that the defendant acted without any reasonable excuse and that he/she also acted intentionally (as to which **see Crime, chapter 1.1**). The offence does not apply where the actions were carried out under a lawful warrant or statutory provision (e.g. the Regulation of Investigatory Powers Act 2000—**see para. 4.12.4**). Similarly, any action carried out in accordance with the terms and conditions of postage will not attract criminal liability here. Delays (but not the opening of mail) caused by industrial action also fall outside this offence.

The offence under s. 84(3) above looks simple enough but requires proof of a number of elements. First, it must be shown that the defendant opened a postal packet (as opposed to delaying it under s. 84(1)). It must also be shown that he/she did so intending 'to act to another person's detriment'—this can be any other person's detriment, not simply the addressee, but it is nevertheless a key feature of the offence. It must also be shown that the defendant knew or reasonably suspected that the postal packet had been incorrectly delivered to him/her. This means that the packet must have been 'delivered'; it would be difficult to show that someone reasonably suspected a packet that is still in transit to have been 'incorrectly delivered' to him/her. As with the general offence under s. 84(1), any opening of postal packets that is done properly in pursuance of a warrant, statutory authority or under the conditions of postage will not be an offence under s. 84(3).

For the further offences of intercepting communications **see para. 4.12.4**.

4.5.7.4 Sending Prohibited Article by Post

OFFENCE: **Sending prohibited article by post—*Postal Services Act 2000, s. 85***

• Triable either way • Twelve months' imprisonment on indictment • Fine summarily

The Postal Services Act 2000, s. 85 states:

(1) A person commits an offence if he sends by post a postal packet which encloses any creature, article or thing of any kind which is likely to injure other postal packets in course of their transmission by post or any person engaged in the business of a postal operator.

(2) Subsection (1) does not apply to postal packets which enclose anything permitted (whether generally or specifically) by the postal operator concerned.

(3) A person commits an offence if he sends by post a postal packet which encloses—

(a) any indecent or obscene print, painting, photograph, lithograph, engraving, cinematograph film or other record of a picture or pictures, book, card or written communication, or

(b) any other indecent or obscene article (whether or not of a similar kind to those mentioned in paragraph (a)).

(4) A person commits an offence if he sends by post a postal packet which has on the packet, or on the cover of the packet, any words, marks or designs which are of an indecent or obscene character.

KEYNOTE

Section 85 creates a number of offences, all concerned with the sending of postal packets via the newly created postal infrastructure. The first offence addresses the sending of things that are likely to harm either other postal packets or postal workers. Evidence that any article is in the course of transmission by post, or has been accepted by a postal operator for transmission by post, will be enough to prove that it is in fact a 'postal packet' (s. 109). This offence will not apply to the sending of things that are permitted by the relevant postal operator.

The other offences under s. 85 apply irrespective of whether the offending packets are permitted by the postal operator and include indecent or obscene contents or packaging.

Whether an article is obscene etc. is a question of fact for the court to determine in each case. That test will not look at the particular views or frailties of the recipient but will be an objective test based on a reasonable bystander (*Kosmos Publications Ltd* v *DPP* [1975] Crim LR 345).

As causing severe shock can amount to an assault, the relevant offences against the person may be considered (**see Crime, chapter 1.7**).

For specific offences of harassment, **see para. 4.5.4.**

4.5.7.5 Obstruction of Postal Service

OFFENCE: **Obstruction—*Postal Services Act 2000, s. 88***

- Triable summarily • Fine

The Postal Services Act 2000, s. 88 states:

(1) A person commits an offence if, without reasonable excuse, he—
(a) obstructs a person engaged in the business of a universal service provider in the execution of his duty in connection with the provision of a universal postal service, or
(b) obstructs, while in any universal postal service post office or related premises, the course of business of a universal service provider.
(2) ...
(3) A person commits an offence if without reasonable excuse, he fails to leave a universal postal service post office or related premises when required to do so by a person who—
(a) is engaged in the business of a universal service provider, and
(b) reasonably suspects him of committing an offence under subsection (1).
(4) A person who commits an offence under subsection (3)—
(a) ...
(b) may be removed by any person engaged in the business of a universal service provider.

KEYNOTE

Section 88 creates two offences relating to obstruction. The first offence involves the general obstruction, without reasonable excuse, of someone engaged in the business of a 'universal service provider'. These providers are broadly organisations empowered under the 2000 Act to carry on many of the services that were formerly provided by the Post Office.

The second offence relates to conduct in a post office or related premises. Such conduct must be shown to have obstructed, without reasonable excuse, *the course of business* of a universal service provider. Therefore, it is not a member of staff who has to be obstructed here, but rather the postal business itself.

Subsection (3) is of more immediate relevance to police officers. This offence is committed if a person fails without reasonable excuse to leave a post office or related premises when required to do so by someone engaged in the provider's business who reasonably suspects the other person of committing one of the obstruction offences under s. 88(1). Anyone failing to leave when properly required to do so under subsection (3) may be removed by the post office staff but also, subsection (5) provides that '*any constable shall on demand remove, or assist in removing, any such person*'. This places a clear duty on—as opposed to just granting a power to—individual police officers to help in removing offenders under these circumstances. It is similar to the powers and obligation placed on police officers in relation to licensed premises (as to which see chapter 4.11).

'Related premises' are any premises belonging to a universal postal service post office or used together with any such post office (s. 88(6)).

4.5.7.6 Malicious Communications

OFFENCE: **Malicious communications—*Malicious Communications Act 1988, s. 1(1)***

- Triable summarily • Six months' imprisonment and/or a fine

The Malicious Communications Act 1988, s. 1 states:

(1) Any person who sends to another person—

(a) a letter, electronic communication or article of any description which conveys—

(i) a message which is indecent or grossly offensive;

(ii) a threat; or

(iii) information which is false and known or believed to be false by the sender; or

(b) any article or electronic communication which is, in whole or part, of an indecent or grossly offensive nature,

is guilty of an offence if his purpose, or one of his purposes, in sending it is that it should, so far as falling within paragraph (a) or (b) above, cause distress or anxiety to the recipient or to any other person to whom he intends that it or its contents or nature should be communicated.

KEYNOTE

The offence is not restricted to threatening or indecent communications and can include giving false information provided that *one* of the sender's purposes in so doing is to cause distress or anxiety. 'Purposes' appears simply to be another way of stating intention in which case this an offence of 'specific intent' (see Crime, chapter 1.1).

In addition to letters, the above offence also covers *any* article; it also covers electronic communications which include any oral or other communication by means of an electronic communications network. This will extend to communications in electronic form such as emails, text messages, pager messages etc. (see s. 1(2A)).

'Sending' will include transmitting.

The relevant distress or anxiety may be intended towards the recipient *or* any other person.

It is clear from s. 1(3) that the offence can be committed by using someone else to send, deliver or transmit a message. This would include occasions where a person falsely reports that someone has been a victim of a crime in order to cause anxiety or distress by the arrival of the police. (For wasting police time, see Crime, chapter 1.14.)

Section 1(1)(b) covers occasions where the article itself is indecent or grossly offensive (such as putting dog faeces through someone's letter box).

4.5.7.7 Defence Regarding Malicious Communications

Section 1(2) of the 1988 Act states:

> A person is not guilty of an offence by virtue of subsection (1)(a)(ii) above if he shows—
> (a) that the threat was used to reinforce a demand made by him on reasonable grounds; and
> (b) that he believed, and had reasonable grounds for believing, that the use of the threat was a proper means of reinforcing the demand.

KEYNOTE

The wording of the statutory defence has been changed (by the Criminal Justice and Police Act 2001) to make the relevant test objective. It will no longer be enough that the person claiming the defence under s. 1(2) believed that he/she had reasonable grounds; the defendant will have to show:

- that there were in fact reasonable grounds for making the demand;
- that he/she believed that the accompanying threat was a proper means of enforcing the demand; and
- that reasonable grounds existed for that belief.

Given the decisions of the courts in similarly worded defences under the Theft Act 1968 (blackmail; see Crime, chapter 1.11), it is unlikely that any demand could be reasonable where agreement to it would amount to a crime.

The defence is intended to cover financial institutions and other commercial concerns who often need to send forceful letters to customers. However, for the offence of unlawfully harassing debtors, see s. 40 of the Administration of Justice Act 1970.

4.5.7.8 Public Communications

OFFENCE: **Improper use of public electronic communications network—*Communications Act 2003, s.127***

- Triable summarily • Six months' imprisonment and/or a fine

The Communications Act 2003, s. 127 states:

> (1) A person is guilty of an offence if he—
> (a) sends by means of a public electronic communications network a message or other matter that is grossly offensive or of an indecent, obscene or menacing character; or
> (b) causes any such message or matter to be so sent.
> (2) A person is guilty of an offence if, for the purpose of causing annoyance, inconvenience or needless anxiety to another, he—
> (a) sends by means of a public electronic communications network, a message that he knows to be false;
> (b) causes such a message to be sent; or
> (c) persistently makes use of a public electronic communications network.

KEYNOTE

These offences, like their predecessors, are designed to deal with 'nuisance' calls. They only apply to 'public' electronic communications networks. These are defined as an electronic communications network provided wholly or mainly for the purpose of making electronic communications services available to members of the public (s. 151) and would therefore not generally include internal calls in a workplace. The wording would apply to the sending of messages via the internet (provided the system used comes within the definition under s. 151).

There is no need to show a particular 'purpose' (intention) on the part of the defendant for the first offence under subs. (1) and that offence is complete if the message is, as a matter of fact, grossly offensive, indecent, obscene or menacing. The offence also covers actions which cause others to send such a message. Unlike the offence under s. 51(2) of the Criminal Law Act 1977 (**see para. 4.5.7.2**), there is no need for any information passed to be 'false'. In determining whether a message is 'grossly offensive', it is the message and not the content that is the basic ingredient of the offence. What constitutes 'grossly offensive' has to be judged by considering the reaction of reasonable people and the standards of an open and just multiracial society (*DPP* v *Collins* [2006] 1 WLR 308).

The second offence under subs. (2) requires that you show the defendant acted with the purpose of causing annoyance, inconvenience or needless anxiety. A person is to be treated as 'persistently misusing' a network or service in any case in which his/her misuse is repeated on a sufficient number of occasions for it to be clear that the misuse represents a pattern of behaviour or practice, or recklessness as to whether persons suffer annoyance, inconvenience or anxiety (s. 128(6)). In assessing these points it is immaterial that the misuse was in relation to a 'network' on some occasions and in relation to a communications 'service' on others, that different networks or services were involved on different occasions or that the people likely to suffer annoyance, inconvenience or anxiety were different on different occasions (s. 128(7)).

This second offence is a 'penalty offence' for the purposes of s. 1 of the Criminal Justice and Police Act 2001 (**see para. 4.4.3**).

Where a number of calls have been made to several different people within the community, the offence of public nuisance may also be considered (**see para. 4.5.6.1**).

4.5.7.9 False Alarms of Fire

OFFENCE: **Making false alarm of fire—*Fire and Rescue Services Act 2004, s. 49***

• Triable summarily • Imprisonment for a term not exceeding 51 weeks and/or a fine (In relation to an offence committed before the commencement of s. 281(5) of the Criminal Justice Act 2003, the reference to 51 weeks is to be read as a reference to three months)

The Fire and Rescue Services Act 2004, s. 49 states:

> (1) A person commits an offence if he knowingly gives or causes to be given a false alarm of fire to a person acting on behalf of a fire and rescue authority.

KEYNOTE

The offence requires proof that the defendant acted 'knowingly' (as opposed to e.g. mistakenly). The offence clearly applies where someone makes a malicious call to a fire and rescue authority. However the wording 'causes to be given' potentially covers the making of a false report to a body other than a fire and rescue authority—e.g. the police—if the person knew that this would result in the police passing that call to the relevant fire and rescue authority.

This offence is a 'penalty offence' for the purposes of s.1 of the Criminal Justice and Police Act 2001 (**see para. 4.4.3**).

4.5.7.10 Unsolicited Publications

It is a summary offence to send unsolicited material or advertising material which describes or illustrates human sexual techniques (s. 4 of the Unsolicited Goods and Services Act 1971). This offence cannot be prosecuted without the consent of the DPP.

4.6 Public Disorder and Terrorism

4.6.1 Introduction

Threats to public order or the 'normal state of society' can arise in many forms, from intimidating and anti-social behaviour to full-scale riots and acts of terrorism. The role of the police in maintaining the normal state of society is both extremely important but also increasingly challenging. It is one thing to provide police officers and auxiliary staff with statutory and common law powers to tackle disorder in all its many forms and, perhaps more importantly, to prevent anticipated disorder in advance; it is quite another to use those powers in a way that is sensitive to the competing needs and expectations of people and the communities in which they live. Although such powers help the police in their efforts to preserve a peaceful state of society, their use is frequently controversial and often confrontational. This area of constitutional law involves balancing the opposing rights of individuals with one another against the wider entitlements and requirements of society—a task that, in practical terms, can seem like trying to satisfy the insatiable.

Although 'public disorder' related, the offences of drunk and disorderly and being found drunk are contained in the chapter dealing with alcohol-related offences (**see paras 4.11.8.9** and **4.11.8.10**).

4.6.2 Breach of the Peace

The lowest level of threat to public order is probably represented in the common law 'complaint' of a breach of the peace. Defined specifically in *R* v *Howell* [1982] QB 416, a breach of the peace generally occurs when an act is done, or threatened to be done:

- which harms a person or, in his/her presence, his/her property; or
- which is likely to cause such harm; or
- which puts someone in fear of such harm.

The common law provides a power of arrest and also the power to intervene and/or detain by force, in order to prevent any action likely to result in a breach of the peace in either public or private places.

Breach of the peace is dealt with by way of complaint and is not a criminal offence (*R* v *County of London Quarter Sessions Appeals Committee, ex parte Metropolitan Police Commissioner* [1948] 1 KB 670). In *Williamson* v *Chief Constable of West Midlands Police* [2003] EWCA Civ 337 the Court of Appeal held that a person arrested for a breach of the peace is not, strictly speaking, in police detention for the purposes of s. 118 of the Police and Criminal Evidence Act 1984 (**see Evidence & Procedure, chapter 2.10**) and the provisions in relation to bail do not apply. A person may be detained and placed before the next available court, or detained until there is no further likelihood of a reoccurrence of the breach of the peace. In *Williamson* it was considered good practice for people arrested and detained for breach of the peace to be treated in accordance with the provisions of PACE, and that they should also be cautioned.

4.6.2.1 Breach of the Peace on Private Premises

A breach of the peace may take place on private premises as well as in public places (*R* v *Chief Constable of Devon and Cornwall, ex parte Central Electricity Generating Board* [1982] QB 458). The police are entitled to enter premises to prevent a breach of the peace and to remain there in order to do so (*Thomas* v *Sawkins* [1935] 2 KB 249). This power has not been affected by the general powers of entry provided by the Police and Criminal Evidence Act 1984 (**see chapter 4.4** and s. 17(6) of the 1984 Act).

Where a breach of the peace takes place on private property, there is no requirement to show that the resulting disturbance affected members of the public outside that property—*McQuade* v *Chief Constable of Humberside Police* [2002] 1 WLR 1347. The presence of a member (or members) of the public is, however, a highly relevant factor when dealing with a breach of the peace (see *McConnell* v *Chief Constable of Greater Manchester Police* [1990] 1 WLR 364).

4.6.2.2 Police Powers are Discretionary

Although the police have a general duty to preserve the Queen's peace, and enjoy common law powers to carry out that duty, they also have a wide discretion as to how they go about that function. The common law powers of the police allow them, where appropriate, to prevent people from travelling to certain locations (e.g. striking miners heading for a working coalfield where their presence would give reasonable grounds to apprehend a breach of the peace (*Moss* v *McLachlan* [1985] IRLR 76)). Such an 'anticipatory' power is, however, exceptional (*Foulkes* v *Chief Constable of Merseyside Police* [1998] 3 All ER 705) (see below) and requires a careful balancing of the individual rights of the people involved against the wider interests of public safety, the maintenance of public order and the prevention of crime. Such exceptional powers to impose anticipatory restrictions on the movement of individuals, falling short of arrest, only arise if there is an imminent threat to public order.

The policing practicalities involved in this careful balancing exercise were considered in *R (On the Application of Laporte)* v *Chief Constable of Gloucestershire* [2006] UKHL 55. That case produced a useful interpretation and examination of a number of operational policing powers. In *Laporte* a lawful assembly had been arranged under the provisions of ss. 12 and 14 of the Public Order Act 1986 (**see para. 4.6.11**) in connection with protests against the war in Iraq. As the result of a stop and search order made under s. 60 of the Criminal Justice and Public Order Act 1994 (**see para. 4.4.4.12**) the police stopped a number of coaches en route to the lawful assembly at Fairford US Air Force base, and then escorted them back to London. Intelligence had been received that the passengers would cause disorder at the base. The Court of Appeal held that the police actions were reasonable to apprehend a breach of the peace. However, the House of Lords ruled that the police had acted unlawfully because a breach of the peace was not imminent when the coaches were stopped. This action interfered with the passengers' rights under Articles 10 and 11 of the European Convention on Human Rights (as to which **see chapter 4.3**) and was disproportionate.

4.6.2.3 Which Parties are Likely to Present Actual Threat?

When exercising discretionary powers to prevent disorder, police officers will be expected to focus their attention on those who are likely to present the actual threat of violence or disorder. This is the approach first taken by the Divisional Court in a case where people preaching on the steps of a church were warned by police that they were antagonising passers-by. Despite the warning, the preachers continued and, as there was an imminent likelihood of a recently gathered crowd attacking them, the preachers were arrested (see below) (*Redmond-Bate* v *DPP* [1999] Crim LR 998). The Divisional Court felt that the approach taken by the police was incompatible with Article 10 of the European Convention on Human Rights and that the officers' attention should have been directed at the crowd from whom the threat to the 'peace' was emanating. The individuals preaching were simply exercising their right to freedom of expression. It was the crowd who, in the court's view, ought to have received the warning and who should have been arrested in the event of their continuing to represent a threat to public order.

However, it will not always be practicable to separate those who are directly and individually presenting a threat to the peace and those who are part of a larger crowd. In *Austin* v *Commissioner of Police of the Metropolis* [2007] EWCA Civ 989 it was held that in extreme and exceptional circumstances it would be lawful for the police to contain demonstrators and members of the public caught up in that demonstration, even though they themselves did not appear to be about to commit a breach of the peace. This would be the case where it was necessary to prevent an imminent breach of the peace by others, and no other means would achieve that.

4.6.2.4 Power of Arrest

A constable or any other person may arrest without warrant any person:

- who is committing a breach of the peace;
- whom he/she reasonably believes will commit a breach of the peace in the immediate future; or
- who has committed a breach of the peace, where it is reasonably believed that a recurrence of the breach of the peace is threatened.

This power of arrest may be exercised on private premises, even where there is no other member of the public present (*R* v *Howell* [1982] QB 416).

In *Bibby* v *Chief Constable of Essex Police* [2000] EWCA Civ 113, the Court of Appeal held that the power of arrest for breach of the peace was wholly exceptional and set out the conditions that must be met before this power should be used. These conditions are:

- there must be the clearest of circumstances and a real and present threat to the peace to justify the arrest
- the threat must be coming from the person who is ultimately arrested
- their conduct must be clearly interfering with the rights of another
- that conduct must be unreasonable.

Even if exercising the power under circumstances where a breach of the peace has not yet occurred, it is enough that a constable uses the wording 'I am arresting you for a breach of the peace' when arresting the person (*R* v *Howell* [1982] QB 416).

4.6.3 The Public Order Acts

Many of the most common offences regulating public disorder and threats to public order were formerly contained in the Public Order Act 1936. This left several key offences, such as riot and affray to the common law. These provisions were felt to be inadequate and the Public Order Act 1986 was passed in an attempt to codify the law in this area.

4.6.4 Riot

OFFENCE: **Riot—*Public Order Act 1986, s. 1***

• Triable on indictment • Ten years' imprisonment and/or a fine

The Public Order Act 1986, s. 1 states:

(1) Where 12 or more persons who are present together use or threaten unlawful violence for a common purpose and the conduct of them (taken together) is such as would cause a person of reasonable firmness present at the scene to fear for his personal safety, each of the persons using unlawful violence for the common purpose is guilty of riot.
(2) It is immaterial whether or not the 12 or more use or threaten unlawful violence simultaneously.
(3) The common purpose may be inferred from conduct.
(4) No person of reasonable firmness need actually be, or be likely to be, present at the scene.
(5) Riot may be committed in private as well as in public places.

KEYNOTE

This offence requires the consent of the DPP before a prosecution can be brought. Although there may be occasions where 12 or more people behave in the way proscribed by s. 1, it still very rare for a charge of riot to be brought. This may have something to do with the provisions of the Riot (Damages) Act 1886 which enables people who have suffered loss or damage during a riot to claim compensation from the local police budget (s. 2) irrespective of whether there has been any proven negligence on the part of the police. This provision attracted a great deal of criticism following the disturbances in Bradford, Oldham and Burnley in 2001 and, in the same year, the lodging of civil claims following disorder at the Yarl's Wood detention centre.

It is not necessary that all 12 people concerned use or threaten unlawful violence at the same time. However, the courts have held that each defendant must be shown to have *used* unlawful violence and not merely threatened to do so (*R* v *Jefferson* [1994] 1 All ER 270). A defendant must be shown to have *intended* to use/threaten violence or to have *been aware* that his/her conduct may have been violent (s. 6(1)).

The offence may be committed in private as well as in a public place. There is no need to prove that a person of reasonable firmness was actually caused to fear for his/her safety, merely that such a person would be caused so to fear (although clearly one way to prove that element would be by the testimony of those witnessing the behaviour).

Although there must be a common purpose, this need not be part of a pre-determined plan, nor be unlawful in itself. A common purpose to get into a rock concert or even the January sales at a high street store could therefore be enough, provided all other elements are present.

4.6.4.1 Violence

Section 8 of the Public Order Act 1986 provides guidance on when conduct will amount to 'violence':

> 'violence' means any violent conduct, so that—
> (a) except in the context of affray, it includes violent conduct towards property as well as violent conduct towards persons, and
> (b) it is not restricted to conduct causing or intended to cause injury or damage but includes any other violent conduct (for example, throwing at or towards a person a missile of a kind capable of causing injury which does not hit or falls short).

KEYNOTE

It has been held that the use of the term 'unlawful' in the 1986 Act has been included to allow for the general defences—such as self-defence (**see Crime, chapter 1.4**)—to be applicable (see *R* v *Rothwell* [1993] Crim LR 626).

4.6.4.2 Drunkenness

The effect of drunkenness on criminal liability generally is discussed in **Crime, chapter 1.4**. However, Parliament has specifically catered for self-induced intoxication, not just for the offence of riot, but in relation to other offences under the 1986 Act by s. 6 which states:

> (5) For the purposes of this section a person whose awareness is impaired by intoxication shall be taken to be aware of that of which he would be aware if not intoxicated, unless he shows either that his intoxication was not self-induced or that it was caused solely by the taking or administration of a substance in the course of medical treatment.
> (6) In subsection (5) 'intoxication' means any intoxication, whether caused by drink, drugs or other means, or by a combination of means.

4.6.5 Violent Disorder

OFFENCE: **Violent disorder—*Public Order Act 1986, s. 2***

- Triable either way • Five years' imprisonment and/or a fine on indictment
- Six months' imprisonment and/or a fine summarily

The Public Order Act 1986, s. 2 states:

> (1) Where 3 or more persons who are present together use or threaten unlawful violence and the conduct of them (taken together) is such as would cause a person of reasonable firmness present at the scene to fear for his personal safety, each of the persons using or threatening unlawful violence is guilty of violent disorder.
> (2) It is immaterial whether or not the 3 or more use or threaten unlawful violence simultaneously.
> (3) No person of reasonable firmness need actually be, or be likely to be, present at the scene.
> (4) Violent disorder may be committed in private as well as in public places.

KEYNOTE

In order to convict any defendant of this offence, you must show that there were three or more people using or threatening violence. In the case of two of the defendants being acquitted, the remaining defendant can still be convicted (*R* v *Mahroof* (1989) 88 Cr App R 317).

The requirements as to the hypothetical effects on an equally hypothetical person of reasonable firmness are the same as for the offence of riot. However, there is no requirement to prove a common purpose.

Again, a defendant must be shown to have *intended* to use/threaten violence or to have *been aware* that his/her conduct may have been violent (s. 6(2)) and the offence may be committed in private as well as in a public place. 'Violence' for these purposes can include violent conduct towards property (s. 8).

4.6.6 Affray

OFFENCE: **Affray—*Public Order Act 1986, s. 3***

- Triable either way • Three years' imprisonment and/or a fine on indictment
- Six months' imprisonment and/or a fine summarily

The Public Order Act 1986, s. 3 states:

(1) A person is guilty of affray if he uses or threatens unlawful violence towards another and his conduct is such as would cause a person of reasonable firmness present at the scene to fear for his personal safety.
(2) Where 2 or more persons use or threaten the unlawful violence, it is the conduct of them taken together that must be considered for the purposes of subsection (1).
(3) For the purposes of this section a threat cannot be made by the use of words alone.
(4) No person of reasonable firmness need actually be, or be likely to be, present at the scene.
(5) Affray may be committed in private as well as in public places.

KEYNOTE

Formerly an offence requiring more than one person, this offence may now be committed by a single defendant although, if he/she acts with another, the conduct of them taken together will be the relevant factor in determining their criminal conduct (s. 3(2)).

The House of Lords has held that, in order to prove the offence of affray, the threat of unlawful violence has to be towards a person(s) present at the scene (*I* v *DPP* [2002] 1 AC 285). Once this element has been proved, it will be necessary to prove the second element, namely whether the defendant's conduct would have caused a hypothetical person present at the scene to fear for his/her personal safety (*R* v *Sanchez* (1996) 160 JP 321 and *R* v *Carey* [2006] EWCA Crim 17).

The threat cannot be made by words alone (s. 3(3)), therefore there must be some action by the defendant—even if that 'action' consists of utilising something else such as a dog to threaten the violence (*R* v *Dixon* [1993] Crim LR 579).

The effect of s. 3(4) is that it is not necessary to show that the defendant's behaviour either was or could have been seen by someone at the time. Contrast this with the lesser offence under s. 5 **(see para. 4.6.9)**.

Although violence is 'not restricted to conduct causing or intended to cause injury or damage but includes any other violent conduct' (s. 8), the expression does not include conduct towards property as it does with the offences under ss. 1 and 2.

Once more, a defendant must be shown to have *intended* to use/threaten violence or to have *been aware* that his/her conduct may have been violent (s. 6(2)).

4.6.7 Fear or Provocation of Violence

OFFENCE: **Fear or provocation of violence—*Public Order Act 1986, s. 4***

- Triable summarily • Six months' imprisonment and/or a fine

OFFENCE: **Racially or religiously aggravated—*Crime and Disorder Act 1998, s. 31(1)(a)***

- Triable either way • Two years' imprisonment and/or a fine on indictment
- Six months' imprisonment and/or a fine summarily

The Public Order Act 1986, s. 4 states:

(1) A person is guilty of an offence if he—
(a) uses towards another person threatening, abusive or insulting words or behaviour, or
(b) distributes or displays to another person any writing, sign or other visible representation which is threatening, abusive or insulting,
with intent to cause that person to believe that immediate unlawful violence will be used against him or another by any person, or to provoke the immediate use of unlawful violence by that person or another, or whereby that person is likely to believe that such violence will be used or it is likely that such violence will be provoked.
(2) An offence under this section may be committed in a public or a private place, except that no offence is committed where the words or behaviour are used, or the writing, sign or other visible representation is distributed or displayed, by a person inside a dwelling and the other person is also inside that or another dwelling.

KEYNOTE

The phrase 'threatening, abusive or insulting' is not defined but it was interpreted by the courts under the Public Order Act 1936. Whether words or behaviour are threatening, abusive or insulting will be a question of fact for the magistrate(s) to decide in each case (see *Brutus* v *Cozens* [1973] AC 854).

As with many of the other public order offences that follow in this chapter, the effect that an individual's rights (such as the right to freedom of expression under Article 10 of the European Convention on Human Rights) will have here is not yet clear. The problems of balancing such freedom of expression with the expectations and sensibilities of ordinary members of society can be seen in other countries where these individual rights have been specifically protected by a written constitution. To paraphrase one American judge in a case involving the use of obscene language by an anti-Vietnam protester, 'it is often true that one person's vulgarity is another person's lyric' (see *Cohen* v *State of California* 403 US 15 (1971) 25).

It is not enough that conduct is 'offensive' but it has been held that masturbation towards a police officer in a public lavatory is capable of being insulting (*Parkin* v *Norman* [1983] QB 92).

'Immediate' unlawful violence does not have to be instantaneous but it must be shown that the defendant's conduct was likely to lead to more than some form of violence at some later date. Therefore publication and sale of material by the author Salman Rushdie, however insulting it may have been to some people, was not enough on its facts to support a charge against the publishers under s 4 (*R* v *Horseferry Road Metropolitan Stipendiary Magistrate, ex parte Siadatan* [1991] 1 QB 260). 'Immediate' here requires some close proximity between the acts of the defendant and the apprehended violence, with no intervening occurrence.

In this, and the s. 4A offence (below), the victim of the racially or religiously aggravated behaviour can be a police officer and the courts have held that police officers are entitled to the same protection under the legislation as anyone else (see *R* v *Jacobs* [2001] 2 Cr App R(s) 38).

There are a number of ways in which this offence can be committed (see below). In all of these, however, there must be the use of threatening/abusive/insulting words or behaviour (or distribution/ display of writing, signs, etc.). This must be carried out with the requisite state of mind set out at s. 6(3) which states:

(3) A person is guilty of an offence under section 4 only if he intends his words or behaviour, or the writing, sign or other visible representation, to be threatening, abusive or insulting, or is aware that it may be threatening, abusive or insulting.

In addition, it must be shown that the person further *intended* to bring about the consequences set out below (at (a) and (b)) or that the consequences (at (c) and (d)) were likely.

The offence was broken down into four component parts in *Winn* v *DPP* (1992) 156 JP 881. For each of these parts it must be shown:

(a) that the defendant:
- intended the person against whom the conduct was directed
- to believe
- that immediate unlawful violence would be used
- either against him/her or against anyone else
- by the defendant or anyone else; *or*

(b) that he/she:
- intended to provoke the immediate use of unlawful violence
- by that person or anyone else; *or*

(c) that:
- the person against whom the words or behaviour (or distribution/display of writing etc.) were directed
- was likely to believe
- that immediate unlawful violence would be used; *or*

(d) that:
- it was likely that immediate unlawful violence would be provoked.

In the case at (a) above, it does not have to be shown that the other person *actually believed* that immediate violence would be used; it has to be shown that the defendant *intended to cause* him/her to believe it (*Swanston* v *DPP* (1997) 161 JP 203).

The person in whom the defendant intends to create that belief must be the same person at whom the conduct is directed (*Loade* v *DPP* [1990] 1 QB 1052). Therefore, if the defendant uses threatening behaviour towards person A, intending that this will cause person B to believe that immediate unlawful violence will be used, the offence under s. 4 is not, without more, made out.

For a full explanation of the meaning of 'racially or religiously aggravated' (see para. 4.5.2).

4.6.7.1 Definition of Dwelling

Under the Public Order Act 1986, s. 8, dwelling is defined as:

> ... any structure or part of a structure occupied as a person's home or as other living accommodation (whether the occupation is separate or shared with others) but does not include any part not so occupied, and for this purpose 'structure' includes a tent, caravan, vehicle, vessel or other temporary or movable structure.

KEYNOTE

Given that the offence at s. 4 can be committed in private (under the restrictions in relation to dwellings by s. 4(2) above), it appears that the offence could be committed by a person sending out emails or other forms of communication from his/her house to other non-dwellings or from his/her place of work to people's houses.

Communal landings which form access routes to separate dwellings have been held not to constitute part of a dwelling even though they could only be entered by way of an entry phone system (*Rukwira* v *DPP* [1993] Crim LR 882).

4.6.8 Intentional Harassment, Alarm or Distress

OFFENCE: **Intentionally causing harassment, alarm or distress—*Public Order Act 1986, s. 4A***

- Triable summarily • Six months' imprisonment and/or a fine

OFFENCE: **Racially or religiously aggravated—*Crime and Disorder Act 1998, s. 31(1)(b)***

- Triable either way • Two years' imprisonment and/or a fine on indictment
- Six months' imprisonment and/or a fine summarily

The Public Order Act 1986, s. 4A states:

(1) A person is guilty of an offence if, with intent to cause a person harassment, alarm or distress, he—
  (a) uses threatening, abusive or insulting words or behaviour, or disorderly behaviour, or
  (b) displays any writing, sign or other visible representation which is threatening, abusive or insulting,

thereby causing that or another person harassment, alarm or distress.

KEYNOTE

For a full explanation of the meaning of 'racially or religiously aggravated', see para. 4.5.2.

For the purpose of the racially or religiously aggravated form of causing fear or provocation of violence, any words used by the defendant have to be construed within the meaning that they are given in England and Wales. In construing those words, the courts should not have any regard to the *defendant's* own racial, national or ethnic origins—or presumably their religious beliefs or lack of such (*R* v *White (Anthony Delroy)* [2001] EWCA Crim 216).

In order to prove this offence you must show that the defendant *intended* to cause harassment, alarm or distress and, it seems, that by so doing, the defendant actually caused some harassment, alarm or distress. In *S* v *DPP* [2008] All ER (D) 119 the defendant took a digital photograph of the complainant and posted it on the internet with a speech bubble and text alleging the complainant had previous convictions for violence. It was several months later that the photograph was shown to the complainant by the police and the Divisional Court held that the time and the circumstances in which it had been brought fully to the attention of the complainant were immaterial.

Harassment, alarm or distress are not defined and it would appear that they are to be given their ordinary everyday meaning. A police officer can be caused such harassment, alarm or distress (*DPP* v *Orum* [1989] 1 WLR 88) and can also be the victim of the racially aggravated form of the offence (see *R* v *Jacobs* [2001]

Cr App R(s) 38), and he/she can feel that harassment, alarm or distress for someone else present (e.g. a child—see *Lodge* v *DPP* [1989] COD 179). Police officers are expected to display a degree of fortitude and, for an officer to be caused harassment, alarm or distress, the conduct complained of must go beyond that which he/she would regularly come across in the ordinary course of police duties.

Whether the use of a particular phrase, in the context and circumstances in which it was used, was intended to cause harassment, alarm or distress for the offences above is a question of fact for the relevant magistrate/jury to decide (see *DPP* v *Weeks* (2000) *The Independent*, 17 July). Consequently, in that case where the defendant was alleged to have called the victim a 'black bastard' during a heated argument over a business transaction, the magistrates were still entitled to find him not guilty of the aggravated s. 4A offence if they were satisfied that the relevant intention was not present.

Posting a threatening, abusive or insulting letter through someone's letter box is not an offence under this section (*Chappell* v *DPP* (1988) 89 Cr App R 82). It may, however, amount to an offence under the Malicious Communications Act 1988 (**see para. 4.5.7.6**).

As with the offence under s. 4, an offence under s. 4A can be committed in a public or private place, but no offence is committed where the words or behaviour are used, etc. by a person inside a dwelling and the person who is harassed, alarmed or distressed is also inside that or another dwelling (s. 4A(2)). For the definition of a 'dwelling' **see para. 4.6.7.1**.

4.6.8.1 Defence

The Public Order Act 1986, s. 4A provides a specific defence:

(3) It is a defence for the accused to prove—
  (a) that he was inside a dwelling and had no reason to believe that the words or behaviour used, or the writing, sign or other visible representation displayed, would be heard or seen by a person outside that or any other dwelling, or
  (b) that his conduct was reasonable.

KEYNOTE

If is for the defendant to prove that one of the elements existed at the time of the offence. The standard of proof here will be that of the balance of probabilities, i.e. that it was more likely than not.

4.6.9 Harassment, Alarm or Distress

OFFENCE: **Harassment, alarm or distress—*Public Order Act 1986, s. 5***
- Triable summarily • Fine

OFFENCE: **Racially or religiously aggravated—*Crime and Disorder Act 1998, s. 31(1)(c)***
- Triable summarily • Fine

The Public Order Act 1986, s. 5 states:

(1) A person is guilty of an offence if he—
  (a) uses threatening, abusive or insulting words or behaviour, or disorderly behaviour, or
  (b) displays any writing, sign or other visible representation which is threatening, abusive or insulting,

within the hearing or sight of a person likely to be caused harassment, alarm or distress thereby.

KEYNOTE

Unlike the other racially or religiously aggravated forms of public order offences, the offence under s. 5 remains triable summarily, even if aggravated by the conditions set out in s. 28 of the Crime and Disorder Act 1998 (s. 31(5)). (For a full explanation of the meaning of 'racially or religiously aggravated', **see para. 4.5.2.**)

In a case where the defendant used the words 'You're fucking Islam' in an aggressive manner towards a Sikh police officer of Asian appearance, the Divisional Court held that the expression itself was almost undeniably abusive if not insulting. The magistrates' court's decision (that there was 'no case to answer') did not disclose any apparent reasons as to why it was of the opinion that the words used were not abusive and insulting and the DPP's appeal was upheld (*R (On the Application of DPP)* v *Humphrey* [2005] EWHC 822).

The racially or religiously aggravated circumstances set out at s. 28(1)(a) of the Crime and Disorder Act 1998 deal with situations where the defendant demonstrates racial or religious hostility at the time of (or immediately before or after) commiting the offence, towards the *victim*. To clarify such situations in relation to the racially or religiously aggravated form of the above offence, s. 31(7) provides that the person 'likely to be caused harassment, alarm or distress' will be treated as the 'victim'. This appears to be a more useful provision than its counterpart in relation to the Criminal Damage Act 1971 (**see Crime, chapter 1.13**).

Note that 'disorderly' is not defined and ought to be given its ordinary everyday meaning. It need not be shown that the disorderly behaviour is itself threatening, abusive or insulting, nor that it brought about any feelings of apprehension in the person to whom it was directed (*Chambers and Edwards* v *DPP* [1995] Crim LR 896). The wording of s. 5 is not limited to rowdy behaviour and will extend to any behaviour that could be construed as threatening, abusive or insulting. 'Insulting' has been held by the Divisional Court to include the actions of a market trader who installed a hidden video camera to film women trying on swimwear (*Vigon* v *DPP* (1998) 162 JP 115).

The discussion above (**see para. 4.6.8**) in relation to intentional harassment, alarm or distress also applies to this offence, except here there needs to be a person within whose sight or hearing the conduct takes place. This requirement was confirmed in *Taylor* v *DPP* [2006] EWHC 1202 where it was held that there must be at least evidence that there was someone who could see, or could hear, at the material time, what the individual was doing. However, there was no requirement for the prosecution to call evidence that that someone did actually hear the words spoken or see the behaviour.

Quashing a conviction under s. 5, the Administrative Court has held that there is a presumption that a defendant's conduct was protected by Article 10 unless and until it is established that a restriction on their freedom of expression was strictly necessary (*Percy* v *DPP* (2002) 166 JP 93). That case involved the defendant defacing an American flag as part of a political protest at a US air base. The court held that ss. 5 and 6 of the Act contained the necessary balance between the right of individual freedom of expression and the right of others not to be insulted and/or distressed. However, on the facts of the case itself, the issues of proportionality had not been properly considered and therefore the defendant's conviction was quashed.

This offence is a 'penalty offence' for the purposes of s. 1 of the Criminal Justice and Police Act 2001 (**see para. 4.4.3**).

As with the offence under s. 4, an offence under s. 5 can be committed in a public place or a private place, but no offence is committed where the words or behaviour are used, etc. by a person inside a dwelling and the other person is also inside that or another dwelling (s. 5(2)). For the definition of a 'dwelling' **see para. 4.6.7.1**.

4.6.9.1 State of Mind

The Public Order Act 1986, s. 6 states:

(4) A person is guilty of an offence under section 5 only if he intends his words or behaviour, or the writing, sign or other visible representation, to be threatening, abusive or insulting, or is aware that it may be threatening, abusive or insulting or (as the case may be) he intends his behaviour to be or is aware that it may be disorderly.

4.6.9.2 Defence

The Public Order Act 1986, s. 5 provides a specific defence:

(3) It is a defence for the accused to prove—
(a) that he had no reason to believe that there was any person within hearing or sight who was likely to be caused harassment, alarm or distress, or
(b) that he was inside a dwelling and had no reason to believe that the words or behaviour used, or the writing sign or other visible representation displayed, would be heard or seen by a person outside that or any other dwelling, or
(c) that his conduct was reasonable.

KEYNOTE

It is for the defendant to prove that one of the elements existed at the time of the offence. The standard of proof here will be that of the balance of probabilities, i.e. that it was more likely than not.

In deciding whether a defendant's conduct was reasonable under s. 5(3)(c) an objective test will be applied (*DPP* v *Clarke* (1991) 94 Cr App R 359).

4.6.9.3 Police Direction to Prevent Harassment

In response to a number of campaigns against individuals believed to be involved in animal experiments, the Criminal Justice and Police Act 2001 gives the police specific powers to prevent the intimidation or harassment of people in their own or others' homes. Situations envisaged by the legislation typically arise where protestors gather outside a house where a particular individual is believed to be. Under such circumstances s. 42 provides the most senior ranking police officer at the scene with discretionary powers to give directions to people in the vicinity. The power arises where:

- the person is outside (or in the vicinity of) any premises that are used by any individual as his/her dwelling, and
- the constable believes, on reasonable grounds, that the person is there for the purpose of representing or persuading the resident (or anyone else)
- that they should not do something they are entitled or required to do or
- that they should do something that they are under no obligation to do, and
- the constable also believes, on reasonable grounds, that the person's presence amounts to, or is likely to result in, the harassment of the resident or is likely to cause alarm or distress to the resident.

Although the premises involved may be in use by any 'individual' (e.g. *not* a company) and the purpose may be to persuade that or any other 'individual', the officer must believe that the ultimate effect will be harassment, alarm or distress of the *resident*. The requirement for 'belief' by the police officer here is greater than mere concern or suspicion. The requirement for reasonable grounds means that their existence or otherwise will be judged objectively and not simply from the personal standpoint of the officer using the power. Nevertheless, the officer is given a great deal of individual discretion in using this power. Given the discretion and the potential impact on the competing rights of all involved, the use and extent of this power must be carefully considered in the light of the principles of the Human Rights Act 1998 (**see chapter 4.3**).

A direction given under s. 42 requires the person(s) to do all such things as the officer specifies as being *necessary* to prevent the harassment, alarm or distress of the resident, including:

(a) a requirement to leave the vicinity of the premises in question, and
(b) a requirement to leave that vicinity and not to return to it within such period as the constable may specify, not being longer than 3 months;

and (in either case) the requirement to leave the vicinity may be to do so immediately or after a specified period of time (s. 42(4)).

The direction may be given orally and, where appropriate, may be given to a group of people together the (s. 42(3)). There is no requirement that the officer giving the direction be in uniform.

The power under s. 42 cannot be used to direct someone to refrain from conduct made lawful under the Trade Union and Labour Relations (Consolidation) Act 1992, s. 220 (peaceful picketing, **see chapter 4.9**).

For further offences and measures in relation to animal experiments **see para. 4.6.16**.

4.6.9.4 Contravening a s. 42 Direction

OFFENCE: **Knowingly contravening a s. 42 direction—*Criminal Justice and Police Act 2001, s. 42(7)***

- Triable summarily • Three months' imprisonment and/or a fine

The Criminal Justice and Police Act 2001, s. 42 states:

(7) Any person who knowingly fails to comply with a requirement in a direction given to him under this section (other than a requirement under subsection (4)(b)) shall be guilty of an offence.

KEYNOTE

The wording of this offence means that you will have to prove a number of key aspects. First, you will need to show that the person acted 'knowingly' in failing to comply with a requirement in a direction and secondly that it was 'given to them'. Generally the best proof of this will be to show that the person had received the direction (and the detail of its extent) personally and that they understood it. Therefore, although the section allows for directions to be given to groups, there may be practical benefits in giving personal directions where circumstances allow.

The reference to subs. (4)(b) means a requirement to leave that vicinity and not to return to it within such period as the constable may specify, not being for a period longer than three months (**see para. 4.6.9.3**).

OFFENCE: **Unlawfully returning to vicinity—*Criminal Justice and Police Act 2001, s. 42(7A)***

• Triable summarily • Imprisonment for a term not exceeding 51 weeks and/or a fine. (In relation to an offence committed before the commencement of s. 281(5) of the Criminal Justice Act 2003 the reference to 51 weeks is to be read as a reference to six months)

The Criminal Justice and Police Act 2001, s. 42 states:

(7A) Any person to whom a constable has given a direction including a requirement under subsection (4)(b) commits an offence if he—
(a) returns to the vicinity of the premises in question within the period specified in the direction beginning with the date on which the direction is given; and
(b) does so for the purpose described in subsection (1)(b).

KEYNOTE

This offence was introduced by the Serious Organised Crime and Police Act 2005, s. 127 following some doubts as to whether a direction issued by a police officer under s. 42 could lawfully direct a person to stay away from the premises in question for anything other than a relatively short period of time. The offence is committed where a person who is subject to a direction to leave the vicinity, returns within a period of up to three months (the precise length of time will be specified by the police officer) for the 'purposes' described at s. 42A(1)(b) **(see para. 4.6.9.5)**—representing to or persuading a person not to do something he/she is entitled to do, or to do something he/she is not obliged to do.

The Criminal Justice and Police Act 2001 also makes specific provision for protecting the directors (and those who live with them) of certain companies involved in sensitive and emotive operations from harassment in their homes or private lives. Under the 2001 Act (see s. 45), an individual who is (or proposes to be) a director, secretary or permanent representative of a relevant company can apply to the Secretary of State for a 'confidentiality order', exempting the individual's personal details from many of the public records that have to be maintained under the Companies Act 1985. This provision is designed to prevent activists who are opposed to the operations of certain research organisations from gaining access to the personal details of the company's officers through public registers.

4.6.9.5 Harassment etc. of Person in Their Home

OFFENCE: **Harassment of a person in their home—*Criminal Justice and Police Act 2001, s. 42A***

• Triable summarily • Imprisonment for a term not exceeding 51 weeks and/or a fine

The Criminal Justice and Police Act 2001, s.42A states:

(1) A person commits an offence if—
(a) that person is present outside or in the vicinity of any premises that are used by any individual ('the resident') as his dwelling;
(b) that person is present there for the purpose (by his presence or otherwise) of representing to the resident or another individual (whether or not one who uses the premises as his dwelling), or of persuading the resident or such another individual—
(i) that he should not do something that he is entitled or required to do; or
(ii) that he should do something that he is not under any obligation to do;
(c) that person—

(i) intends his presence to amount to the harassment of, or to cause alarm or distress to, the resident; or

(ii) knows or ought to know that his presence is likely to result in the harassment of, or to cause alarm or distress to, the resident; and

(d) the presence of that person—

(i) amounts to the harassment of, or causes alarm or distress to, any person falling within subsection (2); or

(ii) is likely to result in the harassment of, or to cause alarm or distress to, any such person.

(2) A person falls within this subsection if he is—

(a) the resident,

(b) a person in the resident's dwelling, or

(c) a person in another dwelling in the vicinity of the resident's dwelling.

KEYNOTE

This offence, created by s.126 of the Serious Organised Crime and Police Act 2005, has a number of elements, each of which must be proved if a successful prosecution is to be brought. The ingredients include:

- **Place**—the defendant must be shown to have been in the relevant place (outside or in the vicinity of a 'dwelling' which has the same meaning as in part 1 of the Public Order Act 1986.
- **Purpose**—the defendant's purpose in being there must be to represent to, or persuade the resident/another individual that he/she should not do something they are entitled/required to do or that he/she should do something that they are not under any obligation to do.
- **Intention/knowledge**—you must prove that the defendant intended his/her presence to amount to harassment of, or to cause alarm or distress to, the resident or that he/she or that he/she knew/ought to have known that his/her presence was likely to have that result.
- **Consequences**—you must show that the defendant's presence amounted to/was likely to result in the harassment of, or causing alarm or distress to, any resident, person in the resident's dwelling, or person in another dwelling in the vicinity of the resident's dwelling.

References in subs. (1)(c) and (d) to a person's presence are references either to his/her presence alone or together with that of any other people who are also present (s. 42A(3)).

For the purposes of this section a person ought to know that his/her presence is likely to result in the harassment of, or to cause alarm or distress to, a resident if a reasonable person in possession of the same information would think that it was likely to have that effect (s. 42A(4)).

'Dwelling' means any structure or part of a structure occupied as a person's home or as other living accommodation (whether the occupation is separate or shared with others) but does not include any part not so occupied (s. 42A(7)).

Further guidance on this section is provided by Home Office Circular 34/2005.

4.6.10 Wearing of Political Uniforms in Public Places

Section 1 of the Public Order Act 1936 prohibits the wearing of uniforms signifying association with any political organisation in a public place or at a public meeting and creates a summary offence to that effect.

Section 2 of the 1936 Act outlaws quasi-military organisations which are trained or organised to usurp the functions of the police or the armed forces, or to display physical force in promoting any political object.

4.6.11 Public Processions and Assemblies

In addition to the sporadic conduct threatening public order considered at the start of this chapter, the organisation of processions and assemblies presents significant policing problems. The law relating to these events is discussed below.

In using the statutory provisions discussed here, it is also useful to note the overlap with other policing powers such as those under s. 60 of the Criminal Justice and Public Order Act 1994 (**see para. 4.4.4.12**). For a further discussion of these preventive powers **see para. 4.6.2.2**.

4.6.11.1 Procession Organiser

The Public Order Act 1986 places certain obligations on the organisers of public processions that are intended:

- to demonstrate support for, or opposition to, the views or actions of any person or body,
- to publicise a cause or campaign, or
- to mark or commemorate an event.

If a public procession is to be held for any of these purposes, the organisers must give written notice—by delivering it to a police station in the relevant police area—unless it is not reasonably practicable to do so (s. 11(1) and (4)).

In the case of a procession that is to begin in Scotland but will cross over into England, the notice must be delivered to a police station in the first police area in England on the proposed route (s. 11(4)(b)).

Under s. 11(3), the notice must specify:

- the date and time of the proposed procession,
- the proposed route, and
- the name and address of the person(s) proposing to organise it.

If such a procession is held without compliance with these requirements, or if a procession takes place on a different date, time or route, each of the people organising it commits a summary offence (s. 11(7)).

As with the offences in relation to the wearing of political uniforms (**see para. 4.6.10**), particular care will need to be taken in utilising the powers under this legislation in light of the protection that is given, both by the European Convention on Human Rights and by the courts, to freedom of speech and assembly.

4.6.11.2 Defence

The Public Order Act 1986, s. 11 states:

> (8) It is a defence for the accused to prove that he did not know of, and neither suspected nor had reason to suspect, the failure to satisfy the requirements or (as the case may be) the difference of date, time or route.
>
> (9) To the extent that an alleged offence turns on a difference of date, time or route, it is a defence for the accused to prove that the difference arose from circumstances beyond his control or from something done with the agreement of a police officer or by his direction.

4.6.11.3 Imposing Conditions on Public Processions

Section 12 of the Public Order Act 1986 allows for conditions to be imposed on public processions. These conditions may be imposed by 'the senior police officer' in each case. For the purposes of s. 12, the 'senior police officer' is:

- in relation to a procession being held or intended to be held where people are assembling to take part in it, *the most senior rank of the police officers present at the scene*;
- in relation to any other intended procession, the chief officer of police.

Therefore, where advance notice of a procession is given, the chief of police may impose conditions on it as set out below. Where the procession has already begun, or where people are gathering to take part in it, the most senior officer present at the scene may impose those conditions.

The chief officer's directions must be in writing (s. 12(3)); the directions of other officers may be given orally, though it will be far easier to prove the relevant offences of failing to comply with those directions if there is some permanent and reliable record of them.

If the senior police officer, having regard to:

- the time or place of the procession *and*
- the circumstances in which it is to be held *and*
- its route/proposed route

'reasonably believes' (**see chapter 4.4**) that it may result in:

- serious public disorder
- serious damage to property *or*
- serious disruption to the life of the community

he/she may give directions imposing such conditions as appear to him/her to be necessary to prevent such disorder, damage or disruption on the organisers or the people taking part (s. 12(1)).

The senior police officer (as defined above) may also give those directions where he/she reasonably believes that the purpose of the person(s) organising the procession is the intimidation of others with a view to compelling them either:

- not to do an act they have a right to do *or*
- to do an act they have a right not to do.

In any of the cases above, the directions may include directions as to the route of the procession or a prohibition on it entering certain public places (s. 12(1)).

4.6.11.4 Offences Regarding Failure to Comply with Conditions

There are three summary offences created in relation to these directions under s. 12(4), (5) and (6). The first two are:

- organising or
- taking part in

a public procession and, in doing so, *knowingly* (**see Crime, chapter 1.1**) failing to comply with a condition imposed under s. 12. In either case it is a defence for the person to show that the circumstances were beyond their control.

The third offence is inciting another (**see Crime, chapter 1.3**) to take part in a public procession in a way which the person incited knows is failing to comply with an imposed condition.

4.6.11.5 Prohibited Processions

Section 13 of the Public Order Act 1986 allows for a public procession to be prohibited, either by the district council on application from the chief constable (outside the City of London or the Metropolitan Police District) or the Commissioner with approval of the Secretary of State.

As with the conditions imposed under s. 12 above, there are three summary offences created in relation to prohibited public processions. The first two offences are committed by people who either organise a public procession which they *know* has been prohibited under s. 13 or who take part in such a procession *knowing* that it has been so prohibited (s. 13(7) and (8)). There is also an offence of a person inciting another to take part in a procession which he/she knows has been prohibited (s. 13(9)).

4.6.11.6 Conditions on Public Assemblies

Section 14 of the Public Order Act 1986 allows for the 'senior police officer' (as defined above) to impose conditions on public assemblies in the same way as public processions.

A public assembly is an assembly of two or more people in a public place that is wholly or partly open to the air (s. 16).

The circumstances under which such conditions may be imposed are the same as for public processions with the added provision that the officer may direct:

- the maximum duration or
- the maximum number of people

as appears necessary to him/her in order to avoid disorder, damage, disruption or intimidation (s. 14(1)).

The chief officer's directions must be given in writing but, as with the offences relating to public processions, it will be easier to prove the offences under s. 14 if there is a reliable record of any directions given by the senior officer. Clearly the imposition of conditions can conflict with the individual rights of affected people and therefore must be shown to be a necessary, and proportionate, interference with those rights (**see chapter 4.3**). Where a chief officer imposes restrictions under these provisions, he/she will have to identify what limb of s. 14(1) was being relied upon and, where appropriate, to identify which of the grounds contained in the legislation was being relied upon. While the reasons given by a chief officer do not have to be given in great detail, they nevertheless have to be sufficient to enable demonstrators to understand why the decision was made and for a court to understand if a decision was reasonable or not (see *R (On the Application of Brehony)* v *Chief Constable of Greater Manchester Police* [2005] EWHC 640).

Summary offences are again created in relation to the organising, taking part or inciting others to take part in a public assembly in each case where the person knowingly fails to comply with a condition imposed under s. 14 (s. 14(4), (5) and (6)). In the cases of people organising or taking part in such an assembly, there is a statutory defence available if the defendant can prove that the failure to comply with the relevant condition arose from circumstances beyond his/her control.

It is important to note that situations envisaged by s. 14 are different from those envisaged by s. 12. One envisages public processions, the other public assemblies. The relevance to police officers of this distinction lies in the conditions that may be imposed under each section. This distinction was considered at length in *DPP* v *Jones* [2002] EWHC 110 by the Administrative Court where demonstrators against the Huntingdon Life Sciences centre were prosecuted for failing to comply with a condition set out in a police notice issued under s. 14. It was held on appeal that some of the conditions imposed were more properly concerned with a public procession and therefore were beyond the police powers under s. 14. Although in *Jones* the offending parts of the police notice were 'severed', leaving the enforceable bits intact, it may be safer to issue two separate notices in appropriate circumstances, one relating to the conditions to be observed by participants in the 'procession' element of an operation and the other imposing conditions on the 'assembly' element.

4.6.11.7 Trespassory Assemblies

The provisions of s. 14 above apply to public assemblies. However, occasions have arisen where the assembly has been *trespassory*, that is, on land which is either private or where there is only a limited right of public access and the permission of the relevant landowner has not been granted. In such instances, s. 14A of the Public Order Act 1986 provides the police with certain powers.

Section 14A allows a chief officer of police (including the Commissioners of the City of London and Metropolitan Police) to apply to the relevant district council for an order prohibiting the holding of trespassory assemblies.

The conditions under which a chief officer may make such an application are where he/she reasonably believes that an assembly is to be held in any district at a place on land to which the public has no right/limited rights of access and that the assembly:

- is likely to be held without the permission of the occupier of the land *or*
- to conduct itself in such a way as to exceed the limits of the public's right of access

and that the assembly may result:

- in serious disruption to the life of the community or
- where the land (or a building/monument on it) is of historical, architectural, archaeological or scientific importance, significant damage to the land, building or monument.

The classic example of such a situation can be found at sites such as Stonehenge.

On receiving the application, the council may—*with the consent of the Secretary of State*—make an order either in the terms of the application or with such modifications as may be approved by the Secretary of State (s. 14A(2)(a)). The order must be in writing or reduced into writing as soon as practicable after being made (s. 14A(8)).

If such an order is made it must not last for more than four days nor must it apply to an area beyond a radius of five miles from a specified centre (s. 14A(6)).

Unlike the amended definition of public assembly generally, an assembly for the above purposes means 20 or more people and 'land' means land in the open air. 'Public' includes a section of the public (see s. 14A(9)).

4.6.11.8 Offences in Relation to Trespassory Assemblies

There are three summary offences in relation to trespassory assemblies in respect of which an order has been passed. These offences, under s. 14B(1), (2) and (3) apply to people who:

- organise or
- take part in

an assembly that they *know* is prohibited by an order under s. 14A *or*

- who incite another to take part in such an assembly.

Even where an order has been passed, there will be a need to show that the assembly was obstructive of the highway or at least that it exceeded the public's general right of access (*DPP* v *Jones* [1999] 2 AC 240).

4.6.11.9 Police Powers Regarding Trespassory Assemblies

Section 14C of the 1986 Act states:

> (1) If a constable in uniform reasonably believes from proceedings that a person is on his way to an assembly within the area to which an order under section 14A applies which the constable reasonably believes is likely to be an assembly which is prohibited by that order, he may, subject to subsection (2) below—
> (a) stop that person, and
> (b) direct him not to proceed in the direction of the assembly.
> (2) The power conferred by subsection (1) may only be exercised within the area to which the order applies.
> (3) A person who fails to comply with a direction under subsection (1) which he knows has been given to him is guilty of an offence.

KEYNOTE

This power allows officers to stop people, though not, it would seem, vehicles (in which case the general power under the Road Traffic Act 1988 must be used). This is the type of non-Police and Criminal Evidence Act 1984 power that may be required to be recorded in the same way as general stop and search powers in accordance with recommendation 61 of the Stephen Lawrence Inquiry. For more detail on these general powers to stop people and vehicles and the recording requirements, **see para. 4.4.4.**

4.6.11.10 Public Meetings

It is an offence to attempt to break up a public meeting.

OFFENCE: **Trying to break up a public meeting—*Public Meeting Act 1908, s. 1***
- Triable summarily • Six months' imprisonment and/or a fine

(No specific power of arrest)

The Public Meeting Act 1908, s. 1 states:

> (1) Any person who at a lawful public meeting acts in a disorderly manner for the purpose of preventing the transaction of the business for which the meeting was called together shall be guilty of an offence and shall on summary conviction be liable to imprisonment for a term not exceeding six months or to a fine not exceeding £1,000 or to both ...
> (2) Any person who incites others to commit an offence under this section shall be guilty of a like offence.

KEYNOTE

If a constable reasonably suspects any person of committing this offence, he/she may, *if requested by the person chairing the meeting*, require the offender to declare his/her name and address immediately. Failing to comply with such a request or giving false details is a summary offence (s. 1(3)).

'Public meeting' is not defined in the 1908 Act. There appears to be no requirement for the meeting to be lawfully assembled.

This offence does not apply to meetings held in relation to the Representation of the People Act 1983, s. 97 (meetings concerned with public elections) (s. 1(4)). In the case of people acting or inciting others to act in a disorderly way at such meetings, there is a specific summary offence under s. 97(1) of the 1983 Act.

4.6.12 Dispersal of Groups

In addition to the organisation of public assemblies, processions and meetings, informal and *ad hoc* gatherings have implications for policing. Although individual rights to freedom of assembly and movement are protected by the European Convention on Human Rights (**see chapter 4.3**), these rights have to be balanced against those of the community at large and, in certain circumstances, the presence of groups can be intimidating.

The Anti-social Behaviour Act 2003 provides further policing powers to deal with such occasions by allowing a senior police officer to authorise the use of powers of dispersal if the relevant conditions are met.

4.6.12.1 Authorisation of Powers

The Anti-social Behaviour Act 2003, s. 30 states:

(1) This section applies where a relevant officer has reasonable grounds for believing—
- (a) that any members of the public have been intimidated, harassed, alarmed or distressed as a result of the presence or behaviour of groups of two or more persons in public places in any locality in his police area (the 'relevant locality'), and
- (b) that anti-social behaviour is a significant and persistent problem in the relevant locality.

(2) The relevant officer may give an authorisation that the powers conferred on a constable in uniform by subsections (3) to (6) are to be exercisable for a period specified in the authorisation which does not exceed 6 months.

KEYNOTE

'Relevant officer' means a police officer of or above the rank of superintendent (s. 36). This officer must be able to show that he/she had reasonable grounds for believing *both* conditions set out at (a) and (b) above were met. If they are met, the relevant officer can then authorise the use of the further powers set out in the paragraphs below.

The 'anti-social behaviour' referred to means behaviour by a person which causes (or is likely to cause) harassment, alarm or distress to one or more other people not of the same household as that person (s. 36).

The definition of public place is also contained in s. 36 and is fairly wide. It includes a highway and any place to which at the material time the public (or any section of it) has access, on payment or otherwise, as of right or by virtue of express or implied permission.

Any authorisation must be in writing, signed by the relevant officer giving it and must specify:

- the relevant locality;
- the grounds on which the authority is given;
- the period during which the relevant powers (conferred by s. 30(3) to (6) below) are exercisable (which is not to exceed six months) (s. 31).

The implications of such an authorisation for the individual rights and freedoms of members of the community mean that further conditions have been attached to the authorising of these powers. For instance, an authorisation may not be given without the consent of the local authority or each local authority whose area includes the whole or part of the relevant locality (s. 31(2)). In addition, the authorisation must be given publicity, either by publishing a notice in a newspaper circulating in the relevant locality or by posting an authorisation notice in some conspicuous place or places within the relevant locality (or both) (s. 31(3)). This publicity must be given *before* the specified date on which the powers of dispersal below are to begin (s. 31(5)).

An authorisation can be withdrawn by the officer who made it or by another officer for that police area of the same or higher rank; however, the local authority must be consulted first.

4.6.12.2 Powers of Dispersal

The Anti-social Behaviour Act 2003, s. 30 states:

> (3) Subsection (4) applies if a constable in uniform has reasonable grounds for believing that the presence or behaviour of a group of two or more persons in any public place in the relevant locality has resulted, or is likely to result, in any members of the public being intimidated, harassed, alarmed or distressed.

KEYNOTE

If the relevant conditions in s. 30(3) are met, a police officer in uniform may give one or more of the specified directions. These directions (set out at s. 30(4)(a) to (c)) are directions:

(a) requiring the people in the group to disperse (either immediately or by such time and in such a way as the officer may specify);
(b) requiring any of those people whose place of residence is not within the relevant locality to leave the relevant locality (or any part of it) either immediately or by such time and in such a way as the officer may specify; and
(c) prohibiting any of those people whose place of residence is not within the relevant locality from returning to the relevant locality (or any part of it) for such period (not exceeding 24 hours) from the giving of the direction as the officer may specify.

The direction under subs. (4) may be given orally, may be given to any person individually or to two or more people together, and may be withdrawn or varied *by the person who gave it* (s. 32(1)).

Note that any reference to the presence or behaviour of a group of people will include a reference to the presence or behaviour of *any one or more* of those people. Therefore it is not necessary to show that the presence or behaviour of all the people in a particular group meets each of the criteria above.

In *R (On the Application of Singh)* v *Chief Constable of West Midlands Police* [2006] EWCA Civ 1118 it was held that the use of dispersal orders, in respect of a group of protesters of two or more persons who were causing harassment, alarm and distress to members of the public, was lawful even though the authorisation order was already in force in respect of unrelated expected anti-social behaviour. In addition it was held that the use of the power did not override the applicants fundamental human rights (European Convention on Human Rights, Articles 9 and 10—see **paras 4.3.12** and **4.3.13** respectively), but was expressly subject to them.

In *Bucknell* v *DPP* [2006] EWHC 1888 two groups totalling about 15 to 20 black and Asian young people had assembled and, although no member of the public had complained, the local beat constable took the view that the presence of the groups was likely to cause intimidation, alarm, harassment or distress to members of the public and issued a direction to them to disperse. It was held that the direction was not a proportionate response because the apparent characterisation of those groups alone was not capable objectively of giving rise to the necessary reasonable belief.

An exception is made (by s. 30(5)) for people engaged in lawful picketing (under s. 220 of the Trade Union and Labour Relations (Consolidation) Act 1992; **see chapter 4.9**) or who are taking part in a lawfully notified and organised public procession under s. 11(1) of the Public Order Act 1986 (**see para. 4.6.11.1**). The powers to give directions will not be available in these specific cases.

This power is among those that can be conferred on a designated person under sch. 4 to the Police Reform Act 2002 (**see chapter 4.2**). In exercising the powers conferred by s. 30(3) to (6), police officers and designated PCSOs must have regard to the Code of Practice (s. 34(5)).

4.6.12.3 Power to Remove Under-16s

A further power, to remove people under 16 to their place of residence, is provided by the Act.

The Anti-social Behaviour Act 2003, s. 30 states:

> (6) If, between the hours of 9pm and 6am, a constable in uniform finds a person in any public place in the relevant locality who he has reasonable grounds for believing—
> (a) is under the age of 16, and
> (b) is not under the effective control of a parent or a responsible person aged 18 or over,
> he may remove the person to the person's place of residence unless he has reasonable grounds for believing that the person would, if removed to that place, be likely to suffer significant harm.

KEYNOTE

This power, while appearing relatively straightforward, presents some practical difficulties. It presupposes a number of things, one of them being that the officer knows the person's place of residence. Additionally, in many cases, 'removing' teenagers to their home address will be far easier said than done. Careful reference will need to be made to the Code of Practice when exercising this power.

In *R (On the Application of W)* v *Metropolitan Police Commissioner* [2006] EWCA Civ 458 it was held that the word 'remove' in s. 30(6) naturally and compellingly means 'take away using reasonable force if necessary'. However, this is not an arbitrary power and, within a designated dispersal area, a constable must only use this power, (a) to protect children under 16 from the physical and social risks of anti-social behaviour by others, or (b) to prevent children from participating in anti-social behaviour themselves.

If this power is used, any local authority whose area includes the whole or part of the relevant locality must be notified of that fact (s. 32(4)).

For the police powers to remove suspected truants, **see Evidence & Procedure, para. 2.6.12.**

4.6.12.4 Knowingly Contravening Direction

OFFENCE: **Knowingly contravening direction—*Anti-social Behaviour Act 2003*, s. 32(2)**

- Triable summarily • Three months' imprisonment and/or a fine

The Anti-social Behaviour Act 2003, s. 32 states:

(2) A person who knowingly contravenes a direction given to him under section 30(4) commits an offence . . .

KEYNOTE

You must show that the person contravened the direction(s) 'knowingly'. Therefore it is important to be able to prove that the direction was lawfully authorised, clearly given and that it was understood by the defendant.

4.6.13 Sporting Events

In addition to the more general offences regulating public order, there are several offences and statutory measures which are specifically aimed at tackling disorder and anti-social behaviour at sporting events. The legislation in this area has developed piecemeal over a number of years and is sprinkled across a number of different Acts. However, one of the more important pieces of football legislation, the Football (Disorder) Act 2000 which amended the Football Spectators Act 1989, significantly altered the powers of courts and police in football-related matters.

These wide powers are discussed in more detail below.

4.6.13.1 Offences under the Football (Offences) Act 1991

OFFENCE: **Misbehaviour at designated football match—*Football (Offences) Act 1991, ss. 2, 3 and 4***

- Triable summarily • Fine

The Football (Offences) Act 1991, ss. 2, 3 and 4 state:

2. It is an offence for a person at a designated football match to throw anything at or towards—
(a) the playing area, or any area adjacent to the playing area to which spectators are not generally admitted, or
(b) any area in which spectators or other persons are or may be present, without lawful authority or lawful excuse (which shall be for him to prove).

3.—(1) It is an offence to engage or take part in chanting of an indecent or racialist nature at a designated football match.
(2) For this purpose—
(a) 'chanting' means the repeated uttering of any words or sounds (whether alone or in concert with one or more others); and
(b) 'of racialist nature means consisting of or including matter which is threatening, abusive or insulting to a person by reason of his colour, race, nationality (including citizenship) or ethnic or national origins.

4. It is an offence for a person at a designated football match to go onto the playing area, or any area adjacent to the playing area to which spectators are not generally admitted, without lawful authority or lawful excuse (which shall be for him to prove).

KEYNOTE

A 'designated' match for these purposes is the same as a 'regulated' match under the Football Spectators Act 1989 (see below).

These offences can be separated into those affecting the playing area and adjacent parts of the ground (ss. 2 and 4) and the offence of indecent or 'racialist' chanting (s. 3).

In the case of the first offence (s. 2), throwing anything at or towards the playing area etc., there is a defence of having lawful authority or lawful excuse (which presumably would cover returning the ball to the field of play). Generally there seem to be few occasions on which a defendant would have lawful authority/reasonable excuse for the behaviour prohibited by s. 2.

Section 4 makes the same savings in relation to lawful authority/reasonable excuse and, in both cases, the burden of proof falls on the defendant. (The *standard* of proof will be that of the balance of probabilities; **see Evidence & Procedure, chapter 2.7**).

For the offence under s. 3, the defendant must be shown to have *repeated* the words or sounds before it can be classed as 'chanting'. The definition under subsection (2) was amended by the Football (Offences and Disorder) Act 1999 to cater for occasions where the offence is committed by one person acting alone.

'Indecent' is not defined and will be a question of fact for the court to decide in all the circumstances.

'Racialist' is a slightly outdated term. The wording of s. 3(2)(b) requires that the chanting *is* rather than might potentially be, threatening, abusive or insulting (compare with the wording under the other general public order offences above). Therefore, although there is no express requirement for a 'victim' of the offence under this section, the best way to prove that element of the offence would be to find someone who was so threatened, abused or insulted by the behaviour.

For an example where the Administrative Court held that shouting 'you're just a town full of Pakis' at supporters from Oldham fell squarely within the definition, see *DPP* v *Stoke on Trent Magistrates Court* [2003] 3 All ER 1086.

Unlike the racially or religiously aggravated offences created by the Crime and Disorder Act 1998, as amended by the Anti-terrorism, Crime and Security Act 2001, religion is not included in the definition.

4.6.13.2 Designated and Regulated Football Matches

Many of the offences and powers relating to football fixtures apply to 'designated' or 'regulated' football matches. These expressions have caused a number of practical anomalies and have been standardised by various statutory instruments. In summary, the expressions generally have the following meaning:

- An association football match (in England and Wales) as described below will be a regulated football match for the purposes of part II of the Football Spectators Act 1989. The description will cover association football matches in which one or both of the participating teams represents a club which is, for the time being, a member (whether a full or associate member) of the Football League, the Football Association Premier League, the Football Conference or the League of Wales, or represents a country or territory.
- An association football match (outside England and Wales) as described below will also be a regulated football match for the purposes of part II of the 1989 Act. The description will cover an association football match involving:
  - a national team appointed by the Football Association to represent England or the Football Association of Wales to represent Wales; or
  - a team representing a club which is, at the time the match is played, a member (whether a full or associate member) of the Football League, the Football Association Premier League, the Football Conference or the League of Wales; or
  - any match involving a country or territory whose football association is for the time being a member of Fédération Internationale de Football Association (FIFA), where the match is part of a competition or tournament organised by or under the authority of FIFA or the Union des Associations Européennes de Football (UEFA), and where the

competition or tournament is one in which the England or Wales national team is eligible to participate or has participated; or

- any match involving a club whose national football association is a member of FIFA, where the match is part of a competition or tournament organised by or under the authority of FIFA or UEFA, and where the competition or tournament is one in which a club from the Football League, the Football Association Premier League, the Football Conference or the League of Wales is eligible to participate or has participated.

4.6.13.3 Banning Orders and Detention

The Football Spectators Act 1989 contains the powers to impose banning orders that exclude offenders from attendance at both domestic and international football matches. There are two ways in which a banning order can be made and the first of these is where a person is convicted of a relevant offence (s. 14A). The relevant offences are set out in sch. 1 to the 1989 Act and include offences relating to drunkenness, violence or threats of violence, or public order offences committed on journeys to or from regulated matches or during the period of such a match. Where a court is considering a banning order there are special provisions allowing evidence that might otherwise be inadmissible to be heard.

Rather than simply having the power to make such orders, courts are under a statutory duty to pass such orders if they are satisfied that there are reasonable grounds to believe that the orders would help prevent violence or disorder at/in connection with a 'regulated football match' (see above). Violence here includes violence towards property and disorder includes stirring up racial hatred (s. 14C of the 1989 Act). If the court does not pass an order, it must state in open court its reasons for not doing so.

The court may adjourn any proceedings in relation to an order even after sentencing the offender and may remand the offender (s. 14A(4A) and (4BA)). Where the offender is remanded on bail he/she may be required not to leave England and Wales before appearing before the court and to surrender his/her passport to a constable (s. 14A(4BB)).

If a magistrates' court fails to make a banning order, the prosecution have a right of appeal to the Crown Court, or to the Court of Appeal where the Crown Court failed to make an order (s. 14A(5A)). If the offender does not appear for any adjourned proceedings, the court may further adjourn the proceedings, or it may issue a warrant for his/her arrest but only after it is satisfied that he/she has had adequate notice of the time and place of the adjourned proceedings (s. 14A(4B) and (4C)).

A banning order may only be made in addition to a sentence imposed by the court but can be passed even if the originating offence is dealt with by way of a conditional or absolute discharge.

The second way of getting a banning order is by way of complaint by the relevant chief officer, or the DPP (s. 14B(1)). On such an application a magistrates' court can make an order if the person has at any time caused or contributed to any violence or disorder in the United Kingdom or elsewhere. The court may impose conditions on banning orders and must require the surrender of the person's passport in connection with regulated football matches outside the United Kingdom (s. 14E(3)). Where proceedings are adjourned, as with the first way of obtaining a banning order, the offender may be remanded and, where bailed, be required to surrender his/her passport (s. 14B(5) and (6)). Again, where the magistrates have failed to make a banning order, the prosecution have a right of appeal to the Crown Court (s. 14D(1A)). Note that 'passport' will be amended to 'travel authorisation' when the provisions of the Identity Cards Act 2006 are in force.

The effect of a banning order, unless a person is detained in legal custody, is that they must initially report to the police station specified within five days of the order being made

(s. 14E(2)). They must also notify the enforcing authority of specified changes to their personal circumstances within seven days of the occurrence of any such changes (s. 14E(2B) and (2C)).

Banning orders made under s. 14A of the 1989 Act (on conviction of a relevant offence) in addition to an immediate sentence of imprisonment will have a minimum of six and a maximum of ten years' duration (s. 14F(3)). Other banning orders made under s. 14A (i.e. where they do not accompany a sentence of immediate imprisonment) have a minimum of three and a maximum of five years' duration (s. 14F(4)). Banning orders made under s. 14B (on complaint by a chief officer of police) have a minimum of three and a maximum of five years' duration (s. 14F(5)). If a banning order has been in effect for at least two-thirds of its period, the person subject to it can apply to the court which passed the order for its termination. The Serious Organised Crime Agency (**see chapter 4.1**) has responsibility for monitoring the movement of football spectators and collating relevant intelligence. The Football Banning Orders Authority is the 'designated authority' for the purposes of the 1989 Act. Under the Football Disorder Act 2000, the Serious Organised Crime Agency is empowered to disclose information for the purposes of the 1989 Act.

International banning orders do not contravene either the general European law on the free movement of people within the European Union, or the European Convention on Human Rights (*Gough* v *Chief Constable of Derbyshire* [2002] QB 1213).

In *Gough*, the Court of Appeal held that there was no absolute right to leave one's country. As banning orders were to be imposed only where there were strong grounds for concluding that the person had a propensity to take part in football hooliganism, the court held that it was appropriate that such people should be subject to a scheme that restricted their ability to indulge in that hooliganism. Like Sexual Offences Prevention Orders (**see Crime, chapter 1.9**) and Anti-social Behaviour Orders (**see chapter 4.5**), banning orders are not criminal charges, nor are the proceedings in applying for them 'criminal' proceedings (*Gough*). However, although the standard of proof is the civil standard in applying for banning orders, that standard is flexible and has to reflect the consequences that would follow if the case for a banning order were made out. In reality, this means that magistrates should apply a standard of proof which is hard to distinguish from the criminal one. If properly made, any interference with an individual's Article 8 rights by a banning order will be justified (under Article 8(2)) as the order is necessary for the prevention of disorder.

4.6.13.4 Failing to Comply with Banning Order

OFFENCE: **Failing to comply with banning order—*Football Spectators Act 1989, s. 14J***

• Triable summarily • Six months' imprisonment and/or a fine

(1) A person subject to a banning order who fails to comply with—
  (a) any requirement imposed by the order, or
  (b) any requirement imposed under section 19(2B) or (2C) below is guilty of an offence.

KEYNOTE

The reference to s. 19(2B) and (2C) is to the power for the enforcing authority to issue written notices requiring individuals to report to police stations and, where relevant, to surrender their passports, in advance of certain matches outside England and Wales.

A number of exemptions are provided for under s. 20. These allow, among other things, for the person on whom an order has been passed to apply for exemption from the duties of the order under special circumstances.

4.6.13.5 Power of Detention

The Football Spectators Act 1989, s. 21A states:

(1) This section and section 21B below apply during any control period in relation to a regulated football match outside England and Wales or an external tournament if a constable in uniform—
   (a) has reasonable grounds for suspecting that the condition in section 14B(2) above is met in the case of a person present before him, and
   (b) has reasonable grounds to believe that making a banning order in his case would help to prevent violence or disorder at or in connection with any regulated football matches.

(2) The constable may detain the person in his custody (whether there or elsewhere) until he has decided whether or not to issue a notice under section 21B below, and shall give the person his reasons for detaining him in writing.
   This is without prejudice to any power of the constable apart from this section to arrest the person.

(3) A person may not be detained under subsection (2) above for more than four hours or, with the authority of an officer of at least the rank of inspector, six hours.

KEYNOTE

The power under s. 21A requires the police officer to be in uniform and may be exercised only in relation to a person who is a British citizen (see s. 21C(1)).

The initial period of detention allowed is a *maximum* of four hours, extendable to a further *maximum* of six hours by an inspector. There is no requirement under this section that the inspector be either present or in uniform. The purpose of the detention is for the officer to decide whether or not to issue a notice (see below).

The condition under s. 14B(2) referred to is that the person has at any time caused or contributed to any violence or disorder in the United Kingdom or elsewhere.

'Control period' means, in relation to a regulated football match outside England and Wales, the period:

(a) beginning five days before the day of the match, and
(b) ending when the match is finished or cancelled

and in relation to an external tournament, means any period described in an order made by the Secretary of State:

(a) beginning five days before the day of the first football match outside England and Wales which is included in the tournament, and
(b) ending when the last football match outside England and Wales which is included in the tournament is finished or cancelled,

but, for the purposes of paragraph (a), any football match included in the qualifying or pre-qualifying stages of the tournament is to be ignored (see s. 14(5) and (6)). An example of a specified 'control period' can be seen in the Football Spectators (European Championship Control Period) Order 2004 (SI 2004/1029), which set the period during which the relevant police powers could be exercised before and after the Euro 2004 championship taking place in Portugal.

References to football matches include matches intended to be played (s. 14(7)). A person who has been detained under subsection (2) above may only be further detained under that subsection in the same control period in reliance on information which was not available to the constable who previously detained him/her; and a person on whom a notice has been served under s. 21B(2) may not be detained under subsection (2) above in the same control period (s. 21A(4)).

4.6.13.6 Service of Notice

The Football Spectators Act 1989, s. 21B states:

(1) A constable in uniform may exercise the power in subsection (2) below if authorised to do so by an officer of at least the rank of inspector.
(2) The constable may give the person a notice in writing requiring him—
  (a) to appear before a magistrates' court at a time, or between the times, specified in the notice,
  (b) not to leave England and Wales before that time (or the later of those times), and
  (c) if the control period relates to a regulated football match outside the United Kingdom or to an external tournament which includes such matches, to surrender his passport to the constable, and stating the grounds referred to in section 21A(1) above.
(3) The times for appearance before the magistrates' court must be within the period of 24 hours beginning with—
  (a) the giving of the notice, or
  (b) the person's detention under section 21A(2) above,
  whichever is the earlier.

KEYNOTE

The power above requires the police officer to be in uniform and the authority of an inspector or above. It applies during any control period in relation to a regulated football match outside England and Wales or an external tournament (as to which, see the Keynote above).

A constable may arrest a person to whom he/she is giving a notice if he/she has reasonable grounds to believe that it is *necessary* to do so in order to ensure that the person complies with the notice (s. 21B(5)).

For the purposes of s. 14B, the notice is to be treated as an application for a banning order made by complaint (s. 21B(4)).

As with the provision for detention under s. 21A, the powers conferred above may be exercised only in relation to a person who is a British citizen (s. 21C(1)).

4.6.13.7 Failure to Comply with Notice under Section 21B

OFFENCE: **Failing to comply with notice—*Football Spectators Act 1989, s. 21C***

- Triable summarily • Six months' imprisonment and/or a fine

The Football Spectators Act 1989, s. 21C states:

(2) A person who fails to comply with a notice given to him under section 21B above is guilty of an offence...

KEYNOTE

The notice must have been lawfully given in order to attract liability for this offence. Where a person who has been given a notice appears before a magistrates' court as required by the notice (whether under arrest or not), the court may remand him/her and the court may require the person not to leave England

and Wales as a condition of bail (s. 21C(3) and (4)). Also, if the control period relates to a regulated football match outside the United Kingdom or to an external tournament which includes such matches, the court can order the person to surrender his/her passport to a police constable, if he/she has not already done so.

4.6.13.8 Offences under the Sporting Events (Control of Alcohol etc.) Act 1985

OFFENCE: **Alcohol on coaches and trains—*Sporting Events (Control of Alcohol etc.) Act 1985, s. 1***

- Triable summarily • Three months' imprisonment and/or a fine (s. 1(3))
- Fine (s. 1(2) and (4))

The Sporting Events (Control of Alcohol etc.) Act 1985, s. 1 states:

(1) This section applies to a vehicle which—
  (a) is a public service vehicle or railway passenger vehicle, and
  (b) is being used for the principal purpose of carrying passengers for the whole or part of a journey to or from a designated sporting event.

(2) A person who knowingly causes or permits alcohol to be carried on a vehicle to which the section applies is guilty of an offence—
  (a) if the vehicle is a public service vehicle and he is the operator of the vehicle or the servant or agent of the operator, or
  (b) if the vehicle is a hired vehicle and he is the person to whom it is hired or the servant or agent of that person.

(3) A person who has alcohol in his possession while on a vehicle to which this section applies is guilty of an offence.

(4) A person who is drunk on a vehicle to which this section applies is guilty of an offence.

KEYNOTE

Section 1 creates a number of offences in relation to public service vehicles and trains being used principally (though not exclusively) to carry passengers for the whole or part of a journey, to or from a designated sporting event.

The offences can be committed by the vehicle operator/hirer or his/her servant or agent provided there is evidence of *knowingly* causing or permitting the carrying of alcohol (for 'cause and permit', see Road Policing, chapter 3.1).

The other offences are committed by people who have alcohol in their 'possession' (as to which, see Crime, chapter 1.6) and by people who are drunk on a relevant vehicle. Generally, any mature and competent witness may give evidence as to drunkenness (see Evidence & Procedure, chapter 2.7).

Section 7(3) provides a power for a police officer to stop a public service vehicle in order to search it where he/she has reasonable grounds to suspect an offence under this section *is being or has been committed* in respect of that vehicle. It also provides a power to search a railway carriage (though not to stop the train) under the same circumstances. The power to search people in those vehicles comes from s. 7(2).

OFFENCE: **Alcohol on other vehicles—*Sporting Events (Control of Alcohol etc.) Act 1985, s. 1A***

- Triable summarily • Three months' imprisonment and/or a fine (s. 1A(3))
- Fine (s. 1A(2) and (4))

The Sporting Events (Control of Alcohol etc.) Act 1985, s. 1A states:

(1) This section applies to a motor vehicle which—
 (a) is not a public service vehicle but is adapted to carry more than 8 passengers, and
 (b) is being used for the principal purpose of carrying two or more passengers for the whole or part of a journey to or from a designated sporting event.
(2) A person who knowingly causes or permits alcohol to be carried on a motor vehicle to which this section applies is guilty of an offence—
 (a) if he is its driver, or
 (b) if he is not its driver but is its keeper, the servant or agent of its keeper, a person to whom it is made available (by hire, loan or otherwise) by its keeper or the keeper's servant or agent, or the servant or agent of a person to whom it is so made available.
(3) A person who has alcohol in his possession while on a motor vehicle to which this section applies is guilty of an offence.
(4) A person who is drunk on a motor vehicle to which this section applies is guilty of an offence.

KEYNOTE

This section creates similar offences to those set out under s. 1 but these relate to mechanically propelled vehicles that are intended or adapted for use on roads and that are adapted to carry more than eight passengers (not being PSVs). For an explanation of each of these terms, **see Road Policing, chapter 3.1**.

For the purposes of the above offences, a vehicle's 'keeper' is the person having the duty to take out a vehicle excise licence for it (s. 1A(5)).

The power to stop and search vehicles and their occupants under s. 7(3) above also applies to an offence under this section.

Power to prohibit sale of alcohol on trains

The Licensing Act 2003, s. 157 states:

(1) A magistrates' court acting for a petty sessions area may make an order prohibiting the sale of alcohol, during such period as may be specified, on any railway vehicle—
 (a) at such station or stations as may be specified, being stations in that area, or
 (b) travelling between such stations as may be specified, at least one of which is in that area.

KEYNOTE

Unlike some other aspects relating to the control of pre- and post-match events, there is no specific restriction on the period over which such an order may be made. However, the court cannot make such an order unless it is satisfied that the order is *necessary* to prevent disorder (s. 157(3)).

A court may only make an order under this section on the application of a senior police officer (s. 157(2)). 'Senior police officer' means a police officer of, or above, the rank of inspector (s. 157(7)).

Where an order is made, the police officer who applied for the order (or, if the chief officer of police of the force in question has designated another senior police officer for the purpose, that other officer) must immediately serve a copy of the order on the train operator (or each train operator) affected by the order (s. 157(4)).

OFFENCE: **Contravening prohibition order for sale of alcohol on trains—*Licensing Act 2003, s. 157(5)***

• Triable summarily • Three months' imprisonment and/or a fine not exceeding £20,000

The Licensing Act 2003, s.157 states:

(5) A person commits an offence if he knowingly—
  (a) sells or attempts to sell alcohol in contravention of an order under this section, or
  (b) allows the sale of alcohol in contravention of such an order.

KEYNOTE

The defendant must be shown to have acted *knowingly*, and proof that the order was properly made and in force so far as that date and location were concerned will be critical.

4.6.13.9 Designated Sporting Event

For the purposes of the Sporting Events (Control of Alcohol etc.) Act 1985, a 'designated' sporting event means an event or proposed event which has been designated or is part of a class designated by order made by the Secretary of State. It also includes events designated under comparable Scottish legislation. Events which are to be held outside Great Britain can also be designated (s. 9).

4.6.13.10 The Sporting Events (Control of Alcohol etc.) Act 1985

OFFENCE: **Alcohol at sports grounds—*Sporting Events (Control of Alcohol etc.) Act 1985, s. 2***

- Triable summarily • Three months' imprisonment and/or a fine (s. 2(1))
- Fine (s. 2(2))

The Sporting Events (Control of Alcohol etc.) Act 1985, s. 2 states:

(1) A person who has alcohol or an article to which this section applies in his possession—
  (a) at any time during the period of a designated sporting event when he is in any area of a designated sports ground from which the event may be directly viewed, or
  (b) while entering or trying to enter a designated sports ground at any time during the period of a designated sporting event at that ground, is guilty of an offence.

(2) A person who is drunk in a designated sports ground at any time during the period of a designated sporting event at that ground or is drunk while entering or trying to enter such a ground at any time during the period of a designated sporting event at that ground is guilty of an offence.

KEYNOTE

The articles to which s. 2 applies are:

- articles capable of causing injury to a person struck by them, being
- bottles, cans or other portable containers (including ones that are crushed or broken), which
- are for holding any drink, and
- are of a kind which are normally discarded or returned to/left to be recovered by the supplier when empty

and include parts of those articles. Any such article that is for holding any medicinal product (within the meaning of the Medicines Act 1968) is excluded from this definition (s. 2(3)).

Section 7(1) provides a power for a constable to enter any part of a ground during a designated sporting event for the purpose of enforcing the provisions of the Act.

Where a person is convicted of an offence under either s. 2(1) or s. 2(2) the court must consider imposing a banning order (see para. 4.6.13.3).

4.6.13.11 Fireworks, Flares and Similar Objects at Sports Grounds and Events

OFFENCE: **Having fireworks, flares etc.—*Sporting Events (Control of Alcohol etc.) Act 1985, s. 2A***

- Triable summarily • Three months' imprisonment and/or a fine

The Sporting Events (Control of Alcohol etc.) Act 1985, s. 2A states:

(1) A person is guilty of an offence if he has an article or substance to which this section applies in his possession—
   (a) at any time during the period of a designated sporting event when he is in any area of a designated sports ground from which the event may be directly viewed, or
   (b) while entering or trying to enter a designated sports ground at any time during the period of a designated sporting event at the ground.

(2) ...

(3) This section applies to any article or substance whose main purpose is the emission of a flare for purposes of illuminating or signalling (as opposed to igniting or heating) or the emission of smoke or a visible gas; and in particular it applies to distress flares, fog signals, and pellets and capsules intended to be used as fumigators or for testing pipes, but not to matches, cigarette lighters or heaters.

(4) This section also applies to any article which is a firework.

KEYNOTE

There is a defence under s. 2A(2) for the person to prove that he/she had possession of the article or substance with lawful authority. 'Possession' is quite a broad concept going beyond 'carrying' (**see Crime, chapter 1.6**).

As with all other offences under the 1985 Act, the powers of entry, search and arrest under s. 7 apply to this offence.

4.6.13.12 Designated Sports Ground

Under s. 9 of the 1985 Act, a 'designated sports ground' means:

(2) ... any place—
   (a) used (wholly or partly) for sporting events where accommodation is provided for spectators, and
   (b) for the time being designated, or of a class designated, by order made by the Secretary of State,

   and an order under this subsection may include provision for determining for the purposes of this Act the outer limit of any designated sports ground.

The period of a 'designated sporting event' is also covered by s. 9:

(4) The period of a designated sporting event is the period beginning two hours before the start of the event or (if earlier) two hours before the time at which it is advertised to start and ending one hour after the end of the event, but—
   (a) where an event advertised to start at a particular time on a particular day is postponed to a later day, the period includes the period in the day on which it is advertised to take place beginning two hours before and ending one hour after that time, and
   (b) where an event advertised to start at a particular time on a particular day does not take place, the period is the period referred to in paragraph (a) above.

KEYNOTE

The Sports Grounds and Sporting Events (Designation) Order 2005 (SI 2005/3204) provides for the classes of sporting events for the purposes of the 1985 Act. These differ slightly from those contained in the Football Spectators Act 1989 (**see para. 4.6.13.2**) and include:

- Association football matches in which one or both of the participating teams represents a club which is for the time being a member (whether a full or associate member) of the Football League, the Football Association Premier League, the Football Conference National Division, the Scottish Football League, or Welsh Premier League, or represents a country or territory.
- Association football matches in competition for the Football Association Cup (other than in a preliminary or qualifying round).
- Association football matches at a sports ground outside England and Wales in which one or both of the participating teams represents a club which is for the time being a member (whether a full or associate member) of the Football League, the Football Association Premier League, the Football Conference National Division, the Scottish Football League, or Welsh Premier League, or represents the Football Association or the Football Association of Wales.

4.6.13.13 Ticket Touts

OFFENCE: **Ticket touts—*Criminal Justice and Public Order Act 1994, s. 166***

- Triable summarily • Fine

The Criminal Justice and Public Order Act 1994, s. 166 states:

(1) It is an offence for an unauthorised person to—
  (a) sell a ticket for a designated football match, or
  (b) otherwise to dispose of such a ticket to another person.
(2) For this purpose—
  (a) a person is 'unauthorised' unless he is authorised in writing to sell or otherwise dispose of tickets for the match by the organisers of the match;
  (aa) a reference to selling a ticket includes a reference to—
    (i) offering to sell a ticket;
    (ii) exposing a ticket for sale;
    (iii) making a ticket available for sale by another;
    (iv) advertising that a ticket is available for purchase; and
    (v) giving a ticket to a person who pays or agrees to pay for some other goods or services or offering to do so;
  (b) a 'ticket' means anything which purports to be a ticket; and
  (c) a 'designated football match' means a football match of a description, or a particular football match, for the time being designated for the purposes of this section by order made by the Secretary of State.

KEYNOTE

Section 166 was amended by the Violent Crime Reduction Act 2006 to update provisions on the sale and disposal of football match tickets by unauthorised persons, to cover ticket touting on the internet and other practices associated with the unauthorised sale and distribution of tickets.

Section 166A, inserted by the 2006 Act, is designed to ensure that the offence in s. 166 is compatible with European Directive 2000/31/EC. It ensures that the provisions in s. 166 do not apply to internet service providers based outside the UK, but makes it an offence for an internet service provider established in the

UK to sell or otherwise dispose of tickets for designated football matches regardless of where the sale etc., takes place.

The power to search on arrest under s. 32 of the Police and Criminal Evidence Act 1984 (**see chapter 4.4**) extends to vehicles that it is believed are being used by ticket touts.

For the purposes of s. 166(2)(c) a 'designated football match' is currently described in the Ticket Touting (Designation of Football Matches) Order 2007 (SI 2007/790). Article 2 of the Order designates association football matches in England and Wales in which one or both participating teams represent a club which is a member of the Football League, Football Association Premier League, Football Conference or League of Wales, or represents a country or territory. Article 2(3) designates association football matches outside England and Wales involving a national team of England or Wales, or a team representing a club which is a member of the Football League, Football Association Premier League, Football Conference or League of Wales, or matches in competitions or tournaments organised by or under the authority of FIFA (Fédération Internationale de Football Association) or UEFA (Union des Associations Européennes de Football), in which any of such English or Welsh domestic or national teams is eligible to participate or has participated.

4.6.14 Terrorism

The Terrorism Act 2000 extended earlier law and powers so that they encompassed all forms of terrorism, both in England and Wales and elsewhere; it also redefined 'terrorism'. Following what is now commonly referred to as the 9/11 attacks on America, the more prominent threat posed by terrorist activity generally, and in particular the attacks in London on 7 and 21 July 2005, Parliament determined the need for further measures which were included in the Terrorism Act 2006.

The following paragraphs set out some of the key features and definitions of the legislation relating to terrorism.

4.6.14.1 Terrorism Act 2000

The Terrorism Act 2000 (as amended) is set out in eight parts. Broadly, these are as follows:

- part I—the definition of terrorism, the repeal of the Prevention of Terrorism (Temporary Provisions) Act 1989 and making of transitional arrangements;
- part II—proscribed organisations and the associated offences;
- part III—terrorist property, fund raising and financial matters;
- parts IV and V—terrorist investigations and police powers;
- part VI—miscellaneous offences;
- part VII—provisions relating to Northern Ireland;
- part VIII—technical provisions.

Given the specialist nature of terrorist investigations and the extent of the revised legislation, it is not appropriate to cover all aspects of counter-terrorist law here. What follows is a summary of some of the key areas of the legislation in so far as they might be encountered by operational police officers in general.

4.6.14.2 Terrorism

Terrorism is defined in s. 1 of the 2000 Act as:

(1) … the use or threat of action where—
 (a) the action falls within subsection (2),

(b) the use or threat is designed to influence the government or an international governmental organisation, or to intimidate the public or a section of the public, and
(c) the use or threat is made for the purpose of advancing a political, religious or ideological cause.

(2) Action falls within this subsection if it—
(a) involves serious violence against a person,
(b) involves serious damage to property,
(c) endangers a person's life, other than that of the person committing the action,
(d) creates a serious risk to the health or safety of the public or a section of the public, or
(e) is designed seriously to interfere with or seriously to disrupt an electronic system.

(3) The use or threat of action falling within subsection (2) which involves the use of firearms or explosives is terrorism whether or not subsection (1)(b) is satisfied.

KEYNOTE

As discussed above, this definition extends far beyond the original boundaries of terrorism defined under the former Prevention of Terrorism (Temporary Provisions) Act 1989 and will now include domestic terrorism. The definition is now so broad that it should be considered when dealing with other, more familiar offences such as blackmail, contamination of goods and threats to kill (as to which, **see Crime**). In fact it is so wide that it technically covers some threats of industrial action (though it would be extraordinary to contemplate using the legislation in that context).

The above definition recognises that terrorist activity may be motivated by religious or ideological reasons rather than simply political ones. The definition also encompasses broad activities (including threats) which, though potentially devastating in their impact on society, may not be overtly violent. Examples of such activity might be interference with domestic water and power supplies or serious disruption of computer networks.

The provision at s. 1(3) means that, where the relevant criminal activity involves the use of firearms or explosives, there is no further need to show that the behaviour was designed to influence the government or to intimidate the public or a section of the public. An example of such activity might be the shooting of a senior military or political figure. A 'firearm' for this purpose includes air weapons (s. 121); it is not clear whether the definition includes imitation firearms (as to which, **see chapter 4.7**).

The reference to 'action' here includes action outside the United Kingdom. Similarly, references to people, property, the public and governments apply to all those features whether in the United Kingdom or elsewhere (s. 1(4)).

4.6.14.3 Proscribed Organisations

Part II of the 2000 Act, as amended by the 2006 Act, allows the Secretary of State to proscribe specific organisations. The most recent list of proscribed organisations contains some of the most active and widely known terrorist groups across the world, including al-Qaeda (see sch. 2 to the Act). However, the fact that a particular organisation does not appear on that list does not necessarily mean that it is not 'proscribed'. This is clear from the case of *R* v *Z* [2005] UKHL 35, where the House of Lords held that the 'Real IRA' was to be regarded as a *part of* a proscribed organisation (namely the IRA), even though it was not specifically named in the relevant section. The main relevance of proscribing an organisation under the 2000 Act is that there are a number of serious terrorist offences arising out of proscribed organisations. In summary, these are:

- belonging or professing to belong to a proscribed organisation (s. 11(1));
- inviting support for a proscribed organisation (s. 12(1));

- arranging or managing (or assisting in doing so) a meeting of three or more people (in public or private) which the defendant knows is:
  - to support a proscribed organisation,
  - to further the activities of a proscribed organisation, or
  - to be addressed by a person who belongs or professes to belong to a proscribed organisation (s. 12(2)) *or* addressing a meeting to encourage support for a proscribed organisation or to further its activities (s. 12(3)).

All of the above offences are punishable by ten years' imprisonment on indictment. The offence under s. 11(1) can be rebutted by a defendant if he/she can prove certain facts. This 'reverse burden of proof' was challenged in *Attorney-General's Reference (No. 4 of 2002), Sheldrake* v *DPP* [2005] 1 AC 264 as imposing a legal burden on the defendant to prove his/her innocence and therefore in breach of the presumption of innocence (Article 6 of the Convention; **see para. 4.3.9**) and also the defendant's freedom of expression (under Article 10; **see para. 4.3.13**). The House of Lords considered the imposition of a legal burden upon the accused under s. 11(2) as neither proportionate nor reasonable and stated that courts should read the subsection as imposing an evidential, as opposed to a persuasive, burden of proof (**see Evidence & Procedure, para. 2.7.4**).

There is a further, summary, offence of wearing an item of clothing, or wearing, carrying or displaying an article in such a way or in such circumstances as to arouse reasonable suspicion that the defendant is a member or supporter of a proscribed organisation (s. 13).

Detailed provisions for organisations to appeal against their proscribed status to an Appeal Commission are contained in sch. 3 to the 2000 Act.

4.6.14.4 Offences under the Terrorism Act 2000

As a general summary, the main offences under the Terrorism Act 2000 include:

- *inviting* another to provide money or other property (s. 15(1));
- *providing* money or other property (s. 15(3));
- *receiving* money or other property (s. 15(2));
- *possessing* money or other property (s. 16(2));
- *arranging* for money or other property to be made available;

in each case intending that, or having reasonable cause to suspect that, it may be used for the purposes of terrorism (ss. 15, 16(2) and 17):

- *using* money or other property for the purposes of terrorism (s. 16(1));
- *concealing, moving or transferring* any terrorist property (s. 18).

Each of these offences is punishable by a maximum of 14 years' imprisonment on indictment (s. 22).

In addition, under s. 19, where a person:

- believes or suspects that another person has committed an offence under any of ss. 15 to 18 and
- bases that belief or suspicion on information which comes to his/her attention in the course of a trade, profession, business or employment

he/she must disclose to a constable as soon as is reasonably practicable that belief or suspicion, and the information on which it is based, otherwise he/she commits an offence punishable with five years' imprisonment.

This offence imposes a duty on banks and other businesses to inform the police without delay where they have suspicions over the activities of individuals with whom they come into contact. The s. 19 offence applies only where the suspicion has arisen in the course of the defendant's *work*. The former offence that tried to impose a similar duty on people who became suspicious in their general day-to-day life has not been replicated in the 2000 Act. There are several provisos and qualifications to the obligations imposed by s. 19.

The Terrorism Act 2000 goes on to create a number of further offences in relation to terrorism. In summary, the key offences are:

- *Directing* the activities of an organisation which is concerned in the commission of acts of terrorism (s. 56). This offence (which is often easier to prove than some of the better known offences) carries a maximum sentence of life imprisonment.
- *Providing or receiving instruction or training* in the making or use of firearms or explosives or radioactive material or weapons designed or adapted for the discharge of any radioactive material, or chemical, biological or nuclear weapons (s. 54).
- *Possessing articles* in circumstances which give rise to a reasonable suspicion that the possession is for a purpose connected with the commission, preparation or instigation of an act of terrorism (s. 57). It must be shown that the defendant(s) possessed extremist material for use in the future to incite the commission of terrorist acts (*R* v *Zafar* [2008] EWCA Crim 184).
- *Collecting or making a record* of information (including photographs and electronic records) of a kind likely to be useful to a person committing or preparing an act of terrorism, or possessing a document or record containing information of that kind (s. 58). The document, etc. concerned must be of a kind that is likely to provide practical assistance to a person, rather than simply encouraging the commission of terrorist acts (*R* v *K* [2008] EWCA Crim 185).
- *Inciting* another person to commit an act of terrorism wholly or partly outside the United Kingdom (s. 59).

4.6.14.5 Offences under the Terrorism Act 2006

For the purposes of the 2006 Act the offences are grouped into three specific areas; encouragement etc. of terrorism; preparation of terrorist acts and terrorist training; offences involving radioactive devices and materials and nuclear facilities and sites.

The offences within the *encouragement etc. of terrorism* group are:

- publishes a statement to encourage the commission, preparation or instigation of acts of terrorism or Convention offences (s. 1(2));
- engages in the dissemination of terrorist publications (s. 2(1)).

For the purposes of both these sections it is necessary to prove that they glorify the act of terrorism and which members of the public could reasonably be expected to infer that what is being glorified is being glorified as conduct that should be emulated by them in existing circumstances. 'Glorification' includes any form of praise or celebration, and cognate expressions are to be construed accordingly (s. 20(2)). The 'Convention offences' mentioned in s. 1(2) are those offences listed in sch. 1 to the Act and include offences in relation to explosives, biological weapons, chemical weapons, nuclear weapons, hostage-taking, hijacking, terrorist funds, etc.

Section 3(1) provides that the offences under ss. 1 and 2 can be committed by publishing a statement electronically, i.e. via the internet. 'Statement' includes a communication of any description, including a communication without words consisting of sounds or images or both (s. 20(6)). The section provides for a notice to be served by a constable on the person electronically publishing the statement declaring that it is, in his/her opinion, unlawfully terrorism-related and requiring its removal or modification (s. 3(3)). The methods for giving such a notice are provided in s. 4 of the Act. The offences under ss. 1 and 2 are punishable on indictment to a term of imprisonment not exceeding seven years or to a fine or both, and summarily to a term of imprisonment not exceeding 12 months or to a fine or both.

The offences within the *preparation of terrorist acts and terrorist training* group are:

- preparation for terrorist acts (s. 5(1));
- providing instruction or training in any of the skills mentioned for the commission or preparation of acts of terrorism or Convention offences (s. 6(1));
- receiving instruction or training in any of the skills mentioned for the commission or preparation of acts of terrorism or Convention offences (s. 6(2));
- attendance at a place used for terrorist training s. 8(1)).

For an offence under s. 5(1) it is irrelevant whether the intention and preparations relate to one or more particular acts of terrorism, acts of terrorism of a particular description or acts of terrorism generally (s. 5(2)). The punishment for an offence under this section is imprisonment for life.

In relation to the offences of providing or receiving instruction or training under s. 6, the skills mentioned include: the making, handling or use of a noxious substance, the use of any method or technique for doing anything capable of being done for the purposes of terrorism, and the design or adaptation for the purposes of terrorism of any method or technique for doing anything. The punishment on indictment for an offence under s. 6(1) and (2) is a term of imprisonment not exceeding ten years or to a fine or both, or on summary conviction to imprisonment for a term not exceeding 12 months or a fine, or both.

The offence under s. 8(1) may be committed either in the United Kingdom or elsewhere. It must be shown that the person either knew or believed that the instruction or training was wholly or partly for purposes connected with the commission or preparation of acts of terrorism, or that the person could not reasonably have failed to understand the purpose of such instruction or training (s. 8(2)). The punishment on indictment for an offence under this section is a term of imprisonment not exceeding ten years or to a fine or both, or on summary conviction to imprisonment for a term not exceeding 12 months or a fine, or both.

The offences within the *offences involving radioactive devices and materials and nuclear facilities and sites* group are:

- making and possession of devices or materials (s. 9(1));
- misuse of devices or material and misuse and damage of facilities (s. 10(1) and (2));
- terrorist threats relating to devices, materials or facilities (s. 11(1) and (2));
- trespassing etc. on nuclear sites (s. 12 which amends s. 128 of the Serious Organised Crime and Police Act 2005).

The offence under s. 9(1) is committed where a person intends using the device or material in the course of or in connection with the commission or preparation of an act of terrorism or for the purposes of terrorism, or of making it available to be so used. The punishment for an offence under this section is imprisonment for life.

A person commits an offence under s. 10(1) if he/she uses a radioactive device or radioactive material in connection with an act of terrorism. For the offence under s. 10(2) the person must use or damage a nuclear facility in a manner which causes a release of radioactive material or creates or increases a risk that such material will be released. The punishment for both these offences is imprisonment for life.

In relation to s. 11(1), this offence deals with a demand for the supply of a radioactive device, radioactive material, a nuclear facility, or for access to such a facility, for himself or another, and supports such a demand with a threat that a reasonable person would assume that there is a real risk of the threat being carried out if the demand is not met. Section 11(2) deals with a threat to use radioactive material, a radioactive device, or use or damage a nuclear facility in a manner that releases radioactive material or creates or increases a risk of its release. The punishment for both these offences is imprisonment for life.

For trespassing, etc. on nuclear sites **see para. 4.10.10**.

Where a person does anything outside the United Kingdom, which would constitute an offence falling within ss. 1, 6, 8 to 11 of the Act, he/she is deemed to be guilty of that offence. This includes conspiracy, incitement, attempt, aiding, abetting, counselling or procuring the commission of such offences. Proceedings for any such offence may be taken at any place in the United Kingdom irrespective of whether the person is a British citizen or, in the case of a company, a company incorporated in a part of the United Kingdom (s. 17). Proceedings for any of the offences may only be instituted in England and Wales with the consent of the DPP. However, where an offence(s) has been committed for a purpose wholly or partly connected with the affairs of another country' the DPP's consent may only be given with the permission of the Attorney-General (s. 19).

4.6.14.6 Disclosure of Information

Section 38B of the Terrorism Act 2000 introduced an offence for failing to disclose information about acts of terrorism to an appropriate authority.

OFFENCE: **Information about acts of terrorism—*Terrorism Act 2000, s. 38B***

- Triable either way • Five years' imprisonment and/or a fine on indictment
- Six months' imprisonment and/or a fine summarily

The Terrorism Act 2000, s. 38B states:

(1) This section applies where a person has information which he knows or believes might be of material assistance—
 (a) in preventing the commission by another person of an act of terrorism, or
 (b) in securing the apprehension, prosecution or conviction of another person, in the United Kingdom, for an offence involving the commission, preparation or instigation of an act of terrorism.

(2) The person commits an offence if he does not disclose the information as soon as reasonably practicable in accordance with subsection (3).

(3) Disclosure is in accordance with this subsection if it is made—
 (a) in England and Wales, to a constable,
 (b) in Scotland, to a constable, or
 (c) in Northern Ireland, to a constable or a member of Her Majesty's forces.

(4) ...

(5) ...

(6) Proceedings for an offence under this section may be taken, and the offence may for the purposes of those proceedings be treated as having been committed, in any place where the person to be charged is or has at any time been since he first knew or believed that the information might be of material assistance as mentioned in subsection (1).

KEYNOTE

This offence was added by the Anti-terrorism, Crime and Security Act 2001, along with other provisions relating to the monitoring of bank accounts (see s. 38A). Unlike some of the Act's other provisions, this offence relates to *any* person who has information which he/she knows or believes might help prevent an act of terrorism or help bring terrorists to justice.

In England and Wales the disclosure must be made to a police officer.

The provisions of s. 38B(6) mean that a person resident in the United Kingdom could be charged with the offence even if he/she was outside the country when he/she became aware of the information.

It is a defence for a person charged with an offence under subsection (2) to prove that he/she had a reasonable excuse for not making the disclosure (s. 38B(4)).

The 2000 Act also provides for two offences designed to prevent 'tipping off', both of which are punishable on indictment with five years' imprisonment. The first such offence generally prohibits:

- the disclosure of anything which is likely to prejudice an investigation resulting from s. 19 above, or
- interference with material which is likely to be relevant to such an investigation (s. 39(4)).

An example of this offence would be where a bank advises the police of some suspicious activity by one of its customers (under its s. 19 duty) and an employee of the bank tips the customer off.

The second offence is more general and applies where a person knows or has reasonable cause to suspect that a constable is conducting (or proposes to conduct) a terrorist investigation. In such circumstances, under s. 39(2), the person commits an offence if he/she:

- discloses to another anything which is likely to prejudice the investigation, or
- interferes with material which is likely to be relevant to the investigation.

For the definition of a 'terrorist investigation', **see chapter 4.4**. There are specific statutory defences available for both of the above offences.

4.6.14.7 Police Powers

The Terrorism Act 2000 provides the police with many wide-ranging powers. These powers specifically exist *in addition* to any more general powers that the police may have and reasonable force may be used in their exercise (s. 114). Nevertheless, given the nature and extent of these powers, the application of the relevant principles under the Human Rights Act 1998 must be adhered to. In relation to the general police powers, it is worth noting that most offences connected with terrorist activity will be arrestable under s. 24 of the Police and Criminal Evidence Act 1984 (**see chapter 4.4**). An important additional power, however, is provided by s. 41 of the Terrorism Act 2000. This section gives a constable a power to arrest without a warrant a person whom he/she reasonably suspects to be 'a terrorist'. The definition of 'a terrorist' here is broadly a person who:

- has committed one of the main terrorism offences under the Act (including ss. 11, 12 and 15 to 18); or
- is or has been concerned in the commission, preparation or instigation of acts of terrorism.

The full definition of 'a terrorist' can be found in s. 40 of the Act.

The detention, treatment and questioning of persons by police officers arrested under s. 41 is contained in HOC 23/2006 and Code H of the PACE Codes of Practice (for a full discussion **see Evidence & Procedure, para. 2.10.7.5**).

One of the benefits of the power under s.41 is the requirement that the officer reasonably suspects the person of being 'a terrorist' rather than suspecting his/her involvement in a specific offence. A further benefit to the police is that a person who has the powers of a constable in one part of the United Kingdom may exercise the power of arrest anywhere in the United Kingdom (s. 41(9)). Similarly, s. 43 gives a constable the power to:

- stop and search a person whom he/she reasonably suspects to be a terrorist to discover whether they have in their possession anything which may constitute evidence that they are a terrorist—note the applicability of the PACE Codes of Practice to these powers (**see chapter 4.4**); and
- seize and retain anything which he/she discovers in the course of the search which he/she reasonably suspects may constitute evidence that the person is a terrorist and a person who has the powers of a constable in one part of the United Kingdom may exercise these powers (in addition to the powers of arrest above) anywhere in the United Kingdom (s. 43(4) and (5)).

Schedule 5 to the 2000 Act (as amended by the 2006 Act) provides for searches, etc. for the purposes of terrorist investigations. Similar to the provisions of the Police and Criminal Evidence Act 1984' the warrants available include specific premises warrants and all premises warrants. In addition, s. 28 of the 2006 Act provides for the issue of a warrant in relation to the search, seizure and forfeiture of terrorist publications.

The 2006 Act also requires the Secretary of State to appoint a person to review the operation of the provisions of the 2000 Act and part 1 of the 2006 Act. Such a review must be conducted at least once in every 12 month period and a copy of the report must be laid before Parliament (s. 36).

4.6.14.8 Explosives

OFFENCE: **Causing explosion likely to endanger life or property—*Explosive Substances Act 1883, s. 2***

- Triable on indictment • Life imprisonment

The Explosive Substances Act 1883, s. 2 states:

> (1) A person who in the United Kingdom or (being a citizen of the United Kingdom and Colonies) in the Republic of Ireland unlawfully and maliciously causes by any explosive substance an explosion of a nature likely to endanger life or to cause serious injury to property shall, whether any injury to person or property has been actually caused or not, be guilty of an offence ...

KEYNOTE

The consent of the Attorney-General (or Solicitor-General) is required before prosecuting this offence (s. 7(1) of the 1883 Act).

'Explosive substance' includes any materials for making any explosive substance; any implement or apparatus used, or intended or adapted to be used for causing or aiding any explosion (s. 9(1)).

The definition of 'explosive' under the Explosives Act 1875 (**see chapter 4.5**) also applies to this offence (see *R* v *Wheatley* [1979] 1 WLR 144). Therefore fireworks and petrol bombs will be covered (*R* v *Bouch* [1983] QB 246). For offences involving fireworks generally, **see chapter 4.5**; for offences involving fireworks at sporting events, **see para. 4.6.13.11**

Other articles which have been held to amount to 'explosive substances' include:

- shotguns (*R* v *Downey* [1971] NI 224);
- electronic timers (*R* v *Berry (No. 3)* [1995] 1 WLR 7);
- gelignite with a fuse and detonator (*R* v *McCarthy* [1964] 1 WLR 196).

You must prove that the act was carried out 'maliciously' (**see Crime, chapter 1.1**).

Sections 73 to 75 of the Explosives Act 1875 provide powers to search for explosives in connection with the above offence.

OFFENCE: **Attempting to cause explosion or keeping explosive with intent—*Explosive Substances Act 1883, s. 3***

- Triable on indictment • Life imprisonment

The Explosive Substances Act 1883, s. 3 states:

(1) A person who in the United Kingdom or a dependency or (being a citizen of the United Kingdom and Colonies) elsewhere unlawfully and maliciously—

(a) does any act with intent to cause, or conspires to cause, by an an explosive substance an explosion of a nature likely to endanger life, or cause serious injury to property, whether in the United Kingdom or the Republic of Ireland, or

(b) makes or has in his possession or under his control an explosive substance with intent by means thereof to endanger life, or cause serious injury to property, whether in the United Kingdom or the Republic of Ireland, or to enable any other person so to do

shall, whether any explosion does or does not take place, and whether any injury to person or property is actually caused or not, be guilty of an offence ...

OFFENCE: **Making or possessing explosive under suspicious circumstances—*Explosive Substances Act 1883, s. 4***

- Triable on indictment • Fourteen years' imprisonment

The Explosive Substances Act 1883, s. 4 states:

(1) Any person who makes or knowingly has in his possession or under his control any explosive substance under such circumstances as to give rise to a reasonable suspicion that he is not making it or does not have it in his possession or under his control for a lawful object, shall, unless he can show that he made it or had it in his possession or under his control for a lawful object, be guilty of felony ...

KEYNOTE

The offence under s. 3 is one of specific intent (**see Crime, chapter 1.1**).

Both of the above offences require the consent of the Attorney-General (or Solicitor-General) before a prosecution can be brought.

It would seem that the wording of these offences requires the prosecution—in cases of 'possession'—to prove that a defendant *had* the relevant article in his/her possession and that he/she *knew* the nature of it (see *R* v *Hallam* [1957] 1 QB 569). This should be contrasted with the usual approach to offences involving 'possession' where the second part (knowledge of the 'quality' of an item) does not need to be shown; **see Crime, chapter 1.6**. However, the concept of 'in your possession' or 'under your control' is a wide one, as illustrated in a case where the defendant had moved out of his property and left homemade bombs and other articles in some boxes with a friend. New tenants in the property had discovered the boxes which later turned up on a rubbish tip. The defendant went to the police station after learning that he was a suspect and he claimed that he had collected the articles many years previously when he was too young to appreciate how dangerous they were. Although he had left the boxes with his friend he was nevertheless convicted of the above offence as he still had the explosives under his control when he left the property (*R* v *Campbell* [2004] EWCA Crim 2309).

'Reasonable suspicion' in this case will be assessed *objectively*, that is, you must prove that the circumstances of the possession or making of the explosive substance would give rise to suspicion in a reasonable and objective bystander (*R* v *Fegan* (1971) 78 Cr App R 189).

Whether a person's purpose in having the items prohibited by these offences is a 'lawful object' will need to be determined in each case (*Fegan*).

There is no need to show any criminal intent or an unlawful purpose on the part of the defendant (see *Campbell*, above).

Sections 73 to 75 of the Explosives Act 1875 provide powers to search for explosives in connection with the above offence.

Gunpowder

Sections 28 to 30 of the Offences Against the Person Act 1861 creates offences of exploding gunpowder to cause bodily injury; throwing or placing gunpowder or corrosive fluid with intent to cause bodily harm; and placing gunpowder or explosives near buildings or vessels with intent to cause bodily injury. The 1861 Act also creates an offence of possessing or making gunpowder or explosives (or other noxious things) with intent to enable any other person to commit an offence under the Act (s. 64). This offence is triable on indictment and carries two years' imprisonment.

4.6.15 The Prevention of Terrorism Act 2005

Following the many high-level legal arguments and cases arising out of the detention of suspected terrorists in 2004, the government introduced further legislation addressing the problem of what to do with such individuals.

The Prevention of Terrorism Act 2005 creates a number of measures that have a significant impact on this area of policing. However, as this is a highly specialised aspect of operational policing, what follows is simply a summary of the key provisions.

4.6.15.1 Control Orders

At the centre of the Act's framework to prevent the threat of terrorism from certain individuals, is the concept of the control order. The Act provides for the making of control orders imposing obligations on those suspected of being involved in terrorism-related activity. In essence these are preventive orders designed to restrict or prevent further involvement by individuals in such activity. While they may include a provision for 'house arrest', control orders are not synonymous with this requirement which was the focus of much publicity in the media. Control orders can be made against any individual suspected of involvement in terrorism-related activity, irrespective of nationality or the particular terrorist 'cause' in which they are believed to be involved.

Control orders may impose a wide range of obligations on an individual, provided they are necessary for purposes connected with preventing or restricting that individual's further involvement in terrorism-related activity. The legislators intend that each order would be specifically tailored to the particular risk presented by the individual against whom it is sought. The type of obligations that could be imposed would include restrictions on:

- possessing certain items or using property;
- the person's movement to or within certain specified areas;
- the person's place of abode;
- the person's communications and associations (see ss. 1 to 4).

Clearly these are highly controversial measures and there is a direct tension between the concept—let alone the content—of a control order and the Human Rights Act 1998 (as to which **see chapter 4.3**). Control orders that do not involve derogation from the European Convention on Human Rights ('non-derogating control orders') will be made by the Secretary of State who must generally seek permission from the court before doing so. This requirement is designed to ensure that the making of such an order involves legal rather than purely political authority. There have been a number of cases in relation to control orders especially concerning their possible breach of Article 5 of the European Convention on Human Rights (right to liberty and security). However, the House of Lords has upheld the legality of control orders but commented on curfew conditions that have been imposed. For example, they considered a maximum curfew of 12 hours would be acceptable and not be in breach of the human right to liberty (*Secretary of State for the Home Department* v *JJ* [2007] UKHL 45, *Secretary of State for the Home Department* v *MB & AF* [2007] UKHL 46, and *Secretary of State for the Home Department* v *E* [2007] UKHL 47).

Where it appears to the Secretary of State that the involvement in terrorism-related activity of which an individual is suspected may have involved the commission of an offence relating to terrorism that would fall to be investigated by a police force, he/she must consult the chief officer of the police force before making or applying for a control order (s. 8(2)).

If a control order is made against an individual, the Secretary of State must inform the chief officer both that the order has been made and that the chief officer has a duty to make sure that the investigation of the individual's conduct with a view to their prosecution for a terrorism offence is kept under review throughout the period during which the control order has effect (s. 8(4)).

OFFENCE: **Contravening control order—*Prevention of Terrorism Act 2005, s. 9***

- Triable either way • Five years' imprisonment and/or a fine on indictment
- Twelve months' imprisonment and/or a fine summarily

The Prevention of Terrorism Act 2005, s. 9 states:

> (1) A person who, without reasonable excuse, contravenes an obligation imposed on him by a control order is guilty of an offence.

KEYNOTE

The above offence requires proof that the individual has contravened *any* obligation imposed under a control order and the absence of reasonable excuse.

There is a further offence involving individuals bound by a control order in relation to their leaving or returning to the United Kingdom (see s. 9(2)). In addition there is an offence of intentionally obstructing the exercise by any person of a power conferred by s. 7(9) (delivery of notice relating to control order) (s. 9(3)).

Arrest and detention pending control order

The Prevention of Terrorism Act 2005, s. 5 states:

(1) A constable may arrest and detain an individual if—
  (a) the Secretary of State has made an application to the court for a derogating control order to be made against that individual; and
  (b) the constable considers that the individual's arrest and detention is necessary to ensure that he is available to be given notice of the order if it is made.

KEYNOTE

A constable who has arrested an individual under this section must take him/her to the designated place *that the constable considers most appropriate* as soon as practicable after the arrest (s. 5(2)).

An individual taken to a designated place under this section may be detained there until the end of 48 hours from the time of their arrest and a court may then extend the period for no more than 48 hours if necessary to ensure that the person is available to be given notice of any derogating control order that is made against them (s. 5(3) and (4)).

A person arrested under this section and taken to a designated place will be in police detention for the purposes of the Police and Criminal Evidence Act 1984 (s. 5(7)) (for the detention and treatment of prisoners generally **see Evidence & Procedure, para. 2.10.7.5**).

4.6.16 Animal Experiments and Vivisection

The activities of anti-vivisection campaigners and others opposed to the 'commercial exploitation' of animals can be significant and serious in policing terms. These activities have led to specific changes in legislation and also significant policing operations to protect individuals who work with animals in certain circumstances. Some activities that are seen as necessary within our society—such as formal animal experiments—rely on secrecy in order to avoid disruption and the intimidation of staff. For this reason the Animals (Scientific Procedures) Act 1986—under which animal experiments are licensed—creates an offence of improperly disclosing information to others (s. 24).

The Serious Organised Crime and Police Act 2005 provides two offences in relation to animal research organisations as outlined below.

4.6.16.1 Activities Relating to Animal Research Organisations

OFFENCE: **Interference with contractual relationships so as to harm animal research organisation—*Serious Organised Crime and Police Act 2005, s. 145(1)***

- Triable either way • Five years' imprisonment and/or a fine on indictment
- Twelve months' imprisonment and/or a fine summarily

The Serious Organised Crime and Police Act 2005, s. 145 states:

(1) A person (A) commits an offence if, with the intention of harming an animal research organisation, he—
  (a) does a relevant act, or
  (b) threatens that he or somebody else will do a relevant act, in circumstances in which that act or threat is intended or likely to cause a second person (B) to take any of the steps in subsection (2).

(2) The steps are—

(a) not to perform any contractual obligation owed by B to a third person (C) (whether or not such non-performance amounts to a breach of contract);
(b) to terminate any contract B has with C;
(c) not to enter into a contract with C.

(3) For the purposes of this section, a 'relevant act' is—
(a) an act amounting to a criminal offence, or
(b) a tortious act causing B to suffer loss or damage of any description;
but paragraph (b) does not include an act which is actionable on the ground only that it induces another person to break a contract with B.

KEYNOTE

To commit this offence the defendant needs to do a relevant act—this means a criminal offence or a tortious act causing loss or damage—or to threaten that they or another will commit a crime or such a tortious act. A tortious act is an act that is a civil wrong but is not a criminal offence. It then needs to be shown that the conduct of the defendant was likely or intended to cause the person against whom the crime/tortious act is committed (or threatened) to fail to perform a contractual obligation, to terminate a contract or to decide not to enter into a contract.

The intent to harm an animal research organisation needs to be proved. 'Animal research organisation' has two specific meanings for the purposes of ss. 145 and 146:

- A person or organisation who is the owner, lessee or licensee of premises constituting or including:
  - a place specified in a licence granted under ss. 4 or 5 of the Animals (Scientific Procedures) Act 1986,
  - a scientific procedure establishment designated under s. 6 of that Act, or
  - a breeding or supplying establishment designated under s. 7 of that Act (s. 148(2)).
- A person or organisation employed or engaged under a contract for services, as:
  - the holder of a personal or project licence granted under the 1986 Act,
  - a person specified under ss. 6(5) or 7(5) of that Act (s. 148(3)).

'Harming' an animal research organisation means to cause such an organisation loss or damage of any description, or to prevent or hinder such an organisation from carrying on any of its activities (s. 145(5)).

By virtue of s. 145(3)(b), no offence is committed if the only relevant tortious act is an inducement to break a contract. This means that no offence is committed by people peacefully arguing, or representing, that one person should cease doing business with another on the basis of the other's involvement with an animal research organisation.

Generally this section does not apply to any act done wholly or mainly in contemplation or furtherance of a trade dispute (s. 145(6)). However, there are some changes to the definition of such a dispute that need to be taken into account (see s. 145(7)).

No proceedings for an offence under either of those sections may be instituted except by or with the consent of the DPP.

Further guidance on the implementation of this section can be found in Home Office Circular 34/2005.

OFFENCE: **Intimidation of persons connected with animal research organisation—*Serious Organised Crime and Police Act 2005, s. 146(1)***

- Triable either way • Five years' imprisonment and/or a fine on indictment
- Twelve months' imprisonment and/or a fine summarily

The Serious Organised Crime and Police Act 2005, s. 146 states:

(1) A person (A) commits an offence if, with the intention of causing a second person (B) to abstain from doing something which B is entitled to do (or to do something which B is entitled to abstain from doing)—

(a) A threatens B that A or somebody else will do a relevant act, and
(b) A does so wholly or mainly because B is a person falling within subsection (2).

KEYNOTE

Subsection (2) is a lengthy and very comprehensive list. In summary, a person falls within this subsection if he/she is:

- an employee or officer of an animal research organisation;
- a student at an educational establishment that is an animal research organisation;
- a lessor or licensor of any premises occupied by an animal research organisation;
- a person with a financial interest in, or who provides financial assistance to, an animal research organisation;
- a customer or supplier of an animal research organisation (s. 146(2)).

A person who is contemplating becoming someone within the categories covered by the third, fourth and fifth bullet points is covered, as is a person who is (or is contemplating becoming) a customer or supplier of such people/organisations.

Employees and employers of someone within the above descriptions are covered, as are people with a financial interest in, or providing financial assistance to the above.

Subsection (2) also extends to spouses, civil partners, friends or relatives, or people known personally to someone within any of the above descriptions.

As with the offence under s. 145, this section does not generally apply to any act done wholly or mainly in contemplation or furtherance of a trade dispute and no proceedings for an offence under either of those sections may be instituted except by or with the consent of the DPP.

For the general offences involving threats and malicious communications **see para. 4.5.7.**

Further guidance on the implementation of this section can be found in Home Office Circular 34/2005.

4.7 Firearms and Gun Crime

4.7.1 Introduction

The Firearms Act 1968 and Firearms (Amendment) Act 1988 regulate the possession, transfer and use of firearms. The Violent Crime Reduction Act 2006 introduced further measures dealing with the misuse of air weapons and imitation firearms and created an offence of using someone to mind a dangerous weapon.

In considering the legislation that follows in this chapter, it is worth bearing in mind the provisions of the Terrorism Act 2000 and, in particular, the offences of providing or receiving instruction in the use of firearms and some other weapons (**see chapter 4.6**). The leading authority giving guidance in relation to sentencing for offences involving firearms is *R* v *Avis* [1998] 1 Cr App R 420. There it was held that there were four questions a sentencing court had to ask itself when assessing the seriousness of a firearms offence:

- what sort of weapon was involved;
- what use had been made of the weapon;
- with what intention did the defendant possess or use the firearm; and
- what was the defendant's record.

All of these issues should arguably be borne in mind when gathering and presenting evidence in firearms cases.

4.7.2 The 'This' Checklist

When considering any situation involving firearms legislation, whether practically or for the purposes of study, it is useful to apply the 'this' checklist.

The 'this' checklist, which is also useful in other areas of law (**see Road Policing, para. 3.6.2**), means asking whether:

- **this** certificate/exemption
- covers **this** person
- for **this** activity
- involving **this** firearm/ammunition
- for **this** purpose.

4.7.2.1 This Certificate/Exemption

The Firearms Act 1968 provides for people to be authorised by certificate to hold, transfer or buy firearms under specified conditions.

The 1968 Act—and the amending legislation—also contains many exemptions, some generally applicable and others very specific.

In each case, whether considering a certificate or other authority, or a possible exemption, it is critical that you establish what conditions apply.

4.7.2.2 This Person

Certificates will authorise the *holder* to do certain things (e.g. to buy firearms); other authorities will allow a wider group of people to do things (e.g. borrow the rifle of a certificate holder). In considering offences it is important to establish exactly which person is authorised or is exempt from any liability.

4.7.2.3 This Activity

Certificates and exemptions never grant unlimited authority to undertake any activity with every firearm or ammunition. Certificates will usually specify whether the holder can have a firearm in his/her '*possession*'; which firearms or ammunition he/she can possess; and whether he/she can *sell* or *transfer* firearms *or* ammunition. Exemptions are the same in that they will not apply to everyone in respect of all activities.

4.7.2.4 This Firearm/Ammunition

In addition to the restrictions on the activity, certificates and exemptions will only apply to particular firearms and/or ammunition. A person authorised to possess a shotgun is not thereby permitted to have an automatic rifle. Similarly, a person who runs a mini rifle range is not thereby given authority to possess mortar shells!

4.7.2.5 This Purpose

Certificates and exemptions will specify the precise purposes for which they apply. For instance, if a certificate allows a person to possess a firearm for slaughtering animals while at the slaughterhouse, that does not permit the possession of the firearm by the slaughterer while at home or travelling to work.

Similarly, some of the general exemptions apply only to the people concerned while they are involved in *the ordinary course of their business*, whether they are registered firearms dealers or members of the armed forces; possession or use of a firearm outside those particular circumstances will not be covered.

4.7.3 Firearms Generally

Section 57 of the Firearms Act 1968 states:

> (1) In this Act, the expression 'firearm' means a lethal barrelled weapon of any description from which any shot, bullet or other missile can be discharged, and includes—
> (a) any prohibited weapon, whether it is such a lethal weapon as aforesaid or not; and
> (b) any component part of such a lethal or prohibited weapon; and
> (c) any accessory to any such weapon designed or adapted to diminish the noise or flash caused by firing the weapon.

KEYNOTE

'Lethal barrelled weapon' is not defined under the 1968 Act.

The way in which the courts have determined whether or not something amounts to such a weapon is by asking:

- Can any shot, bullet or other missile be discharged from the weapon, or
- Could the weapon be adapted so that any shot, bullet or other missile can be discharged?
- If so, is the weapon a 'lethal barrelled' weapon?

(See *Grace* v *DPP* [1989] COD 374.)

A weapon is a lethal barrelled weapon if it is capable of causing injury, irrespective of the intentions of its maker (*Read* v *Donovan* [1947] KB 326). In determining whether a firearm is in fact a lethal barrelled weapon from which missiles can be discharged a court need not consider any specific evidence of someone who has seen the effects of it being fired. Therefore, where magistrates had heard evidence from a gun shop assistant that an air rifle was in working order, they were entitled to conclude that it fell within the definition even though no evidence was given as to the actual effects of the gun being fired (*Castle* v *DPP* (1998) *The Times*, 3 April).

Air pistols (*R* v *Thorpe* [1987] 1 WLR 383), imitation revolvers (*Cafferata* v *Wilson* [1936] 3 All ER 149) and signalling pistols (*Read* v *Donovan*, above) have all been held to be lethal barrelled weapons. That is not to say, however, that they will always be so and each case must be determined in the light of the evidence available.

Although ordinary air weapons not classified as being specially dangerous may not be capable of firing a lethal shot, possession of such a weapon was held, under the former legislation, still to be capable of amounting to an offence under s. 19 (see *Street* v *DPP* (2004) *The Times*, 23 January). In the context of the specific offence under s. 19, this decision has been overtaken in any event by the legislation but it is still of interest in defining the term 'firearm'.

Component parts, such as triggers or barrels, are also included in the definition, as are silencers and accessories to hide the muzzle flash of a weapon. If a defendant is found in possession of a silencer which has been manufactured for a weapon that is also in the defendant's possession, that will be enough to bring it under s. 57(1). If, however, the silencer is made for a different weapon, it may still come under the s. 57 definition but the prosecution will have to show that it could be used with the defendant's weapon and that he/she had it for that purpose. This slightly odd situtation is the result of the Court of Appeal's decision in *R* v *Buckfield* [1998] Crim LR 673. Following that reasoning, a silencer or accessory on its own does not appear to be a firearm for the purposes of s. 57(1). Section 57(1) does not include telescopic sights.

4.7.3.1 Deactivation of Firearms

A weapon may cease to be a firearm if it is deactivated in line with the provisions of the Firearms (Amendment) Act 1988, s. 8 which states:

> For the purposes of the principal Act and this Act it shall be presumed, unless the contrary is shown, that a firearm has been rendered incapable of discharging any shot, bullet or other missile, and has consequently ceased to be a firearm within the meaning of those Acts, if—
>
> (a) it bears a mark which has been approved by the Secretary of State for denoting that fact and which has been made either by one of the two companies mentioned in section 58(1) of the principal Act or by such other person as may be approved by the Secretary of State for the purposes of this section; and
>
> (b) that company or person has certified in writing that work has been carried out on the firearm in a manner approved by the Secretary of State for rendering it incapable of discharging any shot, bullet or other missile.

KEYNOTE

A deactivated weapon must remain in its complete state. Where it is disassembled the parts that are then made available are capable of being reassembled into a working weapon and are therefore component parts of a firearm (*R* v *Ashton* [2007] EWCA Crim 234).

The 'two companies' referred to in s. 8(a) above are the Society of the Mystery of Gunmakers of the City of London and the Birmingham Proof House.

4.7.4 Definitions

The law regulating firearms classifies weapons into several categories, each of which is specifically defined. As with offences under road traffic legislation (**see Road Policing, chapter 3.1**), it is critical that the relevant definition is considered before deciding upon a particular charge or offence.

4.7.4.1 Prohibited Weapon

A prohibited weapon is defined under the Firearms Act 1968, s. 5. The definition formerly covered the more powerful or potentially destructive firearms—and their ammunition—such as automatic weapons and specialist ammunition.

Since the Firearms (Amendment) Acts of 1997, however, s. 5 also covers many small firearms which were formerly covered by other parts of the 1968 Act.

The test as to whether a weapon is a 'prohibited' weapon is a purely objective one and is not affected by the intentions of the defendant. Therefore, where a firearm was capable of successively discharging two or more missiles without repeated pressure on the trigger, that weapon was 'prohibited' irrespective of the intentions of the firearms dealer who was in possession of it (*R* v *Law* [1999] Crim LR 837).

Whereas a firearms certificate is usually needed in order to possess, buy or acquire firearms and ammunition, the authority of the Secretary of State is needed if the firearm or ammunition is a 'prohibited weapon'.

4.7.4.2 List of Prohibited Weapons and Ammunition

The full list of prohibited weapons and ammunition is contained in s. 5(1) and (1A) of the Firearms Act 1968 (**see Blackstone's Criminal Practice 2008, para. B12.50**). This list includes:

- automatic weapons
- most self-loading or pump-action weapons
- any firearm which either has a barrel less than 30 cm in length or is less than 60 cm in length overall, other than an air weapon, a muzzle-loading gun or a firearm designed as signalling apparatus
- most smooth bore revolvers
- any weapon, of whatever description, designed or adapted for the discharge of any noxious liquid, gas or other thing
- any air rifle, air gun or air pistol which uses, or is designed or adapted for use with, a self-contained gas cartridge system
- military weapons and ammunition including grenades and mortars.

KEYNOTE

In relation to weapons designed or adapted for the discharge of any noxious liquid, gas or other thing, taking empty washing-up bottles and filling them with a noxious fluid such as hydrochloric acid does not amount to adapting them, neither is such a thing a 'weapon' for the purposes of s. 5 (*R* v *Formosa*, *R* v *Upton* [1991] 2 QB 1).

An electric 'stun gun' has been held to be a prohibited weapon as it discharges an electric current (*Flack* v *Baldry* [1988] 1 WLR 393) and it continues to be such even if it is not working (*Brown* v *DPP* (1992) *The Times*, 27 March).

Note that s. 5A of the Firearms Act 1968 creates exemptions under the European Council Directive 91/477/EEC on control of the acquisition and possession of weapons [1991] OJ L256/51 which allows people from Member States to possess some prohibited weapons under certain circumstances.

4.7.4.3 Shotguns

A shotgun is defined under s. 1(3)(a) of the Firearms Act 1968. Section 1 (amended by Firearms (Amendment) Act 1988 s. 2) states:

> (3) ...
> (a) a shotgun within the meaning of this Act, that is to say a smooth-bore gun (not being an airgun) which—
> (i) has a barrel not less than 24 inches in length and does not have any barrel with a bore exceeding 2 inches in diameter;
> (ii) either has no magazine or has a non-detachable magazine incapable of holding more than two cartridges; and
> (iii) is not a revolver gun...
>
> (3A) A gun which has been adapted to have such a magazine as is mentioned in subsection (3)(a)(ii) above shall not be regarded as falling within that provision unless the magazine bears a mark approved by the Secretary of State for denoting that fact and that mark has been made, and the adaptation has been certified in writing as having been carried out in a manner approved by him, either by one of the two companies mentioned in section 58(1) of this Act or by such other person as may be approved by him for that purpose.

KEYNOTE

A barrel's length is measured from the muzzle to the point at which the charge is exploded on firing the weapon (s. 57(6)(a) of the 1968 Act).

For the 'two companies' referred to in s. 1(3A) above **see para. 4.7.3.1**.

4.7.4.4 Air Weapons

Air weapons are defined under s. 1(3)(b) of the Firearms Act 1968. In summary these are air rifles, air guns or air pistols which do not fall within s. 5(1) (**see para. 4.7.4.2**) and which are not of a type declared to be specially dangerous. Any air rifle, air gun or air pistol that uses or is designed or adapted for use with a self-contained gas cartridge system *does* fall within the definition of a prohibited weapon at s. 5(1).

Some air weapons are deemed to be specially dangerous and therefore subject to stricter control than conventional air weapons. Those which are subject to this stricter control are those declared to be so by the Secretary of State. Listed in r. 2 of the Firearms (Dangerous Air Weapons) Rules 1969, as amended, they include:

(1) [any] air rifle, air gun or air pistol—
    (a) which is capable of discharging a missile so that the missile has, on being discharged from the muzzle of the weapon, kinetic energy in excess, in the case of an air pistol, of 6ft lb or, in the case of an air weapon other than an air pistol, of 12ft lb, or
    (b) which is disguised as another object.

Note that this does not include a weapon falling within para. (1)(a) above and which is designed for use only when submerged in water (r. 2(2)).

The Violent Crime Reduction Act 2006 amended the Firearms Act 1968 and made it an offence for a person, other than a registered firearms dealer, to sell or transfer an air weapon, or expose such a weapon for sale or transfer, or have possession of such a weapon for sale or transfer (s. 3(1)(c) of the 1968 Act). The 2006 Act increased the age from 17 to 18 for the acquisition or possession of air weapons, and removed the age restriction for firing an air weapon beyond premises.

Section 32 of the 2006 Act also imposed a 'face to face' requirement on trade transactions by persons selling air weapons.

OFFENCE: **Sales of air weapons by way of trade or business to be face to face—*Violent Crime Reduction Act 2006, s. 32***

- Triable summarily • 51 weeks' imprisonment and/or a fine

The Violent Crime Reduction Act 2006, s. 32 states:

(1) This section applies where a person sells an air weapon by way of trade or business to an individual in Great Britain who is not registered as a firearms dealer.
(2) A person is guilty of an offence if, for the purposes of the sale, he transfers possession of the air weapon to the buyer otherwise than at a time when both—
    (a) the buyer, and
    (b) either the seller or a representative of his,
    are present in person.

KEYNOTE

A representative of the seller is a reference to a person who is employed by the seller in his/her business as a registered firearms dealer; a registered firearms dealer who has been authorised by the seller to act on his/her behalf in relation to the sale; or a person who is employed by a person falling within s. 32(3)(b) in his/her business as a registered firearms dealer. This allows an air weapon to be sent from one registered firearms dealer to another to make the final transfer in person to the buyer. It also enables someone to buy an air weapon from a dealer in a distant part of the country without one or other party to the transaction having to make a long journey, while still preserving the safeguards of a face-to-face handover.

4.7.4.5 Section 1 Firearm

There is a group of firearms which, although not a category defined in the 1968 Act, are subject to a number of offences including s. 1 (see below). Firearms which fall into this group are often referred to as 'section 1 firearms' and include all firearms except shotguns (**see para. 4.7.4.3**) and conventional air weapons (**see para. 4.7.4.4**). However, shotguns which have been 'sawn off' (i.e. had their barrels shortened) are section 1 firearms, as are air weapons declared to be 'specially dangerous'.

Section 1 ammunition includes any ammunition for a firearm except:

- cartridges containing five or more shot, none of which is bigger than 0.36 inches in diameter;
- ammunition for an airgun, air rifle or air pistol; and
- blank cartridges not more than one inch in diameter (s. 1(4)).

4.7.4.6 Conversion

Some weapons which began their life as section 1 firearms or prohibited weapons will remain so even after their conversion to a shotgun, air weapon or other type of firearm (see s. 7 of the Firearms (Amendment) Act 1988).

4.7.4.7 Imitation Firearms

Some, though not all, offences which regulate the use of firearms will also apply to *imitation* firearms. Whether they do so can be found either in the specific wording of the offence, or by virtue of the Firearms Act 1982.

Put simply there are two types of imitation firearms:

- general imitations—those which have the appearance of firearms (which are covered by s. 57 of the Firearms Act 1968); and
- imitations of section 1 firearms—those which both have the appearance of a *section 1 firearm* and which can be readily converted into such a firearm (which are covered by ss. 1 and 2 of the Firearms Act 1982).

Where 'imitation firearms' are referred to *in the wording of the offence*, that offence will apply to the first category above, that is, 'anything which has the appearance of being a firearm'. The House of Lords has held that the definition in s. 57 requires the defendant to be carrying a 'thing' which is separate and distinct from him/herself and therefore capable of being possessed (*R* v *Bentham* [2005] 1 WLR 1057). Holding your fingers under your coat and pretending that this is a firearm—as happened in *Bentham*—will not therefore amount to an imitation firearm for the relevant offences. Their Lordships held that an unsevered hand or finger was part of oneself and therefore could not be 'possessed' in the way envisaged by the Act. The 'imitation' must have the appearance of a firearm and it is not necessary for any object to have been constructed, adapted or altered so as to resemble a firearm (*R* v *Williams* [2006] EWCA Crim 1650). In *K* v *DPP* [2006] EWHC 2183 it was held that in some circumstances a realistic toy gun, in this case a plastic ball bearing gun, could become an imitation firearm. Note that this category does not include anything which resembles a prohibited weapon *under s. 5(1)(b)*. Prohibited weapons under s. 5(1)(b) are those which are designed or adapted to discharge noxious liquid etc. (**see para. 4.7.4.2**).

In some other offences, *the definition of the 1982 Act is applicable*. These offences are all offences which involve section 1 firearms, except those under ss. 4(3) and (4), 16 to 20 and 47 of the 1968 Act.

If an offence does not come within either of the circumstances above, it will not apply to an imitation firearm.

Whether or not something has the appearance of being a firearm will be a question of fact for the jury/magistrate(s) to decide in each case.

The Violent Crime Reduction Act 2006, ss. 36 to 41, introduced measures to deal with the misuse of firearms. These sections created the three specific summary offences detailed below.

Section 36 makes it an offence to manufacture, import or sell realistic imitation firearms as defined in s. 38.

Section 39 makes it an offence to manufacture, modify or import an imitation firearm that does not conform to specifications set out in regulations to be made by the Secretary of State.

Section 40 inserted a new s. 24A into the 1968 Act and makes it an offence to sell an imitation firearm to a person under 18. It also makes it an offence for a person under 18 to purchase an imitation firearm (**see para. 4.7.9.2**).

KEYNOTE

For the purposes of the 2006 Act, an 'imitation firearm' is defined as that used in the Firearms Act 1968. A 'realistic imitation firearm' is defined as an imitation firearm which has an appearance that is so realistic as to make it indistinguishable, for all practical purposes, from a real firearm and is neither a deactivated firearm nor itself an antique (s. 38(1)). An imitation firearm will be regarded as distinguishable if its size, shape or principal colour is unrealistic for a real firearm (s. 38(3)). The Violent Crime Reduction Act 2006 (Realistic Imitation Firearms) Regulations 2007 (SI 2007/2606) provide defences for an offence under s. 36, and make provision in connection with the definition of 'realistic imitation firearm' in s. 38, specifying the sizes and colours which are to be regarded as unrealistic for a real firearm.

4.7.5 Possessing etc. Firearm or Ammunition without Certificate

OFFENCE: **Possessing etc. firearm or ammunition without certificate—*Firearms Act, 1968 s. 1***

- Triable either way • Five years' imprisonment and/or a fine on indictment
- Six months' imprisonment and/or a fine summarily

The Firearms Act 1968, s. 1 states:

(1) Subject to any exemption under this Act, it is an offence for a person—
  (a) to have in his possession, or to purchase or acquire, a firearm to which this section applies without holding a firearm certificate in force at the time, or otherwise than as authorised by such a certificate;
  (b) to have in his possession, or to purchase or acquire, any ammunition to which this section applies without holding a firearm certificate in force at the time, or otherwise than as authorised by such a certificate, or in quantities in excess of those so authorised.

KEYNOTE

This offence relates to those firearms described above as section 1 firearms.

If the firearm involved is a sawn-off shotgun, the offence becomes 'aggravated' (under s. 4(4)) and attracts a maximum penalty of seven years' imprisonment.

The Firearms Act 1982 applies to this section and therefore the second definition of 'imitation firearms' at para. 4.7.4.7 above applies here.

The certificate referred to is issued by the chief officer of police under s. 26A. Such certificates may carry significant restrictions on the types of firearms which the holder is allowed, together with the circumstances under which he/she may have them (see s. 44(1) of the Firearms (Amendment) Act 1997).

The purpose of the legislation regulating the licensing of firearms is to provide certainty and consistency in the effective control of such weapons. Therefore the issue of whether a certificate covers a particular category of weapon is a matter of law for the judge to decide and cannot be affected by the intentions or misunderstanding of the defendant (*R* v *Paul* (1998) 95(32) LSG 30).

For the forms to be used in relation to the grant of certificates and permits, see the Firearms Rules 1998 (SI 1998/1941 made under Firearms Act 1968).

A person may hold a European firearms pass or similar document, in which case he/she will be governed by the provision of ss. 32A to 32C of the Firearms Act 1968.

If a person has such a certificate which allows the possession etc. of the firearm in question and under the particular circumstances encountered, no offence is committed.

The Violent Crime Reduction Act 2006 has created a summary offence that restricts the purchase and sale of primers to persons who hold a relevant firearms certificate or who otherwise have lawful authority for having them (s. 35). This relates to the cap-type primers designed for use in metallic ammunition for a firearm, containing a chemical compound that detonates on impact.

4.7.5.1 Possession

As in other areas of criminal law (**see Crime, chapter 1.6**), the meaning of possession is wider here than actual physical custody of the firearm in question. A person can remain in possession of a firearm even if someone else has custody of it (*Sullivan* v *Earl of Caithness* [1976] QB 966).

Possession for the purposes of this offence does not require any specific knowledge on the part of the defendant. For example, if X knows he is in possession of *something* (e.g. a box), then X is in possession of its contents, *even though X does not know what those contents are* (*R* v *Hussain* [1981] 1 WLR 416).

Therefore there is no need to prove that the defendant knew the nature of the thing which he/she possessed in order to prove this offence (and the offence under s. 19, **see para. 4.7.8.7**). If a defendant is carrying a rucksack and that rucksack turns out to contain ammunition for a section 1 firearm, the defendant is 'in possession' of that ammunition irrespective of his/her knowledge—or ignorance—of its presence in the rucksack (see *R* v *Waller* [1991] Crim LR 381 and *R* v *Cremin* [2007] EWCA Crim 666).

4.7.5.2 Acquire

Acquire will include hiring, accepting as a gift and borrowing (s. 57(4) of the Firearms Act 1968).

4.7.5.3 Exemptions

The offence specifies that it is subject to any exemptions under the 1968 Act. There are three main categories of exemption under the firearms legislation:

- General exemptions—listed below.
- European exemptions—these are made under s. 5A to reflect the European Weapons Directive (**see para. 4.7.7.1**).
- Special exemptions—which apply to the provisions affecting prohibited weapons under s. 5 (**see para. 4.7.7.1**).

Many of the exemptions overlap as they follow a fairly common sense approach to the necessary possession and use of firearms/ammunition in the course of work and leisure.

4.7.5.4 General Exemptions

The general exemptions, which apply to the provisions of ss. 1 to 5 of the Firearms Act 1968 are mainly concerned with the various occupations of people whom you might expect to be in contact with firearms in one form or another. They include:

Police permit holders

Under s. 7(1) of the 1968 Act, the chief officer of police may grant a permit authorising the possession of firearms or ammunition under the conditions specified in the permit.

Clubs, athletics and sporting purposes

Section 11 of the 1968 Act provides exemptions for a person:

- borrowing the firearm/ammunition from a certificate holder *for sporting purposes only* (s. 11(1));
- possessing a firearm at an athletic meeting for the purposes of starting races (s. 11(2));
- in charge of a miniature rifle range buying, acquiring or possessing miniature rifles and ammunition, and using them at such a rifle range (s. 11(4));
- who is a member of an approved rifle club, miniature rifle club or pistol club to possess a firearm or ammunition *when engaged as a club member in target practice* (s. 15(1) of the Firearms (Amendment) Act 1988);
- borrowing a shotgun from the occupier of private premises and using it on those premises in the occupier's presence (s. 11(5) of the 1968 Act);
- using a shotgun at a time and place approved by the chief officer of police for shooting at artificial targets (s. 11(6)).

Borrowed rifle on private premises

Section 16 of the Firearms (Amendment) Act 1988 allows a person to borrow a rifle from the occupier of private premises, provided the person is on those premises and in the presence of the occupier (or his/her servant), as long as the occupier holds a certificate and that the borrowing of the rifle complies with that certificate. The person borrowing the rifle may buy or acquire ammunition for it in accordance with the certificate's conditions.

Visitors' permits

Section 17 of the Firearms (Amendment) Act 1988 provides for the issuing of a visitors' permit by a chief officer of police and for the possession of firearms and ammunition by the holder of such a permit.

Visitors' permits will not be issued to anyone without a European firearms pass. It is a summary offence (punishable with six months' imprisonment) to make a false statement in order to get a visitors' permit, and it is a similar offence to fail to comply with any conditions within such a permit (see s. 17(10)).

Antiques as ornaments or curiosities

Section 58(2) of the 1968 Act allows for the sale, buying, transfer, acquisition or possession of antique firearms *as curiosities or ornaments*. Whether a firearm is such an antique will be a question of fact to be determined by the court in each case. Mere belief in the fact that a firearm is an antique will not be enough (*R* v *Howells* [1977] QB 614).

Authorised firearms dealers

Section 8(1) of the 1968 Act provides for registered firearms dealers (or their employees) to possess, acquire or buy firearms or ammunition in the ordinary course of their business without a certificate. If the possession etc. is not in the ordinary course of their business, the exemption will not apply.

> **KEYNOTE**
>
> In addition to the above, other occupations of people exempt include: auctioneers, carriers and warehouse staff; licensed slaughterers; theatrical performers; ships, aircraft or aerodrome equipment; Crown servants; proof houses; and holders of a museums licence.

4.7.6 Shotgun Offences

OFFENCE: **Possessing shotgun without certificate—*Firearms Act 1968, s. 2(1)***

- Triable either way • Five years' imprisonment and/or a fine on indictment
- Six months' imprisonment and/or a fine summarily

The Firearms Act 1968, s. 2 states:

> (1) Subject to any exemption under this Act, it is an offence for a person to have in his possession, or to purchase or acquire, a shotgun without holding a certificate under this Act authorising him to possess shot guns.

> **KEYNOTE**
>
> For the definition of 'shotgun', see para. 4.7.4.3.
>
> The relevant exemptions above will also apply to shotguns.
>
> A shotgun certificate is granted by a chief officer of police under s. 26B of the 1968 Act and will have certain conditions attached to it. A person failing to comply with those conditions commits the following offence:

OFFENCE: **Failing to comply with conditions of shot gun certificate—*Firearms Act 1968, s. 2(2)***

- Triable summarily • Six months' imprisonment and/or a fine

The Firearms Act 1968, s. 2 states:

> (2) It is an offence for a person to fail to comply with a condition subject to which a shot gun certificate is held by him.

The conditions and forms used in relation to the grant of shotgun certificates are contained in the Firearms Rules 1998 (SI 1998/1941) and the Firearms (Amendment) Rules 2005 (SI 2005/3344).

4.7.7 Possessing or Distributing Prohibited Weapons or Ammunition

OFFENCE: **Possessing or distributing prohibited weapons or ammunition—*Firearms Act 1968, s. 5***

- Triable either way • Ten years' imprisonment and/or a fine on indictment
- Six months' imprisonment and/or a fine summarily

The Firearms Act 1968, s. 5 states:

> (1) A person commits an offence if, without the authority of the Secretary of State or the Scottish Ministers, he has in his possession, or purchases, or acquires, or manufactures, sells or transfers [a prohibited weapon or ammunition] ...

KEYNOTE

See para. 4.7.4.1 for prohibited weapons. For 'possession', see para. 4.7.5.1.

'Self-loading' and 'pump-action' mean designed or adapted so that the weapon is either automatically reloaded, or is reloaded by manual operation of the fore-end or forestock (s. 57 of the 1968 Act).

Section 5(7) and (8) provides guidance in determining whether certain arms and ammunition will fall within the descriptions in s. 5, including the fact that any folding or detachable butt-stock of a firearm will not count when measuring the weapon's overall length.

4.7.7.1 Exemptions

The first set of exemptions were discussed in relation to the offence under s. 1 (**see para. 4.7.5.3**); the second and third set are relevant to the offences under s. 5. Those remaining exemptions are:

- European exemptions—exemptions to conform with the European Weapons Directive.
- Special exemptions.

European Weapons Directive

The European Weapons Directive (91/477/EEC) was brought into effect in order to adjust our domestic legislation in line with the expansion of the European internal market. Its effect is to create certain additional savings and exemptions in relation to the possession of, or some transactions in, specified firearms and ammunition by people who have the relevant certificates or who are recognised as collectors under the law of another country.

To this end, s. 5A of the Firearms Act 1968 provides for a number of occasions where the authority of the Secretary of State will not be required to possess or deal with certain weapons under certain conditions.

The main areas covered by s. 5A are:

- authorised collectors and firearms dealers possessing or being involved in transactions of weapons and ammunition;
- authorised people being involved in transactions of particular ammunition used for lawful shooting and slaughtering of animals, the management of an estate or the protection of other animals and humans.

Section 57(4A) of the Firearms Act 1968 makes other provisions in relation to the European directive as an authority for certain uses of firearms.

Special exemptions

The list of special exemptions to the offences involving firearms under s. 5(1)(aba) focuses largely on people in jobs where they will need to come into contact with firearms mainly in connection with animals or leisure activities.

The exemptions include:

- **Slaughterers**—A slaughterer, if entitled under s. 10 of the 1968 Act (**see para. 4.7.5.4**), may possess a slaughtering instrument. In addition, persons authorised by certificate to possess, buy, acquire, sell or transfer slaughtering instruments are exempt from the provisions of s. 5 (s. 2 of the Firearms (Amendment) Act 1997). This is the most common exemption.
- **Humane killing of animals**—A person authorised by certificate to possess, buy or acquire a firearm solely for use in connection with the humane killing of animals may possess, buy, acquire, sell or transfer such a firearm (s. 3 of the Firearms (Amendment) Act 1997). When determining whether a firearm falls within the meaning of a 'humane killer', the definition of a 'slaughtering instrument' under s. 57(4) may be referred to (*R* v *Paul (Benjamin)* (1998) 95(32) LSG 30).
- **Shot pistols for vermin**—A person authorised by certificate to possess, buy or acquire a 'shot pistol' solely for the shooting of vermin, may possess, buy, acquire, sell or transfer such a pistol (s. 4(1) of the Firearms (Amendment) Act 1997). A 'shot pistol' is a smooth-bored gun chambered for .410 cartridges or 9mm rim-fire cartridges (s. 4(2)).
- **Treatment of animals**—A person authorised by certificate to possess, buy or acquire a firearm for use in connection with the treatment of animals may possess, buy, acquire, sell or transfer any firearm or ammunition designed or adapted for the purpose of tranquillising or treating any animal (s. 8 of the Firearms (Amendment) Act 1997). This exemption also applies to offences involving firearms under s. 5(1)(b) and (c) (**see para. 4.7.4.2**).
- **Races at athletic meetings**—A person may possess a firearm at an athletic meeting for the purpose of starting races at that meeting (s. 5(a) of the Firearms (Amendment) Act 1997). Similarly, a person authorised by certificate to possess, buy or acquire a firearm solely for the purposes of starting such races may possess, buy, acquire, sell or transfer a firearm for such a purpose (s. 5(b)).
- **Trophies of war**—A person authorised by certificate to do so may possess a firearm which was acquired as a trophy before 1 January 1946 (s. 6 of the Firearms (Amendment) Act 1997).
- **Firearms of historic interest**—Some firearms are felt to be of particular historical, aesthetic or technical interest. Section 7(4) of the Firearms (Amendment) Act 1997 makes detailed provision for the exemption of such firearms, exemptions which exist in addition to the general exemptions under s. 58 of the Firearms Act 1968 (**see para. 4.7.5.4**). These provisions are set out in the Firearms (Amendment) Act 1997 (Firearms of Historic Interest) Order 1997 (SI 1997/1537) and the Firearms (Amendment) Act 1997 (Transitional Provisions and Savings) Regulations 1997 (SI 1997/1538).
- **Air weapons**—In relation to air weapons with self-contained gas cartridges, owned before 20 January 2004, the owner, if he/she applied for a firearms certificate before 1 April 2004, may retain his/her weapons.

4.7.8 Further Offences

Further to the more straightforward possession offences discussed above, there are a number of important offences where the purpose of the person with the firearm, or the circumstances in which he/she has it, are aggravating factors. These offences are discussed below.

4.7.8.1 Possession with Intent to Endanger Life

OFFENCE: **Possession with intent to endanger life—*Firearms Act 1968, s. 16***

- Triable on indictment • Life imprisonment and/or a fine

The Firearms Act 1968, s. 16 states:

> It is an offence for a person to have in his possession any firearm or ammunition with intent by means thereof to endanger life or to enable another person by means thereof to endanger life, whether any injury has been caused or not.

KEYNOTE

There is no reference to imitation firearms in the wording of the offence, neither does the 1982 Act apply, therefore this offence cannot be committed by possessing an imitation firearm (**see para. 4.7.4.7**).

The offence involves 'possession' (**see para. 4.7.5.1**); there is no need for the firearm to be produced or shown to another.

This is a crime of 'specific intent' (**see Crime, chapter 1.1**). You will have to show an intention by the defendant to behave in a way that he/she knows will in fact endanger the life of another (*R* v *Brown and Ciarla* [1995] Crim LR 327).

That intent does not have to be an immediate one and it may be conditional (e.g. an intent to shoot someone if they do not do as they are asked) (*R* v *Bentham* [1973] QB 357).

The life endangered must be the life of 'another', not the defendant's (*R* v *Norton* [1977] Crim LR 478) but that other person may be outside the UK (*R* v *El-Hakkoui* [1975] 1 WLR 396).

The firearm must provide the means by which life is endangered; it is not enough to have a firearm at the time when life is endangered by some other means (e.g. by dangerous driving).

There may be occasions where self-defence can be raised in answer to a charge under s. 16 of the 1968 Act but these circumstances will be very unusual (see *R* v *Georgiades* [1989] 1 WLR 759). This defence could apply where the defendant is carrying a weapon for his own defence anticipating an imminent attack (*R* v *Salih* [2007] EWCA Crim 2750).

4.7.8.2 Possession with Intent to Cause Fear of Violence

OFFENCE: **Possession with intent to cause fear of violence—*Firearms Act 1968, s. 16A***

- Triable on indictment • Ten years' imprisonment and/or a fine

The Firearms Act 1968, s. 16A (added by Firearms (Amendment) Act 1994, s. 1) states:

> It is an offence for a person to have in his possession any firearm or imitation firearm with intent—
> (a) by means thereof to cause, or
> (b) to enable another person by means thereof to cause,
> any person to believe that unlawful violence will be used against him or another person.

KEYNOTE

This offence includes imitation firearms in the general sense (**see para. 4.7.4.7**).

This is a crime of 'specific intent' (**see Crime, chapter 1.1**).

Section 16A is committed by possession, accompanied by an intention to cause fear of violence at or immediately before the defendant's actions which are designed to cause such fear (*R* v *Goluchowski* [2006] EWCA Crim 1972). There is no need for a firearm/imitation firearm to be produced or shown to anyone, though it must provide the 'means' of the threat. Possession of a firearm/imitation firearm while making a general threat to someone who does not know of its presence is unlikely to fall within this section.

4.7.8.3 Using Firearm to Resist Arrest

OFFENCE: **Using firearm to resist arrest—*Firearms Act 1968, s. 17(1)***

- Triable on indictment • Life imprisonment and/or a fine

The Firearms Act 1968, s. 17 states:

(1) It is an offence for a person to make or attempt to make any use whatsoever of a firearm or imitation firearm with intent to resist or prevent the lawful arrest or detention of himself or another person.

KEYNOTE

If the defendant has the firearm or imitation firearm with them at the time of resisting or preventing an arrest, they commit the offence under s. 18 (**see para. 4.7.8.6**).

The 'firearm' to which s. 17 refers is that defined at **para. 4.7.3**, *except* component parts and silencers/flash diminishers (s. 17(4)).

This offence includes imitation firearms in the general sense (**see para. 4.7.4.7**) but not imitation component parts, etc.

This is a crime of 'specific intent' (**see Crime, chapter 1.1**). It requires proof, not of possession, but of evidence that the defendant made some actual use of the firearm and did so intending to resist/prevent the arrest of themselves or someone else. Any arrest which the defendant intended to prevent/resist must have been 'lawful'.

4.7.8.4 Possessing Firearm while Committing a Schedule 1 Offence

OFFENCE: **Possessing firearm while committing or being arrested for sch. 1 offence—*Firearms Act 1968, s. 17(2)***

- Triable on indictment • Life imprisonment and/or a fine

The Firearms Act 1968, s. 17 states:

(2) If a person, at the time of his committing or being arrested for an offence specified in schedule 1 to this Act, has in his possession a firearm or imitation firearm, he shall be guilty of an offence under this subsection unless he shows that he had it in his possession for a lawful object.

KEYNOTE

This offence may be committed in two ways; either by being in possession of the weapon at the time of committing the sch. 1 offence or by being in possession of it *at the time of being arrested* for such an offence. Clearly in the second case, there may be some time between actually committing the sch. 1 offence and being arrested for it.

Nevertheless, if the defendant is in possession of the firearm at the time of his/her arrest, the offence is committed (unless he/she can show that it was for a lawful purpose).

For this offence, you need to prove that the person *was in possession* of the firearm but not that they actually *had it with them*. This fine but important distinction was reviewed by the Court of Appeal where it was reiterated that the two expressions have different meanings throughout the Act, with possession being a deliberately wider concept than the expression 'has with him' (*R* v *North* [2001] Crim LR 746).

There is no need for the defendant to be subsequently *convicted* of the sch. 1 offence, nor even to prove the elements of it; all that is needed is to show that the defendant, at the time of his/her arrest for a sch. 1 offence, had a firearm/imitation firearm in his/her possession (*R* v *Nelson* [2000] 3 WLR 300).

It is for the defendant to prove that the firearm was in his/her possession for a lawful purpose, presumably on the balance of probabilities (**see Evidence & Procedure, chapter 2.7**).

This offence includes imitation firearms in the general sense (**see para. 4.7.4.7**).

The House of Lords has overturned the decision which allowed a defendant's use of his stiffened fingers beneath his coat to qualify as an imitation firearm for the purposes of the above offence (*R* v *Bentham* [2005] UKHL 18—**see para. 4.7.4.7**). In *Bentham* their Lordships pointed out that the above circumstances may have amounted to 'falsely pretending to have a firearm' but Parliament had not created any such offence.

Schedule 1 offences

The *main* offences listed in sch. 1 are:

- **D**amage—s. 1 of the Criminal Damage Act 1971.
- **A**ssaults and woundings—ss. 20 and 47 of the Offences Against the Person Act 1861, assault police (s. 89 of the Police Act 1996) and civilian custody officers (s. 90(1) of the Criminal Justice Act 1991 and s. 13(1) of the Criminal Justice and Public Order Act 1994).
- **R**ape and other sexual/abduction offences—the following offences under the Sexual Offences Act 2003: s. 1 (rape), s. 2 (assault by penetration), s. 4 (causing a person to engage in sexual activity without consent), where the activity caused involved penetration within subs. (4)(a) to (d) of that section, s. 5 and s. 6 (rape and assault of a child under 13), s. 8 (causing or inciting a child under 13 to engage in sexual activity), where an activity involving penetration within subs. (3)(a) to (d) of that section was caused, s. 30 and s. 31 (sexual activity with/causing or inciting a person with a mental disorder impeding choice), where the touching involved or activity caused penetration within subs. (3)(a) to (d) of that section. Also offences under part I of the Child Abduction Act 1984.
- **T**heft, robbery, burglary, blackmail and taking a conveyance—Theft Act 1968. (**D.A.R.T.**)

Although covering several types of assault, sch. 1 does not extend to wounding/causing grievous bodily harm with intent. Schedule 1 also covers the aiding, abetting or attempting to commit such offences.

For a further explanation of these substantive offences **see Crime**.

4.7.8.5 Trespassing with Firearms

OFFENCE: **Trespassing with firearm in building—*Firearms Act 1968, s. 20(1)***

- Triable either way (unless imitation firearm or air weapon) • Seven years' imprisonment and/or a fine on indictment • Six months' imprisonment and/or a fine summarily

The Firearms Act 1968, s. 20 states:

(1) A person commits an offence if, while he has a firearm or imitation firearm with him, he enters or is in any building or part of a building as a trespasser and without reasonable excuse (the proof whereof lies on him).

KEYNOTE

This offence includes a specific reference to imitation firearms (**see para. 4.7.4.7**).

If the relevant firearm is an imitation or an air weapon, the offence is triable summarily.

This offence can be committed either by entering a building/part of a building or simply by *being* in such a place, in each case as a trespasser while having the firearm. As there is no need for the defendant to have 'entered' the building as a trespasser in every case, the offence might be committed after the occupier has withdrawn any permission for the defendant to be there. (Contrast the offence of trespassing with a weapon of offence; **see chapter 4.8**.)

For a discussion of the elements of entering a building/part of a building as a trespasser, **see Crime, chapter 1.11**.

For the interpretation of 'has with him', **see para. 4.7.8.6**.

It will be for the defendant to prove that he/she had reasonable excuse and the standard of that proof will be judged against the balance of probabilities.

The power of entry and search under s. 47 of the 1968 Act applies to this offence (**see para. 4.7.10**).

OFFENCE: **Trespassing with firearm on land—*Firearms Act 1968, s. 20(2)***

- Triable summarily • Three months' imprisonment and/or a fine

The Firearms Act 1968, s. 20 states:

(2) A person commits an offence if, while he has a firearm or imitation firearm with him, he enters or is on any land as a trespasser and without reasonable excuse (the proof whereof lies on him).

KEYNOTE

The elements of this offence are generally the same as those for the s. 20(1) offence above.

As with the s. 20(1) offence, there is no requirement that the defendant had the firearm/imitation firearm with him/her when entering onto the land (compare with the offence of aggravated burglary under the Theft Act 1968; see **Crime, chapter 1.11**).

'Land' for these purposes will include land covered by water (s. 20(3)).

4.7.8.6 Having Firearm with Intent to Commit Indictable Offence or Resist Arrest

OFFENCE: **Having firearm with intent to commit an indictable offence or resist arrest—*Firearms Act 1968, s. 18(1)***

- Triable on indictment • Life imprisonment and/or a fine

The Firearms Act 1968, s. 18 states:

(1) It is an offence for a person to have with him a firearm or imitation firearm with intent to commit an indictable offence, or to resist arrest or prevent the arrest of another, in either case while he has the firearm or imitation firearm with him.

KEYNOTE

This offence, which overlaps with that under s. 17(1) (**see para. 4.7.8.3**), requires the defendant to have the firearm 'with him'. This is a more restrictive expression than 'possession' (as to which, **see para. 4.7.5.1**), and requires that the firearm is 'readily accessible' to the defendant (e.g. in a car nearby) (*R* v *Pawlicki* [1992] 1 WLR 827).

Where a defendant left a firearm in his house which was a few miles from the scene of the relevant criminal offence, the Court of Appeal held that this was not enough to meet the requirement of 'having with him'—*R* v *Bradish* (2004) LTL 2 April.

Despite this narrower meaning, the defendant does not have to be shown to have been 'carrying' the firearm (*R* v *Kelt* [1977] 1 WLR 1365), a decision which now conflicts with the situation relating to identical statutory expressions under the Theft Act 1968 (**see Crime, chapter 1.11**) and also under the legislation relating to weapons (**see chapter 4.8**).

Intention

This is a crime of 'specific intent' (**see Crime, chapter 1.1**) and, in proving that intent, s. 18 states:

(2) In proceedings for an offence under this section proof that the accused had a firearm or imitation firearm with him and intended to commit an offence, or to resist or prevent arrest, is evidence that he intended to have it with him while doing so.

It is not necessary to show that the defendant intended to *use* the firearm to commit the indictable offence or to prevent/resist the arrest (*R* v *Duhaney* [1998] 2 Cr App R 25). (Contrast the offence under s. 17(1); **see para. 4.7.8.3.**)

The mental element is, however, an essential part of this offence. Therefore, if the defendant only formed the intent as a result of duress (as to which **see Crime, chapter 1.4**), this ingredient will not have been established—
R v *Fisher* [2004] EWCA Crim 1190.

An indictable offence includes an offence triable either way (Interpretation Act 1978).

Section 18 does not appear to require that any arrest be 'lawful' and it may be that Parliament intended for this offence to be broader in that respect than the offence under s. 17.

This offence includes imitation firearms in the general sense (**see para. 4.7.4.7**).

The power of entry and search under s. 47 of the 1968 Act applies to this offence (**see para. 4.7.10**).

4.7.8.7 Having Firearm or Imitation Firearm in Public Place

OFFENCE: **Having firearm/imitation firearm in public place—*Firearms Act 1968, s. 19***

- Triable either way • Seven years' imprisonment and/or a fine on indictment
- Twelve months' imprisonment and/or a fine summarily

The Firearms Act 1968, s. 19 states:

A person commits an offence if, without lawful authority or reasonable excuse (the proof whereof lies on him), he has with him in a public place—
(a) a loaded shot gun,
(b) an air weapon (whether loaded or not),

(c) any other firearm (whether loaded or not) together with ammunition suitable for use in that firearm, or
(d) an imitation firearm.

KEYNOTE

If the weapon is a shotgun it must be loaded. 'Loaded' here means if there is ammunition in the chamber or barrel (or in any magazine or other device) whereby the ammunition can be fed into the chamber or barrel by the manual or automatic operation of some part of the weapon (see s. 57(6)(b)). If the weapon is an imitation firearm (**see para. 4.7.4.7**) or an air weapon the offence is committed by the defendant having it with him/her. In the case of other firearms the offence is committed by the defendant having the firearm with him/her together with ammunition suitable for use in it.

For the meaning of 'has with him', **see para. 4.7.8.6.**

This offence is an 'absolute' offence like s. 1 (**see para. 4.7.5**). Therefore, if you can show that the defendant (X) knew he had something with him and that the 'something' was a loaded shotgun, an air weapon, an imitation firearm, or another firearm with ammunition, the offence is complete (*R* v *Vann* [1996] Crim LR 52). It is for the defendant to show lawful authority or reasonable excuse; possession of a valid certificate does not of itself provide lawful authority for having the firearm/ammunition in a public place (*Ross* v *Collins* [1982] Crim LR 368).

4.7.8.8 Using Someone to Mind a Weapon

OFFENCE: **Using someone to mind a weapon—*Violent Crime Reduction Act 2006, s. 28(1)***

- Triable on indictment • Ten years' imprisonment and/or a fine (firearms, etc.)
- Four years' imprisonment and/or a fine (offensive weapons, etc.)

The Violent Crime Reduction Act 2006, s. 28 states:

(1) A person is guilty of an offence if—
  (a) he uses another to look after, hide or transport a dangerous weapon for him; and
  (b) he does so under arrangements or in circumstances that facilitate, or are intended to facilitate, the weapon's being available to him for an unlawful purpose.
(2) For the purposes of this section the cases in which a dangerous weapon is to be regarded as available to a person for an unlawful purpose include any case where—
  (a) the weapon is available for him to take possession of it at a time and place; and
  (b) his possession of the weapon at that time and place would constitute, or be likely to involve or to lead to, the commission by him of an offence.

KEYNOTE

The offence was introduced by the 2006 Act to close a perceived loophole in the law where people have escaped prosecution by entrusting their weapon to another person, in particular to a child. Using children in this way may risk injury to them and in the longer term draw them into gun and knife crime as a result of their early association with weapons. Using a minor to mind a firearm is an aggravating factor attracting harsher sentences (s. 29(3)(a)).

A 'dangerous weapon' means a firearm other than an air weapon or a component part of, or accessory to, an air weapon; or a weapon to which s. 141 or 141A of the Criminal Justice Act 1988 applies (specified offensive weapons, knives and bladed weapons—**see para. 4.8.6.1**) (s. 28(3)).

4.7.8.9 Firing an Air Weapon Beyond Premises

OFFENCE: **Firing an air weapon beyond premises—*Firearms Act 1968, s. 21A***
• Triable summarily • Fine

The Firearms Act 1968, s. 21A states:

(1) A person commits an offence if—
 (a) he has with him an air weapon on any premises; and
 (b) he uses it for firing a missile beyond those premises.
(2) In proceedings against a person for an offence under this section it shall be a defence for him to show that the only premises into or across which the missile was fired were premises the occupier of which had consented to the firing of the missile (whether specifically or by way of a general consent).

KEYNOTE

This offence was inserted by the Violent Crime Reduction Act 2006 to close a loophole in the law by making it an offence for a person of *any* age to fire an air weapon beyond the boundary of premises. Prior to the introduction of this section the offence only related to persons under the age of 17. Note that a defence is provided to cover the situation where the person shooting has the consent of the occupier of the land over or into which he/she shoots.

4.7.9 Possession or Acquisition of Firearms by Certain People

Sections 21 to 24 of the Firearms Act 1968 place further restrictions on the people who can possess, acquire, receive or otherwise have involvement with firearms. Section 21 deals with people who have been convicted of certain offences while ss. 22 to 24 set out minimum ages in respect of certain firearms and transactions.

Section 21 generally provides that any person who has been sentenced to:

- custody for life, or
- to preventive detention, imprisonment, corrective training, youth custody or detention in a young offender institution for three years or more

must not, *at any time*, have a firearm or ammunition in his/her possession.

Section 21 goes on to provide that any person who has been sentenced to imprisonment, youth custody, detention in a young offender institution or a secure training order for three months or more, *but less than three years*, must not have a firearm or ammunition in his/her possession at any time before the end of a five-year period beginning on the date of his/her release.

Date of release means, for a sentence partly served and partly suspended, the date on which the offender completes the part to be served and, in the case of a person subject to a secure training order, the date on which he/she is released from detention (under the various relevant statutes) or the date halfway through the total specified by the court making the order, whichever is the latest (s. 21(2A)).

A person holding a licence under the Children and Young Persons Act 1933 or a person subject to a recognisance to keep the peace or be of good behaviour with a condition relating to the possession of firearms, must not, *at any time during the licence or the recognisance*, have a firearm or ammunition in his/her possession (s. 21(3)).

Where sentences or court orders are mentioned, their Scottish equivalents will also apply and a person prohibited in Northern Ireland from possessing a firearm/ammunition will also be prohibited in Great Britain (s. 21(3A)).

Section 21 does not apply to imitation firearms as there is no express reference to them in the section and because the reference in the Firearms Act 1982 does not apply (**see para. 4.7.4.7**).

4.7.9.1 Supplying Firearm to Person Prohibited by Section 21

OFFENCE: **Selling or transferring firearm to person prohibited by s. 21—*Firearms Act 1968, s. 21(5)***

- Triable either way • Five years' imprisonment and/or a fine on indictment
- Six months' imprisonment and/or a fine summarily

The Firearms Act 1968, s. 21 states:

> (5) It is an offence for a person to sell or transfer a firearm or ammunition to, or to repair, test or prove a firearm or ammunition for, a person whom he knows or has reasonable ground for believing to be prohibited by this section from having a firearm or ammunition in his possession.

KEYNOTE

Given that all people are presumed to know the law once it is published, it would seem that the knowledge or belief by the defendant would apply to the *convictions of* the other person, not the fact that possession by that person was an offence.

What you must show is knowledge by the defendant or at least *reasonable ground for believing*; this latter requirement is stronger than mere cause to *suspect* (**see chapter 4.4**).

4.7.9.2 Other Restrictions on Possession or Acquisition

In addition to the general provisions relating to possession, acquisition etc., ss. 22 to 24 create a number of summary offences restricting the involvement of people of various ages in their dealings with certain types of firearm and ammunition. The Violent Crime Reduction Act 2006 amended ss. 22 to 24 of the Firearms Act 1968, so that the age limit for the purchase and possession of air weapons is now higher than for other firearms. The 2006 Act also inserted a new s. 24A in relation to the sale and purchase of imitation firearms.

In summary the age restrictions are as follows:

- a person under 18:
  - (i) must not purchase or hire an air weapon or ammunition for an air weapon (s. 22(1)(a));
  - (ii) must not have with them an air weapon or ammunition for an air weapon (s. 22(4)). An exception to this is where the person is under the supervision of another who is at least 21 years old. However, if the person under 18 fires the weapon beyond the relevant premises they will commit an offence under s. 21A (**see para. 4.7.8.9**) and the person supervising them will be guilty of an offence under s. 23(1)). Generally it is not an offence under this section for a person aged 14 or over to have with them an air weapon or ammunition on private premises with the consent of the owner (s. 23(3));

(iii) it is an offence to sell or let on hire an air weapon or ammunition for an air weapon to a person under the age of 18 (s. 24(1)(a)), or to make a gift/part with possession of an air weapon or ammunition for an air weapon to such a person (unless under the permitted circumstances above) (s. 24(4));
(iv) it is an offence to sell an imitation firearm to a person under the age of 18 (s. 24A(2)), or for a person under 18 to purchase one (s. 24A(1)). It is a defence to show that the vendor believed that the purchaser was 18 or over and had reasonable grounds for that belief (s. 24A(3));

- a person under 17:
  (i) must not purchase or hire any firearm or ammunition (s. 22(1)(b)); or
  (ii) it is an offence to sell or let on hire to a person under 17 any firearm or ammunition (s. 24(1)(b));
- a person under 15:
  (i) must not have with them an assembled shotgun unless supervised by a person aged at least 21 or while the shotgun is securely covered so it cannot be fired (s. 22(3)); and
  (ii) it is an offence to make a gift of a shotgun/ammunition to such a person (s. 24(3));
- a person under 14:
  (i) must not have in their possession a section 1 firearm or ammunition (s. 22(2)); and
  (ii) it is an offence to make a gift/part with possession of such a firearm/ammunition to such a person (s. 24(2)) (subject to some exceptions relating to sports and shooting clubs—see s. 11 of the Firearms Act 1968 and s. 15 of the Firearms (Amendment) Act 1988).

There is a further provision creating an offence for a person under 18 who is the holder of a certificate using a firearm for a purpose not authorised by the European Weapons Directive (s. 22(1A)).

This is merely a summary of what are relatively convoluted provisions regarding ages and permitted circumstances. For the full extent of these restrictions and their exemptions, reference should be made to the 1968 and 1988 Acts. Note that s. 24(5) of the Firearms Act 1968 provides that it is a defence to prove that the person charged with an offence believed that other person to be of or over the age mentioned and had reasonable grounds for the belief.

It is a summary offence (punishable by one month's imprisonment and/or a fine) to be in possession of *any* loaded firearm when drunk (s. 12 of the Licensing Act 1872). There is no requirement that the person be in a public place.

4.7.10 Police Powers

Section 47 of the Firearms Act 1968 states:

> (1) A constable may require any person whom he has reasonable cause to suspect—
> (a) of having a firearm, with or without ammunition, with him in a public place; or
> (b) to be committing or about to commit, elsewhere than in a public place, an offence relevant for the purposes of this section,
> to hand over the firearm or any ammunition for examination by the constable.

KEYNOTE

This power has two distinct elements. The first applies where the officer has reasonable cause to suspect that a person has a firearm with him/her in a public place. The second relates to a situation where the officer has reasonable cause to suspect that the person is committing or is about to commit an offence relevant to this section anywhere else.

An 'offence relevant to this section' appears to be an offence unders ss. 18(1), 18(2) and 20 (see s. 47(6)).

It is a summary offence to fail to hand over a firearm when required under this section (s. 47(2)).

In order to exercise this power, a police officer may search the person and may detain him/her for that purpose (s. 47(3)). The officer may also enter *any place* (s. 47(5)).

If the officer has reasonable cause to suspect that:

- there is a firearm in a vehicle in a public place, or
- that a vehicle is being/about to be used in connection with the commission of an 'offence relevant to this section' (see above)

he/she may search the vehicle and, for that purpose, may require the person driving or in control of the vehicle to stop it (s. 47(4)).

The provisions of the PACE Codes of Practice, Code A, will apply to the exercise of these powers of stop and search (**see appendix 4.1**).

For powers of stop and search generally, **see chapter 4.4**.

4.7.10.1 Power to Demand Documentation

Section 48 of the Firearms Act 1968 states:

(1) A constable may demand, from any person whom he believes to be in possession of a firearm or ammunition to which section 1 of this Act applies, or of a shot gun, the production of his firearm certificate or, as the case may be, his shot gun certificate.

KEYNOTE

The demand for the relevant documentation may be made where the police officer 'believes' that a person is in possession of a section 1 firearm or ammunition or a shotgun. There is no requirement that the officer's belief be reasonable.

Where the person fails to:

- produce the relevant certificate or
- show that he/she is not entitled to be issued with such a certificate or
- show that he/she is in possession of the firearm exclusively in connection with recognised purposes (collecting/historical/cultural) under the law of another EU Member State

the officer may demand the production of the relevant valid documentation issued in another member State under any corresponding provisions (s. 48(1A)).

Failing to produce any of the required documents *and* to let the officer read it, or failing to show an entitlement to possess the firearm or ammunition triggers (!) the power of seizure under s. 48(2). It also gives the officer the power to demand the person's name and address. This requirement is similar to the provision under s. 170 of the Road Traffic Act 1988 (duty to give details after an accident; **see Road Policing, chapter 3.4**) where it has been held that the name and address of the person's solicitor would suffice (*DPP* v *McCarthy* [1999] RTR 323). That decision was based on the purpose behind the Road Traffic Act requirement, namely to allow the respective parties to the accident to get in touch with each other in the future. It is suggested that the purpose of the Firearms Act power is a very different one of regulating the possession of weapons and that the furnishing of details of some convenient administrative location for correspondence would not be enough to satisfy the requirements of this section.

If the person refuses to give his/her name or address or gives a false name and address, he/she commits a summary offence (s. 48(3)).

A person from another Member State who is in possession of a firearm and who fails to comply with a demand under s. 48(1A) also commits a separate summary offence (s. 48(4)).

4.7.11 Shortening and Conversion of Firearms

OFFENCE: **Shortening barrel of shotgun to less than 24 inches—*Firearms Act 1968, s. 4(1)***

- Triable either way • Five years' imprisonment and/or a fine on indictment
- Six months' imprisonment and/or a fine summarily

The Firearms Act 1968, s. 4 states:

(1) Subject to this section, it is an offence to shorten the barrel of a shot gun to a length less than 24 inches.

OFFENCE: **Shortening barrel of other smooth-bore section 1 firearm to less than 24 inches—*Firearms (Amendment) Act 1988 s. 6(1)***

- Triable either way • Five years' imprisonment and/or a fine on indictment
- Six months' imprisonment and/or a fine summarily

The Firearms (Amendment) Act 1988, s. 6 states:

(1) Subject to subsection (2) below, it is an offence to shorten to a length less than 24 inches the barrel of any smooth-bore gun to which section 1 of the principal Act applies other than one which has a barrel with a bore exceeding 2 inches in diameter; . . .

OFFENCE: **Converting imitation firearm—*Firearms Act 1968, s. 4(3)***

- Triable either way • Five years' imprisonment and/or a fine on indictment
- Six months' imprisonment and/or a fine summarily

The Firearms Act 1968, s. 4 states:

(3) It is an offence for a person other than a registered firearms dealer to convert into a firearm anything which, though having the appearance of being a firearm, is so constructed as to be incapable of discharging any missile through its barrel.

KEYNOTE

The relevant definitions are considered at para. 4.7.4.

The first two offences are concerned with the shortening of barrels while the third involves conversion of anything which has the appearance of a firearm so that it can be fired. Registered firearms dealers (see para. 4.7.5.4) are excluded from the wording of the conversion offence. They are also exempted by ss. 4(2) and 6(2) from the relevant offences involving shortening barrels provided the shortening is done *for the sole purpose* of replacing a defective part of the barrel *so as to produce a new barrel having an overall length of at least 24 inches.*

The length of the barrel of a weapon will be measured from its muzzle to the point at which the charge is exploded (s. 57(6)(a) of the 1968 Act).

Once the shortening or conversion has taken place, the nature of the firearm will have changed (e.g. from a shotgun into a section 1 firearm or from an imitation into a real firearm), in which case the person will also commit the relevant possession offences unless he/she has the appropriate authorisation.

4.7.12 Restrictions on Transfer of Firearms

The Firearms (Amendment) Act 1997 created a number of offences concerned with the transfer, lending, hiring etc. of firearms and ammunition.

In brief, a person 'transferring' (that is, selling, letting on hire, lending or giving) a section 1 firearm or ammunition to another must:

- produce a certificate or permit entitling him/her to do so (s. 32(2)(a)),
- he/she must comply with all the conditions of that certificate or permit (s. 32(2)(b)), and
- the transferor must personally hand the firearm or ammunition over to the receiver (s. 32(2)(c)).

The 1997 Act also requires any person who is the holder of a certificate or permit who is involved in such a transfer (which includes a lending of the firearm/ammunition for a period exceeding 72 hours) to give notice to the chief officer of police who granted the certificate or permit (s. 33(2)).

Notice is also required of certificate or permit holders where a firearm is lost, deactivated or destroyed or where ammunition is lost, or where firearms are sold outside Great Britain (see ss. 34 and 35).

OFFENCE: **Failing to comply with requirements—*Firearms (Amendment) Act 1997, ss. 32–35***

• Section 1 firearm/ammunition: triable either way • Five years' imprisonment and/or a fine on indictment; six months' imprisonment and/or a fine summarily • Shotguns: triable summarily • Six months' imprisonment and/or a fine

OFFENCE: **Trade transactions by person not registered as firearms dealer—*Firearms Act 1968, s. 3(1)***

• Triable either way • Five years' imprisonment and/or a fine on indictment • Six months' imprisonment and/or a fine summarily

The Firearms Act 1968, s. 3 states:

(1) A person commits an offence if, by way of trade or business, he—
 (a) manufactures, sells, transfers, repairs, tests or proves any firearm or ammunition to which section 1 of this Act applies, or a shot gun;
 (b) exposes for sale or transfer, or has in his possession for sale, transfer, repair, test or proof any such firearm or ammunition, or a shot gun, or
 (c) sells or transfers an air weapon, exposes such a weapon for sale or transfer or has such a weapon in his possession for sale or transfer,

without being registered under this Act as a firearms dealer.

KEYNOTE

A registered firearms dealer is a person who, by way of trade or business, manufactures, sells, transfers, repairs, tests or proves firearms or ammunition to which s. 1 of this Act applies, or shotguns, or sells or transfers air weapons.

If the person undertakes the repair, proofing etc. of a s. 1 firearm or ammunition or a shotgun otherwise than as a trade or business, he/she commits an offence (carrying the same punishment as the s. 3(1) offence above) under s. 3(3) unless he/she can point to some authorisation under the Act allowing him/her to do so.

Section 3 goes on to create further either way offences of selling or transferring a firearm or ammunition to someone other than a registered firearms dealer or someone otherwise authorised under the Act to buy or acquire them and of falsifying certificates with a view to acquiring firearms. These offences also carry the same punishment as the s. 3(1) offence above.

Registration is under s. 33 of the 1968 Act.

'Transferring' is also defined under s. 57(4) and includes letting on hire, giving, lending and parting with possession.

Section 9(2) of the 1968 Act exempts auctioneers from the restrictions on selling and possessing for the purposes of sale of firearms and ammunition where the auctioneer has a permit from the chief officer of police. There are further defences provided by s. 9 (for carriers and warehouse staff) and also under s. 8 (transfer to people authorised to possess firearms without a certificate).

4.7.13 Other Offences under the Firearms Acts

The Firearms (Amendment) Act 1988 introduced two summary offences punishable with three months' imprisonment and/or a fine, to ensure compliance with the European Weapons Directive (91/477/EEC): s. 18(6) (firearms dealer failing to enter particulars in the register kept under s. 40 of the 1968 Act of firearms acquired for export to another member state); and s. 18A(6) (failing to notify the purchase and acquisition of firearms in other member states).

The Firearms (Amendment) Act 1997 makes further provision for notification to be given to the relevant chief officer of police of the transfer of s. 1 firearms or shotguns (including the lending of shotguns to certain people for a period of more than 72 hours—see s. 33). In addition, the Act requires that all such transfers and transfers of ammunition for s. 1 firearms, must be carried out in person (see s. 32). Each section goes on to create summary offences for failing to comply with these obligations.

Other summary offences under the 1968 and 1988 Acts include:

- A firearms dealer failing to send the required notification within 48 hours to the chief officer of police, after selling a firearm or shotgun acquired for export (s. 18(5) of the 1988 Act).
- Selling certain ammunition to a person who is not a registered firearms dealer and is not permitted to have the relevant weapon for the ammunition (s. 5(2) of the 1988 Act).
- A pawnbroker taking a section 1 firearm or ammunition as a pawn (s. 3(6) of the 1968 Act).
- Any person selling or transferring any firearm or ammunition or carrying out repairs or tests on such for another person who is drunk or of unsound mind (s. 25 of the 1968 Act).

4.7.14 Documentation

The enforcement of the firearms legislation depends heavily on the possession and production of the relevant documents and ss. 30A to 30D of the Firearms Act 1968 allow for the revocation or partial revocation of certificates by chief officers of police. There are therefore many offences which deal with the application for and obtaining of documents, the falsification of records and documents and the failure to maintain proper records. The offences under the Firearms Act 1968 are under ss. 29(3), 30D(3), 38(8), 39(1) to (3), 40(5) and 52(2)(c), **see Blackstone's Criminal Practice 2008, para. B12.3.**

There is also an offence under s. 12(2) of the Firearms (Amendment) Act 1988 of failing to comply with a notice from the chief officer of police for the surrender of a certificate. This is a summary offence punishable with three months' imprisonment and/or a fine.

There are further summary offences which were created to ensure compliance with the European Weapons Directive (see ss. 32B(5), 32C(6), 42A(3) and 48(4) of the Firearms Act 1968).

4.8 Weapons

4.8.1 Introduction

The carrying of weapons has become an issue of considerable concern over recent years. This is particularly true of 'knife enabled crime' and the recent number of high profile murders involving young people where the murder weapon has been a knife.

In considering the different offences and restrictions, it is important to look at the *particular weapons* covered by each piece of legislation, together with the *particular activity* that Parliament has sought to control.

Although it is convenient to refer to the *possession* of offensive weapons, that word has a wide meaning which goes beyond the expressions used in most offences involving the carrying of weapons.

When considering this area, it is important to remember that the carrying of weapons is a very different thing from the use of weapons. This is why simply picking up a handy object and hitting someone with it will not usually amount to an offence under the relevant legislation dealing with carrying of weapons.

It is also useful to bear in mind the differences between offensive weapons and *weapons of offence*. The latter are specifically concerned with the entry onto premises as a trespasser and are slightly wider in their definition than offensive weapons.

4.8.2 Having Offensive Weapon in Public Place

OFFENCE: **Having offensive weapon in public place—*Prevention of Crime Act 1953, s. 1(1)***

- Triable either way • Four years' imprisonment and/or a fine on indictment
- Six months' imprisonment and/or a fine summarily

The Prevention of Crime Act 1953, s. 1 states:

> (1) Any person who without lawful authority or reasonable excuse, the proof whereof shall lie on him, has with him in any public place any offensive weapon shall be guilty of an offence.

KEYNOTE

'Lawful authority' means those occasions where people from time to time are required to carry weapons as a matter of duty, such as police officers or members of the armed forces (*Bryan* v *Mott* (1976) 62 Cr App R 71). Security guards carrying truncheons, even if required to do so by their contracts of employment, are not covered (*R* v *Spanner* [1973] Crim LR 704). If someone does not fall into this—very limited—group, he/she may still have a 'reasonable excuse' for having the weapon with him/her.

'Reasonable excuse' may arise from a number of circumstances. People having tools with them in the course of their trade (e.g. craft knives for fitting carpets or hammers for carpentry) may have a 'reasonable excuse' (see *Ohlson* v *Hylton* [1975] 1 WLR 724). If a person passing the scene of a recent disturbance sees a weapon lying on the ground and he/she picks it up and puts it in his/her car intending to take it to the nearest police station, those circumstances would amount to a reasonable excuse for having the weapon with him/her.

The issues arising out of reasonable excuses under this offence overlap greatly with those of 'good reason' under the Criminal Justice Act 1988 offence below (**see para. 4.8.3.1**) and the two should be read together to make any sense of the many decisions. Along with harassment (**see chapter 4.5**) and the breathalyser laws (**see Road Policing**), this area of criminal legislation has provided some of the most extensive litigation in recent years, to the point that most arguments open to even the most creative defendants have been tried. Nevertheless, magistrates retain a wide degree of discretion in what they accept as a 'reasonable excuse' and the cases below do *not* mean that this discretion is fettered and that the courts must follow this reasoning in every case—*DPP* v *Patterson* [2004] EWHC 2744 (magistrates' court finding that a defendant in possession of a butterfly knife in a shopping centre because 'he needed it for feeding and stabling horses' and had meant to deposit it in a safe place that day but had not had the chance to do so, had a 'reasonable excuse'). Against that background, however, the following situations have been considered and pronounced upon by the courts:

- Not being aware that you have an offensive weapon with you is *not* a reasonable excuse in itself (*R* v *Densu* [1998] 1 Cr App R 400).
- Neither is forgetting that you have a weapon with you (*R* v *Lorimer* [2003] EWCA Crim 721) generally, or forgetting that there is one in the car you are driving (*R* v *McCalla* (1988) 87 Cr App 372).
- However, where a taxi driver was found with a piece of wood and a cosh in the back of his cab where they had been left by passengers earlier in the week, the Court of Appeal held that his forgetting to remove the weapons might have been accepted as a reasonable excuse and the question should have been left for the jury (*R* v *Glidewell* (1999) 163 JP 557).
- Under the Criminal Justice Act offence below, however, there can be circumstances where forgetfulness could be relevant to the defence of 'good reason' (e.g. where it results from illness or medication)—*Bayliss* v *DPP* [2003] ACD 56.

Some of these decisions are more evidential niceties surrounding matters for summing up than policing issues but they might at least explain to bewildered officers/victims the odd acquittal when it happens.

It is not reasonable to have a weapon with you as *a general precaution* in case you are attacked (*Evans* v *Hughes* [1972] 1 WLR 1452). It may, however, be reasonable to have a weapon if you have good grounds to anticipate an unprovoked or unlawful attack (e.g. for a person guarding cash transits—see *Malnik* v *DPP* [1989] Crim LR 451).

Having a weapon for some other reason may amount to a reasonable excuse and whether or not it does so is a matter of fact for the court/jury to decide (see e.g. *Houghton* v *Chief Constable of Greater Manchester Police* (1987) 84 Cr App R 319 where the defendant was in 'fancy dress' costume as a police officer and had a truncheon with him as part of the costume—held to amount to 'reasonable excuse').

The burden of proving the reasonable excuse or lawful authority rests with the defendant, but only when the prosecution have established that the defendant had an offensive weapon with him/her at the time. That burden of proof will be judged against the balance of probabilities and not 'beyond a reasonable doubt' (**see Evidence & Procedure, chapter 2.7**).

4.8.2.1 'Has With Him'

This expression (which is also discussed in relation to firearms, **see chapter 4.7**) shows that the offence is designed to prevent the carrying of weapons; it is not an offence of *intention* and the reported decisions of the courts have consistently reflected that fact.

This is most apparent where an 'innocent' article is used offensively. In *Ohlson* v *Hylton* [1975] 1 WLR 724 the defendant had a bag of tools with him in the course of his trade. He produced a hammer from the bag and used it to hit someone. The court held that, as he had formed the intention to use the hammer *after* it came into his possession, the offence was not made out. Although the court accepted that there might be times where a later intention to use an innocent article offensively would amount to an offence under the 1953 Act, the main purpose of the law was to prevent people from arming themselves with weapons. Similar decisions have been reached in relation to picking up a discarded knife during a fight (*Bates* v *Bulman* [1979] 1 WLR 1190), brandishing a jack taken from a car (*R* v *Dayle* [1974] 1 WLR 181) and using a penknife—which the defendant happened to be carrying—to stab someone who attacked him (*R* v *Humphreys* [1977] Crim LR 225).

Some confusion has been caused in this area by the different interpretations of the expression 'has with him' in relation to firearms offences (**see chapter 4.7**).

The fact that the offence is not one of intention is supported by the decisions on 'reasonable excuse' above; the reasonable excuse must relate to the *carrying* of the weapon or article and not the *intention* of the person carrying it (*R* v *Jura* [1954] 1 QB 503).

It is possible for more than one person to have the same weapon 'with them', provided you can show that they knew of its existence in the hands of another at the time (*R* v *Edmonds* [1963] 2 QB 142).

You must show that the defendant knew that he/she had *something* with him/her and that the 'something' was, in fact, an offensive weapon (*R* v *Cugullere* [1961] 1 WLR 858). For a similar situation regarding 'possession' of drugs, **see Crime, chapter 1.6**.

4.8.2.2 Public Place

Section 1 of the 1953 Act states:

> (4) In this section 'public place' includes any highway and any other premises or place to which at the material time the public have or are permitted to have access, whether on payment or otherwise...

KEYNOTE

What is a public place is a question of fact, but whether it is capable of being a public place is a question of law (*R* v *Hanrahan* [2004] EWCA Crim 2943).

4.8.2.3 Offensive Weapon

Section 1(4) of the 1953 Act also states:

> ...'offensive weapon' means any article made or adapted for use for causing injury to the person, or intended by the person having it with him for such use by him or by some other person.

KEYNOTE

Offensive weapons fall into three categories for the purposes of this offence, namely articles:

- made for causing injury (offensive weapons *per se*);
- adapted for causing injury; and
- intended by the person who has it, for causing injury.

(For the definition of a 'weapon of offence' used in aggravated burglary, **see para. 4.8.5 and Crime, chapter 1.11**.)

Offensive weapons *per se* are those which have been manufactured for use for causing injury and include truncheons, PR-24 batons and bayonets. A swordstick has been held to be such a weapon (*R* v *Butler* [1988] Crim LR 695) as have flick-knives (*R* v *Simpson* [1983] 1 WLR 1494) and butterfly knives (*DPP* v *Hynde* [1998] 1 WLR 1222). In *Hynde* the court took notice of the fact that butterfly knives were outlawed under the Criminal Justice Act 1988 (**see para. 4.8.6**) in deciding that such knives were clearly 'made' for causing injury. In *R* v *R* [2007] EWCA Crim 3312, the Court of Appeal held that a pair of combat gloves containing powdered lead/sand in the knuckle area were designed or adapted as an offensive weapon.

Once it has been shown that the article in question was in fact an offensive weapon, there is no need for the prosecution to show any intention to use it for causing injury (*Davis* v *Alexander* (1970) 54 Cr App R 398).

Weapons *adapted* for causing injury can include virtually anything. Whether something has in fact been so adapted is a question of fact for the court/jury to decide in each case. Bottles or glasses which have been broken in order to create a jagged edge have been held to be 'adapted' (*R* v *Simpson* [1983] 1 WLR 1494), so too has a potato with razor blades protruding from it (*R* v *Williamson* (1978) 67 Cr App R 35). If the article itself has not been altered in any physical way (such as by putting ammonia in a 'Jif' lemon to squirt in people's eyes—*R* v *Formosa* [1991] 2 QB 1), it has not been adapted.

It is still unclear whether the adaptation has to be to cause injury to *another* person or whether its capacity for self-inflicted injury (as in a suicide attempt) is enough. It is submitted that, as it is the *adaptation* of the article which is relevant, and not the *intention* of the person carrying it, the ultimate 'victim' is irrelevant (see *Bryan* v *Mott* (1976) 62 Cr App R 71).

Weapons *intended* to be used for causing injury can also include virtually anything. Here the intention of the person carrying it *is relevant* and you must prove an intention to cause injury (as to intention generally, **see Crime, chapter 1.1**). An intention to cause shock can be enough to satisfy this condition (see the memorably named *R* v *Rapier* (1980) 70 Cr App R 17) but simply using the article to scare potential attackers away will not (see the less menacingly named *R* v *Snooks* [1997] Crim LR 230). To an extent this overlaps with the issues of 'reasonable excuse' and 'has with him' discussed above. In *C* v *DPP* [2001] EWHC Admin 1093 the court held that it was necessary to examine how closely the adoption of the relevant object and the intention to use it occurred, along with the circumstances in which the offence took place.

4.8.3 Having Bladed or Pointed Article in Public Place

OFFENCE: **Having bladed or sharply pointed article in public place—*Criminal Justice Act 1988, s. 139(1)***

- Triable either way • Four years' imprisonment and/or a fine on indictment
- Six months' imprisonment and/or a fine summarily

The Criminal Justice Act 1988, s. 139 states:

(1) Subject to subsections (4) and (5) below, any person who has an article to which this section applies with him in a public place shall be guilty of an offence.

KEYNOTE

This offence applies to any sharply pointed article or article having a blade. Folding pocket knives are excluded unless the cutting edge of the blade exceeds three inches (7.62 cm). If the knife is a lock-knife, it will be covered by this offence irrespective of whether the blade is actually locked open at the time (*Harris* v *DPP* [1993] 1 WLR 82).

Whether an article falls within the parameters of s. 139 is a question of law for the judge/magistrate(s) to determine (*R* v *Deegan* [1998] 2 Cr App R 121—a case that concerned the carrying of a folding pocket-knife that *was* locked open). In *R* v *Davis* [1998] Crim LR 564 the Court of Appeal reiterated that the question of whether an article was 'bladed' or not was a matter of law for the judge to decide. In that case the defendant had been carrying a screwdriver which, the prosecution contended, was a 'bladed' article capable of causing injury. The court decided that the test to be applied in such cases was not whether the 'bladed' article was capable of causing injury, but whether it had a cutting edge. Deciding whether or not an article was caught by the provisions of s. 139 was not a matter of interpreting the ordinary English word 'blade', but required the straightforward construction of the statute. This decision does not mean that a screwdriver can *never* fall within the type of article outlawed under s. 139 and if the screwdriver is pointed or it has been sharpened, it may still be caught by the above offence. There is no requirement for the item to be sharp as long as it has a blade. In *Brooker* v *DPP* (2005) 169 JP 368, a blunt butter knife was held to fall within s. 139.

The fact that an article prohibited under s. 139 is part of something that has other innocuous features (e.g. a utility tool or 'Swiss army knife'), does not save it from falling under this offence if the other ingredients are present (see *R* v *Giles* [2003] EWCA Crim 1287).

'Has with him' is discussed above (**see para. 4.8.2.1**). The need to prove that the defendant was aware that he/she had the weapon with them for this offence was re-affirmed by the Court of Appeal in *R* v *Daubney* (2000) 164 JP 519.

'Public place' is similar to that under the Prevention of Crime Act 1953 (**see para. 4.8.2.2**). The front garden of a house has been held *not* to be a public place for the purposes of this offence even where that garden is very narrow and the defendant would be able to inflict injuries on passers by from within it (*R* v *Roberts* [2004] 1 WLR 181). It must also be determined whether public access was implied or tolerated (*Harriott* v *DPP* [2005] All ER (D) 28 May).

Note that there is a specific offence relating to the carrying of weapons on school premises (**see para. 4.8.4**).

4.8.3.1 Defences

The defendant may show that he/she had 'good reason' or 'lawful authority' for having the article in a public place (s. 139(4) and (5)). Lawful authority is discussed above; good reason is similar to reasonable excuse (**see para. 4.8.2**), also discussed above. This approach was confirmed by the Court of Appeal in *R* v *Emmanuel* [1998] Crim LR 347 where it accepted that 'good reason' could include self-defence. Again it will be for the defendant to prove this authority or reason on the balance of probabilities and, again, forgetting that you have the article with you is not a general defence (*DPP* v *Gregson* (1992) 96 Cr App R 240).

Under s. 139 of the Criminal Justice Act 1988 there is a 'strong public interest' in bladed articles not being carried in public without good reason. The Divisional Court so held, finding that the requirement on the defendant to prove a good reason for having the relevant article (a lock-knife) is not an infringement of human rights legislation—*Lynch* v *DPP* [2002] 2 All ER 854. The Court of Appeal went on to consider the relevant issues here in *R* v *Matthews* [2004] QB 690. There it was held that the plain and ordinary meaning of s. 139(4) and (5) was that these provisions imposed a persuasive burden on the defendant, not merely an evidential burden (see Evidence & Procedure, chapter 2.7). As such, the defence made an inroad into Article 6(2) but, because the defendant is the only person who knows why he/she has a bladed article in a public place, there is an objective justification for this burden being imposed on a defendant. Such a measure was proportionate and struck a fair balance between the general interest of the community and the individual's rights.

The courts and commentators have had lots of debates about forgetfulness in this context and the relevance of 'forgetting' you have a knife or other article with you. The issues were summarised by the Court of Appeal in *R* v *Jolie* [2004] 1 Cr App R 3. While it is clear that forgetfulness alone cannot be a 'good reason', from a policing perspective the main thing is to gather any evidence that the defendant had the article with them in a public place and to record any explanation given. Whether the defendant had a 'good reason' (which might include forgetfulness combined with other circumstances) is then a matter for them and the court.

A defendant may also show that he/she has the article:

- for use at work, e.g. joiners, chefs, gardeners etc.;
- for religious reasons, e.g. members of the Sikh religion having a *kirpan*;
- as part of any national costume—such as someone in Highland Dress with a *skean dhu*.

In *Mohammed* v *Chief Constable of South Yorkshire* [2002] EWHC 406 the court held that the defendant did not have possession of a meat cleaver for use at his place of work; he had it for the purpose of rendering it possible to use it at work. He had taken the cleaver on a Saturday night intending, he claimed, to have it sharpened the following Monday. It was considered that there was no reason for him not to have taken the cleaver on the Monday, taking it directly to be sharpened. His appeal was dismissed.

Strangely, whether or not an article is for the uses or reasons set out above appears to be a question of *fact* (see *R* v *Manning* [1998] Crim LR 198).

4.8.4 Weapons on School Premises

OFFENCE: **Having bladed or sharply pointed article on school premises—*Criminal Justice Act 1988, s. 139A(1)***

- Triable either way • Four years' imprisonment and/or a fine on indictment
- Six months' imprisonment and/or a fine summarily

The Criminal Justice Act 1988, s. 139A states:

(1) Any person who has an article to which section 139 of this Act applies with him on school premises shall be guilty of an offence.

KEYNOTE

'Has with him' is much narrower than 'possession', **see chapter 4.7 and also Crime, chapter 1.6.**

'School premises' means land used for the purposes of a school *excluding any land occupied solely as a dwelling by a person employed at the school.* This means that the provisions would not apply to someone found in the garden of a caretaker's house if that house was occupied solely as a dwelling by the school caretaker.

'School', under the Education Act 1996, s. 4, means:

(1) . . . an educational institution which is outside the further education sector and the higher education sector and is an institution for providing—
(a) primary education;
(b) secondary education, or
(c) both primary and secondary education,
whether or not the institution also provides further education.

This offence applies to the same articles as those covered under s. 139(1), **see para. 4.8.3.**

OFFENCE: **Having offensive weapon on school premises—*Criminal Justice Act 1988, s. 139A(2)***

- Triable either way • Four years' imprisonment and/or a fine on indictment
- Six months' imprisonment and/or a fine summarily

The Criminal Justice Act 1988, s. 139A states:

(2) Any person who has an offensive weapon within the meaning of section 1 of the Prevention of Crime Act 1953 with him on school premises shall be guilty of an offence.

KEYNOTE

For the purposes of this offence, 'offensive weapons' fall into the three categories discussed at **para. 4.8.2.3.**

'Has with him', 'school premises' and 'school' are all discussed above.

4.8.4.1 Defences

The defences are the same as for s. 139(1) (**see para. 4.8.3.1**), although in relation to a s. 139A(1) offence, it is a defence for the person charged to prove that they had the article or weapon in question for educational purposes (see s. 139A(4)(b)).

4.8.4.2 Power of Entry

The Criminal Justice Act 1988, s. 139B states:

(1) A constable may enter school premises and search those premises and any person on those premises for—
(a) any article to which section 139 of this Act applies, or
(b) any offensive weapon within the meaning of section 1 of the Prevention of Crime Act 1953,
if he has reasonable grounds for suspecting that an offence under section 139A of this Act is being, or has been, committed.

(2) If in the course of a search under this section a constable discovers an article or weapon which he has reasonable grounds for suspecting to be an article or weapon of a kind described in subsection (1) above, he may seize and retain it.

(3) The constable may use reasonable force, if necessary, in the exercise of the power of entry conferred by this section.

KEYNOTE

Note that the Violent Crime Reduction Act 2006 reduced the threshold for a constable to exercise his/her powers of entry and search from 'reasonable grounds for believing' to 'reasonable grounds for suspecting'.

The power of search under this provision is covered by the Police and Criminal Evidence Act 1984 Codes of Practice (**see chapter 4.4**).

4.8.4.3 Power of Members of Staff to Search School Pupils for Weapons

Section 550AA of the Education Act 1996 states:

(1) A member of the staff of a school who has reasonable grounds for suspecting that a pupil at the school may have with him or in his possessions—
  (a) an article to which section 139 of the Criminal Justice Act 1988 applies (knives and blades etc.), or
  (b) an offensive weapon (within the meaning of the Prevention of Crime Act 1953),

  may search that pupil or his possessions for such articles and weapons.

(2) A search under this section may be carried out only where—
  (a) the member of the staff and the pupil are on the premises of the school; or
  (b) they are elsewhere and the member of the staff has lawful control or charge of the pupil.

(3) A person may carry out a search under this section only if—
  (a) he is the head teacher of the school; or
  (b) he has been authorised by the head teacher to carry out the search.

KEYNOTE

A person carrying out a search of a pupil may only require the removal of outer clothing, must be of the same sex and must carry out the search in the presence of another member of staff also of the same sex as the pupil (s. 550AA(5)). A pupil's possessions may not be searched under this section except in their presence and in the presence of another member of the staff (s. 550AA(6)). If any offensive weapon, knife or bladed weapon is found it may be seized and retained (s. 550AA(7)). As much force as is reasonable may be used in exercising this power (s. 550AA(8)). Any article seized must be delivered to a police constable as soon as reasonably practicable, and the Police (Property) Act 1897 will apply to its disposal (s. 550AA(9) and (10)).

Similar powers of search and seizure are provided for members of staff at higher education institutions (Further and Higher Education Act 1992, s. 85B), and for members of staff at attendance centres (Violent Crime Reduction Act 2006, s. 47).

The Department for Education and Skills (DfES) has published a draft guidance document which is aimed at all maintained schools, including pupil referral units, when they consider whether or not to screen pupils or use the search power provided. The guidance, which can be found on the DfES website (www.dfes.gov.uk), contains several references to the police.

4.8.5 Trespassing with Weapon of Offence

As a further complication, there is another offence relating to weapons, namely that under the Criminal Law Act 1977. As opposed to the carrying of weapons in public, or the carrying of them on school premises, this offence is concerned with preventing people *trespassing* with weapons in much the same way as aggravated burglary.

OFFENCE: **Trespassing with weapon of offence—*Criminal Law Act 1977, s. 8(1)***

- Triable summarily • Three months' imprisonment and/or a fine

The Criminal Law Act 1977, s. 8 states:

(1) A person who is on any premises as a trespasser, after having entered as such, is guilty of an offence if, without lawful authority or reasonable excuse, he has with him on the premises any weapon of offence.

KEYNOTE

The definition of 'weapon of offence' is the same as that for aggravated burglary (**see Crime, chapter 1.11**), namely any article made or adapted for use for causing injury to or incapacitating a person, or intended by the person having it with him/her for that use (s. 8(2)).

This offence is restricted to a person who has entered the relevant premises as a trespasser. It does not therefore extend to a person who, having entered lawfully, then becomes a trespasser for whatever reason (e.g. because the occupier has told him/her to leave).

'Premises' for this purpose means:

- any building or
- any part of a building under separate occupation
- any land adjacent to and used/intended for use in connection with a building
- the site comprising any building(s) together with ancillary land
- any fixed structure
- any movable structure, vehicle or vessel designed or adapted for residential purposes (s. 12 of the 1977 Act).

There are specific offences of trespassing on land or in buildings with firearms (**see chapter 4.7**).

For a further discussion of the meaning of 'has with him', 'trespasser' and 'made, adapted or intended', **see Crime, chapter 1.11**.

4.8.6 Manufacture and Sale of Weapons

In addition to the controls on the carrying of weapons, there are also restrictions on the sale, manufacture, hire and buying of some weapons. The legislation is aimed at restricting the supply of such weapons and their availability in England and Wales. As such, they are mainly concerned with manufacture, sale, offering for sale etc. and should not be confused with offences of *carrying* such weapons (which are dealt with above).

Some of the offences relate to *possession* for the purpose of sale, hire etc.; this is a much wider term than that used in the carrying offences ('has with him') and is discussed in greater detail in the context of drugs (**see Crime, chapter 1.6**) and firearms (**see chapter 4.7**).

OFFENCE: **Manufacture, sale or hire of weapons—*Restriction of Offensive Weapons Act 1959, s. 1(1)***

- Triable summarily • Six months' imprisonment and/or a fine

The Restriction of Offensive Weapons Act 1959, s. 1 states:

(1) Any person who manufactures, sells or hires or offers for sale or hire or exposes or has in his possession for the purpose of sale or hire, or lends or gives to any other person—

(a) any knife which has a blade which opens automatically by hand pressure applied to a button, spring or other device in or attached to the handle of the knife, sometimes known as a 'flick knife' or 'flick gun'; or

(b) any knife which has a blade which is released from the handle or sheath thereof by the force of gravity or the application of centrifugal force and which, when released, is locked in place by means of a button, spring, lever, or other device, sometimes known as a 'gravity knife',

shall be guilty of an offence...

OFFENCE: **Manufacture, sale and hire of offensive weapons—*Criminal Justice Act 1988, s. 141(1)***

- Triable summarily • Six months' imprisonment and/or a fine

The Criminal Justice Act 1988, s. 141 states:

(1) Any person who manufactures, sells or hires or offers for sale or hire, exposes or has in his possession for the purpose of sale or hire, or lends or gives to any other person, a weapon to which this section applies shall be guilty of an offence...

KEYNOTE

The importation of the weapons described in these offences is also prohibited (under s. 141(2) and (4) respectively).

4.8.6.1 Weapons Covered by Section 141

The weapons to which the 1988 Act applies are set out in the schedule to the Criminal Justice Act 1988 (Offensive Weapons) Order 1988 (SI 1988/2019) (**see Blackstone's Criminal Practice 2008, para. B12.141**). The weapons listed include knuckledusters, swordsticks, some telescopic truncheons, butterfly knives, samurai swords and a whole range of martial arts weapons.

KEYNOTE

The courts take notice of the fact that a weapon has been outlawed under this legislation in deciding whether or not it is 'made' for causing injury under the Prevention of Crime Act 1953 (**see para. 4.8.2.3**).

There are a number of defences provided that include, Crown servants and visiting forces (s. 141(5) to (7)), transactions made by or to museums and galleries (s. 141(8) to (11)), theatrical performances/rehearsals, and the production of films or television programmes (s. 141(11A) and (11B)). For the purpose of these defences the onus is on the defendant to provide sufficient evidence and the contrary is not proved beyond reasonable doubt (s. 141(11C)).

4.8.7 Knives

Although some knives will fall into the categories of offence covered above, there are further restrictions which apply to knives generally.

4.8.7.1 Sale of Knives etc. to Persons under 18

OFFENCE: **Selling, knives and articles to under 18's—*Criminal Justice Act 1988, s. 141A***

- Triable summarily • Six months' imprisonment and/or a fine

The Criminal Justice Act 1988, s. 141A states:

(1) Any person who sells to a person under the age of eighteen years an article to which this section applies shall be guilty of an offence ...
(2) Subject to subsection (3) below, this section applies to—
(a) any knife, knife blade or razor blade,
(b) any axe, and
(c) any other article which has a blade or which is sharply pointed and which is made or adapted for use for causing injury to the person.
(3) This section does not apply to any article described in—
(a) section 1 of the Restriction of Offensive Weapons Act 1959,
(b) an order made under section 141(2) of this Act, or
(c) an order made by the Secretary of State under this section.

KEYNOTE

This offence does not apply to folding pocket knives with a cutting edge not exceeding three inches (7.62 cm), neither does it apply to certain types of razor blade in a cartridge where not more than 2 mm of blade is exposed (Criminal Justice Act 1988 (Offensive Weapons) (Exemption) Order 1996 (SI 1996/3064)).

4.8.7.2 Defence

Section 141A of the 1988 Act states:

(4) It shall be a defence for a person charged with an offence under subsection (1) above to prove that he took all reasonable precautions and exercised all due diligence to avoid the commission of the offence.

4.8.7.3 Unlawful Marketing of Knives

OFFENCE: **Unlawful marketing of knives—*Knives Act 1997, s. 1***

- Triable either way • Two years' imprisonment and/or a fine on indictment
- Six months' imprisonment and/or a fine summarily

The Knives Act 1997, s. 1 states:

(1) A person is guilty of an offence if he markets a knife in a way which—
(a) indicates, or suggests, that it is suitable for combat; or
(b) is otherwise likely to stimulate or encourage violent behaviour involving the use of the knife as a weapon.

KEYNOTE

'Knife' for this purpose means any instrument which has a blade *or* which is sharply pointed (s. 10 of the 1997 Act).

Marketing will include selling, hiring, offering or exposing for sale or hire and possessing it for those purposes (s. 1(4)).

'Indicates or suggests' is a very loose concept requiring no *mens rea* on the part of the defendant (however, see defences below).

'Suitable for combat' means suitable for use as a weapon for inflicting injury to anyone *or causing them to fear injury*, and 'violent behaviour' means an unlawful act inflicting injury *or causing a person to fear injury* (s. 10). The elements in italics (author's emphasis) show that the legislation is intended to address the fear of the use of knives as well as their actual use.

The suggestion that knives are suitable for combat may be express or it may be implied by the name given to a product (e.g. 'commando') or by the packaging or advertisement relating to it (s. 1(3)). Therefore such packaging or advertising material, together with any surrounding advertisements, can be produced in evidence.

4.8.7.4 Defences

The Knives Act 1997, ss. 3 and 4 state:

3.—(1) It is a defence for a person charged with an offence under section 1 to prove that—
(a) the knife was marketed—
(i) for use by the armed forces of any country;
(ii) as an antique or curio; or
(iii) as falling within such other category (if any) as may be prescribed;
(b) it was reasonable for the knife to be marketed in that way; and
(c) there were no reasonable grounds for suspecting that a person into whose possession the knife might come in consequence of the way in which it was marketed would use it for an unlawful purpose.

...

4.—(1) It is a defence for a person charged with an offence under section 1 to prove that he did not know or suspect, and had no reasonable grounds for suspecting, that the way in which the knife was marketed—
(a) amounted to an indication or suggestion that the knife was suitable for combat; or
(b) was likely to stimulate or encourage violent behaviour involving the use of the knife as a weapon...

KEYNOTE

The defences at s. 3 require the person to show that the knife was marketed/the material published:

- for one of the uses at s. 3(1)(a)(i) to (iii) and s. 3(2)(a)(i) to (iii) *and*
- that it was reasonable to market it in that way *and*
- that there were no reasonable grounds for suspecting that a person would use the knife for an unlawful purpose.

The defences at s. 4 require the person to show that he/she:

- did not know or suspect, or
- *have any reasonable grounds to suspect*
- that the marketing/the marketing material amounted to an indication or even a *suggestion* that the knife was suitable for combat *or*

- was likely to stimulate or encourage violent behaviour involving the use of the knife as a weapon.

There is also the general defence under s. 4(3) for the person to show that he/she took *all* reasonable precautions and exercised *all* due diligence to avoid committing the offence.

In each of these cases, the standard of proof will be against the balance of probabilities (**see Evidence & Procedure, chapter 2.7**).

Section 5 allows a court to issue a warrant for the entry onto premises and for the search, seizure and removal of knives (or materials where an offence under s. 2 is involved—**see para. 4.8.7.5**). Any knives or publications which have been seized and removed by a constable under a warrant issued under this section may be retained until the conclusion of proceedings against the suspect (s. 5(4)).

4.8.7.5 Publications Relating to Knives

OFFENCE: **Publications relating to knives—*Knives Act 1997, s. 2(1)***

- Triable either way • Two years' imprisonment and/or a fine on indictment
- Six months' imprisonment and/or a fine summarily

The Knives Act 1997, s. 2 states:

(1) A person is guilty of an offence if he publishes any written, pictorial or other material in connection with the marketing of any knife and that material—
  (a) indicates, or suggests, that the knife is suitable for combat; or
  (b) is otherwise likely to stimulate or encourage violent behaviour involving the use of the knife as a weapon.

The Knives Act 1997, s. 3 states:

(2) It is a defence for a person charged with an offence under section 2 to prove that—
  (a) the material was published in connection with marketing a knife—
    (i) for use by the armed forces of any country;
    (ii) as an antique or curio; or
    (iii) as falling within such other category (if any) as may be prescribed;
  (b) it was reasonable for the knife to be marketed in that way; and
  (c) there were no reasonable grounds for suspecting that a person into whose possession the knife might come in consequence of the publishing of the material would use it for an unlawful purpose.

The Knives Act 1997, s. 4 states:

(2) It is a defence for a person charged with an offence under section 2 to prove that he did not know or suspect, and had no reasonable grounds for suspecting, that the material—
  (a) amounted to an indication or suggestion that the knife was suitable for combat; or
  (b) was likely to stimulate or encourage violent behaviour involving the use of the knife as a weapon.

KEYNOTE

This offence is aimed at the publishers of advertisements rather than those who are involved in the sale and marketing of knives. The defences are shown above.

A search warrant may be issued under s. 5 for relevant publications (**see para. 4.8.7.4**).

4.8.8 Crossbows

Even though they might fit into some of the other offences discussed above, crossbows are also subject to specific legislation.

OFFENCE: **Selling or letting on hire crossbow to person under 18—*Crossbows Act 1987, s. 1***

- Triable summarily • Six months' imprisonment and/or a fine

The Crossbows Act 1987, s. 1 states:

> A person who sells or lets on hire a crossbow or a part of a crossbow to a person under the age of eighteen is guilty of an offence, unless he believes him to be eighteen years of age or older and has reasonable ground for the belief.

OFFENCE: **Purchase or hire of crossbow by person under 18—*Crossbows Act 1987, s. 2***

- Triable summarily • Fine

The Crossbows Act 1987, s. 2 states:

> A person under the age of eighteen who buys or hires a crossbow or a part of a crossbow is guilty of an offence.

OFFENCE: **Person under 18 having crossbow—*Crossbows Act 1987, s. 3***

- Triable summarily • Fine

The Crossbows Act 1987, s. 3 states:

> A person under the age of eighteen who has with him—
> (a) a crossbow which is capable of discharging a missile, or
> (b) parts of a crossbow which together (and without any other parts) can be assembled to form a crossbow capable of discharging a missile,
> is guilty of an offence, unless he is under the supervision of a person who is twenty-one years of age or older.

KEYNOTE

The offence under s. 3 again relates to a person 'having with him' (see para. 4.8.2.1) and it only applies to a crossbow which is capable of firing a missile or the parts of one which can be assembled to do so. If the crossbow has a 'draw weight' (the force required to pull back the cord to load it) of less than 1.4 kg, the provisions of the Act do not apply.

In each of the above cases the court may order forfeiture of the crossbow or parts of a crossbow.

4.8.8.1 Power of Search and Seizure

The Crossbows Act 1987, s. 4 states:

> (1) If a constable suspects with reasonable cause that a person is committing or has committed an offence under section 3, the constable may—
> (a) search that person for a crossbow or part of a crossbow;
> (b) search any vehicle, or anything in or on any vehicle, in or on which the constable suspects with reasonable cause there is a crossbow, or part of a crossbow, connected with the offence.

KEYNOTE

This power of search is governed by PACE Codes of Practice, Code A (**see appendix 4.1**). For a full discussion of police powers to stop and search, **see chapter 4.4**.

A police officer may detain a person or vehicle for the purpose of a search under this power (s. 4(2)).

Anything that appears to be a crossbow or part of a crossbow to the officer found during the search may be seized (s. 4(3)).

For the purposes of exercising the powers above, a police officer may enter any land other than a dwelling house (s. 4(4)).

PART THREE

General Police Duties

4.9 Civil Disputes

4.9.1 Introduction

Although most civil disputes, by definition, do not involve the core functions of the police, there are occasions when the involvement of the police is necessary. The most common are 'domestic' disputes (usually involving close friends, partners and relatives) and trade disputes. The effects of the Human Rights Act 1998 and the increased focus on the State's positive duty to protect some of the competing rights of individuals (**see chapter 4.3**) has meant that the police are increasingly being brought into what appear to be essentially private disputes. Other common sources of civil dispute are addressed under **chapters 4.5 and 4.10**.

4.9.2 Domestic Disputes

A 'domestic' dispute may involve a whole range of infringements of the criminal law, from a breach of the peace (**see chapter 4.6**), to serious assault and homicide (**see Crime, chapters 1.7 and 1.5** respectively).

Each of these is dealt with in other areas of this work, together with any attendant powers of entry and arrest (**see chapter 4.4**).

There are also occasions where police officers become involved in enforcing what are in effect civil matters in relation to *matrimonial* or *family* domestic disputes. Generally these occasions will come about where one party is subject to a court order preventing them from doing certain acts, acts which they nevertheless go on to carry out.

The area of domestic violence has received a great deal of political and legislative attention over recent years. A number of important changes were made to this area of the law by the Domestic Violence, Crime and Victims Act 2004 and most of the provisions contained in the Act are now in force. The Association of Chief Police Officers has issued a policy document setting out the approach to be adopted where police officers are personally involved in domestic violence, and advocating a 'presumption towards dismissal' where an officer is convicted of a domestic violence-related offence. In addition, any officer whose conduct is found to have fallen below the required standard (**see para. 4.1.11.4**) in respect of domestic violence/abuse, can expect to be dismissed or required to resign, despite not having attracted a criminal conviction.

4.9.2.1 Court Orders

Any court having jurisdiction over family law matters can make an order under the Family Law Act 1996.

4.9.2.2 The Family Law Act 1996

The Family Law Act 1996 consolidated many aspects of the law regulating family proceedings. Part IV of the Act makes provisions for family homes and for dealing with domestic violence.

4.9.2.3 Non-Molestation Orders

Section 42 of the 1996 Act provides for 'non-molestation' orders. Section 42 states:

(1) In this Part a 'non-molestation order' means an order containing either or both of the following provisions—
  (a) provision prohibiting a person ('the respondent') from molesting another person who is associated with the respondent;
  (b) provision prohibiting the respondent from molesting a relevant child.

(2) The court may make a non-molestation order—
  (a) if an application for the order has been made (whether in other family proceedings or without any other family proceedings being instituted) by a person who is associated with the respondent; or
  (b) if in any family proceedings to which the respondent is a party the court considers that the order should be made for the benefit of any other party to the proceedings or any relevant child even though no such application has been made.

KEYNOTE

Non-molestation orders can be applied for even though no other proceedings have been begun and such orders do not relate just to spouses or former partners; they apply to anyone who is 'associated' with the respondent.

Under s. 62, a person is 'associated' with another person if:

(3) ...
  (a) they are or have been married to each other;
  (aa) they are or have been civil partners of each other;
  (b) they are cohabitants or former cohabitants;
  (c) they live or have lived in the same household, otherwise than merely by reason of one of them being the other's employee, tenant, lodger or boarder;
  (d) they are relatives;
  (e) they have agreed to marry one another (whether or not that agreement has been terminated);
  (eza) they have entered a civil partnership agreement (as defined by section 73 of the Civil Partnership Act 2004) (whether or not that agreement has been terminated);
  (ea) they have or have had an intimate personal relationship with each other which is or was of significant duration;
  (f) in relation to any child, they are both persons falling within subsection (4); or
  (g) they are parties to the same family proceedings (other than proceedings under this Part).

(4) A person falls within this subsection in relation to a child if—
  (a) he is a parent of the child; or
  (b) he has or has had parental responsibility for the child.

In deciding whether or not to make such an order, the court must consider all the circumstances, including the need to secure the health, safety and well-being of the applicant or any relevant child (s. 42(5)).

4.9.2.4 Breach of a Non-Molestation Order

OFFENCE: **Breach of a non-molestation order—Family Law Act 1996, s. 42A**
- Triable either way • Five years' imprisonment and/or a fine on indictment • Twelve months' imprisonment and/or a fine summarily

The Family Law Act 1996, s. 42A states:

(1) A person who without reasonable excuse does anything that he is prohibited from doing by a non-molestation order is guilty of an offence.
(2) In the case of a non-molestation order made by virtue of s. 45(1), a person can be guilty of an offence under this section only in respect of conduct engaged in at a time when he was aware of the existence of the order.

KEYNOTE

This section, introduced by the Domestic Violence, Crime and Victims Act 2004, made the breach of a non-molestation order a criminal offence. Consequently, this provides a power of arrest for the breach of a non-molestation order under the provisions of s. 24(1) of the Police and Criminal Evidence Act 1984.

In relation to s. 42A(2), non-molestation orders made by virtue of s. 45(1) are *ex parte* orders where the respondent has not been present at the proceedings when the order was made.

4.9.3 Trade Disputes

Most of the conditions regulating trade disputes can be found in the Trade Union and Labour Relations (Consolidation) Act 1992.

The areas which have historically created the greatest need for police involvement arise from the differences between those who wish to exercise their right to strike and those who wish to continue to work.

4.9.3.1 Picketing

Section 220 of the 1992 Act states:

(1) It is lawful for a person in contemplation or furtherance of a trade dispute to attend—
  (a) at or near his own place of work, or
  (b) if he is an official of a trade union, at or near the place of work of a member of the union whom he is accompanying and whom he represents,

  for the purpose only of peacefully obtaining or communicating information, or peacefully persuading any person to work or abstain from working.
(2) If a person works or normally works—
  (a) otherwise than at any one place, or
  (b) at a place the location of which is such that attendance there for a purpose mentioned in subsection (1) is impracticable,

  his place of work for the purposes of that subsection shall be any premises of his employer from which he works or from which his work is administered.
(3) In the case of a worker not in employment where—
  (a) his last employment was terminated in connection with a trade dispute, or
  (b) the termination of his employment was one of the circumstances giving rise to a trade dispute,

  in relation to that dispute his former place of work shall be treated for the purposes of subsection (1) as being his place of work.

(4) A person who is an official of a trade union by virtue only of having been elected or appointed to be a representative of some of the members of the union shall be regarded for the purposes of subsection (1) as representing only those members; but otherwise an official of a union shall be regarded for those purposes as representing all its members.

KEYNOTE

Section 220 effectively restricts lawful picketing to 'primary' picketing outside the person's own place of work.

If there is a real danger of any offence (such as a public order offence, **see chapter 4.6**) being committed, then pickets have no right to attend the place in question under s. 220 (*Piddington* v *Bates* [1961] 1 WLR 162).

The power for police officers to give directions to people in the vicinity of someone's dwelling (under the Criminal Justice and Police Act 2001, s. 42) does not apply to any conduct made lawful by s. 220 above (**see para. 4.6.9.3**). Given the restrictions on just what conduct s. 220 allows, there may be occasions where the Criminal Justice and Police Act power could be used in connection with a trade dispute.

Although s. 220 does not place any restriction on the numbers of pickets, if they gather in large enough numbers, there may be a presumption that the pickets intend to intimidate others (*Broome* v *DPP* [1974] AC 587).

Section 220 does not authorise pickets to enter onto private land (*British Airports Authority* v *Ashton* [1983] 1 WLR 1079).

A person's place of work does not include new premises of an employer who has moved since dismissing the people picketing (*News Group Newspapers Ltd* v *SOGAT'82 (No. 2)* [1987] ICR 181).

For the Code of Practice on Picketing, see the Code of Practice (Picketing) Order 1992 (SI 1992/476 made under Employment Act 1980 s. 3). The contents of this Order may now need to be reviewed in the light of the Human Rights Act 1998 and the incorporation of the European Convention into the law of England and Wales (**see chapter 4.3**). In particular, the recommended numbers for pickets may be an unreasonable infringement of Article 11.

Note that the police powers to disperse groups under s. 30 of the Anti-social Behaviour Act 2003 do not apply to people picketing lawfully under the above provisions (**see para. 4.6.12.2**).

4.9.3.2 Meaning of 'Trade Dispute'

Section 244 of the 1992 Act states:

(1) In this Part a 'trade dispute' means a dispute between workers and their employer which relates wholly or mainly to one or more of the following—
- (a) terms and conditions of employment, or the physical conditions in which any workers are required to work;
- (b) engagement or non-engagement, or termination or suspension of employment or the duties of employment, of one or more workers;
- (c) allocation of work or the duties of employment between workers or groups of workers;
- (d) matters of discipline;
- (e) a worker's membership or non-membership of a trade union;
- (f) facilities for officials of trade unions; and
- (g) machinery for negotiation or consultation, and other procedures, relating to any of the above matters, including the recognition by employers or employers' associations of the right of a trade union to represent workers in such negotiation or consultation or in the carrying out of such procedures.

KEYNOTE

'Employment' includes any relationship whereby one person personally does work or performs services for another. 'Worker', in relation to a dispute with an employer, means a worker employed by that employer, or a person who has ceased to be so employed if his/her employment was terminated in connection with the dispute, or if the termination of his/her employment was one of the circumstances giving rise to the dispute (s. 244(5)).

4.9.3.3 Use of Violence or Intimidation

OFFENCE: **Intimidation or annoyance by violence or otherwise—*Trade Union and Labour Relations (Consolidation) Act 1992, s. 241***

- Triable summarily • Six months' imprisonment and/or a fine

The Trade Union and Labour Relations (Consolidation) Act 1992, s. 241 states:

(1) A person commits an offence who, with a view to compelling another person to abstain from doing or to do any act which that person has a legal right to do or abstain from doing, wrongfully and without legal authority—

(a) uses violence to or intimidates that person or his spouse or civil partner or children, or injures his property,

(b) persistently follows that person about from place to place,

(c) hides any tools, clothes or other property owned or used by that person, or deprives him of or hinders him in the use thereof,

(d) watches or besets the house or other place where that person resides, works, carries on business or happens to be, or the approach to any such house or place, or

(e) follows that person with two or more other persons in a disorderly manner in or through any street or road.

KEYNOTE

'With a view to compelling' means with intent to compel. This is therefore an offence of 'specific intent' (see Crime, chapter 1.1).

'Wrongfully' means a civil wrong.

Although the breach of a contract is generally not a criminal offence, this section imposes a duty on some contracted personnel not to breach their contract under certain conditions.

For this offence you would have to show that the person acted wilfully and maliciously (see Crime, chapter 1.1); you would also have to show knowledge or reasonable cause to believe that the listed consequences would apply. This would clearly create practical difficulties and this offence is likely to be very rarely used.

For the general offence of harassment and intimidation of someone at their home see para. 4.6.9.3.

4.10 Offences Relating to Land and Premises

4.10.1 Introduction

The law regulating the relationship between landlord and occupier falls largely within the province of 'civil' law. There are, however, a number of occasions and circumstances where the interests of landowners and occupiers conflict. Under some such circumstances the threat to public order, property or proprietary rights is considered to need the protection of the criminal law.

4.10.2 Criminal Trespass

The law of trespass, as with that of landlord and tenant, is generally dealt with as civil law and, contrary to the many notices that appear on premises, trespass is not usually a matter for prosecution.

Whether it be civil or criminal, trespass involves an interference with someone's occupation of land or premises. This chapter is concerned with four main aspects of such interference, namely:

- aggravated trespass (which can include common as well as private land)
- interfering with the rights of occupiers/intending occupiers
- trespassing during court order
- nuisances on educational premises
- trespassing on designated sites.

4.10.3 Aggravated Trespass

In the wake of several well-publicised encounters between police officers and groups of people who either had trespassed, or intended to trespass, on someone else's land, Parliament created a number of criminal offences (in the Criminal Justice and Public Order Act 1994). It also created specific police powers to deal with such occasions.

These powers have recently been extended to include trespassing in or on buildings as well as on land in the open air.

The types of trespass addressed by the 1994 Act can be categorised into four main groups:

- trespassing with the intention of disrupting or obstructing a lawful activity, or intimidating those engaged in it;

- two or more people trespassing with the purpose of residing on the land;
- 20 or more people attending a 'rave';
- residing in vehicles on land.

4.10.4 Trespass intending to Obstruct, Disrupt or Intimidate

OFFENCE: **Trespass intending to obstruct, disrupt or intimidate—*Criminal Justice and Public Order Act 1994, s. 68***

- Triable summarily • Three months' imprisonment and/or a fine

The Criminal Justice and Public Order Act 1994, s. 68 states:

(1) A person commits the offence of aggravated trespass if he trespasses on land and, in relation to any lawful activity which persons are engaging in or are about to engage in on that or adjoining land, does there anything which is intended by him to have the effect—
   (a) of intimidating those persons or any of them so as to deter them or any of them from engaging in that activity,
   (b) of obstructing that activity, or
   (c) of disrupting that activity.

(2) Activity on any occasion on the part of a person or persons on land is 'lawful' for the purposes of this section if he or they may engage in the activity on the land on that occasion without committing an offence or trespassing on the land.

KEYNOTE

Examples of the sort of conduct envisaged would be environmental activists disrupting a building programme or saboteurs disrupting a fox hunt (see *Winder* v *DPP* (1996) 160 JP 713).

This is an offence of specific intent (**see Crime, chapter 1.1**) rather than consequence. Therefore what must be shown is the defendant's intention to bring about the effects set out at s. 68(1)(a)–(c). There is no need to specify which of the intended activities (i.e. deterring, obstructing or disrupting) in any charge and use of all three expressions is not bad for duplicity (*Nelder* v *DPP* (1988) *The Times*, 11 June). However, proof is required of both the trespassing on land *and* of some overt act, other than the trespassing, which was intended to have the effects set out at s. 68(1)(a) to (c) (see *DPP* v *Barnard* [2000] Crim LR 371).

The activity of the defendant can include 'anything' provided it was accompanied by the relevant intention.

In order to establish the offence of aggravated trespass under s. 68, you must prove that the defendant had committed the act(s) complained of in the physical presence of a person engaged or about to engage in the lawful activity with which the defendant wished to interfere (*DPP* v *Tilly* (2002) 166 JP 22).

The lawful activity that people are engaging in (or are about to engage in) must also take place (be proposed to take place) on the same land or on adjoining land.

Under s. 68(5) land does not include land forming part of a highway unless it is:

- a footpath, bridleway or byway open to all traffic or road used as a public path (as defined by s. 54 of the Wildlife and Countryside Act 1981) or
- a cycle track under the Highways Act 1980 or the Cycle Tracks Act 1984.

Lawful activity is defined at s. 68(2) and is a very wide concept. Arguments as to the lawfulness of activities such as protesting or canvassing support for a given cause are strengthened with the advent of the Human Rights Act 1998 (as to which, **see chapter 4.3**). This point has been determined in the context of anti-war protestors where it was argued that the war against Iraq was illegal and therefore the activities carried out by staff at airbases were also unlawful. The House of Lords determined that for the purposes of s. 68(2), an act of aggression against another State or a general crime against peace did not constitute an offence contrary to the law of England and Wales (*R* v *Jones* [2006] UKHL 16)—(see also *Ayliffe* v *DPP* [2006] QB 227).

For a discussion of the offence of obstructing highways and the effect of the Human Rights Act 1998, see Road Policing, chapter 3.8.

4.10.4.1 Police Powers

The Criminal Justice and Public Order Act 1994, s. 69 states:

(1) If the senior police officer present at the scene reasonably believes—
 (a) that a person is committing, has committed or intends to commit the offence of aggravated trespass on land; or
 (b) that two or more persons are trespassing on land and are present there with the common purpose of intimidating persons so as to deter them from engaging in a lawful activity or of obstructing or disrupting a lawful activity,

he may direct that person or (as the case may be) those persons (or any of them) to leave the land.

(2) A direction under subsection (1) above, if not communicated to the persons referred to in subsection (1) by the police officer giving the direction, may be communicated to them by any constable at the scene.

KEYNOTE

Although this power requires the senior officer present at the scene to have a reasonable *belief* (a narrower concept than mere suspicion) as to the circumstances set out at s. 69(1)(a) or (b), the power is available as a preventive measure and as a means of dealing with the incident after it has happened. In this respect it is far wider than the power of arrest above.

The direction to leave the land may be communicated to the relevant people by any police officer at the scene and there is no requirement for either officer to be in uniform.

OFFENCE: **Failure to leave or re-entry when directed to leave—*Criminal Justice and Public Order Act 1994, s. 69(3)***

- Triable summarily • Three months' imprisonment and/or a fine

The Criminal Justice and Public Order Act 1994, s. 69 states:

(3) If a person knowing that a direction under subsection (1) above has been given which applies to him—
 (a) fails to leave the land as soon as practicable, or
 (b) having left again enters the land as a trespasser within the period of three months beginning with the day on which the direction was given,

he commits an offence ...

KEYNOTE

In order to prove this offence it must be shown that the person knew of the direction and that it applied to him/her. Clearly the easiest way of ensuring both elements would be to serve a written notice on the person at the same time as communicating the direction to leave and to record any response.

4.10.4.2 Defence

The Criminal Justice and Public Order Act 1994, s. 69 states:

(4) In proceedings for an offence under subsection (3) it is a defence for the accused to show—
(a) that he was not trespassing on the land, or
(b) that he had a reasonable excuse for failing to leave the land as soon as practicable or, as the case may be, for again entering the land as a trespasser.

4.10.5 Trespassing for Purpose of Residence

OFFENCE: **Two or more people trespassing for purpose of residence—*Criminal Justice and Public Order Act 1994, s. 61***

- Triable summarily • Three months' imprisonment and/or a fine

The Criminal Justice and Public Order Act 1994, s. 61 states:

(1) If the senior police officer present at the scene reasonably believes that two or more persons are trespassing on land and are present there with the common purpose of residing there for any period, that reasonable steps have been taken by or on behalf of the occupier to ask them to leave and—
(a) that any of those persons has caused damage to the land or to property on the land or used threatening, abusive or insulting words or behaviour towards the occupier, a member of his family or an employee or agent of his, or
(b) that those persons have between them six or more vehicles on the land,
he may direct those persons, or any of them, to leave the land and to remove any vehicles or other property they have with them on the land.
(2) Where the persons in question are reasonably believed by the senior police officer to be persons who were not originally trespassers but have become trespassers on the land, the officer must reasonably believe that the other conditions specified in subsection (1) are satisfied after those persons became trespassers before he can exercise the power conferred by that subsection.
(3) A direction under subsection (1) above, if not communicated to the persons referred to in subsection (1) by the police officer giving the direction, may be communicated to them by any constable at the scene.

KEYNOTE

The key features of this section can be broken down into two parts. First, the senior officer present at the scene must have a reasonable belief that:

- at least two people *are trespassing* on land *and*
- that they are there with the common purpose of residing there *and*
- that reasonable (though not *all* reasonable) steps have been taken by/on behalf of the occupier to ask them to leave.

If this is the case, the senior officer must also have a reasonable belief that:

- *any* of those people have caused damage to the land or to property on the land *or*
- *any* of those people have used threatening, abusive or insulting words or behaviour towards the occupier or a member of the occupier's family or staff or one of his/her agents *or*
- those people have between them six or more vehicles on the land.

If all the conditions under the first heading, together with any of the conditions under the second are met the officer may direct the people to leave the land and to take their vehicles and other property with them.

Most of the terms used in this section are defined under s. 61(9). 'Land' does not include buildings other than agricultural buildings or scheduled monuments. It also has the same restrictions in relation to highways as those set out under s. 68 above.

The damaging of property includes the deposit of any substance capable of polluting the land and property for the purposes of damage has the same meaning as under the Criminal Damage Act 1971 (**see Crime, chapter 1.13**).

'Vehicles' do not have to be in a fit state for use on a road and can include a chassis or body (with or without wheels) appearing to have formed part of a vehicle. They also include caravans (as defined under the Caravan Sites and Control of Development Act 1960).

A person may be regarded as having a purpose of residing on land even though he/she has a home elsewhere.

Where the land concerned is 'common land', any references to trespassing will be construed as acts that are an infringement of the rights of the occupier or 'commoners' rights'. Where the public has access to that common land, references to the occupier will include the local authority (s. 61(7)).

If the people concerned were not originally trespassers (e.g. because they were given limited permission to be there), the senior officer present must have a reasonable belief that the relevant conditions above came about after the people became trespassers.

Again, the direction to leave the land may be communicated to the relevant parties by any police officer at the scene and there is no requirement for either officer to be in uniform.

Following confusion that this section had been replaced by the insertion of s. 62A of the Act (**see para. 4.10.6**), a letter from the Home Office provided guidance on the use of s. 61. This guidance advises that the police must be able to demonstrate that all eviction and enforcement decisions are 'proportionate' in weighing individual harm against the wider public interest. The guidance further states that the use of this section is not prohibited by the Race Relations Act 1976 as amended by the Race Relations (Amendment) Act 2000, providing that the police are able to show that they have properly considered the race and equalities implications of their policies and actions in relation to unauthorised encampments and unauthorised development by gypsies and Irish travellers, and can demonstrate that their policies and actions are proportionate bearing in mind all the circumstances of the case.

4.10.5.1 Failure to Follow Direction to Leave

OFFENCE: **Failure to leave when directed—*Criminal Justice and Public Order Act 1994, s. 61(4)***

• Triable summarily • Three months' imprisonment and/or a fine

The Criminal Justice and Public Order Act 1994, s. 61 states:

> (4) If a person knowing that a direction under subsection (1) above has been given which applies to him—
> (a) fails to leave the land as soon as reasonably practicable, or
> (b) having left again enters the land as a trespasser within the period of three months beginning with the day on which the direction was given,
> he commits an offence ...

KEYNOTE

The requirements as to proof of knowledge here are the same as those under s. 69 above. This offence is the same as that under s. 69 with the exception of the word *reasonably* before practicable. This suggests that the law provides more latitude to people directed to leave the land under s. 61 than under s. 69, a suggestion that is also borne out by the wording of the respective defences.

In a case involving travellers trespassing on local authority land, the Administrative Court has had the opportunity to review the compatibility of a s. 61 direction with the European Convention on Human Rights and to set out some views which will be of use to operational officers considering making s. 61 directions. The court held as follows:

- Section 61 has to be construed narrowly because it creates a criminal offence (see below). As the fear of arrest can induce compliance with the direction even in someone who has an arguable justification for remaining on the land, it has to be construed all the more narrowly.
- Parliament could not have intended to impose criminal sanctions on trespassers who *complied* with requests to leave.
- The natural reading of s. 61(1) and (4) (see below) is that a direction amounts to an order to trespassers to leave—with their vehicles—as soon as reasonably practicable after the giving of the direction.
- When taking the operational decision to give a s. 61 direction, the police officer in this case was entitled to assume that the local authority had not, by its decision to evict trespassers, breached the Convention.
- Article 3 (subjecting a person to inhuman or degrading treatment—**see para. 4.3.6**) has no application to a s. 61 direction.
- Similarly, Article 6 (right to a fair trial—**see para. 4.3.9**) is concerned with procedure, not substantive law and is therefore not infringed by the 'criminalisation of trespass' in this way.
- The financial charges that could be made for the removal, retention, disposal or destruction of vehicles (under s. 67 of the Act) are not a 'penalty' making it a 'criminal process' but a civil debt.
- The exercise of power under s. 61 of the Act does not necessarily infringe Article 8 (right to private life—**see para. 4.3.11**) (see also *South Buckinghamshire District Council* v *Porter* [2002] 1 WLR 1359).
- The concept of 'home' in Article 8 involves a continuity that had been absent in the traveller's claim in this particular case.
- A trespasser is still free to enjoy his/her property—just not on the trespassed land. Therefore Protocol 1, Article 1 (**see para. 4.3.19**) is not necessarily infringed by s. 61.

Section 61 is therefore compatible with the Convention *per se*. However, the *actual* direction given *was*, in *R (On the Application of Fuller & Secretary of State for the Home Department)* v *Chief Constable of Dorset Police* [2003] QB 480, held to be unlawful because:

- insufficient opportunity was given to ensure compliance with the local authority's request that the land be vacated, and
- the direction did not require departure immediately or as soon as reasonably practicable, but simply gave a date for vacant possession.

4.10.5.2 Defence

The Criminal Justice and Public Order Act 1994, s. 61 states:

(6) In proceedings for an offence under this section it is a defence for the accused to show—
  (a) that he was not trespassing on the land, or
  (b) that he had a reasonable excuse for failing to leave the land as soon as reasonably practicable or, as the case may be, for again entering the land as a trespasser.

4.10.5.3 Power of Seizure

If a direction has been given under s. 61 and a police officer reasonably suspects that any person to whom it applies has, without reasonable excuse:

- failed to remove any vehicle on the land which appears to the officer to belong to him/her or to be in his/her possession or under his/her control, or

- entered the land as a trespasser with a vehicle within the period of three months beginning with the day when the direction was given

the officer may seize and remove the vehicle (s. 62).

4.10.6 Trespassing for Purpose of Residence with Vehicle(s) when Alternative Site Available

Section 62A of the Criminal Justice and Public Order Act 1994 creates a power for a senior police officer to direct people to leave land and remove any vehicle or other property with them on that land.

Section 62A states:

(1) If the senior police officer present at a scene reasonably believes that the conditions in subsection (2) are satisfied in relation to a person and land, he may direct the person—
   (a) to leave the land;
   (b) to remove any vehicle and other property he has with him on the land.
(2) The conditions are—
   (a) that the person and one or more others ('the trespassers') are trespassing on the land;
   (b) that the trespassers have between them at least one vehicle on the land;
   (c) that the trespassers are present on the land with the common purpose of residing there for any period;
   (d) if it appears to the officer that the person has one or more caravans in his possession or under his control on the land, that there is a suitable pitch on a relevant caravan site for that caravan or each of those caravans;
   (e) that the occupier of the land or a person acting on his behalf has asked the police to remove the trespassers from the land.

KEYNOTE

As with the powers under s. 61, the key features of this section can be broken down into component parts. First, the senior officer present at the scene must have a reasonable belief that:

- at least two people *are trespassing* on the land;
- that they have at least one vehicle between them; and
- that they are there with the common purpose of residing there for any period;
- that the occupier (or person acting on their behalf) has asked the police to remove the trespassers from the land.

If it appears that a person has one or more caravans in their possession or under their control on the land, there is a further condition requiring the senior officer to consult with the local authority and ascertain that there is a suitable pitch on a relevant caravan site for that caravan or each of those caravans (see s. 62A(4) and (5)).

If the above conditions are satisfied, the senior officer can direct the people to leave the land and to remove any vehicles and other property they have with them.

This direction may be communicated to the person by any constable at the scene (s. 62A(3)) and there is no requirement that the officer giving the direction be in uniform.

A person may be regarded as having a 'purpose of residing' in a place even if they have a home elsewhere (s. 62E(8)).

'Vehicle' has the same meaning as under s. 61 (see para. 4.10.5).

'Land' does not generally include buildings here (except for ancient monuments and certain specific types of agricultural buildings—see s. 62E).

4.10.6.1 Failure to Follow Direction to Leave

OFFENCE: **Failure to comply with direction under section 62A—*Criminal Justice and Public Order Act 1994, s. 62B***

- Triable summarily • Three months' imprisonment and/or a fine

The Criminal Justice and Public Order Act 1994, s. 62B states:

(1) A person commits an offence if he knows that a direction under section 62A(1) has been given which applies to him and—
  (a) he fails to leave the relevant land as soon as reasonably practicable, or
  (b) he enters any land in the area of the relevant local authority as a trespasser before the end of the relevant period with the intention of residing there.

KEYNOTE

This section has two limbs. The first makes it an offence to fail to comply with a direction properly given under s. 62A as soon as reasonably practicable. The second limb makes it an offence, within the relevant period (three months of the direction being given—s.62B(2)), to return to any land in the area of the relevant local authority as a trespasser with the intention of residing there.

There is a defence under subs. (5) if the defendant was not a trespasser or if he/she had a reasonable excuse for failing to leave or for returning to the relevant land, or if he/she was under 18 and living with a parent or guardian when the direction was given (s. 62B(5)).

4.10.7 People Attending a Rave

OFFENCE: **Failing to leave land when directed: 'raves'—*Criminal Justice and Public Order Act 1994, s. 63***

- Triable summarily • Three months' imprisonment and/or a fine

The Criminal Justice and Public Order Act 1994, s. 63 states:

(2) If, as respects any land, a police officer of at least the rank of superintendent reasonably believes that—
  (a) two or more persons are making preparations for the holding there of a gathering to which this section applies,
  (b) ten or more persons are waiting for such a gathering to begin there, or
  (c) ten or more persons are attending such a gathering which is in progress,
  he may give a direction that those persons and any other persons who come to prepare or wait for or to attend the gathering are to leave the land and remove any vehicles or other property which they have with them on the land.

(3) A direction under subsection (2) above, if not communicated to the persons referred to in subsection (2) by the police officer giving the direction, may be communicated to them by any constable at the scene.

(4) Persons shall be treated as having had a direction under subsection (2) above communicated to them if reasonable steps have been taken to bring it to their attention.

(5) ...

KEYNOTE

Whereas the powers to direct people to leave land above can be exercised by the senior police officer present at the scene, the power under s. 63 is restricted to an officer of at least superintendent rank.

Again, the officer must have a reasonable belief that one of the circumstances set out in s. 63(2) applies in respect of any land in the open air. Those circumstances are that:

- at least two people are making preparations for the holding of a relevant gathering; *or*
- at least ten people are waiting for such a gathering to begin or are attending such a gathering which is in progress.

Where this is the case, the officer may direct those people, together with any others who come to prepare, wait for or attend the gathering, to leave the land and to take their property with them.

Given the practical constraints on communicating with people at an open air 'rave', s. 63 makes provision for the communication of a direction to leave. If reasonable steps have been taken to bring the direction to the attention of the people concerned, s. 63(4) provides that the relevant person will be taken to have received it. Therefore a person cannot later argue that he/she had not been able to hear or understand the direction when it was given.

In common with the other sections above, the direction to leave the land may be communicated to the relevant people by any police officer at the scene and there is no requirement for the officer to be in uniform.

4.10.7.1 Type of Gathering

The elements of the type of gathering to which s. 63 applies are as follows:

> (1) This section applies to a gathering on land in the open air of 20 or more persons (whether or not trespassers) at which amplified music is played during the night (with or without intermissions) and is such as, by reason of its loudness and duration and the time at which it is played, is likely to cause serious distress to the inhabitants of the locality; and for this purpose—
> (a) such a gathering continues during intermissions in the music and, where the gathering extends over several days, throughout the period during which amplified music is played at night (with or without intermissions); and
> (b) 'music' includes sounds wholly or predominantly characterised by the emission of a succession of repetitive beats.
>
> (1A) This section also applies to a gathering if—
> (a) it is a gathering on land of 20 or more persons who are trespassing on the land; and
> (b) it would be a gathering of a kind mentioned in subsection (1) above if it took place on land in the open air.

There are two specific offences arising out of a direction under s. 63—failing to leave/returning to the land within seven days of the direction and making preparations to return or attending a gathering within 24 hours of the direction being given. These are set out below.

4.10.7.2 Failure to Follow Directions

OFFENCE: **Failure to comply with directions under section 63—*Criminal Justice and Public Order Act 1994, s. 63***

- Triable summarily • Three months' imprisonment and/or a fine

The Criminal Justice and Public Order Act 1994, s. 63 states:

> (6) If a person knowing that a direction has been given which applies to him—
> (a) fails to leave the land as soon as reasonably practicable, or
> (b) having left again enters the land within the period of 7 days beginning with the day on which the direction was given,
>
> he commits an offence ...

...

(7A) A person commits an offence if—

(a) he knows that a direction under subsection (2) above has been given which applies to him, and

(b) he makes preparations for or attends a gathering to which this section applies within the period of 24 hours starting when the direction was given.

KEYNOTE

In each of the above cases you will need to show that the defendant knew that the direction applied to him or her. For the practicalities of communicating any direction **see the Keynote in para. 4.10.7.**

The offence under subs. (6) deals with failing to leave/returning to the *land*, while that under subs. (7A) deals with preparing to attend or attending a *gathering*, in each case where a direction has been properly given.

4.10.7.3 Defence

The Criminal Justice and Public Order Act 1994, s. 63 states:

(7) In proceedings for an offence under subsection (6) above it is a defence for the accused to show that he had a reasonable excuse for failing to leave the land as soon as reasonably practicable or, as the case may be, for again entering the land.

4.10.7.4 Power of Entry

Section 64 provides that if a superintendent or above reasonably believes that circumstances justifying the giving of a direction under s. 63 above exist, he/she may authorise any police officer to enter the relevant land for the purposes of:

- ascertaining whether such circumstances exist and
- to exercise any power conferred by s. 63 or
- to exercise the power of seizure below (s. 64).

The power of seizure arises if a direction has been given under s. 63 and a police officer reasonably suspects that any person to whom it applies has, without reasonable excuse:

- failed to remove any vehicle or sound equipment on the land which appears to the officer to belong to him/her or to be in his/her possession or under his/her control, or
- entered the land as a trespasser with a vehicle within the period of seven days beginning with the day when the direction was given

the officer may seize and remove the vehicle or equipment (provided it does not belong to an exempt person) (s. 64(4) and (5)).

4.10.7.5 Exemptions

The directions will not apply to 'exempt persons' (s. 63(5) of the 1994 Act). Such people include the occupier of the land, any member of his/her family or his/her employees/agents, or anyone whose home is situated on the land (s. 63(10)).

The directions will not apply to a gathering in relation to a licensable activity within s. 1(1)(c) of the Licensing Act 2003 carried on under and in accordance with an authorisation within the meaning of s. 136 of that Act (as to which **see para. 4.11.2**).

4.10.7.6 Powers to Stop People from Proceeding to 'Raves'

Under s. 65 of the 1994 Act, if a police officer in uniform reasonably believes that a person is on his/her way to a relevant gathering (as defined above) in relation to which a direction under s. 63(2) is in force, the officer may stop that person and direct him/her not to proceed in the direction of the gathering.

OFFENCE: **Failing to comply with direction not to proceed—*Criminal Justice and Public Order Act 1994, s. 65(4)***

- Triable summarily • Fine

The Criminal Justice and Public Order Act 1994, s. 65 states:

(4) If a person knowing that a direction under [s. 65(1)] has been given to him fails to comply with that direction, he commits an offence.

KEYNOTE

This power may only be exercised at a place within five miles of the boundary of the site of the gathering (s. 65(2)).

Unlike the other directions discussed above, this one must be given by a police officer in uniform. The power does not appear to authorise the stopping of vehicles and therefore the general power under the Road Traffic Act 1988 would need to be used.

For the general provisions in relation to the stopping of people and vehicles, see chapter 4.4.

4.10.8 Residing in Vehicles on Land

In addition to the powers set out above, the Criminal Justice and Public Order Act 1994 gives local authorities powers to deal with people living in vehicles on certain land.

OFFENCE: **Failure to leave land when directed: residing in vehicles—*Criminal Justice and Public Order Act 1994, s. 77***

- Triable summarily • Fine

The Criminal Justice and Public Order Act 1994, s. 77 states:

(1) If it appears to a local authority that persons are for the time being residing in a vehicle or vehicles within that authority's area—
   (a) on any land forming part of a highway;
   (b) on any other unoccupied land; or
   (c) on any occupied land without the consent of the occupier,

   the authority may give a direction that those persons and any others with them are to leave the land and remove the vehicle or vehicles and any other property they have with them on the land.

(2) Notice of a direction under subsection (1) must be served on the persons to whom the direction applies, but it shall be sufficient for this purpose for the direction to specify the land and (except where the direction applies to only one person) to be addressed to all occupants of the vehicles on the land, without naming them.

(3) If a person knowing that a direction under subsection (1) above has been given which applies to him—
   (a) fails, as soon as practicable, to leave the land or remove from the land any vehicle or other property which is the subject of the direction, or

(b) having removed any such vehicle or property again enters the land with a vehicle within the period of three months beginning with the day on which the direction was given,

he commits an offence . . .

KEYNOTE

This offence is committed after notice has been served by a local authority. Sections 77 to 79 make provision for the manner in which the notices are to be served. A direction in the notice is operative in relation to people who return to the land with their vehicles within three months of the serving of the notice (s. 77(4)).

A person can be regarded as 'residing' on land notwithstanding that he/she has a home elsewhere (s. 77(6)).

4.10.8.1 Defence

The Criminal Justice and Public Order Act 1994, s. 77 states:

(5) In proceedings for an offence under this section it is a defence for the accused to show that his failure to leave or to remove the vehicle or other property as soon as practicable or his re-entry with a vehicle was due to illness, mechanical breakdown or other immediate emergency.

4.10.8.2 Removal Order

A local authority may apply to a magistrates' court for a removal order if people continue to reside in their vehicles on land in contravention of a notice under s. 77 of the 1994 Act (s. 78(1)).

The local authority can enforce the order by entering onto the land in question and taking such steps as are mentioned in the order. Before doing so, however, the local authority must give the owner of the land and the occupiers 24 hours' notice of its intention (unless the names and addresses cannot be ascertained after reasonable enquiries) (s. 78(3)).

4.10.8.3 Interim Possession Orders

Wilful obstruction of anyone executing such an order is a summary offence, punishable by a fine (s. 78(4)).

Under certain circumstances, a court may make an interim possession order when land is occupied by trespassers. Any person who is in occupation of those premises at the time such an order is served is, by the Criminal Justice and Public Order Act 1994, s. 76(6), to be treated for the purposes of the following offences as 'trespassers'.

OFFENCE: **Trespassing during interim possession order—*Criminal Justice and Public Order Act 1994, s. 76***

- Triable summarily • Six months' imprisonment and/or a fine

The Criminal Justice and Public Order Act 1994, s. 76 states:

(1) This section applies where an interim possession order has been made in respect of any premises and served in accordance with rules of court; and references to 'the order' and 'the premises' shall be construed accordingly.

(2) Subject to subsection (3), a person who is present on the premises as a trespasser at any time during the currency of the order commits an offence.

(3) No offence under subsection (2) is committed by a person if

(a) he leaves the premises within 24 hours of the time of service of the order and does not return; or

(b) a copy of the order was not fixed to the premises in accordance with rules of court.

(4) A person who was in occupation of the premises at the time of service of the order but leaves them commits an offence if he re-enters the premises as a trespasser or attempts to do so after the expiry of the order but within the period of one year beginning with the day on which it was served.

KEYNOTE

For the power of entry without warrant for this offence, **see para. 4.4.13.**

This offence is complete when the person is present as a trespasser during the currency of the order. There is no need to prove any further *actus reus* and there is no requirement for any *mens rea* (**see Crime, chapter 1.1**). Therefore, in practice, the person has got 24 hours from the time of service of the order to get out and stay out to avoid committing this offence. If the copy of the notice was not fixed to the premises as required, there will be no offence.

Section 75 creates several either way offences in relation to the making of false or misleading statements in order to obtain or resist the making of an interim possession order.

OFFENCE: **Making false statement to obtain interim possession order—*Criminal Justice and Public Order Act 1994, s. 75***

- Triable either way • Two years' imprisonment and/or a fine on indictment
- Six months' imprisonment and/or a fine summarily

The Criminal Justice and Public Order Act 1994, s. 75 states:

(1) A person commits an offence if, for the purpose of obtaining an interim possession order, he—
  (a) makes a statement which he knows to be false or misleading in a material particular; or
  (b) recklessly makes a statement which is false or misleading in a material particular.
(2) A person commits an offence if, for the purpose of resisting the making of an interim possession order, he—
  (a) makes a statement which he knows to be false or misleading in a material particular; or
  (b) recklessly makes a statement which is false or misleading in a material particular.

4.10.9 Other Offences involving Premises

There are several specific offences and provisions relating to various types of premises that impact on day-to-day policing.

4.10.9.1 Depriving Residential Occupier

OFFENCE: **Depriving residential occupier—*Protection from Eviction Act 1977, s. 1***

- Triable either way • Two years' imprisonment and/or a fine on indictment
- Six months' imprisonment and/or a fine summarily

The Protection from Eviction Act 1977, s. 1 (amended by the Housing Act 1988, s. 9) states:

(2) If any person unlawfully deprives the residential occupier of any premises of his occupation of the premises or any part thereof, or attempts to do so, he shall be guilty of an offence unless he proves that he believed, and had reasonable cause to believe, that the residential occupier had ceased to reside in the premises.
(3) If any person with intent to cause the residential occupier of any premises—
  (a) to give up the occupation of the premises or any part thereof; or
  (b) to refrain from exercising any right or pursuing any remedy in respect of the premises or part thereof;

does acts likely to interfere with the peace or comfort of the residential occupier or members of his household, or persistently withdraws or withholds services reasonably required for the occupation of the premises as a residence, he shall be guilty of an offence.

(3A) Subject to subsection (3B) below, the landlord of a residential occupier or an agent of the landlord shall be guilty of an offence if—

(a) he does acts likely to interfere with the peace or comfort of the residential occupier or members of his household, or

(b) he persistently withdraws or withholds services reasonably required for the occupation of the premises in question as a residence,

and (in either case) he knows, or has reasonable cause to believe, that that conduct is likely to cause the residential occupier to give up the occupation of the whole or part of the premises or to refrain from exercising any right or pursuing any remedy in respect of the whole or part of the premises.

KEYNOTE

The first two offences can be committed by 'any person', whereas the offence under s. 1(3A) can only be committed by a landlord or his/her agent.

Where these offences are committed by a 'body corporate' (e.g. a company), then the company's officers may be guilty as well as the company itself (s. 1(6)).

Thankfully—from a police perspective—the Court of Appeal has refused to find that a duty of care is owed by the police to an assured tenant to prevent that tenant's eviction without the necessary court order in breach of the Protection from Eviction Act 1977 (*Cowan* v *Chief Constable of Avon & Somerset* [2002] HLR 44).

The actions envisaged by s. 1(2) are those which amount to an eviction for any length of time (*R* v *Yuthiwattana* (1984) 80 Cr App R 55), while anything less (e.g. changing the locks of an entrance door while the residential occupier is out) would amount to an offence under s. 1(3) (*Costelloe* v *Camden London Borough Council* [1986] Crim LR 249).

A caravan may amount to 'premises' for these offences (*Norton* v *Knowles* [1969] 1 QB 572).

Under s. 1 of the 1977 Act 'residential occupier' means:

(1) ... in relation to any premises, ... a person occupying the premises as a residence, whether under a contract or by virtue of any enactment or rule of law giving him the right to remain in occupation or restricting the right of any other person to recover possession of the premises.

4.10.9.2 Defence to Depriving Residential Occupier

In addition to the defence provided by s. 1(2) above, there is a specific defence to an offence under s. 1(3A):

(3B) A person shall not be guilty of an offence under subsection (3A) above if he proves that he had reasonable grounds for doing the acts or withdrawing or withholding the services in question.

4.10.9.3 Using or Threatening Violence to Secure Entry

OFFENCE: **Using or threatening violence to secure entry to premises—*Criminal Law Act 1977, s. 6(1)***

- Triable summarily • Six months' imprisonment and/or a fine

The Criminal Law Act 1977, s. 6 states:

(1) Subject to the following provisions of this section, any person who, without lawful authority, uses or threatens violence for the purpose of securing entry into any premises for himself or for any other person is guilty of an offence, provided that—

(a) there is someone present on those premises at the time who is opposed to the entry which the violence is intended to secure; and
(b) the person using or threatening the violence knows that that is the case.

KEYNOTE

This offence is not restricted to occasions involving 'residential occupiers'.

It is immaterial whether the violence used/threatened is against a person or property, or whether the purpose of the entry is to gain possession of the premises or any other purpose (s. 6(4)).

The fact that a person has any right or interest in premises will not constitute 'lawful authority' to use violence to secure entry into those premises (s. 6(2)).

For the power of entry for this offence, **see para. 4.4.13**.

For police powers in relation to intimidation and harassment of individuals within their homes, **see chapter 4.6**.

4.10.9.4 Defence to Using or Threatening Violence to Secure Entry

The Criminal Law Act 1977, s. 6 states:

(1A) Subsection (1) above does not apply to a person who is a displaced residential occupier or a protected intending occupier of the premises in question or who is acting on behalf of such an occupier; and if the accused adduces sufficient evidence that he was, or was acting on behalf of, such an occupier he shall be presumed to be, or to be acting on behalf of, such an occupier unless the contrary is proved by the prosecution.

(2) Subject to subsection (1A) above, the fact that a person has any interest in or right to possession or occupation of any premises shall not for the purposes of subsection (1) above constitute lawful authority for the use or threat of violence by him or anyone else for the purpose of securing his entry into those premises.

A 'displaced residential occupier' is defined at s. 12, which states:

(3) Subject to subsection (4) below, any person who was occupying any premises as a residence immediately before being excluded from occupation by anyone who entered those premises, or any access to those premises, as a trespasser is a displaced residential occupier of the premises for the purposes of this Part of this Act so long as he continues to be excluded from occupation of the premises by the original trespasser or by any subsequent trespasser.

(4) A person who was himself occupying the premises in question as a trespasser immediately before being excluded from occupation shall not by virtue of subsection (3) above be a displaced residential occupier of the premises for the purposes of this Part of this Act.

KEYNOTE

The definition of a 'protected intending occupier' (s. 12A) must be one of the longest definitions in criminal law (if not criminal history) and takes up an entire page of the Act! The gist of it is that it will include someone with a freehold or leasehold interest in the premises which has at least two years left to run; where the person needs the premises for his/her own occupation as a residence; where he/she is excluded from those premises by a trespasser and where he/she has documentation to prove his/her right to occupy the premises. (For a full discussion, **see Blackstone's Criminal Practice 2008, para. B13.27.**)

4.10.9.5 Failing to Leave

OFFENCE: **Failing to leave premises—*Criminal Law Act 1977, s. 7***

- Triable summarily • Six months' imprisonment and/or a fine

The Criminal Law Act 1977, s. 7 states:

> (1) Subject to the following provisions of this section and to section 12A(9) below, any person who is on any premises as a trespasser after having entered as such is guilty of an offence if he fails to leave those premises on being required to do so by or on behalf of—
> (a) a displaced residential occupier of the premises; or
> (b) an individual who is a protected intending occupier of the premises.

KEYNOTE

Sections 7 and 12A of the 1977 Act provide defences in relation to s. 7(1). It is a defence for the accused to prove that he/she believed that the person requiring him/her to leave the premises was not a person as described in s. 7(1)(a) or (b), or that the premises were used mainly for non-residential purposes and he/she was not on any part of the premises used wholly or mainly for residential purposes (s. 7(2) and (3)).

Section 12A provides that it is a defence for the accused to prove that the person making the requirement for the accused to leave did not produce a written statement specifying his/her interest in the premises (s. 12A(2)(d) or (4)(d)), or a certificate or licence from a protected intending occupier in relation to his/her right to tenancy or occupancy of the premises (s. 12A(6)(d)).

4.10.9.6 Found on Enclosed Premises

It is a summary offence under s. 4 of the Vagrancy Act 1824 for any person to be found in or upon any dwelling house, warehouse, coach house, stable or outhouse or in any inclosed yard, garden or area for *any unlawful purpose*. The unlawful purpose must be to commit some specific criminal offence as opposed to simply trespassing and a purely immoral purpose, and without more will not suffice (*Hayes* v *Stevenson* (1860) 3 LT 296).

Where the defendant is found on the relevant premises, he/she can be arrested elsewhere (*R* v *Lumsden* [1951] 2 KB 513). Where a defendant was found in the garden of a house peering through the window at a woman inside intending to frighten her, his conduct was held to amount to an 'unlawful purpose' (*Smith* v *Chief Superintendent of Woking Police Station* (1983) 76 Cr App R 234). Had there not been any intention to frighten, the 'unlawful' purpose would probably not have been made out.

An area may still be 'inclosed' even though there are spaces left in between buildings, arches etc. for access (*Goodhew* v *Morton* [1962] 1 WLR 210). Railway sidings have been held not to amount to 'inclosed' premises and the essential feature of yards and similar enclosed areas for the purposes of this offence would appear to be that they are small pieces of land ancillary to a building (see *Quatromini* v *Peck* [1972] 1 WLR 1318). However, a room within an office building has been held not to amount to an inclosed area for the purposes of this offence (*Talbot* v *Oxford City Justices* [2000] 1 WLR 1102). It appears from the findings of the Divisional Court in *Talbot* that the expression 'inclosed' relates only to yards, gardens and areas in the open air. If the defendant is found in a *building* then that building must be a 'dwelling house, warehouse, coach house, stable or outhouse' before the offence under s. 4 can be applied.

There is no need to show that the person intended to carry out the relevant criminal offence at the time or at that particular place. If the person is found in a building and either intends to commit certain offences there or had that intention when entering, the relevant offences of burglary may well apply (**see Crime, chapter 1.11**).

4.10.9.7 Housing and Accommodation

In some cases the policing problems presented within a particular area will arise directly or indirectly from the area's housing. Among the legislation available to the relevant agencies in this regard is the Housing Act 1996, which is itself reinforced by the Housing Act 2004, providing local authorities with a range of significant powers where use of premises or the state of the property itself presents a nuisance or hazard to the physical or mental health of others.

Injunctions

Under s. 153A of the 1996 Act, as amended by the Police and Justice Act 2006, a court may, on the application of a relevant landlord, grant an anti-social behaviour injunction if:

> the person against whom the injunction is sought is engaging, has engaged or threatens to engage in housing-related conduct capable of causing a nuisance or annoyance to:
> (a) a person with a right (of whatever description) to reside in or occupy housing accommodation owned or managed by a relevant landlord,
> (b) a person with a right (of whatever description) to reside in or occupy other housing accommodation in the neighbourhood of housing accommodation mentioned in paragraph (a),
> (c) a person engaged in lawful activity in, or in the neighbourhood of, housing accommodation mentioned in paragraph (a), or
> (d) a person employed (whether or not by a relevant landlord) in connection with the exercise of a relevant landlord's housing management functions.

It is immaterial where conduct to which this section applies occurs, and an anti-social behaviour injunction prohibits the person from engaging in any such conduct as described above.

KEYNOTE

This section allows social landlords (which may include local authorities) to obtain injunctions against a wide range of persons, not just residents, in order to protect other residents, visitors and their own staff. It also applies to situations where the conduct in question is capable of causing nuisance or annoyance (even if a complaint has not been received), but which directly or indirectly affects the landlord's management of its housing stock.

Other injunctions are also available to social landlords. This includes where a person engages in conduct, which consists of, or involves using, or threatening to use, housing accommodation for an unlawful purpose (s. 153B). Where the court considers that the conduct relates to the use or threatened use of violence, or that there is a significant risk of harm to a person mentioned in s. 153A(3)(a)–(d) (above), it may include a provision prohibiting the person from entering or being in any premises or area specified in the injunction, and may also attach a power of arrest.

4.10.9.8 Nuisance on Educational Premises

There has been increasing concern over recent years that schools and their premises are particularly vulnerable to crime and the fear of crime. There are two main areas of behaviour in relation to school premises which the law seeks to regulate; the carrying of certain weapons and the creation of nuisance or disturbance.

For the law relating to the carrying of weapons on school premises, **see para. 4.8.4.**

In relation to nuisances on educational premises, the Education Act 1996 applies to premises that provide primary or secondary education (or both) and which are maintained by a local education authority or are grant-maintained.

OFFENCE: **Causing or permitting nuisance—*Education Act 1996, s. 547(1)***

- Triable summarily • Fine

The Education Act 1996, s. 547 states:

(1) Any person who without lawful authority is present on premises to which this section applies and causes or permits nuisance or disturbance to the annoyance of persons who lawfully use those premises (whether or not any such persons are present at the time) [shall be guilty of an offence].

KEYNOTE

This offence is designed to deal with many types of nuisance, from using school playing fields inappropriately to interrupting lessons and lectures.

To be guilty of the above offence the defendant must be on the relevant premises without lawful authority and have caused (been directly responsible for bringing about) or permitted a nuisance or disturbance.

This provision applies to playing fields and other premises for outdoor recreation of the relevant institution including playgrounds (s. 547(2)).

Police powers

Subsection (3) of the Act states:

(3) If—
(a) a police constable or
(b) ..., a person whom [the appropriate authority has] authorised to exercise the power conferred by this subsection,
has reasonable cause to suspect that any person is committing or has committed an offence under this section, he may remove him from the premises in question.

KEYNOTE

The nuisance or disturbance may have finished by the time the police officer gets to the premises but the wording of the subsection allows for the removal of the offender provided there is reasonable cause to suspect that he/she committed the offence.

4.10.10 Trespassing on Designated Sites

The Serious Organised Crime and Police Act 2005 provides that various public access rights, as provided by the Countryside and Rights of Way Act 2000 in England and Wales, are not exercisable in relation to land forming part of a protected site.

OFFENCE: **Trespassing on designated sites—*Serious Organised Crime and Police Act 2005, s. 128(1)***

- Triable summarily • Imprisonment for a term not exceeding 51 weeks and/or a fine

The Serious Organised Crime and Police Act 2005, s. 128 states:

(1) A person commits an offence if he enters, or is on, any protected site in England and Wales . . . as a trespasser.

(1A) In this section 'protected site' means—

(a) a nuclear site; or

(b) a designated site.

KEYNOTE

A *nuclear* site means so much of any premises in respect of which a nuclear site licence (within the meaning of the Nuclear Installations Act 1965) is for the time being in force as lies within the outer perimeter of the protection provided for those premises (s. 128(1B)). Nuclear sites were included within this section as a result of the Terrorism Act 2006 provisions.

A *designated site* is one which the Secretary of State has so designated for the purposes of this section if—

- it is comprised in Crown land; or
- it is comprised in land belonging to Her Majesty in her private capacity or to the immediate heir to the Throne in his/her private capacity; or
- it appears to the Secretary of State that it is appropriate to designate the site in the interests of national security (s. 128(3)).

A 'designated site' means a site specified or described in an order made by the Secretary of State (s. 128(2)), and a schedule of the these sites is contained in the Serious Organised Crime and Police Act 2005 (Designated Sites) Order 2005 (SI 2005/3447). Such a 'site' means the whole or part of any building or buildings, or any land, or both (s. 128(8)(a)).

It is a defence for a person charged with an offence under this section to prove that he/she did not know, and had no reasonable cause to suspect, that the site in relation to which the offence is alleged to have been committed was a protected site (s. 128(4)).

For the purposes of this section a person who is on any protected site as a trespasser does not cease to be a trespasser by virtue of being allowed time to leave the site (s. 128(7)).

4.11 Licensing, Offences Relating to Alcohol, and Gambling

4.11.1 Introduction

The sale, supply and consumption of alcohol, along with the proper control and management of relevant premises, has a significant part of everyday policing. The provisions of the Licensing Act 2003 include the law in relation to the sale and supply of alcohol and a clear and enforceable regulation over the provision of certain types of public entertainment. Some of the aims of the 2003 Act included providing the police with powers to deal with alcohol-related disorder and for licensed premises to be dealt with quickly and effectively.

The second part of this chapter provides an overview of the provisions of the Gambling Act 2005.

All police forces have departments that deal with the licensing of premises for both the sale or supply of alcohol and gambling. Consequently, this chapter only provides a brief overview of those matters dealt with by these departments and concentrates on the specific offences and powers contained within the relevant legislation.

4.11.2 Licensable Activities

The Licensing Act 2003, s. 1 states:

(1) For the purposes of this Act the following are licensable activities—
 (a) the sale by retail of alcohol,
 (b) the supply of alcohol by or on behalf of a club to, or to the order of, a member of the club,
 (c) the provision of regulated entertainment, and
 (d) the provision of late night refreshment.

KEYNOTE

The concept of licensable activities is critical to much of the framework set up by the 2003 Act.

Note that by simply calling itself a 'club', an organisation will not necessarily fall into the relevant provisions—in order to be a 'qualifying club' the organisation will need to be in the control or ownership of its members. If it is not, any supply of alcohol will be by retail.

For an explanation of 'regulated entertainment' see para. 4.11.8.1.

A person provides (unless exempt) late night refreshment if at any time between the hours of 11.00 pm and 5.00 am, he/she supplies hot food or hot drink to members of the public, or a section of the public, on or from any premises, whether for consumption on or off the premises, or at any time between those hours when members of the public, or a section of the public, are admitted to any premises, he/she supplies, or holds him/herself out as willing to supply, hot food or hot drink to any persons, or to persons of a particular description, on or from those premises, whether for consumption on or off the premises. Those exempt include people staying at hotels, guest houses, campsites, etc. (sch. 2).

There are specific restrictions on the sale or supply of alcohol from vehicles and from garages and other 'excluded' related premises.

4.11.2.1 General Exemptions to Licensable Activities

There is a whole series of exemptions to the above definition of 'licensable activities'. These include activities: aboard an aircraft, hovercraft or railway vehicle engaged on a journey; aboard a vessel on an international journey, at an approved wharf at a designated port or hoverport; at premises permanently or temporarily occupied for the purposes of the armed forces; at premises exempt for national security purposes; at such other place as may be prescribed (ss. 173 to 175).

4.11.2.2 Authorisation of Licensable Activities

The Licensing Act 2003, s. 2 states:

(1) A licensable activity may be carried on—
  (a) under and in accordance with a premises licence (see Part 3), or
  (b) in circumstances where the activity is a permitted temporary activity by virtue of Part 5.

KEYNOTE

Carrying on a licensable activity other than in accordance with a premises licence, club premises certificate or temporary event notice will be an offence under s. 136 (see para. 4.11.8.2).

More than one authority can cover the same premises (s. 2(3)). This would allow, for example, a qualifying club to have a premises licence in addition to its club premises certificate, enabling the club to supply members of the public with alcohol on certain open days.

The different authorities can be held by different people.

Throughout the Act 'premises' means any place and includes a vehicle, vessel or movable structure (s. 193).

4.11.2.3 Powers of Entry

The Act creates a number of powers for police officers and other authorised people to enter and inspect premises, to investigate licensable activities, to investigate offences and to require production of documents.

One such power is the power of entry to investigate licensable activities.

Entry to investigate licensable activities

Where a constable or an authorised person has reason to believe that any premises are being, or are about to be, used for a licensable activity, they may enter the premises with a view to seeing whether the activity is being, or is to be, carried on under and in accordance with an authorisation (s. 179(1)).

A person exercising the power conferred by this section may, if necessary, use reasonable force (s. 179(3)).

A consistent requirement within the Act's provisions is that an authorised person exercising the powers conferred on them must, if so requested, produce evidence of their authority to exercise the power.

There is a separate power of entry where there is a club premises certificate (**see para. 4.11.5.1**) and the above power does *not* apply to such premises if there is no other authorisation in force (s. 179(7)).

Power of entry to investigate offences

Another power of entry exists, not simply to ensure compliance with the Act's framework regarding licensable activities, but specifically to investigate offences in relation to the premises.

Under s. 180, a constable may enter and search any premises in respect of which he/she has reason to believe that an offence under this Act has been, is being or is about to be committed.

A constable exercising a power conferred by this section may, if necessary, use reasonable force.

4.11.3 Licensing Authorities

The bodies which comprise the licensing authorities for the purposes of the Licensing Act 2003 include councils of a district, county or county borough within England and Wales (s. 3(1)).

The purpose of the system of licensing for licensable activities is to promote four fundamental objectives ('the licensing objectives'). These objectives, contained in s. 4(2), are:

(a) the prevention of crime and disorder;
(b) public safety;
(c) the prevention of public nuisance; and
(d) the protection of children from harm.

KEYNOTE

The four licensing objectives aim to ensure that the carrying on of licensable activities on or from premises is done in the public interest. The third licensing objective, the prevention of public nuisance, will not extend to every activity which annoys another person but will cover behaviour which, when balanced against the public interest, is found to be unacceptable. The fourth licensing objective relates to harm to children beyond matters relating to physical safety.

Licensing authorities can bring proceedings for offences under the Licensing Act except for an offence under s. 147A (persistently selling alcohol to children) (s. 186(2)).

4.11.4 The Licensing System

The 2003 Act sets out a single licensing system that governs all premises used for licensable activities. Discussed below are the key licensing authorisations contained within the Act. These are:

- Premises licences
- Personal licences

- Club premises certificates
- Temporary event notices.

For the purposes of this part of the Act, s. 14 provides that the 'supply of alcohol' means:

(a) the sale by retail of alcohol, or
(b) the supply of alcohol by or on behalf of a club to, or to the order of, a member of the club.

4.11.4.1 Premises Licence

The premises licence is a central feature of the Act's framework and recurs in a number of its provisions. A 'premises licence' means a licence in respect of any premises, which authorises them to be used for one or more licensable activities (s. 11).

Section 16 of the Act provides that the following persons may apply for a premises licence:

(a) a person who carries on, or proposes to carry on, a business which involves the use of the premises for the licensable activities to which the application relates,
(b) a person who makes the application pursuant to—
  (i) any statutory function discharged by that person which relates to those licensable activities, or
  (ii) any function discharged by that person by virtue of Her Majesty's prerogative,
(c) a recognised club,
(d) a charity,
(e) the proprietor of an educational institution,
(f) a health service body,
(g) a person who is registered under Part 2 of the Care Standards Act 2000 in respect of an independent hospital,
(h) the chief officer of police of a police force in England and Wales,
(i) a person of such other description as may be prescribed.

KEYNOTE

In relation to s. 16(b)(ii) above, an example would be a body exercising functions by virtue of a royal charter.

An individual may not apply for a premises licence unless he/she is aged 18 or over (s. 16(2)).

Any application for a premises licence must be accompanied by an operating schedule. The operating schedule must set out various details relating to the operation of the premises when carrying on licensable activities. These details include the licensable activities to be carried out, the proposed hours of opening etc., the duration of the licence (if it is to have a fixed term), details about the individual (if any) who is to act as the designated premises supervisor, details of whether alcohol is to be supplied (if at all) for on-sales, off-sales or both, and a statement of how the applicant intends to promote the licensing objectives. For example, the arrangements to be put in place to prevent crime and disorder, such as door security (s. 17(4)).

A constable or an authorised person may require production of a premises licence or a certified copy of it (s. 57(5)), and a person who fails, without reasonable excuse, to produce the licence, or certified copy, commits a summary offence (s. 57(7)).

4.11.4.2 Conditions

Premises licences will generally be subject to certain conditions. They will vary according to the application but, where a premises licence authorises the supply of alcohol, there will be some mandatory conditions. For instance, the premises licence will name a designated premises supervisor who holds a valid personal licence (as to which **see para. 4.11.4.4**).

Every supply of alcohol under a premises licence must be made by a personal licence holder or a person authorised by such a holder (see s. 19).

One important condition of a premises licence may be a requirement for door supervision. Where this condition applies, the person carrying out the function must be authorised to carry out that activity by a licence granted under the Private Security Industry Act 2001, or be entitled to carry out that activity by virtue of s. 4 of that Act (s. 21(1) of the Licensing Act 2003).

4.11.4.3 Review of Premises Licence

Section 51 of the Act makes provision for an interested party or responsible authority to apply to a relevant licensing authority for a review of the premises licence. For example, a local resident may consider that the measures taken by the licensee to prevent public nuisance are insufficient and request that they be reviewed. Similarly, the police may consider that the measures put in place to prevent crime and disorder are not being effective and need to be reviewed.

Section 53A, inserted by the Violent Crime Reduction Act 2006, provides for an accelerated review of licensed premises by a licensing authority, and the attaching of temporary conditions to a premises licence pending a full review of the licence. The procedure provides for a senior police officer (of or above the rank of superintendent) to certify to a licensing authority that he/she considers licensed premises to be associated with serious crime and/or serious disorder. On receiving the application the licensing authority will be obliged to consider within 48 hours whether it is necessary to take interim steps pending a full review of the licence which must take place within 28 days.

KEYNOTE

The interim steps that a licensing authority may take include modifications of the conditions of a licence (e.g. requiring at risk pubs/clubs to search for offensive weapons or use toughened glass); the exclusion of the sale of alcohol; the removal of the designated premises supervisor from the licence; or the suspension of the licence (s. 53B).

The Licensing Act 2003 (Summary Review of Premises Licences) Regulations 2007 (SI 2007/2502) detail the procedure involved with such a review of licensed premises.

4.11.4.4 Personal Licences

The supply of alcohol is regulated generally by the granting of a personal licence to an individual. The Licensing Act 2003, s. 111 states:

> (1) In this Act 'personal licence' means a licence which—
> (a) is granted by a licensing authority to an individual, and
> (b) authorises that individual to supply alcohol, or authorise the supply of alcohol, in accordance with a premises licence.
>
> (2) In subsection (1)(b) the reference to an individual supplying alcohol is to him—
> (a) selling alcohol by retail, or
> (b) supplying alcohol by or on behalf of a club to, or to the order of, a member of the club.

KEYNOTE

The licensing of individuals is separate from the licensing of premises and enables personal licence holders to move from one set of premises to another.

A mainstay of the personal licensing system is the ability to refuse to grant, or to suspend/revoke the licence as a result of applicant's or licensee's previous character or other conduct.

A personal licence, which is valid for ten years, must be held by the designated premises supervisor and more than one individual at the licensed premises may hold a personal licence. It is not necessary for all staff to be licensed, but all supplies of alcohol under a premises licence must be made by or under the authority of a personal licence holder.

A constable or an authorised person may require production of a personal licence (s. 135(2)), and a person who fails without reasonable excuse to produce the licence commits a summary offence (s. 135(4)).

4.11.5 Clubs

The 2003 Act provides for arrangements for qualifying clubs to carry on certain licensable activities (known as 'qualifying club activities') at their premises. Clubs falling within this category will include the Royal British Legion, Working Men's Clubs, cricket and rugby clubs. These clubs are treated differently from other venues because they carry on activities from private premises (to which access is accordingly restricted) and because alcohol and regulated entertainment are provided otherwise than for profit. Generally 'nightclubs' will not fall within this category.

There are five main conditions provided by s. 62 that apply for a club to qualify as a qualifying club:

- persons are not admitted to any of the privileges of membership without an interval of at least two days between nomination or application and their admission;
- persons becoming members without prior nomination or application may not be admitted to the privileges of membership without an interval of at least two days between their becoming members and their admission;
- the club is established and conducted in good faith as a club;
- the club has at least 25 members; and
- alcohol is not supplied, or intended to be supplied, to members on the premises otherwise than by or on behalf of the club.

4.11.5.1 Club Premises Certificate

The Licensing Act 2003 Act established a system of club premises certificates, issued by the relevant licensing authority, which authorise a qualifying club to carry on qualifying club activities. Qualifying clubs have a special status under licensing law; clubs holding certificates will be exempted from the requirement for any member or employee to hold a personal licence to supply or sell alcohol to members or guests. The general offence of supplying alcohol to people under 18 applies in clubs as it does elsewhere.

KEYNOTE

An interested party, responsible authority, or club member, may apply for a review of the club premises certificate. However, the authority may reject the review if it is not relevant to any of the licensing objectives or the application is considered frivolous, vexatious or repetitious (s. 87).

A constable or an authorised person may require production of a club premises certificate (or a certified copy of it) (s. 94(7)), and a person who fails, without reasonable excuse, to produce the certificate (or certified copy) commits a summary offence (s. 94(9)).

A constable may also enter and search the club premises where he/she has reasonable cause to believe that an offence under s. 4(3)(a), (b) or (c) of the Misuse of Drugs Act 1971 (supplying or offering to supply, or being concerned in supplying or making an offer to supply, a controlled drug), has been, is being, or is about to be, committed there (**see Crime, chapter 1.6**). The constable may use reasonable force if necessary.

4.11.5.2 Other Powers of Entry

Where a club premises certificate has effect in respect of any premises, a constable may enter and search the premises if he or she has reasonable cause to believe:

- that an offence under s. 4(3)(a), (b) or (c) of the Misuse of Drugs Act 1971 (supplying or offering to supply, or being concerned in supplying or making an offer to supply, a controlled drug) has been, is being, or is about to be, committed there (as to which **see Crime, chapter 1.6**), or
- that there is likely to be a breach of the peace there (**see chapter 4.6**).

The constable may use reasonable force if necessary (s. 97).

4.11.6 Permitted Temporary Activities

The Licensing Act 2003 makes provision for a system that allows people ('premises users') to carry out licensable activities on a temporary basis, subject to various conditions and limits attaching to the number of events that may be permitted. Different limits apply depending on whether or not the person carrying out the licensable activities holds a personal licence and the frequency of use of the premises. Examples of circumstances under which an individual might make use of the arrangements could include a publican engaged to run a temporary bar for a wedding at a venue not licensed for the sale of alcohol, or an individual not being the holder of a personal licence who may wish to run a bar and provide a band at a party to celebrate a significant anniversary.

4.11.6.1 Temporary Event Notices

Section 100 of the 2003 Act provides that where it is proposed to use premises for one or more licensable activities during a period not exceeding 96 hours, an individual ('the premises user') may give to the relevant licensing authority notice of that proposal (a 'temporary event notice'). The premises user must be at least 18 years old.

KEYNOTE

Section 100(4) and (5) provide that the temporary event notice must be in a form prescribed in regulations by the Secretary of State and set out certain details about the proposed event:

(a) the licensable activities that are to be carried out;
(b) the total length of the event—which must not exceed 96 hours;
(c) the times the licensable activities are to be carried out;

(d) the maximum number of people to be allowed on the premises at any one time—which must be less than 500;
(e) whether any alcohol sales are to be made for consumption on or off the premises (or both);
(f) any other information that may be prescribed by regulations.

The notice must include a condition that all supplies of alcohol will be made by, or under the authority of, the premises user (s. 100(6)), and the temporary event notice must be given to the licensing authority at least ten working days before the event (s. 100(7)).

A constable or an authorised officer may, at any reasonable time, enter the premises to which a temporary event notice relates, to assess the likely effect of the notice on the promotion of the crime prevention objective (s. 108(1)). A person commits an offence if he/she intentionally obstructs an authorised officer exercising a power conferred by this section (s. 108(3)).

Where a temporary event notice has been issued and the premises are being used for a licensable activity, the premises user must ensure a copy of the notice is prominently displayed at the premises, or be in possession of the notice, or the possession of some other person on the premises who has been nominated by the premises user. In the latter case, a notice to that effect must be displayed at the premises. The premises user is guilty of a summary offence if he/she does not comply with these requirements (s. (109(4)). Failure to produce a temporary event notice when required by a constable or authorised person is also a summary offence (s. 109(8)).

4.11.6.2 Police Objections

A copy of the temporary event notice must also be given to the relevant chief officer of police no later than ten working days before the day on which the event period specified in the notice begins. If the police are of the view that allowing the event to proceed would undermine the crime prevention objective, they must notify (an objection notice) the premises user and the relevant licensing authority, stating their reasons, no later than 48 hours after receipt of the copy of the notice (s. 104).

The licensing authority is then required to hold a hearing and, if it upholds the objection from the police, issues a counter-notice to the premises user informing him/her that the event cannot proceed (s. 105). However, provision is also made for the police and premises user to agree to modify the temporary event notice in such a way that it no longer undermines the promotion of the crime prevention objective (s. 106).

4.11.7 Relaxation of Opening Hours for Special Occasions

The Licensing Act 2003, s. 172(1) provides that the Secretary of State may make an order to provide for premises with a premises licence or club premises certificate to open for specified, generally extended, hours on special occasions, for example, on the occasion of a Royal Jubilee.

Any such order may make provision generally in relation to premises in one or more specified areas, make different provision in respect of different days, or make different provision in respect of different licensable activities (s. 172(3)).

4.11.7.1 Dancing and Live Music in Certain Small Premises

Among the many exemptions to the general licensing framework, the Act makes special provision for dancing and live music in certain small premises.

Where a premises licence authorises the supply of alcohol for consumption on the premises, and the provision of music entertainment, there are exemptions if those premises are used primarily for the supply of alcohol for consumption on the premises and have a permitted capacity of not more than 200 people (see s. 177).

The exceptions and exemptions under this section rely heavily on 'double negatives' and various qualifications before they apply. Essentially, they mean that certain licensing authority-imposed conditions of the premises licence which relate to the provision of the music entertainment will not have effect in small premises putting on live music and dancing under some very specific circumstances. In practice the full wording of s. 177 should be referred to, along with any relevant regulations.

4.11.8 Offences

The main offences with which police officers will be involved are contained in the 2003 Act. These follow a fairly common-sense approach imposing requirements and obligations on those people who could have acted to prevent the relevant conduct or who could have made the relevant request, e.g. of a disorderly person to leave.

Like many regulated activities, the Licensing Act framework relies on documentation and certification for its effective operation. Therefore there are several offences arising out of the making of false statements in that context. For instance, knowingly or recklessly making a false statement in connection with an application for the grant or renewal of a premises licence, club premises certificate or personal licence will be a summary offence under s. 158, along with other false statements relating to reviews, transfers and renewals of various documents. For the more serious criminal offence arising out of false statements and documents, **see Crime, chapter 1.12**.

4.11.8.1 Regulated Entertainment

Licensing the provision of regulated entertainment is another key feature of the 2003 Act and detailed guidance on this provision is contained in sch. 1 to the Act.

Regulated entertainment covers entertainment, provided solely or partly for members of the public, or exclusively to club members and their guests, or for which a charge is made, which is provided for profit (which will include raising money for charities).

The forms of entertainment regulated by the Act includes:

- plays, including both performance and rehearsal;
- films, or any exhibition of moving pictures;
- all indoor sporting events;
- outdoor boxing and wrestling matches;
- performance of live music and the playing of recorded music;
- performance of dance.

Schedule 1 provides a number of exemptions to regulated entertainment, for example, entertainment at a garden fete, Morris dancing (or dancing of a similar nature), and entertainment provided on vehicles in motion.

4.11.8.2 Unauthorised Licensable Activities

OFFENCE: **Unauthorised licensable activities—*Licensing Act 2003, s. 136***

- Triable summarily • Six months' imprisonment and/or a fine up to £20,000

The Licensing Act 2003, s. 136 states:

> (1) A person commits an offence if—
> (a) he carries on or attempts to carry on a licensable activity on or from any premises otherwise than under and in accordance with an authorisation, or
> (b) he knowingly allows a licensable activity to be so carried on.

KEYNOTE

This offence requires that the person carried on (or attempted to carry on) the licensable activity (as to which see para. 4.11.2) *either* in a manner not authorised by or in accordance with an appropriate authorisation, or *knowingly* allowing the activity to be carried on in that way. Therefore the element of knowledge on the part of the defendant is essential in any case where he/she is not directly involved.

If the relevant authorisation (e.g. a premises licence) has certain conditions attached and they are not adhered to, this offence would be committed.

'Authorisation' here means a premises licence, a club premises certificate or a temporary event notice in respect of which the relevant conditions have been met. While some offences apply only to 'relevant premises', the above is wider than that and applies to any premises.

Where the licensable activity in question is the provision of regulated entertainment (see para. 4.11.8.1), a person will generally not commit an offence under this section if their only involvement in the provision of the entertainment is that they played the music, performed the dance etc. (see s. 136(2)).

The statutory defence of due diligence applies to this offence (see para. 4.11.8.4).

4.11.8.3 Exposing Alcohol for Unauthorised Sale

OFFENCE: **Exposing alcohol for unauthorised sale—*Licensing Act 2003, s. 137***

- Triable summarily • Six months' imprisonment and/or a fine up to £20,000

The Licensing Act 2003, s. 137 states:

> (1) A person commits an offence if, on any premises, he exposes for sale by retail any alcohol in circumstances where the sale by retail of that alcohol on those premises would be an unauthorised licensable activity.
> (2) For that purpose a licensable activity is unauthorised unless it is under and in accordance with an authorisation.

KEYNOTE

This offence concerns retail sales of alcohol on premises where to do so lawfully would ordinarily require some form of authorisation. There is no requirement for the person to have done so 'knowingly' or with any particular state of mind, neither is there a need for any *sale* actually to have taken place, and the exposing for sale under the relevant circumstances makes the offence complete.

While some offences apply only to 'relevant premises', the above is wider than that and applies to any premises.

There is a further summary offence (punishable by a fine) for a person to have in their possession or under their control alcohol which they intend to sell by retail or supply by or on behalf of a club to a member of the club in circumstances where that activity would be an unauthorised licensable activity (see s. 138). The statutory defence of due diligence applies to both these offences (see para. 4.11.8.4).

The court by which a person is convicted of either of these offences may order the alcohol in question (and any container), to be forfeited and either destroyed or dealt with in such other manner as the court may order (s. 137(4)).

'Sale by retail' is specifically defined in s. 192. In essence it excludes wholesale transactions made with people (including personal licence holders) in the course of their trade and sales for consumption off the premises.

4.11.8.4 Defence of Due Diligence

The Licensing Act 2003 contains a specific defence of 'due diligence', and s.139 states:

(1) In proceedings against a person for an offence to which subsection (2) applies, it is a defence that—
  (a) his act was due to a mistake, or to reliance on information given to him, or to an act or omission by another person, or to some other cause beyond his control, and
  (b) he took all reasonable precautions and exercised all due diligence to avoid committing the offence.

KEYNOTE

The offences to which this defence applies are:

- s. 136(1)(a) (carrying on unauthorised licensable activity);
- s. 137 (exposing alcohol for unauthorised sale); or
- s. 138 (keeping alcohol on premises for unauthorised sale).

The defence of due diligence has two limbs and both (a) and (b) must be shown for it to apply.

4.11.8.5 Allowing Disorderly Conduct on Licensed Premises

OFFENCE: **Allowing disorderly conduct on licensed premises etc.—*Licensing Act 2003, s. 140***

- Triable summarily • Fine

The Licensing Act 2003, s. 140 states:

(1) A person to whom subsection (2) applies commits an offence if he knowingly allows disorderly conduct on relevant premises.
(2) This subsection applies—
  (a) to any person who works at the premises in a capacity, whether paid or unpaid, which authorises him to prevent the conduct,
  (b) in the case of licensed premises, to—
    (i) the holder of a premises licence in respect of the premises, and
    (ii) the designated premises supervisor (if any) under such a licence,
  (c) in the case of premises in respect of which a club premises certificate has effect, to any member or officer of the club which holds the certificate who at the time the conduct takes place is present on the premises in a capacity which enables him to prevent it, and
  (d) in the case of premises which may be used for a permitted temporary activity by virtue of Part 5, to the premises user in relation to the temporary event notice in question.

KEYNOTE

The above offence is very widely drafted and covers all the various people set out at subs. (2)(a) to (d). It will be important to note the distinctions between the roles of these people. In the case of licensed premises (and premises which may be used for a permitted temporary activity by virtue of part 5), the requirements are fairly straightforward. In such cases the holder of the premises licence, the designated premises supervisor (see para. 4.11.4) or the premises user respectively will be liable and it will only be necessary to prove that they *knowingly* allowed disorderly conduct on relevant premises. In the case of premises where a club premises certificate is in effect, it will be necessary, in addition, to show that the defendant was present on the premises and in a capacity that enabled him/her to prevent the conduct.

Whether the conduct involved was disorderly will be a question of fact to be decided in all the circumstances.

'Relevant premises' means licensed premises, premises in respect of which there is in force a club premises certificate, and premises which may be used for a permitted temporary activity by virtue of part 5 (s. 159).

4.11.8.6 Sale of Alcohol to a Person who is Drunk

OFFENCE: **Sale of alcohol to a person who is drunk—*Licensing Act 2003, s. 141***
- Triable summarily • Fine

The Licensing Act 2003, s. 141 states:

(1) A person to whom subsection (2) applies commits an offence if, on relevant premises, he knowingly—
  (a) sells or attempts to sell alcohol to a person who is drunk, or
  (b) allows alcohol to be sold to such a person.

(2) This subsection applies—
  (a) to any person who works at the premises in a capacity, whether paid or unpaid, which gives him authority to sell the alcohol concerned,
  (b) in the case of licensed premises, to—
    (i) the holder of a premises licence in respect of the premises, and
    (ii) the designated premises supervisor (if any) under such a licence,
  (c) in the case of premises in respect of which a club premises certificate has effect, to any member or officer of the club which holds the certificate who at the time the sale (or attempted sale) takes place is present on the premises in a capacity which enables him to prevent it, and
  (d) in the case of premises which may be used for a permitted temporary activity by virtue of Part 5, to the premises user in relation to the temporary event notice in question.

KEYNOTE

As with the previous offence under s. 140, the offence is very widely drafted and covers all the various people set out at paras (2)(a) to (d). It will be important to note the distinctions between the roles of these people.

In addition, this offence is not restricted to retail sales and will cover all sales, including those for consumption off the premises.

This section applies in relation to the supply of alcohol by or on behalf of a club to, or to the order of, a member of the club as it applies in relation to the sale of alcohol (s. 141(3)).

'Relevant premises' means licensed premises, premises in respect of which there is in force a club premises certificate, and premises which may be used for a permitted temporary activity by virtue of part 5 (s. 159).

The people to whom this offence applies are those in the roles that would allow them to take the appropriate action in preventing the offence.

4.11.8.7 Obtaining Alcohol for a Person who is Drunk

OFFENCE: **Obtaining alcohol for a person who is drunk—*Licensing Act 2003, s. 142***

- Triable summarily • Fine

The Licensing Act 2003, s. 142 states:

(1) A person commits an offence if, on relevant premises, he knowingly obtains or attempts to obtain alcohol for consumption on those premises by a person who is drunk.

KEYNOTE

'Relevant premises' means licensed premises, premises in respect of which there is in force a club premises certificate, and premises which may be used for a permitted temporary activity by virtue of part 5 (s. 159).

The requirement to show that the defendant acted *knowingly* is critical to prove this offence.

The intended consumption must be on the premises where the alcohol is obtained/attempted to be obtained.

4.11.8.8 Failure to Leave Licensed Premises

OFFENCE: **Failure to leave licensed premises etc.—*Licensing Act 2003, s. 143***

- Triable summarily • Fine

The Licensing Act 2003, s. 143 states:

(1) A person who is drunk *or* disorderly commits an offence if, without reasonable excuse—
  (a) he fails to leave relevant premises when requested to do so by a constable or by a person to whom subsection (2) applies, or
  (b) he enters or attempts to enter relevant premises after a constable or a person to whom subsection (2) applies has requested him not to enter.
(2) This subsection applies—
  (a) to any person who works at the premises in a capacity, whether paid or unpaid, which gives him authority to sell the alcohol concerned,
  (b) in the case of licensed premises, to—
    (i) the holder of a premises licence in respect of the premises, and
    (ii) the designated premises supervisor (if any) under such a licence,
  (c) in the case of premises in respect of which a club premises certificate has effect, to any member or officer of the club which holds the certificate who is present on the premises in a capacity which enables him to make such a request, and
  (d) in the case of premises which may be used for a permitted temporary activity by virtue of Part 5, to the premises user in relation to the temporary event notice in question.

KEYNOTE

The above offence requires that the person concerned is shown to be *either* drunk *or* disorderly (contrast the offence under the Criminal Justice Act 1967, see para. 4.11.8.9).

The absence of a reasonable excuse is an important ingredient in this offence, and it should be shown that the request to leave/not to enter was both heard and understood by the defendant.

On being requested to do so by a person to whom subs. (2) applies, a constable must:

- help to expel from relevant premises a person who is drunk or disorderly;
- help to prevent such a person from entering relevant premises (s. 143(4)).

Note that, if requested to do so by one of the above people, a police officer is under a duty (rather than simply having a power) to help them expel anyone who is drunk or disorderly. The wording of the section means that police officers are also under a similar duty to help to prevent such a person from entering relevant premises.

'Relevant premises' means licensed premises, premises in respect of which there is in force a club premises certificate, and premises which may be used for a permitted temporary activity by virtue of part 5 (s. 159).

The people to whom this offence applies are those identified within some other offences under the Act and cover the capacity of person who would be allowed to make the relevant request.

4.11.8.9 Drunk and Disorderly

OFFENCE: **Drunk and disorderly—*Criminal Justice Act 1967, s. 91(1)***

- Triable summarily • Fine

The Criminal Justice Act 1967, s. 91 states:

(1) Any person who in any public place is guilty, while drunk, of disorderly behaviour and shall be liable ...

KEYNOTE

To prove this offence you must show that the defendant was both drunk and disorderly. The drunkenness must be as a result of excessive consumption of *alcohol*; if the person's state is caused by some other intoxicant (e.g. glue solvents), the offence is not made out (*Neale* v *R. M. J. E. (a minor)* (1985) 80 Cr App R 20). The same ruling applies to a person 'found drunk' in a public place (*Lanham* v *Rickwood* (1984) 148 JP 737 (see para. 4.11.8.10). This can be contrasted with the situation in relation to drink driving cases (see Road Policing, chapter 3.5) where unfitness to drive can arise from drugs as well as alcohol.

'Drunkenness' here means where the defendant has taken intoxicating liquor (alcohol) to an extent that affects his/her steady self-control (per Goff LJ in *Neale*).

Where there are *several* causes of a person's incapacitated state, one of which is alcohol, a court can find that the person was in fact 'drunk', even though some additional intoxicant had an exacerbating effect on his/her loss of 'steady self-control'.

This offence is not committed where a person did not commit any disorderly act until after their arrest (*H* v *DPP* (2006) 170 JP 4).

This offence is a 'penalty offence' for the purposes of s. 1 of the Criminal Justice and Police Act 2001 (see para. 4.4.3).

Where a person is arrested for committing this offence, under the powers contained within s. 24 of the Police and Criminal Evidence Act 1984, a constable may take them to an approved treatment centre for alcoholism (a 'detoxification' centre) and he/she will be treated as being in lawful custody for the purposes of that journey (see s. 34(1) of the Criminal Justice Act 1972).

The conduct of passengers who are drunk on an aircraft has a potential impact on the safety of the aircraft and the people therein, therefore they can be dealt with under s. 61 of the Civil Aviation Act 1982 and the relevant regulations made thereunder (see e.g. *R* v *Tagg* [2002] 1 Cr App R 2 and Air Navigation Order 2005 (SI 2005/1970, part 5) made under Civil Aviation Act 1982 and the Airports Act 1986).

4.11.8.10 Found Drunk

OFFENCE: **Being found drunk—*Licensing Act 1872, s. 12***

- Triable summarily • Fine

The Licensing Act 1872, s. 12 states:

> Every person found drunk in any highway or other public place, whether a building or not, or on any licensed premises, shall be liable . . .

KEYNOTE

This offence is committed if a person is on the highway or public place and shown to be drunk. It does not matter that the person is there only briefly or of his/her own volition.

'Other public place' will include all places to which the public have access (whether on payment or otherwise).

The offence has been held to apply to the licensee when found drunk on the licensed premises, even when those premises were not open to the public (see *Evans* v *Fletcher* (1926) 135 LT 153).

The drunkenness must be as a result of excessive consumption of *alcohol*; if the person's state is caused by some other intoxicant, e.g. glue solvents, the offence is not made out (*Lanham* v *Rickwood* (1984) 148 JP 737). The same ruling applies to a person who is disorderly whilst drunk.

This offence is a 'penalty offence' for the purposes of s. 1 of the Criminal Justice and Police Act 2001 (see para. 4.4.3).

On arresting a person for this offence, under the powers contained in s. 24 of the Police and Criminal Evidence Act 1984, a police officer may, if he/she thinks fit, take the person to an approved treatment centre under s. 34 of the Criminal Justice Act 1972. During the journey to such a treatment centre the person will be deemed to be in lawful custody. Section 34 does not allow a person to be detained at the centre and does not preclude any charge being brought in relation to the offence.

For the offence of being drunk in charge of a mechanically propelled vehicle (under s. 4 of the Road Traffic Act 1988), see Road Policing, chapter 3.5, and the offence of being drunk in possession of a firearm (under s. 12 of the 1872 Act), see para. 4.7.9.2.

4.11.9 Children

The Licensing Act 2003 makes provision for offences and breaches of the regulatory framework with the protection of children as one of its primary objectives. The Act left in place the offence of giving alcohol to a child under five years old (s. 5 of the Children and Young Persons Act 1933), except on a doctor's order, or in cases of sickness, apprehended sickness or other urgent cause.

4.11.9.1 Unaccompanied Children Prohibited from Certain Premises

OFFENCE: **Unaccompanied children prohibited from certain premises—*Licensing Act 2003, s. 145***

- Triable summarily • Fine

The Licensing Act 2003, s. 145 states:

> (1) A person to whom subsection (3) applies commits an offence if—
>
> (a) knowing that relevant premises are within subsection (4), he allows an unaccompanied child to be on the premises at a time when they are open for the purposes of being used for the supply of alcohol for consumption there, or

(b) he allows an unaccompanied child to be on relevant premises at a time between the hours of midnight and 5 a.m. when the premises are open for the purposes of being used for the supply of alcohol for consumption there.

(2) ...

(3) This subsection applies—

(a) to any person who works at the premises in a capacity, whether paid or unpaid, which authorises him to request the unaccompanied child to leave the premises,

(b) in the case of licensed premises, to—

(i) the holder of a premises licence in respect of the premises, and

(ii) the designated premises supervisor (if any) under such a licence,

(c) in the case of premises in respect of which a club premises certificate has effect, to any member or officer of the club which holds the certificate who is present on the premises in a capacity which enables him to make such a request, and

(d) in the case of premises which may be used for a permitted temporary activity by virtue of Part 5, to the premises user in relation to the temporary event notice in question.

KEYNOTE

The two limbs to this offence are either:

- that the child is unaccompanied on the premises at a time when they are open for the purposes of supplying alcohol for consumption on those premises, and the defendant knows that the premises fall within subs. (4); or
- that the child is unaccompanied on the premises at a time between midnight and 5 am when the premises are being so used.

The people to whom this offence applies are those identified within other offences under the Act and cover the roles that would allow the person to take the appropriate action in preventing the presence of children in the way prohibited.

'Child' means an individual aged under 16 (s. 145(2)(a)).

A child is unaccompanied if they are not in the company of an individual aged 18 or over (s. 145(2)(b)).

Relevant premises are within subs. (4) if:

- they are exclusively or primarily used for the supply of alcohol for consumption on the premises; or
- they are open for the purposes of being used for the supply of alcohol for consumption on the premises by virtue of part 5 (permitted temporary activities) and, at the time the temporary event notice in question has effect, they are exclusively or primarily used for such supplies (s. 145(4)).

'Supply of alcohol' means the sale by retail of alcohol, or the supply of alcohol by or on behalf of a club to, or to the order of, a member of the club (s. 145(10)).

No offence is committed if the unaccompanied child is on the premises solely for the purpose of passing to or from some other place to or from which there is no other convenient means of access or egress (s. 145(5)).

As with some other offences, there are specific defences where the person is charged as a result of their own conduct and where the conduct is that of someone else.

4.11.9.2 Defence

Where a person is charged with an offence under this section by *reason of his own conduct*, it is a defence that:

- he believed that the unaccompanied child was aged 16 or over or that an individual accompanying him was aged 18 or over, *and*
- either:
  - he had taken all reasonable steps to establish the individual's age, or

- ♦ nobody could reasonably have suspected from the individual's appearance that he was aged under 16 or, as the case may be, under 18.

Where a person is charged with an offence under this section *by reason of the act or default of some other person*, it is a defence that the person charged exercised all due diligence to avoid committing it (s. 145(6) and (8)).

A person will have taken all reasonable steps to establish an individual's age if:

- he/she asked the individual for evidence of their age, and
- the evidence would have convinced a reasonable person (s. 145(7)).

4.11.9.3 Sale of Alcohol to Children

OFFENCE: **Sale of alcohol to children—*Licensing Act 2003, s. 146***

- Triable summarily • Fine

The Licensing Act 2003, s. 146 states:

(1) A person commits an offence if he sells alcohol to an individual aged under 18.
(2) A club commits an offence if alcohol is supplied by it or on its behalf—
 (a) to, or to the order of, a member of the club who is aged under 18, or
 (b) to the order of a member of the club, to an individual who is aged under 18.
(3) A person commits an offence if he supplies alcohol on behalf of a club—
 (a) to, or to the order of, a member of the club who is aged under 18, or
 (b) to the order of a member of the club, to an individual who is aged under 18.

KEYNOTE

The main offence under subs. (1) is straightforward and covers any type of 'selling' of alcohol to people under 18 *anywhere* (not just on licensed premises).

As with some other offences there are specific defences where the person is charged as a result of their own conduct or where the conduct is that of someone else.

4.11.9.4 Defence

Where a person is charged with an offence under this section *by reason of his own conduct*, it is a defence that:

- he believed that the individual was aged 18 or over, and
- either:
  - ♦ he had taken all reasonable steps to establish the individual's age, or
  - ♦ nobody could reasonably have suspected from the individual's appearance that he was aged under 18.

Where a person is charged with an offence under this section *by reason of the act or default of some other person*, it is a defence that the person charged exercised all due diligence to avoid committing it (s. 146(4) and (6))

A person will have taken all reasonable steps to establish an individual's age if:

- he/she asked the individual for evidence of their age, and
- the evidence would have convinced a reasonable person (s. 146(5)).

4.11.9.5 Allowing the Sale of Alcohol to Children

OFFENCE: **Allowing the sale of alcohol to children—*Licensing Act 2003, s. 147***

- Triable summarily • Fine

The Licensing Act 2003, s. 147 states:

(1) A person to whom subsection (2) applies commits an offence if he knowingly allows the sale of alcohol on relevant premises to an individual aged under 18.
(2) This subsection applies to a person who works at the premises in a capacity, whether paid or unpaid, which authorises him to prevent the sale.
(3) A person to whom subsection (4) applies commits an offence if he knowingly allows alcohol to be supplied on relevant premises by or on behalf of a club—
(a) to or to the order of a member of the club who is aged under 18, or
(b) to the order of a member of the club, to an individual who is aged under 18.

KEYNOTE

The offences above require proof that the person *knowingly* allowed the sale (or, in the case of subs. (3), the supply) to a person under 18. Unlike the offence under s. 146 (**see para. 4.11.9.3**), the offence at s.147 relates to 'relevant premises'. These are licensed premises, premises in respect of which there is in force a club premises certificate, and premises which may be used for a permitted temporary activity by virtue of part 5 (s. 159).

So far as the second offence relating to clubs (under s. 147(3)) is concerned, subs. (4) to which it refers applies:

- a person who works on the premises in a capacity, whether paid or unpaid, which authorises him/her to prevent the supply, and
- any member or officer of the club who at the time of the supply is present on the relevant premises in a capacity which enables him/her to prevent it.

Every local weights and measures authority in England and Wales has a statutory duty to enforce within its area the above provisions so far as they apply to sales of alcohol made on or from premises to which the public have access, and a weights and measures inspector may make (or authorise any person to make on his/her behalf) test purchases of goods for the purpose of determining whether those provisions are being complied with (s. 154).

4.11.9.6 Persistently Selling Alcohol to Children

OFFENCE: **Persistently selling alcohol to children—*Licensing Act 2003, s. 147A***

- Triable summarily • Fine

The Licensing Act 2003, s. 147A states:

(1) A person is guilty of an offence if—
(a) on 3 or more different occasions within a period of 3 consecutive months alcohol is unlawfully sold on the same premises to an individual aged under 18;
(b) at the time of each sale the premises were either licensed premises or premises authorised to be used for a permitted temporary activity by virtue of Part 5; and
(c) that person was a responsible person in relation to the premises at each such time.
(2) For the purposes of this section alcohol sold to an individual aged under 18 is unlawfully sold to him if—
(a) the person making the sale believed the individual to be aged under 18; or
(b) that person did not have reasonable grounds for believing the individual to be aged 18 or over.

(3) For the purposes of subsection (2) a person has reasonable grounds for believing an individual to be aged 18 or over only if—
  (a) he asked the individual for evidence of his age and that individual produced evidence that would have convinced a reasonable person; or
  (b) nobody could reasonably have suspected from the individual's appearance that he was aged under 18.

KEYNOTE

This offence requires the sale to be 'unlawful' and explains the meaning of this in subs. (2). The 'premises' are licensed premises where a person holds a premises licence or is the premises user in respect of a temporary event notice by reference to which the premises are authorised to be used for a permitted temporary activity by virtue of part 5 (s. 147A(4)). The individual aged under 18, to whom the sale is made, can be the same person or others (subs. (5)), and the same sale may not be counted in respect of different offences (subs. (6)).

The following will be admissible as evidence that there has been an unlawful sale of alcohol to an individual aged under 18 on any premises on any occasion: the conviction, caution or payment of a fixed penalty for an offence under s. 146 (s. 147A(7)).

In addition to a fine, a premises licence can be suspended for up to three months in so far as it authorises the sale of alcohol (s. 147B).

Where there is evidence that a person has committed the offence of persistently selling alcohol to children, a senior police officer may give a closure notice in respect of the premises concerned (see para. 4.11.9.16).

4.11.9.7 Sale of Liqueur Confectionery to Children

OFFENCE: **Sale of liqueur confectionery to children under 16—*Licensing Act 2003, s. 148***

- Triable summarily • Fine

The Licensing Act 2003, s. 148 states:

(1) A person commits an offence if he—
  (a) sells liqueur confectionery to an individual aged under 16, or
  (b) supplies such confectionery, on behalf of a club—
    (i) to or to the order of a member of the club who is aged under 16, or
    (ii) to the order of a member of the club, to an individual who is aged under 16.

KEYNOTE

A club itself commits an offence if liqueur confectionery is supplied by it or on its behalf to or to the order of a member of the club who is aged under 16, or to the order of a member of the club, to an individual who is aged under 16 (s. 148(2)).

While most 'liqueur confectionery' will be obvious in practice, it has a very specific definition based on the weight of the confectionery, and the relative strength and volume of the alcohol (see s. 191). This element will need to be proved in any prosecution.

The above offence is not limited to 'retail' sales.

As with other age-related offences under the Act, the two specific defences—where the person is charged as a result of their own conduct and where the conduct is that of someone else—apply.

4.11.9.8 Defence

Where a person is charged with an offence under this section *by reason of his own conduct*, it is a defence that:

- he believed that the individual was aged 16 or over, and
- either:
  - he had taken all reasonable steps to establish the individual's age, or
  - nobody could reasonably have suspected from the individual's appearance that he was aged under 16.

Where a person is charged with an offence under this section *by reason of the act or default of some other person*, it is a defence that the person charged exercised all due diligence to avoid committing it (s. 148(3) and (5)).

Again, a person will have taken all reasonable steps to establish an individual's age if:

- he/she asked the individual for evidence of their age, and
- the evidence would have convinced a reasonable person (s. 148(4)).

4.11.9.9 Purchase of Alcohol by or on behalf of Children

OFFENCE: **Purchase of alcohol by or on behalf of children—*Licensing Act 2003, s. 149***

- Triable summarily • Fine

The Licensing Act 2003, s. 149 states:

(1) An individual aged under 18 commits an offence if—
  (a) he buys or attempts to buy alcohol, or
  (b) where he is a member of a club—
    (i) alcohol is supplied to him or to his order by or on behalf of the club, as a result of some act or default of his, or
    (ii) he attempts to have alcohol supplied to him or to his order by or on behalf of the club.
(2) ...
(3) A person commits an offence if—
  (a) he buys or attempts to buy alcohol on behalf of an individual aged under 18, or
  (b) where he is a member of a club, on behalf of an individual aged under 18 he—
    (i) makes arrangements whereby alcohol is supplied to him or to his order by or on behalf of the club, or
    (ii) attempts to make such arrangements.
(4) A person ('the relevant person') commits an offence if—
  (a) he buys or attempts to buy alcohol for consumption on relevant premises by an individual aged under 18, or
  (b) where he is a member of a club—
    (i) by some act or default of his, alcohol is supplied to him, or to his order, by or on behalf of the club for consumption on relevant premises by an individual aged under 18, or
    (ii) he attempts to have alcohol so supplied for such consumption.

KEYNOTE

This wide offence covers all forms of under-18-year-olds buying (or trying to buy) alcohol or someone else doing it for them.

Subsection (1) does not apply where the individual buys or attempts to buy the alcohol at the request of a constable, or a weights and measures inspector who is acting in the course of his/her duty (s. 149(2)).

The offence at subs. (4) does not apply where:

- the relevant person is aged 18 or over,
- the individual is aged 16 or 17,
- the alcohol is beer, wine or cider,
- its purchase or supply is for consumption at a table meal on relevant premises, and
- the individual is accompanied at the meal by an individual aged 18 or over (s. 149(5)).

'Table meal' here means a meal eaten by a person seated at a table (or at a counter or other structure which serves the purpose of a table) and is not used for the service of refreshments for consumption by people who are not seated at such a table or structure (s. 159).

Where a person is charged with an offence under subs. (3) or (4) it is a defence that they had no reason to suspect that the individual was aged under 18 (s. 149(6)).

4.11.9.10 Consumption of Alcohol by Children

OFFENCE: **Consumption of alcohol by children—*Licensing Act 2003, s. 150***
- Triable summarily • Fine

The Licensing Act 2003, s. 150 states:

(1) An individual aged under 18 commits an offence if he knowingly consumes alcohol on relevant premises.
(2) A person to whom subsection (3) applies commits an offence if he knowingly allows the consumption of alcohol on relevant premises by an individual aged under 18.
(3) This subsection applies—
 (a) to a person who works at the premises in a capacity, whether paid or unpaid, which authorises him to prevent the consumption, and
 (b) where the alcohol was supplied by a club to or to the order of a member of the club, to any member or officer of the club who is present at the premises at the time of the consumption in a capacity which enables him to prevent it.

KEYNOTE

These offences address the consumption of alcohol by under-18-year-olds on relevant premises.

'Relevant premises' are generally licensed premises, in respect of which there is in force a club premises certificate, and premises which may be used for a permitted temporary activity by virtue of part 5 (s. 159).

Subsections (1) and (2) do not apply where:

- the individual is aged 16 or 17;
- the alcohol is beer, wine or cider;
- its consumption is at a table meal on relevant premises; and
- the individual is accompanied at the meal by an individual aged 18 or over (s. 150(4)).

4.11.9.11 Delivering Alcohol to Children

OFFENCE: **Delivering alcohol to children—*Licensing Act 2003, s. 151***
- Triable summarily • Fine

The Licensing Act 2003, s. 151 states:

(1) A person who works on relevant premises in any capacity, whether paid or unpaid, commits an offence if he knowingly delivers to an individual aged under 18—
 (a) alcohol sold on the premises, or

(b) alcohol supplied on the premises by or on behalf of a club to or to the order of a member of the club.

(2) A person to whom subsection (3) applies commits an offence if he knowingly allows anybody else to deliver to an individual aged under 18 alcohol sold on relevant premises.

(3) This subsection applies to a person who works on the premises in a capacity, whether paid or unpaid, which authorises him to prevent the delivery of the alcohol.

(4) A person to whom subsection (5) applies commits an offence if he knowingly allows anybody else to deliver to an individual aged under 18 alcohol supplied on relevant premises by or on behalf of a club to or to the order of a member of the club.

(5) This subsection applies—

(a) to a person who works on the premises in a capacity, whether paid or unpaid, which authorises him to prevent the supply, and

(b) to any member or officer of the club who at the time of the supply in question is present on the premises in a capacity which enables him to prevent the supply.

KEYNOTE

These offences require proof that the defendant—who must be working on the relevant premises—acted *knowingly*. The person can be working on the premises in any capacity, paid or not, and does not have to be bar staff, licence holder etc.

Where:

- the alcohol is delivered at a place where the buyer (or person supplied) lives or works, or
- the individual aged under 18 works on the relevant premises in a capacity (whether paid or unpaid) which involves the delivery of alcohol, or
- the alcohol is sold or supplied for consumption on the relevant premises,

the offences do not apply (see s. 151(6)).

4.11.9.12 Sending a Child to Obtain Alcohol

OFFENCE: **Sending a child to obtain alcohol—*Licensing Act 2003, s. 152***

- Triable summarily • Fine

The Licensing Act 2003, s. 152 states:

(1) A person commits an offence if he knowingly sends an individual aged under 18 to obtain—

(a) alcohol sold or to be sold on relevant premises for consumption off the premises, or

(b) alcohol supplied or to be supplied by or on behalf of a club to or to the order of a member of the club for such consumption.

KEYNOTE

This offence—which again requires proof of the defendant's acting *knowingly*—has several exceptions.

For the purposes of this section, it is immaterial whether the individual aged under 18 is sent to obtain the alcohol from the relevant premises or from other premises from which it is delivered in pursuance of the sale or supply (s. 152(2)).

The offence will not be committed where the individual aged under 18 works on the relevant premises in a capacity, whether paid or unpaid, which involves the delivery of alcohol (s. 152(3)).

The offence will not be committed where the individual buys or attempts to buy the alcohol at the request of a constable or a weights and measures inspector who is acting in the course of his/her duty (s. 152(4)).

4.11.9.13 Prohibition of Unsupervised Sales by Children

OFFENCE: **Prohibition of unsupervised sales by children—*Licensing Act 2003, s. 153***

- Triable summarily • Fine

The Licensing Act 2003, s. 153 states:

> (1) A responsible person commits an offence if on any relevant premises he knowingly allows an individual aged under 18 to make on the premises—
> (a) any sale of alcohol, or
> (b) any supply of alcohol by or on behalf of a club to or to the order of a member of the club,
> unless the sale or supply has been specifically approved by that or another responsible person.

KEYNOTE

This offences addresses a responsible person *knowingly* allowing an under-18-year-old to make sales or supplies of alcohol on relevant premises.

'Responsible person' means:

- in relation to licensed premises:
  - the holder of a premises licence in respect of the premises,
  - the designated premises supervisor (if any) under such a licence, or
  - any individual aged 18 or over who is authorised for the purposes of this section by such a holder or supervisor,
- in relation to premises in respect of which there is in force a club premises certificate, any member or officer of the club present on the premises in a capacity which enables him to prevent the supply in question, and
- in relation to premises which may be used for a permitted temporary activity by virtue of part 5:
  - the premises user, or
  - any individual aged 18 or over who is authorised for the purposes of this section by the premises user (s. 153(4)).

'Relevant premises' are generally the same premises as those set out under the various descriptions of 'responsible person' above (see s. 159).

The offence is not committed where:

- the alcohol is sold or supplied for consumption with a table meal,
- it is sold or supplied in premises which are being used for the service of table meals (or in a part of any premises which is being so used), *and*
- the premises are (or the part is) not used for the sale or supply of alcohol otherwise than to persons having table meals there and for consumption by such a person as an ancillary to their meal (s. 153(2)).

4.11.9.14 Confiscation of Alcohol when Person under 18 may be involved

The Confiscation of Alcohol (Young Persons) Act 1997, s. 1 states:

> (1) Where a constable reasonably suspects that a person in a relevant place is in possession of alcohol, and that either—
> (a) he is under the age of 18; or
> (b) he intends that any of the alcohol should be consumed by a person under the age of 18 in that or any other relevant place; or
> (c) a person under the age of 18 who is, or has recently been, with him has recently consumed alcohol in that or any other relevant place,

the constable may require him to surrender anything in his possession which is, or which the constable reasonably believes to be, alcohol or a container for such alcohol and to state his name and address.

(1A) But a constable may not under subsection (1) require a person to surrender any sealed container unless the constable reasonably believes that the person is, or has been, consuming, or intends to consume alcohol in any relevant place.

KEYNOTE

This is a discretionary power for police officers to exercise as they deem fit in accordance with general human rights principles and, in particular, Article 1 of the First Protocol (**see chapter 4.3**).

It is unusual that the wording of the section says 'either', then goes on to give *three* instances where the power will be available. However, if one of the instances at s. 1(1)(a) to (c) applies, the police officer may require the person concerned to:

- surrender anything that is, or that the officer reasonably *believes* (a narrower expression than 'suspects') to be, alcohol or a container for such alcohol, and
- state his/her name and address.

The wording of this section is similar to that relating to powers to confiscate items in a designated public place (**see para. 4.11.10**). There is no requirement for the officer to be in uniform.

The requirement for the person to state his/her name and *his/her own address* appears to be quite specific. A similar provision under s. 170 of the Road Traffic Act 1988 (duty to give details after an accident; **see Road Policing, chapter 3.4**), has been satisfied where the person concerned gave the name and address of his solicitor (*DPP* v *McCarthy* [1999] RTR 323). However, as the above power will affect mostly young people, it would seem unlikely that anything less than their own personal details would satisfy the requirements of this section. It is an important point, because failure to comply with either requirement under s. 1(1) triggers the power of arrest under s. 1(5) (see below).

Under s. 1(2), the officer may dispose of *anything* surrendered to him/her in answer to the making of such a requirement. This wide discretionary power is not limited to alcohol and the officer could dispose of any other drink surrendered under this section (see HC Official Report SC C, 12 February 1997).

4.11.9.15 Failure to Surrender Items believed to be Alcohol

OFFENCE: **Failing to surrender alcohol—*Confiscation of Alcohol (Young Persons) Act 1997, s 1(3)***

- Triable summarily • Fine

The Confiscation of Alcohol (Young Persons) Act 1997, s. 1 states:

(3) A person who fails without reasonable excuse to comply with a requirement imposed on him under subsection (1) commits an offence.

KEYNOTE

Where a constable imposes a requirement on a person under s. 1(1) above, he/she must inform that person of his/her suspicion and that to fail without reasonable excuse to comply with such a requirement is an offence (s. 1(4)).

Under s. 1(6), a 'relevant place' is:

- any public place, other than licensed premises; or
- any place, other than a public place, to which that person has unlawfully gained access;

and for this purpose a place is a public place if, at the material time, the public or any section of the public has access to it—on payment or otherwise—as of right or by virtue of express or implied permission. Therefore the power may be exercised in any public place (as defined above) not being 'licensed premises'. It may also be exercised in any other place that is not a public place to which the person has gained access unlawfully. This second expression suggests that the person must, as a matter of fact, have gained access to the place unlawfully—as opposed to the officer simply 'suspecting' or 'believing' that to be the case. It also suggests that, if the person was originally in the place lawfully but was later asked to leave, the power would not apply as the person's access would not have been 'unlawfully gained'. The section does not provide the police officer with a power of entry or a power to search.

The 1997 Act provides a useful power which might be considered in relation to events such as parties and 'raves' (**see chapter 4.10**).

4.11.9.16 Closure Notices for Persistently Selling Alcohol to Children

Section 169A of the Licensing Act 2003, provides that a senior police officer (of the rank of superintendent or higher), or an inspector of weights and measures, may give a closure notice where there is evidence that a person has committed the offence of persistently selling alcohol to children at the premises in question (**see para. 4.11.9.6**), and he/she considers that the evidence is such that there would be a realistic prospect of conviction if the offender was prosecuted for it. A closure notice can only be given within three months of the last offence (s. 169A(9)).

A closure notice will propose a prohibition on sales of alcohol at the premises in question for a period not exceeding 48 hours, and will offer the opportunity to discharge all criminal liability in respect of the alleged offence by the acceptance of the prohibition proposed in the notice (s. 169A(2)). The premises licence holder will have fourteen days to decide whether or not to accept the proposed prohibition or to elect to be tried for the offence (s. 169A(4)). Where the licence holder decides to accept the prohibition, it must take effect not less than fourteen days after the date on which the notice was served at a time specified in the closure notice (s. 169A(5)).

A closure notice may be served on the premises to which it applies only by being handed by a constable or trading standards officer to a person on the premises who appears to the constable or trading standards officer to have control of or responsibility for the premises (s. 169A(7)). The closure notice can only be served at a time when licensable activities are being carried on at the premises.

4.11.10 Alcohol Consumption in Designated Public Places

The Criminal Justice and Police Act 2001 introduced a statutory framework to regulate the drinking of alcohol in certain public places and to reinforce existing licensing laws.

Home Office Circular 13/2007, *The Local Authorities (Alcohol Consumption in Designated Public Places) Regulations 2007*, provides guidance on the use of Designated Public Places Orders issued by local authorities.

4.11.10.1 Orders by Local Authorities

Under s. 13 of the 2001 Act, local authorities may identify public places within their area if they are satisfied that:

- nuisance or annoyance to members of the public (or section of the public), or
- disorder

has been associated with the consumption of alcohol in that place. This expression '*has been associated*' is a fairly loose one which does not appear to impose a particularly heavy burden on the local authority, who will clearly rely on evidence from the police in establishing whether such a situation exists. 'Public place' here means any place to which the public (or a section of the public) has access, on payment or otherwise, as of right or by virtue of any express or implied permission (s. 16(1)).

Once it is satisfied that one of the relevant conditions applies to a public place, the local authority may make an order (under s. 13(2)) designating that place.

Although the 2001 Act allows places to be designated either by specific reference (e.g. to their street name), or by description, premises in respect of which a premises licence, club premises licence or temporary event notice is in force cannot be 'designated public places'. This applies when alcohol is actually being sold or supplied in accordance with the licence or notice and for another 30 minutes thereafter (s. 14).

4.11.10.2 Police Powers

Where a constable reasonably believes that a person:

- is, or has been consuming
- or intends to consume
- alcohol
- in a designated public place,

the constable may require the person:

- not to consume in that place anything which is, or *which the constable reasonably believes to be*, alcohol;
- to surrender anything in his/her possession which is, *or which the constable reasonably believes to be*, alcohol or a container for alcohol (other than a sealed container),

and the constable may dispose of anything so surrendered in such a manner as he/she considers appropriate (s. 12).

Although there is nothing to prevent the use of this power when dealing with people under 18 years of age, there is a power designed specifically in relation to young people (**see para. 4.11.9.14**).

Any offence under s. 12 (see below) is a 'penalty offence' for the purposes of s. 1 of the Criminal Justice and Police Act 2001 (**see para. 4.4.3**).

4.11.10.3 Failing to Comply with Requirement in Designated Public Place

OFFENCE: **Failing to comply with requirement—*Criminal Justice and Police Act 2001, s. 12(4)***

- Triable summarily • Fine

The Criminal Justice and Police Act 2001, s. 12(4) states:

> A person who fails without reasonable excuse to comply with a requirement imposed on him under subsection (2) commits an offence.

KEYNOTE

This offence will not be made out if the person has a 'reasonable excuse' for not complying. Although there is no requirement for the officer to be in uniform, *the officer imposing the requirement* must tell the person that the above behaviour will amount to an offence. Failure to do so will almost certainly provide the person with a defence.

4.11.10.4 Directions to Individuals who Represent a Risk of Disorder

The Violent Crime Reduction Act 2006 provides the police with a power to issue a direction to an individual to leave a locality to minimise the risk of alcohol-related crime or disorder arising and/or taking place. Section 27 of the Act states:

> (1) If the test in subsection (2) is satisfied in the case of an individual aged 16 or over who is in a public place, a constable in uniform may give a direction to that individual—
> (a) requiring him to leave the locality of that place; and
> (b) prohibiting the individual from returning to that locality for such period (not exceeding 48 hours) from the giving of the direction as the constable may specify.
>
> (2) That test is—
> (a) that the presence of the individual in that locality is likely, in all the circumstances, to cause or to contribute to the occurrence of alcohol-related crime or disorder in that locality, or to cause or to contribute to a repetition or continuance there of such crime or disorder; and
> (b) that the giving of a direction under this section to that individual is necessary for the purpose of removing or reducing the likelihood of there being such crime or disorder in that locality during the period for which the direction has effect or of there being a repetition or continuance in that locality during that period of such crime or disorder.
>
> (3) A direction under this section—
> (a) must be given in writing;
> (b) may require the individual to whom it is given to leave the locality in question either immediately or by such time as the constable giving the direction may specify;
> (c) must clearly identify the locality to which it relates;
> (d) must specify the period for which the individual is prohibited from returning to that locality;
> (e) may impose requirements as to the manner in which that individual leaves the locality, including his route; and
> (f) may be withdrawn or varied (but not extended so as to apply for a period of more than 48 hours) by a constable.

KEYNOTE

A constable may not give a direction that prevents a person from having access to a place where he/she, resides or works, is attending education or training, receiving medical treatment, is under an obligation imposed under any enactment, or by the order of a court or tribunal (s. 27(4)).

The constable giving a direction must record the terms of the direction and locality to which it relates, the name of the person to whom it is given, the time it is given, and the specified period (s. 27(5)).

OFFENCE: **Failing to comply with a direction—*Violent Crime Reduction Act 2006, s. 27(6)***

- Triable summarily • Fine

The Violent Crime Reduction Act 2006, s. 27(6) states:

> A person who fails to comply with a direction under this section is guilty of an offence.

4.11.10.5 Designation of Alcohol Disorder Zones

Alcohol disorder zones seek to address problems within an area where other interventions provided by the Licensing Act 2003 and the Violent Crime Reduction Act 2006 have been tried but not solved the problem.

The Violent Crime Reduction Act 2006, ss. 15 to 20, provides a local authority with the power to designate, with the consent of the police, a locality as an alcohol disorder zone where there is a problem with alcohol-related nuisance and disorder. The police may also make application to the local authority for a locality to be so designated.

Local authorities are required to give notice of their intention to designate a particular zone following which there is a period of 28 days' consultation where all interested parties can make representations about the proposal.

KEYNOTE

There is a power for local authorities to impose charges on holders of premises licences allowing the sale by retail of alcohol and on holders of club premises certificates allowing the supply of alcohol to members and their guests. Charges can be imposed if licensed premises and clubs do not implement an action plan, prepared by the local authority and designed to address the alcohol-related problem, within eight weeks of publication of the plan.

As part of the action plan, licensed premises may be asked to fund extra service provision, for example, extra late-night transport. If premises fail to implement the action plan, then charges can be levied at a nationally set rate, reflecting the cost of initiatives that are used by the local authority to tackle the problem. A designation will be subject to a three-monthly review of its appropriateness.

Note that the Local Authorities (Alcohol Disorder Zones) Regulations 2008, which will implement ss. 15 to 20, are currently in draft form but it is anticipated these will come into force in the near future.

4.11.10.6 Drinking Banning Orders

When in force, s. 1 of the Violent Crime Reduction Act 2006 will provide for a civil order, a drinking banning order, which is designed to protect persons and their property from criminal or disorderly conduct by an individual while he/she is under the influence of alcohol.

The 2006 Act will provide powers for persons aged 16 and over who are responsible for alcohol-related disorder to be excluded from licensed premises in a defined geographic area for a given length of time under a drinking banning order. Other relevant prohibitions may also be included in the order. Such orders must be for not less than two months and not more than two years in duration.

KEYNOTE

Orders may be made on the application (by way of complaint) of the police or local authority to a magistrates' court that an individual has engaged in criminal or disorderly conduct while under the influence of alcohol, and that such an order is necessary to protect other persons from further conduct by him/her of that kind while he/she is under the influence of alcohol (s. 3(2)).

The magistrates' court may also make a drinking banning order where a person aged 16 or over is convicted of an offence and at the time of its commission was under the influence of alcohol.

Provision is made for the duration of an order to be reduced if an individual satisfactorily completes an approved course to address his/her alcohol misuse behaviour (s. 2(3)).

OFFENCE: **Breach of a drinking banning order—*Violent Crime Reduction Act 2006, s. 11(1)***
- Triable summarily • Fine

The Violent Crime Reduction Act 2006, s. 11(1) states:

> If the subject of a drinking banning order or of an interim order does, without reasonable excuse, anything that he is prohibited from doing by the order, he is guilty of an offence.

4.11.11 Closure Orders for Licensed Premises

The Licensing Act 2003 introduced further police powers to tackle disorder and disturbance connected with certain licensed premises. Although these powers are relatively straightforward, the legislation is complicated by the fact that there are two separate types of closure order: one for some (though not all) licensed premises and the other for *unlicensed* premises.

The following provisions amount to a significant interference with a number of key individual European Convention rights (**see chapter 4.3**) and, as such, the Human Rights Act 1998 considerations should be borne firmly in mind at each stage.

4.11.11.1 Orders to Close Premises in Area Experiencing Disorder

The Licensing Act 2003, s.160 states:

> (1) Where there is or is expected to be disorder in any petty sessions area, a magistrates' court acting for the area may make an order requiring all premises—
> (a) which are situated at or near the place of the disorder or expected disorder, and
> (b) in respect of which a premises licence or a temporary event notice has effect,
> to be closed for a period, not exceeding 24 hours, specified in the order.

KEYNOTE

This provision can be used either where disorder is taking place in an area or where it is expected.

A magistrates' court may make an order under this section only on the application of a police officer who is of the rank of superintendent or above (s. 160(2)). It may only do so if it is satisfied that such an order is *necessary* to prevent disorder (s. 160(3)).

A constable may use such force as may be necessary for the purpose of closing premises ordered to be closed under this section (s. 160(7)).

OFFENCE: **Contravening closure order—*Licensing Act 2003, s. 160***
- Triable summarily • Fine

The Licensing Act 2003, s. 160 states:

> (4) Where an order is made under this section, a person to whom subsection (5) applies commits an offence if he knowingly keeps any premises to which the order relates open, or allows any such premises to be kept open, during the period of the order.

KEYNOTE

This subsection applies:

- in the case of licensed premises, to:
  - the holder of a premises licence in respect of the premises, and
  - the designated premises supervisor (if any) under such a licence;
- in the case of premises in respect of which a temporary event notice has effect, to the premises user in relation to that notice;
- in the case of any other specified premises, to any manager of those premises (s. 160(5)).

Proof that the person acted *knowingly* is an essential element of this offence. Proof that the order was properly made and in force so far as that date and location were concerned will also be an essential part of any prosecution.

4.11.11.2 Closure Orders for Identified Premises

The Licensing Act 2003, s. 161 states:

(1) A senior police officer may make a closure order in relation to any relevant premises if he reasonably believes that—
  (a) there is, or is likely imminently to be, disorder on, or in the vicinity of and related to, the premises and their closure is necessary in the interests of public safety, or
  (b) a public nuisance is being caused by noise coming from the premises and the closure of the premises is necessary to prevent that nuisance.

KEYNOTE

As with the previous order under s. 160, this power can be used where disorder is happening or anticipated (although the requirement here is for any potential disorder to be imminent). The disorder—present or anticipated—can be on the premises or in the vicinity *and* related to them, and the order can be made where their closure is *necessary* in the interests of public safety. The order can also be made where a public nuisance is being caused by noise from the premises and their closure is necessary to prevent it.

An order made under this section may only require relevant premises to be closed for a period not exceeding 24 hours beginning with the coming into force of the order (s. 161(2)). It comes into force at the time *any* constable gives notice of it to an appropriate person who is connected with any of the activities to which the disorder or nuisance relates (s. 161(5)).

The expression 'relevant premises' for the purposes of closure orders is slightly different from other sections in the Act and means premises in respect of which a premises licence or a temporary event notice has effect (s. 161(8)).

'Appropriate person' includes any person who holds a premises licence in respect of the premises, any designated premises supervisor under such a licence, and a manager of the premises (s. 171(5)).

A 'senior police officer' for this purpose is a police officer of, or above, the rank of inspector (s. 161(8)). In determining whether to make a closure order in respect of any premises, that police officer must have regard, in particular, to the conduct of each appropriate person in relation to the disorder or nuisance (s. 161(3)).

A closure order must:

- specify the premises to which it relates;
- specify the period for which the premises are to be closed;

- specify the grounds on which it is made; and
- state the effects of the court and extension procedures under ss.162 to 168 (s. 161(4)).

The 'responsible senior police officer' (i.e. the senior police officer who made the order, or another senior police officer designated for the purpose by the chief officer of police for the police area in which the premises are situated) *must* cancel a closure order and any extension of it if he/she no longer reasonably believes that closure is necessary for the purposes under s. 161(1)(a) or (b)—(see s. 163(2)).

In other cases, the 'responsible senior police officer' *may* cancel a closure order and any extension of it at any time after the making of the order, but *before* a magistrates' court has determined whether to exercise its powers under s. 165(2) in respect of the order and any extension of it (s. 163(1)).

Where a closure order (and any extension of it) is cancelled under this section, the responsible senior police officer must give notice of the cancellation to an appropriate person connected with any of the activities related to the disorder (or anticipated disorder) or nuisance in respect of which the closure order was made (s. 163(3)).

A constable may use such force as may be necessary for the purposes of closing premises in compliance with a closure order (s. 169).

4.11.11.3 Application to Court

As soon as reasonably practicable after a closure order comes into force in respect of any relevant premises, the responsible senior police officer *must* apply to a relevant magistrates' court for it to consider the order and any extension of it (s. 164(1)).

Where the application is made in respect of licensed premises, the responsible senior officer must also notify the relevant licensing authority:

- that a closure order has come into force;
- of the contents of the order and of any extension of it; and
- of the application under subs. (1) (s. 164(2)).

As soon as reasonably practicable after receiving an application, the magistrates' court must hold a hearing to consider whether it is appropriate to exercise any of its relevant powers in relation to the closure order (or any extension), and decide whether to exercise them (s. 165(1)).

Generally the court has powers to revoke the order, to add conditions or exceptions to it, or to leave the order in place until it has carried out a review of the order under s. 167.

Any person aggrieved by a decision of a magistrates' court under s. 165 may appeal to the Crown Court against the decision (s. 166).

OFFENCE: **Contravening closure order—*Licensing Act 2003, s. 161***

- Triable summarily • s. 161(6) offence—fine • s. 165(7) offence—three months' imprisonment and/or a fine not exceeding £20,000

The Licensing Act 2003 states:

> 161(6) A person commits an offence if, without reasonable excuse, he permits relevant premises to be open in contravention of a closure order or any extension of it.
>
> ...
>
> 165(7) A person commits an offence if, without reasonable excuse, he permits relevant premises to be open in contravention of [a magistrates' court order].

KEYNOTE

There is no requirement for the defendant to have acted *knowingly* here, only that he/she acted without reasonable excuse in permitting the premises to be open. Proof that the order was properly made (either by the police or the court), and in force so far as that date and location were concerned, will be critical.

Clearly there are practical reasons why certain people will need to be allowed to come and go from the premises. The legislation takes account of this and specifies when premises will be regarded as being open. Basically, relevant premises are 'open' if someone other than a person who works at, manages, holds a licence for or usually lives at the premises enters the premises and

- they buy or are otherwise supplied with food, drink or anything usually sold on the premises, or
- while they are on the premises, the premises are used for the provision of regulated entertainment (see s. 171).

4.11.11.4 Extension of Closure Order

Where, before the end of the period for which relevant premises are to be closed under a closure order or any extension of it (the 'closure period'), the responsible senior police officer reasonably believes that:

- a relevant magistrates' court will not have determined whether to exercise its powers under s. 165(2) in respect of the closure order, and any extension of it, by the end of the closure period, and
- the following conditions for an extension are satisfied,

he/she may extend the closure period for a further period not exceeding 24 hours beginning with the end of the previous closure period (s. 162).

The conditions referred to are:

- in the case of an order made under s. 161(1)(a), closure is necessary in the interests of public safety because of disorder or likely disorder on, or in the vicinity of and related to, the premises;
- in the case of an order made under s. 161(1)(b), closure is necessary to ensure that no public nuisance is, or is likely to be, caused by noise coming from the premises.

An extension in relation to any relevant premises comes into force when *any* constable gives notice of it to an appropriate person connected with any of the activities to which the disorder or nuisance relates or is expected to relate, but the extension does not come into force *unless the notice is given before the end of the previous closure period* (see s. 162(3) and (4)).

4.11.11.5 Review of Closure Orders

The Act makes extensive provisions for the review of closure orders and imposes a number of obligations on the courts and the licensing authority in this regard. In particular, the authority must reach a determination on the review no later than 28 days after the day on which it receives notification of a closure order from a magistrates' court (see s. 167). Detailed regulations regarding these duties and obligations, including the relevant hearings, are set out in statutory instruments. Among the things that can be done in the course of such a review is the amendment, suspension or revocation of the relevant premises licence.

4.11.11.6 Closure Orders for Unlicensed Premises

The key distinction between these orders and the ones relating to licensed premises is that, in the latter case, the police can make the order while, in the circumstances below, the police simply issue a notice which may lead to a magistrate's order being made.

Where a constable is satisfied that any premises (including land or any place whether covered or not):

- *are being* used or
- *have been* used within the last 24 hours
- for the unlicensed sale/exposure for sale
- of alcohol
- for consumption on or in the vicinity of the premises

he/she may serve a closure notice (s. 19 of the Criminal Justice and Police Act 2001). Note that the above power is available to any police officer of any rank. These powers may also be exercised by the relevant local authority.

The closure notice must specify the alleged use of the premises, the grounds on which it has been issued and the steps that are required to be taken; it must also state the consequences of the notice (as set out in s. 20 of the Criminal Justice and Police Act 2001).

The closure notice must be served by the officer making it (compare the procedure for closure orders above). The notice *must* be served on the person having control of, or responsibility for the activities carried on at the premises; it must also be served on any person occupying another part of any building or other structure of which the premises form part *if* the constable reasonably believes that, at the time of serving the notice, that person's access would be impeded by the making of a closure order resulting from the notice (s. 19(3) and (4)). This is to alert neighbours and adjoining occupiers of the possibility that an order may be made which restricts access to their property.

The notice *may* also be served on anyone else having such control or responsibility or an interest (i.e. a leaseholder, owner or occupier) in the premises (s. 19(5)). The closure notice can be cancelled by serving a cancellation notice and any cancellation will take effect as soon as the cancellation notice is served on at least one of the above people.

'Serving' of notices for all these purposes will include leaving them at, or posting them to, the person's proper address (s. 27 of the 2001 Act).

Where a closure notice has been served, any police officer or local authority may make a complaint to a magistrate no less than seven days after service of the notice (but within six months) seeking a closure order. This effectively gives the owner or person in control etc. of the premises seven days to cease selling alcohol. If the officer (or local authority) is satisfied that this has ceased and there is no reasonable likelihood of the premises being so used again in the future, no complaint can be made to a magistrate (s. 20(3)).

On receiving a complaint under s. 20, a magistrate may summons anyone served with a closure notice to answer the complaint. Thereafter, the court may make an order requiring the premises to be closed immediately to the public and to remain closed until the police or local authority issue a certificate that the need for the order has ceased. The court can also make other conditions within the order, including a requirement that any defendant pay money into court (see generally s. 21). Sections 23 and 24 of the 2001 Act make provision for applications and complaints against closure orders.

4.11.11.7 Enforcement of a Closure Order

Where a closure order has been made, a constable or authorised person may (if necessary using reasonable force) enter the premises concerned at any reasonable time and, having so entered, do anything reasonably necessary to secure compliance with the order (s. 25(1)). If required by or on behalf of the owner or occupier, or person in charge of the premises, the constable or authorised person must produce evidence of their identity and authority before entering the premises (s. 25(2)).

Intentionally obstructing a constable or authorised person in the exercise of these—very wide—powers is, as you would expect, a summary offence (s. 25(3)). Similarly, permitting premises to be open in contravention of an order is an offence in the same way as the offence under s. 161(6) of the Licensing Act 2003 above, as is failing to comply with a closure order generally (see s. 25). The provisions for corporate liability set out in relation to the closure order for licensed premises above also apply to orders relating to unlicensed premises (see s. 26).

4.11.12 Keeping of Smuggled Goods

OFFENCE: **Keeping of smuggled goods—*Licensing Act 2003, s. 144***
- Triable summarily • Fine

The Licensing Act 2003, s. 144 states:

(1) A person to whom subsection (2) applies commits an offence if he knowingly keeps or allows to be kept, on any relevant premises, any goods which have been imported without payment of duty or which have otherwise been unlawfully imported.

(2) This subsection applies—
  (a) to any person who works at the premises in a capacity, whether paid or unpaid, which gives him authority to prevent the keeping of the goods on the premises,
  (b) in the case of licensed premises, to—
    (i) the holder of a premises licence in respect of the premises, and
    (ii) the designated premises supervisor (if any) under such a licence,
  (c) in the case of premises in respect of which a club premises certificate has effect, to any member or officer of the club which holds the certificate who is present on the premises at any time when the goods are kept on the premises in a capacity which enables him to prevent them being so kept, and
  (d) in the case of premises which may be used for a permitted temporary activity by virtue of Part 5, to the premises user in relation to the temporary event notice in question.

KEYNOTE

This offence was primarily created in an attempt to control the influx of tobacco and alcohol products on which the relevant duty had not been paid, but it is far wider than that.

The requirement that the defendant acted *knowingly* is an essential element of this offence.

The court by which a person is convicted of this offence may order the goods in question (and any container for them) to be forfeited and either destroyed or dealt with in such other manner as the court may order (s. 144(4)).

4.11.13 Gambling

The Gambling Act 2005 reformed the law on gambling and contains a regulatory system to govern the provision of all gambling in Great Britain, other than the National Lottery and spread betting.

4.11.13.1 Licensing Authorities

The Gambling Act 2005 provides that the licensing authorities mirror those contained in the Licensing Act 2003, i.e. councils of a district, county or county borough within England and Wales (s. 2). However, responsibility for granting gaming and betting permissions will be shared between the Gambling Commission and licensing authorities.

The 2005 Act, s. 1, contains three licensing objectives which underpin the functions that the Commission and licensing authorities will perform. These objectives are central to the new regulatory regime created by the Act. They are:

- protecting children and other vulnerable people from being harmed or exploited by gambling;
- preventing gambling from being a source of crime or disorder, being associated with crime or disorder, or being used to support crime; and
- ensuring that gambling is conducted in a fair and open way.

KEYNOTE

In relation to the first objective, the Act does this through a number of specific offences that prevent children and young people from being given access to inappropriate or harmful gambling opportunities. In particular, it will be an offence to invite or permit a child or a young person to gamble contrary to the provisions of the Act (see para. 4.11.13.7).

4.11.13.2 The Gambling Commission

The Gambling Commission consists of a chairman and other commissioners appointed by the Secretary of State (s. 20 and sch. 4).

The Commission is required to issue one or more codes of practice for the purpose of ensuring gambling is fair and open, protecting children and other vulnerable persons from harm and exploitation, and making assistance available to persons affected by problems relating to gambling (s. 24). It may investigate whether an offence has been committed under the Act and may institute criminal proceedings (s. 28).

4.11.13.3 The Licensing System

There are four categories of licence under the Gambling Act licensing regime: operating licences, personal licences, premises licences, and temporary use of premises notices.

Operating licences, granted by the Gambling Commission, are one of the principal forms of authorisation under the Act for the lawful provision of facilities for gambling. There are ten different kinds of operating licences for the various forms of gambling facilities, e.g. to operate a casino, to provide facilities for betting, or to act as a betting intermediary (s. 65).

Personal licences are granted by the Gambling Commission and are relevant to operating licence holders who will be required to use personnel who hold a personal licence (s. 127).

Licences need to be held by those directly providing the facilities for gambling, such as a croupier, or those who perform certain functions in a gambling operation but do not actually themselves provide the facilities, such as a compliance officer. Not everyone who works in the gambling industry needs a personal licence.

Premises licences are granted by local authorities and include casino premises, bingo premises, betting premises, adult gaming centres and family entertainment centres.

The holder of an operating licence may give notice in writing (a 'temporary use notice') that he/she intends temporarily to use premises (e.g. hotels, exhibition centres or entertainment venues), and the activity that he/she wishes to provide must be the same activity authorised under the terms of the operating licence (s. 214).

4.11.13.4 Providing Gambling or Premises Without Permission

The 2005 Act provides two comprehensive offences: providing facilities for gambling (s. 33), or using premises for gambling (s. 37), in either case without the appropriate permission. Such permission may come from a licence, permit, or registration granted pursuant to the Act or from an exemption given by the Act. Section 33 does not apply to the provision of facilities for a lottery (s. 34), or to making a gaming machine available for use (s. 35).

4.11.13.5 Definition of Gambling

Gambling means gaming, betting, or participating in a lottery (s. 3), and unlike the previous legislation the 2005 Act provides defintions of both gaming and betting.

'Gaming' and 'game of chance' are defined by s. 6 of the 2005 Act, which states:

(1) In this Act 'gaming' means playing a game of chance for a prize.
(2) In this Act 'game of chance'—
  (a) includes—
    (i) a game that involves both an element of chance and an element of skill,
    (ii) a game that involves an element of chance that can be eliminated by superlative skill, and
    (iii) a game that is presented as involving an element of chance, but
  (b) does not include a sport.

KEYNOTE

A person can play a game of chance even if there are no other players, or the actions of a computer stand in for another player. This means that gaming on a machine or with virtual games is within the scope of the Act (s. 6(3)).

Private gaming is not unlawful as long as no charge is made for participation, that it is equal chance gaming, and does not occur in a place to which the public have access, whether or not on payment (s. 296 and sch. 15).

Betting is defined by s. 9 of the 2005 Act, which states:

(1) In this Act 'betting' means making or accepting a bet on—
  (a) the outcome of a race, competition or other event or process,
  (b) the likelihood of anything occurring or not occurring, or
  (c) whether anything is or is not true.

KEYNOTE

Betting includes bets on races, competitions, or events that have occurred in the past (s. 9(2) and (3)).

Section 4 of the Act provides the meaning of 'remote gambling' as gambling in which persons participate by the use of remote communication, including the internet, telephone, television, radio, or any kind of electronic or other technology for facilitating communication,

Betting is not unlawful if it is 'domestic betting' where the transaction takes place on premises in which each party to the transaction lives, or 'workers' betting' if the transaction is made between persons each of whom is employed under a contract of employment with the same employer (sch. 15).

4.11.13.6 Protection of Children and Young Persons

For the purposes of the Gambling Act 2005, any person aged less than 16 years is defined as a child, and any person aged 16 years or more, but who is not yet 18, is defined as a young person (s. 45).

4.11.13.7 Principal Offences: Children and Young Persons

A number of specific offences in relation to children and young persons are contained in the 2005 Act and these include:

- inviting, causing or permitting a child or young person to gamble: participation by young persons in gambling (ss. 46 and 48)
- inviting children or young persons to enter premises: young persons entering premises (ss. 47 and 49)
- young persons providing facilities for gambling (s. 50)
- employment of children and young persons to provide facilities for gambling; for lottery or football pools; on bingo and club premises; on premises with gaming machines; in a casino (ss. 51 to 55)
- inviting, causing or permitting a child to participate in a lottery (s. 56)
- inviting, causing or permitting a child to participate in football pools (s. 57)
- return of any money (stake) paid by children or young persons (s. 58)
- inviting, causing or permitting a child or young person below a specified age to use a category D gaming machine (s. 59)

KEYNOTE

Generally, people under 18 years of age are not permitted to gamble. There are some exceptions to this general prohibition, for example, young persons may participate in all forms of private and non-commercial gaming and betting, they may also use Category D gaming machines (those with the lowest stakes and prizes (see para. 4.11.13.8), and young persons may participate in lotteries and pool betting football.

Section 63 provides a defence for a person charged with any of the above offences to prove he/she took all reasonable steps to determine the individual's age and reasonably believed that the individual was not a child or young person.

Where a child or young person is required by a constable, enforcement officer, or authorised person, to perform a function in an enforcement operation, nothing done by that child or young person, or the person making the requirement, will be unlawful (s. 64).

4.11.13.8 Gaming Machines

Section 235 of the 2005 Act provides a definition of a gaming machine as a machine that is designed or adapted for use by individuals to gamble (whether or not it can be used for other purposes).

Gaming machines are divided into categories, with different entitlements set out to use the various categories. Section 236 requires the Secretary of State to define, in regulations, four classes of gaming machine, known as categories A, B, C and D. Category B can also be sub-divided into further sub-categories. The categorisation refers to the particular facilities for gambling that are offered on the machine, namely:

- the maximum amounts that can be paid to use the machine;
- the value or nature of the prize delivered as a result of its use;
- the nature of the gambling for which the machine is used; or
- the types of premises on which it can be used.

Category D gaming machines have the lowest levels of charge and prizes that increase in value up to Category A, where there are no limits as to charges and prizes.

4.11.13.9 Alcohol Licensed Premises, Clubs and Fairs

Part 12 of the 2005 Act provides certain gaming allowances, and additional authorisation procedures for gaming and gaming machines for:

- members' clubs;
- commercial clubs;
- miners' welfare institutes;
- alcohol licensed premises; and
- travelling fairs.

In relation to alcohol licensed premises these are premises licensed to supply alcohol for consumption on the premises under part 3 of the Licensing Act 2003 (**see para. 4.11.4**). The premises must contain a bar at which alcohol is served for consumption on the premises. This means that premises such as restaurants, which do not have a bar for serving drinks to customers, are not included.

The gaming and gaming machine exemptions conferred by the 2005 Act only apply at those times when alcohol is authorised to be sold at the premises. Section 279 authorises the provision of gaming facilities on alcohol licensed premises, provided the gaming complies with certain conditions. These conditions are:

- the facilities are limited to equal chance gaming;
- stakes and prizes for the gaming must not exceed any prescribed limits;
- no amount may be deducted or levied from amounts staked or won;
- no participation fees may be charged;
- the games played may only take place on one set of alcohol licensed premises, i.e. there may not be any linking of games between premises; and
- children and young people must be excluded from the gaming.

Alcohol licensed premises may have up to two Category C or D gaming machines (s. 282). This authorisation only applies if the person who holds the relevant alcohol licence has notified the licensing authority of his/her intention to make gaming machines available, and has paid the required notification fee. Further Category C or D gaming machines may be made available in alcohol licensed premises (in addition to the two machines authorised under s. 282) in accordance with a permit known as a licensed premises gaming machine permit (s. 283). The permit will specify the number of gaming machines authorised.

4.11.13.10 Police Powers

Part 15 of the Act deals with the inspection rights and powers that are provided for the police, Commission enforcement officers, and local authority officers to carry out their functions under the Act.

These powers include rights of entry to premises for the purposes of inspection and compliance, and the production of relevant licences. Section 323 provides that a constable may use reasonable force for the purpose of entering premises in pursuance of any power provided, and a person commits an offence if without reasonable excuse he/she obstructs, or fails to cooperate with, a constable, enforcement officer or authorised person who is exercising or seeking to exercise a power under the Act (s. 326).

4.12 Offences and Powers Relating to Information

4.12.1 Introduction

This chapter considers the offences and powers concerned with accessing computer programs and also the handling of personal data held on such programs. In considering what follows in this chapter, it is worth noting the specific police powers in relation to gaining access to stored data, particularly where the data is encrypted in some form (**see chapter 4.4**).

In addition, this chapter also considers the provisions of the Regulation of Investigatory Powers Act 2000 in relation to the interception of communication and the covert acquisition of information about people.

4.12.1.1 Freedom of Information Act 2000

The 2000 Act gives people a general right to access information that is being held by public authorities and is being phased in over five years. Introducing the general right of access to information held by public authorities (subject to a number of exceptions and conditions), the Act also imposes a duty on those public authorities to disclose certain types of information. The Act also creates the office of Information Commissioner whose remit extends to the provisions of the Data Protection Act 1998 (as to which, **see para. 4.12.3**). Public authorities such as the police, the Crown Prosecution Service and government departments, along with National Health Service bodies, schools and colleges are required to draw up a publication scheme setting out their specific plans for making certain types of information available. Under proposed timetables for implementation the police had to set out their publication schemes by June 2003.

The Act creates a default position of a general right of access to information that is recorded and held by public authorities. Within days of its being brought into effect, the Act and its provisions were utilised by the news media to access formerly undisclosed documents and archives revealing a whole range of decisions, reports and data. That is not to say, however, that anyone can simply apply to the police or other criminal justice agencies for disclosure of everything held in their records, and the Act imposes a number of significant exemptions and qualifications on this general 'right to know'. These exemptions and qualifications usually arise from either the nature or the quantity of the material sought.

The Act's provisions are detailed and extensive, and in practice reference should be made to both the Act itself and any relevant local/national policy. The government has also produced a number of guidance documents to assist organisations to meet their obligations and understand the relevant exemptions under the statutory scheme. It is beyond the scope of this Manual to address the Act's provisions in any detail. However, so far as general policing is concerned, the following are among the key areas:

- Any 'person' (including a representative organisation or person who is not a UK national) can make a request for information (in writing) and, if they do so, they are generally entitled to be informed (in writing) whether the public authority holds specified information and to have that information communicated to them (s. 1). There is a payment scheme in operation and any request must be accompanied by the relevant fee if required by the public authority.
- The public authority is under a duty to comply with properly made requests within specified time limits (see s. 10). The authority must also provide advice and assistance to the person applying unless there is an exemption or the application is repeated or vexatious.
- There are significant exemptions to the duty of disclosure and assistance. There is a general exemption where, in all the circumstances of the case, the public interest in withholding the information outweighs that of disclosing it (s. 2). In addition, there is a very practical exemption arising from the limit placed on the cost of obtaining the information sought. Clearly there are internal costs associated with assimilating and disclosing large amounts of information and, if that cost exceeds the appropriate fee payable by the applicant, the public authority will usually be exempt from complying. There is also a whole range of material that will be classed—under part II of the Act—as being 'absolutely exempt'. This includes information the disclosure of which would be prejudicial to law enforcement, national security or defence. There are also many other qualified areas whereby the information is absolutely exempt, such as information attracting legal professional privilege, investigations conducted by public authorities and health and safety.

Applications regarding personal information will need to comply with the relevant parts of the Data Protection framework (as to which **see para. 4.12.3**).

4.12.1.2 Duty to Share Information

Under the provisions of the Criminal Justice Act 2003, a number of public agencies have a duty to share information in relation to violent or dangerous offenders.

This duty arises under the Multi-Agency Public Protection Arrangements (MAPPAs), the primary obligations of which are imposed on 'responsible authorities'. These authorities are the chief officer of police, the local probation board and the Home Secretary (see s. 325(1)).

The primary duty is for the responsible authority to establish arrangements, in cooperation with other listed bodies, for the purpose of assessing and managing risks posed by those convicted of certain violent or sexual offences. Those other listed bodies include youth offending teams, local education and housing authorities, NHS authorities and some registered social landlords.

MAPPAs involve the sharing of information about offenders across agencies, though due regard needs to be given to other legislative requirements such as the Data Protection Act 1998. Statutory guidance is issued by the Secretary of State under s. 325(8) of the 2003 Act and can be accessed on the <www.probation.homeoffice.gov.uk> website under MAPPA Guidance 2007.

4.12.2 Offences under the Computer Misuse Act 1990

The Computer Misuse Act 1990 was enacted to address the growth in the use of computers and the inadequacy of the existing legislation (such as the Theft Act 1968 and the Criminal Damage Act 1971, as to which **see Crime**) in dealing with offences involving computers, such as 'hacking'.

When in force, the Police and Justice Act 2006 will introduce amendments to the 1990 Act to ensure the UK's compliance with the European Union Framework Decision on Attacks Against Information Systems. This compliance requires that penalties relating to 'hacking' into computer systems, unauthorised access to computer material, and the intentional serious hindering of a computer system, reflect the seriousness of the criminal activities that can be involved in committing these offences.

4.12.2.1 Unauthorised Access to Computer Materials

OFFENCE: **Unauthorised access to computer material ('hacking')—*Computer Misuse Act 1990, s. 1***

- Triable summarily • Six months' imprisonment and/or a fine

The Computer Misuse Act 1990, s. 1 states:

(1) A person is guilty of an offence if—
 (a) he causes a computer to perform any function with intent to secure access to any program or data held in any computer;
 (b) the access he intends to secure is unauthorised; and
 (c) he knows at the time when he causes the computer to perform the function that that is the case.
(2) The intent a person has to have to commit an offence under this section need not be directed at—
 (a) any particular program or data;
 (b) a program or data of any particular kind; or
 (c) a program or data held in any particular computer.

KEYNOTE

This offence involves 'causing a computer to perform any function', which means more than simply looking at material on a screen or having any physical contact with computer hardware. In the latter case an offence of criminal damage may be appropriate. Any attempt to log on would involve getting the computer to perform a function (even if the function is to deny you access!). 'Computer' is not defined and therefore must be given its ordinary meaning. Given the multiple functions of many electronic devices such as mobile phones, this could arguably bring them within the ambit of the Act.

As this is a summary offence it cannot be 'attempted' in the sense of the Criminal Attempts Act 1981 (**see Crime, chapter 1.3**). However, the wording of the substantive offence covers virtually every activity, including the switching on of the computer and many activities which would ordinarily be classed as 'merely preparatory'.

Any access must be 'unauthorised'. If the defendant is authorised to *access* a computer, albeit for restricted purposes, then it was originally held that he/she did not commit this offence if he/she then *used* any information for some other unauthorised purpose (e.g. police officers using data from the Police National Computer for private gain (*DPP* v *Bignell* [1998] 1 Cr App R 1)). However, this case was overruled by the House of Lords where an employee of American Express accessed accounts that fell outside her normal scope of work and passed on the information to credit card forgers. Their Lordships held that, although she was authorised to access certain data generally, she was not authorised to access the specific data involved—*R* v *Bow Street Metropolitan Stipendiary Magistrate, ex parte Government of the USA* [2000] 2 AC 216. This case still illustrates that the purpose of the Act is to address unauthorised access as opposed to unauthorised use of data and behaviour such as looking over a computer operator's shoulder to read what is on their screen would not be covered (for offences covering the protection of data, **see para. 4.12.3**).

In order to prove the offence under s. 1 you must show that the defendant intended to secure access to the program or data. This is therefore an offence of 'specific intent' (**see Crime, chapter 1.1**) and lesser forms of *mens rea* such as recklessness will not do.

You must also show that the defendant knew the access was unauthorised.

Section 11(2) of the 1990 Act states that proceedings for an offence under s. 1 must be brought within a period of six months from the date on which evidence sufficient in the opinion of the prosecutor to warrant the proceedings comes to his/her knowledge. It has been held that anyone actively involved in the making or prosecuting of a charge (e.g. the officer in charge of the investigation) can be 'the prosecutor' for this purpose and that the expression is not restricted to the CPS (*Morgans* v *DPP* [1999] 1 WLR 968). It was also held that the time limit began from the date when sufficient evidence to warrant a prosecution had actually come to the knowledge of the prosecutor, i.e. when the evidence was assembled by the officer in charge of the case. It did not mean the point at which the prosecutor *formed the opinion* that the evidence was sufficient. This meant that, where the papers from the case had been assembled but the officer in charge had gone sick, leaving a long delay before the CPS was able to form the opinion that there was sufficient evidence to warrant proceedings, the proceedings were 'out of time' and the defendant's conviction was quashed.

The Privacy and Electronic Communications (EC Directive) Regulations 2003 (SI 2003/2426) regulate the use of cookies and internet tracking devices, along with the use of unsolicited email and text messages. These regulations came into force in December 2003 and guidance in their extent and practical effect has been prepared by the Office of the Information Commissioner.

When in force, the Police and Justice Act 2006 will increase the penalty for the offence under this section and make it a 'triable either way' offence. This will mean that the powers under s. 8 (power of justice of the peace to authorise entry and search of premises), s. 17 (entry for purpose of arrest, etc), s. 18 (general power of seizure, etc.), and s. 32 (search upon arrest) of the Police and Criminal Evidence Act 1984 will be applied to this offence.

4.12.2.2 Definition of Terms

The 1990 Act defines a number of its terms at s. 17 which states:

(2) A person secures access to any program or data held in a computer if by causing a computer to perform any function he—
   (a) alters or erases the program or data;
   (b) copies or moves it to any storage medium other than that in which it is held or to a different location in the storage medium in which it is held;
   (c) uses it; or
   (d) has it output from the computer in which it is held (whether by having it displayed or in any other manner);

and references to access to a program or data (and to an intent to secure such access) shall be read accordingly.

(3) For the purposes of subsection (2)(c) above a person uses a program if the function he causes the computer to perform—
   (a) causes the program to be executed; or
   (b) is itself a function of the program.

(4) For the purposes of subsection (2)(d) above—
   (a) a program is output if the instructions of which it consists are output; and

(b) the form in which any such instructions or any other data is output (and in particular whether or not it represents a form in which, in the case of instructions, they are capable of being executed or, in the case of data, it is capable of being processed by a computer) is immaterial.

(5) Access of any kind by any person to any program or data held in a computer is unauthorised if—

(a) he is not himself entitled to control access of the kind in question to the program or data; and

(b) he does not have consent to access by him of the kind in question to the program or data from any person who is so entitled

but this subsection is subject to section 10.

(6) References to any program or data held in a computer include references to any program or data held in any removable storage medium which is for the time being in the computer; and a computer is to be regarded as containing any program or data held in any such medium.

(7) A modification of the contents of any computer takes place if, by the operation of any function of the computer concerned or any other computer—

(a) any program or data held in the computer concerned is altered or erased; or

(b) any program or data is added to its contents;

and any act which contributes towards causing such a modification shall be regarded as causing it.

(8) Such a modification is unauthorised if—

(a) the person whose act causes it is not himself entitled to determine whether the modification should be made; and

(b) he does not have consent to the modification from any person who is so entitled.

KEYNOTE

Securing access will therefore include:

- altering or erasing a program or data;
- copying or moving a program or data to a new storage medium;
- using data or having it displayed or 'output' in any form from the computer in which it is held.

Under s. 17(5) access is 'unauthorised' if the person is neither entitled to control that type of access to a program or data, nor does he/she have the consent of any person who is so entitled. The provision under s. 17(5)(a) was the basis for the decision in *Bow Street* above. This definition does not affect the powers available to any 'enforcement officers', i.e. police officers or other people charged with a duty of investigating offences (s. 10).

For the powers of a police officer to seize data contained on a computer, see chapter 4.4.

A modification will also take place if, by the operation of *any* computer (not just the one being 'misused') any program or data in the computer concerned is altered, erased or added. A modification is 'unauthorised' if the person whose act causes it is neither entitled to determine whether that modification should be made, nor has the consent of anyone who is so entitled.

4.12.2.3 Unauthorised Access to Computers with Intent

OFFENCE: **Unauthorised access with intent to commit arrestable offence—*Computer Misuse Act 1990, s. 2***

- Triable either way • Five years' imprisonment and/or a fine on indictment
- Six months' imprisonment and/or a fine summarily

The Computer Misuse Act 1990, s. 2 states:

(1) A person is guilty of an offence under this section if he commits an offence under section 1 above ('the unauthorised access offence') with intent—

(a) to commit an offence to which this section applies; or

(b) to facilitate the commission of such an offence (whether by himself or by any other person); and the offence he intends to commit or facilitate is referred to below in this section as the further offence.

(2) This section applies to offences—
  (a) for which the sentence is fixed by law; or
  (b) for which a person of twenty-one years of age or over (not previously convicted) may be sentenced to imprisonment for a term of five years (or, in England and Wales, might be so sentenced but for the restrictions imposed by section 33 of the Magistrates' Courts Act 1980).

(3) It is immaterial for the purposes of this section whether the further offence is to be committed on the same occasion as the unauthorised access offence or on any future occasion.

(4) A person may be guilty of an offence under this section even though the facts are such that the commission of the further offence is impossible.

KEYNOTE

The defendant must be shown to have had the required intent at the time of the access or other *actus reus* (see Crime, chapter 1.2).

The intended further offence does not have to be committed at the same time, but may be committed in future (e.g. where the data is used to commit an offence of blackmail or to secure the transfer of funds from a bank account).

The provision as to impossibility (s. 2(4)) means that a person would still commit the offence if he/she tried, say, to access the bank account of a person who did not in fact exist (for impossibility generally, see Crime, chapter 1.3).

4.12.2.4 Unauthorised Modification of Computer Material

OFFENCE: **Unauthorised modification of computer material—*Computer Misuse Act 1990, s. 3***

- Triable either way • Five years' imprisonment and/or a fine on indictment
- Six months' imprisonment and/or a fine summarily

The Computer Misuse Act 1990, s. 3 states:

(1) A person is guilty of an offence if—
  (a) he does any act which causes an unauthorised modification of the contents of any computer; and
  (b) at the time when he does the act he has the requisite intent and the requisite knowledge.

(2) For the purposes of subsection (1)(b) above the requisite intent is an intent to cause a modification of the contents of any computer and by so doing—
  (a) to impair the operation of any computer;
  (b) to prevent or hinder access to any program or data held in any computer; or
  (c) to impair the operation of any such program or the reliability of any such data.

(3) The intent need not be directed at—
  (a) any particular computer;
  (b) any particular program or data or a program or data of any particular kind; or
  (c) any particular modification or a modification of any particular kind.

(4) For the purposes of subsection (1)(b) above the requisite knowledge is knowledge that any modification he intends to cause is unauthorised.

(5) It is immaterial for the purposes of this section whether an unauthorised modification or any intended effect of it of a kind mentioned in subsection (2) above is, or is intended to be, permanent or merely temporary.

(6) For the purposes of the Criminal Damage Act 1971 a modification of the contents of a computer shall not be regarded as damaging any computer or computer storage medium unless its effect on that computer or computer storage medium impairs its physical condition.

KEYNOTE

This offence covers a whole range of behaviour provided that the defendant is shown to have had the required intent *and* knowledge at the time.

Causing a computer to record that information came from one source when it in fact came from another clearly affects the reliability of that information for the purposes of s. 3. This was made clear by the Divisional Court in a case involving the unauthorised use of international emails from within the computer network of a New York-based company which provided financial information (*Zezev* v *USA*; *Yarimaka* v *Governor of HM Prison Brixton* [2002] 2 CR App R 33).

Implanting viruses would be caught by s. 3.

The purpose of s. 3(6) was to avoid future convictions such as that in *Cox* v *Riley* (1986) 83 Cr App R 54 where the defendant deleted information from a computer card and was convicted of criminal damage (as to which, **see Crime, chapter 1.13**).

For the general powers of seizure (including powers to 'sift' under the Criminal Justice and Police Act 2001) **see chapter 4.4**.

When in force, the Police and Justice Act 2006 will change the wording of s. 3, increase the penalty for the offence and insert two new offences under s. 3A.

4.12.3 The Data Protection Act 1998

The Data Protection Act 1998 affects all international corporations, companies, partnerships and sole traders irrespective of whether they are businesses or not-for-profit organisations. If information is kept on a living person they must comply with the Act and if they process information in certain circumstances they must register with the Information Commissioner.

In essence the Act imposes three key obligations on 'data controllers', who are defined as the people who (alone or jointly) determine the purposes for which, and the manner in which, any personal data are, or are to be, processed (s. 1(1)). The three obligations are:

- Personal data must not be processed unless and until the relevant data controller has registered the details set out at s. 16.
- Data controllers must register with the Commissioner and notify him/her of any changes in the details set out at s. 16.
- Data controllers must comply with the data protection principles set out in sch. 1 to the Act (**see para. 4.12.3.2**).

Section 16 of the Act deals with the 'registrable particulars' required in relation to a data controller, for example, his/her name and address, description of the personal data being, or to be, processed, etc.

Processing personal data without registration and failing to notify the Commissioner of any relevant changes are offences which are triable either way, and punishable on indictment with unlimited fines.

Restrictions are also placed on the storage of, and access to, certain data in 'relevant filing systems'. This means that structured sets of information filed manually, as opposed to being stored on a computer, will also potentially fall within the provisions of the Act.

Individuals are entitled to be given information and explanation by the relevant data controller about some of the personal data held about them, the identity of the source of it and, in certain circumstances, to be informed as to some of the decision-making processes involved in its use.

The Information Commissioner has overall responsibility to ensure that personal data are protected in observance with the Act as well as having similar responsibilities in relation to the Freedom of Information Act 2000 (**see para. 4.12.1.1**). The Commissioner provides guidance and information, resolves complaints, and prosecutes those who commit offences under the Act. The Director of Public Prosecutions may also prosecute offences or give his/her consent to such prosecutions.

Most police organisations have Data Protection Officers and their advice should be sought in every case.

4.12.3.1 Personal Data and Sensitive Personal Data

Section 1 of the 1998 Act states:

> (1) In this Act, unless the context otherwise requires—'data' means information which—
> (a) is being processed by means of equipment operating automatically in response to instructions given for that purpose,
> (b) is recorded with the intention that it should be processed by means of such equipment,
> (c) is recorded as part of a relevant filing system or with the intention that it should form part of a relevant filing system, or
> (d) does not fall within paragraph (a), (b) or (c) but forms part of an accessible record as defined by section 68, or
> (e) is recorded information held by a public authority and does not fall within any of paragraphs (a) to (d).

The Data Protection Act 1998 seeks to protect 'personal data', that is,

> data which relate to a living individual who can be identified—(a) from those data, or (b) from those data and other information which is in the possession of, or is likely to come into the possession of, the data controller, and includes any expression of opinion about the individual and any indication of the intentions of the data controller or any other person in respect of the individual (s. 1(1)).

KEYNOTE

One of the effects of this legislation, combined with Article 8 and Article 10 of the European Convention on Human Rights (**see chapter 4.3**), has been to move closer to what might be called a 'law of privacy', previously unrecognised in English and Welsh law.

In *Johnson* v *Medical Defence Union Ltd (No. 2)* [2007] EWCA Civ 262 it was held that the compilation of information from various manual and electronic files in a computer-related document is not necessarily the creation of data capable of being processed under s. 1(1).

The individual must be capable of being identified from the data that the data controller has or is likely to get. This does not mean that the person's name and/or address must be known. If it is possible to distinguish the individual from other people (e.g. by email addresses which contain the person's name or from CCTV film of them) then it may be that the above test is satisfied.

The definition of personal data would apply to data held on police computers about suspected and convicted offenders and may well apply to other similar paper records. Personal data held on the PNC clearly fall within this category (see *R* v *Rees* [2000] LTL 20 October).

The 1998 Act makes special provision in relation to 'sensitive personal data' which it defines (at s. 2) as:

> ... personal data consisting of information as to—
> (a) the racial or ethnic origin of the data subject,
> (b) his political opinions,
> (c) his religious beliefs or other beliefs of a similar nature,
> (d) whether he is a member of a trade union (within the meaning of the Trade Union and Labour Relations (Consolidation) Act 1992),
> (e) his physical or mental health or condition,
> (f) his sexual life,
> (g) the commission or alleged commission by him of any offence, or
> (h) any proceedings for any offence committed or alleged to have been committed by him, the disposal of such proceedings or the sentence of any court in such proceedings.

4.12.3.2 Data Protection Principles

A crucial element in the 1998 Act is the data protection principles set out at sch. 1. As well as introducing the principles, s. 4 makes it clear that it is the duty of the relevant 'data controller' to comply with those principles wherever they apply. Part I of sch. 1 sets out the principles as being:

> 1. Personal data shall be processed fairly and lawfully and, in particular, shall not be processed unless—
>   (a) at least one of the conditions in Schedule 2 is met, and
>   (b) in the case of sensitive personal data, at least one of the conditions in Schedule 3 is also met.
> 2. Personal data shall be obtained only for one or more specified and lawful purposes, and shall not be further processed in any manner incompatible with that purpose or those purposes.
> 3. Personal data shall be adequate, relevant and not excessive in relation to the purpose or purposes for which they are processed.
> 4. Personal data shall be accurate and, where necessary, kept up to date.
> 5. Personal data processed for any purpose or purposes shall not be kept for longer than is necessary for that purpose or those purposes.
> 6. Personal data shall be processed in accordance with the rights of data subjects under this Act.
> 7. Appropriate technical and organisational measures shall be taken against unauthorised or unlawful processing of personal data and against accidental loss or destruction of, or damage to, personal data.
> 8. Personal data shall not be transferred to a country or territory outside the European Economic Area unless that country or territory ensures an adequate level of protection for the rights and freedoms of data subjects in relation to the processing of personal data.

4.12.3.3 Offences and Exemptions

Section 55 of the 1998 Act creates certain offences and limited exemptions from the first data protection principle and the provisions of s. 7 (**see para. 4.12.3.2**). Section 55 states:

> (1) A person must not knowingly or recklessly, without the consent of the data controller—
>   (a) obtain or disclose personal data or the information contained in personal data, or
>   (b) procure the disclosure to another person of the information contained in personal data.
> (2) Subsection (1) does not apply to a person who shows—
>   (a) that the obtaining, disclosing or procuring—
>   (i) was necessary for the purpose of preventing or detecting crime, or
>   (ii) was required or authorised by or under any enactment, by any rule of law or by the order of a court,

(b) that he acted in the reasonable belief that he had in law the right to obtain or disclose the data or information or, as the case may be, to procure the disclosure of the information to the other person,

(c) that he acted in the reasonable belief that he would have had the consent of the data controller if the data controller had known of the obtaining, disclosing or procuring and the circumstances of it, or

(d) that in the particular circumstances the obtaining, disclosing or procuring was justified as being in the public interest.

(3) A person who contravenes subsection (1) is guilty of an offence.

KEYNOTE

It is an offence under this section to sell personal data if they have been obtained in contravention of subs. (1) (s. 55(4)), and also an offence to offer for sale personal data if they have been obtained in contravention of subs. (1) or have been subsequently obtained in contravention of that subsection (s. 55(5)).

If an organisation fails to renew its registration despite reminders to do so, it can be reasonably inferred that the organisation was aware of its omission and that its continued holding and use of personal data 'knowingly' or 'recklessly' is in breach of the relevant provisions (*Information Commissioner* v *Islington London Borough Council* [2003] LGR 38).

4.12.4 The Regulation of Investigatory Powers Act 2000

The 2000 Act addresses the interception of communications and the covert acquisition of information about people. The Act is intended to make sure that these activities, when carried out by public authorities (as opposed to the journalists referred to above), are subjected to a robust statutory framework which allows for proper independent control and monitoring. A further reason for the legislation is the need for such practices to conform to the European Convention on Human Rights, particularly since the former regulatory provisions were held to be inadequate in this regard (see *Khan* v *United Kingdom* [2000] Crim LR 684).

The 2000 Act appears in five parts:

- part I—the interception of communications and the acquisition/disclosure of data;
- part II—surveillance and use of covert human intelligence sources (informers, agents and undercover officers);
- part III—the investigation of electronic data (e.g. encrypted files);
- part IV—the supervision of investigatory powers and Codes of Practice;
- part V—miscellaneous provisions.

4.12.4.1 Purpose of the Act

The main purpose of the 2000 Act is to control the use of surveillance and Covert Human Intelligence Sources operations by public authorities. Breach of the Act's provisions in a policing context will have three main consequences. The first consequence is that any evidence obtained may be excluded by any court or tribunal as being unfair. The second consequence is that the breach may give rise to proceedings under the relevant police conduct regulations (as to which, **see chapter 4.1**). A third consequence is that a person may make a claim before the Investigatory Powers Tribunal in London. Such a claim can generally be made where the conduct complained of occurred within one year of the complaint, though the Tribunal may consider claims outside this time limit. Claims made to the Tribunal will be separated into those relating to an alleged infringement of a person's human rights by the intelligence services, the police and HM Revenue and Customs and those falling into broader, non-human-rights cases against other public agencies. The Tribunal will investigate whether the relevant authority has carried out any activities in relation to the complainant, their communications or property and, if so, whether the proper authorities were obtained. The Tribunal will then consider whether the complaint or claim is justified and will advise the person whether or not it has found in their favour as soon as possible. If it finds in the person's favour, the Tribunal *may* provide a summary of its findings and, after hearing representations from the person, order such remedial action as it considers appropriate (see generally the Investigatory Powers Tribunal Rules 2000 (SI 2000/2665)). Leaflets advising people how to bring a claim before a Tribunal are available from HMSO.

On a further practical note, most, if not all, police services have an identified bureau or department that deal centrally with the procedures under the 2000 Act and any queries as to the practical implementation of what follows in this section should be directed to them. Under s. 71 of the Act, the Secretary of State must draw up Codes of Practice and these must be taken into account by anyone exercising powers or authority given by the Act (s. 72). Breach of the Codes of Practice is not of itself an offence but the Codes will be admissible in evidence. Although the rest of this chapter sets out some of the key *legal* features, the Codes of Practice make significant additions (particularly in the requirements for authorisation levels) to the practical implementation of the Act and should be referred to in any practical context.

4.12.4.2 Independence and Safeguards

Taking the regulatory framework first, part IV of the 2000 Act provides for a number of independent public appointments, giving the relevant postholders clear duties and powers. The Chief Surveillance Commissioner and the Interception Commissioner are among the key postholders tasked with ensuring the proper supervision of the Act and currently these posts are held by very senior judges. Other appointments include ordinary and assistant Surveillance Commissioners and these posts will generally be held by circuit judges or their equivalent. Part IV also sets up a tribunal with a very wide remit to consider, among other things, complaints arising from the application of the Act.

4.12.4.3 Surveillance and Human Intelligence Sources

Part II of the 2000 Act sets up a system for the authorisation and monitoring of various methods of surveillance and the use of 'covert human intelligence sources'. These activities, which are a significant feature of modern crime management, were formerly governed by agreed codes of conduct and guidelines. Now, in the wake of the Human Rights Act 1998, they have been placed on a firm statutory footing. Failure to follow the statutory requirements will render the relevant public authority liable to an action for breaching the 1998 Act and will also risk any evidence that has been obtained as a result being excluded by the courts.

Part II deals with three main types of activity by the police (and other investigators), namely:

- covert human intelligence sources
- directed surveillance and
- intrusive surveillance (s. 26(1)).

Although only the first of these expressly uses the word 'covert' for the nature of the activity, it is relevant to *all three* of these areas. Part II is concerned with *covert* activity and so, as a general rule, if it is not covert, it is not covered.

Some law enforcement activities fall outside the scope of the Act—an example is 'property interference' which is a very intrusive form of intelligence gathering such as attaching listening devices within people's homes. This type of activity is covered by part III of the Police Act 1997 and is beyond the scope of this Manual.

For a discussion of the issues relating to disclosure of evidence obtained through covert operations, **see Evidence & Procedure, chapters 2.7 and 2.9.**

4.12.4.4 Covert Human Intelligence Sources

The 2000 Act introduces the concept of a 'covert human intelligence source' (CHIS). As with the legislation regulating surveillance (see below), it is the *covert* nature of this type of activity that the Act is concerned with. This is because of the effect of such activity on an individual's rights under the European Convention *when carried out by public authorities* (e.g. the police). As the decided cases show (**see Crime, chapter 1.3**), the use of human intelligence sources has been a significant feature of crime detection and management for many years. However, the various types of activity involving informers, test purchasers and undercover operatives have not been subjected to open statutory regulation. The lack of clear legal regulation of such activity raises the risk of incompatibility with the European Convention and, with the arrival of the Human Rights Act 1998, a robust statutory framework was needed if the activities of the police and other agencies in this area were to avoid fundamental challenge. It is worth noting that, apart from the many other considerations of using CHIS, the police owe a duty to take reasonable care to avoid unnecessary disclosure to the general public of information which an informant has given to them—*Swinney* v *Chief Constable of Northumbria Police (No. 2)* (1999) *The Times*, 25 May.

What is a CHIS?

Broadly, a covert human intelligence source is someone who establishes or maintains a relationship with another person for the *covert* purpose of:

- obtaining information
- providing access to information

or who *covertly* discloses information obtained by the use of such a relationship.

The full definition is set out in s. 26(8) of the 2000 Act. Clearly this definition would cover the types of police operation involved in the decided cases discussed in **Crime, chapter 1.3**. A purpose is 'covert' here only if the relationship (and the subsequent disclosure of information) is conducted in a manner that is calculated to ensure that one of the parties is unaware of that purpose (see s. 26(9)). Therefore the definition would not usually apply to members of the public generally supplying information to the police. Similarly, people who have come across information in the ordinary course of their jobs who suspect criminal activity (such as bank staff, local authority employees, etc.) do not have a covert relationship with the police simply by passing on information. Great care will be needed, however, if the person supplying the information is asked by the police to do something further in order to develop or enhance it. Any form of direction or tasking by the police in this way could make the person a CHIS and thereby attract all the statutory provisions and safeguards.

Practically there are two broad areas to be considered when considering covert human intelligence sources: 'use' of a CHIS and acting as a CHIS. Both areas are strictly controlled by the legislation and require the relevant authorisation if they are to be lawful. 'Using' a CHIS includes inducing, asking or assisting someone to act as such and obtaining information by means of such a source (s. 26(7)(b)).

Generally, covertly recording conversations and other personal information about a particular person will amount to some form of 'surveillance' (and therefore will be governed by the strict rules regulating such operations: see below). However, such use of a CHIS will not amount to 'surveillance' (s. 48(3)).

Who can authorise a CHIS?

Section 27 of the 2000 Act provides that activity involving a CHIS will be lawful for all purposes if it is carried out in accordance with a properly granted authorisation. Such authorisation can cover activity in the United Kingdom or elsewhere.

The people who can grant authorisations for a CHIS are prescribed by s. 30 and the relevant order(s) made by the Secretary of State. The power to authorise the use of a CHIS extends to public authorities far beyond the police (see sch. 1 to the Act). The Regulation of Investigatory Powers (Directed Surveillance and Covert Human Intelligence Sources) Order 2003 (SI 2003/3171), as amended, sets out the relevant people who can authorise the activities of a CHIS. The schedule to the Order identifies the relevant roles and ranks of people in a whole series of public authorities, from the Serious Organised Crime Agency to the Egg Marketing Inspectorate! In the case of police services in England and Wales, the relevant rank is superintendent and above. However, where

- it is not reasonably practicable
- to have the application considered
- by someone of that rank in the same organisation
- having regard to the urgency of the case

then an inspector may generally give the relevant authorisation (see r. 6 of the Order). As with other parts of the Act, however, the Codes of Practice place further restrictions on this area and must be consulted. For example, in the case of a juvenile CHIS or a situation where the CHIS may obtain confidential material, the Code does not allow an inspector to give the relevant authority. Given that this issue will most commonly arise where the police are trying to adduce evidence obtained by a CHIS, it will normally fall to the officer seeking the authorisation to prove that all the above ingredients were in fact present.

How long will an authorisation last?

Unless it is renewed, the authorisation given by a superintendent will ordinarily cease to have effect after 12 months beginning on the day that it was granted (s. 43(3)(b)). If that authorisation was given orally by the superintendent in an urgent case, it will only last for 72 hours unless renewed (s. 43(3)(a)(i)).

Where the case was urgent and the authority was given by an inspector, it will cease to have effect 72 hours later unless renewed (s. 43(3)(a)).

Special provisions exist where the CHIS is under 18 (see below).

A single authorisation can cover more than one regulated activity (e.g. the use of surveillance—see below—and the use of a CHIS) but they operate independently of each other. This means that when one authorisation lapses, any other authorisation made at the same time does not necessarily end as well.

When and how can a CHIS be used?

A designated person must not authorise any activity by a CHIS unless he/she believes it is necessary:

- for the purpose of preventing or detecting crime or of preventing disorder
- in the interests of national security, public safety or the economic well-being of the United Kingdom
- for the purposes of protecting health or collecting or assessing any tax, duty, etc.
- for any other purpose specified by an order made by the Secretary of State

and that to do so is proportionate to what is sought to be achieved (s. 29).

It will not be enough for a designated person to show that he or she thought the use of a CHIS would be very useful or productive in achieving one of the above purposes; he/she must *believe* that is both *necessary* and *proportionate* to the legitimate objective of the operation. Both the requirements for necessity and proportionality are key features of the European Convention. In *R* v *Winter* [2007] WLR (D) 314 it was held the police must act within the statutory provisions and not go beyond what was acceptable. Police conduct that brought about state-created crime was not acceptable except where the accused took the opportunity to break the law of his/her own free will, unless that conduct brought the administration of justice into disrepute.

Generally, the authorisation must be given in writing but, in urgent cases involving superintendents' authority, it may be given orally (s. 43(1)).

In addition to the requirements surrounding authorisation, the 2000 Act makes provisions for the independent management and supervision of a CHIS. A Code of Practice, together with a number of statutory instruments set out clear guidelines for the control and monitoring of CHIS activities and the keeping of records (see, for example, the Regulation of Investigatory Powers (Source Records) Regulations 2000 (SI 2000/2725)). These provisions set out detailed requirements which replace any former rules governing the recruitment and handling of informants. This regulatory framework sets out specific conditions in relation to the deployment of different types of CHIS, from undercover operatives who change their entire identity in order to infiltrate criminal organisations, to 'decoys' who have no direct communication with suspects.

The Code of Practice sets out the requirements of key personnel in the recruitment and management of CHIS such as *handlers* (broadly the person dealing with, directing, monitoring and recording the activities of the CHIS) and *controllers* (the person with the relevant experience who oversees the use of the CHIS); it also defines some core activity that will be caught by the legislation such as the 'tasking' and 'cultivation' of a CHIS.

In addition, the Code sets out the form and content of the records that must be kept when applying for, authorising, using and maintaining a relationship with a CHIS. Among other things, these records will contain the confidential details of the CHIS's true identity, their given name or reference and a risk assessment of their deployment. Details of payments or rewards made along with all information provided by the CHIS must also be recorded.

Very strict controls have been put in place where the CHIS is under 18 years of age (see the Regulation of Investigatory Powers Act (Juveniles) Order 2000 (SI 2000/2793)). One such control is the time for which a written authorisation will last; in the case of a juvenile it is reduced from 12 months to one month. Further restrictions are imposed by the Code of Practice.

For the specific statutory provisions relating to 'test purchases' of alcohol by people under 18, **see chapter 4.11**.

This discussion is merely a summary of the key aspects of this legislation. To find the full extent of the powers and duties under part II, the statutory text should be used, along with the relevant Code of Practice in force at the time.

4.12.4.5 Covert Surveillance

Along with the deployment of CHIS, covert surveillance has become a vital method of obtaining evidence and intelligence in the reduction of crime and the investigation of offences. Surveillance will only be covert for the purposes of part II of the 2000 Act if it is carried out in a manner that is calculated to ensure that people subject to it are unaware that it is (or might be) taking place (see s. 26(9)). Surveillance includes monitoring, observing, listening to and recording people and their conversations, activities and communications (see s. 48(2)). So, if the police are monitoring a person's movements and are trying to do it without that person knowing, the activities will usually amount to 'covert' surveillance. General monitoring of a particular area such as a shopping precinct by CCTV will not usually be covert and therefore will not be caught by the provisions of part II. There are, however, exceptions (see below). The proper use of covert TV detector equipment is neither directed nor intrusive surveillance (s. 26(6)).

For the practical considerations when gathering evidence from observation points, **see Evidence & Procedure, chapter 2.9.**

Directed surveillance

It can be seen from s. 26(1) that there are two particular types of surveillance for the purposes of part II—'directed' and 'intrusive'. It is clear from the wording of s. 26 that surveillance must be one or the other; it cannot be both. Why does it matter? Because the controls surrounding *intrusive* surveillance are far tighter than those imposed on *directed* surveillance. If surveillance is:

- covert (but not 'intrusive'—see below)
- for the purposes of a specific investigation or specific operation
- likely to result in the obtaining of private information about a person (including information about their family life)
- whether or not that person has been specifically identified for the purposes of the investigation/operation, and
- not carried out in immediate response to events/circumstances where it would not be reasonably practicable to seek prior authorisation

it will generally be 'directed' surveillance (s. 26(2)).

Therefore, if in the example cited above, the police *specifically* use the CCTV camera in connection with a planned operation or they are covertly filming an area in a way that is likely to result in the obtaining of private information about someone, these may amount to directed surveillance. On the other hand, if a police officer in immediate pursuit of a suspect conceals himself/herself behind an obstacle in order to watch that person briefly, this would not amount to directed surveillance—because the activity was carried out in immediate response to events/circumstances where it would not have been reasonably practicable to seek prior authorisation.

Note that the *use* of CCTV footage, even if lawfully obtained in the first instance, can potentially give rise to a serious infringement of a person's right to private and family life (under Article 8 of the European Convention—**see chapter 4.3**) and its disclosure should be carefully considered in every case (see *Peck* v *United Kingdom* (Application No. 44647/98) ECHR [2003] EMLR 15).

The interception of a communication in the course of its transmission by a postal or telecommunication system will be 'directed' surveillance if the communication is sent or intended to be received by someone who has consented to its interception and there is no interception warrant (as to which, see below) (s. 48(4)). However, the use of a CHIS (see above) to record or obtain information will not usually amount to 'surveillance' (s. 48(3)).

Authorising directed surveillance

Directed surveillance must be authorised by a designated person (see below) and the authorisation can cover activity in the United Kingdom or elsewhere. The person must not grant the authorisation unless he/she believes that it is *proportionate* to what is sought to be achieved and *necessary* on the specified grounds (s. 28). These specified grounds are the same as those for 'communications data' (see s. 22) with the exception that there is no provision for emergency actions.

The people who can grant authorisations for directed surveillance are prescribed by s. 30 and the relevant order(s) made by the Secretary of State. The power to authorise directed surveillance extends to other public authorities (see sch. 1 to the 2000 Act). The Regulation of Investigatory Powers (Directed Surveillance and Covert Human Intelligence Sources) Order 2003 (SI 2003/3171) as amended, sets out the relevant roles and ranks of the people in those public authorities who can authorise directed surveillance. In the case of police services, the relevant rank will generally be superintendent and above. However, where it is not reasonably practicable:

- to have the application considered
- by someone of that rank in the same organisation
- having regard to the urgency of the case

then an inspector may give the relevant authorisation (see r. 6 of the Order).

Authorisations must generally be made in writing but, in urgent cases, a superintendent may give an oral authorisation (s. 43(1)(a)).

Additional procedural safeguards are made by the Codes of Practice. For instance, if the material sought by the surveillance is subject to legal privilege, is confidential personal information or some journalistic material, the authority of the relevant chief officer will be needed.

How long will an authorisation last?

Unless it is renewed, the authorisation given by a superintendent will ordinarily cease to have effect after three months beginning on the day that it was granted (s. 43(3)(c)). If that authorisation was given orally by the superintendent in an urgent case, it will only last for 72 hours unless renewed (s. 43(3)(a)(i)).

Where the case was urgent and the authority was given by an inspector, it will cease to have effect 72 hours later unless renewed (s. 43(3)(a)).

Intrusive surveillance

Intrusive surveillance is broadly what it says—surveillance activity that immediately intrudes on someone's private life (as protected by Article 8 of the European Convention, **see chapter 4.3**). The statutory regulation of this activity is concerned as much with the intrusive *effects* of such surveillance as the means by which they are carried out and is designed to keep such intrusions by public authorities to an absolute minimum. If surveillance is:

- covert,
- carried out in relation to anything taking place on any *residential premises* or in any *private vehicle*, and

- involves the presence of an individual on the premises or in the vehicle, or is carried out by means of a surveillance device

it will generally be 'intrusive' surveillance (s. 26(3)).

The definition of residential premises extends much wider than a conventional home. Covert rural surveillance operations and the use of specialist devices in houses or hotel rooms will generally fall into the category of intrusive surveillance. In addition to the activities authorised under part II of the 2000 Act, the Police Act 1997 makes further provision governing the interference with property for the purposes of evidence/intelligence. These highly specialised areas of property interference are beyond the scope of this Manual.

The elements of intrusive surveillance listed above require the presence of people or devices on the relevant premises/vehicle. However, if the surveillance:

- involves a surveillance device and
- relates to activities taking place on residential premises or in private vehicles
- but without the device being present on the premises or in, on or under the vehicle

it will still be 'intrusive' if that device *consistently* provides information of the same quality and detail as might be expected from a device that was actually present on the premises or in the vehicle (s. 26(5)). An example would be long-range audio equipment monitoring conversations or powerful lenses used to watch people inside a house and giving the same quality and detail of image as if a camera had been placed in the premises. This is in keeping with the aims of part II of the Act in this area, namely to minimise the intrusive effects of such surveillance on people's legitimate right to conduct their private and family life without interference from the State.

Surveillance carried out by means of a device for the purpose of providing information about the location of a vehicle (e.g. a tracking device) is not 'intrusive' (s. 26(4)(a)).

Authorising intrusive surveillance

Given the type of activity that is covered by this category, the restrictions on its authorisation are very tight. In addition, many types of activity under this heading will involve applications for 'multiple' authorisations and specialist advice must be sought.

Generally, the person who will authorise intrusive surveillance by the intelligence services, the armed forces and other specified bodies is the Secretary of State. In relation to the police (including the armed services police) the authority will be sought from senior authorising officers. Broadly these will be chief officers, the Commissioners/Assistant Commissioners of the Metropolitan and City of London Police and the Director-General of the Serious Organised Crime Agency (SOCA) (s. 32). Provision is also made for authorisations by designated deputies in some cases. In keeping with the tenor of the Act, these officers must not grant the relevant authorisation unless they believe that it is necessary and proportionate to do so:

- in the interests of national security;
- for the purpose of preventing or detecting 'serious crime', for example, offences for which a person aged 21 or over could reasonably expect to be sentenced to at least three years' imprisonment on his/her first offence, or offences resulting in substantial financial gain, involving the use of violence or a large number of people pursuing a common purpose (s. 81(3));
- for the purpose of safeguarding the economic well-being of the United Kingdom.

These are very similar to the grounds on which an interception warrant may be authorised (see below). The 2000 Act makes detailed provision for the recording and notification of authorisations. Anyone granting a police, SOCA or Revenue and Customs authorisation for intrusive surveillance must notify a Surveillance Commissioner (as to which, see above) in writing as soon as reasonably practicable (s. 35). This is because, except in urgent cases, the authorisation will not take effect until the Surveillance Commissioner has approved it and given written notification to that effect to the authorising officer (s. 36). The purpose behind this process is to make the system open to independent scrutiny and monitoring, largely in satisfaction of the requirements of the Human Rights Act 1998. Surveillance Commissioners can quash or revoke authorisations and order the destruction of certain records and materials obtained by intrusive surveillance. Senior authorising officers may appeal against decisions of Surveillance Commissioners to the Chief Surveillance Commissioner.

As in the case of directed surveillance, authorisations last for three months and urgent authorisations granted, for example, by an Assistant Chief Constable last for 72 hours. Authorisations can be renewed before they cease to have effect provided that the criteria for authorisation are still satisfied.

4.12.4.6 Interception of Communications

The interception of communications is relevant to police operations for two reasons—first, because there are several substantive offences caught by this area (including listening in to police communications) but, more importantly, because the interception and monitoring of some communications have become important tools for the police and other investigatory bodies, particularly in proving a defendant's involvement in some of the incomplete offences covered by this chapter. Also, of increasing importance, is the interception of communications for intelligence-gathering purposes, particularly when monitoring terrorism and organised crime.

OFFENCE: **Unlawful interception of public communications—*Regulation of Investigatory Powers Act 2000, s. 1(1)***

- Triable either way • Two years' imprisonment and/or a fine on indictment
- Fine summarily

The Regulation of Investigatory Powers Act 2000, s. 1(1) states:

> (1) It shall be an offence for a person intentionally and without lawful authority to intercept, at any place in the United Kingdom, any communication in the course of its transmission by means of—
> (a) a public postal service; or
> (b) a public telecommunication system.

KEYNOTE

This offence is similar to the former offence under the Interception of Communications Act 1985 (which it repeals). It cannot be prosecuted without the prior authority of the DPP.

The offence relates to public postal services and public telecommunication systems. Broadly, these are:

- Public postal service—any postal service which is offered or provided to the public in any part of the United Kingdom.
- Public telecommunication system—the parts of a public telecommunications service that are located within the United Kingdom.

The full definition is set out at s. 2(1). Under the former offence under the 1985 Act, interception of a communication between a cordless handset and the base set of a domestic telephone was held to fall outside the concept of a 'public' system, even though the line ultimately connected with a public system (*R* v *Effik* [1995] 1 AC 309). Under such circumstances there would now probably be an offence under s. 1(2) (see below).

To prove this offence you must show that the defendant acted intentionally and without lawful authority. For a full discussion of the concept of intent, **see Crime, chapter 1.1**.

For the statutory provisions governing 'lawful authority' here, see below.

As in other parts of the Act, special provision is made for international mutual assistance.

4.12.4.7 What Amounts to Interception?

What amounts to 'interception' is set out in s. 2(2) of the 2000 Act. This generally provides that a person only intercepts a communication in the course of its transmission by a telecommunication system if he/she:

- modifies or interferes with the system or its operation
- monitors transmissions made by means of the system or by wireless telegraphy to or from apparatus comprised in the system

so as to make some or all of the contents of the communication available to a person other than the sender or intended recipient *while the communication is being transmitted*.

A communication is 'being transmitted' for the purposes of this offence when it is stored on the system for the intended recipient to collect or access (s. 2(7)). This means that email messages awaiting collection/access by the intended recipient are still 'being transmitted', as are unreceived or uncollected pager messages.

Again, the full definition can be found in s. 2 of the 2000 Act. The expression *'in the course of its transmission'* is critical in applying the extent of the definition of interception. In a case where a listening device installed by the police in the defendant's car had recorded the defendant speaking on his mobile phone, the Court of Appeal held that this did not amount to an 'interception', and mere eavesdropping on a conversation between one person at one end of a mobile telephone or two people face-to-face could not constitute communication in the course of transmission. The listening device in question did not distinguish between what the defendant said to people present in the car and what he said into the phone. The Court held that the wording of the Act denoted some *interference* with, or *abstraction* of, a *signal* during the process of transmission. Simply recording a voice that happened to be talking into a phone at the time did not therefore amount to an interception (*R* v *Allsopp* [2005] EWCA Crim 703; see also *R* v *E (Admissibility: Covert Listening Device)* [2004] 1 WLR 3279). In addition, the Court of Appeal held that, in this context, the 2000 Act was compatible with both the European Data Protection Directive (Directive 97/66 EC) and Article 8 of the European Convention on Human Rights (**see para. 4.3.11**).

There is no equivalent definition for the interception of postal communications and this will presumably be a question of fact to be addressed on the merits of each case. Having set out what the offence covers, the Act goes on to specify particular activities that will *not* be caught by this section. These include:

- the interception of any communication broadcast for general reception—this covers broadcasts such as television and radio; it does not extend to pagers and mobile phone communications and these *are* covered by the Act;
- the interception of certain types of 'traffic data'—this means certain types of information that are needed to deliver or route the communication.

OFFENCE: **Unlawful interception of private communications—*Regulation of Investigatory Powers Act 2000, s. 1(2)***

- Triable either way • Two years' imprisonment and/or a fine on indictment
- Fine summarily

The Regulation of Investigatory Powers Act 2000, s. 1(2) states:

(2) It shall be an offence for a person—

(a) intentionally and without lawful authority, and

(b) otherwise than in circumstances in which his conduct is excluded by subsection (6) from criminal liability under this subsection,

to intercept, at any place in the United Kingdom, any communication in the course of its transmission by means of a private telecommunication system.

KEYNOTE

This offence had no equivalent under the Interception of Communications Act 1985. Like the offence under s. 1(1), this offence also requires the authority of the DPP before being prosecuted.

Although sharing many of the other features of the offence under s. 1(1), this offence applies only to the interception of a communication that is being transmitted by a private telecommunication system.

A 'private telecommunication system' is defined at s. 2(1). Generally, it must satisfy the following criteria. It must be:

- attached (directly or indirectly) to a public telecommunication system (see above); and
- have apparatus comprised in it which is located in the United Kingdom and used for attaching it to that public telecommunication system.

Therefore a privately owned office telephone system in England and Wales which is locally attached to a public telecommunication system would now come under s. 1. So too would the type of police station payphone which was routed via the internal telephone system in *R* v *Ahmed* [1995] Crim LR 246 (under the former provisions, these types of telephone system fell outside the statutory controls preventing interception of calls). Interestingly, one of the earliest cases in this area of alleged human rights infringement within the United Kingdom arose out of the tapping of a senior police officer's telephone calls by her employer (*Halford* v *United Kingdom* (Application 20605/92) (1997) 24 EHRR 523).

As with the s. 1(1) offence, the above offence requires proof of intention and also the absence of lawful authority (as to which, see below). However, it contains a further stipulation that the interception is not excluded by s. 1(6). Subsection (6) exempts some interception of communications where the interceptor has a right to control the operation or use of the system or has the consent of such a person to intercept the communication. This means the right to authorise or forbid the operation of the system (*R* v *Stanford* [2006] EWCA Crim 258). The sort of interception envisaged here is where organisations intercept and monitor communications made on their telecommunication systems. Monitoring and recording communications in this way is permitted by the Telecommunications (Lawful Business Practice) (Interception of Communications) Regulations 2000 (SI 2000/2699). In addition the Data Protection Commissioner has issued a code of conduct for employers, setting out conditions that should be observed when monitoring employee's communications at work.

Returning to the above offence. Bottom line? You must show that the person intercepted the communication intentionally, without lawful authority and under circumstances that are not exempted by s. 1(6).

Lawful authority is discussed below.

4.12.4.8 Lawful Authority

Under s. 1(5), conduct has lawful authority for the purposes of the s. 1 offences above if it falls into one of three areas:

- conduct in accordance with any statutory power (apart from this section) for the purpose of obtaining information or of taking possession of any document or other property in relation to any *stored communication*;
- conduct authorised under s. 3 or 4; or
- conduct in accordance with a warrant under s. 5.

The conduct authorised by the warrant must be proportionate to what is sought to be achieved by it (s. 5(2)(b)).

Each of these three areas is considered below.

Stored communication

The first exception referred to above relates to occasions where the person is exercising a statutory power other than s. 1 of the 2000 Act for the purpose of obtaining information or taking possession of any document or other property *in relation to any stored communication*. The example given by the Home Office of such a situation is where police officers have recovered a pager from a person in custody and they apply to a circuit judge for an order under sch. 1 to the Police and Criminal Evidence Act 1984 to access its messages.

Conduct authorised under section 3 or 4

Section 3 of the 2000 Act authorises certain *types of interception* without the need for a warrant. In general, it covers interception where:

- both the sender and intended recipient have consented or the person intercepting has reasonable grounds to believe they have both consented;
- either the sender or intended recipient have consented and surveillance by means of that interception has been authorised under part II (as to which, see below)—this might cover the situation where the police are monitoring threatening telephone calls made to a victim or calls made in connection with blackmail demands;
- the interception is by/on behalf of the provider of the postal or telecommunications service for purposes connected with it (examples of this conduct would include postal workers who need to open mail in order to return it to the sender);
- the person is authorised under the Wireless Telegraphy Act 2006, s. 48 (as to which, see below).

Section 4 of the 2000 Act generally sets out occasions where *other authorities* might permit the interception of certain communications without the need for a warrant such as communications to/from prisons and high security psychiatric hospitals. Section 4 also makes provision for interception of communications involving people who are (or are believed to be) outside the United Kingdom.

Interception warrants

Section 5 of the 2000 Act allows the Secretary of State to issue interception warrants under certain, very stringent, conditions. Section 5(2) says that the Secretary of State must not issue an interception warrant unless he/she *believes* that the warrant is *necessary* and proportionate:

- in the interests of national security;

- for the purpose of preventing or detecting 'serious crime', for example, offences for which a person aged 18 or over could reasonably expect to be sentenced to at least three years' imprisonment on his/her first offence, or offences resulting in substantial financial gain, involving the use of violence or a large number of people pursuing a common purpose (s. 81(3));
- for the purpose of safeguarding the economic well-being of the United Kingdom (where the relevant acts or intentions relate to people outside the United Kingdom (s. 5(3));
- for the purpose of 'international mutual assistance'.

Note that, emphasised in italics above, it is not enough that the Secretary of State 'suspects' that these threats or needs exist, nor that he/she considers that an interception warrant might be useful, valuable or effective. The Secretary of State must believe that the warrant is necessary for one of the purposes set out. The wording used in s. 5 is in accordance with Article 8 of the European Convention (as to which, **see chapter 4.3**). Furthermore, the Secretary of State must consider whether the information that is sought under the application for a warrant could be obtained by other means (s. 5(4)). In urgent cases an interception may be signed by a senior official who has been expressly authorised to do so by the Secretary of State (s. 7).

As a general rule, most interception warrants are valid for three months unless cancelled (s. 9). Interception warrants issued in urgent cases by a senior official last for five working days only (s. 9(1) and (6)(a)). The Terrorism Act 2006 has amended s. 9 in relation to an interception warrant endorsed by the Secretary of State; where the issue of a warrant is believed to be necessary on the grounds falling within s. 5(3), the warrant is valid for six months from the date of issue (s. 9(6)(ab)).

You can apply for an interception warrant only if you are doing so on behalf of one of the people set out in s. 6(2). These people include the Commissioner of the Metropolitan Police, the Director-General of SOCA and various chief officers of the intelligence and Revenue and Customs services.

The 2000 Act makes several provisions relating to the providers of communications services (telecommunications companies, etc.) and imposes duties on them to help implement the execution of interception warrants. It also goes on to provide a system of general safeguards against abuse or misuse of the powers in relation to interception of communications.

Intercepted information is usually collated for intelligence rather than evidential purposes. With this is mind, and in order to protect both the sources and content of any intercepted communications, the 2000 Act imposes a general prohibition on disclosing such information in evidence, or generally raising any matters which are likely to reveal the existence (or absence) of a warrant. The prohibition extends, not only to the existence/absence of warrants, but also to any reference in any proceedings that tends to suggest a relevant person (e.g. police officers, investigators or telecommunications staff) has done a relevant act (such as applying for a warrant). The general ban on any use of this type of information for evidential purposes or in connection with criminal proceedings is subject to a number of exceptions, including proceedings for an offence under s. 19 (see below) and in connection with a prosecutor's duty of disclosure under certain circumstances. These are fairly technical evidential points and can be found in full in ss. 17 and 18.

However, if a prosecution is based on the position that the contents of an intercepted call were transmitted via a *private* telecommunications system, carried out with the consent of the relevant person, a defendant can still argue that the interception had occurred in a *public* telecommunications system. This, it has been held, is essential to the fairness of any proceedings and s. 17 does not prevent the defendant from raising the issue (*Attorney-General's Reference (No. 5 of 2002)* [2004] UKHL 40).

If enacted, the Interception of Communications (Admissibility of Evidence) Bill will, with the permission of a court, permit the introduction of interception evidence and evidence of communications data in cases involving serious crime and offences relating to terrorism.

4.12.4.9 Unauthorised Disclosures

The 2000 Act creates the following offence:

OFFENCE: **Unauthorised disclosures—*Regulation of Investigatory Powers Act 2000, s. 19***

- Triable either way • Five years' imprisonment and/or a fine on indictment
- Six months' imprisonment and/or a fine summarily

The Regulation of Investigatory Powers Act 2000, s. 19 states:

(1) Where an interception warrant has been issued or renewed, it shall be the duty of every person falling within subsection (2) to keep secret all the matters mentioned in subsection (3).
(2) The persons falling within this subsection are—
(a) the persons specified in section 6(2);
(b) every person holding office under the Crown;
(c) every member of the staff of the Serious Organised Crime Agency;
(ca) every member of the Scottish Crime and Drugs Enforcement Agency;
(e) every person employed by or for the purposes of a police force;
(f) persons providing postal services or employed for the purposes of any business of providing such a service;
(g) persons providing public telecommunications services or employed for the purposes of any business of providing such a service;
(h) persons having control of the whole or any part of a telecommunication system located wholly or partly in the United Kingdom.
(3) Those matters are—
(a) the existence and contents of the warrant and of any section 8(4) certificate in relation to the warrant;
(b) the details of the issue of the warrant and of any renewal or modification of the warrant or of any such certificate;
(c) the existence and contents of any requirement to provide assistance with giving effect to the warrant;
(d) the steps taken in pursuance of the warrant or of any such requirement; and
(e) everything in the intercepted material, together with any related communications data.
(4) A person who makes a disclosure to another of anything that he is required to keep secret under this section shall be guilty of an offence ...

KEYNOTE

This offence carries a far greater sentence than the offences of unlawful interception of communications. It is clearly intended to apply to police officers and others involved in an investigation, and it extends to support staff as well.

It will be a defence for a person charged with this offence to show that he/she could not reasonably have been expected, after first becoming aware of the matter disclosed, to take steps to prevent the disclosure (s. 19(5)). Nevertheless, this offence imposes a very clear duty on the people set out above. The offence makes no specific requirement as to state of mind.

Further defences exist for some communications with professional legal advisers and other proper communications with the Interception of Communications Commissioner.

4.12.4.10 Wireless Telegraphy

The unauthorised interception of radio communications is a summary offence under s. 48 of the Wireless Telegraphy Act 2006, and a similar offence under the previous legislation was used where defendants had deliberately tuned in to police radio messages (*DPP* v *Waite* [1997] Crim LR 123).

The Regulation of Investigatory Powers Act 2000 now greatly restricts the ability of a designated person to authorise interception of wireless telegraphy but this type of interception is outside the scope of this Manual.

4.12.4.11 Communications Data

Chapter II of the 2000 Act deals with the concept of 'communications data'. This is broadly information that relates to the use of the particular communications service but not the *content* of the communication itself. The full definition can be found in s. 21(4).

Examples of communications data would include:

- itemised telephone bills
- telephone subscriber details
- addresses or other marks on the outside of postal packages and letters.

Access to this type of data is clearly useful to the investigation of crime and the gathering of criminal intelligence. However, in line with the European Convention, this activity must be regulated by clear and accessible legal rules.

Chapter II deals with the obtaining and disclosure of this communications data; it does not apply to any *interception* of such data while the communication is being transmitted (as to which, see above).

Section 22 sets out the circumstances when, and the purposes for which such communications data may be obtained. In order to obtain communications data the designated person (see below) must *believe* it is *necessary* to obtain the data:

- for the purpose of preventing or detecting crime or preventing disorder;
- in the interests of national security, public safety or the economic well-being of the United Kingdom;
- for the purposes of protecting health or collecting or assessing any tax, duty, etc.;
- in an emergency, for the purpose of preventing (or mitigating) death, injury or damage to a person's physical or mental health;
- to assist investigations into alleged miscarriages of justice;
- for the purpose of assisting in identifying any person who has died otherwise than as a result of crime, or who is unable to identify him/herself because of a physical or mental condition, other than one resulting from crime, or obtaining information about the next of kin or other connected persons of such a person or about the reason for his/her death or condition;
- for any other purpose specified by an order made by the Secretary of State;

and that to do so is *proportionate* to what is sought to be achieved.

Both the requirements for necessity and proportionality are key features of the European Convention.

Note that, although the requirements for *necessity* are the same here as for interception warrants, the grounds contain significant differences. In particular, a much wider class of people can authorise the obtaining of communications data under chapter II and there is no stipulation that 'serious crime' is involved.

The 'designated person' who can authorise communications data to be obtained is the person holding a specified rank or office in one of the relevant public authorities. Those public authorities here include police forces, the SOCA, HM Revenue and Customs and any other public authority specified by the Secretary of State in appropriate regulations. The data can be obtained by an authorised person collecting it him/herself or by serving a notice on the holder of the data requiring him/her to comply with the terms of the notice.

Additional public authorities, specified for the purposes of s. 25 to acquire communications data under the provisions in Chapter II of the Act, are set out in the Regulation of Investigatory Powers (Communications Data) Order 2003 (SI 2003/3172) as amended. That Order specifies those individuals within each public authority (and the public authorities already listed in the Act) who are entitled to acquire communications data; it also puts restrictions on the grounds on which they may acquire communications data and the types of communications data they can acquire.

The format for recording authorisations and notices is set out in s. 23. Generally any such authorisations or notices will last for one month unless cancelled or renewed.

Under the Anti-terrorism, Crime and Security Act 2001 the Secretary of State may make Codes of Practice for the retention and storage of communications data (Retention of Communications Data (Code of Practice) Order 2003 (SI 2003/3175)).

This discussion is merely a summary of the key aspects of this legislation. To find the full extent of the powers and duties under the Act, the statutory text should be used along with the relevant Code of Practice in force at the time.

4.13 Diversity, Discrimination and Equality

4.13.1 Introduction

This chapter sets out in brief summary the key features of the law relating to diversity, discrimination and equality in the workplace. This area of employment law is very specialised and, on occasions, very sensitive. So far as the police are concerned, equality and diversity are among some of the most important and sensitive issues.

The specific legislation governing each area of diversity is overseen by the Commission for Equality and Human Rights (CEHR). The CEHR was established by the Equality Act 2006 to replace the previous three separate commissions (Equal Opportunities Commission, Commission for Racial Equality, and the Disability Rights Commission). In addition to undertaking the work of the three previous commissions the CEHR also assumes responsibility for promoting equality and combating unlawful discrimination in three new strands, namely sexual orientation, religion or belief, and age. It also has responsibility for the promotion of human rights. The CEHR is required to promote understanding of the importance of human rights and encourage public authorities to comply with s. 6 of the Human Rights Act 1998, which prohibits them from acting in a way which is incompatible with the Convention rights (**see chapter 4.3**).

The Equality Act 2006 makes it unlawful to discriminate on the grounds of religion or belief in the provision of goods, facilities and services, education, the use and disposal of premises, and the exercise of public functions. A similar provision is also provided in relation to discrimination on the grounds of sexual orientation. In addition, the 2006 Act has created a duty on public authorities to promote equality of opportunity between women and men ('the gender duty'), and prohibits sex discrimination and harassment in the exercise of public functions.

Most police organisations have employee relations or human resources departments to help both managers and employees in these fields. The police staff associations, together with other groups such as the National Black Police Association, will also provide help in ensuring that the spirit of this legislation is observed at work.

Most police organisations also have grievance procedures to deal with issues of equality in an informal setting. Although there is a growing array of legislative provisions to protect the rights of various groups within the workplace, recourse to the law is not the only—or even the best—solution to issues of diversity. The government has introduced further legislation aimed at averting litigation through the courts and employment tribunals and encouraging local resolution.

In most circumstances, a chief officer will now be liable for most of the actions of his/her staff in the course of their duties (**see chapter 4.1**). Generally, this concept of 'vicarious liability' for acts committed by people in the course of their work is passed up the chain to their employer. As *public office holders*, police officers are not 'employees' of their chief officers and therefore there are occasions where chief officers have not been held vicariously liable for wrongful acts committed by their police staff. This situation has attracted some criticism, particularly in the area of race relations. Under the Race Relations Act 1976 as it originally stood, chief officers had been held not to be vicariously liable for the discriminatory behaviour of their officers (see *R* v *Farah* (1996) *The Times*, 17 October). Similarly, there has been a lack of clarity as to which public authorities are covered by the provisions of the 1976 Act. As a result of these anomalies, highlighted in a number of cases, not least the inquiry into the death of Stephen Lawrence, the government introduced the Race Relations (Amendment) Act 2000 (see below). Increasingly, employment legislation is being drafted in a way that applies its provisions to police officers and their chief constables/police authorities *as if* they were in an employer–employee relationship. Further evidence of this trend can be seen in the recent extension to the Disability Discrimination Act 1995 (**see para. 4.13.7**). The Police Reform Act 2002 also broadened the vicarious liability of chief officers for the conduct of their officers (**see chapter 4.1**).

While these issues may now have been resolved, there was, until recently, still uncertainty as to the extent of a chief officer's liability under the Sex Discrimination Act 1975 for the individual acts of his/her officers and the same arguments that preceded the Race Relations (Amendment) Act 2000 could be raised (for these arguments, see *Chief Constable of Bedfordshire* v *Liversidge* [2002] ICR 1135). However, the introduction of secondary legislation (see below) has now placed the whole area of discrimination on a much clearer footing.

4.13.1.1 Discrimination in Code of Conduct for Police Officers

It is worth noting that discrimination and victimisation are included in the Code of Conduct for police officers (**see chapter 4.1**). Where acts amounting to discrimination take place outside the workplace, the employer and employees may still be caught within the framework of the legislation. So, for instance, where police officers engage in inappropriate sexual behaviour towards a colleague at a work-related social function, a tribunal may be entitled to hold that the function was an extension of the workplace and so hold the chief officer liable for the acts of his/her officers at that function (see *Chief Constable of Lincolnshire* v *Stubbs* [1999] IRLR 81). Similarly, the actions (or inaction) of a fellow officer or supervisor are capable of attracting personal liability to that individual under a claim for discrimination in addition to any claim that the victim might have against the relevant chief officer (see *AM* v *WC* [1999] ICR 1218) though this is an area that is still far from clear.

4.13.2 The Law

There are four main sources of primary legislation which deal with equality and discrimination:

- Race Relations Act 1976
- Sex Discrimination Act 1975
- Equal Pay Act 1970
- Disability Discrimination Act 1995.

All of these Acts deal with matters which fall under the heading of employment law as that is the main area of their concern.

In addition to this legislation, the role of European law in this area is of considerable significance and, as well as case law from the European Court of Justice, includes European Directives such as the Equal Pay Directive (75/117/EEC), the Equal Treatment (Employment) Directive (76/207/EEC and 2002/73/EC); the Equal Treatment Framework Directive (2000/78/EC), and a Consolidating Directive (2006/54/EC). The last Directive deals with the implementation of the principle of equal opportunities and equal treatment of men and women in matters of employment and occupation throughout the European Community.

There are other pieces of legislation, such as those specific offences under the Public Order Acts (**see chapter 4.6**) which are aimed at discriminatory behaviour by anyone under certain circumstances. There are also offences under the Code of Conduct (**see chapter 4.1**) which deal with other forms of discriminatory behaviour by police officers in the course of their duties.

Generally, however, there is no overall legal restriction on discriminatory behaviour. There is no 'Equal Opportunities Act' and the United Kingdom has no written constitution protecting the individual from being discriminated against other than in the circumstances described in this chapter and the specific provisions made under the European Convention on Human Rights (**see chapter 4.3**). It is worth noting that although Article 14 of the Convention gives individuals a right not to be discriminated against on certain grounds, this right exists alongside the other Convention rights and applies to the way in which *those rights* are protected; it does not grant a free-standing right not to be discriminated against. One of the cornerstones of the European Community, however, is the achievement of equality of treatment for individuals of each Member State within the Community. European law has had a significant influence on the impact of equal opportunities and discrimination (at least on the grounds of sex) in England and Wales.

The purpose of the two main Acts, the Race Relations Act 1976 and the Sex Discrimination Act 1975, was summed up by Waite LJ in *Jones* v *Tower Boot Company Ltd* [1997] 2 All ER 406:

> The legislation . . . broke new ground in seeking to work upon the minds of men and women and thus affect their attitude to the social consequences of differences between the sexes or the distinction of skin colour. Its general thrust was educative, persuasive, and where necessary coercive . . .

His Lordship went to on to say how, against this background, the courts would not adopt a technical or restrictive approach when interpreting the law in this area.

4.13.2.1 Procedure

The procedure relating to claims made against employers was significantly altered by the Employment Rights (Dispute Resolution) Act 1998. The 1998 Act renamed industrial tribunals 'employment tribunals' to convey their function more clearly. The Act went on to make provision for regulations permitting tribunals to determine cases without a full hearing or, at times, without a hearing at all under certain circumstances. It also made provisions for 'compromise agreements' made by relevant independent advisers—as opposed to just qualified lawyers—and set out a class of individuals, to be known as 'legal officers' who carry out some of the more straightforward functions currently carried out by tribunal chairpersons.

4.13.3 The Race Relations Act 1976

The Race Relations Act 1976 deals with racial discrimination, the first type of discrimination to be prohibited in England and Wales.

Under s. 3, the 1976 Act aims to control discrimination (**see para. 4.13.10**) on grounds of:

- colour
- race
- nationality
- ethnic or national origins.

The meaning of 'nationality' here is wider than the normal 'legal' meaning and has been held by the Scottish Court of Session to include citizenship acquired at birth (*Souster* v *BBC Scotland* [2001] IRLR 150). As such, an English applicant can be discriminated against by a Scottish employer on the grounds of his/her nationality as occurred in the *Souster* case where the BBC replaced the applicant as a commentator on its 'Rugby Special' with someone of Scottish origin.

Ethnic group is a broad definition which may include any group with a shared culture or history (**see chapter 4.5**). It does not include Rastafarians (*Crown Suppliers* v *Dawkins* [1993] ICR 517). Speakers of a particular language (e.g. Welsh) are not an 'ethnic' group *per se* (*Gwynedd County Council* v *Jones* [1986] ICR 833); it would need to be shown that such people belonged to a group with a shared culture or history before they come under the provisions of the 1976 Act.

The Act has been amended in two main ways since its inception. The first is by the amending Act set out in the next paragraph; the second is by the Race Relations Act 1976 (Amendment) Regulations 2003 (SI 2003/1626). The Regulations came into force in July 2003 and make several extensions to the Act in a number of areas including the meaning of indirect discrimination (as to which **see para. 4.13.10.2**), the inclusion of harassment as a specific category of unlawful treatment (as to which **see para. 4.13.10.3**) and the broadening of the Act's ambit to cover organisations and people that were formerly excluded.

4.13.4 The Race Relations (Amendment) Act 2000

As discussed above, the Race Relations Act 1976 made it unlawful to discriminate against others on the grounds of race in relation to certain areas, namely employment, training and education, the provision of goods, facilities and services and some other specific activities. The 1976 Act did not extend to all functions of public authorities. In addition, the Act made employers vicariously liable for some discriminatory actions of their employees but, as police officers are not *employees*, this extended liability did not apply to chief officers in relation to the actions of their police staff (see *R* v *Farah* (1996) *The Times*, 17 October). These were two principal reasons why the 1976 Act was felt to be in need of amendment. The latter reason was given increased impetus by the recommendations of the Report of the Inquiry into the death of Stephen Lawrence (Cm 4262-I). The Race Relations (Amendment) Act 2000 addresses both of these issues.

Interestingly, the Employment Appeal Tribunal was not persuaded that the concept of 'institutional racism' as levelled against the Metropolitan Police Service (MPS) in the

Stephen Lawrence Inquiry was related to the statutory definition of race discrimination and refused to accept that the MPS could generally be regarded in this context as having been racist at the time covered by the Report for the purposes of bringing discrimination claims against it—*Commissioner of Police for the Metropolis* v *Hendricks* [2003] All ER 654.

4.13.4.1 Public Authorities

The Race Relations (Amendment) Act 2000 inserted ss. 19B to 19F into the 1976 Act. These provisions together with the 2003 Regulations above generally make it unlawful for a public authority to discriminate against or harass a person on grounds of race in carrying out any of its functions. 'Public authority' here follows the definition used in the Human Rights Act 1998 (**see chapter 4.3**) and clearly includes the police. The Act allows for some exemptions and these include (controversially) a limited exemption where the person discriminates on grounds of nationality or ethnic/national origins and, in doing so, is properly acting on behalf of a Minister of the Crown in relation to immigration or nationality functions (see s. 19D).

Under s. 71 of the 1976 Act, specific public authorities are now under a general duty to have due regard to the need to eliminate unlawful discrimination and to promote equality of opportunity and good relations between people of different racial groups. Police forces (Home Office and others), chief officers and police authorities are under a statutory duty to publish Race Equality Schemes setting out how they intend to fulfil their duties under s. 71(1) of the Act. These Schemes must include details of those functions and policies that they have assessed as being relevant to the performance of their duties under s. 71(1) and their arrangements for:

- assessing and consulting on the likely impact of those proposed policies on the promotion of race equality
- monitoring policies for adverse impact on the promotion of race equality
- publishing the results of such assessments and consultation
- ensuring public access to information and services and
- training staff

(see the Race Relations Act 1976 (Statutory Duties) Order 2001 (S1 2001/3458 made under the Race Relations Act 1976, s. 71)).

Section 71 also empowers the CEHR to issue codes of practice to help public authorities in carrying out their duties in this area. As with many such codes, a breach of the code would not be actionable on its own but it would certainly provide significant evidence in support of a claim against a public authority. The CEHR is also given the power to issue and enforce compliance notices to public authorities in respect of this statutory duty.

4.13.4.2 Extension of Police Liability

The Race Relations (Amendment) Act 2000 inserted new ss. 76A and 76B into the original 1976 Act. This addition makes a police authority and chief officers liable for acts *done by them* to a police constable (which includes special constables and cadets); it also makes chief officers vicariously liable for racially discriminatory acts by such constables under their direction or control. This largely puts the police service on the same footing as other 'employers' and 'employees'. As a result, the statutory defence provided by the 1976 Act (under s. 32) that an employer took reasonable steps to prevent the acts of discrimination complained of will also be available to chief officers.

4.13.5 The Sex Discrimination Act 1975

The Sex Discrimination Act 1975 is aimed at preventing discrimination on the grounds of sex or marital status, and also has a Code of Practice to support it.

The 1975 Act makes it unlawful to discriminate on the grounds of a person's sex (s. 1) or marital status (s. 3). The provisions apply in favour of both men and women equally (s. 2); they do not, however, operate equally in respect of married and single people and an employer may provide greater benefits for employees who are married.

The Equality Act 2006 has inserted a new s. 21A into the 1975 Act which makes it unlawful for a public authority to discriminate or commit acts of harassment on grounds of sex when carrying out its functions. This means that ministers, local authorities, the police, other governmental organisations and private bodies which have functions of a public nature are not permitted to discriminate or harass on the grounds of a person's sex when exercising their public functions.

The 2006 Act has also inserted a new s. 76A into the 1975 Act, imposing on public authorities a duty to promote equality of opportunity between men and women ('the gender duty'); similar duties are imposed by the Race Relations Act 1976 and the Disability Discrimination Act 1995.

The Act has been extended by three sets of regulations. The Sex Discrimination Act 1975 (Amendment) Regulations 2003 (SI 2003/1657) clarified the applicability of the Act's provisions to police officers. The legislation now treats constables under the employment of their chief officer for the purposes of making that chief officer liable for unlawful acts done in the performance (or purported performance) of the constable's functions. This amendment to the law was necessary as a result of some common law decisions involving police officers and their chief officers' liability (see *Chief Constable of Bedfordshire* v *Liversidge* [2002] ICR 1135).

The Employment Equality (Sex Discrimination) Regulations 2005 (SI 2005/2467), made under the European Communities Act 1972, implemented some of the requirements of Council Directive 2002/73/EC. This Directive deals with the definition of indirect discrimination (**see para. 4.13.10.2**), harassment (**see para. 4.13.10.3**) and genuine occupational requirements (**see para. 4.13.11.1**). It also amends the 1975 Act by clarifying that discrimination on the grounds of pregnancy and maternity leave is unlawful sex discrimination.

The Sex Discrimination Act 1975 (Amendment) Regulations 2008 (SI 2008/656) give full effect to Council Directive 2002/73/EC in relation to the definitions of harassment and discrimination on the grounds of pregnancy or maternity leave, and so far as it relates to terms and conditions during maternity leave. The amended definition of discrimination on the grounds of pregnancy or maternity leave eliminates the requirement of a comparator who is not pregnant or not on maternity leave, as the case may be (r. 2), i.e. without reference to how she would have been treated had she not become pregnant or exercised a right to maternity leave. Regulation 3 enables claims of harassment to be made by someone who is not subjected to the unwanted conduct him/herself but the effect of which nonetheless violates his/her dignity or creates an intimidating, etc. environment for him/her. The Regulations also make it unlawful for an employer to fail to take reasonably practicable steps to protect employees from harassment by third parties where such harassment is known to have occurred on at least two other occasions (r. 4).

The Regulations also generally prohibit sex discrimination after the end of an employment-type relationship in line with the Equal Treatment Directive.

4.13.6 The Equal Pay Act 1970

The Equal Pay Act 1970 requires that men and women who do the same type of work receive the same rewards. In *Chief Constable of West Midlands Police* v *Blackburn* [2007] UKEAT 007 07 1112, it was held that where police officers needed to work hours compatible with their child care responsibilities they were not entitled to the special payments received by officers working 24/7 shift patterns. The Employment Equality (Sex Discrimination) Regulations 2005 (SI 2005/2467) extend the 1970 Act to include office-holders (reg. 35), and amends the Act to set out the extent to which it is discriminatory to pay a woman less than she would otherwise have been paid due to pregnancy or maternity leave (reg. 36).

A new s. 76A(2), inserted into the Sex Discrimination Act 1975 by the Equality Act 2006, now places a duty on public authorities also to eliminate unlawful discrimination in relation to the Equal Pay Act 1970.

4.13.7 The Disability Discrimination Act 1995

The Disability Discrimination Act 1995, which was significantly extended by the Disability Discrimination Act 2005, makes it unlawful to discriminate against people on grounds of disability.

A person is 'disabled' for the purposes of the Act if they have a physical or mental impairment which has a substantial and long-term adverse effect on their ability to carry out normal day-to-day activities (s. 1).

Again there are exceptions which may be justified. In *Hart* v *Chief Constable of Derbyshire Constabulary* (2008) IDA 847 EAT a police officer was unable to undertake confrontational duties to pass her probation as a PC because she was disabled from a back injury. The Employment Appeal Tribunal decided she was discriminated against but the police force was justified in refusing to make the adjustment as confrontational duties were an essential part of an officer's job (see also *Chief Constable of Lincolnshire* v *Weaver* (2008) UKEAT 0622 07 1903). However, under the 1995 Act employers and others are required to make 'reasonable adjustments' to prevent disabled people from being put at a substantial disadvantage when compared with others (s. 6).

The 1995 Act was extended by the Disability Discrimination Act 1995 (Amendment) Regulations 2003 (SI 2003/1673) which provided that for the purposes of part 2 of the Act police officers were to be treated as employees of their chief officer (**see chapter 4.1** for a discussion of the background to, and significance of, the employment status of police officers).

Given the context in which many policing roles occur and the various physical and mental demands made on police officers generally, the defence of justification can be expected to cover a significant range of duties and tasks. Clearly there will be occasions where it is simply not possible or practicable for a person with a given disability to carry out the full requirements of a role—even with adjustments. Consequently the Act allows for a statutory 'defence' of justification in such cases (**see para. 4.13.11.3**). However, the extension of the Disability Discrimination Act 1995 to cover police officers marks an important development in this area of discrimination law. The Disability Discrimination Act 2005 amended and extended the 1995 Act and included: making it unlawful for operators of transport vehicles to discriminate against disabled people, making it easier for disabled people to rent property and for tenants to make disability-related adaptations; making sure that private clubs with 25 or more members cannot keep disabled people out just because they have a disability; extending protection to cover people who have HIV, cancer and multiple sclerosis from the moment they are diagnosed; ensuring that discrimination law covers all the activities of the public sector; and requiring public bodies to promote equality of opportunity for disabled people. This last requirement places a duty on public authorities to ensure better performance in relation to eliminating disability discrimination. The duty is imposed by the Disability Discrimination (Public Authorities) (Statutory Duties) Regulations 2005 (SI 2005/2966) which require public authorities to publish a Disability Equality Scheme (reg. 2), and report annually on the implementation of their Scheme (reg. 4). A Code of Practice on the duty to promote disability equality was published by the Disability Rights Commission (now the Equality and Human Rights Commission), and is entitled *The Duty to promote Disability Equality: Statutory Code of Practice.*

The TUC publishes a guide to disability equality, entitled *Disability and Work: A Trade Union Guide to the Law and Practice,* and the Home Office, in conjunction with local forces, produces a best practice document intended to assist police forces in the production of their Disability Equality Schemes (*Disability in the Police Service—Best Practice Principles*).

4.13.8 Subsequent Extensions to Areas of Discrimination

Areas which were not directly covered by the original legislation in the context of discrimination included:

- religious belief
- sexual orientation
- age.

Taking these in order, religion means any religion, belief means any religious or philosophical belief, a reference to religion includes a reference to lack of religion, and a reference to belief includes a reference to lack of belief (reg. 2 of the Employment Equality (Religion or Belief) Regulations 2003 (SI 2003/1660) as amended by the Equality Act 2006). The 2003 Regulations implemented Council Directive 2000/78/EC and make it unlawful to discriminate on the grounds of religion or belief in the fields of employment or vocational training. Both direct and indirect discrimination are covered, as are victimisation and harassment (**see para. 4.13.10**).

Outside the employment context, the Anti-terrorism, Crime and Security Act 2001 introduced statutory measures to protect groups with reference to their religious beliefs (**see chapter 4.5**). The Equality Act 2006 has provided that discrimination on the grounds of religion or belief in the provision of goods, facilities and services is unlawful (s. 46). In addition, the 2006 Act also makes it unlawful to discriminate in relation to: selling and letting premises (s. 47), the admission and exclusion of school pupils (s. 49), in the exercise of the functions of public authorities (s. 52), to operate, adopt or maintain a practice which results in unlawful discrimination (s. 53), publishing an advertisement intending to discriminate unlawfully (s. 54), or to instruct, cause or induce, or attempt to cause or induce, another person to discriminate unlawfully (s. 55).

Any claim for unlawful discrimination is dealt with in the county court by way of proceedings in tort for breach of statutory duty (s. 66). Proceedings must be brought either within six months of the alleged unlawful act, or if later, with the permission of the court (s. 69). However, many cases of systematic harassment will constitute continuing discrimination for as long as they last (*Hendricks* v *Commissioner of Police for the Metropolis* [2003] IRLR 96).

For example, a claimant was dismissed for gross misconduct by his employer after it was alleged that he had used his holiday entitlement and taken a week's unpaid leave—in each case without authority—to make a pilgrimage to Mecca. The employee claimed that he had sought permission but, having received no reply from his employer, his manager told him to assume it had been approved. On returning from the pilgrimage, he was suspended without pay and dismissed. The Employment Tribunal found his case to have been proved and awarded him £10,000 (*Khan (Mohammed Sajwal)* v *NIC Hygiene* (2005) 17 January, unreported).

Discrimination on the grounds of sexual orientation is covered by the Employment Equality (Sexual Orientation) Regulations 2003 (SI 2003/1661), as amended. These Regulations implement Council Directive 2000/78/EC and make it unlawful to discriminate on grounds of sexual orientation in employment and vocational training and apply to direct and indirect discrimination, victimisation, and harassment. 'Sexual orientation' means a sexual orientation towards people of the same sex, people of the opposite sex, or to both people of the same sex and the opposite sex (reg. 2). Specific provision is made for police constables (reg. 11).

Section 81 of the Equality Act 2006 provides a power under which the Secretary of State can make regulations that prohibit sexual orientation discrimination, including indirect discrimination, victimisation, and harassment. The regulations may make provision similar to those for religion or belief, where the regulations may prohibit—either generally or in specified circumstances—discrimination in the provision of goods, facilities and services; the exercise of public functions; education; and the disposal of premises. In addition, the regulations will be able to prohibit discriminatory advertisements and instructing or causing discrimination or harassment.

The Civil Partnership Act 2004 also makes it unlawful to discriminate against same-sex couples in a civil partnership.

The Employment Equality (Age) Regulations 2006 are a direct result of the age discrimination strand of the European Employment Directive 2000/78/EC. These Regulations deal with age discrimination in relation to such matters as recruitment, promotion, training, retirement and unfair dismissal. They also include provisions relating to service-related benefits and occupational pensions as well as removing age limits for Statutory Sick Pay, Statutory Maternity Pay, Statutory Adoption Pay and Statutory Paternity Pay.

While there are now broad similarities across many of the protected categories, the specific definitions, qualifications and exemptions under the relevant regulations must be considered in each case.

4.13.9 Gender Reassignment and Recognition

Many of the provisions of the Sex Discrimination Act 1975 have been extended to cover discrimination on the grounds of gender reassignment in employment and vocational training. These extensions were made by the Sex Discrimination (Gender Reassignment) Regulations 1999 (SI 1999/1102 made under European Communities Act, s. 2) in response to a case in the European Court of Justice (*P* v *S and Cornwall County Council* (case C-13/94) [1996] All ER (EC) 397). Gender reassignment means a process which is undertaken under medical supervision for the purpose of reassigning a person's sex by changing physiological or other characteristics of sex (reg. 2(3)). The Regulations only extend the provisions of some sections of the 1975 Act and include a number of concessions and exemptions.

Taking time off work in order to undergo reassignment surgery attracts the protection of the Act and is to be treated as a special category of absence.

The employment of transsexuals as police officers has caused the police service some difficulties. In a case arising before the Sex Discrimination (Gender Reassignment) Regulations 1999 (SI 1999/1102 made under European Communities Act, s. 2), a transsexual applicant was turned down by a police force on the basis that she would not be able to perform all the duties of a constable—in particular the searching of prisoners. The force claimed a genuine occupational qualification for discriminating against transsexuals in this way and the Employment Appeal Tribunal (EAT) upheld its appeal against a finding of unlawful discrimination (*Chief Constable of West Yorkshire Police* v *A* [2002] IRLR 103).

In *A* above, the EAT referred to the established legal principle that gender in law is set at birth—if you are born male, you remain male and vice versa (see *Corbett* v *Corbett* [1970] 2 WLR 1306). The EAT went on to find that a police force could not condone a police officer searching someone of the opposite sex in contravention of the PACE Codes of Practice (**see chapter 4.4**) even if that officer's true 'legal' gender could be concealed by their general appearance and dress. Although the number of occasions when such an officer might be called upon to carry out a search in this way were few and far between, the EAT did not accept that they were 'minimal' or 'negligible' considerations. The EAT also held that the Regulations did not amount to an absolute bar on a transsexual ever being a police constable and therefore they were not incompatible with the Equal Treatment Directive (No. 76/207).

However, following the decision of the European Court of Human Rights in *Goodwin* v *United Kingdom* [2002] IRLR 664, the Court of Appeal held that it was no longer possible in the context of employment to regard a transsexual in these circumstances as being anything other than female. Although there might be public interest considerations that outweighed the interests of an individual applicant to the police service and a chief officer might decide on the balance of those interests not to appoint such a person, such circumstances were held not to exist in the case of *A* and the decision of the EAT was eventually overturned (*A* v *Chief Constable of West Yorkshire and the Secretary of State for Work and Pensions* [2004] UKHL 21).

In response to the above common law developments the Gender Recognition Act 2004 was passed. The Act's primary purpose is to allow people who have changed their sex to be legally recognised.

Under the Act, anyone who has attained 18 years of age may apply for their new gender identity to be recognised in the United Kingdom. Applications will be submitted to a special panel whose terms of appointment are set out in sch. 1 to the Act.

All applications must be supported by evidence of the person's gender 'dysphoria', and submitted via two medical practitioners or a medical practitioner and a psychologist, in each case who are subject matter experts in this field.

Successful applications will result in the issuing of a certificate after which the person will, for most legal purposes, be regarded as having the new gender; however, this will not affect their status as the mother or father of a child. It will allow the person to bring discrimination claims within their 'new' gender (e.g. former males bringing claims for sex discrimination against females). Where the applicant is married at the time, an interim certificate will be issued until the marriage is annulled, and the various conditions attaching to such certificates can be found in sch. 2.

The Secretary of State will maintain a Gender Recognition Register recording certification of changes, although the register will not (unlike, for instance, the register of births and marriages) be open to general public inspection.

4.13.10 Discrimination

Discrimination in the context of this chapter may come about in four main ways:

- directly
- indirectly
- harassment
- by victimisation

In the context of disability discrimination (as to which **see para. 4.13.7**) discrimination is slightly different. For example, disability discrimination occurs when:

- for a reason which relates to a person's disability, their employer treats them less favourably than they treat (or would treat) others to whom the reason does not or would not apply; or
- fails to comply with a duty of reasonable adjustment imposed by Disability Discrimination Act 1995, s. 4A; and
- the employer cannot show that this treatment is justified.

Examples of the duty to make reasonable adjustments would include adapting keyboards or providing laptops and adapting access points to buildings.

It is also worth noting that, in many cases of discrimination within an employment context, the legislation provides protection from acts of discrimination even after the employment relationship has ended.

4.13.10.1 Direct Discrimination

This type of discrimination generally happens when one person is treated less favourably than another on the protected grounds (e.g. his/her racial origin, marital status, sex, religion or belief etc.). The key elements here are the 'treatment' of the person and the fact that such treatment was 'less favourable' than it would have been had the person not fallen into that particular group. Treatment will generally involve dealing with or behaving towards someone—as opposed to simply talking in a derogatory fashion *about* them (see e.g. *De Souza* v *Automobile Association* [1986] ICR 514). Treatment can be shown by a continuing state of affairs as well as a particular act (*Owusu* v *London Fire & Civil Defence Authority* [1995] IRLR 574—employer continually failing to re-grade appellant's post).

It must be shown that the treatment was made *on the grounds* of or *by reason* of the person's belonging to a protected group or having the protected characteristics. Like the test of 'causation' in criminal law (as to which, **see Crime, chapter 1.2**), the 'but for' test is helpful here, i.e. asking whether the person would have received the same treatment as others *but for* their sex, race, etc. In determining whether a person has been so treated the courts will not look at the motive of an employer or individual, only at the cause of the treatment (see *R* v *Birmingham City Council, ex parte Equal Opportunities Commission* [1989] AC 1155—more boys than girls allocated places at a school).

It can be seen that these elements of discrimination (so-called 'positive discrimination', e.g. deliberately favouring applications for jobs from one sex over the other) would generally be unlawful because treating people of one sex *more* favourably necessarily involves treating people from the other sex *less* favourably. A notable exception to the general principle that 'positive discrimination' is unlawful can be found in the Sex Discrimination (Election Candidates) Act 2002 which allows political parties (if they wish to do so) to adopt selection measures in order to reduce inequality in the numbers of men and women elected as candidates. Positive discrimination as described here should be contrasted with positive action (as to which, **see para. 4.13.11.2**).

Claims in the courts and tribunals for direct discrimination are rare. Examples of such have included:

- getting someone to carry out unpleasant tasks or duties (*Ministry of Defence* v *Jeremiah* [1980] QB 87)
- rescinding an officer's posting on the grounds of force policy that spouses should not work in the same Division because neither officer would be competent or compellable as witnesses against each other (*Graham* v *Chief Constable of Bedfordshire Constabulary* [2002] IRLR 239)
- treating a police officer of one racial group, who was under investigation for disciplinary matters, differently from another officer under such investigation belonging to a different racial group (*Virdi* v *Commissioner of Police for the Metropolis* (2000) LTL 5 February)
- acceding to a request by a customer not to be served by someone of a particular colour (*Eldridge & Barbican Car Hire Ltd* v *Zhang* (2001) LTL 10 May),

in each case as a result of their membership of a protected group.

Note that the legal basis of the concept of discrimination does not allow for stereotyping—even if the stereotyping is accurate. This position has been reaffirmed by the House of Lords in *R (On the Application of European Roma Centre)* v *Immigration Officer at Prague Airport* [2005] 2 WLR 1. In that case the policy of treating asylum applications from Roma people more sceptically than those of non-Romas (and therefore subjecting them to longer and more searching interviews), was held to be unlawful. As the judgment says: 'the object of the legislation is to ensure that each person is treated as an individual and not assumed to be like other members of the group', and this general principle applies *even where it can be demonstrated that most members of a specific group in fact have those characteristics.*

Legislation that treats same-sex couples differently from unmarried heterosexual couples is open to challenge under Article 14 of the European Convention on Human Rights (**see chapter 4.3**), either by requiring the relevant court or tribunal to interpret the law in a way that is compatible with the Convention or by seeking a declaration of incompatibility. Until the provisions of the Civil Partnership Act 2004 came into force it was easier to discriminate between same-sex couples and *married* heterosexual couples, largely because the courts accepted differences in treatment between married and unmarried couples generally. The 2004 Act makes it illegal to discriminate against same-sex couples in a civil partnership.

4.13.10.2 Indirect Discrimination

Broadly speaking, indirect discrimination involves applying the same conditions to all relevant people (e.g. job applicants or employees), but in circumstances where a person belonging to the protected group is disadvantaged. For instance, if an employer imposes a requirement on all employees to work on certain days and at certain times, it may be that this requirement puts people of a certain nationality, sex or religious belief at a disadvantage when compared with other employees (for an earlier example see *Walker (J.H.) Ltd* v *Hussain* [1996] IRLR 11). This would raise an initial inference of indirect discrimination. This inference is not the end of the matter and in some cases the legislation allows an employer or other respondent to demonstrate justification of their actions.

This concept was first altered by the introduction of the Sex Discrimination (Indirect Discrimination and Burden of Proof) Regulations 2001 (SI 2001/2660) and then was followed by the regulations relating to race, sexual orientation and religion referred to above.

While there are some differences in specific aspects of discrimination law, as a very general rule indirect discrimination will now occur if:

- a person or organisation (R) in the relevant context applies a provision, criterion or practice equally and
- that provision, criterion or practice puts people in the protected group at a disadvantage when compared to others and
- it puts a person (A) at that disadvantage and
- R cannot show their actions to be a proportionate means of achieving a legitimate aim.

The practical effect of this in a sex discrimination context was summarised by the Employment Appeal Tribunal in *Barton* v *Investec Henderson Crosthwaite Securities Ltd* [2003] IRLR 332. Following the reasoning of the Tribunal in that case, in order to discharge the burden of proof, an employer must prove on the balance of probabilities that the treatment of the applicant was 'in no sense whatsoever' on the grounds of sex, race or other protected category. This approach has been endorsed by the Court of Appeal (*Wong* v *Igen Ltd (formerly Leeds Careers Guidance)* [2005] EWCA Civ 142). In essence, the employee must make out an initial case of discrimination by showing facts which could—in the absence of an adequate explanation—amount to less favourable treatment on the prohibited ground (such as sex or race). Once the employee has done this it must be assumed that there is no adequate explanation and the burden of showing one moves squarely to the employer.

Earlier decisions of the courts based on the disproportionate effect of generally applied requirements serve to illustrate the nature of indirect discrimination. So, for instance, the fact that someone can *physically* comply with a criterion (e.g. a woman could decide not to have children in order to comply with an age requirement in a promotion system) does not mean that it falls outside the legislation. What the courts have looked at is the person's *practical* ability to comply. In *Mandla* v *Dowell Lee* [1983] 2 AC 548, the fact that the complainant could physically remove his turban and cut his hair in order to comply with his chosen school's admission policy did not prevent that policy from being indirectly discriminatory. The House of Lords said that the test of whether someone could comply with a condition would be taken to mean, 'could he/she comply in practice or in a way that was consistent with the customs and cultural conditions of the group?'

A further example of indirect discrimination can be seen in the case of *London Underground Ltd* v *Edwards (No. 2)* [1998] IRLR 364. Despite the fact that a managerial policy only had an adverse effect on one woman train driver among a total of 24 woman drivers, the fact that *all* 2,023 male drivers could comply with it made the policy discriminatory. While 100 per cent of males could comply with the policy, which related to rostering of duties, only 95.2 per cent of females were able to do so. Accordingly, the Court of Appeal held that the policy discriminated indirectly against the applicant who was unable to continue in her job as a result.

Even where the difference between the number of female police officers unable to comply with a practice (e.g. a shift system) compared with male police officers is only a few per cent (or vice versa), an employment tribunal can find that a disparate effect has been established and that indirect sex discrimination has occurred (*Chief Constable of Avon & Somerset Constabulary* v *Chew* [2002] Emp LR 370).

Other examples of indirect discrimination would include:

- requiring all employees to work within 'normal office hours' (*Bhudi* v *IMI Refiners* [1994] IRLR 204)
- requiring all workers to have short hair—thereby making it more difficult for some groups such as Sikhs to comply (*Mandla* v *Dowell Lee*, above)

- denying a police officer access to operational duties as a result of a colour vision deficiency where the condition was not objectively justifiable in relation to those duties but where the condition *was* shown to affect a greater percentage of males than females (*Webster* v *Chief Constable of Hertfordshire Constabulary*, 2000, unreported).

Note that Article 14 of the European Convention on Human Rights does not make express provision for *indirect* discrimination (**see chapter 4.3** and *R (On the Application of Barber)* v *Secretary of State for Work and Pensions* [2002] 2 FLR 1181).

4.13.10.3 Harassment

The Race Relations Act 1976 contains a specific definition of harassment which outlaws unwanted conduct on the grounds of race or ethnic or national origins which violates the person's dignity or which creates an intimidating, hostile, degrading, humiliating or offensive environment (see ss. 3A and 4). The specific legislation addressing other areas of discrimination (e.g. disability, sexual orientation and religious belief) contains similar provisions.

Harassment was not originally a separate category of discrimination and came under the general heading of sex discrimination. However, in 2005 the Sex Discrimination Act 1975 was amended to include definitions of 'harassment' and 'sexual harassment' to conform to the Equal Treatment Directive (2002/73/EC). Sexual harassment is basically unwanted conduct of a sexual nature, or other conduct based on sex affecting the dignity of women and men at work (see *Wadman* v *Carpenter Farrer Partnership* [1993] IRLR 374). This can include verbal remarks, written comments and physical contact. However, some of the case law in this area is confusing. For instance, a case involving offensive and obscene remarks made by a supervisor to both male and female colleagues on a training course, was held by the Employment Appeal Tribunal as not amounting to sex discrimination. The EAT did not accept that a man using offensive words of a sexual nature in conversation with a woman amounts to discrimination *unless* it can be shown that this was less favourable treatment than the man would have used to another man in a comparable situation (*Brumfitt* v *Ministry of Defence* [2005] IRLR 4). Nevertheless, in another case with a different presiding judge, the EAT held that male colleagues downloading pornography and displaying it on their screens in an open-plan office was less favourable treatment, even in the absence of any complaint from the female colleague who subsequently brought an action for sex discrimination (*Moonsar* v *Fiveways Express Transport Ltd* [2005] IRLR 9). Most equal opportunities policies include some reference to this type of behaviour and grievance procedures take account of sexual harassment as if it were a separate heading; there are plans within the European Union legislative programme to make this a separate category of less favourable treatment.

Harassment is also a criminal offence (**see chapter 4.5**) and, if anxiety or shock caused to another person is sufficiently serious, a charge of assault may be brought (**see Crime, chapter 1.7**).

4.13.10.4 Victimisation

Victimisation is a type of discrimination and therefore only attracts protection in the same circumstances as the other discrimination provisions of the various Acts.

People often refer to having been 'victimised' at work in the sense that they have been singled out or persecuted in some way. While this treatment may contain elements of discrimination and other unlawful conduct, it is not the same as victimisation in the statutory sense used here.

In other words, it will not be enough for an employee to claim that he/she has been 'picked on' in some way; they will have to show that they belong to a protected group of people and have thereby been discriminated against.

A person is discriminated against by way of 'victimisation' under s. 2 of the Race Relations Act 1976, s. 4 of the Sex Discrimination Act 1975, s. 55 of the Disability Discrimination Act 1995, and s. 45 of the Equality Act 2006 if they are treated less favourably than another person is (or would be) treated in the same circumstances with regard to any action covered by any of those Acts because the person:

- brought or intends to bring proceedings against any person under any of those Acts;
- has given or provided or intends to give or provide evidence or information in connection with proceedings brought by any person under any of those Acts;
- otherwise did anything under or by reference to the Acts with regard to any person (e.g. provided advice to someone as to his/her rights);
- has alleged that any person has done anything which would amount to a contravention of those Acts (whether or not the allegation specifically so states); or
- because the discriminator knows or suspects that the person victimised has done or intends to do any of the things set out above.

These listed actions above are generally referred to as 'protected acts'. The test to be applied in assessing whether or not victimisation has taken place is, 'was the real reason for the victim's treatment the fact that he/she had carried out a protected act?' (see the House of Lords' decision in *Chief Constable of West Yorkshire Police* v *Khan* [2001] 1 WLR 1947).

The legislation relating to other specific types of discrimination such as religious belief and sexual orientation contain their own elements of protection from victimisation on a similar basis and reference should be made to them as appropriate.

The protection from victimisation does not extend to treatment of a person by reason of any allegation that the person makes falsely and not in good faith.

Where the person victimised has (or had) a disability, that disability is to be disregarded when deciding whether or not he/she has been treated 'less favourably' than another person in the same circumstances.

In proving victimisation, the person must show that less favourable treatment occurred as a result of his/her involvement in the protected action described, that is, applying the 'but for' test (see *Aziz* v *Trinity Street Taxis Ltd* [1989] QB 463).

However, once this can be established, the concept of victimisation is very wide and can even give rise to an action against a former employer *after* you have ceased to work for them (see *Metropolitan Police Service* v *Shoebridge* (2004) ICR 1690).

4.13.11 Exceptions and Defences

There are a number of exceptions and defences to the provisions of the various Acts and Regulations discussed above. As with other defences and exceptions, not all of them apply to all types of behaviour and it is necessary to refer to the relevant legislation in each case. Below are some of the more common exceptions and defences.

4.13.11.1 Genuine Occupational Qualification

The most frequently encountered defence to acts made unlawful by the Race Relations Act 1976 and the Sex Discrimination Act 1975 is that of 'genuine occupational qualification' (GOQ).

In each case the GOQ defence only applies to:

- recruitment,
- refusing employment, and
- affording access to promotion, training, etc.

The principle behind the GOQ defence is that, in certain jobs and roles, there may well be a legitimate reason demanded by that job/role for the relevant person to be a particular sex or to belong to a particular racial group. Such occasions are generally concerned with:

- preserving decency and privacy (e.g. public lavatory attendants),
- authenticity (e.g. actors/actresses in plays), or
- the provision of personal services.

Exceptions to unlawful discrimination can be found in a number of areas under the relevant Acts and statutory instruments, though there are far more potential exceptions to discrimination on the grounds of sex and sexual orientation than for reasons of race, religion or belief.

4.13.11.2 Positive Action

In order to encourage members of particular groups to follow training courses, employers and other bodies may discriminate in their provision of training opportunities under certain circumstances.

Positive action may in some circumstances be permitted where there is a legitimate need within a particular area of work or where it is necessary to train people from specified protected groups to fill certain jobs. These areas are provided for in the specific legislation and are beyond the general scope of this Manual.

Efforts made under these circumstances are positive *action* and should not be confused with positive *discrimination* or *affirmative* action as used in the United States and elsewhere. Affirmative action in that sense (whereby people are selected in preference to others solely on the basis of their membership of a certain minority group) is unlawful in England and Wales. Consequently, an attempt to recruit female police officers into a specialist department by excluding male applicants was held to be unlawful in *Jones* v *Chief Constable of Northamptonshire Police* (1999) *The Times*, 1 November.

4.13.11.3 Justification

The concept of justification in relation to disability is an important but unusual one. Under the Disability Discrimination Act 1995 (as to which **see para. 4.13.7**), the definition of discrimination itself contains a reference to the inability of the alleged discriminator to 'justify' their treatment of the relevant person. Justification is an important balancing provision within the disability discrimination framework as it reflects the operational and practical realities of the workplace or relevant area. However, less favourable treatment of a disabled person will only be justified if the reason is both 'material to the circumstances' and 'substantial'. Therefore the reason has to relate to the specific circumstances of the case and must not be trivial or minor. In addition, less favourable treatment cannot be justified where the employer is under a duty to make a reasonable adjustment but fails to do so, unless the treatment would have been justified even after that adjustment. In *Paterson* v *Commissioner of Police of the Metropolis* [2007] IRLR 763, a police officer diagnosed as suffering from mild dyslexia was held to be a disabled person within the meaning of s. 1 of the 1995 Act.

The Code of Practice gives examples of a clerical worker with a learning disability who cannot sort papers quite as quickly as some of his colleagues or one who is turned down for a job because of a severe facial disfigurement solely on the ground that other employees would be uncomfortable working alongside him. In both of these examples the Code suggests the reason would not meet the criteria for 'justification' and the employer would be acting unlawfully.

4.13.12 Maternity and Parental Leave

In addition to the protection which appears in the above enactments, women and men have other statutory protection in relation to pregnancy and childbirth. These include:

- rights to unpaid time off work
- protection against dismissal
- rights to maternity pay and leave
- rights to paternity pay and leave
- rights to return to work.

These and other protections are contained in the Employment Rights Act 1996 (as amended), and the Work and Families Act 2006. The 2006 Act has changed the law in this area whereby it has:

- extended the maximum period for statutory maternity pay, maternity allowance and statutory adoption pay;
- provided employees (generally fathers) with a new entitlement to take leave to care for a child and to receive pay while they are on leave, if certain conditions are met;
- widened the scope of the existing law on flexible working;
- increased, on one occasion, the maximum amount of a week's pay which may be taken into account in the calculation of certain payments (e.g. redundancy payments);
- made new provisions about annual leave.

Most of the legislation in relation to maternity and parental leave is driven by European law and is outside the scope of this Manual. Guidance on the agreed policies for maternity leave, etc., for police officers is contained in Home Office Circular 33/2003 and adoption leave policy in Home Office Circular 1/2007.

The Trades Union Congress has also produced a risk assessment guide for new and expectant mothers that sets out the steps to be taken by employers who employ any women of childbearing age and who carry out work that could involve any risk.

Appendix 4.1

PACE Code of Practice for the Exercise by Police Officers of Statutory Powers of Stop and Search; Police Officers and Police Staff of Requirements to Record Public Encounters (Code A)

This code applies to any search by a police officer and the requirement to record public encounters taking place after midnight on 31 January 2008.

General

This code of practice must be readily available at all police stations for consultation by police officers, police staff, detained persons and members of the public.

The notes for guidance included are not provisions of this code, but are guidance to police officers and others about its application and interpretation. Provisions in the annexes to the code are provisions of this code.

This code governs the exercise by police officers of statutory powers to search a person or a vehicle without first making an arrest. The main stop and search powers to which this code applies are set out in Annex A, but that list should not be regarded as definitive. [See Note 1] In addition, it covers requirements on police officers and police staff to record encounters not governed by statutory powers. This code does not apply to:

(a) the powers of stop and search under;
 (i) Aviation Security Act 1982, section 27(2);
 (ii) Police and Criminal Evidence Act 1984, section 6(1) (which relates specifically to powers of constables employed by statutory undertakers on the premises of the statutory undertakers).

(b) searches carried out for the purposes of examination under Schedule 7 to the Terrorism Act 2000 and to which the Code of Practice issued under paragraph 6 of Schedule 14 to the Terrorism Act 2000 applies.

1 Principles governing stop and search

1.1 Powers to stop and search must be used fairly, responsibly, with respect for people being searched and without unlawful discrimination. The Race Relations (Amendment) Act 2000 makes it unlawful for police officers to discriminate on the grounds of race, colour, ethnic origin, nationality or national origins when using their powers.

1.2 The intrusion on the liberty of the person stopped or searched must be brief and detention for the purposes of a search must take place at or near the location of the stop.

1.3 If these fundamental principles are not observed the use of powers to stop and search may be drawn into question. Failure to use the powers in the proper manner reduces their effectiveness. Stop and search can play an important role in the detection and prevention of crime, and using the powers fairly makes them more effective.

1.4 The primary purpose of stop and search powers is to enable officers to allay or confirm suspicions about individuals without exercising their power of arrest. Officers may be required to justify the use or authorisation of such powers, in relation both to individual searches and the overall pattern of their activity in this regard, to their supervisory officers or in court. Any misuse of the powers is likely to be harmful to policing and lead to mistrust of the police. Officers must also be able to explain their actions to the member of the public searched. The misuse of these powers can lead to disciplinary action.

1.5 An officer must not search a person, even with his or her consent, where no power to search is applicable. Even where a person is prepared to submit to a search voluntarily, the person must not be searched unless the necessary legal power exists, and the search must be in accordance with the relevant power and the provisions of this Code. The only exception, where an officer does not require a specific power, applies to searches of persons entering sports grounds or other premises carried out with their consent given as a condition of entry.

2 Explanation of powers to stop and search

2.1 This code applies to powers of stop and search as follows:

(a) powers which require reasonable grounds for suspicion, before they may be exercised; that articles unlawfully obtained or possessed are being carried, or under Section 43 of the Terrorism Act 2000 that a person is a terrorist;

(b) authorised under section 60 of the Criminal Justice and Public Order Act 1994, based upon a reasonable belief that incidents involving serious violence may take place or that people are carrying dangerous instruments or offensive weapons within any locality in the police area;

(c) authorised under section 44(1) and (2) of the Terrorism Act 2000 based upon a consideration that the exercise of one or both powers is expedient for the prevention of acts of terrorism;

(d) powers to search a person who has not been arrested in the exercise of a power to search premises (see Code B paragraph 2.4).

Searches requiring reasonable grounds for suspicion

2.2 Reasonable grounds for suspicion depend on the circumstances in each case. There must be an objective basis for that suspicion based on facts, information, and/or intelligence which are relevant to the likelihood of finding an article of a certain kind or, in the case of searches under section 43 of the Terrorism Act 2000, to the likelihood that the person is a terrorist. Reasonable suspicion can never be supported on the basis of personal factors alone without reliable supporting intelligence or information or some specific behaviour by the person concerned. For example, a person's race, age, appearance, or the fact that the person is known to have a previous conviction, cannot be used alone or in combination with each other as the reason for searching that person. Reasonable suspicion cannot be based on generalisations or stereotypical images of certain groups or categories of people as more likely to be involved in criminal activity. A person's religion cannot be considered as reasonable grounds for suspicion and should never be considered as a reason to stop or stop and search an individual.

2.3 Reasonable suspicion can sometimes exist without specific information or intelligence and on the basis of some level of generalisation stemming from the behaviour of a person. For example, if an officer encounters someone on the street at night who is obviously trying to hide something, the officer may (depending on the other surrounding circumstances) base such suspicion on the fact that this kind of behaviour is often linked to stolen or prohibited articles being carried. Similarly, for the purposes of section 43 of the Terrorism Act 2000, suspicion that a person is a terrorist may arise from the person's behaviour at or near a location which has been identified as a potential target for terrorists.

2.4 However, reasonable suspicion should normally be linked to accurate and current intelligence or information, such as information describing an article being carried, a suspected offender, or a person who has been seen carrying a type of article known to have been stolen recently from premises in the area. Searches based on accurate and current intelligence or information are more likely to be effective. Targeting searches in a particular area at specified crime problems increases their effectiveness and minimises inconvenience to law-abiding members of the public. It also helps in justifying the use of searches both to those who are searched and to the public. This does not however prevent stop and search powers being exercised in other locations where such powers may be exercised and reasonable suspicion exists.

2.5 Searches are more likely to be effective, legitimate, and secure public confidence when reasonable suspicion is based on a range of factors. The overall use of these powers is more likely to be effective when up to date and accurate intelligence or information is communicated to officers and they are well-informed about local crime patterns.

2.6 Where there is reliable information or intelligence that members of a group or gang habitually carry knives unlawfully or weapons or controlled drugs, and wear a distinctive item of clothing or other means of identification to indicate their membership of the group or gang, that distinctive item of clothing or other means of identification may provide reasonable grounds to stop and search a person. [See *Note 9*]

2.7 A police officer may have reasonable grounds to suspect that a person is in innocent possession of a stolen or prohibited article or other item for which he or she is empowered to search. In that case the officer may stop and search the person even though there would be no power of arrest.

2.8 Under section 43(1) of the Terrorism Act 2000 a constable may stop and search a person whom the officer reasonably suspects to be a terrorist to discover whether the person is in possession of anything which may constitute evidence that the person is a terrorist. These searches may only be carried out by an officer of the same sex as the person searched.

2.9 An officer who has reasonable grounds for suspicion may detain the person concerned in order to carry out a search. Before carrying out a search the officer may ask questions about the person's behaviour or presence in circumstances which gave rise to the suspicion. As a result of questioning the detained person, the reasonable grounds for suspicion necessary to detain that person may be confirmed or, because of a satisfactory explanation, be eliminated. [See *Notes 2* and *3*] Questioning may also reveal reasonable grounds to suspect the possession of a different kind of unlawful article from that originally suspected. Reasonable grounds for suspicion however cannot be provided retrospectively by such questioning during a person's detention or by refusal to answer any questions put.

2.10 If, as a result of questioning before a search, or other circumstances which come to the attention of the officer, there cease to be reasonable grounds for suspecting that an article is being carried of a kind for which there is a power to stop and search, no search may take place. [See *Note 3*] In the absence of any other lawful power to detain, the person is free to leave at will and must be so informed.

2.11 There is no power to stop or detain a person in order to find grounds for a search. Police officers have many encounters with members of the public which do not involve detaining people against their will. If reasonable grounds for suspicion emerge during such an encounter, the officer may search the person, even though no grounds existed when the encounter began. If an officer is detaining someone for the purpose of a search, he or she should inform the person as soon as detention begins.

Searches authorised under section 60 of the Criminal Justice and Public Order Act 1994

2.12 Authority for a constable in uniform to stop and search under section 60 of the Criminal Justice and Public Order Act 1994 may be given if the authorising officer reasonably believes:

(a) that incidents involving serious violence may take place in any locality in the officer's police area, and it is expedient to use these powers to prevent their occurrence, or

(b) that persons are carrying dangerous instruments or offensive weapons without good reason in any locality in the officer's police area.

2.13 An authorisation under section 60 may only be given by an officer of the rank of inspector or above, in writing, specifying the grounds on which it was given, the locality in which the powers may be exercised and the period of time for which they are in force. The period authorised shall be no longer than appears reasonably necessary to prevent, or seek to prevent incidents of serious violence, or to deal with the problem of carrying dangerous instruments or offensive weapons. It may not exceed 24 hours. [See *Notes 10–13*]

2.14 If an inspector gives an authorisation, he or she must, as soon as practicable, inform an officer of or above the rank of superintendent. This officer may direct that the authorisation shall be extended for a further 24 hours, if violence or the carrying of dangerous instruments or offensive weapons has occurred, or is suspected to have occurred, and the continued use of the powers is considered necessary to prevent or deal with further such activity. That direction must also be given in writing at the time or as soon as practicable afterwards. [See *Note 12*]

Powers to require removal of face coverings

2.15 Section 60AA of the Criminal Justice and Public Order Act 1994 also provides a power to demand the removal of disguises. The officer exercising the power must reasonably believe that someone is wearing an item wholly or mainly for the purpose of concealing identity. There is also a power to seize such items where the officer believes that a person intends to wear them for this purpose. There is no power to stop and search for disguises. An officer may seize any such item which is discovered when exercising a power of search for something else, or which is being carried, and which the officer reasonably believes is intended to be used for concealing anyone's identity. This power can only be used if an authorisation under section 60 or an authorisation under section 60AA is in force.

2.16 Authority for a constable in uniform to require the removal of disguises and to seize them under section 60AA may be given if the authorising officer reasonably believes that activities may take place in any locality in the officer's police area that are likely to involve the commission of offences and it is expedient to use these powers to prevent or control these activities.

2.17 An authorisation under section 60AA may only be given by an officer of the rank of inspector or above, in writing, specifying the grounds on which it was given, the locality in which the powers may be exercised and the period of time for which they are in force. The period authorised shall be no longer than appears reasonably necessary to prevent, or seek to prevent the commission of offences. It may not exceed 24 hours. [See *Notes 10–13*]

2.18 If an inspector gives an authorisation, he or she must, as soon as practicable, inform an officer of or above the rank of superintendent. This officer may direct that the authorisation shall be extended for a further 24 hours, if crimes have been committed, or is suspected to have been committed, and the continued use of the powers is considered necessary to prevent or deal with further such activity. This direction must also be given in writing at the time or as soon as practicable afterwards. [See *Note 12*]

Searches authorised under section 44 of the Terrorism Act 2000

2.19 An officer of the rank of assistant chief constable (or equivalent) or above, may give authority for the following powers of stop and search under section 44 of the Terrorism Act 2000 to be exercised in the whole or part of his or her police area if the officer considers it is expedient for the prevention of acts of terrorism:

(a) under section 44(1) of the Terrorism Act 2000, to give a constable in uniform power to stop and search any vehicle, its driver, any passenger in the vehicle and anything in or on the vehicle or carried by the driver or any passenger; and

(b) under section 44(2) of the Terrorism Act 2000, to give a constable in uniform power to stop and search any pedestrian and anything carried by the pedestrian.

An authorisation under section 44(1) may be combined with one under section 44(2).

2.20 If an authorisation is given orally at first, it must be confirmed in writing by the officer who gave it as soon as reasonably practicable.

2.21 When giving an authorisation, the officer must specify the geographical area in which the power may be used, and the time and date that the authorisation ends (up to a maximum of 28 days from the time the authorisation was given). [See *Notes 12* and *13*]

2.22 The officer giving an authorisation under section 44(1) or (2) must cause the Secretary of State to be informed, as soon as reasonably practicable, that such an authorisation has been given. An authorisation which is not confirmed by the Secretary of State within 48 hours of its having been given, shall have effect up until the end of that 48 hour period or the end of the period specified in the authorisation (whichever is the earlier). [See *Note 14*]

2.23 Following notification of the authorisation, the Secretary of State may:

(i) cancel the authorisation with immediate effect or with effect from such other time as he or she may direct;

(ii) confirm it but for a shorter period than that specified in the authorisation; or

(iii) confirm the authorisation as given.

2.24 When an authorisation under section 44 is given, a constable in uniform may exercise the powers:

(a) only for the purpose of searching for articles of a kind which could be used in connection with terrorism (see paragraph 2.25);

(b) whether or not there are any grounds for suspecting the presence of such articles.

2.24A When a Community Support Officer on duty and in uniform has been conferred powers under Section 44 of the Terrorism Act 2000 by a Chief Officer of their force, the exercise of this power must comply with the requirements of this Code of Practice, including the recording requirements.

2.25 The selection of persons stopped under section 44 of Terrorism Act 2000 should reflect an objective assessment of the threat posed by the various terrorist groups active in Great Britain. The powers must not be used to stop and search for reasons unconnected with terrorism. Officers must take particular care not to discriminate against members of minority ethnic groups in the exercise of these powers. There may be circumstances, however, where it is appropriate for officers to take account of a person's ethnic origin in selecting persons to be stopped in response to a specific terrorist threat (for example, some international terrorist groups are associated with particular ethnic identities). [See *Notes 12* and *13*]

2.26 The powers under sections 43 and 44 of the Terrorism Act 2000 allow a constable to search only for articles which could be used for terrorist purposes. However, this would not prevent a search being carried out under other powers if, in the course of exercising these powers, the officer formed reasonable grounds for suspicion.

Powers to search in the exercise of a power to search premises

2.27 The following powers to search premises also authorise the search of a person, not under arrest, who is found on the premises during the course of the search:

(a) section 139B of the Criminal Justice Act 1988 under which a constable may enter school premises and search the premises and any person on those premises for any bladed or pointed article or offensive weapon; and
(b) under a warrant issued under section 23(3) of the Misuse of Drugs Act 1971 to search premises for drugs or documents but only if the warrant specifically authorises the search of persons found on the premises.

2.28 Before the power under section 139B of the Criminal Justice Act 1988 may be exercised, the constable must have reasonable grounds to believe that an offence under section 139A of the Criminal Justice Act 1988 (having a bladed or pointed article or offensive weapon on school premises) has been or is being committed. A warrant to search premises and persons found therein may be issued under section 23(3) of the Misuse of Drugs Act 1971 if there are reasonable grounds to suspect that controlled drugs or certain documents are in the possession of a person on the premises.

2.29 The powers in paragraph 2.27(a) or (b) do not require prior specific grounds to suspect that the person to be searched is in possession of an item for which there is an existing power to search. However, it is still necessary to ensure that the selection and treatment of those searched under these powers is based upon objective factors connected with the search of the premises, and not upon personal prejudice.

3 Conduct of searches

3.1 All stops and searches must be carried out with courtesy, consideration and respect for the person concerned. This has a significant impact on public confidence in the police. Every reasonable effort must be made to minimise the embarrassment that a person being searched may experience. [See *Note 4*]

3.2 The co-operation of the person to be searched must be sought in every case, even if the person initially objects to the search. A forcible search may be made only if it has been established that the person is unwilling to co-operate or resists. Reasonable force may be used as a last resort if necessary to conduct a search or to detain a person or vehicle for the purposes of a search.

3.3 The length of time for which a person or vehicle may be detained must be reasonable and kept to a minimum. Where the exercise of the power requires reasonable suspicion, the thoroughness and extent of a search must depend on what is suspected of being carried, and by whom. If the suspicion relates to a particular article which is seen to be slipped into a person's pocket, then, in the absence of other grounds for suspicion or an opportunity for the article to be moved elsewhere, the search must be confined to that pocket. In the case of a small article which can readily be concealed, such as a drug, and which might be concealed anywhere on the person, a more extensive search may be necessary. In the case of searches mentioned in paragraph 2.1(b), (c), and (d), which do not require reasonable grounds for suspicion, officers may make any reasonable search to look for items for which they are empowered to search. [See *Note 5*]

3.4 The search must be carried out at or near the place where the person or vehicle was first detained. [See *Note 6*]

3.5 There is no power to require a person to remove any clothing in public other than an outer coat, jacket or gloves except under section 45(3) of the Terrorism Act 2000 (which empowers a constable conducting a search under section 44(1) or 44(2) of that Act to require a person to remove headgear and footwear in public) and under section 60AA of the Criminal Justice and Public Order Act 1994 (which empowers a constable to require a person to remove any item worn to conceal identity). [See *Notes 4* and *6*] A search in public of a person's clothing which has not been removed must be restricted to superficial examination of outer garments. This does not, however, prevent an officer from placing his or her hand inside the pockets of the outer clothing, or feeling round the inside of collars, socks and shoes if this is reasonably necessary in the circumstances to look for the object of the search or to remove and examine any item reasonably suspected to be the object of the search. For the same reasons, subject to the restrictions on the removal of headgear, a person's hair may also be searched in public (see paragraphs 3.1 and 3.3).

3.6 Where on reasonable grounds it is considered necessary to conduct a more thorough search (e.g. by requiring a person to take off a T-shirt), this must be done out of public view, for example, in a police van unless paragraph 3.7 applies, or police station if there is one nearby. [See *Note 6*] Any search involving the removal of more than an outer coat, jacket, gloves, headgear or footwear, or any other item concealing identity, may only be made by an officer of the same sex as the person searched and may not be made in the presence of anyone of the opposite sex unless the person being searched specifically requests it. [See *Notes 4, 7* and *8*]

3.7 Searches involving exposure of intimate parts of the body must not be conducted as a routine extension of a less thorough search, simply because nothing is found in the course of the initial search. Searches involving exposure of intimate parts of the body may be carried out only at a nearby police station or other nearby location which is out of public view (but not a police vehicle). These searches must be conducted in accordance with paragraph 11 of Annex A to Code C except that an intimate search mentioned in paragraph 11(f) of Annex A to Code C may not be authorised or carried out under any stop and search powers. The other provisions of Code C do not apply to the conduct and recording of searches of persons detained at police stations in the exercise of stop and search powers. [See *Note 7*]

Steps to be taken prior to a search

3.8 Before any search of a detained person or attended vehicle takes place the officer must take reasonable steps to give the person to be searched or in charge of the vehicle the following information:

(a) that they are being detained for the purposes of a search

(b) the officer's name (except in the case of enquiries linked to the investigation of terrorism, or otherwise where the officer reasonably believes that giving his or her name might put him or her in danger, in which case a warrant or other identification number shall be given) and the name of the police station to which the officer is attached;

(c) the legal search power which is being exercised; and

(d) a clear explanation of:

(i) the purpose of the search in terms of the article or articles for which there is a power to search; and

(ii) in the case of powers requiring reasonable suspicion (see paragraph 2.1(a)), the grounds for that suspicion; or

(iii) in the case of powers which do not require reasonable suspicion (see paragraph 2.1(b), and (c)), the nature of the power and of any necessary authorisation and the fact that it has been given.

3.9 Officers not in uniform must show their warrant cards. Stops and searches under the powers mentioned in paragraphs 2.1(b), and (c) may be undertaken only by a constable in uniform.

3.10 Before the search takes place the officer must inform the person (or the owner or person in charge of the vehicle that is to be searched) of his or her entitlement to a copy of the record of the search, including his entitlement to a record of the search if an application is made within 12 months, if it is wholly impracticable to make a record at the time. If a record is not made at the time the person should also be told how a copy can be obtained (see section 4). The person should also be given information about police powers to stop and search and the individual's rights in these circumstances.

3.11 If the person to be searched, or in charge of a vehicle to be searched, does not appear to understand what is being said, or there is any doubt about the person's ability to understand English, the officer must take reasonable steps to bring information regarding the person's rights and any relevant provisions of this Code to his or her attention. If the person is deaf or cannot understand English and is accompanied by someone, then the officer must try to establish whether that person can interpret or otherwise help the officer to give the required information.

4 Recording requirements

4.1 An officer who has carried out a search in the exercise of any power to which this Code applies, must make a record of it at the time, unless there are exceptional circumstances which would make this wholly impracticable (e.g. in situations involving public disorder or when the officer's presence is urgently required elsewhere). If a record is not made at the time, the officer must do so as soon as practicable afterwards. There may be situations in which it is not practicable to obtain the information necessary to complete a record, but the officer should make every reasonable effort to do so.. [See *Note 21.*]

4.2 A copy of a record made at the time must be given immediately to the person who has been searched. The officer must ask for the name, address and date of birth of the person searched, but there is no obligation on a person to provide these details and no power of detention if the person is unwilling to do so.

4.3 The following information must always be included in the record of a search even if the person does not wish to provide any personal details:

(i) the name of the person searched, or (if it is withheld) a description;
(ii) a note of the person's self-defined ethnic background; [*See Note 18*]
(iii) when a vehicle is searched, its registration number; [*See Note 16*]
(iv) the date, time, and place that the person or vehicle was first detained;
(v) the date, time and place the person or vehicle was searched (if different from (iv));
(vi) the purpose of the search;
(vii) the grounds for making it, or in the case of those searches mentioned in paragraph 2.1(b) and (c), the nature of the power and of any necessary authorisation and the fact that it has been given; [*See Note 17*]
(viii) its outcome (e.g. arrest or no further action);
(ix) a note of any injury or damage to property resulting from it;
(x) subject to paragraph 3.8(b), the identity of the officer making the search. [*See Note 15*]

4.4 Nothing in paragraph 4.3 (x) or 4.10A requires the names of police officers to be shown on the search record or any other record required to be made under this code in the case of enquiries linked to the investigation of terrorism or otherwise where an officer reasonably believes that recording names might endanger the officers. In such cases the record must show the officers' warrant or other identification number and duty station.

4.5 A record is required for each person and each vehicle searched. However, if a person is in a vehicle and both are searched, and the object and grounds of the search are the same, only one record need be completed. If more than one person in a vehicle is searched, separate records for each search of a person must be made. If only a vehicle is searched, the name of the driver and his or her self-defined ethnic background must be recorded, unless the vehicle is unattended.

4.6 The record of the grounds for making a search must, briefly but informatively, explain the reason for suspecting the person concerned, by reference to the person's behaviour and/or other circumstances.

4.7 Where officers detain an individual with a view to performing a search, but the search is not carried out due to the grounds for suspicion being eliminated as a result of questioning the person detained, a record must still be made in accordance with the procedure outlined in Paragraph 4.12.

4.8 After searching an unattended vehicle, or anything in or on it, an officer must leave a notice in it (or on it, if things on it have been searched without opening it) recording the fact that it has been searched.

4.9 The notice must include the name of the police station to which the officer concerned is attached and state where a copy of the record of the search may be obtained and where any application for compensation should be directed.

4.10 The vehicle must if practicable be left secure.

4.10A When an officer makes a record of the stop electronically and is unable to produce a copy of the form at the time, the officer must explain how the person can obtain a full copy of the record of the stop or search and give the person a receipt which contains:

- a unique reference number and guidance on how to obtain a full copy of the stop or search;
- the name of the officer who carried out the stop or search (unless paragraph 4.4 applies); and
- the power used to stop and search them. [See Note 21]

Recording of encounters not governed by Statutory Powers

4.11 Not used.

4.12 When an officer requests a person in a public place to account for themselves, i.e. their actions, behaviour, presence in an area or possession of anything, a record of the encounter must be completed at the time and a copy given to the person who has been questioned. The record must identify the name of the officer who has made the stop and conducted the encounter. This does not apply under the exceptional circumstances outlined in paragraph 4.1 of this code.

4.13 This requirement does not apply to general conversations such as when giving directions to a place, or when seeking witnesses. It also does not include occasions on which an officer is seeking general information or questioning people to establish background to incidents which have required officers to intervene to keep the peace or resolve a dispute.

4.14 A separate record need not be completed when:

— stopping a person in a vehicle when an HORT/1 form, a Vehicle Defect Rectification Scheme Notice, or aFixed Penalty Notice is issued. It also does not apply when a specimen of breath is required under Section 6 of the Road Traffic Act 1988.

— stopping a person when a Penalty Notice is issued for an offence.

4.15 Officers must inform the person of their entitlement to a copy of a record of the encounter.

4.16 The provisions of paragraph 4.4 of this code apply equally when the encounters described in 4.12 and 4.13 are recorded.

4.17 The following information must be included in the record

(i) the date, time and place of the encounter;
(ii) if the person is in a vehicle, the registration number;
(iii) the reason why the officer questioned that person; [See *Note 17*]
(iv) a note of the person's self-defined ethnic background; [See *Note 18*]
(v) the outcome of the encounter.

4.18 There is no power to require the person questioned to provide personal details. If a person refuses to give their self-defined ethnic background, a form must still be completed, which includes a description of the person's ethnic background. [See Note 18]

4.19 A record of an encounter must always be made when the criteria set out in 4.12 have been met. If the criteria are not met but the person requests a record, the officer should provide a copy of the form but record on it that the encounter did not meet the criteria. The officer can refuse to issue the form if he or she reasonably believes that the purpose of the request is deliberately aimed at frustrating or delaying legitimate police activity. [See *Note 20*]

4.20 All references to officers in this section include police staff designated as Community Support Officers under section 38 of the Police Reform Act 2002.

5 Monitoring and supervising the use of stop and search powers

5.1 Supervising officers must monitor the use of stop and search powers and should consider in particular whether there is any evidence that they are being exercised on the basis of stereotyped images or inappropriate generalisations. Supervising officers should satisfy themselves that the practice of officers under their supervision in stopping, searching and recording is fully in accordance with this Code. Supervisors must also examine whether the records reveal any trends or patterns which give cause for concern, and if so take appropriate action to address this

5.2 Senior officers with area or force-wide responsibilities must also monitor the broader use of stop and search powers and, where necessary, take action at the relevant level.

5.3 Supervision and monitoring must be supported by the compilation of comprehensive statistical records of stops and searches at force, area and local level. Any apparently disproportionate use of the powers by particular officers or groups of officers or in relation to specific sections of the community should be identified and investigated.

5.4 In order to promote public confidence in the use of the powers, forces in consultation with police authorities must make arrangements for the records to be scrutinised by representatives of the community, and to explain the use of the powers at a local level. [See *Note 19*].

Notes for Guidance

Officers exercising stop and search powers

1 *This code does not affect the ability of an officer to speak to or question a person in the ordinary course of the officer's duties without detaining the person or exercising any element of compulsion. It is not the purpose of the code to prohibit such encounters between the police and the community with the co-operation of the person concerned and neither does it affect the principle that all citizens have a duty to help police officers to prevent crime and discover offenders. This is a civic rather than a legal duty; but when a police officer is trying to discover whether, or by whom, an offence has been committed he or she may question any person from whom useful information might be obtained, subject to the restrictions imposed by Code C. A person's unwillingness to reply does not alter this entitlement, but in the absence of a power to arrest, or to detain in order to search, the person is free to leave at will and cannot be compelled to remain with the officer.*

2 *In some circumstances preparatory questioning may be unnecessary, but in general a brief conversation or exchange will be desirable not only as a means of avoiding unsuccessful searches, but to explain the grounds for the stop/search, to gain cooperation and reduce any tension there might be surrounding the stop/search.*

3 *Where a person is lawfully detained for the purpose of a search, but no search in the event takes place, the detention will not thereby have been rendered unlawful.*

4 *Many people customarily cover their heads or faces for religious reasons—for example, Muslim women, Sikh men, Sikh or Hindu women, or Rastarfarian men or women. A police officer cannot order the removal of a head or face covering except where there is reason to believe that the item is being worn by the individual wholly or mainly for the purpose of disguising identity, not simply because it disguises identity. Where there may be religious sensitivities about ordering the removal of such an item, the officer should permit the item to be removed out of public view. Where practicable, the item should be removed in the presence of an officer of the same sex as the person and out of sight of anyone of the opposite sex .*

5 *A search of a person in public should be completed as soon as possible.*

6 *A person may be detained under a stop and search power at a place other than where the person was first detained, only if that place, be it a police station or elsewhere, is nearby. Such a place should be located within a reasonable travelling distance using whatever mode of travel (on foot or by car) is appropriate. This applies to all searches under stop and search powers, whether or not they involve the removal of clothing or exposure of intimate parts of the body (see paragraphs 3.6 and 3.7) or take*

place in or out of public view. It means, for example, that a search under the stop and search power in section 23 of the Misuse of Drugs Act 1971 which involves the compulsory removal of more than a person's outer coat, jacket or gloves cannot be carried out unless a place which is both nearby the place they were first detained and out of public view, is available. If a search involves exposure of intimate parts of the body and a police station is not nearby, particular care must be taken to ensure that the location is suitable in that it enables the search to be conducted in accordance with the requirements of paragraph 11 of Annex A to Code C.

7 *A search in the street itself should be regarded as being in public for the purposes of paragraphs 3.6 and 3.7 above, even though it may be empty at the time a search begins. Although there is no power to require a person to do so, there is nothing to prevent an officer from asking a person voluntarily to remove more than an outer coat, jacket or gloves (and headgear or footwear under section 45(3) of the Terrorism Act 2000) in public.*

8 *Where there may be religious sensitivities about asking someone to remove headgear using a power under section 45(3) of the Terrorism Act 2000, the police officer should offer to carry out the search out of public view (for example, in a police van or police station if there is one nearby).*

9 *Other means of identification might include jewellery, insignias, tattoos or other features which are known to identify members of the particular gang or group.*

Authorising officers

10 *The powers under section 60 are separate from and additional to the normal stop and search powers which require reasonable grounds to suspect an individual of carrying an offensive weapon (or other article). Their overall purpose is to prevent serious violence and the widespread carrying of weapons which might lead to persons being seriously injured by disarming potential offenders in circumstances where other powers would not be sufficient. They should not therefore be used to replace or circumvent the normal powers for dealing with routine crime problems. The purpose of the powers under section 60AA is to prevent those involved in intimidatory or violent protests using face coverings to disguise identity.*

11 *Authorisations under section 60 require a reasonable belief on the part of the authorising officer. This must have an objective basis, for example: intelligence or relevant information such as a history of antagonism and violence between particular groups; previous incidents of violence at, or connected with, particular events or locations; a significant increase in knife-point robberies in a limited area; reports that individuals are regularly carrying weapons in a particular locality; or in the case of section 60AA previous incidents of crimes being committed while wearing face coverings to conceal identity.*

12 *It is for the authorising officer to determine the period of time during which the powers mentioned in paragraph 2.1 (b) and (c) may be exercised. The officer should set the minimum period he or she considers necessary to deal with the risk of violence, the carrying of knives or offensive weapons, or terrorism. A direction to extend the period authorised under the powers mentioned in paragraph 2.1(b) may be given only once. Thereafter further use of the powers requires a new authorisation. There is no provision to extend an authorisation of the powers mentioned in paragraph 2.1(c); further use of the powers requires a new authorisation.*

13 *It is for the authorising officer to determine the geographical area in which the use of the powers is to be authorised. In doing so the officer may wish to take into account factors such as the nature and venue of the anticipated incident, the number of people who may be in the immediate area of any possible incident, their access to surrounding areas and the anticipated level of violence. The officer should not set a geographical area which is wider than that he or she believes necessary for the purpose of preventing anticipated violence, the carrying of knives or offensive weapons, acts of terrorism, or, in the case of section 60AA, the prevention of commission of offences. It is particularly important to ensure that constables exercising such powers are fully aware of where they may be used. If the area specified is smaller than the whole force area, the officer giving the authorisation should specify either the streets which form the boundary of the area or a divisional boundary within the force area. If the power is to be used in response to a threat or incident that straddles police force areas, an officer from each of the forces concerned will need to give an authorisation.*

14 *An officer who has authorised the use of powers under section 44 of the Terrorism Act 2000 must take immediate steps to send a copy of the authorisation to the National Joint Unit, Metropolitan Police Special Branch, who will forward it to the Secretary of State. The Secretary of State should be informed of the reasons for the authorisation. The National Joint Unit will inform the force concerned, within 48 hours of the authorisation being made, whether the Secretary of State has confirmed or cancelled or altered the authorisation.*

Recording

15 *Where a stop and search is conducted by more than one officer the identity of all the officers engaged in the search must be recorded on the record. Nothing prevents an officer who is present but not directly involved in searching from completing the record during the course of the encounter.*

16 *Where a vehicle has not been allocated a registration number (e.g. a rally car or a trials motorbike) that part of the requirement under 4.3(iii) does not apply.*

17 *It is important for monitoring purposes to specify whether the authority for exercising a stop and search power was given under section 60 of the Criminal Justice and Public Order Act 1994, or under section 44(1) or 44(2) of the Terrorism Act 2000.*

18 *Officers should record the self-defined ethnicity of every person stopped according to the categories used in the 2001 census question listed in Annex B. Respondents should be asked to select one of the five main categories representing broad ethnic groups and then a more specific cultural background from within this group. The ethnic classification should be coded for recording purposes using the coding system in Annex B. An additional "Not stated" box is available but should not be offered to respondents explicitly. Officers should be aware and explain to members of the public, especially where concerns are raised, that this information is required to obtain a true picture of stop and search activity and to help improve ethnic monitoring, tackle discriminatory practice, and promote effective use of the powers. If the person gives what appears to the officer to be an "incorrect" answer (e.g. a person who appears to be white states that they are black), the officer should record the response that has been given. Officers should also record their own perception of the ethnic background of every person stopped and this must be done by using the PNC/Phoenix classification system. If the "Not stated" category is used the reason for this must be recorded on the form.*

19 *Arrangements for public scrutiny of records should take account of the right to confidentiality of those stopped and searched. Anonymised forms and/or statistics generated from records should be the focus of the examinations by members of the public.*

20 *Where an officer engages in conversation which is not pertinent to the actions or whereabouts of the individual (e.g. does not relate to why the person is there, what they are doing or where they have been or are going) then issuing a form would not meet the criteria set out in paragraph 4.12. Situations designed to impede police activity may arise, for example, in public order situations where individuals engage in dialogue with the officer but the officer does not initiate or engage in contact about the person's individual circumstances.*

21 *In situations where it is not practicable to provide a written record of the stop or stop and search at that time, the officer should consider providing the person with details of the station to which the person may attend for a record. This may take the form of a simple business card, adding the date of the stop or stop and search.*

Definition of Offensive Weapon

22 *'Offensive weapon' is defined as any article made or adapted for use for causing injury to the person, or intended by the person having it with him for such use or by someone else. There are three categories of offensive weapons: those made for causing injury to the person; those adapted for such a purpose; and those not so made or adapted, but carried with the intention of causing injury to the person. A firearm, as defined by section 57 of the Firearms Act 1968, would fall within the definition of offensive weapon if any of the criteria above.*

ANNEX A—SUMMARY OF MAIN STOP AND SEARCH POWERS

THIS TABLE RELATES TO STOP AND SEARCH POWERS ONLY. INDIVIDUAL STATUTES BELOW MAY CONTAIN OTHER POLICE POWERS OF ENTRY, SEARCH AND SEIZURE

Power	Object of search	Extent of search	Where exercisable
Unlawful articles general			
1. Public Stores Act 1875, s6	HM Stores stolen or unlawfully obtained	Persons, vehicles and vessels	Anywhere where the constabulary powers are exercisable
2. Firearms Act 1968, s47	Firearms	Persons and vehicles	A public place, or anywhere in the case of reasonable suspicion of offences of carrying firearms with criminal intent or trespassing with firearms
3. Misuse of Drugs Act 1971, s23	Controlled drugs	Persons and vehicles	Anywhere
4. Customs and Excise Management Act 1979, s163	Goods: (a) on which duty has not been paid; (b) being unlawfully removed, imported or exported; (c) otherwise liable to forfeiture to HM Customs and Excise	Vehicles and vessels only	Anywhere
5. Aviation Security Act 1982, s27(1)	Stolen or unlawfully obtained goods	Airport employees and vehicles carrying airport employees or aircraft or any vehicle in a cargo area whether or not carrying an employee	Any designated airport
6. Police and Criminal Evidence Act 1984, s1	Stolen goods; articles for use in certain Theft Act offences; offensive weapons, including bladed or sharply-pointed articles (except folding pocket knives with a bladed cutting edge not exceeding 3 inches); prohibited possession of a category 4 (display grade) firework, any person under 18 in possession of an adult firework in a public place.	Persons and vehicles	Where there is public access

Power	Object of search	Extent of search	Where exercisable
	Criminal Damage: Articles made, adapted or intended for use in destroying or damaging property	Persons and vehicles	Where there is public access
Police and Criminal Evidence Act 1984, s6(3) (by a constable of the United Kingdom Atomic Energy Authority Constabulary in respect of property owned or controlled by British Nuclear Fuels plc)	HM Stores (in the form of goods and chattels belonging to British Nuclear Fuels plc)	Persons, vehicles and vessels	Anywhere where the constabulary powers are exercisable
7. Sporting events (Control of Alcohol etc.) Act 1985, s7	Intoxicating liquor	Persons, coaches and trains	Designated sports grounds or coaches and trains travelling to or from a designated sporting event
8. Crossbows Act 1987, s4	Crossbows or parts of crossbows (except crossbows with a draw weight of less than 1.4 kilograms)	Persons and vehicles	Anywhere except dwellings
9. Criminal Justice Act 1988 s139B	Offensive weapons, bladed or sharply pointed article	Persons	School premises
Evidence of game and wildlife offences			
10. Poaching Prevention Act 1862, s2	Game or poaching equipment	Persons and vehicles	A public place
11. Deer Act 1991, s12	Evidence of offences under the Act	Persons and vehicles	Anywhere except dwellings
12. Conservation of Seals Act 1970, s4	Seals or hunting equipment	Vehicles only	Anywhere
13. Badgers Act 1992, s11	Evidence of offences under the Act	Persons and vehicles	Anywhere
14. Wildlife and Countryside Act 1981, s19	Evidence of wildlife offences	Persons and vehicles	Anywhere except dwellings
Other			
15. Terrorism Act 2000, s.43	*Evidence of liability to arrest under section 41 of the Act*	Persons	Anywhere

Power	Object of search	Extent of search	Where exercisable
16. Terrorism Act 2000, s.44(1)	Articles which could be used for a purpose connected with the commission, preparation or instigation of acts of terrorism	*Vehicles, driver and passengers*	Anywhere within the area or locality authorised under subsection (1)
17. Terrorism Act 2000, s.44(2)	*Articles which could be used for a purpose connected with the commission, preparation or instigation of acts of terrorism*	*Pedestrians*	Anywhere within the area of locality authorised
18. Paragraphs 7 and 8 of Schedule 7 to the Terrorism Act 2000	*Anything relevant to determining if a person being examined falls within paragraph 2(1)(a) to (c) of Schedule 5*	Persons, vehicles, vessels etc.	*Ports and airports*
19. Section 60 Criminal Justice and Public Order Act 1994 , *as amended by s.8 of the Knives Act 1997*	Offensive weapons or dangerous instruments to prevent incidents of serious violence *or to deal with the carrying of such items*	Persons and vehicles	Anywhere within a locality authorised under subsection (1)

ANNEX B—SELF-DEFINED ETHNIC CLASSIFICATION CATEGORIES

White	**W**
A. White—British	W1
B. White—Irish	W2
C. Any other White background	W9
Mixed	**M**
D. White and Black Caribbean	M1
E. White and Black African	M2
F. White and Asian	M3
G. Any other Mixed Background	M9
Asian/Asian—British	**A**
H. Asian—Indian	A1
I. Asian—Pakistani	A2
J. Asian—Bangladeshi	A3
K. Any other Asian background	A9
Black/Black—British	**B**
L. Black—Caribbean	B1
M. Black African	B2
N. Any other Black background	B9

Other	**O**
O. Chinese	O1
P. Any other	O9
Not Stated	**NS**

ANNEX C—SUMMARY OF POWERS OF COMMUNITY SUPPORT OFFICERS TO SEARCH AND SEIZE

The following is a summary of the search and seizure powers that may be exercised by a community support officer (CSO) who has been designated with the relevant powers in accordance with Part 4 of the Police Reform Act 2002.

When exercising any of these powers, a CSO must have regard to any relevant provisions of this Code, including section 3 governing the conduct of searches and the steps to be taken prior to a search.

1. Powers to stop and search not requiring consent

Designation	Power conferred	Object of Search	Extent of Search	Where Exercisable
Police Reform Act 2002, Schedule 4, paragraph 15	*(a) Terrorism Act 2000, s.44(1)(a) and (d) and 45(2);*	Items intended to be used in connection with terrorism.	(a) Vehicles or anything carried in or on the vehicle and anything carried by driver or passenger.	Anywhere within area of locality authorised and in the company and under the supervision of a constable.
	(b) Terrorism Act 2000, s.44 (2)(b) and 45(2).		(b) Anything carried by a pedestrian.	

2. Powers to search requiring the consent of the person and seizure

A CSO may detain a person using reasonable force where necessary as set out in Part 1of Schedule 4 to the Police Reform Act 2002. If the person has been lawfully detained, the CSO may search the person provided that person gives consent to such a search in relation to the following:

Designation	Power conferred	Object of Search	Extent of Search	Where Exercisable
Police Reform Act 2002, Schedule 4, paragraph 7A	(a) Criminal Justice and Police Act 2001, s12(2)	a) Alcohol or a container for alcohol	a) Persons	a) Designated public place

Designation	Power conferred	Object of Search	Extent of Search	Where Exercisable
	(b) Confiscation of Alcohol (Young Persons) Act 1997, s1	b) Alcohol	b) Persons under 18 years old	b) Public place
	(c) Children and Young Persons Act 1933, section 7(3)	(c) Tobacco or cigarette papers	(c) Persons under 16 years old found smoking	(c) Public place

3. Powers to search not requiring the consent of the person and seizure

A CSO may detain a person using reasonable force where necessary as set out in Part 1 of Schedule 4 to the Police Reform Act 2002. If the person has been lawfully detained, the CSO may search the person without the need for that person's consent in relation to the following:

Designation	Power conferred	Object of Search	Extent of Search	Where Exercisable
Police Reform Act 2002, Schedule 4, paragraph 2A	Police and Criminal Evidence Act 1984, s.32	a) Objects that might be used to cause physical injury to the person or the CSO. b) Items that might be used to assist escape.	Persons made subject to a requirement to wait.	Any place where the requirement to wait has been made.

4. Powers to seize without consent

This power applies when drugs are found in the course of any search mentioned above.

Designation	Power conferred	Object of Seizure	Where Exercisable
Police Reform Act 2002, Schedule 4, paragraph 7B	*Police Reform Act 2002, Schedule 4, paragraph 7B*	Controlled drugs in a person's possession.	Any place where the person is in possession of the drug.

Appendix 4.2

PACE Code of Practice for Searches of Premises by Police Officers and the Seizure of Property found by Police Officers on Persons or Premises (Code B)

This Code applies to applications for warrants made after midnight 31 January 2008 and to searches and seizures taking place after midnight on 31 January 2008.

1 Introduction

1.1 This Code of Practice deals with police powers to:
- search premises
- seize and retain property found on premises and persons

1.1A These powers may be used to find:
- property and material relating to a crime
- wanted persons
- children who abscond from local authority accommodation where they have been remanded or committed by a court

1.2 A justice of the peace may issue a search warrant granting powers of entry, search and seizure, e.g. warrants to search for stolen property, drugs, firearms and evidence of serious offences. Police also have powers without a search warrant. The main ones provided by the Police and Criminal Evidence Act 1984 (PACE) include powers to search premises:
- to make an arrest
- after an arrest

1.3 The right to privacy and respect for personal property are key principles of the Human Rights Act 1998. Powers of entry, search and seizure should be fully and clearly justified before use because they may significantly interfere with the occupier's privacy. Officers should consider if the necessary objectives can be met by less intrusive means.

1.4 In all cases, police should:
- exercise their powers courteously and with respect for persons and property
- only use reasonable force when this is considered necessary and proportionate to the circumstances

1.5 If the provisions of PACE and this Code are not observed, evidence obtained from a search may be open to question.

2 General

2.1 This Code must be readily available at all police stations for consultation by:

- police officers
- police staff
- detained persons
- members of the public

2.2 The *Notes for Guidance* included are not provisions of this Code.

2.3 This Code applies to searches of premises:

(a) by police for the purposes of an investigation into an alleged offence, with the occupier's consent, other than:

- routine scene of crime searches;
- calls to a fire or burglary made by or on behalf of an occupier or searches following the activation of fire or burglar alarms or discovery of insecure premises;
- searches when *paragraph 5.4* applies;
- bomb threat calls;

(b) under powers conferred on police officers by PACE, sections 17, 18 and 32;

(c) undertaken in pursuance of search warrants issued to and executed by constables in accordance with PACE, sections 15 and 16. See *Note 2A*;

(d) subject to *paragraph 2.6*, under any other power given to police to enter premises with or without a search warrant for any purpose connected with the investigation into an alleged or suspected offence. See *Note 2B*.

For the purposes of this Code, 'premises' as defined in PACE, section 23, includes any place, vehicle, vessel, aircraft, hovercraft, tent or movable structure and any offshore installation as defined in the Mineral Workings (Offshore Installations) Act 1971, section 1. See *Note 2D*

2.4 A person who has not been arrested but is searched during a search of premises should be searched in accordance with Code A. See *Note 2C*

2.5 This Code does not apply to the exercise of a statutory power to enter premises or to inspect goods, equipment or procedures if the exercise of that power is not dependent on the existence of grounds for suspecting that an offence may have been committed and the person exercising the power has no reasonable grounds for such suspicion.

2.6 This Code does not affect any directions of a search warrant or order, lawfully executed in England or Wales that any item or evidence seized under that warrant or order be handed over to a police force, court, tribunal, or other authority outside England or Wales. For example, warrants and orders issued in Scotland or Northern Ireland, see *Note 2B(f)* and search warrants issued under the Criminal Justice (International Co-operation) Act 1990, section 7.

2.7 When this Code requires the prior authority or agreement of an officer of at least inspector or superintendent rank, that authority may be given by a sergeant or chief inspector authorised to perform the functions of the higher rank under PACE, section 107.

2.8 Written records required under this Code not made in the search record shall, unless otherwise specified, be made:

- in the recording officer's pocket book ('pocket book' includes any official report book issued to police officers) or
- on forms provided for the purpose

2.9 Nothing in this Code requires the identity of officers, or anyone accompanying them during a search of premises, to be recorded or disclosed:

(a) in the case of enquiries linked to the investigation of terrorism; or

(b) if officers reasonably believe recording or disclosing their names might put them in danger.

In these cases officers should use warrant or other identification numbers and the name of their police station. Police staff should use any identification number provided to them by the police force. See *Note 2E*

2.10 The 'officer in charge of the search' means the officer assigned specific duties and responsibilities under this Code. Whenever there is a search of premises to which this Code applies one officer must act as the officer in charge of the search. See *Note 2F*

2.11 In this Code:

(a) 'designated person' means a person other than a police officer, designated under the Police Reform Act 2002, Part 4 who has specified powers and duties of police officers conferred or imposed on them. See *Note 2G*.

(b) any reference to a police officer includes a designated person acting in the exercise or performance of the powers and duties conferred or imposed on them by their designation.

(c) a person authorised to accompany police officers or designated persons in the execution of a warrant has the same powers as a constable in the execution of the warrant and the search and seizure of anything related to the warrant. These powers must be exercised in the company and under the supervision of a police officer. See *Note 3C*.

2.12 If a power conferred on a designated person:

(a) allows reasonable force to be used when exercised by a police officer, a designated person exercising that power has the same entitlement to use force;

(b) includes power to use force to enter any premises, that power is not exercisable by that designated person except:

(i) in the company and under the supervision of a police officer; or

(ii) for the purpose of:

- saving life or limb; or
- preventing serious damage to property.

2.13 Designated persons must have regard to any relevant provisions of the Codes of Practice.

Notes for guidance

2A PACE sections 15 and 16 apply to all search warrants issued to and executed by constables under any enactment, e.g. search warrants issued by a:

(a) justice of the peace under the:

- *Theft Act 1968, section 26—stolen property;*
- *Misuse of Drugs Act 1971, section 23—controlled drugs;*
- *PACE, section 8—evidence of an indictable offence;*
- *Terrorism Act 2000, Schedule 5, paragraph 1;*

(b) a Circuit judge under:

- *PACE, Schedule 1;*
- *Terrorism Act 2000, Schedule 5, paragraph 11.*

2B Examples of the other powers in paragraph 2.3(d) include:

(a) Road Traffic Act 1988, section 6E(1) giving police power to enter premises under section 6E(1) to:

- *require a person to provide a specimen of breath; or*
- *arrest a person following*
  - *— a positive breath test;*
  - *— failure to provide a specimen of breath;*

(b) Transport and Works Act 1992, section 30(4) giving police powers to enter premises mirroring the powers in (a) in relation to specified persons working on transport systems to which the Act applies;

(c) Criminal Justice Act 1988, section 139B giving police power to enter and search school premises for offensive weapons, bladed or pointed articles;

(d) Terrorism Act 2000, Schedule 5, paragraphs 3 and 15 empowering a superintendent in urgent cases to give written authority for police to enter and search premises for the purposes of a terrorist investigation;

(e) Explosives Act 1875, section 73(b) empowering a superintendent to give written authority for police to enter premises, examine and search them for explosives;

(*f*) *search warrants and production orders or the equivalent issued in Scotland or Northern Ireland endorsed under the Summary Jurisdiction (Process) Act 1881 or the Petty Sessions (Ireland) Act 1851 respectively for execution in England and Wales.*

2C *The Criminal Justice Act 1988, section 139B provides that a constable who has reasonable grounds to believe an offence under the Criminal Justice Act 1988, section 139A has or is being committed may enter school premises and search the premises and any persons on the premises for any bladed or pointed article or offensive weapon. Persons may be searched under a warrant issued under the Misuse of Drugs Act 1971, section 23(3) to search premises for drugs or documents only if the warrant specifically authorises the search of persons on the premises.*

2D *The Immigration Act 1971, Part III and Schedule 2 gives immigration officers powers to enter and search premises, seize and retain property, with and without a search warrant. These are similar to the powers available to police under search warrants issued by a justice of the peace and without a warrant under PACE, sections 17, 18, 19 and 32 except they only apply to specified offences under the Immigration Act 1971 and immigration control powers. For certain types of investigations and enquiries these powers avoid the need for the Immigration Service to rely on police officers becoming directly involved. When exercising these powers, immigration officers are required by the Immigration and Asylum Act 1999, section 145 to have regard to this Code's corresponding provisions. When immigration officers are dealing with persons or property at police stations, police officers should give appropriate assistance to help them discharge their specific duties and responsibilities.*

2E *The purpose of paragraph 2.9(b) is to protect those involved in serious organised crime investigations or arrests of particularly violent suspects when there is reliable information that those arrested or their associates may threaten or cause harm to the officers or anyone accompanying them during a search of premises. In cases of doubt, an officer of inspector rank or above should be consulted.*

2F *For the purposes of paragraph 2.10, the officer in charge of the search should normally be the most senior officer present. Some exceptions are:*

(*a*) *a supervising officer who attends or assists at the scene of a premises search may appoint an officer of lower rank as officer in charge of the search if that officer is:*
- *more conversant with the facts;*
- *a more appropriate officer to be in charge of the search;*

(*b*) *when all officers in a premises search are the same rank. The supervising officer if available must make sure one of them is appointed officer in charge of the search, otherwise the officers themselves must nominate one of their number as the officer in charge;*

(*c*) *a senior officer assisting in a specialist role. This officer need not be regarded as having a general supervisory role over the conduct of the search or be appointed or expected to act as the officer in charge of the search.*

Except in (c), nothing in this Note diminishes the role and responsibilities of a supervisory officer who is present at the search or knows of a search taking place.

2G *An officer of the rank of inspector or above may direct a designated investigating officer not to wear a uniform for the purposes of a specific operation.*

3 Search warrants and production orders

(a) Before making an application

3.1 When information appears to justify an application, the officer must take reasonable steps to check the information is accurate, recent and not provided maliciously or irresponsibly. An application may not be made on the basis of information from an anonymous source if corroboration has not been sought. See *Note 3A*

3.2 The officer shall ascertain as specifically as possible the nature of the articles concerned and their location.

3.3 The officer shall make reasonable enquiries to:

(i) establish if:
- anything is known about the likely occupier of the premises and the nature of the premises themselves;

- the premises have been searched previously and how recently;

(ii) obtain any other relevant information.

3.4 An application:

(a) to a justice of the peace for a search warrant or to a Circuit judge for a search warrant or production order under PACE, Schedule 1 must be supported by a signed written authority from an officer of inspector rank or above:

Note: If the case is an urgent application to a justice of the peace and an inspector or above is not readily available, the next most senior officer on duty can give the written authority.

(b) to a circuit judge under the Terrorism Act 2000, Schedule 5 for

- a production order;
- search warrant; or
- an order requiring an explanation of material seized or produced under such a warrant or production order

must be supported by a signed written authority from an officer of superintendent rank or above.

3.5 Except in a case of urgency, if there is reason to believe a search might have an adverse effect on relations between the police and the community, the officer in charge shall consult the local police/community liaison officer:

- before the search; or
- in urgent cases, as soon as practicable after the search

(b) Making an application

3.6 A search warrant application must be supported in writing, specifying:

(a) the enactment under which the application is made, see *Note 2A;*

(b) (i) whether the warrant is to authorise entry and search of:

- one set of premises; or
- if the application is under PACE section 8, or Schedule 1, paragraph 12, more than one set of specified premises or all premises occupied or controlled by a specified person, and

(ii) the premises to be searched;

(c) the object of the search, see *Note 3B;*

(d) the grounds for the application, including, when the purpose of the proposed search is to find evidence of an alleged offence, an indication of how the evidence relates to the investigation;

(da) where the application is under PACE section 8, or Schedule 1, paragraph 12 for a single warrant to enter and search:

(i) more than one set of specified premises, the officer must specify each set of premises which it is desired to enter and search

(ii) all premises occupied or controlled by a specified person, the officer must specify;

- as many sets of premises which it is desired to enter and search as it is reasonably practicable to specify
- the person who is in occupation or control of those premises and any others which it is desired to search
- why it is necessary to search more premises than those which can be specified
- why it is not reasonably practicable to specify all the premises which it is desired to enter and search

(db) whether an application under PACE section 8 is for a warrant authorising entry and search on more than one occasion, and if so, the officer must state the grounds for this and whether the desired number of entries authorised is unlimited or a specified maximum.

(e) there are no reasonable grounds to believe the material to be sought, when making application to a:

(i) justice of the peace or a Circuit judge consists of or includes items subject to legal privilege;

(ii) justice of the peace, consists of or includes excluded material or special procedure material;

Note: this does not affect the additional powers of seizure in the Criminal Justice and Police Act 2001, Part 2 covered in paragraph 7.7, see Note 3B;

(f) if applicable, a request for the warrant to authorise a person or persons to accompany the officer who executes the warrant, see *Note 3C.*

3.7 A search warrant application under PACE, Schedule 1, paragraph 12(a), shall if appropriate indicate why it is believed service of notice of an application for a production order may seriously prejudice the investigation. Applications for search warrants under the Terrorism Act 2000, Schedule 5, paragraph 11 must indicate why a production order would not be appropriate.

3.8 If a search warrant application is refused, a further application may not be made for those premises unless supported by additional grounds.

Notes for guidance

3A The identity of an informant need not be disclosed when making an application, but the officer should be prepared to answer any questions the magistrate or judge may have about:

- *the accuracy of previous information from that source*
- *any other related matters*

3B The information supporting a search warrant application should be as specific as possible, particularly in relation to the articles or persons being sought and where in the premises it is suspected they may be found.The meaning of 'items subject to legal privilege', 'excluded material' and 'special procedure material' are defined by PACE, sections 10, 11 and 14 respectively.

3C Under PACE, section 16(2), a search warrant may authorise persons other than police officers to accompany the constable who executes the warrant. This includes, e.g. any suitably qualified or skilled person or an expert in a particular field whose presence is needed to help accurately identify the material sought or to advise where certain evidence is most likely to be found and how it should be dealt with. It does not give them any right to force entry, but it gives them the right to be on the premises during the search and to search for or seize property without the occupier's permission.

4 Entry without warrant—particular powers

(a) Making an arrest etc

4.1 The conditions under which an officer may enter and search premises without a warrant are set out in PACE, section 17. It should be noted that this section does not create or confer any powers of arrest. See other powers in *Note 2B(a).*

(b) Search of premises where arrest takes place or the arrested person was immediately before arrest

4.2 When a person has been arrested for an indictable offence, a police officer has power under PACE, section 32 to search the premises where the person was arrested or where the person was immediately before being arrested.

(c) Search of premises occupied or controlled by the arrested person

4.3 The specific powers to search premises occupied or controlled by a person arrested for an indictable offence are set out in PACE, section 18. They may not be exercised, except if section 18(5) applies, unless an officer of inspector rank or above has given written authority. That authority should only be given when the authorising officer is satisfied the necessary grounds exist. If possible the authorising officer should record the authority on the Notice of Powers and Rights and, subject to *paragraph 2.9*, sign the Notice. The record of the grounds for the search and the nature of the evidence sought as required by section 18(7) of the Act should be made in:

- the custody record if there is one, otherwise
- the officer's pocket book, or
- the search record

5 Search with consent

5.1 Subject to *paragraph 5.4*, if it is proposed to search premises with the consent of a person entitled to grant entry the consent must, if practicable, be given in writing on the Notice of Powers and Rights before the search. The officer must make any necessary enquiries to be satisfied the person is in a position to give such consent. See *Notes 5A* and *5B*

5.2 Before seeking consent the officer in charge of the search shall state the purpose of the proposed search and its extent. This information must be as specific as possible, particularly regarding the articles or persons being sought and the parts of the premises to be searched. The person concerned must be clearly informed they are not obliged to consent and anything seized may be produced in evidence. If at the time the person is not suspected of an offence, the officer shall say this when stating the purpose of the search.

5.3 An officer cannot enter and search or continue to search premises under *paragraph 5.1* if consent is given under duress or withdrawn before the search is completed.

5.4 It is unnecessary to seek consent under *paragraphs 5.1* and *5.2* if this would cause disproportionate inconvenience to the person concerned. See *Note 5C*

Notes for guidance

5A In a lodging house or similar accommodation, every reasonable effort should be made to obtain the consent of the tenant, lodger or occupier. A search should not be made solely on the basis of the landlord's consent unless the tenant, lodger or occupier is unavailable and the matter is urgent.

5B If the intention is to search premises under the authority of a warrant or a power of entry and search without warrant, and the occupier of the premises co-operates in accordance with paragraph 6.4, there is no need to obtain written consent.

5C Paragraph 5.4 is intended to apply when it is reasonable to assume innocent occupiers would agree to, and expect, police to take the proposed action, e.g. if:

- *a suspect has fled the scene of a crime or to evade arrest and it is necessary quickly to check surrounding gardens and readily accessible places to see if the suspect is hiding*
- *police have arrested someone in the night after a pursuit and it is necessary to make a brief check of gardens along the pursuit route to see if stolen or incriminating articles have been discarded*

6 Searching premises—general considerations

(a) Time of searches

6.1 Searches made under warrant must be made within three calendar months of the date of the warrant's issue.

6.2 Searches must be made at a reasonable hour unless this might frustrate the purpose of the search.

6.3 When the extent or complexity of a search mean it is likely to take a long time, the officer in charge of the search may consider using the seize and sift powers referred to in *section 7*.

6.3A A warrant under PACE, section 8 may authorise entry to and search of premises on more than one occasion if, on the application, the justice of the peace is satisfied that it is necessary to authorise multiple entries in order to achieve the purpose for which the warrant is issued. No premises may be entered or searched on any subsequent occasions without the prior written authority of an officer of the rank of inspector who is not involved in the investigation. All other warrants authorise entry on one occasion only.

6.3B Where a warrant under PACE section 8, or Schedule 1, paragraph 12 authorises entry to and search of all premises occupied or controlled by a specified person, no premises which are not specified in the warrant may be entered and searched without the prior written authority of an officer of the rank of inspector who is not involved in the investigation.

(b) Entry other than with consent

6.4 The officer in charge of the search shall first try to communicate with the occupier, or any other person entitled to grant access to the premises, explain the authority under which entry is sought and ask the occupier to allow entry, unless:

(i) the search premises are unoccupied;

(ii) the occupier and any other person entitled to grant access are absent;

(iii) there are reasonable grounds for believing that alerting the occupier or any other person entitled to grant access would frustrate the object of the search or endanger officers or other people.

6.5 Unless *sub-paragraph 6.4(iii)* applies, if the premises are occupied the officer, subject to *paragraph 2.9*, shall, before the search begins:

(i) identify him or herself, show their warrant card (if not in uniform) and state the purpose of and grounds for the search;

(ii) identify and introduce any person accompanying the officer on the search (such persons should carry identification for production on request) and briefly describe that person's role in the process.

6.6 Reasonable and proportionate force may be used if necessary to enter premises if the officer in charge of the search is satisfied the premises are those specified in any warrant, or in exercise of the powers described in *paragraphs 4.1* to *4.3*, and if:

(i) the occupier or any other person entitled to grant access has refused entry;

(ii) it is impossible to communicate with the occupier or any other person entitled to grant access; or

(iii) any of the provisions of *paragraph 6.4* apply.

(c) Notice of Powers and Rights

6.7 If an officer conducts a search to which this Code applies the officer shall, unless it is impracticable to do so, provide the occupier with a copy of a Notice in a standard format:

(i) specifying if the search is made under warrant, with consent, or in the exercise of the powers described in *paragraphs 4.1* to *4.3*. Note: the notice format shall provide for authority or consent to be indicated, see *paragraphs 4.3* and *5.1*;

(ii) summarising the extent of the powers of search and seizure conferred by PACE;

(iii) explaining the rights of the occupier, and the owner of the property seized;

(iv) explaining compensation may be payable in appropriate cases for damages caused entering and searching premises, and giving the address to send a compensation application, see *Note 6A*;

(v) stating this Code is available at any police station.

6.8 If the occupier is:

- present, copies of the Notice and warrant shall, if practicable, be given to them before the search begins, unless the officer in charge of the search reasonably believes this would frustrate the object of the search or endanger officers or other people

- not present, copies of the Notice and warrant shall be left in a prominent place on the premises or appropriate part of the premises and endorsed, subject to *paragraph 2.9* with the name of the officer in charge of the search, the date and time of the search

The warrant shall be endorsed to show this has been done.

(d) Conduct of searches

6.9 Premises may be searched only to the extent necessary to achieve the object of the search, having regard to the size and nature of whatever is sought.

6.9A A search may not continue under:

- a warrant's authority once all the things specified in that warrant have been found
- any other power once the object of that search has been achieved

6.9B No search may continue once the officer in charge of the search is satisfied whatever is being sought is not on the premises. See *Note 6B*. This does not prevent a further search of the same premises if additional grounds come to light supporting a further application for a search warrant or exercise or further exercise of another power. For example, when, as a result of new information, it is believed articles previously not found or additional articles are on the premises.

6.10 Searches must be conducted with due consideration for the property and privacy of the occupier and with no more disturbance than necessary. Reasonable force may be used only when necessary and proportionate because the co-operation of the occupier cannot be obtained or is insufficient for the purpose. See *Note 6C*

6.11 A friend, neighbour or other person must be allowed to witness the search if the occupier wishes unless the officer in charge of the search has reasonable grounds for believing the presence of the person asked for would seriously hinder the investigation or endanger officers or other people. A search need not be unreasonably delayed for this purpose. A record of the action taken should be made on the premises search record including the grounds for refusing the occupier's request.

6.12 A person is not required to be cautioned prior to being asked questions that are solely necessary for the purpose of furthering the proper and effective conduct of a search, see Code C, *paragraph 10.1(c)*. For example, questions to discover the occupier of specified premises, to find a key to open a locked drawer or cupboard or to otherwise seek co-operation during the search or to determine if a particular item is liable to be seized.

6.12A If questioning goes beyond what is necessary for the purpose of the exemption in Code C, the exchange is likely to constitute an interview as defined by Code C, *paragraph 11.1A* and would require the associated safeguards included in Code C, *section 10.*

(e) Leaving premises

6.13 If premises have been entered by force, before leaving the officer in charge of the search must make sure they are secure by:

- arranging for the occupier or their agent to be present
- any other appropriate means

(f) Searches under PACE Schedule 1 or the Terrorism Act 2000, Schedule 5

6.14 An officer shall be appointed as the officer in charge of the search, see *paragraph 2.10*, in respect of any search made under a warrant issued under PACE Act 1984, Schedule 1 or the Terrorism Act 2000, Schedule 5. They are responsible for making sure the search is conducted with discretion and in a manner that causes the least possible disruption to any business or other activities carried out on the premises.

6.15 Once the officer in charge of the search is satisfied material may not be taken from the premises without their knowledge, they shall ask for the documents or other records concerned. The officer in charge of the search may also ask to see the index to files held on the premises, and the officers conducting the search may inspect any files which, according to the index, appear to contain the material sought. A more extensive search of the premises may be made only if:

- the person responsible for them refuses to:
  — produce the material sought, or
  — allow access to the index
- it appears the index is:
  — inaccurate, or
  — incomplete
- for any other reason the officer in charge of the search has reasonable grounds for believing such a search is necessary in order to find the material sought

Notes for guidance

6A Whether compensation is appropriate depends on the circumstances in each case. Compensation for damage caused when effecting entry is unlikely to be appropriate if the search was lawful, and the force used can be shown to be reasonable, proportionate and necessary to effect entry. If the wrong premises are searched by mistake everything possible should be done at the earliest opportunity to allay any sense of grievance and there should normally be a strong presumption in favour of paying compensation.

6B It is important that, when possible, all those involved in a search are fully briefed about any powers to be exercised and the extent and limits within which it should be conducted.

6C In all cases the number of officers and other persons involved in executing the warrant should be determined by what is reasonable and necessary according to the particular circumstances.

7 Seizure and retention of property

(a) Seizure

7.1 Subject to *paragraph 7.2*, an officer who is searching any person or premises under any statutory power or with the consent of the occupier may seize anything:

(a) covered by a warrant

(b) the officer has reasonable grounds for believing is evidence of an offence or has been obtained in consequence of the commission of an offence but only if seizure is necessary to prevent the items being concealed, lost, disposed of, altered, damaged, destroyed or tampered with

(c) covered by the powers in the Criminal Justice and Police Act 2001, Part 2 allowing an officer to seize property from persons or premises and retain it for sifting or examination elsewhere

See *Note 7B*

7.2 No item may be seized which an officer has reasonable grounds for believing to be subject to legal privilege, as defined in PACE, section 10, other than under the Criminal Justice and Police Act 2001, Part 2.

7.3 Officers must be aware of the provisions in the Criminal Justice and Police Act 2001, section 59, allowing for applications to a judicial authority for the return of property seized and the subsequent duty to secure in section 60, see *paragraph 7.12(iii)*.

7.4 An officer may decide it is not appropriate to seize property because of an explanation from the person holding it but may nevertheless have reasonable grounds for believing it was obtained in consequence of an offence by some person. In these circumstances, the officer should identify the property to the holder, inform the holder of their suspicions and explain the holder may be liable to civil or criminal proceedings if they dispose of, alter or destroy the property.

7.5 An officer may arrange to photograph, image or copy, any document or other article they have the power to seize in accordance with *paragraph 7.1*. This is subject to specific restrictions on the examination, imaging or copying of certain property seized under the Criminal Justice and Police Act 2001, Part 2. An officer must have regard to their statutory obligation to retain an original document or other article only when a photograph or copy is not sufficient.

7.6 If an officer considers information stored in any electronic form and accessible from the premises could be used in evidence, they may require the information to be produced in a form:

- which can be taken away and in which it is visible and legible; or
- from which it can readily be produced in a visible and legible form

(b) Criminal Justice and Police Act 2001: Specific procedures for seize and sift powers

7.7 The Criminal Justice and Police Act 2001, Part 2 gives officers limited powers to seize property from premises or persons so they can sift or examine it elsewhere. Officers must be careful they only exercise these powers when it is essential and they do not remove any more material than necessary. The removal of large volumes of material, much of which may not ultimately be retainable, may have serious implications for the owners, particularly when they are involved in business or activities such as journalism or the provision of medical services. Officers must carefully consider if removing copies or images of relevant material or data would be a satisfactory alternative to removing originals. When originals are taken, officers must be prepared to facilitate the provision of copies or images for the owners when reasonably practicable. See *Note 7C*

7.8 Property seized under the Criminal Justice and Police Act 2001, sections 50 or 51 must be kept securely and separately from any material seized under other powers. An examination under section 53 to determine which elements may be retained must be carried out at the earliest practicable time, having due regard to the desirability of allowing the person from whom the property was seized, or a person with an interest in the property, an opportunity of being present or represented at the examination.

7.8A All reasonable steps should be taken to accommodate an interested person's request to be present, provided the request is reasonable and subject to the need to prevent harm to, interference with, or unreasonable delay to the investigatory process. If an examination proceeds in the absence of an interested person who asked to attend or their representative, the officer who exercised the relevant seizure power must give that person a written notice of why the examination was carried out in those circumstances. If it is necessary for security reasons or to maintain confidentiality officers may exclude interested persons from decryption or other processes which facilitate the examination but do not form part of it. See *Note 7D*

7.9 It is the responsibility of the officer in charge of the investigation to make sure property is returned in accordance with sections 53 to 55. Material which there is no power to retain must be:

- separated from the rest of the seized property
- returned as soon as reasonably practicable after examination of all the seized property

7.9A Delay is only warranted if very clear and compelling reasons exist, e.g. the:

- unavailability of the person to whom the material is to be returned
- need to agree a convenient time to return a large volume of material

7.9B Legally privileged, excluded or special procedure material which cannot be retained must be returned:

- as soon as reasonably practicable
- without waiting for the whole examination

7.9C As set out in section 58, material must be returned to the person from whom it was seized, except when it is clear some other person has a better right to it. See *Note 7E*

7.10 When an officer involved in the investigation has reasonable grounds to believe a person with a relevant interest in property seized under section 50 or 51 intends to make an application under section 59 for the return of any legally privileged, special procedure or excluded material, the officer in charge of the investigation should be informed as soon as practicable and the material seized should be kept secure in accordance with section 61. See *Note 7C*

7.11 The officer in charge of the investigation is responsible for making sure property is properly secured. Securing involves making sure the property is not examined, copied, imaged or put to any other use except at the request, or with the consent, of the applicant or in accordance with the directions of the appropriate judicial authority. Any request, consent or directions must be recorded in writing and signed by both the initiator and the officer in charge of the investigation. See *Notes 7F* and *7G*

7.12 When an officer exercises a power of seizure conferred by sections 50 or 51 they shall provide the occupier of the premises or the person from whom the property is being seized with a written notice:

(i) specifying what has been seized under the powers conferred by that section;

(ii) specifying the grounds for those powers;

(iii) setting out the effect of sections 59 to 61 covering the grounds for a person with a relevant interest in seized property to apply to a judicial authority for its return and the duty of officers to secure property in certain circumstances when an application is made;

(iv) specifying the name and address of the person to whom:

- notice of an application to the appropriate judicial authority in respect of any of the seized property must be given;
- an application may be made to allow attendance at the initial examination of the property.

7.13 If the occupier is not present but there is someone in charge of the premises, the notice shall be given to them. If no suitable person is available, so the notice will easily be found it should either be:

- left in a prominent place on the premises
- attached to the exterior of the premises

(c) Retention

7.14 Subject to *paragraph 7.15*, anything seized in accordance with the above provisions may be retained only for as long as is necessary. It may be retained, among other purposes:

(i) for use as evidence at a trial for an offence;

(ii) to facilitate the use in any investigation or proceedings of anything to which it is inextricably linked, see *Note 7H*;

(iii) for forensic examination or other investigation in connection with an offence;

(iv) in order to establish its lawful owner when there are reasonable grounds for believing it has been stolen or obtained by the commission of an offence.

7.15 Property shall not be retained under *paragraph 7.14(i), (ii)* or *(iii)* if a copy or image would be sufficient.

(d) Rights of owners etc

7.16 If property is retained, the person who had custody or control of it immediately before seizure must, on request, be provided with a list or description of the property within a reasonable time.

7.17 That person or their representative must be allowed supervised access to the property to examine it or have it photographed or copied, or must be provided with a photograph or copy, in either case within a reasonable time of any request and at their own expense, unless the officer in charge of an investigation has reasonable grounds for believing this would:

(i) prejudice the investigation of any offence or criminal proceedings; or

(ii) lead to the commission of an offence by providing access to unlawful material such as pornography;

A record of the grounds shall be made when access is denied.

Notes for guidance

7A *Any person claiming property seized by the police may apply to a magistrates' court under the Police (Property) Act 1897 for its possession and should, if appropriate, be advised of this procedure.*

7B *The powers of seizure conferred by PACE, sections 18(2) and 19(3) extend to the seizure of the whole premises when it is physically possible to seize and retain the premises in their totality and practical considerations make seizure desirable. For example, police may remove premises such as tents, vehicles or caravans to a police station for the purpose of preserving evidence.*

7C *Officers should consider reaching agreement with owners and/or other interested parties on the procedures for examining a specific set of property, rather than awaiting the judicial authority's determination. Agreement can sometimes give a quicker and more satisfactory route for all concerned and minimise costs and legal complexities.*

7D *What constitutes a relevant interest in specific material may depend on the nature of that material and the circumstances in which it is seized. Anyone with a reasonable claim to ownership of the material and anyone entrusted with its safe keeping by the owner should be considered.*

7E *Requirements to secure and return property apply equally to all copies, images or other material created because of seizure of the original property.*

7F *The mechanics of securing property vary according to the circumstances; "bagging up", i.e. placing material in sealed bags or containers and strict subsequent control of access is the appropriate procedure in many cases.*

7G *When material is seized under the powers of seizure conferred by PACE, the duty to retain it under the Code of Practice issued under the Criminal Procedure and Investigations Act 1996 is subject to the provisions on retention of seized material in PACE, section 22.*

7H *Paragraph 7.14 (ii) applies if inextricably linked material is seized under the Criminal Justice and Police Act 2001, sections 50 or 51. Inextricably linked material is material it is not reasonably practicable to separate from other linked material without prejudicing the use of that other material in any investigation or proceedings. For example, it may not be possible to separate items of data held on computer disk without damaging their evidential integrity. Inextricably linked material must not be examined, imaged, copied or used for any purpose other than for proving the source and/or integrity of the linked material.*

8 Action after searches

8.1 If premises are searched in circumstances where this Code applies, unless the exceptions in *paragraph 2.3(a)* apply, on arrival at a police station the officer in charge of the search shall make or have made a record of the search, to include:

(i) the address of the searched premises;

(ii) the date, time and duration of the search;

(iii) the authority used for the search:

- if the search was made in exercise of a statutory power to search premises without warrant, the power which was used for the search:
- if the search was made under a warrant or with written consent;
  - — a copy of the warrant and the written authority to apply for it, see paragraph 3.4; or
  - — the written consent;

shall be appended to the record or the record shall show the location of the copy warrant or consent.

(iv) subject to *paragraph 2.9*, the names of:

- the officer(s) in charge of the search;
- all other officers and any authorised persons who conducted the search;

(v) the names of any people on the premises if they are known;

(vi) any grounds for refusing the occupier's request to have someone present during the search, see *paragraph 6.11;*

(vii) a list of any articles seized or the location of a list and, if not covered by a warrant, the grounds for their seizure;
(viii) whether force was used, and the reason;
(ix) details of any damage caused during the search, and the circumstances;
(x) if applicable, the reason it was not practicable;
  (a) to give the occupier a copy of the Notice of Powers and Rights, see *paragraph 6.7*;
  (b) before the search to give the occupier a copy of the Notice, see *paragraph 6.8*;
(xi) when the occupier was not present, the place where copies of the Notice of Powers and Rights and search warrant were left on the premises, see *paragraph 6.8*.

8.2 On each occasion when premises are searched under warrant, the warrant authorising the search on that occasion shall be endorsed to show:
(i) if any articles specified in the warrant were found and the address where found;
(ii) if any other articles were seized;
(iii) the date and time it was executed and if present, the name of the occupier or if the occupier is not present the name of the person in charge of the premises:
(iv) subject to paragraph 2.9, the names of the officers who executed it and any authorised persons who accompanied them;
(v) if a copy, together with a copy of the Notice of Powers and Rights was:
- handed to the occupier; or
- endorsed as required by paragraph 6.8; and left on the premises and where.

8.3 Any warrant shall be returned within three calendar months of its issue or sooner on completion of the search(es) authorised by that warrant, if it was issued by a:
- justice of the peace, to the designated officer for the local justice area in which the justice was acting when issuing the warrant; or
- judge, to the appropriate officer of the court concerned,

9 Search registers

9.1 A search register will be maintained at each sub-divisional or equivalent police station. All search records required under *paragraph 8.1* shall be made, copied, or referred to in the register. See *Note 9A*

Note for guidance

9A Paragraph 9.1 also applies to search records made by immigration officers. In these cases, a search register must also be maintained at an immigration office. See also Note 2D

Appendix 4.3

PACE Code of Practice for the Statutory Power of Arrest by Police Officers (Code G)

This Code applies to any arrest made by a police officer after midnight on 31 December 2005

1 Introduction

1.1 This Code of Practice deals with statutory power of police to arrest persons suspected of involvement in a criminal offence.

1.2 The right to liberty is a key principle of the Human Rights Act 1998. The exercise of the power of arrest represents an obvious and significant interference with that right.

1.3 The use of the power must be fully justified and officers exercising the power should consider if the necessary objectives can be met by other, less intrusive means. Arrest must never be used simply because it can be used. Absence of justification for exercising the powers of arrest may lead to challenges should the case proceed to court. When the power of arrest is exercised it is essential that it is exercised in a non- discriminatory and proportionate manner.

1.4 Section 24 of the Police and Criminal Evidence Act 1984 (as substituted by section 110 of the Serious Organised Crime and Police Act 2005) provides the statutory power of arrest. If the provisions of the Act and this Code are not observed, both the arrest and the conduct of any subsequent investigation may be open to question.

1.5 This code of practice must be readily available at all police stations for consultation by police officers and police staff, detained persons and members of the public.

1.6 The notes for guidance are not provisions of this code.

2 Elements of Arrest under section 24 PACE

2.1 A lawful arrest requires two elements:

A person's involvement or suspected involvement or attempted involvement in the commission of a criminal offence;

AND

Reasonable grounds for believing that the person's arrest is necessary.

2.2 Arresting officers are required to inform the person arrested that they have been arrested, even if this fact is obvious, and of the relevant circumstances of the arrest in relation to both elements and to inform the custody officer of these on arrival at the police station. See Code C paragraph 3.4.

Involvement in the commission of an offence'

2.3 A constable may arrest without warrant in relation to any offence, except for the single exception listed in Note for Guidance 1. A constable may arrest anyone:

- who is about to commit an offence or is in the act of committing an offence
- whom the officer has reasonable grounds for suspecting is about to commit an offence or to be committing an offence

- whom the officer has reasonable grounds to suspect of being guilty of an offence which he or she has reasonable grounds for suspecting has been committed
- anyone who is guilty of an offence which has been committed or anyone whom the officer has reasonable grounds for suspecting to be guilty of that offence.

Necessity criteria

2.4 The power of arrest is only exercisable if the constable has reasonable grounds for believing that it is necessary to arrest the person. The criteria for what may constitute necessity are set out in paragraph 2.9. It remains an operational decision at the discretion of the arresting officer as to:

- what action he or she may take at the point of contact with the individual;
- the necessity criterion or criteria (if any) which applies to the individual; and
- whether to arrest, report for summons, grant street bail, issue a fixed penalty notice or take any other action that is open to the officer.

2.5 In applying the criteria, the arresting officer has to be satisfied that at least one of the reasons supporting the need for arrest is satisfied.

2.6 Extending the power of arrest to all offences provides a constable with the ability to use that power to deal with any situation. However applying the necessity criteria requires the constable to examine and justify the reason or reasons why a person needs to be taken to a police station for the custody officer to decide whether the person should be placed in police detention.

2.7 The criteria below are set out in section 24 of PACE as substituted by section 110 of the Serious Organised Crime and Police Act 2005. The criteria are exhaustive. However, the circumstances that may satisfy those criteria remain a matter for the operational discretion of individual officers. Some examples are given below of what those circumstances may be.

2.8 In considering the individual circumstances, the constable must take into account the situation of the victim, the nature of the offence, the circumstances of the suspect and the needs of the investigative process.

2.9 The criteria are that the arrest is necessary:

(a) to enable the name of the person in question to be ascertained (in the case where the constable does not know, and cannot readily ascertain, the person's name, or has reasonable grounds for doubting whether a name given by the person as his name is his real name)

(b) correspondingly as regards the person's address

an address is a satisfactory address for service of summons if the person will be at it for a sufficiently long period for it to be possible to serve him or her with a summons; or, that some other person at that address specified by the person will accept service of the summons on their behalf.

(c) to prevent the person in question—

(i) causing physical injury to himself or any other person;

(ii) suffering physical injury;

(iii) causing loss or damage to property;

(iv) committing an offence against public decency (only applies where members of the public going about their normal business cannot reasonably be expected to avoid the person in question); or

(v) causing an unlawful obstruction of the highway;

(d) to protect a child or other vulnerable person from the person in question

(e) to allow the prompt and effective investigation of the offence or of the conduct of the person in question.

This may include cases such as:

(i) Where there are reasonable grounds to believe that the person:

- has made false statements;
- has made statements which cannot be readily verified;
- has presented false evidence;
- may steal or destroy evidence;
- may make contact with co-suspects or conspirators;

- may intimidate or threaten or make contact with witnesses;
- where it is necessary to obtain evidence by questioning; or

(ii) when considering arrest in connection with an indictable offence, there is a need to:
- enter and search any premises occupied or controlled by a person
- search the person
- prevent contact with others
- take fingerprints, footwear impressions, samples or photographs of the suspect

(iii) ensuring compliance with statutory drug testing requirements.

(f) to prevent any prosecution for the offence from being hindered by the disappearance of the person in question.

This may arise if there are reasonable grounds for believing that
- if the person is not arrested he or she will fail to attend court
- street bail after arrest would be insufficient to deter the suspect from trying to evade prosecution

3 Information to be given on Arrest

(a) Cautions—when a caution must be given (taken from Code C section 10)

3.1 A person whom there are grounds to suspect of an offence (see Note 2) must be cautioned before any questions about an offence, or further questions if the answers provide the grounds for suspicion, are put to them if either the suspect's answers or silence, (i.e. failure or refusal to answer or answer satisfactorily) may be given in evidence to a court in a prosecution. A person need not be cautioned if questions are for other necessary purposes e.g.:

(a) solely to establish their identity or ownership of any vehicle;
(b) to obtain information in accordance with any relevant statutory requirement;
(c) in furtherance of the proper and effective conduct of a search, e.g. to determine the need to search in the exercise of powers of stop and search or to seek cooperation while carrying out a search;
(d) to seek verification of a written record as in *Code C paragraph 11.13*;
(e) when examining a person in accordance with the Terrorism Act 2000, Schedule 7 and the Code of Practice for Examining Officers issued under that Act, Schedule 14, paragraph 6.

3.2 Whenever a person not under arrest is initially cautioned, or reminded they are under caution, that person must at the same time be told they are not under arrest and are free to leave if they want to.

3.3 A person who is arrested, or further arrested, must be informed at the time, or as soon as practicable thereafter, that they are under arrest and the grounds for their arrest, see *Note 3*.

3.4 A person who is arrested, or further arrested, must also be cautioned unless:
(a) it is impracticable to do so by reason of their condition or behaviour at the time;
(b) they have already been cautioned immediately prior to arrest as in *paragraph 3.1*.
(c) Terms of the caution (Taken from Code C section 10)

3.5 The caution, which must be given on arrest, should be in the following terms:

"You do not have to say anything. But it may harm your defence if you do not mention when questioned something which you later rely on in Court. Anything you do say may be given in evidence."

See *Note 5*

3.6 Minor deviations from the words of any caution given in accordance with this Code do not constitute a breach of this Code, provided the sense of the relevant caution is preserved. See *Note 6*

3.7 When, despite being cautioned, a person fails to co-operate or to answer particular questions which may affect their immediate treatment, the person should be informed of any relevant consequences and that those consequences are not affected by the caution. Examples are when a person's refusal to provide:

- their name and address when charged may make them liable to detention;
- particulars and information in accordance with a statutory requirement, e.g. under the Road Traffic Act 1988, may amount to an offence or may make the person liable to a further arrest.

4 Records of Arrest

(a) General

4.1 The arresting officer is required to record in his pocket book or by other methods used for recording information:
- the nature and circumstances of the offence leading to the arrest
- the reason or reasons why arrest was necessary
- the giving of the caution
- anything said by the person at the time of arrest

4.2 Such a record should be made at the time of the arrest unless impracticable to do. If not made at that time, the record should then be completed as soon as possible thereafter.

4.3 On arrival at the police station, the custody officer shall open the custody record (see paragraph 1.1A and section 2 of Code C). The information given by the arresting officer on the circumstances and reason or reasons for arrest shall be recorded as part of the custody record. Alternatively, a copy of the record made by the officer in accordance with paragraph 4.1 above shall be attached as part of the custody record. See *paragraph 2.2* and *Code C paragraphs 3.4 and 10.3.*

4.4 The custody record will serve as a record of the arrest. Copies of the custody record will be provided in accordance with paragraphs 2.4 and 2.4A of Code C and access for inspection of the original record in accordance with paragraph 2.5 of Code C.

(b) Interviews and arrests

4.5 Records of interview, significant statements or silences will be treated in the same way as set out in sections 10 and 11 of Code C and in Code E (tape recording of interviews).

Notes for guidance

1 *The powers of arrest for offences under sections 4(1) and 5(1) of the Criminal Law Act 1967 require that the offences to which they relate must carry a sentence fixed by law or one in which a first time offender aged 18 or over could be sentenced to 5 years or more imprisonment.*

2 *There must be some reasonable, objective grounds for the suspicion, based on known facts or information which are relevant to the likelihood the offence has been committed and the person to be questioned committed it.*

3 *An arrested person must be given sufficient information to enable them to understand they have been deprived of their liberty and the reason they have been arrested, e.g. when a person is arrested on suspicion of committing an offence they must be informed of the suspected offence's nature, when and where it was committed. The suspect must also be informed of the reason or reasons why arrest is considered necessary. Vague or technical language should be avoided.*

4 *Nothing in this Code requires a caution to be given or repeated when informing a person not under arrest they may be prosecuted for an offence. However, a court will not be able to draw any inferences under the Criminal Justice and Public Order Act 1994, section 34, if the person was not cautioned.*

5 *If it appears a person does not understand the caution, the people giving it should explain it in their own words.*

6 *The powers available to an officer as the result of an arrest—for example, entry and search of premises, holding a person incommunicado, setting up road blocks—are only available in respect of indictable offences and are subject to the specific requirements on authorisation as set out in the 1984 Act and relevant PACE Code of Practice.*

Appendix 4.4

Powers of Police Community Support Officers

Police Community Support Officers

Part 1 of Schedule 4 to the Police Reform Act 2002—Police Community Support Officers

Each of the following paragraphs will only apply if the designation specifically applies it to the Police Community Support Officer (PCSO) concerned.

Power to issue fixed penalty notices—paragraph 1

(1) Where a designation applies this paragraph to any person, that person shall have the powers specified in sub-paragraph (2) in relation to any individual who he has reason to believe has committed a relevant fixed penalty offence at a place within the relevant police area.

(2) Those powers are the following powers so far as exercisable in respect of a relevant fixed penalty offence—

- (a) the powers of a constable in uniform and of an authorised constable to give a penalty notice under Chapter 1 of Part 1 of the Criminal Justice and Police Act 2001 (fixed penalty notices in respect of offences of disorder);
- (aa) the power of a constable to give a penalty notice under section 444A of the Education Act 1996 (penalty notice in respect of failure to secure regular attendance at school of registered pupil);
- (ab) the power of a constable to give a penalty notice under section 105 of the Education and Inspections Act 2006 (penalty notice in respect of presence of excluded pupil in public place);
- (b) the power of a constable in uniform to give a person a fixed penalty notice under section 54 of the Road Traffic Offenders Act 1988 (fixed penalty notices) in respect of an offence under section 72 of the Highway Act 1835 (riding on a footway) committed by cycling;
- (c) . . .
- (ca) the power of an authorised officer of a local authority to give a notice under section 43(1) of the Anti-social Behaviour Act 2003 (penalty notices in respect of graffiti or fly-posting); and
- (d) the power of an authorised officer of a litter authority to give a notice under section 88 of the Environmental Protection Act 1990 (fixed penalty notices in respect of litter); and
- (e) the power of an authorised officer of a primary or secondary authority, within the meaning of section 59 of the Clean Neighbourhoods and Environment Act 2005, to give a notice under that section (fixed penalty notices in respect of offences under dog control orders).

(2A) The reference to the powers mentioned in sub-paragraph (2)(a) does not include those powers so far as they relate to an offence under the provisions in the following list—

section 1 of the Theft Act 1968,

section 87 of the Environmental Protection Act 1990.

(3) In this paragraph 'relevant fixed penalty offence', in relation to a designated person, means an offence which—
   (a) is an offence by reference to which a notice may be given to a person in exercise of any of the powers mentioned in sub-paragraph (2)(a) to (e); and
   (b) is specified or described in that person's designation as an offence he has been designated to enforce under this paragraph.

(4) In its application to an offence which is an offence by reference to which a notice may be given to a person in exercise of the power mentioned in sub-paragraph (2)(aa), sub-paragraph (1) shall have effect as if for the words from 'who he has reason to believe' to the end there were substituted 'in the relevant police area who he has reason to believe has committed a relevant fixed penalty offence'.

Power to require name and address—paragraph 1A

(1) This paragraph applies if a designation applies it to any person.

(2) Such a designation may specify that, in relation to that person, the application of sub-paragraph (3) is confined to one or more only (and not to all) relevant offences or relevant licensing offences, being in each case specified in the designation.

(3) Subject to sub-paragraph (4), where that person has reason to believe that another person has committed a relevant offence in the relevant police area, or a relevant licensing offence (whether or not in the relevant police area), he may require that other person to give him his name and address.

(4) In its application to an offence which is an offence by reference to which a notice may be given to a person in exercise of the power mentioned in sub-paragraph (2)(aa) or (ab), sub-paragraph (1) shall have effect as if for the words from 'who he has reason to believe' to the end there were substituted 'in the relevant police area who he has reason to believe has committed a relevant fixed penalty offence'.

(5) A person who fails to comply with a requirement under sub-paragraph (3) is guilty of an offence and shall be liable, on summary conviction, to a fine not exceeding level 3 on the standard scale.

(6) In its application to an offence which is an offence by reference to which a notice may be given to a person in exercise of the power mentioned in paragraph 1(2)(aa), sub-paragraph (3) of this paragraph shall have effect as if for the words 'has committed a relevant offence in the relevant police area' there were substituted 'in the relevant police area has committed a relevant offence'.

(7) In this paragraph, 'relevant offence', 'relevant licensing offence' and 'relevant byelaw' have the meaning given in paragraph 2 (reading accordingly the references to 'this paragraph' in paragraph 2(6)).

Power to detain—paragraph 2

(1) This paragraph applies if a designation applies it to any person.

(2) A designation may not apply this paragraph to any person unless a designation also applies paragraph 1A to him.

(3) Where, in a case in which a requirement under paragraph 1A(3) has been imposed on another person—
   (a) that other person fails to comply with the requirement, or
   (b) the person who imposed the requirement has reasonable grounds for suspecting that the other person has given him a name or address that is false or inaccurate,

   the person who imposed the requirement may require the other person to wait with him, for a period not exceeding thirty minutes, for the arrival of a constable.

   This sub-paragraph does not apply if the requirement was imposed in connection with a relevant licensing offence mentioned in paragraph (a), (c) or (f) of sub-paragraph (6A) believed to have been committed on licensed premises (within the meaning of the Licensing Act 2003).

(3A) Where—

(a) a designation applies this paragraph to any person ('the CSO'); and

(b) by virtue of a designation applying paragraph 1A to the CSO, the CSO has the power to impose a requirement under sub-paragraph (3) of that paragraph in relation to an offence under a relevant byelaw,

the CSO shall also have any power a constable has under the relevant byelaw to remove a person from a place.

(3B) Where a person to whom this paragraph applies ('the CSO') has reason to believe that another person is committing an offence under section 3 or 4 of the Vagrancy Act 1824, and requires him to stop doing whatever gives rise to that belief, the CSO may, if the other person fails to stop as required, require him to wait with the CSO, for a period not exceeding thirty minutes, for the arrival of a constable.

(4) A person who has been required under sub-paragraph (3) or (3B) to wait with a person to whom this paragraph is applied may, if requested to do so, elect that (instead of waiting) he will accompany the person imposing the requirement to a police station in the relevant police area.

(4A) If a person has imposed a requirement under sub-paragraph (3) or (3B) on another person ('P'), and P does not make an election under sub-paragraph (4), the person imposing the requirement shall, if a constable arrives within the thirty-minute period, be under a duty to remain with the constable and P until he has transferred control of P to the constable.

(4B) If, following an election under sub-paragraph (4), the person imposing the requirement under sub-paragraph (3) or (3B) ('the CSO') takes the person upon whom it is imposed ('P') to a police station, the CSO—

(a) shall be under a duty to remain at the police station until he has transferred control of P to the custody officer there;

(b) until he has so transferred control of P, shall be treated for all purposes as having P in his lawful custody; and

(c) for so long as he is at the police station, or in its immediate vicinity, in compliance with, or having complied with, his duty under paragraph (a), shall be under a duty to prevent P's escape and to assist in keeping P under control.

(5) A person who—

(a) ...

(b) makes off while subject to a requirement under sub-paragraph (3) or (3B), or

(c) makes off while accompanying a person to a police station in accordance with an election under sub-paragraph (4),

is guilty of an offence and shall be liable, on summary conviction, to a fine not exceeding level 3 on the standard scale.

(6) In this paragraph 'relevant offence', in relation to a person to whom this paragraph applies, means any offence which is—

(a) a relevant fixed penalty offence for the purposes of the application of paragraph 1 to that person; or

(aa) an offence under section 32(2) of the Anti-social Behaviour Act 2003; or

(ab) an offence committed in a specified park which by virtue of section 2 of the Parks Regulation (Amendment) Act 1926 is an offence against the Parks Regulation Act 1872; or

(ac) an offence under section 3 or 4 of the Vagrancy Act 1824; or

(ad) an offence under a relevant byelaw; or

(b) an offence the commission of which appears to that person to have caused—

(i) injury, alarm or distress to any other person; or

(ii) the loss of, or any damage to, any other person's property;

but a designation applying this paragraph to any person may provide that an offence is not to be treated as a relevant offence by virtue of paragraph (b) unless it satisfies such other conditions as may be specified in the designation.

(6A) In this paragraph 'relevant licensing offence' means an offence under any of the following provisions of the Licensing Act 2003—
(a) section 141 (otherwise than by virtue of subsection (2)(c) or (3) of that section);
(b) section 142;
(c) section 146(1);
(d) section 149(1)(a), (3)(a) or (4)(a);
(e) section 150(1);
(f) section 150(2) (otherwise than by virtue of subsection (3)(b) of that section);
(g) section 152(1) (excluding paragraph (b)).

(6B) In this paragraph 'relevant byelaw' means a byelaw included in a list of byelaws which—
(a) have been made by a relevant body with authority to make byelaws for any place within the relevant police area; and
(b) the chief officer of the police force for the relevant police area and the relevant body have agreed to include in the list.

(6C) The list must be published by the chief officer in such a way as to bring it to the attention of members of the public in localities where the byelaws in the list apply.

(6D) A list of byelaws mentioned in sub-paragraph (6B) may be amended from time to time by agreement between the chief officer and the relevant body in question, by adding byelaws to it or removing byelaws from it, and the amended list shall also be published by the chief officer as mentioned in sub-paragraph (6C).

(6E) A relevant body for the purposes of sub-paragraph (6B) is—
(a) in England, a county council, a district council, a London borough council or a parish council; or in Wales, a county council, a county borough council or a community council;
(b) the Greater London Authority;
(c) Transport for London;
(d) a metropolitan county passenger transport authority established under section 28 of the Local Government Act 1985;
(e) any body specified in an order made by the Secretary of State.

(6F) An order under sub-paragraph (6E)(e) may provide, in relation to any body specified in the order, that the agreement mentioned in sub-paragraph (6B)(b) and (6D) is to be made between the chief officer and the Secretary of State (rather than between the chief officer and the relevant body).

(7) ...

(8) The application of any provision of this paragraph by paragraph 3(2), 3A(2), 7A(8) or 7C(2) has no effect unless a designation has applied this paragraph to the CSO in question.

Powers to search individuals and to seize and retain items—paragraph 2A

(1) Where a designation applies this paragraph to any person, that person shall (subject to sub-paragraph (3)) have the powers mentioned in sub-paragraph (2) in relation to a person upon whom he has imposed a requirement to wait under paragraph 2(3) or (3B) (whether or not that person makes an election under paragraph 2(4)).

(2) Those powers are the same powers as a constable has under section 32 of the 1984 Act in relation to a person arrested at a place other than a police station—
(a) to search the arrested person if the constable has reasonable grounds for believing that the arrested person may present a danger to himself or others; and to seize and retain anything he finds on exercising that power, if the constable has reasonable grounds for believing that the person being searched might use it to cause physical injury to himself or to any other person;
(b) to search the arrested person for anything which he might use to assist him to escape from lawful custody; and to seize and retain anything he finds on exercising that power (other than an item subject to legal privilege) if the constable has reasonable grounds for believing that the person being searched might use it to assist him to escape from lawful custody.

(3) If in exercise of the power conferred by sub-paragraph (1) the person to whom this paragraph applies seizes and retains anything by virtue of sub-paragraph (2), he must—
(a) tell the person from whom it was seized where inquiries about its recovery may be made; and
(b) comply with a constable's instructions about what to do with it.

Power to require name and address of person acting in an anti-social manner—paragraph 3

(1) Where a designation applies this paragraph to any person, that person shall, in the relevant police area, have the powers of a constable in uniform under section 50 to require a person whom he has reason to believe to have been acting, or to be acting, in an anti-social manner (within the meaning of section 1 of the Crime and Disorder Act 1998 (anti-social behaviour orders)) to give his name and address.
(2) Sub-paragraphs (3) to (5) of paragraph 2 apply in the case of a requirement imposed by virtue of sub-paragraph (1) as they apply in the case of a requirement under paragraph 1A(3).

Power to require name and address: road traffic offences—paragraph 3A

(1) Where a designation applies this paragraph to any person, that person shall, in the relevant police area, have the powers of a constable—
(a) under subsection (1) of section 165 of the Road Traffic Act 1988 to require a person mentioned in paragraph (c) of that subsection who he has reasonable cause to believe has committed, in the relevant police area, an offence under subsection (1) or (2) of section 35 of that Act (including that section as extended by paragraphs 11B(4) and 12(2) of this Schedule) to give his name and address; and
(b) under section 169 of that Act to require a person committing an offence under section 37 of that Act (including that section as extended by paragraphs 11B(4) and 12(2) of this Schedule) to give his name and address.
(2) Sub-paragraphs (3) to (5) of paragraph 2 apply in the case of a requirement imposed by virtue of sub-paragraph (1) as they apply in the case of a requirement under paragraph 1A(3).
(3) The reference in section 169 of the Road Traffic Act 1988 to section 37 of that Act is to be taken to include a reference to that section as extended by paragraphs 11B(4) and 12(2) of this Schedule.

Power to use reasonable force to detain person—paragraphs 4, 4ZA and 4ZB

(1) Sub-paragraph (3) applies where a designation—
(a) applies this paragraph to a person to whom any or all of paragraphs 1 to 3 are also applied; and
(b) sets out matters in respect of which that person has the power conferred by this paragraph.
(2) The matters that may be set out in a designation as matters in respect of which a person has the power conferred by this paragraph shall be confined to—
(a) offences that are relevant penalty notice offences for the purposes of the application of paragraph 1 to the designated person;
(b) offences that are relevant offences or relevant licensing offences for the purposes of the application of paragraph 1A or 2 to the designated person; and
(c) behaviour that constitutes acting in an anti-social manner (within the meaning of section 1 of the Crime and Disorder Act 1998 (anti-social behaviour orders)).
(3) In any case in which a person to whom this paragraph applies has imposed a requirement on any other person under paragraph 1A(3) or 3(1) in respect of anything appearing to him to be a matter set out in the designation, he may use reasonable force to prevent that other person from making off and to keep him under control while he is either—
(a) subject to a requirement imposed in that case by the designated person under sub-paragraph (3) of paragraph 2; or

(b) accompanying the designated person to a police station in accordance with an election made in that case under sub-paragraph (4) of that paragraph.

Where a designation applies this paragraph to any person, that person may, if he has imposed a requirement on any person to wait with him under paragraph 2(3B) or by virtue of paragraph 7A(8) or 7C(2)(a), use reasonable force to prevent that other person from making off and to keep him under control while he is either—

(a) subject to that requirement; or

(b) accompanying the designated person to a police station in accordance with an election made under paragraph 2(4).

Where a designation applies this paragraph to any person, that person, if he is complying with any duty under sub-paragraph (4A) or (4B) of paragraph 2, may use reasonable force to prevent P (as identified in those sub-paragraphs) from making off (or escaping) and to keep him under control.

Power to disperse groups and remove young persons to their place of residence—paragraphs 4A and 4B

Where a designation applies this paragraph to any person, that person shall, within the relevant police area, have the powers which, by virtue of an authorisation under section 30 of the Anti-social Behaviour Act 2003, are conferred on a constable in uniform by section 30(3) to (6) of that Act (power to disperse groups and remove persons under 16 to their place of residence).

(1) Where a designation applies this paragraph to any person, that person shall, within the relevant police area, have the power of a constable under section 15(3) of the Crime and Disorder Act 1998 (power to remove child to their place of residence).

(2) Section 15(1) of that Act shall have effect in relation to the exercise of that power by that person as if the reference to a constable in that section were a reference to that person.

(3) Where that person exercises that power, the duty in section 15(2) of that Act (duty to inform local authority of contravention of curfew notice) is to apply to him as it applies to a constable.

Power to remove truants [and excluded pupils] to designated premises etc—paragraph 4C

Where a designation applies this paragraph to any person, that person shall—

(a) as respects any area falling within the relevant police area and specified in a direction under section 16(2) of the Crime and Disorder Act 1998, but

(b) only during the period specified in the direction,

have the powers conferred on a constable by *section 16(3) of that Act (power to remove truant found in specified area to designated premises or to the school from which truant is absent)* [section 16(3) or (3ZA) of that Act (power to remove truant or excluded pupil found in specified area to designated premises or, in case of truant, to the school from which he is absent)].

NB Paragraph 4C has been amended but the amendments are only in force for England, not Wales (so far). The text which applies to Wales is italicised; that which applies only to England is in square brackets.

Powers relating to alcohol consumption in designated public places—paragraph 5

Where a designation applies this paragraph to any person, that person shall, within the relevant police area, have the powers of a constable under section 12 of the Criminal Justice and Police Act 2001 (alcohol consumption in public places)—

(a) to impose a requirement under subsection (2) of that section; and

(b) to dispose under subsection (3) of that section of anything surrendered to him;

and that section shall have effect in relation to the exercise of those powers by that person as if the references to a constable in subsections (1) and (5) were references to that person.

Power to serve closure notice for licensed premises persistently selling to children—paragraph 5A

Where a designation applies this paragraph to any person, that person shall have—

(a) within the relevant police area, and

(b) if it appears to him as mentioned in subsection (7) of section 169A of the Licensing Act 2003 (closure notices served on licensed premises persistently serving children),

the capacity of a constable under that subsection to be the person by whose delivery of a closure notice that notice is served.

Power to confiscate alcohol—paragraph 6

Where a designation applies this paragraph to any person, that person shall, within the relevant police area, have the powers of a constable under section 1 of the Confiscation of Alcohol (Young Persons) Act 1997 (confiscation of intoxicating liquor)—

(a) to impose a requirement under subsection (1) of that section; and

(b) to dispose under subsection (2) of that section of anything surrendered to him;

and that section shall have effect in relation to the exercise of those powers by that person as if the references to a constable in subsections (1) and (4) (but not the reference in subsection (5) (arrest)) were references to that person.

Power to confiscate alcohol—paragraph 7

Where a designation applies this paragraph to any person, that person shall, within the relevant police area, have—

(a) the power to seize anything that a constable in uniform has a duty to seize under subsection (3) of section 7 of the Children and Young Persons Act 1933 (seizure of tobacco etc from young persons); and

(b) the power to dispose of anything that a constable may dispose of under that subsection;

and the power to dispose of anything shall be a power to dispose of it in such manner as the police authority may direct.

Search and seizure powers: alcohol and tobacco—paragraph 7A

(1) Where a designation applies this paragraph to any person ('the CSO'), the CSO shall have the powers set out below.

(2) Where—

(a) in exercise of the powers referred to in paragraph 5 or 6 the CSO has imposed, under section 12(2) of the Criminal Justice and Police Act 2001 or under section 1 of the Confiscation of Alcohol (Young Persons) Act 1997, a requirement on a person to surrender alcohol or a container for alcohol;

(b) that person fails to comply with that requirement; and

(c) the CSO reasonably believes that the person has alcohol or a container for alcohol in his possession,

the CSO may search him for it.

(3) Where—

(a) in exercise of the powers referred to in paragraph 7 the CSO has sought to seize something which by virtue of that paragraph he has a power to seize;

(b) the person from whom he sought to seize it fails to surrender it; and

(c) the CSO reasonably believes that the person has it in his possession,

the CSO may search him for it.

(4) The power to search conferred by sub-paragraph (2) or (3)—

(a) is to do so only to the extent that is reasonably required for the purpose of discovering whatever the CSO is searching for; and

(b) does not authorise the CSO to require a person to remove any of his clothing in public other than an outer coat, jacket or gloves.

(5) A person who without reasonable excuse fails to consent to being searched is guilty of an offence and shall be liable, on summary conviction, to a fine not exceeding level 3 on the standard scale.
(6) A CSO who proposes to exercise the power to search a person under sub-paragraph (2) or (3) must inform him that failing without reasonable excuse to consent to being searched is an offence.
(7) If the person in question fails to consent to being searched, the CSO may require him to give the CSO his name and address.
(8) Sub-paragraph (3) of paragraph 2 applies in the case of a requirement imposed by virtue of sub-paragraph (7) as it applies in the case of a requirement under paragraph 1A(3); and sub-paragraphs (4) to (5) of paragraph 2 also apply accordingly.
(9) If on searching the person the CSO discovers what he is searching for, he may seize it and dispose of it.

Powers to seize and detain: controlled drugs—paragraphs 7B and 7C

(1) Where a designation applies this paragraph to any person ('the CSO'), the CSO shall, within the relevant police area, have the powers set out in sub-paragraphs (2) and (3).
(2) If the CSO—
  (a) finds a controlled drug in a person's possession (whether or not the CSO finds it in the course of searching the person by virtue of any paragraph of this Part of this Schedule being applied to the CSO by a designation); and
  (b) reasonably believes that it is unlawful for the person to be in possession of it,

  the CSO may seize it and retain it.
(3) If the CSO—
  (a) finds a controlled drug in a person's possession (as mentioned in sub-paragraph (2)); or
  (b) reasonably believes that a person is in possession of a controlled drug,

  and reasonably believes that it is unlawful for the person to be in possession of it, the CSO may require him to give the CSO his name and address.
(4) If in exercise of the power conferred by sub-paragraph (2) the CSO seizes and retains a controlled drug, he must—
  (a) if the person from whom it was seized maintains that he was lawfully in possession of it, tell the person where inquiries about its recovery may be made; and
  (b) comply with a constable's instructions about what to do with it.
(5) A person who fails to comply with a requirement under sub-paragraph (3) is guilty of an offence and shall be liable, on summary conviction, to a fine not exceeding level 3 on the standard scale.
(6) In this paragraph, 'controlled drug' has the same meaning as in the Misuse of Drugs Act 1971.

(1) Sub-paragraph (2) applies where a designation applies this paragraph to any person ('the CSO').
(2) If the CSO imposes a requirement on a person under paragraph 7B(3)—
  (a) sub-paragraph (3) of paragraph 2 applies in the case of such a requirement as it applies in the case of a requirement under paragraph 1A(3); and
  (b) sub-paragraphs (4) to (5) of paragraph 2 also apply accordingly.

Park trading offences—paragraph 7D

(1) This paragraph applies if—
  (a) a designation applies it to any person ('the CSO'), and
  (b) the CSO has under paragraph 2(3) required another person ('P') to wait with him for the arrival of a constable.
(2) If the CSO reasonably suspects that P has committed a park trading offence, the CSO may take possession of anything of a non-perishable nature which—
  (a) P has in his possession or under his control, and
  (b) the CSO reasonably believes to have been used in the commission of the offence.

(3) The CSO may retain possession of the thing in question for a period not exceeding 30 minutes unless P makes an election under paragraph 2(4), in which case the CSO may retain possession of the thing in question until he is able to transfer control of it to a constable.
(4) In this paragraph 'park trading offence' means an offence committed in a specified park which is a park trading offence for the purposes of the Royal Parks (Trading) Act 2000.

Power of entry to save life or limb or prevent serious damage to property—paragraph 8

Where a designation applies this paragraph to any person, that person shall have the powers of a constable under section 17 of the 1984 Act to enter and search any premises in the relevant police area for the purpose of saving life or limb or preventing serious damage to property.

Power of entry to investigate licensing offences—paragraph 8A

(1) Where a designation applies this paragraph to any person, that person shall have the powers of a constable under section 180 of the Licensing Act 2003 to enter and search premises other than clubs in the relevant police area, but only in respect of a relevant licensing offence (as defined for the purposes of paragraph 2).
(2) Except as mentioned in sub-paragraph (3), a person to whom this paragraph applies shall not, in exercise of the power conferred by sub-paragraph (1), enter any premises except in the company, and under the supervision, of a constable.
(3) The prohibition in sub-paragraph (2) does not apply in relation to premises in respect of which the person to whom this paragraph applies reasonably believes that a premises licence under Part 3 of the Licensing Act 2003 authorises the sale of alcohol for consumption off the premises.

Power to seize vehicles used to cause alarm—paragraph 9

(1) Where a designation applies this paragraph to any person—
    (a) that person shall, within the relevant police area, have all the powers of a constable in uniform under section 59 of this Act which are set out in subsection (3) of that section; and
    (b) references in that section to a constable, in relation to the exercise of any of those powers by that person, are references to that person.
(2) A person to whom this paragraph applies shall not enter any premises in exercise of the power conferred by section 59(3)(c) except in the company, and under the supervision, of a constable.

Powers to deal with abandoned vehicles—paragraph 10

Where a designation applies this paragraph to any person, that person shall have any such powers in the relevant police area as are conferred on persons designated under that section by regulations under section 99 of the Road Traffic Regulation Act 1984 (c 27) (removal of abandoned vehicles).

Power to stop vehicle for testing—paragraph 11

Where a designation applies this paragraph to any person, that person shall, within the relevant police area, have the power of a constable in uniform to stop a vehicle under subsection (3) of section 67 of the Road Traffic Act 1988 for the purposes of a test under subsection (1) of that section.

Power to stop cycles—paragraph 11A

(1) Subject to sub-paragraph (2), where a designation applies this paragraph to any person, that person shall, within the relevant police area, have the power of a constable in uniform under section 163(2) of the Road Traffic Act 1988 to stop a cycle.

(2) The power mentioned in sub-paragraph (1) may only be exercised by that person in relation to a person who he has reason to believe has committed an offence under section 72 of the Highway Act 1835 (riding on a footway) by cycling.

Power to control traffic for purposes other than escorting a load of exceptional dimensions—paragraph 11B

(1) Where a designation applies this paragraph to any person, that person shall have, in the relevant police area—
   (a) the power of a constable engaged in the regulation of traffic in a road to direct a person driving or propelling a vehicle to stop the vehicle or to make it proceed in, or keep to, a particular line of traffic;
   (b) the power of a constable in uniform engaged in the regulation of vehicular traffic in a road to direct a person on foot to stop proceeding along or across the carriageway.

(2) The purposes for which those powers may be exercised do not include the purpose mentioned in paragraph 12(1).

(3) Where a designation applies this paragraph to any person, that person shall also have, in the relevant police area, the power of a constable, for the purposes of a traffic survey, to direct a person driving or propelling a vehicle to stop the vehicle, to make it proceed in, or keep to, a particular line of traffic, or to proceed to a particular point on or near the road.

(4) Sections 35 and 37 of the Road Traffic Act 1988 (offences of failing to comply with directions of constable engaged in regulation of traffic in a road) shall have effect in relation to the exercise of the powers mentioned in sub-paragraphs (1) and (3), for the purposes for which they may be exercised and by a person whose designation applies this paragraph to him, as if the references to a constable were references to him.

(5) A designation may not apply this paragraph to any person unless a designation also applies paragraph 3A to him.

Power to control traffic for purposes of escorting a load of exceptional dimensions—paragraph 12

(1) Where a designation applies this paragraph to any person, that person shall have, for the purpose of escorting a vehicle or trailer carrying a load of exceptional dimensions either to or from the relevant police area, the power of a constable engaged in the regulation of traffic in a road—
   (a) to direct a vehicle to stop;
   (b) to make a vehicle proceed in, or keep to, a particular line of traffic; and
   (c) to direct pedestrians to stop.

(2) Sections 35 and 37 of the Road Traffic Act 1988 (offences of failing to comply with directions of constable engaged in regulation of traffic in a road) shall have effect in relation to the exercise of those powers for the purpose mentioned in sub-paragraph (1) by a person whose designation applies this paragraph to him as if the references to a constable engaged in regulation of traffic in a road were references to that person.

(3) The powers conferred by virtue of this paragraph may be exercised in any police area in England and Wales.

(4) In this paragraph 'vehicle or trailer carrying a load of exceptional dimensions' means a vehicle or trailer the use of which is authorised by an order made by the Secretary of State under section 44(1)(d) of the Road Traffic Act 1988.

Power to carry out road checks—paragraph 13

Where a designation applies this paragraph to any person, that person shall have the following powers in the relevant police area—
   (a) the power to carry out any road check the carrying out of which by a police officer is authorised under section 4 of the 1984 Act (road checks); and

(b) for the purpose of exercising that power, the power conferred by section 163 of the Road Traffic Act 1988 (power of police to stop vehicles) on a constable in uniform to stop a vehicle.

Power to place traffic signs—paragraph 13A

(1) Where a designation applies this paragraph to any person, that person shall have, in the relevant police area, the powers of a constable under section 67 of the Road Traffic Regulation Act 1984 to place and maintain traffic signs.
(2) Section 36 of the Road Traffic Act 1988 (drivers to comply with traffic directions) shall apply to signs placed in the exercise of the powers conferred by virtue of sub-paragraph (1).

Cordoned areas—paragraph 14

Where a designation applies this paragraph to any person, that person shall, in relation to any cordoned area in the relevant police area, have all the powers of a constable in uniform under section 36 of the Terrorism Act 2000 (enforcement of cordoned area) to give orders, make arrangements or impose prohibitions or restrictions.

Power to stop and search in authorised areas—paragraph 15

(1) Where a designation applies this paragraph to any person—
   (a) that person shall, in any authorised area within the relevant police area, have all the powers of a constable in uniform by virtue of section 44(1)(a) and (d) and (2)(b) and 45(2) of the Terrorism Act 2000 (powers of stop and search)—
      (i) to stop and search vehicles;
      (ii) to search anything in or on a vehicle or anything carried by the driver of a vehicle or any passenger in a vehicle;
      (iii) to search anything carried by a pedestrian; and
      (iv) to seize and retain any article discovered in the course of a search carried out by him or by a constable by virtue of any provision of section 44(1) or (2) of that Act;

   and
   (b) the references to a constable in subsections (1) and (4) of section 45 of that Act (which relate to the exercise of those powers) shall have effect in relation to the exercise of any of those powers by that person as references to that person.
(2) A person shall not exercise any power of stop, search or seizure by virtue of this paragraph except in the company, and under the supervision, of a constable.

Photographing of persons arrested, detained or given fixed penalty notices—paragraph 15ZA

Where a designation applies this paragraph to any person, that person shall, within the relevant police area, have the power of a constable under section 64A(1A) of the 1984 Act (photographing of suspects etc) to take a photograph of a person elsewhere than at a police station.

Investigating Officers

Part 2 of Schedule 4 to the Police Reform Act 2002—Investigating Officers

Each of the following paragraphs will only apply if the designation specifically applies it to the Investigating Officer concerned.

Search warrants—paragraph 16

Where a designation applies this paragraph to any person—

(a) he may apply as if he were a constable for a warrant under section 8 of the 1984 Act (warrants for entry and search) in respect of any premises whether in the relevant police area or not;

(b) the persons to whom a warrant to enter and search any such premises may be issued under that section shall include that person;

(c) that person shall have the power of a constable under section 8(2) of that Act in any premises in the relevant police area to seize and retain things for which a search has been authorised under subsection (1) of that section;

(d) section 15 of that Act (safeguards) shall have effect in relation to the issue of such a warrant to that person as it has effect in relation to the issue of a warrant under section 8 of that Act to a constable;

(e) section 16 of that Act (execution of warrants) shall have effect in relation to any warrant to enter and search premises that is issued (whether to that person or to any other person), but in respect of premises in the relevant police area only, as if references in that section to a constable included references to that person;

(f) section 19(6) of that Act (protection for legally privileged material from seizure) shall have effect in relation to the seizure of anything by that person by virtue of sub-paragraph (c) as it has effect in relation to the seizure of anything by a constable;

(g) section 20 of that Act (extension of powers of seizure to computerised information) shall have effect in relation the power of seizure conferred on that person by virtue of sub-paragraph (c) as it applies in relation to the power of seizure conferred on a constable by section 8(2) of that Act;

(h) section 21(1) and (2) of that Act (provision of record of seizure) shall have effect in relation to the seizure of anything by that person in exercise of the power conferred on him by virtue of sub-paragraph (c) as if the references to a constable and to an officer included references to that person; and

(i) sections 21(3) to (8) and 22 of that Act (access, copying and retention) shall have effect in relation to anything seized by that person in exercise of that power, or taken away by him following the imposition of a requirement by virtue of sub-paragraph (g)—

    (i) as they have effect in relation to anything seized in exercise of the power conferred on a constable by section 8(2) of that Act or taken away by a constable following the imposition of a requirement by virtue of section 20 of that Act; and

    (ii) as if the references to a constable in subsections (3), (4) and (5) of section 21 included references to a person to whom this paragraph applies.

Warrants for stolen goods—paragraph 16A

Where a designation applies this paragraph to any person—

(a) the persons to whom a warrant may be addressed under section 26 of the Theft Act 1968 (search for stolen goods) shall, in relation to persons or premises in the relevant police area, include that person; and

(b) in relation to such a warrant addressed to him, that person shall have the powers under subsection (3) of that section.

Misuse of Drugs Act 1971—paragraph 16B

Where a designation applies this paragraph to any person, subsection (3), and (to the extent that it applies subsection (3)) subsection (3A), of section 23 of the Misuse of Drugs Act 1971 (powers to search and obtain evidence) shall have effect as if, in relation to premises in the relevant police area, the reference to a constable included a reference to that person.

Access to excluded and special procedure material—paragraph 17

Where a designation applies this paragraph to any person—

(a) he shall have the powers of a constable under section 9(1) of the 1984 Act (special provisions for access) to obtain access, in accordance with Schedule 1 to that Act and the following provisions of this paragraph, to excluded material and special procedure material;

(b) that Schedule shall have effect for the purpose of conferring those powers on that person as if—

  (i) the references in paragraphs 1, 4, 5, 12 and 13 of that Schedule to a constable were references to that person; and

  (ii) the references in paragraphs 12 and 14 of that Schedule to premises were references to premises in the relevant police area (in the case of a specific premises warrant) or any premises, whether in the relevant police area or not (in the case of an all premises warrant);

(bb) section 15 of that Act (safeguards) shall have effect in relation to the issue of any warrant under paragraph 12 of that Schedule to that person as it has effect in relation to the issue of a warrant under that paragraph to a constable;

(bc) section 16 of that Act (execution of warrants) shall have effect in relation to any warrant to enter and search premises that is issued under paragraph 12 of that Schedule (whether to that person or to any other person), but in respect of premises in the relevant police area only, as if references in that section to a constable included references to that person;

(c) section 19(6) of that Act (protection for legally privileged material from seizure) shall have effect in relation to the seizure of anything by that person in exercise of the power conferred on him by paragraph 13 of Schedule 1 to that Act as it has effect in relation to the seizure of anything under that paragraph by a constable;

(d) section 20 of that Act (extension of powers of seizure to computerised information) shall have effect in relation the power of seizure conferred on that person by paragraph 13 of Schedule 1 to that Act as it applies in relation to the power of seizure conferred on a constable by that paragraph;

(e) section 21(1) and (2) of that Act (provision of record of seizure) shall have effect in relation to the seizure of anything by that person in exercise of the power conferred on him by paragraph 13 of Schedule 1 to that Act as if the references to a constable and to an officer included references to that person; and

(f) sections 21(3) to (8) and 22 of that Act (access, copying and retention) shall have effect in relation to anything seized by that person in exercise of that power or taken away by him following the imposition of a requirement by virtue of sub-paragraph (d), and to anything produced to him under paragraph 4(a) of Schedule 1 to that Act—

  (i) as they have effect in relation to anything seized in exercise of the power conferred on a constable by paragraph 13 of that Schedule or taken away by a constable following the imposition of a requirement by virtue of section 20 of that Act or, as the case may be, to anything produced to a constable under paragraph 4(a) of that Schedule; and

  (ii) as if the references to a constable in subsections (3), (4) and (5) of section 21 included references to a person to whom this paragraph applies.

Entry and search after arrest—paragraph 18

Where a designation applies this paragraph to any person—

(a) he shall have the powers of a constable under section 18 of the 1984 Act (entry and search after arrest) to enter and search any premises in the relevant police area and to seize and retain anything for which he may search under that section;

(b) subsections (5) and (6) of that section (power to carry out search before arrested person taken to police station and duty to inform senior officer) shall have effect in relation to any exercise by that person of those powers as if the references in those subsections to a constable were references to that person;

(c) section 19(6) of that Act (protection for legally privileged material from seizure) shall have effect in relation to the seizure of anything by that person by virtue of sub-paragraph (a) as it has effect in relation to the seizure of anything by a constable;

(d) section 20 of that Act (extension of powers of seizure to computerised information) shall have effect in relation the power of seizure conferred on that person by virtue of sub-paragraph (a) as it applies in relation to the power of seizure conferred on a constable by section 18(2) of that Act;
(e) section 21(1) and (2) of that Act (provision of record of seizure) shall have effect in relation to the seizure of anything by that person in exercise of the power conferred on him by virtue of sub-paragraph (a) as if the references to a constable and to an officer included references to that person; and
(f) sections 21(3) to (8) and 22 of that Act (access, copying and retention) shall have effect in relation to anything seized by that person in exercise of that power or taken away by him following the imposition of a requirement by virtue of sub-paragraph (d)—
  (i) as they have effect in relation to anything seized in exercise of the power conferred on a constable by section 18(2) of that Act or taken away by a constable following the imposition of a requirement by virtue of section 20 of that Act; and
  (ii) as if the references to a constable in subsections (3), (4) and (5) of section 21 included references to a person to whom this paragraph applies.

General power of seizure—paragraph 19

Where a designation applies this paragraph to any person—
(a) he shall, when lawfully on any premises in the relevant police area, have the same powers as a constable under section 19 of the 1984 Act (general powers of seizure) to seize things;
(b) he shall also have the powers of a constable to impose a requirement by virtue of subsection (4) of that section in relation to information accessible from such premises;
(c) subsection (6) of that section (protection for legally privileged material from seizure) shall have effect in relation to the seizure of anything by that person by virtue of sub-paragraph (a) as it has effect in relation to the seizure of anything by a constable;
(d) section 21(1) and (2) of that Act (provision of record of seizure) shall have effect in relation to the seizure of anything by that person in exercise of the power conferred on him by virtue of sub-paragraph (a) as if the references to a constable and to an officer included references to that person; and
(e) sections 21(3) to (8) and 22 of that Act (access, copying and retention) shall have effect in relation to anything seized by that person in exercise of that power or taken away by him following the imposition of a requirement by virtue of sub-paragraph (b)—
  (i) as they have effect in relation to anything seized in exercise of the power conferred on a constable by section 19(2) or (3) of that Act or taken away by a constable following the imposition of a requirement by virtue of section 19(4) of that Act; and
  (ii) as if the references to a constable in subsections (3), (4) and (5) of section 21 included references to a person to whom this paragraph applies.

Access and copying in the case of things seized by constables—paragraph 20

Where a designation applies this paragraph to any person, section 21 of the 1984 Act (access and copying) shall have effect in relation to anything seized in the relevant police area by a constable or by a person authorised to accompany him under section 16(2) of that Act as if the references to a constable in subsections (3), (4) and (5) of section 21 (supervision of access and photographing of seized items) included references to a person to whom this paragraph applies.

Arrest at a police station for another offence—paragraph 21

(1) Where a designation applies this paragraph to any person, he shall have the power to make an arrest at any police station in the relevant police area in any case where an arrest—
  (a) is required to be made under section 31 of the 1984 Act (arrest for a further offence of a person already at a police station); or
  (b) would be so required if the reference in that section to a constable included a reference to a person to whom this paragraph applies.

(2) Section 36 of the Criminal Justice and Public Order Act 1994 (consequences of failure by arrested person to account for objects etc) shall apply (without prejudice to the effect of any designation applying paragraph 23) in the case of a person arrested in exercise of the power exercisable by virtue of this paragraph as it applies in the case of a person arrested by a constable.

Power to transfer persons into custody of investigating officers—paragraph 22

(1) Where a designation applies this paragraph to any person, the custody officer for a designated police station in the relevant police area may transfer or permit the transfer to him of a person in police detention for an offence which is being investigated by the person to whom this paragraph applies.

(2) A person into whose custody another person is transferred under sub-paragraph (1)—
  (a) shall be treated for all purposes as having that person in his lawful custody;
  (b) shall be under a duty to keep that person under control and to prevent his escape; and
  (c) shall be entitled to use reasonable force to keep that person in his custody and under his control.

(3) Where a person is transferred into the custody of a person to whom this paragraph applies, in accordance with sub-paragraph (1), subsections (2) and (3) of section 39 of the 1984 Act shall have effect as if—
  (a) references to the transfer of a person in police detention into the custody of a police officer investigating an offence for which that person is in police detention were references to that person's transfer into the custody of the person to whom this paragraph applies; and
  (b) references to the officer to whom the transfer is made and to the officer investigating the offence were references to the person to whom this paragraph applies.

Powers in respect of detained persons—paragraph 22A

Where a designation applies this paragraph to any person, he shall be under a duty, when in the course of his employment he is present at a police station—
  (a) to assist any officer or other designated person to keep any person detained at the police station under control; and
  (b) to prevent the escape of any such person,

and for those purposes shall be entitled to use reasonable force.

Power to require arrested person to account for certain matters—paragraph 23

Where a designation applies this paragraph to any person—

(a) he shall have the powers of a constable under sections 36(1)(c) and 37(1)(c) of the Criminal Justice and Public Order Act 1994 to request a person who—
  (i) has been arrested by a constable, or by any person to whom paragraph 21 applies, and
  (ii) is detained at any place in the relevant police area,

  to account for the presence of an object, substance or mark or for the presence of the arrested person at a particular place; and

(b) the references to a constable in sections 36(1)(b) and (c) and (4) and 37(1)(b) and (c) and (3) of that Act shall have effect accordingly as including references to the person to whom this paragraph is applied.

Extended powers of seizure—paragraph 24

Where a designation applies this paragraph to any person—

(a) the powers of a constable under Part 2 of the Criminal Justice and Police Act 2001 (c 16) (extension of powers of seizure) that are exercisable in the case of a constable by reference to a power of a constable that is conferred on that person by virtue of the provisions of this Part of this Schedule shall be exercisable by that person by reference to that power to the same extent as in the case of a constable but in relation only to premises in the relevant police area and things found on any such premises; and

(b) section 56 of that Act (retention of property seized by a constable) shall have effect as if the property referred to in subsection (1) of that section included property seized by that person at any time when he was lawfully on any premises in the relevant police area.

Persons accompanying investigating officers—paragraph 24A

(1) This paragraph applies where a person ('an authorised person') is authorised by virtue of section 16(2) of the 1984 Act to accompany an investigating officer designated for the purposes of paragraph 16 (or 17) in the execution of a warrant.

(2) The reference in paragraph 16(h) (or 17(e)) to the seizure of anything by a designated person in exercise of a particular power includes a reference to the seizure of anything by the authorised person in exercise of that power by virtue of section 16(2A) of the 1984 Act.

(3) In relation to any such seizure, paragraph 16(h) (or 17(e)) is to be read as if it provided for the references to a constable and to an officer in section 21(1) and (2) of the 1984 Act to include references to the authorised person.

(4) The reference in paragraph 16(i) (or 17(f)) to anything seized by a designated person in exercise of a particular power includes a reference to anything seized by the authorised person in exercise of that power by virtue of section 16(2A) of the 1984 Act.

(5) In relation to anything so seized, paragraph 16(i)(ii) (or 17(f)(ii)) is to be read as if it provided for—

- (a) the references to the supervision of a constable in subsections (3) and (4) of section 21 of the 1984 Act to include references to the supervision of a person designated for the purposes of paragraph 16 (or paragraph 17), and
- (b) the reference to a constable in subsection (5) of that section to include a reference to such a person or an authorised person accompanying him.

(6) Where an authorised person accompanies an investigating officer who is also designated for the purposes of paragraph 24, the references in sub-paragraphs (a) and (b) of that paragraph to the designated person include references to the authorised person.

Accredited Employees

Schedule 5 to the Police Reform Act 2002—accredited employees

Each of the following paragraphs will only apply if the designation specifically applies it to the employee accredited under an authorised Community Safety Accreditation Scheme, established and maintained under s. 40.

Power to issue fixed penalty notices—paragraph 1

The powers below may be conferred on an Accredited Employee in relation to any individual who the employee has reason to believe has committed a relevant fixed penalty offence at a place within the relevant police area. Those powers are:

(a) the power of a constable in uniform to give a person a fixed penalty notice under s. 54 of the Road Traffic Offenders Act 1988 (fixed penalty notices—**see para. 4.4.3**) in respect of an offence under s. 72 of the Highway Act 1835 (riding on a footway) committed by cycling;

(aa) the powers of a constable in uniform to give a penalty notice under chapter 1 of part 1 of the Criminal Justice and Police Act 2001 (fixed penalty notices in respect of offences of disorder) except in respect of an offence under s. 12 of the Licensing Act 1872 or s. 91 of the Criminal Justice Act 1967 or notices under s. 1 of the Theft Act 1968, s. 1(1) of the Criminal Damage Act 1971 or s. 87 of the Environmental Protection Act 1990;

(ab) the power of a constable to give a penalty notice under s. 444A of the Education Act 1996 (penalty notice in respect of failure to secure regular attendance at school of registered pupil) (**see Evidence & Procedure**);

(ac) the power of a constable to give a penalty notice under section 105 of the Education and Inspections Act 2006 (penalty notice in respect of presence of excluded pupil in public place);
(b) the power of an authorised officer of a local authority to give a notice under s. 4 of the Dogs (Fouling of Land) Act 1996 (fixed penalty notices in respect of dog fouling—**see chapter 4.5**);
(c) the power of an authorised officer of a litter authority to give a notice under s. 88 of the Environmental Protection Act 1990 (fixed penalty notices in respect of litter—**see chapter 4.5**);
(ca) the power of an authorised officer of a local authority to give a notice under s. 43(1) of the Anti-social Behaviour Act 2003 (penalty notice in respect of graffiti or fly-posting—**see Crime**), (para. 1(2));
(d) the power of an authorised officer of a primary or secondary authority, within the meaning of section 59 of the Clean Neighbourhoods and Environment Act 2005, to give a notice under that section (fixed penalty notices in respect of offences under dog control orders).

'Relevant fixed penalty offence' = an offence which—

- is an offence by reference to which a notice may be given to a person in exercise of any of the powers mentioned in (a) to (d) above; and
- is specified or described in the Accredited Employee's accreditation as an offence he/she has been accredited to enforce (para. 1(3)).

The Secretary of State may extend the above powers under para. 1(2)(A) beyond simply issuing fixed penalty notices (see sch. 4, para. 15A).

Power to require giving of name and address—paragraph 2

Under this paragraph, where an Accredited Employee has reason to believe that another person has committed a relevant offence in the relevant police area, he/she may require that other person to give his/her name and address. 'Relevant offence' = any offence which is—

- a relevant fixed penalty offence for the purposes of the application of paragraph 1 above; or
- an offence under s. 3 or 4 of the Vagrancy Act 1824; or
- an offence the commission of which appears to the Accredited Employee to have caused—
  (i) injury, alarm or distress to any other person; or
  (ii) the loss of, or any damage to, any other person's property (para. 2(3)).

Note that an accreditation applying this paragraph to an Accredited Employee may provide that an offence is not to be treated as a 'relevant offence' unless some other specified conditions are satisfied.

Power to require name and address of person acting in an anti-social manner—paragraph 3

Under this paragraph an Accredited Employee will, in the relevant police area, have the powers of a constable in uniform under s. 50 to require a person whom he/she has reason to believe to have been acting, or to be acting, in an anti-social manner (within the meaning of s. 1 of the Crime and Disorder Act 1998—Anti-Social Behaviour Orders—**see chapter 4.5**) to give his/her name *and* address (para. 3(1)).

Power to require name and address: road traffic offences—paragraph 3A

Under this paragraph an Accredited Employee will, in the relevant police area, have the following powers of a constable under the Road Traffic Act 1988 to require the person to give their name and address:

(a) under s. 165(1)—a person whom he/she has reasonable cause to believe has committed an offence under s. 35(1) or (2) of that Act (failing to comply with directions) in the relevant police areas (**see Road Policing, para. 3.6.2.6**) and

(b) under s. 169—a person committing an offence under s. 37 of that Act (pedestrian failing to comply with directions).

Powers relating to alcohol consumption in designated public places—paragraph 4

Under this paragraph an Accredited Employee will have the powers of a constable under s. 12 of the Criminal Justice and Police Act 2001 (alcohol consumption in public places—**see para. 4.11.10.2**) in the relevant police area—

(a) to impose a requirement under subsection (2) of that section; and

(b) to dispose under subsection (3) of that section of anything surrendered to him/her;

and that section will have effect in relation to the exercise of those powers by that Accredited Employee as if the references to a constable in subsections (1) and (5) were references to the Accredited Employee.

Power to confiscate alcohol—paragraph 5

Under this paragraph an Accredited Employee will have the powers of a constable under s. 1 of the Confiscation of Alcohol (Young Persons) Act 1997 (confiscation of alcohol—**see chapter 4.11**) in the relevant police area—

(a) to impose a requirement under subsection (1) of that section; and

(b) to dispose under subsection (2) of that section of anything surrendered to him/her;

and that section shall have effect in relation to the exercise of those powers by that Accredited Employee as if the references to a constable in subsections (1) and (4) (but not the reference in subsection (5) (power of arrest)) were references to the Accredited Employee.

Power to confiscate tobacco—paragraph 6

Under this paragraph an Accredited Employee will have within the relevant police area—

(a) the power to seize anything that a constable in uniform has a duty to seize under subsection (3) of s. 7 of the Children and Young Persons Act 1933 (seizure of tobacco etc. from young persons); and

(b) the power to dispose of anything that a constable may dispose of under that subsection;

and the power to dispose of anything shall be a power to dispose of it in such manner as the Accredited Employee's employer may direct.

Powers to deal with abandoned vehicles—paragraph 7

Under this paragraph an Accredited Employee will have all such powers in the relevant police area as are conferred on people accredited under that section by regulations under s. 99 of the Road Traffic Regulation Act 1984 (removal of abandoned vehicles—**see Road Policing**).

Power to stop vehicles for testing—paragraph 8

Under this paragraph an Accredited Employee will have the power of a constable in uniform to stop a vehicle under s. 67(3) the Road Traffic Act 1988 (**see Road Policing**) within the relevant police area for the purposes of a test under s. 67(1) of that section.

Power to stop cycles—paragraph 8A

Under this paragraph an Accredited Employee will, within the relevant police area, have the power of a constable in uniform under s. 163(2) of the Road Traffic Act 1988 to stop a cycle, in relation to a person whom he has reason to believe has committed an offence under s. 72 of the Highway Act 1835 (riding on a footway) by cycling (**see Road Policing**).

Power to control traffic (purposes *other than* escorting load of exceptional dimensions)—paragraph 8B

Under this paragraph an Accredited Employee will, in the relevant police area, have the power of a constable engaged in the regulation of traffic in a road:

(a) to direct a person driving or propelling a vehicle to stop the vehicle, or

(b) to make it proceed in, or keep to, a particular line of traffic

and the power of a constable in uniform engaged in the regulation of vehicular traffic to direct a person on foot to stop proceeding along or across the carriageway.

Paragraph 8B(2) prevents these powers from being for the purposes of escorting loads of exceptional dimensions (as to which see para. 9).

Where their designation authorises it, an Accredited Employee under this paragraph will, in the relevant police area, have the powers of a constable for the purposes of a traffic survey to direct a person driving or propelling a vehicle to stop the vehicle, to make it proceed in, or keep to, a particular line of traffic or to proceed to a particular point on or near a road (para. 8B(3)).

Sections 35 and 37 of the Road Traffic Act 1988 (offences of failing to comply with direction—**see Road Policing, para. 3.6.2.6**) will apply to a direction lawfully given by an appropriately Accredited Employee (para. 8B(4)).

This paragraph can only be applied to an Accredited Employee where their accreditation contains the powers in para. 3A (power to require name and address for road traffic offences) (para. 8B(5)).

Power to control traffic for purposes of escorting a load of exceptional dimensions—paragraph 9

Under this paragraph an Accredited Employee will have, for the purpose of escorting a vehicle or trailer carrying a load of exceptional dimensions either to or from the relevant police area, the power of a constable engaged in the regulation of traffic in a road—

(a) to direct a vehicle to stop;

(b) to make a vehicle proceed in, or keep to, a particular line of traffic; and

(c) to direct pedestrians to stop (para. 9(1)).

Sections 35 and 37 of the Road Traffic Act 1988 (offences of failing to comply with directions of constable engaged in regulation of traffic in a road—**see Road Policing**) will have effect in relation to the exercise of those powers by an Accredited Employee as if the references to a constable engaged in regulation of traffic in a road were references to that Accredited Employee (para. 9(2)) and will have effect in any police area in England and Wales (para. 9(3)).

'Vehicle or trailer carrying a load of exceptional dimensions' = a vehicle or trailer the use of which is authorised by an order made by the Secretary of State under s. 44(1)(d) of the Road Traffic Act 1988 (para. 9(4)).

Index

A

D

F

G

H

I

M

Q

R

S

T

U

V

W

Y